Lecture Notes in Computer Science   6166

Commenced Publication in 1973
Founding and Former Series Editors:
Gerhard Goos, Juris Hartmanis, and Jan van Leeuwen

Sara Foresti   Sushil Jajodia (Eds.)

Data and Applications Security and Privacy XXIV

24th Annual IFIP WG 11.3 Working Conference
Rome, Italy, June 21-23, 2010
Proceedings

 Springer

Volume Editors

Sara Foresti
DTI – Università degli Studi di Milano
via Bramante, 65, 26013 Crema (CR), Italy
E-mail: sara.foresti@unimi.it

Sushil Jajodia
CSIS – George Mason University
4400 University Drive, Fairfax, VA 22030-4422, USA
E-mail: jajodia@gmu.edu

Library of Congress Control Number: 2010928333

CR Subject Classification (1998): C.2, D.4.6, K.6.5, E.3, H.4, H.3

LNCS Sublibrary: SL 3 – Information Systems and Application, incl. Internet/Web
and HCI

ISSN	0302-9743
ISBN-10	3-642-13738-5 Springer Berlin Heidelberg New York
ISBN-13	978-3-642-13738-9 Springer Berlin Heidelberg New York

springer.com

© IFIP International Federation for Information Processing 2010
Printed in Germany

Typesetting: Camera-ready by author, data conversion by Scientific Publishing Services, Chennai, India
Printed on acid-free paper   06/3180

Foreword from the Program Chairs

These proceedings contain the papers selected for presentation at the 24th Annual IFIP WG 11.3 Working Conference on Data and Applications Security and Privacy held in Rome, Italy.

In response to the call for papers 61 papers were submitted to the conference. These papers were evaluated on the basis of their significance, novelty, and technical quality. Each paper was reviewed by at least three members of the Program Committee. The Program Committee meeting was held electronically, with intensive discussion over a period of two weeks. Of the papers submitted, 18 full papers and 11 short papers were selected for presentation at the conference. The conference program also includes an invited talk by Prof. Francesco Pizzetti, President of the Italian Privacy Authority, and a panel.

There is a long list of people who volunteered their time and energy to put together the conference and who deserve acknowledgment. Thanks to all the members of the Program Committee, and the external reviewers, for all their hard work in evaluating and discussing papers. We are also very grateful to all those people who worked for the organization of the conference: Pierangela Samarati (General Chair), Cosimo Comella (General Co-chair), Claudio Ardagna (Publicity Chair), and Eros Pedrini for collating this volume.

Last, but certainly not least, our thanks go to all the authors who submitted papers and all the attendees. We hope you find the proceedings stimulating.

June 2010

Sara Foresti
Sushil Jajodia

Foreword from the General Chair

It is my pleasure to welcome you to the proceedings of the 24th Annual IFIP WG 11.3 Working Conference on Data and Applications Security and Privacy held in Rome, Italy. The conference, hosted for the first time in Rome, offered an outstanding technical program, including one keynote, one panel, 18 full papers, and 11 short papers.

An event like this does not just happen; it depends on the volunteer efforts of a host of individuals. I wish to express my sincere appreciation to all the people who volunteered their time and energy to put together the conference and make it possible. First of all I would like to thank the Program Chairs, Sara Foresti and Sushil Jajodia, and the members of the Program Committee for selecting the technical papers for presentation. I would also like to thank Prof. Francesco Pizzetti, President of the Italian Privacy Authority, for delivering the keynote speech. I am also grateful to all those people who ensured a smooth organization process: Cosimo Comella, for serving as General Co-chair and working with me in the organization of the conference; Angela Di Carlo, for all her help in the organization and local arrangements; Vijay Atluri and Sabrina De Capitani di Vimercati, Chair and Vice Chair of IFIP WG 11.3, for their support; Claudio Ardagna for taking care of publicity; and Eros Pedrini for maintaining the website and for collating the proceedings volume.

Special thanks are due to: the Italian Privacy Authority for its support and for hosting the event; the Department of Information Technology of the University for its support; the Italian Association for Information Processing (AICA) for its financial support and for providing help in the secretarial and registration process.

Last, but certainly not least, my thanks to all the attendees. I hope you enjoy reading the conference proceedings.

June 2010   Pierangela Samarati

Organization

General Chair

Pierangela Samarati   Università degli Studi di Milano, Italy

General Co-chair

Cosimo Comella   Garante per la Protezione dei Dati Personali, Italy

Program Chairs

Sara Foresti   Università degli Studi di Milano, Italy
Sushil Jajodia   George Mason University, USA

Publicity Chair

Claudio A. Ardagna   Università degli Studi di Milano, Italy

IFIP WG 11.3 Chair

Vijay Atluri   Rutgers University, USA

Program Committee

Claudio A. Ardagna	Università degli Studi di Milano, Italy
Vijay Atluri	Rutgers University, USA
Steve Barker	King's College London, UK
Joachim Biskup	Technische Universität Dortmund, Germany
Marina Blanton	University of Notre Dame, USA
David Chadwick	University of Kent, UK
Frédéric Cuppens	TELECOM Bretagne, France
Nora Cuppens-Boulahia	TELECOM Bretagne, France
Anupam Datta	Carnegie Mellon University, USA
Sabrina De Capitani di Vimercati	Università degli Studi di Milano, Italy
Josep Domingo-Ferrer	Universitat Rovira i Virgili, Spain
Eduardo B. Fernandez	Florida Atlantic University, USA
Simone Fischer-Hübner	Karlstad University, Sweden
Simon N. Foley	University College Cork, Ireland
Keith B. Frikken	Miami University, USA

Johannes Gehrke	Cornell University, USA
Joe Giordano	Utica College, USA
Ehud Gudes	Ben-Gurion University, Israel
Ragib Hasan	Johns Hopkins University, USA
Sokratis K. Katsikas	University of Piraeus, Greece
Michiharu Kudo	IBM Tokyo Research, Japan
Yingjiu Li	Singapore Management University, Singapore
Peng Liu	Pennsylvania State University, USA
Javier Lopez	University of Malaga, Spain
Emil C. Lupu	Imperial College London, UK
Ashwin Machanavajjhala	Cornell University, USA
Martin S. Olivier	University of Pretoria, South Africa
Stefano Paraboschi	Università degli Studi di Bergamo, Italy
Wolter Pieters	University of Twente, The Netherlands
Indrajit Ray	Colorado State University, USA
Indrakshi Ray	Colorado State University, USA
Kui Ren	Illinois Institute of Technology, USA
Pierangela Samarati	Università degli Studi di Milano, Italy
Divesh Shrivastava	AT&T Labs Research, USA
Anoop Singhal	Nat. Inst. of Standards and Technology, USA
Traian M. Truta	Northern Kentucky University, USA
Jaideep S. Vaidya	Rutgers University, USA
Lingyu Wang	Concordia University, Canada
Duminda Wijesekera	George Mason University, USA
Xiaokui Xiao	Nanyang Technological University, Singapore
Meng Yu	Western Illinois University, USA
Bo Zhu	Concordia University, Canada

External Reviewers

Isaac Agudo	Jingqiang Lin
Meriam Benghorbel	Wen Ming Liu
Stefan Berthold	Pablo Najera
Kevin Chiew	Bo Qin
André van Cleeff	Ruben Rios
Yehia El Rakaiby	Boris Rozenberg
William Fitzgerald	Jun Shao
Ge Fu	Michal Sramka
Nurit Gal-Oz	Manachai Toahchoodee
Joaquin Garcia-Alfaro	Qianhong Wu
Xiaoyun He	Yan Yang
Hans Hedbom	Junfeng Yu
Fengjun Li	Lei Zhang
Yan Li	Benwen Zhu

Table of Contents

Policy Definition and Enforcement

Trust and Identity Management

Short Papers

Generalizing PIR for Practical Private Retrieval of Public Data

Shiyuan Wang, Divyakant Agrawal, and Amr El Abbadi

Department of Computer Science, UC Santa Barbara
{sywang,agrawal,amr}@cs.ucsb.edu

Abstract. Private retrieval of public data is useful when a client wants to query a public data service without revealing the query to the server. Computational Private Information Retrieval (*c*PIR) achieves complete privacy for clients, but is deemed impractical since it involves expensive computation on all the data on the server. Besides, it is inflexible if the server wants to charge the client based on the service data that is exposed. *k*-Anonymity, on the other hand, is flexible and cheap for anonymizing the querying process, but is vulnerable to privacy and security threats. We propose a practical and flexible approach for the private retrieval of public data called *Bounding-Box* PIR (*bb*PIR). Using *bb*PIR, a client specifies both privacy requirements and a service charge budget. The server satisfies the client's requirements, and achieves overall good performance in computation and communication. *bb*PIR generalizes *c*PIR and *k*-Anonymity in that the bounding box can include as much as all the data on the server or as little as just *k* data items. The efficiency of *bb*PIR compared to *c*PIR and the effectiveness of *bb*PIR compared to *k*-Anonymity are verified in extensive experimental evaluations.

1 Introduction

We consider a special query called *private retrieval of public data*, in which a client retrieves data from a public server using some of its private data as predicates, while not revealing the exact values of the private data in the query. A typical example is privacy-preserving location based services [1,2], in which the private data is a single geographic location point, and the public data contains all possible points of interests within its neighborhood. A more general and promising use is in personalized search and recommendation services through big internet information service providers, such as Google, Yahoo, and Microsoft. Users need these public services in their daily lives, but they are concerned that their personal information might be disclosed or compromised. For example, a researcher with a potentially new idea does not want to reveal her exact idea to Google when she is searching for "prior art".

Currently, the privacy of queries is not properly protected by service providers, mainly because there are no strong business incentives for the service providers to pay for the potentially expensive costs brought by enhancing client privacy. Therefore, we consider a service model, in which the server can charge the client

S. Foresti and S. Jajodia (Eds.): Data and Applications Security XXIV, LNCS 6166, pp. 1–16, 2010.

based on the size of the public data exposed to the client as a result of the private retrieval. The size of the exposed data depends on the private retrieval protocol and is generally larger than the size of the answer to the query.

To enable practical query privacy in the above service model, we have the following desiderata for a private retrieval solution:

1. *Practical.* The solution should try to minimize the *communication* overhead between a client and the server as well as the *computation* overhead. Given that queries may be issued from client devices with limited capabilities, the solution should not impose sophisticated requirements on the client.
2. *Flexible privacy and reasonable charge.* A client can specify the required degree of privacy and the desired charge limit. The server can charge the client per query according to the private retrieval protocol which they agree on. The solution should make sure that the server satisfies a client's privacy specification and does not overcharge.

The two closest studies which could be adapted for developing a possible solution to this problem are *k-Anonymity* [3] and *Computational Private Information Retrieval* (*cPIR*) [4]. *k*-Anonymity has been used in privacy-preserving location based services [1], where the location point of a user is blurred into a cloaked region consisting of at least k nearby user locations and the server returns the nearest points of interests to the cloaked region. The parameter k serves as a configurable degree of privacy. Similarly in the more general setting of private retrieval, one could insert into the private query some random data that is close to the private data in the query, such that a private data item cannot be identified from at least k data items. Then the server returns all the public data that matches the anonymized private data, which is exposed to the client and thus chargeable. However, a potential security threat with *k*-Anonymity is that both the client query and the server answer, although anonymized for protecting the client's privacy, are in plain text that can be seen by a third party. The privacy of *k*-Anonymity for numeric data has also been questioned by a number of proposals [5,6,7] for potential *proximity breach*: the real private data and the blurred data could be so close that the server can conclude with probability $1/k$ that the private data is in a narrow range.

Computational Private Information Retrieval (*cPIR*) [8] retrieves a bit from a public bit string on a server without revealing to the server the position of the desired bit under some intractability assumption. To achieve the most balanced performance for both communication and computation costs, the *cPIR* protocol requires the public data to be organized as a matrix. It achieves computationally complete privacy by incurring expensive computations over all public data on the server, and keeps the data communication secure by transmitting random information hiding vectors. The exposed, chargeable data is only a column of the public data matrix. Due to its expensive computation costs on the server, even the *cPIR* technique with the least expensive operation, modular multiplication [8], is criticized as being up to two orders of magnitude less efficient than simply transferring the entire data from the server to the client [9].

To achieve the above mentioned desiderata and seek a trade-off between the cost of retrieval and the degree of privacy, we propose a generalized private retrieval approach called *Bounding-Box* PIR (*bb*PIR) that unifies both k-Anonymity and cPIR. The public service data is organized as a matrix as in cPIR. A client anonymizes her private query data in a rectangle called *bounding box*, whose range corresponds to a sub matrix of the public data matrix. The size of the bounding box is determined by the client's privacy requirement and desired charge limit. The area of the bounding box determines the privacy that the client can achieve, the larger the area, the higher the privacy obtained, but with higher computation and communication costs, and vice versa.

Compared to k-Anonymity, *bb*PIR is secure in data communication between a client and the server, because it transfers the information hidden in a bounding box instead of plain text data. Moreover, *bb*PIR does not suffer from proximity breach as much as k-Anonymity, because the bounding box includes data values that are not close to the query value. Compared to cPIR, *bb*PIR is more practical because of its lower computation cost. At one extreme, *bb*PIR degenerates into k-Anonymity if the range of the bounding box is a single column on the public data matrix. At the other extreme, *bb*PIR becomes cPIR if the range of the bounding box is the entire public data matrix.

The rest of the paper is organized as follows. Section 2 reviews the related work. Section 3 briefly explains cPIR. Section 4 describes our data model. Section 5 presents the proposed *bb*PIR approach. Section 6 experimentally evaluates *bb*PIR. Section 7 concludes the paper.

2 Related Work

Our work on private retrieval of public data is inspired by the research on Private Information Retrieval, k-Anonymity and privacy-preserving location based services.

Private Information Retrieval (PIR) derives from the following theoretical problem: Given a database which stores a binary string $x = x_1...x_n$ of length n, a client wants to retrieve x_i privately such that the database does not learn i. Chor et al. [10] first introduced the PIR problem and provided solutions for multiple database servers. Observing that a database server is often restricted to perform only polynomial-time computations, Kushilevitz and Ostrovsky proposed a single database, computational PIR solution [8], which we refer to as cPIR in the paper. Follow-up single database cPIR proposals improve the communication overhead, as surveyed in [4], but they use even more expensive operations than the modular multiplications used in [8], as pointed out by Sion and Carbunar [9], thus are not feasible for practical applications. Williams and Sion [11] attempt to make cPIR practical by using oblivious RAM. However, their approach is designed for problem settings where client data is outsourced to the server, thus is not applicable in our context.

k-Anonymity is a widely adopted privacy policy. It generalizes or suppresses the values of data records such that each record is indistinguishable among at least k records with close values in the released private data [3]. In some contexts, the basic principle of k-Anonymity is not sufficient to protect data privacy, for example in a group of data with little diversity or high similarity. Therefore, a number of proposals designed new privacy principles to enhance the privacy of k-Anonymity [12,13,5,6,7]. However, they are not easy to apply in the private retrieval of public data applications. Besides, they share the same security threat as k-Anonymity: all the communication contents can be seen by a third party.

Mokbel et al. [1] use k-Anonymity to implement query privacy in location based services, in which the anonymization of user location points is done on a third party server. Ghinita et al. [2] argue that a third party anonymizer is not needed if cPIR is used. Our bbPIR can also be applied in privacy-preserving location based services. It incurs less costs than cPIR and does not need a third party anonymizer.

3   Background on cPIR

cPIR is designed to retrieve a single bit in a large matrix privately [8]. It relies on the computational intractability of *Quadratic Residuosity*. Let N be a natural number, and $Z_N^* = \{x | 1 \leq x \leq N, gcd(N, x) = 1\}$. x is a *quadratic residue* (QR) mod N if $\exists y \in Z_N^*$ s.t. $y^2 = x$ mod N. Otherwise, x is a *quadratic nonresidue* (QNR) mod N [14]. The problem becomes most difficult if $N = p_1 \cdot p_2$, where p_1 and p_2 are distinct large primes with equal number of bits, $m/2$. Let $Z_N^{+1} = \{x \in Z_N^* | (\frac{x}{N}) = 1\}$. The *Quadratic Residuosity Assumption* (QRA) states that for $x \in Z_N^{+1}$, without knowing p_1 and p_2 in advance, the probability of distinguishing x between a QR and a QNR is negligible for large enough number of bits, m [8].

However, determining whether the number x is a QR or a QNR is much easier if knowing p_1 and p_2. Based on *Euler's theorem* [14], x is a QR if and only if

$$x^{(p_1-1)/2} \ mod \ p_1 = 1 \ \wedge \ x^{(p_2-1)/2} \ mod \ p_2 = 1 \tag{1}$$

and a QNR otherwise.

Let n be the total number of public data items (bits in this case). The public data is organized into an $s \times t$ binary matrix M (choose $s = t = \lceil \sqrt{n} \rceil$ for balanced communication cost between the client and the server). Let (e, g) be the two dimensional address of the bit queried by the client (Refer to Table 1 for a summary of our notations). The cPIR protocol is as follows:

1. Initially, the client sends to the server an m-bit number N which is the product of two random $m/2$-bit primes p_1 and p_2.
2. To retrieve entry (e, g) in M, the client generates a vector of t m-bit random numbers in Z_N^{+1}, $y = [y_1, ..., y_t]$, s.t. y_g is a QNR and all other y_i $(i \neq g)$ are QR. It sends the vector y to the server.
3. The server computes for each row i of M a modular product $z_i = \Pi_{j=1}^t w_{i,j}$, where $w_{i,j} = y_j^2$ if $M_{i,j} = 0$, and $w_{i,j} = y_j$ if $M_{i,j} = 1$.

4. The server sends to the client $z_1, ..., z_s$.
5. The client determines that $M_{e,g} = 0$ if z_e is a QR, and $M_{e,g} = 1$ if z_e is a QNR.

For example in Fig. 1, the client sends $N = 35$ to the server initially. When the client wants to retrieve the bit at $M_{2,3}$, she generates a vector y for the second row of the matrix, where y_3 is a QNR 17, and $y_1 = 4$, $y_2 = 16$, $y_4 = 11$ are QR. Upon receiving y, the server computes for each row of the matrix a modular product z_i, e.g. $z_2 = (4^2 \times 16 \times 17 \times 11^2)$ mod $35 = 17$. Since $z_2 = 17$ is a QNR, when the client receives the vector z from the server, she obtains $M_{2,3} = 1$.

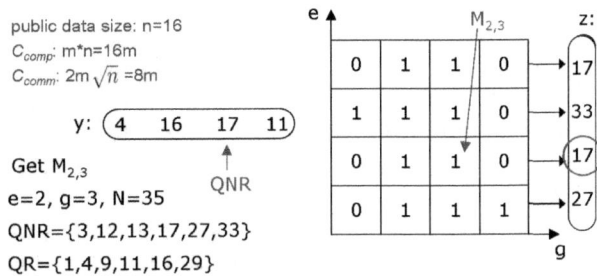

Fig. 1. *c*PIR Example

Note that the server can not figure out if a y_i or z_i is a QR or a QNR, because the server does not know p_1 and p_2, but the client can. In step 5, the client is able to interpret every $M_{i,g}$ ($1 \le i \le s$) by analyzing the corresponding z_i. Thus by running one round of *c*PIR, all s bits in the column of the requested bit entry are exposed to the client and become chargeable.

Table 1. Summary of Notations

Notation	Description
k	for k-Anonymity
n	total number of public data items
m	modulus bit size
$N = p_1 \cdot p_2$	modulus, product of two $m/2$-bit primes p_1 and p_2
s, t	number of rows, columns in the public data matrix
$M_{s \times t}$	public data matrix
(e, g)	address of the client request entry on M
y	client query vector of m-bit random numbers
z	server answer vector of m-bit random numbers
b	number of bits in each data item
ρ	upper bound of privacy breach probability
μ	upper bound of server charge
P_{brh}	privacy breach probability
C_{srv}	server charge
C_{comm}, C_{comp}	communication and server computation cost
r, c	number of rows, columns in a query bounding box
w	minimum number of keys in a bin of a histogram

4   Data Model

We generalize the standard cPIR model in several ways. We consider a (key, address, value) data store, where each value is a b-bit data item. The public data of size n is organized in an $s \times t$ matrix M ($s = t = \lceil \sqrt{n} \rceil$ by default). Each public data item x has a numeric key KA that determines the two dimensional address of x in M. x is only accessible through its address. The public data are sorted by KA in ascending order and then put in M columnwise from the leftmost column to the rightmost column. Two query types are supported for the retrieval of x: *query by address* and *query by key*. The latter is translated to *query by address* in the retrieval.

A client can specify her privacy requirement and desired charge budget (ρ, μ), where ρ is a privacy breach limit (the upper bound probability that a requested item can be identified by the server), and μ is a server charge limit (the upper bound of the number of items that are exposed to the client for one requested item). For example, in the case of k-Anonymity, $\rho = 1/k$, $\mu \geq k$. For a public data set of size n, the best achievable privacy (the minimum ρ) is $1/n$. Similarly, the maximum charge that a client can incur is n ($\mu \leq n$), when the entire data is communicated to the client.

Based on the desiderata in Sect. 1, we keep track of four important metrics: (1) *Communication Cost* C_{comm}, the cost of data communication between the client and the server in terms of number of bits, including the client query and the server answer. (2) *Computation Cost* C_{comp}, the computation cost of private retrieval on the server in terms of the number of involved public data bits. The computation cost on the client is not considered here, because it is generally much smaller than the computation cost on the server, as later shown in our experiment results. (3) *Privacy Breach Probability* P_{brh}, the probability that the server can figure out a requested item, $P_{brh} \leq \rho$. (4) *Server Charge* C_{srv}, the number of interpretable public data items retrieved from the server, $C_{srv} \leq \mu$. We refer to the first two metrics as the *performance* metrics, and the last two metrics as the *quality of service* metrics.

In the case of k-Anonymity, given that we transmit k bits for anonymizing one requested bit, $C_{comm} = 2 \cdot k$ (the client query and the server answer), $C_{comp} = k$, $P_{brh} = 1/k$ and $C_{srv} = k$. k-Anonymity can satisfy any privacy requirement and charge budget (ρ, μ) s.t. $\rho \cdot \mu \geq 1$. In the case of cPIR to retrieve one bit, the client query (row vector y) and the server answer (column vector z) are both vectors of $\lceil \sqrt{n} \rceil$ m-bit numbers, and m-bit modular multiplication is applied on all the data in M. Therefore, all the above metric values are fixed: $C_{comm} = m \cdot (t + s) = 2 \cdot m \cdot \lceil \sqrt{n} \rceil$, $C_{comp} = m \cdot n$, $P_{brh} = 1/(s \cdot t) \leq 1/n$ and $C_{srv} = s = \lceil \sqrt{n} \rceil$. As an example, the top left of Fig. 1 shows the calculated C_{comm} and C_{comp} for the private retrieval of one bit (e.g. $M_{2,3}$) on a 4×4 matrix with $n = 16$ bits. cPIR can satisfy any privacy requirement and charge budget (ρ, μ) s.t. $\rho \geq 1/n$, $\mu \geq \lceil \sqrt{n} \rceil$.

5   Bounding-Box PIR

From the above analysis on cPIR and k-Anonymity, we can see that they are not flexible enough to satisfy any user desired quality of service, and they do not achieve overall good performance on all the metrics. A new practical approach for the private retrieval of public data which achieves both user desired flexibility and overall good performance is thus needed. To design such an approach, we need the security and privacy of cPIR, as well as the flexibility and computation performance of k-Anonymity. On the other hand, we should reduce the impractical costs of cPIR, and mitigate the threats of plain text communication and proximity privacy breach of k-Anonymity. Hence, we propose a private retrieval approach called *Bounding-Box PIR* (*bb*PIR), which unifies and seeks a practical tradeoff between cPIR and k-Anonymity.

The basic idea of *bb*PIR is to use a bounding box BB (an $r \times c$ rectangle corresponding to a sub-matrix of M) as an anonymized range around the address of item x requested by the client, and then apply cPIR on the bounding box. *bb*PIR finds an appropriately sized bounding box that satisfies the privacy request ρ, and achieves overall good performance in terms of Communication and Computation Costs without exceeding the Server Charge limit μ for each retrieved item.

Since *bb*PIR operates on an $r \times c$ sub-matrix of M instead of the entire matrix M as in cPIR, its client query (row vector y) is a vector of c m-bit numbers, its server answer (column vector z) is a vector of r m-bit numbers, and m-bit modular multiplication is applied on all the data in the sub-matrix. Therefore, $C_{comm}(bb\text{PIR})$ is proportional to $m \cdot c$ and $m \cdot r$. $C_{comp}(bb\text{PIR})$ is proportional to the area of the bounding box, $m \cdot r \cdot c$. $P_{brh}(bb\text{PIR})$ equals the ratio of one entry out of the bounding box, $1/(r \cdot c)$. $C_{srv}(bb\text{PIR})$ is the number of rows in the sub-matrix, r, because similar to cPIR, a client can interpret the data within the same column.

We start by supporting *query by address* in Sect. 5.1, assuming that the client knows the exact address of the entry on M to retrieve. Then for practical purposes, in Sect. 5.2 we relax this assumption and support *query by key* by using a public data histogram published by the server. We focus on private retrieval of one item, based on which more complex private queries can be supported.

5.1   Query by Address

*bb*PIR is similar to cPIR in that it retrieves one bit at a time. In order to retrieve a b bit item x, *bb*PIR can be repeated b times. The client query, row vector y, can be reused b times on b bits of x. Only the server answer, column vector z, needs to be re-calculated for each of the b bits. Therefore, the Communication Cost $C_{comm} = m \cdot c + m \cdot b \cdot r$. Since m-bit modular multiplication will be applied on each bit of the $r \cdot c$ items in the bounding box, the Computation Cost $C_{comp} = m \cdot b \cdot r \cdot c$.

We have two constraints based on the client's requirement (ρ, μ): $P_{brh} \leq \rho$, and $C_{srv} = r \leq \mu$. Choose BB to be the minimum bounding box that satisfies the privacy breach limit ρ. It is easy to see that its area $|BB| = r \cdot c = \lceil 1/\rho \rceil$, and the minimum Computation Cost $C_{comp} = m \cdot b \cdot r \cdot c = m \cdot b \cdot \lceil 1/\rho \rceil$. Then the goal is to minimize the Communication Cost $C_{comm} = m \cdot c + m \cdot b \cdot r$ without exceeding the charge limit μ, which is equivalent to minimizing $(c + b \cdot r)$. Because $min\,(c + b \cdot r)$ is achieved when $c = b \cdot r$, given that $r \cdot c = \lceil 1/\rho \rceil$, $r = \lceil \sqrt{1/(\rho \cdot b)} \rceil$, $c = \lceil \sqrt{b/\rho} \rceil$. Since $r \leq \mu$ must hold, $min\,(c + b \cdot r)$ depends on whether $\mu \geq \lceil \sqrt{1/(\rho \cdot b)} \rceil$. The bbPIR protocol is described as follows:

1. Initially, the client sends to the server an m-bit number N which is the product of two random $m/2$-bit primes p_1 and p_2, and the dimensions of the bounding box BB of area $\lceil 1/\rho \rceil$. The number of rows and columns, r and s in the bounding box BB are decided as follows:
   If $\mu \geq \lceil \sqrt{1/(\rho \cdot b)} \rceil$, set

$$r = \lceil \sqrt{1/(\rho \cdot b)} \rceil, \ c = \lceil \sqrt{b/\rho} \rceil \tag{2}$$

   Otherwise, set

$$r = min(\mu, \lceil 1/\rho \rceil, s), \ c = min(\lceil 1/(\rho \cdot r) \rceil, t) \tag{3}$$

2. To retrieve entry (e, g) in M, the client first places BB on M with the above defined dimensions r, c, s.t. BB covers (e, g), and BB is within the address space of M.
3. The client generates a vector of c m-bit random numbers in Z_N^{+1}, $y = [y_1, ..., y_c]$, s.t. y_g is a QNR and all other y_i $(i \neq g)$ are QR. It sends the coordinates of BB and vector y to the server.
4. The server computes for each row i of the sub-matrix BB a modular product $z_i = \Pi_{j=1}^{c} w_{i,j}$, where $w_{i,j} = y_j^2$ if $M_{i,j} = 0$, and $w_{i,j} = y_j$ if $M_{i,j} = 1$.
5. The server sends to the client $z_1, ..., z_r$.
6. The client determines that $M_{e,g} = 0$ if z_e is a QR, and $M_{e,g} = 1$ if z_e is a QNR.
7. Repeat steps 4-6 to obtain the remaining bits of the requested item in (e, g).

Figure 2 illustrates the same example query as in Fig. 1, retrieving $M_{2,3}$ from a 4×4 bit matrix M. Suppose a client specifies $\rho = 1/4, \mu = 2$, then a 2×2 bounding box suffices to satisfy her requirements. The placement of the bounding box BB is flexible, as long as it covers $M_{2,3}$. Compared to Fig. 1, because the sizes of vectors y and z are reduced, the computation and communication costs are reduced proportionally.

A comparison of k-Anonymity, cPIR and bbPIR for the private retrieval of one item on the performance and the quality of service metrics are shown in Table 2. We omit the constant cost for sending N, the size and coordinates of the bounding box in step 1 and step 2.

Compared to k-Anonymity, bbPIR is able to achieve better privacy for the same charge or a lower charge for the same privacy. Compared to cPIR, generally if $\rho > 1/n, r \cdot c < n, c + r < 2 \cdot \lceil \sqrt{n} \rceil$, the communication cost, computation cost and charge of bbPIR are all lower than those of cPIR. If we make the bounding

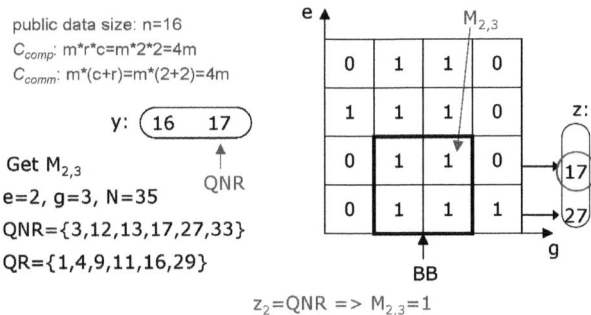

public data size: n=16

C_{comp}: m*r*c=m*2*2=4m

C_{comm}: m*(c+r)=m*(2+2)=4m

y: (16   17)

Get $M_{2,3}$

e=2, g=3, N=35

QNR={3,12,13,17,27,33}

QR={1,4,9,11,16,29}

z_2=QNR => $M_{2,3}$=1

Fig. 2. *bb*PIR Example: Private Retrieval of One Bit

box a single column, i.e. $r = k$ and $c = 1$, there is no point in using the m-bit random number to hide the column g, and bbPIR degenerates into k-Anonymity. If we set $r = c = \lceil \sqrt{n} \rceil$, bbPIR degenerates into cPIR. By determining the dimensions r, c of BB in step 1, bbPIR is able to satisfy any privacy requirement $\rho \geq 1/n$ and charge limit $\mu < s$. It is thus much more flexible than k-Anonymity and cPIR.

Table 2. Comparisons on Private Retrieval of One Item

Method	k-Anonymity	cPIR	bbPIR	bbPIR ($c = r = \sqrt{k}$)
C_{comm}	$2 \cdot b \cdot k$	$m \cdot \lceil \sqrt{n} \rceil + m \cdot b \cdot \lceil \sqrt{n} \rceil$	$m \cdot (c + b \cdot r)$	$m \cdot (1 + b) \cdot \sqrt{k}$
C_{comp}	$b \cdot k$	$m \cdot b \cdot n$	$m \cdot b \cdot r \cdot c$	$m \cdot b \cdot k$
P_{brh}	$1/k$	$1/n$	$1/(r \cdot c)$	$1/k$
C_{srv}	k	$\lceil \sqrt{n} \rceil$	r	$\sqrt{k}$

5.2   Query by Key

In the above formulation, we assume that clients know the exact address of the requested entry, (e, g). However in practice, *query by key* is more common. In this case, the exact knowledge of how the public data is organized on the server is not available. Clients have to figure out the address of the requested item, (e, g), from the requested key.

In fact, the same problem also exists in cPIR. Unfortunately, it has largely been ignored by the PIR community. One proposal enables *query by key* by building an index structure for mapping a keyword to a physical address on the server and processing a query by an oblivious walk on the index [15]. This oblivious walk requires running as many as $O(b \cdot logn)$ rounds of PIR, and consequently incurs high communication and computation costs. Although extra communication and computation costs are not avoidable for translating query keys to addresses, we would like an efficient and privacy-aware way of translation. We also want to avoid trusting a third party.

The basic idea for our solution is that the server publishes a one-dimensional histogram, H, on the key field KA and the dimensions of the public data matrix M, s and t. The histogram is only published to authorized clients. The publishing process, which occurs infrequently, is encrypted for security. When a client issues a query, she calculates an address range for the queried entry by searching the bin of H where the query data falls.

Assume a predefined threshold w, which is the minimum number of keys in each bin of the histogram. To simplify address translation, we require $w \leq s$. Consecutive keys are allocated in the bins of H by scanning M columnwise from left to right. If $w \cdot (\lfloor s/w \rfloor - 1)$ keys have been scanned in the current column on M, assign the next $s - w \cdot (\lfloor s/w \rfloor - 1)$ keys to a new bin and proceed to a new column. Otherwise, assign the next w keys to a new bin. At the end of this process, the bins in H are matched onto M, and H is transformed into an $\lfloor s/w \rfloor \times t$ matrix, HM. For example, if we have 25 keys and a 5×5 matrix M, for $w = 2$, we assign the first two keys in one bin and the last three keys in another bin for each column. The result, HM, is a 2×5 matrix with 10 bins, as illustrated in Fig. 3.

Knowing the organization of HM, the client is able to calculate the address of the requested entry on HM, (e', g'). The address range of the corresponding entries on M is $[(e' - 1) \cdot w + 1, e' \cdot w] \times [g', g']$ for $e' < \lfloor s/w \rfloor$, or $[(e' - 1) \cdot w + 1, s] \times [g', g']$ for $e' = \lfloor s/w \rfloor$. One advantage of $w \leq s$ is that we only need to run bbPIR once to obtain all

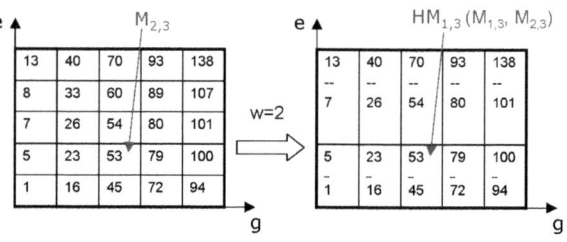

Fig. 3. Example of Locating By Histogram

the entries in the address range of the requested bin. As an example of query by key through the histogram in Fig. 3, if a client requests the item with key 53, she first finds 53 in the 5th bin of H, corresponding to entry $HM_{1,3}$ on HM. Then she runs bbPIR once to obtain the entries in $HM_{1,3}$, where she finds the answer $M_{2,3}$.

Note that $r \geq w$ must hold. bbPIR in query by key can satisfy any privacy and charge specification (ρ, μ) s.t. $\rho \geq 1/n$ and $\mu \geq w$.

6   Experimental Evaluation

Our experiments evaluate the *performance* and the *quality of service* (metrics defined in Sect. 4) of bbPIR against cPIR and k-Anonymity for private retrieval queries. Maintaining the overall proximity philosophy of privacy-preserving location based services [1], as well as the generalization approach of k-Anonymity based data publishing [16,17], the k-Anonymity private retrieval method is implemented by sending a consecutive range of data items that covers the original private query item, which are specified by the lower end of the range and k.

We implemented the three private retrieval methods in C++. We ran a majority of the experiments on an extended data set generated from a real data set, Adult [18]. The Adult database has 32561 records with 15 attributes of categorical or numeric data types. We kept its first 3 attributes and generated 10^6 records by randomly picking attribute values from the original 32561 records. Then the total number of data items, n, is 10^6, and the number of bits for each data item, b, is 208. Only for the experiment on proximity privacy of numeric data (Sect. 6.2), we used a synthetic data set of size 10^6. All the default values in the experiments are listed in Table 3. For each value or range of a variant to test, we ran 100 random queries and reported the average results. The queries are *query by address* by default. In Sect. 6.3 we specifically study *query by key*. Our testbed is a Linux server with Intel 2.40GHz CPU and 3GB memory, running Federal Core 8 OS. The experiment results demonstrate that *bb*PIR is practical for safeguarding client query privacy as well as the server's business revenue.

Table 3. Default Values in Experiments

Variant	Default Value
n	10^6
b	208
s, t, $C_{srv}(c\text{PIR})$	10^3
k, $C_{srv}(k\text{-Anonymity})$	10^3
$P_{brh}(c\text{PIR})$	10^{-6}
ρ, $P_{brh}(bb\text{PIR})$, $P_{brh}(k\text{-Anonymity})$	10^{-3}
μ, $C_{srv}(bb\text{PIR})$	50
m	1024

6.1   Effects of Privacy and Charge Specification

In the following two experiments, we study the effects of the privacy breach limit, ρ ($1/k$ in k-Anonymity), and the charge limit, μ (k in k-Anonymity), on *bb*PIR and k-Anonymity. We do not show the client computation times here, since they are almost negligible compared to server computation times.

Recall that a potential security threat with k-Anonymity is that the data communication between the client and the server is in plain text and can be seen by a third party eavesdropper. In k-Anonymity, the client query, in plain text, is an address range of the anonymized entries, which does not give a third party any useful information without knowing M. But if the server answer is also in plain text, a third party will know the exact result contents sent by the server. Thus to provide k-Anonymity the same security level as *bb*PIR, we applied a popular public key encryption algorithm, RSA, on the server answer of k-Anonymity. We denote the security enhanced k-Anonymity as k-Anonymity (RSA) and abbreviate it as k-A (RSA). Please refer to our technical report [19] for more details on the analysis of its computation and communication costs.

In the first experiment, we fixed $\mu = 50$, and varied ρ ($1/k$) in 5 ranges, $(0, 10^{-4})$, $[10^{-4}, 10^{-3})$, $[10^{-3}, 10^{-2})$, $[10^{-2}, 10^{-1})$ and $[10^{-1}, 1)$. For each range,

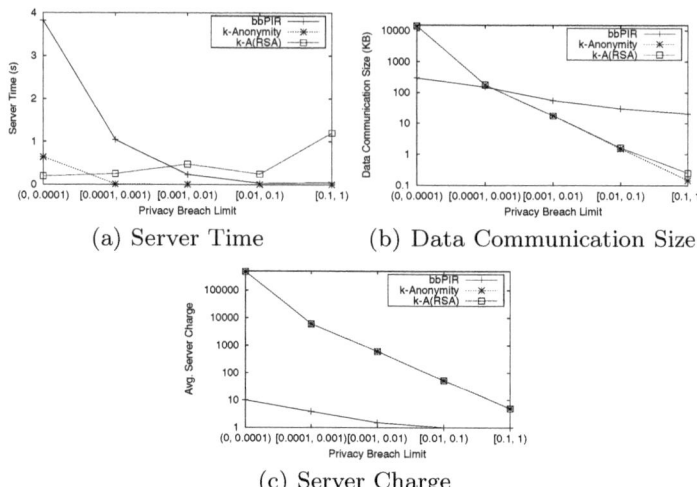

(a) Server Time   (b) Data Communication Size

(c) Server Charge

Fig. 4. Comparison of bbPIR, k-Anonymity and k-A (RSA). Vary ρ $(1/k)$, and Fix $\mu = 50$.

we mimiced requests from different clients by randomly generating 100 values of ρ in the range, and running 100 queries. We then took the average results. Figure 4 demonstrates a general trend that a lower privacy requirement (a higher ρ and a correspondingly lower k value) reduces both computation and communication costs for bbPIR and k-Anonymity. However, as demonstrated in Fig. 4(a), higher ρ (and corresponding lower k) values do not reduce the server computation time of k-A (RSA), because they do not impact the computational complexity of RSA encryption. For the same privacy breach limit, k-Anonymity usually incurs more server charges than bbPIR as seen in Fig. 4(c), which is not appealing to most internet users. k-Anonymity (RSA) has the exact same server charge as k-Anonymity, and almost does not incur additional communication cost, so the two curves of k-A (RSA) and k-Anonymity overlap in Fig. 4(b) and Fig. 4(c).

In the second experiment, we fixed $\rho = 10^{-3}$, and varied μ (k) in 5 ranges, $(1, 5)$, $[5, 10)$, $[10, 50)$, $[50, 100)$ and $[100, 200)$. Similar to the above, we generated 100 values of μ and ran 100 queries in each range. In contrast to the effects of ρ, larger values of μ do not result in better performance, as seen in Fig. 5. The performance of bbPIR remains constant in Fig. 5(b) and Fig. 5(c), because ρ is fixed, according to Formula (2) in Sect. 5.1, the dimensions of the bounding box are fixed regardless of different charges. For the same charge limit, we can see in Fig. 5(c) that both k-Anonymity and k-A (RSA) cannot reach the same privacy as in bbPIR, and their real privacy breach probabilities $P_{brh} > 10^{-3}$. Similar to the previous experiment on ρ, k-A (RSA) achieves the same privacy as k-Anonymity, and almost does not incur additional communication cost, so the two curves of k-Anonymity (RSA) and k-Anonymity overlap in Fig. 5(b) and Fig. 5(c).

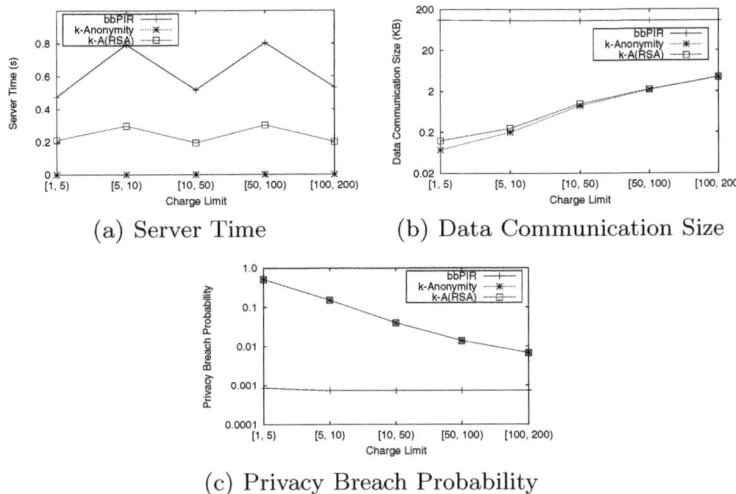

(a) Server Time

(b) Data Communication Size

(c) Privacy Breach Probability

Fig. 5. Comparison of bbPIR, k-Anonymity and k-A (RSA). Vary μ (k), and Fix $\rho = 10^{-3}$.

6.2 Proximity Privacy of Numeric Data

In this experiment, we specifically study the proximity privacy of bbPIR and k-Anonymity on numeric data. As pointed out in [5,6,7], there should be enough difference between the data items in an anonymized range (in a bounding box in the case of bbPIR) under a privacy breach probability P_{brh}, which we call *neighborhood difference*, otherwise the private data can be determined in a narrow range with probability P_{brh}.

Instead of using the non-numeric Adult data set, we generated a synthetic data set with 10^6 numeric data keys and values, which follow a Zipf distribution and are in the range of $[0.0, 1.0]$. We measured the neighborhood difference as the absolute difference between the maximum and minimum values in an anonymized range (or in a bounding box) following [5]. We fixed $\mu = 50$, and varied ρ ($1/k$) from 10^{-4} to 10^{-1}. Since the bounding box used in bbPIR contains both the data items whose values are close to each other in a column and the data items whose values are far away in different columns of the matrix, the neighborhood difference in bbPIR is almost more than 100 times the difference in k-Anonymity for $\rho < 0.1$ as seen in Fig. 6. The results suggest that bbPIR is much more resistant to proximity inference attack on numeric data than k-Anonymity. Our technical report [19] also discusses the tradeoff of an alternative k-Anonymity implementation by sending $k-1$ dummy retrieval requests.

6.3 Effects of Query by Key

Finally we study the costs of *query by key* (QBK) compared to the costs of *query by address* (QBA) in bbPIR. As discussed in Sect. 5.2, clients have to calculate

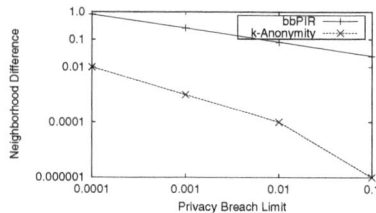

Fig. 6. Comparison of bbPIR and k-Anonymity. Vary ρ, and Fix $\mu = 50$.

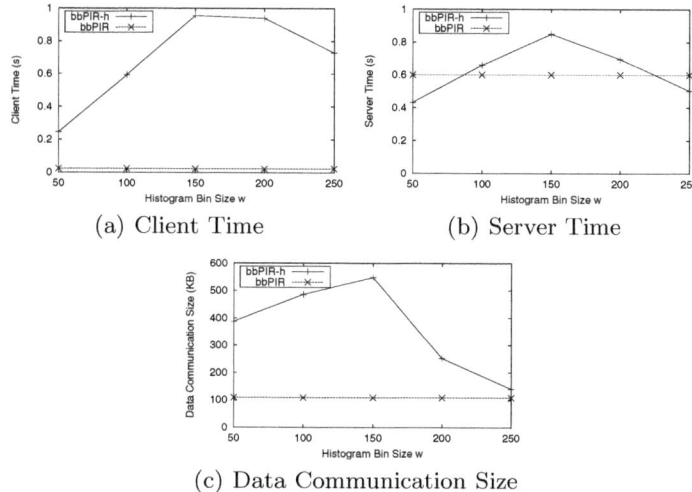

(a) Client Time

(b) Server Time

(c) Data Communication Size

Fig. 7. Comparison of QBK (bbPIR-h) and QBA (bbPIR). Vary Histogram Bin Size w, and Fix $\rho = 10^{-3}$.

an address range of the requested key, and retrieve all the data items whose keys fall in that range. Interpreting all these items could lead to additional costs on the client, so we need to specifically study the client computation times here.

The size of the requested address range is determined by the minimum number of keys in each bin of the server published histogram, w. We varied w from 50 to 250, set $\mu = w$ (since $\mu \geq w$ must hold) for QBK, fixed $\mu = 50$ for QBA, and fixed $\rho = 10^{-3}$ for both query types. We used the extended Adult data set as public data and generated numeric keys for each record. The comparison result of QBK and QBA, denoted as bbPIR-h and bbPIR respectively, is shown in Fig. 7. For Fig. 7, it is interesting to note that the computation and communication costs of QBK are not monotone functions of w. The reason for this behavior can be explained as follows. Since ρ is fixed, the area of the bounding box is fixed. As w increases, the number of rows in the bounding box, r, increases, and contrarily, the number of columns in the bounding box, c, decreases. The related computation and communication costs change with both r and c, so they increase and then decrease as in Fig. 7. More details are explained in [19]. However, consistently QBK increases the computation and communication costs. These overheads are still reasonable, as query by key provides a practical solution to the impractical assumption of cPIR, i.e., that the client knows *a priori* the exact location of the requested data items.

7 Conclusion

Enabling practical private retrieval of public data is useful for privacy aware internet services, but has not received much attention in the database community. Computational Private Information Retrieval (cPIR) achieves complete privacy for a client, but is deemed impractical due to its expensive computations involving the entire public data. On the other hand, k-Anonymity based private retrieval achieves cheap computation and communication, but is subject to the threats of proximity breach and insecure communication, as well as inflexibility between privacy and charge constraints.

To design a practical approach for private retrieval of public data on single server settings, we followed the cPIR approach to achieve privacy and security, and adopted the principle of flexible privacy from k-Anonymity. We proposed an approach called *Bounding-Box* PIR (*bb*PIR). *bb*PIR generalizes cPIR by adjusting a bounding box which trades complete privacy for flexible partial privacy, but bounds computation and communication costs. Given an internet business service model where clients can specify their privacy requirements and service charge budgets (ρ, μ), *bb*PIR is able to achieve lower charges or higher privacy compared to k-Anonymity. We also designed a practical low cost solution for enabling retrieval by keys instead of retrieval by addresses of the matrix. The experimental results confirmed the efficiency and effectiveness of our proposals.

Acknowledgement

This work is partially supported by NSF Grant IIS-0847925. We wish to thank Gabriel Ghinita for providing us his cPIR implementation.

References

1. Mokbel, M.F., Chow, C.Y., Aref, W.G.: The new casper: A privacy-aware location-based database server. In: ICDE, pp. 1499–1500 (2007)
2. Ghinita, G., Kalnis, P., Khoshgozaran, A., Shahabi, C., Tan, K.L.: Private queries in location based services: anonymizers are not necessary. In: SIGMOD Conference, pp. 121–132 (2008)
3. Sweeney, L.: k-anonymity: A model for protecting privacy. International Journal of Uncertainty, Fuzziness and Knowledge-Based Systems 10(5), 557–570 (2002)
4. Ostrovsky, R., Skeith III, W.E.: A survey of single-database private information retrieval: Techniques and applications. In: Okamoto, T., Wang, X. (eds.) PKC 2007. LNCS, vol. 4450, pp. 393–411. Springer, Heidelberg (2007)

5. Zhang, Q., Koudas, N., Srivastava, D., Yu, T.: Aggregate query answering on anonymized tables. In: ICDE, pp. 116–125 (2007)
6. LeFevre, K., DeWitt, D.J., Ramakrishnan, R.: Workload-aware anonymization. In: KDD, pp. 277–286 (2006)
7. Li, J., Tao, Y., Xiao, X.: Preservation of proximity privacy in publishing numerical sensitive data. In: SIGMOD Conference, pp. 473–486 (2008)
8. Kushilevitz, E., Ostrovsky, R.: Replication is not needed: Single database, computationally-private information retrieval. In: FOCS, pp. 364–373 (1997)
9. Sion, R., Carbunar, B.: On the computational practicality of private information retrieval. In: Network and Distributed System Security Symposium (2007)
10. Chor, B., Kushilevitz, E., Goldreich, O., Sudan, M.: Private information retrieval. J. ACM 45(6), 965–981 (1998)
11. Williams, P., Sion, R.: Usable private information retrieval. In: Network and Distributed System Security Symposium (2008)
12. Machanavajjhala, A., Gehrke, J., Kifer, D., Venkitasubramaniam, M.: l-diversity: Privacy beyond k-anonymity. In: ICDE 24 (2006)
13. Li, N., Li, T., Venkatasubramanian, S.: t-closeness: Privacy beyond k-anonymity and l-diversity. In: ICDE, pp. 106–115 (2007)
14. `http://marauder.millersville.edu/~bikenaga/numbertheory/numbertheorynotes.html`: Number theory notes
15. Chor, B., Gilboa, N., Naor, M.: Private information retrieval by keywords. Technical Report TRCS 0917, Department of Computer Science, Technian (1997)
16. Sweeney, L.: Achieving k-anonymity privacy protection using generalization and suppression. International Journal of Uncertainty, Fuzziness and Knowledge-Based Systems 10(5), 571–588 (2002)
17. LeFevre, K., DeWitt, D.J., Ramakrishnan, R.: Incognito: Efficient full-domain k-anonymity. In: SIGMOD Conference, pp. 49–60 (2005)
18. Asuncion, A., Newman, D.: UCI machine learning repository (2007), `http://www.ics.uci.edu/~mlearn/MLRepository.html`
19. Wang, S., Agrawal, D., Abbadi, A.E.: Generalizing pir for practical private retrieval of public data. Technical Report 2009-16, Department of Computer Science, UCSB (2009)

A Logic of Privacy

Steve Barker[1] and Valerio Genovese[2,3]

[1] Dept Computer Science, King's College London
[2] Dept Computer Science University of Luxembourg
[3] Dipartimento di Informatica University of Torino

Abstract. We consider the problem of developing an abstract meta-model of access control in terms of which policies for protecting a principal's private information may be specified. Our concern is with developing the formal foundations of our conceptual model. For both the specific access control models and privacy policies, which may be defined in terms of the meta-model, we adopt a combining approach: we combine access control concepts to form the meta-model and we use a fibred logic for the formal foundations. Our approach enables data subjects to specify flexibly what access controls they wish to apply on their personal data and it provides a formal foundation for policies that are defined in terms of the meta-model.

1 Introduction

For several emerging applications there is a requirement that individual entities be able to choose flexibly what of their data should be accessible to whom, for what purpose, and in what circumstances. As a simple example, an entity may wish to control the release of its history of purchasing, that is held by e-traders, to telemarketers of an e-trader's choosing. The idea of entities having more control over the release of their information has been recognized, in general terms, by Westin [1] and for particular technologies [2] and applications [3].

An important research question applies: how can entities be provided with a formally well-founded framework for defining flexibly the privacy policies that they wish to apply on access to *their* data?

The problem of helping to preserve the privacy of an entity's personal data has recently received attention (see, for example, the work on P3P [4], EPAL [5], Hippocratic databases [6], and XACML [7]). Moreover, researchers in the access control community have proposed various "privacy-aware" access control models (see, for example, the work on P-RBAC [8,9]). Although these approaches allow data subjects to express some controls on access to their personal information, we argue that, to differing extents, they do not provide sufficient expressive power for individually tailored privacy policies, they fail to accommodate adequately some important concepts (e.g., trust and delegation), and, they lack adequate formal foundations. The work by Barth et al. [10] avoids some of the shortcomings of existing proposals on privacy management. Specifically, Barth et al. adopt a well-defined conceptual basis (*contextual integrity*) and they develop a sound formal basis (from temporal logic and the *Logic of Privacy and*

S. Foresti and S. Jajodia (Eds.): Data and Applications Security XXIV, LNCS 6166, pp. 17–32, 2010.

Utility (LPU)) in terms of which a range of privacy policies may be grounded. We adopt a similar methodological position to Barth et al., but we propose a different conceptual base and different logical foundations, which we will argue have certain attractions.

The principal contribution described in this paper is the proposal of a methodology for specializing access control models for privacy purposes and the development of a formal language and semantics for privacy policies that is based on fibred logic [11]. Specifically, we propose a fibred logic formulation of our meta-model of access control, $\mathcal{M}$, from [12]; we denote the privacy-enhanced form of $\mathcal{M}$ by $\mathcal{M}^P$ (where P stands for "privacy"). We demonstrate how privacy-enhanced access control policies may be derived from $\mathcal{M}^P$ by specializing and combining the relations and logical axioms that we introduce to define this meta-model. Our main objective is to extend the notion of category, first introduced by us in [12], to allow categories to be defined using arbitrary logical formulas that may be expressed in a variety of logic languages (e.g., first-order logic, intuitionistic logic, ... and even SQL). For this, we need to develop formal foundations that are quite different to those described in [12]. Specifically, we describe a variant of predicate Fibred Logic and an enhanced form of our Fibred Security Language (FSL) [13], which enables us to use a range of modalities in representations of privacy policies that are derived from our meta-model.

Although we recognize their importance in privacy-enhanced access control, due to space constraints, we will not consider obligations, audit policies, and hierarchies of objects or of purposes. We assume that data is stored and transmitted securely and that sound methods for the authentication of data subjects, controllers and recipients are employed.

The remainder of the discussion is organized in the following way. In Section 2, we describe the basic syntactic notions on which our approach is based. In Section 3, we present details on our privacy logic. In Section 4, we formally describe the core relations and axioms of the meta-model that we specialize for privacy and which can be specialized in multiple ways for different, specific privacy-enhanced access control models and policies. In Section 5, we show how privacy-enhanced access control policies can be represented in terms of our meta-model, by specializing and combining the relations and axioms that the meta-model includes. In Section 6, we discuss related work. In Section 7, conclusions are drawn and further work is suggested.

2   Language Issues and FSL

In this section, we describe the language for formulating the meta-model and specialized instances of it. We only describe the basic syntax and semantic notions (the minimum details to make the paper self-contained).

The key sets of constants in the universe of discourse that we admit are as follows: -A countable set $\mathcal{C}$ of categories, where c_0, c_1, ... are used to denote arbitrary category identifiers. -A countable set $\mathcal{K}_{ds}$ of data subjects and a countable set of K_{du} of data users (requesters for access) where κ_0, κ_1, ... are used for (key) identification. -A countable set $\mathcal{A}$ of named atomic *actions*, where a_0, a_1, ... are used to denote arbitrary action identifiers. -A countable set $\mathcal{R}$ of *resource identifiers*, where r_0, r_1, ... denote arbitrary resources, $r(t_1, \ldots, t_n)$ is an arbitrary n-place relation and t_i $(1 \leq i \leq n)$ is a term, a function, a constant or a variable. -A countable set $\mathcal{P}$ of *purposes*, where p_0, p_1, ... are used to denote arbitrary purpose identifiers. -A countable set of meta-policy identifiers; for example, c (for closed policies), o (for open policies), do (for a denials override policy), ... -A countable set $\mathcal{T}$ of *time points*, $\tau_0, \tau_1, \ldots$ -A countable set $\mathcal{E}$ of *event identifiers*, $e_0, e_1, \ldots$

A major difference to the work in [12] is to change the notion of category, the most fundamental element in our ontology. In [12], a category is used as a proper name to simply refer to a category of entities; the term category being interpreted as "being synonymous with, for example, a type, a sort, a class, a division, a domain." In this paper, category is not merely a proper name; it is a viewed as a well-formed logical formula (that may be expressed in first-order, modal, intuitionistic, ... terms) that defines the membership of the category. The reader is referred to [12] for a fuller account of our original notion of category and for its comparison with the work we describe in this paper.

The notion of purpose is also key in privacy; data subjects must be able to specify what of their personal data may be stored by a data controller and for what purposes this personal data may be used by requesters of access to the data. We discuss our interpretation of purpose more fully below. Two special time points will be important in our treatment: 0 denotes the start of time and ∞ is an arbitrary maximal future time. We assume that various comparison operators exist on times $\{<, \leq, \geq, >\}$, with their usual interpretation e.g., $t_1 \leq t_2$ iff time point t_1 is earlier than or the same time point as t_2. Although we refer to time points, the approach that we describe enables various temporal frameworks to be accommodated (by combining temporal logics). Times and events allow us to provide a degree of dynamacy in the framework that we develop.

In the formulation of the rules that we will use to represent access control models and policies, variables will appear in the upper case and constants in the lower case. The only exception to this will be when we use (lower-case) x and y to refer specifically to types of categories.

As the access control logic that we propose is intended for use in distributed scenarios, we need to be able to express delegation among principals. Our logic is therefore centered, like the access control logics of [14] and [15], on formulas such as "A **says** s" where A represents a principal, s represents a statement (a request, a delegation of authority, or some other utterance), and **says** is a modality. It is important to note that it is possible to derive that A **says** s even when A does not directly utter s. For example, when the principal A is a user and one of its programs includes s in a message, then we may have A says s, if the program has been delegated by A. In this case, A says s means that A has caused s to be said, that s has been said on A's behalf, or that A supports s.

We assume that such assertions are understood by a reference monitor in charge of making decisions on access to a resource r. The reference monitor may implement the policy that a particular data requester A is authorized to perform action a on resource r that contains "private data". This policy may be represented by the formula: $(A$ says $do\_on(a, r)) \rightarrow do\_on(a, r)$, which expresses that A **controls** $do\_on(a, r)$.[1] Similarly, a request for the operation a on r from a principal B may be represented by the formula: B says $do\_on(a, r)$. The goal of the reference monitor is to prove that these two formulas imply $do\_on(a, r)$, and to grant access if the implication can be demonstrated. While proving $do\_on(a, r)$, the reference monitor does not need to prove that the principal B controls $do\_on(a, r)$. Rather, it may exploit relations between A and B and certain other facts. For example, the reference monitor may know that B has been delegated by A, and, thus, that B speaks for A as concerns $do\_on(a, r)$:

$$(B \text{ says } do\_on(a, r)) \rightarrow (A \text{ says } do\_on(a, r))$$

3   An Axiomatization of Privacy

Having introduced the basic language details in the previous section, we now describe the details of the logic language that we use for representing privacy-enhanced access control models and policies.

Our logic is based on a variant of the work described in [16] and extends FSL by adding a privacy context modality, where $[p]\varphi$ has the reading:

"φ holds under the purpose p".

P-FSL formulas are expressed in the following way:

Definition 1 (P-FSL).

$$\varphi ::= F(x_1, \ldots, x_n) \mid \neg\varphi \mid \varphi \vee \varphi \mid \varphi \wedge \varphi \mid \varphi \rightarrow \varphi \mid \varphi(x) \text{ says } \varphi \mid [p]\varphi \mid \rho(\varphi(x), \psi(y))$$

The expression, $\varphi(x)$ says ψ should be read as: "The group composed of all of the principals that satisfy $\varphi(x)$ *supports* the assertion *assert* ψ". In this view, the ρ operator describes a general relationship between groups. In line with [17], we write $\varphi(x)$ **controls** ψ as shorthand for $(\varphi(x)$ says $\psi) \rightarrow \psi$.

Definition 2 (Axiomatization). *The axiomatization consists of all axioms of intuitionistic propositional logic plus axioms and rules for the* **says** *modality.*

All axioms and rules of First-Order Logic	*(FOL)*
If $\vdash \psi$ then $\vdash \varphi(x)$ says ψ	*(N)*
$\vdash \varphi(x)$ says $(\psi \rightarrow \psi') \rightarrow$	
$(\varphi(x)$ says $\psi \rightarrow \varphi(x)$ says $\psi')$	*(K)*
$\vdash \forall x(\varphi_1(x) \leftrightarrow \varphi_2(x)) \rightarrow$	
$(\varphi_1(x)$ says $\psi \leftrightarrow \varphi_2(x)$ says $\psi)$	*(Ex)*
$\vdash (\psi \rightarrow \psi') \rightarrow \varphi(x)$ says $\psi \rightarrow \varphi(x)$ says ψ'	*(Md)*
If $\vdash \psi$ then $\vdash [p]\psi$	*(N^p)*
$\vdash [p]\varphi \rightarrow [q][p]\varphi$	*(4^{p,q})*
$\vdash [p](\psi \rightarrow \psi') \rightarrow [p]\psi \rightarrow [p]\psi'$	*(K^p)*
$\vdash \forall x(\varphi_1(x) \leftrightarrow \varphi_2(x)) \rightarrow \rho(\varphi_1(x), \varphi_2(x))$	*(ρ)*

---

[1] In this view. with A **controls** ψ we express that A has a direct permission to do ψ.

Notice that the (ρ) axiom states that the relation ρ is reflexive, i.e., if two formulas φ_1 and φ_2 describe the same group then they are in relation w.r.t. ρ.

Definition 3. *A first-order P-FSL constant domain model is a tuple* $\mathcal{M} = \langle W, N, D, \theta, I \rangle$ *where:*

- D *is a non-empty set, called the* **domain**[2].
- W *is a set of states.*
- $N : W \times \mathcal{P}(D) \rightarrow \mathcal{P}(\mathcal{P}(W))$ *is a neighborhood function that given a state s and a set of principals T, it associates a family of sets of states (called neighborhoods). The intuition is that at each state $N(w,T)$ is the set of propositions, (i.e. the set of states), that are supported by the group of principals T.*
- $\theta : P \rightarrow \mathcal{P}(W)$ *is a mapping from purposes to a subset of states. We say that that $P' \in \theta(p)$ is the set of states that must be considered in the context of purpose p.*
- I *is a classical first-order interpretation function where for each n-ary predicate symbol F and each state w, $I(F,w) \subseteq D^n$.*

We require the neighborhood function N to satisfy the following properties:

(a) If $X \in N(w,T)$ and $X \subseteq Y$, then $Y \in N(w,T)$
(b) If $X \in N(w,T)$ and $Y \in N(w,T)$, then $X \cap Y \in N(w,T)$
(c) $W \in N(w,T)$

Intuitively, given a set of principals $T \subseteq D$, $N(w,T)$ is the set of propositions (i.e., the set of states), that T supports at state w. As shown in [18], conditions (a), (b) and (c) ensure that **says** is a normal modality (i.e., validates axiom K).

The satisfaction relation $\models$ is inductively defined in terms of an *interpretation* $\mathcal{M}, w$ and a valuation σ, which assigns objects to individual variables.

- $\mathcal{M}, w \models_\sigma F(x_1, \ldots, x_n)$ iff $\langle \sigma(x_1), \ldots, \sigma(x_n) \rangle \in I(F,w)$ for each n-place predicate symbol.
- $\mathcal{M}, w \models_\sigma \neg\varphi$ iff $\mathcal{M}, w \not\models_\sigma \varphi$
- $\mathcal{M}, w \models_\sigma \varphi \vee \psi$ iff $\mathcal{M}, w \models_\sigma \varphi$ or $\mathcal{M}, w \models_\sigma \psi$.
- $\mathcal{M}, w \models_\sigma \varphi \wedge \psi$ iff $\mathcal{M}, w \models_\sigma \varphi$ and $\mathcal{M}, w \models_\sigma \psi$
- $\mathcal{M}, w \models_\sigma \varphi \rightarrow \psi$ iff $\mathcal{M}, w \models_\sigma \varphi$ implies $\mathcal{M}, w \models_\sigma \psi$
- $\mathcal{M}, w \models_\sigma \forall x \varphi$ iff for every element $d \in D$ we have $\mathcal{M}, w \models_{\sigma[d/x]} \varphi$
- $\mathcal{M}, w \models_\sigma \varphi(x)$ says ψ iff $(\varphi)^{\mathcal{M},\sigma} \in N(w,U)$, where $U = \{d \in D \mid \mathcal{M}, w \models_{\sigma[d/x]} \varphi(x)\}$
- $\mathcal{M}, w \models_\sigma [p]\varphi$ iff for all $t \in \Theta(p)$, $\mathcal{M}, t \models \varphi$
- $\mathcal{M}, w \models \rho(\varphi(x), \psi(y))$ iff $\langle U, U' \rangle \in I(\rho, w)$, where $U = \{d \in D \mid \mathcal{M}, w \models_{\sigma[d/x]} \varphi(x)\}$ and $U' = \{d \in D \mid \mathcal{M}, w \models_{\sigma[d/y]} \psi(y)\}$

---

[2] For the sake of readability we identify the domain as the set of all principals, if needed P-FSL can be easily extended to cope with different sorts (e.g., principals, time points, purposes, ...).

When it is clear from the context, we will omit σ as index of $\models$. A formula φ is true in a model $\mathcal{M}$ ($\mathcal{M} \models \varphi$) if, for every state w, $\mathcal{M}, w \models \varphi$. A formula is valid ($\models \varphi$) if it is true in all models. A formula φ is a logical consequence of a set of formulae $\Gamma = \{\gamma_1, \ldots, \gamma_n\}$ ($\Gamma \models \varphi$), if for every $\mathcal{M}, w$ $\mathcal{M}, w \models \bigwedge_{1 \leq i \leq n} \gamma_i$ implies $\mathcal{M}, w \models \varphi$.

Theorem 1 (Soundness of P-FSL Axiomatization). *Every theorem deducible from the axiomatic proof system of Definition 2 is valid with respect to the semantics.*

$$\text{If } \vdash \varphi \text{ then } \models \varphi$$

Proof. By cases on axioms and rules of P-FSL.

It should be noted that P-FSL is, in its full generality, undecidable because it is a extension of first-order modal logic (albeit a conservative one). P-FSL must be understood as providing a general formal framework for studying abstract access control models and, in our case, privacy-enhanced access control models. The undecidability of the logic stems from its high expressive power. However, in relation to access control in practice, many of the features that make first-order logic undecidable are not necessary, like infinite domains, unlimited quantification or an unlimited number of free variables in formulas. As we will see, the expressivity needed to interpret the relations of the abstract access control model $\mathcal{M}^P$ is a restriction of first-order modal logic in which we do not have explicit quantification and formulas have at most one free variable. In [19], the above mentioned restriction is shown to be decidable. More generally, the language of first-order modal logic with two variables (without any restriction on quantification) is decidable with polynomial time complexity with respect to satisfiability.

4   The Model $\mathcal{M}^P$

In the previous section, we established the basic language and axiomatic details. We now consider the specific details that are required for our general meta-model for privacy-enhanced access control and its representation in P-FSL. We wish to accommodate data subjects, data controllers, denials of access, an interpretation of purpose, contextual accessibility criteria and the flexible specification of permitted recipients of a data subject's personal data. For that, the following core relations are included in our meta-model, $\mathcal{M}^P$: -$\mathcal{PCA}$, a 4-ary relation, $\mathcal{K}_{ds} \times \mathcal{K}_{du} \times \mathcal{C} \times \mathcal{P}$. -$\mathcal{ARCA}$, a 5-ary relation, $\mathcal{K}_{ds} \times \mathcal{A} \times \mathcal{R} \times \mathcal{C} \times \mathcal{P}$. -$\mathcal{ARCD}$, a 5-ary relation, $\mathcal{K}_{ds} \times \mathcal{A} \times \mathcal{R} \times \mathcal{C} \times \mathcal{P}$. -$\mathcal{PAR}$, a 3-ary relation, $\mathcal{K}_{du} \times \mathcal{A} \times \mathcal{R}$. -$\mathcal{PRM}$, a 3-ary relation, $\mathcal{K}_{ds} \times \mathcal{R} \times \mathcal{MP}$.

The (informal) semantics of the n-ary tuples in $\mathcal{PCA}$, $\mathcal{ARCA}$, $\mathcal{ARCD}$, $\mathcal{PAR}$, and $\mathcal{PRM}$ are, respectively, defined thus: $(\kappa_{ds}, \kappa_{du}, c, p) \in \mathcal{PCA}$ iff a data user $\kappa_{du} \in \mathcal{K}_{du}$ is assigned to the category $c \in \mathcal{C}$ for the purpose $p \in \mathcal{P}$ according to the data subject κ_{ds}. $(\kappa_{ds}, a, r, c, p) \in \mathcal{ARCA}$ iff the permission (a, r) is assigned to the category $c \in \mathcal{C}$ for the purpose $p \in \mathcal{P}$ according to the data subject κ_{ds}. $(\kappa_{ds}, a, r, c, p) \in \mathcal{ARCD}$ iff a the permission (a, r) is denied to the category $c \in \mathcal{C}$

for the purpose $p \in \mathcal{P}$ according to the data subject κ_{ds}. $(\kappa_{du}, a, r) \in \mathcal{PAR}$ iff a data user $\kappa_{du} \in \mathcal{K}_{du}$ is authorized to perform the action $a \in \mathcal{A}$ on the resource $r \in \mathcal{R}$. $(\kappa_{ds}, r, m) \in \mathcal{PRM}$ iff the data subject κ_{ds} "controls" access to the resource $r \in \mathcal{R}$ and κ_{ds} asserts that the meta-policy $m \in \mathcal{MP}$ applies to access on the resource r.

The semantics of the *pca*, *arca*, *arcd* and *prm* relations can be formally defined in P-FSL via the "says" operator [17] (where $\leftrightarrow$ is "is equivalent to").

- $\models k_{ds}$ says $([p]\varphi_c(k_{du})) \leftrightarrow (k_{ds}, k_{du}, c, p) \in \mathcal{PCA}$
- $\models k_{ds}$ says $([p](\varphi_c(x) \textbf{ controls } do\_on(a, r))) \leftrightarrow (k_{ds}, a, r, c, p) \in \mathcal{ARCA}$
- $\models k_{ds}$ says $([p](\neg(\varphi_c(x) \textbf{ controls } do\_on(a, r)))) \leftrightarrow (k_{ds}, a, r, c, p) \in \mathcal{ARCD}$
- $\models k_{du} \textbf{ controls } do\_on(a, r) \leftrightarrow (k_{du}, a, r) \in \mathcal{PAR}$
- $\models prm(k_{ds}, r, m) \leftrightarrow (k_{ds}, r, m) \in \mathcal{PRM}$

Here, $\varphi_c(x)$ is intended to be the P-FSL formula with one free variable x that maps category c in the meta-model $\mathcal{M}^P$. In the above mapping, most of the relations of $\mathcal{M}^P$ (with the exception of *prm*) are interpreted over *says* and *controls* operators. In relation to [12], we extend the notion of categories from constants to first-order formulas that identify a collection of principals.[3] Notice also that, by viewing purposes as modal contexts, we can map entire formulas under a specific purpose because in the wff $[p]\varphi$, φ can be *anything*, not just a relation. For instance, delegation may be expressed under a specific purpose $[p](bob$ says $\psi \rightarrow admin$ says $\psi)$.

In what follows, the reader is reminded that variables in rules appear in the upper case and are implicitly universally quantified; constants are in the lower case.

The elements in the set $\mathcal{PAR}$ are defined in terms of $\mathcal{PRM}$, $\mathcal{PCA}$, and a specification of a particular meta-policy m, which itself is defined with respect to $\mathcal{ARCA}$ or $\mathcal{ARCD}$. In P-FSL, the rules defining *par* for different meta-policies (closed (c), open (o), and denials-override (do)) are:

$prm(\kappa_{ds}, R, c) \wedge (\kappa_{ds}$ says $[P]C(\kappa_{du})) \wedge$
$(\kappa_{ds}$ says $[P]C(x) \textbf{ controls } do\_on(A, R)) \rightarrow \kappa_{du} \textbf{ controls } do\_on(A, R)$.
$prm(\kappa_{ds}, R, o) \wedge (\kappa_{ds}$ says $[P]C(\kappa_{du})) \wedge$
$\neg(\kappa_{ds}$ says $\neg[P](C(x) \textbf{ controls } do\_on(A, R))) \rightarrow \kappa_{du} \textbf{ controls } do\_on(a, r)$.
$prm(\kappa_{ds}, R, do) \wedge (\kappa_{ds}$ says $[P]C(\kappa_{ds}) \textbf{ controls } do\_on(A, R)) \wedge$
$\neg(\kappa_{ds}$ says $\neg[P](C(x) \textbf{ controls } do\_on(A, R))) \rightarrow \kappa_{du} \textbf{ controls } do\_on(a, r)$.

The above rules should be read as *axiom schemas* that hold for every formula φ representing a category. In this view the upper case in $C(x)$ stands for a second-order quantification (i.e., over formulas).

For representing hierarchies of categories in our meta-model, the following definition is included as part of the axiomatization of the model (where '_' denotes an anonymous variable and *dc* is a "directly contains" relation cf. [12]):

---

[3] As shown in [13], by viewing categories as types we can generalize roles (as in RT) as special instances of categories.

$$dc(C, \_) \rightarrow \rho(C, C).$$
$$dc(\_, C) \rightarrow \rho(C, C).$$
$$dc(C', C'') \rightarrow \rho(C', C'').$$
$$dc(C', C''') \wedge \rho(C''', C'') \rightarrow \rho(C', C'').$$

Authorizations may be defined, quite generally, thus (the meta-policy here being closed, as denoted by c where c is short for "closed" policy):

$$prm(K_{ds}, R, c) \wedge K_{ds} \text{ says } C(K_{du}) \wedge \rho(C, C') \wedge$$
$$K_{ds} \text{ says } [C(x) \textbf{ controls } do\_on(A, R)] \rightarrow K_{du} \text{ says } do\_on(A, R)$$

That is, a data user (requester) K_{du} has A access on resource R if a data subject K_{ds}, which controls access to personal data, says that K_{du} is assigned to a category C that inherits the A privilege on R, to which a closed meta-policy on access applies, from a category C' such that $\rho(C, C')$ holds i.e., C is "senior to" C' in a partial ordering of categories.

The careful reader will have noted that what we are defining is a general logic for a family of privacy-enhanced access control models that may be derived from $\mathcal{M}^P$. The meta-model $\mathcal{M}^P$ may be specialized in multiple ways by, for instance, a policy author admitting different or additional sorts (e.g., times) in the relations from our core set, to allow for specific requirements to be met. On this point, it is important to note that, for our definition of $\mathcal{PAR}$, existential quantification on purposes is important; rather than having a purpose sort as part of the definition of authorization, as in the case of purpose-based access control as that term is interpreted in [20], we treat purpose existentially. On this interpretation, purpose specifications are relevant only in terms of the relationship between a data subject and a data controller: the data subject decides what of its data may be released by the data controller for what purpose. A requester K_{du} has A access on R if for *some* purpose K_{du} has A access on R as a consequence of there being a requester-category assignment and a permission-category assignment that implies that this authorization should hold. Of course, a policy author may instead require a data requester to state explicitly the purpose for the access (cf. the notion of intended purpose from [20]). In that case, a purpose parameter may be added to the *par* relation. The explicit specification of purpose implicitly eliminates the existential quantification that the 3-place form of *par* assumes. The different options available to the policy author reflect the different positions the policy author may adopt on, for example, the interpretation of purpose (e.g., whether the purpose of a request is an intention in the mind of the requester that need not be made explicit), what epistemic commitments are required of the requester (e.g., are requester's required to know for what specific purposes a specific data subject has allowed a specific action to be performed on a specific resource that they control access to), etc. Our formulation is based on what we perceive to be a minimal collection of useful relations where by minimal we mean minimal in terms of the arity of relations as well as their number. As previously stated, a policy author is expected to specialize the meta-model as required.

It must also be noted that a data subject may also be free to decide what specific variant of *par*, and other core relations of $\mathcal{M}^P$, are to be used to access their data. Compelling data subjects to use a particular form of *par* runs counter to our intention of allowing data subjects to define the controls applicable to their data and compelling policy authors to use a particular interpretation of $\mathcal{M}^P$ would be counter to the methodological position that we have argued for.

Constraints on categories may also be flexibly specified in terms of the core predicates of our meta-model and are expressed in P-FSL as statements of the following general form (where $\perp$ read as "is inconsistent" and $c \in \mathcal{C}$ and $c' \in \mathcal{C}$ are constants that denote specific categories): $\varphi_c(P) \wedge \varphi_{c'}(P) \to \perp$. For example, the constraint

$$K_{ds} \text{ says } [P]\varphi_c(K_{du}) \ \wedge \ K_{ds} \text{ says } [P']\varphi_c(K_{du}) \ \wedge \ P \neq P' \to \perp.$$
$$K_{ds} \text{ says } [P](\varphi_c(x) \text{ \textbf{controls} } do\_on(write, r)) \ \wedge$$
$$K_{ds} \text{ says } [P](\varphi_c(x) \text{ \textbf{controls} } do\_on(write, r')) \to \perp.$$

represents that exactly one data user K_{du} may be assigned by a data subject K_{ds} to a category c for a specific purpose (a "separation of categories" constraint) and that *write* privilege on the pair of resources (r, r') is impossible for all categories of data subjects and for all purposes (a "separation of privileges" constraint).

Particular privacy-enhanced access control models can be (and are expected to be) defined within the general axiomatic framework that we have described by specializing predicates and axioms. For example, to accommodate purpose with subject-specified access controls in status-based access control [21], the axioms of $\mathcal{M}^P$ may be simply specialized thus (with the above definition of ρ assumed, with E denoting an event, with C in this case being a category that combines ascribed and action statuses, and with definitions of *pca_init* and *pca_term* omitted):

$$C(P) \wedge \rho(C(x), C'(y)) \ \wedge C'(y) \text{ \textbf{controls} } do\_on(A, R) \to P \text{ \textbf{controls} } do\_on(A, R).$$
$$current\_time(T) \wedge happens(E, T_s) \ \wedge agent(E, P) \ \wedge \ act(E, A) \wedge T_s < T \ \wedge$$
$$pca\_init(E, P, A, C, T_s, T) \ \wedge \ \neg ended\_pca(P, C, T_s, T) \to C(P).$$
$$happens(E', T') \wedge agent(E', P) \ \wedge \ act(E', A') \ \wedge \ T_s < T' \wedge T' \leq T \ \wedge$$
$$pca\_term(E', P, A', C, T_s, T) \ \to \ ended\_pca(P, C, T_s, T).$$

5 Privacy Policies in $\mathcal{M}^P$ by P-FSL

In the previous section, we gave an axiomatization of a general class of "privacy enhanced" access control models. In this section, we consider the representation of privacy-enhanced access control policies by specialization and combination of the core relations and axioms of $\mathcal{M}^P$, which can also be multiply interpreted.

We first introduce an additional technical component: annotated rules. An annotated rule φ, which is used by a data controller in the *specification* of a policy, may be annotated with Δ to represent that a data subject is permitted by the controller to delete or modify φ; the annotation $\neg\Delta$ is used to specify that φ cannot be changed by a data subject in an access policy. In the latter case, a data subject κ_{ds} is still free to insert rules of κ_{ds}'s choosing, but, not surprisingly, only for data that refers to κ_{ds}. Annotations of elements other than rules (e.g., terms) are possible but we omit the details on this. It is also important to note that, as we are concerned about access controls on a data subject's personal data, we assume that the information resource to be accessed by data requesters will contain a personal identifier of a data subject to which the data refers.

The first example that we give is of privacy policy formulation in P-FSL that relates to medical informatics scenario.

Example 1. Consider the following policy of the Virginia Hospital Center (VHC) on the confidentiality of patient data:

> *For the purposes of operating on a patient, the patient's full medical history, which includes the patient's identifier, name, date-of-birth, and history of illnesses, can be seen by any member of the category surgeon (sur) for the purpose of operating (op). The patient's identifier, name, date of birth and diagnosed illnesses in the past six months may be disclosed to the category of non-surgical staff (nss) for the purpose of providing diagnostic support (ds). The pca definitions used by VHC are defined non-locally at v_1. A closed access control policy is to apply to the release of all data. The access control policy as it relates to data subjects generally is maintained by the VHC administrator denoted by κ_c.*

Suppose that the databases used by VHC include an 8-place relation *pat* (where *pat* is short for patient) that is defined at v_2 and includes details of the patient's identifier, the patient's name, date of birth, illness, room number (at the hospital), contact number (at the hospital), time of admittance and time of discharge:

$$pat(Id, Name, DoB, Illness, Rm, Pno, Admit, Discharge).$$

To represent their requirements, VHC's policy on the release of patient information may be represented as a privacy policy, which is simply derived from the $\mathcal{M}^P$ model, thus (where *sct* is short for system clock time):

$\neg\Delta : v_1$ says $(\kappa_c$ says $[P]C(K_{du}) \rightarrow \kappa_c$ says $[P]C(K_{du}))$.
$\neg\Delta : v_2$ says $pat(K_{ds}, V, W, X, Y, Z, T1, T2) \wedge sct(T) \wedge T1 \geq 0 \wedge T \leq \infty \rightarrow$
        κ_c says $[op](sur(x)$ **controls** $do\_on(read, pat(K_{ds}, V, W, X, Y, Z, T1, T2)))$.
$\neg\Delta : v_2$ says $pat(K_{ds}, V, W, X, Y, Z, T1, T2) \wedge sct(T) \wedge month(T, M)$
                                            $\wedge\ month(T1, M1) \wedge M1 \geq M - 6 \rightarrow$
        κ_c says $[ds](nss(x)$ **controls** $do\_on(read, pat(K_{ds}, V, W, X, \_, \_, \_, \_)))$.
$\neg\Delta : prm(K_{ds}, R, c) \wedge K_{ds}$ says $[P]C(K_{du}) \wedge$
K_{ds} says $[P](C(x)$ **controls** $do\_on(read, R)) \rightarrow K_{du}$ **controls** $do\_on(read, R)$.

From the example above, it should be noted that κ_c is the controller of VHC's privacy policy. If any data subject were to have the freedom to change VHC's policy then the data subject could deny access to data users that need to have information on the data subject in order to perform an action of benefit to the data subject (e.g., diagnosing a patient's illness). Nevertheless, the data subject does have the freedom to add to VHC's privacy policy specification in order to represent personal requirements on the release of their data. The next example demonstrates this.

Example 2. Consider the wishes of the individual patient κ_β in relation to VHC's policy on the disclosure of patient information:

> *I agree to the hospital's policy on the release of my personal information for the purpose of operating. However, I also wish some of this information to be accessible to the category of data users that I call family. Specifically, the category family is defined by me (non-locally) at v_3 and I want members of family to be able to access (and only access) my name, bedside phone number, and room number for the purpose of contacting me while I am in hospital (a purpose that I denote by ct, as shorthand for contact).*

To capture κ_β's individual access control requirements, κ_β adds the following definitions:

$$prm(\kappa_\beta, pat(\kappa_\beta, V, W, X, Y, Z, T1, T2), c).$$
$$v_2 \text{ says } pat(\kappa_\beta, V, W, X, Y, Z, T1, T2) \rightarrow$$
$$\kappa_\beta \text{ says } [ct]family(x) \text{ } \mathbf{controls} \text{ } do\_on(read, pat(\kappa_\beta, V, \_, \_, Y, Z, \_, \_)).$$

κ_β then adds the following *pca* definition to VHC's policy to express his required access controls applicable to his family contacts (where f_mbr is short for "family member"):

$$v_3 \text{ says } (f\_mbr(\kappa_\beta, K_{du}) \rightarrow \kappa_\beta \text{ says } [ct]family(K_{du}))$$

Consider next an example of our approach for privacy policy formulation in the context of an e-commerce scenario.

Example 3. Suppose that *ACo* are an on-line trading company that specify the following policy on the confidentiality of customer transaction data that they hold:

> *Our preferred policy is to store a complete history of each customer's purchase transactions (the items bought, the number bought and when); we retain this information indefinitely and make it available at all times to suppliers of our choosing for the purpose of future marketing (f_mkt). Any company that we call a supplier is assigned to the category that we call sup. We assign suppliers, for the purpose f_mkt, from the time at which the supplier is first approved by us. A closed meta-policy is to apply on all forms of data release by default.*

The databases that are used by *ACo* include a 3-place relation *sp* (short for suppliers), and a history of customer transactions is recorded in a 4-place relation, *tr* (short for transactions):

$$sp(SupId, Name, From). \text{ } tr(CustId, Item, Number, Purchase\_Time).$$

We assume that the definitions of predicates in *sp* and *tr* are, respectively, found at v_6, and v_7. The *pca*, *arca* and *prm* definitions are assumed to be stored locally.

To define their access policy on the release of a customer's personal data, ACo can express their requirements in P-FSL thus:

$\Delta : v_6$ says $sp(K_{du}, N, T1) \wedge sct(T) \wedge T1 \leq T \rightarrow (\kappa_c$ says $[f\_mkt]sup(K_{du}))$.
$\Delta : v_7$ says $tr(K_{ds}, X, N, Z) \wedge sct(T) \wedge T \geq 0 \wedge T \leq \infty \rightarrow$
$\qquad\qquad \kappa_c$ says $[f\_mkt](sup(x)$ **controls** $do\_on(read, tr(K_{ds}, Y, N, Z)))$.
$\Delta : subject(K_{ds}) \wedge K_{ds} \neq K_{du} \wedge \neg prm(K_{ds}, tr(K_{ds}, Y, N, Z), c) \rightarrow$
$\qquad\qquad\qquad\qquad\qquad\qquad\qquad prm(\kappa_c, tr(K_{ds}, Y, N, Z), c)$.
$\Delta : prm(K_{ds}, R, c) \wedge K_{ds}$ says $[P]C(K_{du}) \wedge$
K_{ds} says $[P](C(x)$ **controls** $do\_on(read, R)) \rightarrow K_{du}$ **controls** $do\_on(read, R)$.

Next, suppose that κ_ϕ is a customer with ACo and prefers to define its own access controls on its transaction history. On that, suppose that the following access policy issues arise for κ_ϕ on the confidentiality and use of its data that is held by ACo:

> *I will allow my purchase history to be accessed but only by your suppliers that I have recorded as having a status of pr for "premium". My purchase history can only be released to suppliers of yours that satisfy my principals that I categorize as pr, I will only allow access to my transaction data as it relates to the purchase of nuts and the number of nuts bought by me (as I am only interested in nut-related purchases and data users may want to know if I am a "major purchaser"). Moreover, I do not want any release of my transaction data to any supplier for f_mkt purposes if my stock level of nuts, as recorded in stock(item, quantity) at v_{50}, is greater than 100 units and I will only release my transaction history since 2009/01/01 and only until 2010/03/31 (after which time I will not be making any nut-related purchases so there is no reason for my data to be accessible to any external recipients after this time).*

Assuming that the binary relation $status$ is stored at v_8 (and is used to map users to statuses, like pr), to represent the requirements, κ_ϕ's specialization of ACo's privacy-enhanced policy can be represented thus:

κ_c says $[f\_mkt]sup(K_{du}) \wedge v_8$ says $st(K_{du}, pr) \rightarrow \kappa_\phi$ says $[f\_mkt]sup(K_{du})$.
v_7 says $tr(\kappa_\phi, nut, N, T) \wedge T \geq 20090101 \wedge T \leq 20100331 \wedge$
v_{50} says $stock(nut, Q) \wedge Q > 100 \rightarrow$
κ_ϕ says $[f\_mkt](sup(x)$ **controls** $do\_on(read, tr(\kappa_\phi, nut, N, \_)))$.
$prm(\kappa_\phi, tr(\kappa_\phi, Y, N, Z), c)$.

It should be noted from the example above that temporal accessibility constraints and the conditions on access that are defined in terms of notions like stock levels allow for dynamic privacy-enhanced policies to be formulated by κ_ϕ on the release and use of its personal data. Hence, privacy-enhanced policies can change automatically in response to events and without requiring explicit policy modification. Moreover, κ_ϕ freely specifies the sources of access control information *of its choosing* to define allowed forms of access to *its data* (cf. the use of $st/2$ for status).

6   Related Work

The work that we have discussed in this paper is related to that described in [12]. In [12], a formalization of category-based access control is given in terms of identification-based logic programs, which extend the expressive power of the logic programs used in the Flexible Authorization Framework [22] and conceptual notions (e.g., by introducing the notion of category as a generalization of "role" and allowing for distributed trust management). The logic language that we describe in this paper allows for categories that may be defined by formulas in multiple logic languages (including logic programming languages). Our approach differs from [12] in terms of its focus on privacy enhancement in meta-model terms and to both [22] and [12] in that we adopt a combining logic approach and a richer combining model/policy approach.

Issues in privacy policy management have been addressed in the work on P3P [4], EPAL [5], and Hippocratic databases [6]. However, each of these approaches is a particular approach. In contrast, we derive particular cases from the generality of our approach (as we showed by demonstrating how a range of instances of $\mathcal{M}^P$ may be developed as models or policies that can be formulated in P-FSL). P-RBAC [8] also has the attraction of combining access control and privacy as we do. Nevertheless, it is our view that enhancing a *particular* form of access control model for personal data protection, RBAC in the case of P-RBAC, introduces a problem that is common in existing work: the problem of unduly constraining the control that individual data subjects have for managing access to their data. Even though the notion of "role" can be given a quite general interpretation, "role" remains a particular instance of the more general notion of category [12] and category, being more general than "role", offers greater flexibility to data subjects defining access controls on their data. Similarly, although Fischer-Hubner's task-based privacy-oriented access control model [23] is a useful contribution to the literature on access controls on personal data, our approach differs significantly, not least by focusing on a meta-model of access control from which an axiomatic base can be developed that allows for specific models and policies to be derived as particular instances. The work by Byun et al. [20] on Purpose-based Access Control is related to ours in that a formally well-defined framework for privacy protection is described. However, as we previously explained, Byun et al.'s PBAC is a particular interpretation of privacy-based access control whereas our approach is intended to be understood as a "universal" interpretation that admits multiple particular interpretations, e.g., of authorization (cf. the discussion on treating purpose existentially or explicitly in relation to $\mathcal{PAR}$).

Our proposal has been firmly grounded in fibred logic and specifically P-FSL. Related approaches do not necessarily have the same well-defined foundational semantics that our approach offers. It is, for instance, already well known that the P3P proposal has some troublesome semantic features (so ambiguous and inconsistent P3P policies may be specified) and EPAL has an operational semantics that is dependent on rule order. Moreover, although XACML has a privacy profile, XACML, in its full generality, does not have the type of well-defined semantics on which our approach is grounded.

The work of Barth et al. [10] is related to ours in some important respects. Barth et al. provide an abstract model of privacy that is founded upon a well-defined conceptual basis (*contextual integrity*) and a well-defined formal basis (linear temporal logic and the *Logic of Privacy and Utility (LPU)*) from which a wide range of privacy policies may be formulated. Along similar lines, we have tried to provide a well-defined conceptual base (i.e., $\mathcal{M}^P$) and a well-defined formal basis (fibring and P-FSL) from which a range of privacy policies may be formulated. However, the emphasis in Barth et al.'s work is on protection of the flow of personal information, violations of the normative behaviors that members of a role are expected to adhere to, and a logical formulation of a framework that makes use of LPU. In contrast, our concern is to provide a unified framework in which privacy is treated as an aspect of access control. We base our conceptual framework on the general notion of category and we have also been concerned with actions in general (not just communication actions). For our formal foundations, we use fibring to admit the possibility of formulating models and policies in various logics and for defining categories in various logics. The idea of treating, in our approach, information flows in relation to communications in the context of norms, as Barth et al. propose, is an interesting matter for further work.

P-FSL shares with ABLP [17] the core operators *says* and *controls* and can be seen as an extension of ABLP in various ways. ABLP is a propositional logic whereas P-FSL adopts a first-order language that is more expressive and permits us to embed the abstract meta-model $\mathcal{M}^P$ into P-FSL. Moreover, P-FSL proposes a more fine-grained notion of compound principals, in fact ABLP has ad-hoc operators to combine atomic principals in order to express joint supports (e.g., $A \wedge B$ says ψ means that principal A and principal B *jointly* supports ψ to hold) while in P-FSL groups of principals are described by means of first-order formulas with one free variable. In this view, *every* formula of the language can be used to describe a set of principals.[4] Finally, P-FSL proposes a completely new semantics with respect to existing access control logics, which is grounded on fibring and using neighborhood functions to give semantics to the *says* operator.

7 Conclusions and Further Work

We have described an approach that provides users with flexible means for defining the access policies that they require to hold on their "private" data. For that, we introduced a general, abstract access control model $\mathcal{M}^P$, which enables data subjects to conceptualize notions. Our meta-model can be specialized by data subjects in multiple ways so that it may be used to represent a range of access control models and privacy-enhanced access control policies. We formally defined the elements of our meta-model and we expressed privacy policies in P-FSL. We provide a general axiomatic framework that may be specialized by users in multiple ways to represent their individual privacy policy requirements.

---

[4] In [16] it is shown how this feature can be exploited to represent separation of duties in a compact way, a representation that it is not possible by using ABLP language.

Our use of P-FSL and fibred logic enables us to develop a formal foundation for a range of privacy-enhanced access control models and policies and permits complex categories of subjects to be flexibly defined in various logics.

On specifics, we note that our meta-model is essentially based on the use of just five basic relations (the *pca*, *arca*, *arcd*, *par* and *prm* relations) to which "higher-level" *contains*, *controls* and *says* relations are added. Application-specific predicates and non-logical axioms may also be added to the core sets of meta-model features (which may be variously specialized) in order to enable data subjects to define specific privacy-enhanced access control models and policies to satisfy their particular requirements on the protection and exploitation of their data. Providing data subjects with a simple, high-level, implementation-independent, expressive framework for formulating their individual requirements on releases of their personal data is a start towards addressing the key open question of how to provide means that might enable data subjects "to choose freely under what circumstances and to what extent they will expose themselves, their attitudes, and their behavior, to others" [1].

Future work includes to incorporate the notion of obligations and hierarchies of purposes in our model, to build in auditing procedures, to investigate norm-based interpretations of categories and to investigate the use of standard implementation languages, like SQL, for category definition. The focus of this paper has been on the development of semantic notions. In future work, we intend to investigate relevant proof-theoretic notions, like proving meta-theoretic properties of policies that are expressed in P-FSL.

Acknowledgements. Valerio Genovese is supported by the National Research Fund, Luxembourg. The authors thank the reviewers for their comments, which proved to be helpful for improving the clarity of the paper.

References

1. Westin, A.: Privacy and Freedom. Atheneum, New York (1967)
2. Berners-Lee, T.: The semantic web will build in privacy (2009), http://news.cnet.com
3. Simons, W., Mandl, K., Kohane, I.: The PING personally controlled electronic medical record system: Technical architecture. Journal of the American Medical Informatics Association 12(1), 45–54 (2005)
4. Cranor, L.F.: P3p: Making privacy policies more useful. IEEE Security & Privacy 1(6), 50–55 (2003)
5. Backes, M., Dürmuth, M., Karjoth, G.: Unification in privacy policy evaluation - translating EPAL into Prolog. In: POLICY, pp. 185–188 (2004)
6. LeFevre, K., Agrawal, R., Ercegovac, V., Ramakrishnan, R., Xu, Y., DeWitt, D.J.: Limiting disclosure in hippocratic databases. In: VLDB, pp. 108–119 (2004)
7. Anderson, A.H.: A comparison of two privacy policy languages: EPAL and XACMl. In: SWS, pp. 53–60 (2006)
8. Ni, Q., Trombetta, A., Bertino, E., Lobo, J.: Privacy-aware role based access control. In: SACMAT, pp. 41–50 (2007)

9. Ni, Q., Bertino, E., Lobo, J., Calo, S.B.: Privacy-aware role-based access control. IEEE Security & Privacy 7(4), 35–43 (2009)
10. Barth, A., Datta, A., Mitchell, J.C., Nissenbaum, H.: Privacy and contextual integrity: Framework and applications. In: IEEE Symposium on Security and Privacy, pp. 184–198 (2006)
11. Gabbay, D.M.: Fibring logics. Oxford University Press, Oxford (1999)
12. Barker, S.: The next 700 access control models or a unifying meta-model? In: SACMAT, pp. 187–196 (2009)
13. Barker, S., Boella, G., Gabbay, D.M., Genovese, V.: A meta-model of access control in a fibred security language. Studia Logica 92(3), 437–477 (2009)
14. Lampson, B.W., Abadi, M., Burrows, M., Wobber, E.: Authentication in distributed systems: Theory and practice. ACM Trans. Comput. Syst. 10(4), 265–310 (1992)
15. Li, N., Grosof, B.N., Feigenbaum, J.: Delegation logic: A logic-based approach to distributed authorization. ACM Trans. Inf. Syst. Secur. 6(1), 128–171 (2003)
16. Genovese, V., Gabbay, D.M., Boella, G., van der Torre, L.: FSL – fibred security language. In: Boella, G., Noriega, P., Pigozzi, G., Verhagen, H. (eds.) Normative Multi-Agent Systems. Number 09121 in Dagstuhl Seminar Proceedings, Dagstuhl, Germany, Schloss Dagstuhl - Leibniz-Zentrum fuer Informatik, Germany (2009)
17. Abadi, M., Burrows, M., Lampson, B.W., Plotkin, G.D.: A calculus for access control in distributed systems. ACM Trans. Program. Lang. Syst. 15(4), 706–734 (1993)
18. Chellas, B.: Modal logic an introduction. Cambridge University Press, Cambridge (1980)
19. Gabbay, D., Kurucz, A., Wolter, F., Zakharyaschev, M.: Many-Dimensional Modal Logics: Theory and Applications. Elsevier - Studies in Logic (2003)
20. Byun, J.W., Bertino, E., Li, N.: Purpose based access control of complex data for privacy protection. In: SACMAT, pp. 102–110 (2005)
21. Barker, S., Sergot, M.J., Wijesekera, D.: Status-based access control. ACM Trans. Inf. Syst. Secur. 12(1) (2008)
22. Jajodia, S., Samarati, P., Sapino, M., Subrahmaninan, V.: Flexible support for multiple access control policies. ACM TODS 26(2), 214–260 (2001)
23. Fischer-Hubner, S.: IT-Security and Privacy. Springer, Heidelberg (2001)

Understanding Privacy Risk of Publishing Decision Trees*

Zutao Zhu and Wenliang Du

Department of Electrical Engineering and Computer Science
Syracuse University, Syracuse, NY 13244, USA
{zuzhu,wedu}@syr.edu

Abstract. Publishing decision trees can provide enormous benefits to
the society. Meanwhile, it is widely believed that publishing decision
trees can pose a potential risk to privacy. However, there is not much
investigation on the privacy consequence of publishing decision trees. To
understand this problem, we need to quantitatively measure privacy risk.

Based on the well-established maximum entropy theory, we have developed a systematic method to quantify privacy risks when decision
trees are published. Our method converts the knowledge embedded in
decision trees into equations and inequalities (called constraints), and
then uses nonlinear programming tool to conduct maximum entropy estimate. The estimate results are then used to quantify privacy. We have
conducted experiments to evaluate the effectiveness and performance of
our method.

1 Introduction

Decision tree is a powerful data mining tool that has been widely used for classification and prediction in many areas, including financial industry, military af-
fairs, medical research, artificial intelligent, etc. Decision trees can also be used
in data publishing, i.e., instead of publishing the raw data, data owners can publish the decision trees built from their raw data. This type of data sharing and
dissemination can bring tremendous benefits to the society.

A critical concern faced by data publishing is privacy, because many of the
data contain personal information. Decision trees, a form of aggregate information derived from the original dataset, can surely achieve a better privacy
preservation than publishing the original data. However, as long as a decision
tree is still useful, certain degree of private information is still embedded in it.
It is well known that data mining results, such as decision trees and association
rules, can lead to potential privacy breach, but it is not well understood how
much private information is actually disclosed by a published decision tree. In
other words, it is still an open problem to quantitatively measure how much
private information is disclosed by decision trees.

---

* This work has partially supported by Awards No. 0618680 from the United States
National Science Foundation.

S. Foresti and S. Jajodia (Eds.): Data and Applications Security XXIV, LNCS 6166, pp. 33–48, 2010.

1.1   Motivation

We briefly introduce the decision tree, followed by two examples to demonstrate the potential privacy risk caused by the published decision trees.

Decision Tree. Consider table D_1 in Figure 1(a), which has four attributes *Education*, *Country*, *Gender*, and *Salary*. Attribute *Salary* is treated as sensitive and the data publishers want to ensure that no adversary can infer the salary of any individual with a relatively high confidence. We call this attribute a *Sensitive-Attribute* (SA). The other three attributes are often used to identify an individual. They are called *Quasi-Identifier* (QI) attributes. Usually, they can be acquired by the adversary from other sources [1]. Combined with the external data set, such as the voter registration list, an adversary can use *linking attack* [1, 2] to infer the salary of an individual. QIID refers to a distinct combination of QI attributes, i.e., if two people have identical QI values, their QIIDs will be the same. We use it simply for presentation purposes.

QIID	Education	Country	Gender	Salary
q_1	Masters	USA	Female	$\leq 50K$
q_2	Masters	USA	Male	$> 50K$
q_3	Masters	Canada	Male	$\leq 50K$
q_3	Masters	Canada	Male	$\leq 50K$
q_4	Masters	Canada	Female	$\leq 50K$
q_4	Masters	Canada	Female	$> 50K$
q_5	Doctorate	Canada	Female	$> 50K$
q_5	Doctorate	Canada	Female	$> 50K$
q_6	Doctorate	USA	Male	$\leq 50K$
q_6	Doctorate	USA	Male	$> 50K$
q_7	Doctorate	USA	Female	$> 50K$

(a) Microdata D_1 (b) Decision tree for D_1

Fig. 1. Dataset and Decision Tree

Figure 1(b) is a decision tree inducted from the data depicted in Figure 1(a) using ID3 [3] algorithm. Each circle is an internal node, which denotes a test on an attribute. The most informative attribute is selected as the test attribute depending on the attribute selection measure. Branches from a circle denote the outcome of the test. Each rectangle is a leaf node, which holds a class label. The number of tuples a and the misclassified tuples b are listed in the form of "a/b" for each leaf node. The tree predicts whether a person earns less than 50K based on the education, country, and gender information. For any tuple X whose class label is unknown, we can test the attribute values of X against the decision tree. We can trace a path from the root node to a leaf node. The leaf node has the class prediction for X. For instance, the path p, $N_1 \rightarrow N_3 \rightarrow L_4$, states that the probability that the female doctorates earn more than 50K is 100%.

Privacy Issues. As long as a decision tree contains useful aggregate information so that it can be used to predict future data, certain degree of private individual information for the training data is still embedded in it. For the path p: $N_1 \rightarrow N_3 \rightarrow L_4$ that is induced from the training dataset D_1, not only can it predict future tuples, but also disclose the salary information of some tuples in D_1.

We assume that the class attribute of the tree contains sensitive information and adversaries have the QI part of the data in Figure 1(a). Also, we assume that adversaries know that the domain of $Salary$ is $\{\leq 50K, > 50K\}$. Based on these assumptions, adversaries can learn the private information of others:

For the perfect classified nodes, such as L_3 and L_4, the private information (salary) for q_3, q_5, and q_7 is completely disclosed. For example, we can infer that the salaries of q_5 and q_7 are $> 50K$ because q_5 and q_7 are female doctorates. If q_7 is linked to Alice according to the external data source, such as the voter's registration list, her salary is disclosed. Other leaf nodes are not perfectly classified; they only carry aggregate information for a group of individuals. Do they only describe the aggregate information as it labels in the leaf node? For example, the leaf node L_5 is label with "$> 50K$ (2.0/1.0)". Do we only learn that the probability that the male doctorates earn more than 50K is 50%? The answer is NO. In the following example, we show that the adversaries can derive more information when the internal (i.e. non-leaf) nodes are taken into consideration.

Example 1. Figure 2(b) is a decision tree built from the dataset depicted in Figure 2(a) using ID3 [3] algorithm. Surprisingly, having the above assumptions, we can derive the sensitive value for each tuple with 100% confidence. From the leaf nodes L_1 and L_2 in Figure 2(b), we can derive that the sensitive values for q_1 and q_4 in Figure 2(a) are $\leq 50K$ and $> 50K$, respectively. For the leaf node L_3, we learn that the sensitive value of q_2 and q_3 are different. One is $\leq 50K$ and the other is $> 50K$. We make a guess. If the SA of q_2 were $> 50K$ and the SA of q_3 were $\leq 50K$, *Education* would have been selected as the splitting attribute for the internal node N_1 because the split on *Education* can lead to the most informative result. Masters would have all been classified to $> 50K$ while doctorates $\leq 50K$. The decision tree would have been built as Figure 2(c). However, *Age* is the selected attribute instead. This indicates that our guess is incorrect, and therefore, the SA of q_2 is $\leq 50K$ and the SA of q_3 is $> 50K$.

QIID	Age	Education	Salary
q_1	Youth	Doctorate	$\leq 50K$
q_1	Youth	Doctorate	$\leq 50K$
q_2	Senior	Masters	$\leq 50K$
q_3	Senior	Doctorate	$> 50K$
q_4	MiddleAge	Masters	$> 50K$
q_4	MiddleAge	Masters	$> 50K$

(a) Microdata D_2 (b) Real decision tree   (c) Unreal decision tree

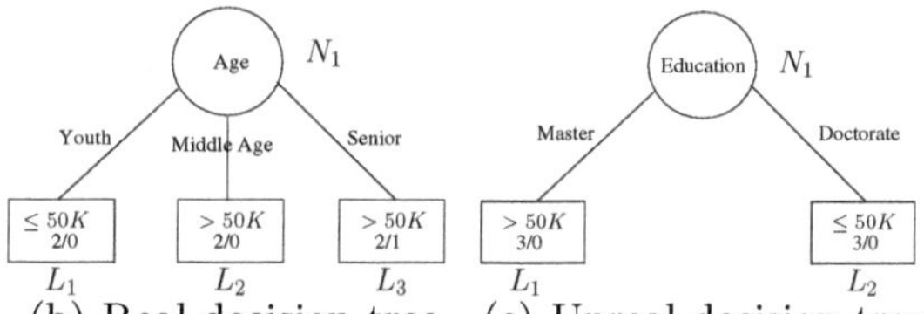

Fig. 2. Dataset and decision trees for Example 1

Example 1 shows that an individual of a group does not necessarily follow the aggregate information of the group. We can capture more precise information for a single one than what is labeled in the leaf nodes, when some analysises are performed.

Challenges. For a simple data set and a simple decision tree, we can use manual deduction as above to derive private information. In a realistic scenario, the dataset often have many tuples and decision trees can become quite complicated. It is infeasible to manually derive private information like what we have done in the previous examples. We need a *systematic* method to analyze privacy; the analysis results will help us understand the privacy risk of decision-tree publishing, and thus improve our practice in data publishing. Once the data publishers understand the privacy situation, they can take actions to preserve it rather than directly publishing a raw tree. Some decision trees are published simply because privacy is not placed enough emphasis on. Therefore, we want to study the open problem: *how much private information the adversaries can infer from the published decision tree given the above assumptions?*

We face two challenges to understand the privacy risk of a published decision tree. First, we have to formulate the information in the leaf nodes. There are many forms of a decision tree: some may publish the accurate error rate as well as the class label while some only have the class label. We need to find a generic formulation to accommodate the various types of information. Second, we need to capture the explicit information in the internal nodes. That is, the most informative attribute is selected.

1.2   Overview of Our Approach

We model the privacy quantification as a Non-Linear Programming (NLP) problem, in which $P(SA \mid QI)$ for each QI and SA combination is represented by a variable. We formulate all the knowledge available to adversaries as linear and nonlinear equations (or inequalities) of these variables. We call them the constraints. Estimating $P(SA \mid QI)$ now becomes finding the values for these variables such that all the constraints are satisfied. Very likely, many solutions exist. However, we are not interested in finding just any solution, we are interested in finding a solution that achieves the most unbiased estimate of $P(SA \mid QI)$. This is exactly what can be achieved by using the maximum entropy theory.

Based on this well-established theory, we propose a systematic method to quantify the privacy disclosure risk in decision trees. The focus of this method is how to formulate constraints from all the information available to adversaries. Once the constraints are formulated, finding the maximum entropy solution is given to software tools that are called *solvers*. There are a number of powerful solvers (in particular, non-linear programming solvers) that we can choose. With this systematic method, we are not only able to analyze privacy disclosure risk in a decision tree; more importantly, we are able to help data publishers reduce their privacy risk when publishing their decision trees.

The rest of the paper is organized as follows. The related work is reviewed in Section 2. Section 3 formally defines the problem. Section 4 presents our main method. Section 5 evaluates our method using a real dataset. Section 6 concludes the paper and describes the future work.

2   Related Work

Privacy-preserving data publishing (PPDP) has been extensively studied in the literatures. The goal of PPDP is to publish a disguised version of the original data, such that the private information of the original data is preserved, while the data are still useful. Several methods have been proposed, including generalization [4,5,6], bucketization [7,8], and randomization [9,10,11].

Understanding privacy is one of the essential tasks in PPDP. The goal of this research is to develop metrics to quantify privacy in data publishing. A number of metrics have been proposed, including K-anonymity [4], L-diversity [12], (α, k)-anonymity [13], t-Closeness [14], and m-invariance [15]. Our work fits into this line of studies. The major difference between our work and others is two-fold. First, instead of proposing a new metric, we focus on computing the conditional probability between QI attributes and SA attributes, i.e., $P(SA \mid QI)$. This conditional probability is a building block for most of the existing metrics. Once we can compute this probability, we can adopt the existing metrics to quantify privacy. Second, the existing privacy metrics are intended for data publishing, while the method proposed in this paper targets the publishing of decision trees. Computing $P(SA \mid QI)$ from a dataset (disguised in most cases) is significantly different from computing the same probability from the decision trees.

The privacy consequence of data mining results is studied by Kantarcioglu et al. [16]. This work tries to understand when data mining results violate privacy. The assumption of the work is that the classifier is kept invisible from adversaries, and adversaries can only request an instance be classified by the owner of a classifier, without knowing other information about the classifier. Although this model has its own merit in the client/server model, where mining results are kept at a sever, the scenario it models is quite different from ours. In our work, decision trees are fully accessible to adversaries. Their work performs a black-box analysis while ours is a white-box analysis.

Another area closely related to PPDP addresses how multiple parties can conduct data mining using their joint data, without disclosing to each other their private data. This line of research uses secure multi-party computation (SMC) protocols to protect private information [17,18]. What is not addressed by SMC studies is how much private information is actually disclosed by the computation results. SMC guarantees that no one in the protocol knows more than what they can derive from the results; however, the results themselves might disclose enough private information. Analyzing how much private information is disclosed by decision trees is exactly the objective of this paper.

Applying the maximum entropy model to estimate privacy is first explored by Du et al. in [19]. They discuss the effect of background knowledge in privacy-preserving data publishing. The work here is dedicated to solve a significantly different problem, that is, to understand the privacy breach when a decision tree is published. Besides, the modeling processes differ far from each other. In [19], all the constraints are explicit according to the disguised dataset. For decision trees, not only do we need to consider the information explicitly in decision trees, we also need to consider the implicit information in decision trees that might cause privacy disclosure.

Another feature of our work is that we do exploit the knowledge about decision-tree building algorithm when deriving private information from a published decision tree. Exploiting the knowledge about algorithms to find private information has also been pursued in several existing studies. Wong et al. [20] explore that adversaries can take advantage of this feature to perform *minimality attack*. Similar attacks are also described by Zhang et al. in [21], and Zhu et al. in [22]. These attacks are based on the information that is not published, but is implied from the published information. Our work follows a similar approach, but the way how we exploit the knowledge of algorithms is quite different from the existing work.

3 Problem Formulation

Assumptions. We make several assumptions in this paper. We assume that the training set consists of two parts: QI attributes and SA attributes. The QI part consists of the information that can also be obtained from other sources. The SA part consists of the information that the data owner wants to protect. This is a general assumption in the field of PPDP. We assume that adversaries have all the data of the QI attributes. This assumption is made because the information in the QI part can be usually obtained via other means [4]. Although in practice, attackers might not know every QI value, this assumption allows us to conduct analysis on the worse-case scenario. For the sake of simplicity in this paper, we assume that there is one SA attribute in the training set, and this attribute is used as the class attribute in a decision tree. We assume that adversaries have the knowledge of the domain of the sensitive attributes, i.e., they know all the possible values of the sensitive attributes. In a decision tree, all the leaf nodes have class labels which are SA values. It is reasonable to make this assumption.

Measuring Privacy. How successful the adversaries can derive an individual's correct SA value depends on the intrinsic conditional probability between QI and SA attributes, i.e., $P(SA \mid QI, \mathcal{O})$, where $\mathcal{O}$ represents all the information available to the adversaries. In most of the existing studies, $\mathcal{O}$ consists of the information from sanitized datasets [4, 12, 13, 14, 7]. In our study, it also comes from the decision trees. For the sake of simplicity, we omit $\mathcal{O}$ from our notation, and only use $P(SA \mid QI)$ in the rest of the paper. Our privacy quantification task can be formally defined as the following:

Problem 1. Let D be the training data set that is used to generate the decision tree(denoted as Ω). Let variable X represent SA attributes, and variable Q represent QI attributes. Given Ω and the QI part of all the tuples in D, derive $P(X \mid Q)$ for all the combinations of Q and X values.

The value of $P(X \mid Q)$ is the primitive behind all the existing privacy measures, i.e., as long as we can compute this conditional probability, we can calculate the existing privacy metrics, such as L-diversity [12], (α, k)-anonymity [13], etc.

Maximum Entropy Modeling. The problem to measure privacy boils down to estimate the distribution of $P(X \mid Q)$, i.e., to assign a probability value to every variable $p(x \mid q)$, where $x \in X$ and $q \in Q$. Such assignment must be consistent with the decision trees that are published. Very likely, there are more than one distributions (we call them solutions) that are consistent with the published decision trees. However, we can only choose one among these distributions; the question is which one should be used to quantify privacy.

There are many ways to choose among these solutions. One way is to choose the most informative solution. For example, we can choose a solution that has $p(x \mid q) = 1$ for many x's and q's, as long as it is consistent with the published decision tree. If we use this solution to quantify privacy, the privacy score will not be very good, because for these people with $QI = q$, there is no uncertainty at all for the SA attribute. Therefore, the uncertainty of this solution is low. The question is whether selecting this solution is fair. If we have multiple choices, one having a higher uncertainty and the other a lower uncertainty, to choose a solution with lower uncertainty actually assumes some information we do not possess, and is thus biased. The maximum entropy theory answers the above question quite nicely. It says that based on the given information, the most unbiased estimate of a distribution is the one that maximizes the entropy [23]. Based on this principle, our problem becomes finding a distribution of $P(X \mid Q)$, such that the following conditional entropy $H(X \mid Q)$ is maximized:

$$H(X \mid Q) = - \sum_{Q,X} P(Q)P(X \mid Q) \log P(X \mid Q).$$

Obviously, when there are no constraints, the uniform distribution is the solution that maximizes the entropy. However, the published decision trees do give us a lot of constraints, i.e., the estimated distribution must be consistent with the tree structure, information at the leaf nodes, information at the internal nodes, etc.

To apply the maximum entropy theory to estimate $P(X \mid Q)$, we need to translate all the available knowledge into equations and inequalities using the word of $P(X \mid Q)$. The translation results become our constraints. With these constraints, we can model our privacy quantification problem as the following:

Definition 1. *(Maximum Entropy Modeling) Finding an assignment for $P(X \mid Q)$ for each combination of Q and X, such that the entropy $H(X \mid Q)$ is maximized, while all the constraints k_1, ..., k_n are satisfied, where constraint k_i is obtained via information that we have on decision tree mining process and results.*

Maximum entropy modeling problem is a special case of the NLP problem. There are sophisticated tools that can be used to solve NLP problems, such as KNITRO [24].

4   Deriving Constraints from Decision Tree Classifiers

To apply the Maximum Entropy theory to estimate the information disclosure, we need to understand where we can derive constraints; namely, we need to understand what adversaries know. They obviously know the published decision tree; it is quite likely that they also know the underlying algorithm used to build the decision tree, in particular, the attribute selection measure (e.g. Information Gain or Gini Index). Moreover, we assume that adversaries know the QI part of the training dataset. Therefore, the source of the constraints can be categorized into the following: the leaf nodes of the decision tree, the internal nodes which encode the attribute selection measure, and the QI part of the dataset.

In the following subsections, we describe how to derive constraints from these three sources. We use the example depicted in Figure 1(a) and 1(b) to help us explain our ideas in this section. We frequently use the following two terminologies in our explanation. An *attribute prefix* of a node V in a decision tree is a conjunction of attribute assignments that represents the path from the root to V. We use Λ to denote attribute prefix. A conjunction expression is said to be a *full conjunction expression* if it contains all the QI attributes of the dataset. Without causing any confusion, we simply call it *full expression*. For example, the attribute prefix of the node L_1 in Figure 1(b) is $\Lambda = (Education = Masters) \wedge (Country = USA)$. Λ is not a full expression because it does not contain all the QI attributes.

It should be noted that in our maximum entropy model, we need the entire QI attributes in our constraints, not a subset of it, i.e., each Q in our variable $P(X \mid Q)$ must be a full expression. We show how to represent $P(X \mid \Lambda)$ (where Λ is not a full expression) using $P(X \mid Q)$, where Q's are full expressions. Let Λ represent an attribute prefix of a node V. Let $q_1, \ldots, q_n$ be all the full-expression QIs that satisfy Λ, i.e., they share the same attribute prefix values. For example, if $\Lambda = (Education = Masters) \wedge (Country = USA)$, q_1 and q_2 in Figure 1(a) satisfy Λ because their *Education* and *Country* attributes satisfy Λ. Based on the conditional probability definition, we have the following:

$$P(X \mid \Lambda) = \frac{\sum_{i=1}^{n} P(X \mid q_i) P(q_i)}{P(\Lambda)}. \tag{1}$$

$P(\Lambda)$ and $P(q_i)$ are constants that are known to the adversaries [1]. Armed with Equation (1), we will not pay attention to whether Λ is a full expression or not in the rest of this paper.

4.1   Leaf Nodes

The most obvious source of privacy disclosure in a published decision tree is the leaf nodes, because leaf nodes contain a lot of information, including class labels and sometimes error rates (the error rate indicates the percentage of the misclassified tuples for each leaf node). We show how to derive constraints with or without error rates.

---

[1] We assume that adversaries know the QI part of the training dataset.

When error rates are published in a decision tree, the percentage of the correctly classified tuples becomes known. Let e represent the error rate of a leaf node whose attribute prefix is Λ, and let C be the class label of this leaf node. We can derive the following constraint (we call it *rate-constraint*):

$$P(C \mid \Lambda) = (1 - e).$$

Furthermore, the fact that C is selected as the class label indicates that C is the most frequent class among all the classes. Therefore, we can infer that within any leaf node, the percentage of tuples with class label C is larger than those with other class labels. Namely, we have the following constraint (called *label-constraint*):

$$P(C \mid \Lambda) \geq P(W \mid \Lambda), \quad \text{for } \forall \, W \neq C.$$

For example, according to the leaf node L_4 in Figure 1(b), the attribute prefix Λ is {Education $=$ Doctorate and Gender $=$ Female}, and two q_5 tuples and one q_7 tuple in Figure 1(a) are included in L_4. Because the number of mis-classified tuples in L_4 is 0, the error rate e of L_4 is 0. Since the class label is "$> 50K$", we can derive the following rate-constraint:

$$P(> 50K \mid \Lambda) = 1, \quad \text{or } P(\leq 50K \mid \Lambda) = 0,$$

and the following label-constraint:

$$P(\,> 50\text{K} \mid \Lambda) \geq P(\leq 50\text{K} \mid \Lambda).$$

Note that in the above example, the label-constraint is redundant. Actually, when there are only two class values, the rate-constraint always implies the label-constraint, because if C is the selected class label for a leaf node, we know $P(C \mid \Lambda)$ is always ≥ 0.5, larger than the other class value that is not selected. However, when there are more than two class values, the error rate might be larger than $P(C \mid \Lambda)$. Therefore, the rate-constraint alone does not always capture the fact that $P(C \mid \Lambda)$ is the largest among all the class values; the label-constraint captures that.

In practice, data publishers might not publish the error rates, i.e., each leaf node is only assigned a class label without a corresponding error rate. In this case, adversaries can only infer the *label-constraint*, not the *rate-constraint*.

4.2   Internal Nodes

In a decision tree, the internal nodes do not seem to contain much information that can lead to privacy disclosure, but actually, they do: the fact that a specific attribute is used as the partition attribute can tell us some information about the training dataset. To use this fact in our maximum entropy model, we need to derive constraints from these internal nodes.

In a decision tree, each internal node represents a subset of tuples that share the same values for certain attributes; these attributes and their values are encoded by the path from the root to this internal node. We use the attribute prefix Λ to represent these attributes and their values (not including the node that is to be splitted). Generally speaking, in decision-tree induction algorithms, at each internal node, an attribute needs to be selected to further partition the records contained in the internal node. The goal of the selection measure is to find the best way to split the tuples such that the expected *impurity* score of the partition is minimized. The following notations are commonly used in decision-tree algorithms.

- $I(\Lambda)$: Impurity score of the node that corresponds to Λ.
- $I(\Lambda, A = A_i)$: impurity score of the node that corresponds to Λ and $A = A_i$. Without causing confusions, we shorten $I(\Lambda, A = A_i)$ as $I(\Lambda, A_i)$.
- $E(\Lambda, A)$: Expected impurity score of using attribute A to partition the node that corresponds to Λ. $E(\Lambda, A)$ is computed using the following formula:

$$E(\Lambda, A) = \sum_{i=1}^{|A|} I(\Lambda, A_i). \tag{2}$$

According to the attribute selection method in the decision tree induction algorithm, the attribute having the best impurity score will be selected as the splitting attribute for the node. Therefore, by seeing that T is the selected attribute at an internal node (say N), we know that the expected impurity score achieved by using T to partition node N is less than that using any other candidate attribute. Let Λ be the attribute prefix of the node N, and let Ψ represent the candidate attributes at node N. We have the following constraint, called *internal-constraint*:

$$E(\Lambda, T) \leq E(\Lambda, W), \quad \text{for } \forall W \in \Psi - \{T\}. \tag{3}$$

The actual computation of expected impurity depends on how impurity is measured. Several methods have been used to measure *impurity*, including entropy [3, 25] and Gini impurity [26]. In the following, we instantiate Inequality (3) for both entropy-based and Gini impurity measures. At the end, we will get a set of constraints that will be integrated into our Maximum Entropy model.

(1) Gini Impurity Measure. Gini impurity depends on squared probabilities of membership for each target category in the node, which is used by the CART algorithm [26]. Its minimum, zero, is reached when all cases of a node fall into the same category, i.e., the purest case. Gini impurity for a branch that corresponds to Λ and $A = A_i$ is computed in the following formula:

$$I(\Lambda, A_i) = \frac{|D_{\Lambda,A_i}|}{|D_\Lambda|} (1 - \sum_{j=1}^{|C|} P(C_j \mid \Lambda, A_i)^2), \tag{4}$$

where the term $|D_{\Lambda,A_i}|/|D_\Lambda|$ is the weight of the i-th partition.

In our maximum entropy modeling, $P(C_j \mid \Lambda, A_i)$ in the above equation is unknown to adversaries because it is a combination of several variables that are what adversaries want to estimate. Although adversaries cannot estimate these values directly, they can use the information from internal nodes to capture the relationship among these variables. The relationship is captured in Inequality (3) after we combine Equations (4) and (2) together.

We use an example to illustrate the constraints derived from internal nodes. Assume that Gini Index measure is used to generate the tree depicted in Figure 1(b). For the internal node N_2 in Figure 1(b), *Country* and *Gender* are the candidate attributes because *Education* has been used in N_1. Since *Country* is the selected attribute, the Gini Index impurity deduction of *Country* is larger than that of *Gender*. That is, the expected impurity score of *Country* is less than that of *Gender*.

Let Λ be *Education* = *Masters*; C_1 be *Country* = *USA*; C_2 be *Country* = *Canada*; G_1 be *Gender* = *Female*; G_2 be *Gender* = *Male*; Let variable p_{i0} represent $P(\leq 50K \mid q_i)$, and let variable p_{i1} represent $P(> 50K \mid q_i)$, where i ranges from 1 to 4 in our example because q_1, q_2, q_3, and q_4 satisfy Λ. For the *Country* attribute, we have the following:

$$I(\Lambda, C_1) = \frac{1}{3}\left[1 - \frac{(p_{10}+p_{20})^2}{2^2} - \frac{(p_{11}+p_{21})^2}{2^2}\right],$$

$$I(\Lambda, C_2) = \frac{2}{3}\left[1 - \frac{(p_{30}+p_{40})^2}{2^2} - \frac{(p_{31}+p_{41})^2}{2^2}\right].$$

For the *Gender* attribute, similarly, we can get $I(\Lambda, G_1)$ and $I(\Lambda, G_2)$. Using Inequality (3), we have the following *internal-constraint*:

$$I(\Lambda, C_1) + I(\Lambda, C_2) \leq I(\Lambda, G_1) + I(\Lambda, G_2).$$

(2) Entropy-based Impurity Measure. Entropy is used to measure the impurity of a node in some decision tree mining algorithms, such as ID3 and C4.5 [25]. Information gain is based on the concept of entropy used in the information theory. The entropy of the *i*-th branch of a partition using attribute A can be calculated as the following:

$$I(\Lambda, A_i) = \frac{|D_{\Lambda, A_i}|}{|D_\Lambda|} \sum_{j=1}^{|C|} -P(C_j \mid \Lambda, A_i) \log P(C_j \mid \Lambda, A_i).$$

Similar to the Gini Index measure, we combine the above equation with Equation (2) for each candidate attribute, and then we apply the results to Inequality (3), which captures the relationships among several variables corresponding the the internal node.

4.3   Deriving Constraints from Quasi-Identifiers

In our maximum entropy modeling, each variable $P(X \mid Q)$ is a conditional probability, so they must satisfy all the constraints imposed on probabilities. For example, the sum of all conditional probabilities given a specific q_i should be 1. We need to explicitly provide these constraints, so the solutions of our maximum entropy modeling will be meaningful with regard to probabilities. Similar to [22], we have the following *QI-constraints*:

$$\sum_{i=1}^{m} P(X = x_i \mid Q = q) = 1. \tag{5}$$

If the distribution of SA values are also published along with the decision tree, adversaries will know $P(X = x)$, so we will have the following *SA-constraints*:

$$\sum_{i=1}^{n} P(q_i \mid X = x) = \sum_{i=1}^{n} \frac{P(X = x \mid q_i)P(q_i)}{P(X = x)} = 1,$$

where $P(X = x)$ is the probability of x in the training data set.

5   Experiments

To demonstrate how much sensitive information is disclosed by decision tree classifiers, we evaluate our proposed method using the Adults dataset from the UC Irvine Machine Learning Repository [2]. We use the same setting described in [22]. However, we choose the "Education" attribute as the class attribute. As a result, we have a dataset D, which has 30162 records, with 4480 distinct QI values and 16 distinct SA values. Therefore, we have 4480 *QI-constraints*. We use Gini Index and Information Gain measures to build two decision trees. The number of *rate-constraints*, *label-constraints*, and *internal-constraints* are 518, 7770, 1097, for Gini Index; and 2983, 44745, 3307, for Information Gain, respectively. Our ME method is implemented using C++ and Oracle 9i. All experiments are run on an Intel(R) Pentium(R)-D machine with 3.00 GHz CPU and 4GB physical memory. We use the KNITRO software package [24] to solve our Maximum Entropy Estimation problem.

The output of the program is the estimate of $P(SA \mid QI)$ for all combinations of SA and QI values, based on the information provided by the published decision tree. The closer our estimate is to the original distribution, the more private information is disclosed via the published decision tree. We measure such closeness at two different levels: individual level and overall level, as is described in [22]. They are

$$\mathrm{D}_{individual} = \sum_{x \in SA} P(x|q) \log \frac{P(x|q)}{P^*(x|q)},$$

$$\mathrm{D}_{overall} = \sum_{q \in QI} [P(q) \cdot \sum_{x \in SA} P(x|q) \log \frac{P(x|q)}{P^*(x|q)}],$$

respectively, where $P^*(X \mid Q = q)$ is the *estimated individual distribution*, and $P(X \mid Q = q)$ is the original distribution.

The above two divergence values allow us to understand information disclosure at two different levels. With $D_{individual}$, we can conduct privacy studies for the worst-case scenario, because it allows us to see the result at the individual level; with $D_{overall}$, we can conduct privacy studies for the average-case scenario. As we will show in our experiments, they can tell different things.

The Effect of the Error Rate. Some decision tree mining tools provide accurate error rates and some do not. From the privacy perspective, decision trees with error rates definitely reveal more private information. The overall divergences with and without error rates are plotted in Figure 3. The overall divergence without error rate is much larger than that with error rate; this is true for both Gini Index and Information Gain. However, the impact on information-gain-based decision trees is much more severe than that on gini-index-based decision trees. Generally speaking, with error rate, more private information is disclosed. The reason is that the solution space with error rates is the subset of that of without error rate. More specific information can help the NLP solver to find solutions that are closer to the original distribution. Therefore, the overall divergence is smaller.

---

[2] http://archive.ics.uci.edu/ml/

Fig. 3. The effect of error rate

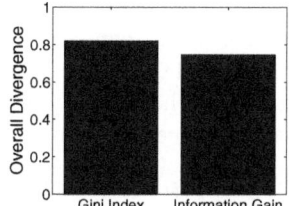

Fig. 4. The effect of selection measure

Case	x_{10}	x_{11}	x_{20}	x_{21}	x_{30}	x_{31}	x_{40}	x_{41}	D_o	D_i^{q2}	D_i^{q3}
S_O	1	0	1	0	0	1	0	1	N/A	N/A	N/A
S_A	1	0	0.5	0.5	0.5	0.5	0	1	0.231	0.693	0.693
S_B	1	0	0.815	0.185	0.815	0.185	0	1	0.068	0.205	0.205

Fig. 5. Impact of the internal nodes for Example 1

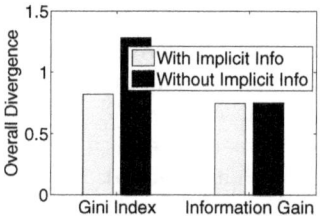

Fig. 6. Effect of implicit information

Top-K	Difference of KL_1 and KL_2	KL_1	KL_2
1	1.492	0.971	2.463
2	1.371	1.156	2.527
3	1.305	0.942	2.247
4	1.304	0.399	1.703
5	1.262	1.170	2.432
6	1.247	1.187	2.435
7	1.197	1.419	2.616
8	1.195	1.253	2.448
9	1.191	1.441	2.632
10	1.144	1.744	2.888

Fig. 7. Top-10 difference of KL-divergence(KL_1:with Implicit)

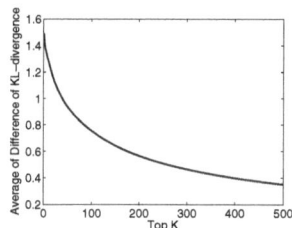

Fig. 8. Impact of individual divergence

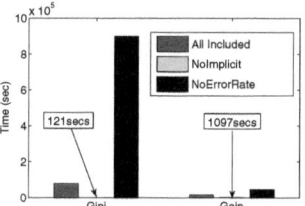

Fig. 9. Running time

The Effect of Attribute Selection Measure. In Section 4.2, we learn that constraints derived from different attribute selection measures are different according to the attribute selection measures. We would like to see whether there is any difference on privacy disclosure between these attribute selection measures. In particular, we would like to study the difference between the Gini Index measure and the Information Gain measure. We assume that error rates are provided. The results are plotted in Figure 4.

From the results, we do see that the overall divergence using gini index is larger from that using information gain. However, there are many factors that cause such a difference, including height of the decision trees, utility of the trees, etc. A comprehensive comparisons of the privacy disclosure between these two measures is beyond the scope of this paper. The goal of this experiment is to show that using our method, data publishers can measure the privacy consequence of their to-be-published decision trees, regardless of what selection method is used.

The Effect of Implicit Information. We have conducted experiments to compare the difference on privacy between with and without implicit information. In the "with" case, we include the internal-constraints while in the "without" case, we exclude the internal-constraints.

First of all, we apply our ME method on Example 1 to illustrate the importance of the implicit information in the decision tree classifier. We have 8 combinations of $P(SA \mid QI)$ since we have 4 distinct QIs and 2 distinct SAs. S_A, S_B are the solutions without and with implicit information, respectively. The original distribution is denoted as S_O. S_A, S_B, and S_O are all listed in Figure 5, where x_{i0} and x_{i1} are the conditional probabilities for q_i whose SA is "$\leq 50K$" and "$> 50K$", respectively. We also list the overall divergence in the D_o column. From the results, we can see that S_B–the results using implicit information–has a smaller overall divergence, and is thus a more accurate estimate.

We also conduct our experiments using the Adult dataset D; we use both the Gini Index measure and the Information Gain measure. In each experiment, we get two estimates, one of which is with the implicit information, the other of which is without the implicit information. In Figure 6, we draw the overall divergences for the two estimations with respect to the real distribution. There is obvious difference for the Gini Index measure. Surprisingly, it shows that there is no major difference for the overall divergences for the Information Gain measure.

To gain a better understanding, we proceed to analyze the *individual divergence* of the result for Information Gain measure. We measure the *individual divergence* between the real distribution and the estimated distribution for each individual QI value. We list the 10 most significant individual divergences in Figure 7, where KL_1 is the individual divergence between the original probabilities and the estimated probabilities when implicit information at internal nodes is used; KL_2 is the corresponding individual divergence when implicit information is not used. From Figure 7, we can clearly tell that KL_1 is significantly smaller than KL_2. For example, in the fourth row in Figure 7, the individual divergence for this QI with the implicit information is 0.399 while that for without the implicit information is 1.703, about 77 percent lower. To fully understand how the implicit information affects the privacy at individual level, we average the top K largest difference between the individual divergences obtained with and without the internal-constraints. The results are plotted in Figure 8; they show that the average impact of the internal-constraint decreases. That is why we do not see much difference if we only measure overall divergence.

Performance. To understand the performance of our proposed method, we conduct two sets of experiments to learn the running time and the memory usage of our ME method. One is for the Gini Index measure while the other is for the

Information Gain measure. In each set, "All Included" means all the constraints are included, with the error rate and the implicit information; "NoImplicit" means no implicit information is included; "NoErrorRate" means no error rate is published. The running time is shown in Figure 9. We find that it is more time-consuming for the Information Gain measure to get the solution than for the Gini Index measure. Intuitively, in Information Gain measure, we need to perform the logarithm computation while in Gini Index, multiplication is performed. Logarithm computation is much more costly. Moreover, we also find that the memory usage of the Information Gain measure (2.5G) is much larger than that of the Gini Index measure (1.2G). This difference is caused by logarithm computation and the different number of constraints. We have observed that the total running time for "All Included" is far less than that of "NoErrorRate". This is because the search space for "All Included" is much smaller than that of "NoErrorRate" due to the fact that the former search space is a subset of the latter. On the other hand, we find out that the total running time for "All Included" is more than that of "NoImplicit". Without the internal-constraints, our solver only has linear constraints to evaluate. Solvers usually run much slower if there are non-linear constraints, such as those derived from implicit information.

6   Conclusion and Future Work

We propose a systematic method to quantitatively measure the private information disclosed by decision tree classifiers. Our method is based on a well-established principle, the Maximum Entropy Principle. We model both leaf nodes and internal nodes as constraints. We then feed these constraints to a Non-Linear Programming software to find the maximum entropy estimate. Our experiments have shown that the proposed method is quite effective.

We also realize that in building decision trees, the training dataset is only a subset (e.g. two third) of the original dataset; as long as we do not publish the information about this subset, adversaries do not know which tuples from the dataset are selected as training data. Although adversaries can still use Maximum Entropy to conduct estimate, the accuracy of the estimate will be affected. We plan to study how the training data selection process affect the privacy of decision trees.

Several other directions can also be followed in our future work. One direction is to extend this method to deal with other data mining results. Another interesting direction is to develop methods to disguise the decision tree mining results, such that the privacy requirements are satisfied, while at the same time, the utility of the published results is not sacrificed too much.

References

1. Samarati, P.: Protecting respondents' identities in microdata release. IEEE transactions on Knowledge and Data Engineering 13(6) (2001)
2. Sweeney, L.: k-anonymity: a model for protecting privacy. International Journal on Uncertainty, Fuzziness, and Knowlege-Based Systems 10(5) (2002)

3. Quinlan, J.R.: Induction of decision trees. Machine Learning 1 (1986)
4. Samarati, P., Sweeney, L.: Protecting privacy when disclosing information: k-anonymity and its enforcement through generalization and suppression. Technical report (1998)
5. LeFevre, K., DeWitt, D.J., Ramakrishnan, R.: Incognito:efficient full-domain k-anonymity. In: Proceedings of the 2005 ACM SIGMOD, June 12–16 (2005)
6. Bayardo, R.J., Agrawal, R.: Data privacy through optimal k-anonymization. In: ICDE 2005 (2005)
7. Xiao, X., Tao, Y.: Anatomy: Simple and effective privacy preservation. In: VLDB 2006 (2006)
8. Martin, D.J., Kifer, D., Machanavajjhala, A., Gehrke, J.E., Halpern, J.: Worst case background knowledge. In: ICDE 2007 (2007)
9. Agrawal, R., Srikant, R.: Privacy-preserving data mining. In: SIGMOD 2000, Dallas, TX USA, May 15–18, pp. 439–450 (2000)
10. Rizvi, S., Haritsa, J.R.: Maintaining data privacy in association rule mining. In: Proceedings of the 28th VLDB Conference, Hong Kong, China (2002)
11. Evfimievski, A., Srikant, R., Agrawal, R., Gehrke, J.: Privacy preserving mining of association rules. In: KDD 2002 (2002)
12. Machanavajjhala, A., Gehrke, J.E., Kifer, D., Venkitasubramaniam, M.: L-diversity: Privacy beyond k-anonymity. In: ICDE 2006 (2006)
13. Wong, R.C.W., Li, J., Fu, A.W.C., Wang, K.: (α, k)-anonymity: An enhanced k-anonymity model for privacy-preserving data publishing. In: KDD 2006 (2006)
14. Li, N., Li, T.: t-closeness: Privacy beyond k-anonymity and l-diversity. In: ICDE 2007 (2007)
15. Xiao, X., Tao, Y.: m-invariance: Towards privacy preserving re-publication of dynamic datasets. In: SIGMOD 2007 (2007)
16. Kantarcioglu, M., Jin, J., Clifton, C.: When do data mining results violate privacy? In: KDD 2004 (2004)
17. Vaidya, J., Clifton, C.: Privacy-preserving decision trees over vertically partitioned data
18. Wright, R., Yang, Z.: Privacy-preserving bayesian network structure computation on distributed heterogeneous data. In: KDD 2004 (2004)
19. Du, W., Teng, Z., Zhu, Z.: Privacy-MaxEnt: Integrating background knowledge in privacy quantification. In: SIGMOD 2008 (2008)
20. Wong, R., Fu, A., Wang, K., Pei, J.: Minimality attack in privacy preserving data publishing. In: VLDB 2007 (2007)
21. Zhang, L., Jajodia, S., Brodsky, A.: Information disclosure under realistic assumptions: Privacy versus optimality. In: CCS 2007 (2007)
22. Zhu, Z., Wang, G., Du, W.: Deriving private information from association rule mining results. In: ICDE 2009 (2009)
23. Jaynes, E.T.: Information theory and statistical mechanics. Physical Review 106(4), 620–630 (1957)
24. Byrd, R., Nocedal, J., Waltz, R.: Knitro: An integrated package for nonlinear optimization. In: di Pillo, G., Roma, M. (eds.) Large-Scale Nonlinear Optimization, pp. 35–59. Springer, Heidelberg (2006)
25. Quinlan, J.R.: C4.5: Programs for Machine Learning. Morgan Kaufmann Publishers, San Francisco (1993)
26. Breiman, L., Friedman, J., Stone, C.J., Olshen, R.A.: Classification and Regression Trees. Chapman Hall/CRC (1984)

Secure Outsourcing of DNA Searching via Finite Automata

Marina Blanton and Mehrdad Aliasgari

Department of Computer Science and Engineering, University of Notre Dame,
{mblanton,maliasga}@cse.nd.edu

Abstract. This work treats the problem of error-resilient DNA searching via oblivious evaluation of finite automata, where a client has a DNA sequence, and a service provider has a pattern that corresponds to a genetic test. Error-resilient searching is achieved by representing the pattern as a finite automaton and evaluating it on the DNA sequence, where privacy of both the pattern and the DNA sequence must be preserved. Interactive solutions to this problem already exist, but can be a burden on the participants. Thus, we propose techniques for secure outsourcing of finite automata evaluation to computational servers, which do not learn any information. Our techniques are applicable to any type of finite automata, but the optimizations are tailored to DNA searching.

1   Introduction

The need to protect private or sensitive information about an individual is widely recognized. Recent advances in bioinformatics and biomedical science promise great potential in our ability to understand and compute over genome data, but the DNA of an individual is highly sensitive data. In recent years, several publications appeared that allow for computing over DNA data in a private manner with the purpose of identifying ancestry relationships or genetic predisposition. In particular, results are known for sequence comparisons that compute the edit-distance [1,2], error-resilient pattern matching based on finite automata (FA) evaluation [3,4], and specific DNA-based ancestry testing [5].

DNAs or DNA fragments used in such computations are large in size. For that reason, recent work [2,6] concentrated on improving the efficiency of such protocols, but they still remain resource-intensive. Thus, if a customer would like to engage in a private computation that uses her DNA, she might not have computational resources or bandwidth to carry out the protocol. When this is the case, it is natural to consider outsourcing the computation to powerful servers or a large distributed network such as a computational grid. Obviously, in such a setting the privacy of all sensitive inputs (the customer's DNA, the service provider's tests, etc.) must be preserved from the participating servers.

Results for privacy-preserving outsourcing of the edit distance computation of two strings are known [7,8], but outsourcing of more general type of computation over DNA via finite automata has remained unexplored. Thus, the focus of this work is on secure outsourcing of oblivious evaluation of a finite automaton on

S. Foresti and S. Jajodia (Eds.): Data and Applications Security XXIV, LNCS 6166, pp. 49–64, 2010.
© IFIP International Federation for Information Processing 2010

a private input. We use the work of Troncoso-Pastoriza et al. that pioneered techniques for oblivious finite automata evaluation (OFAE) [3] as a starting point for out solution and develop techniques for outsourcing such computations.

Using FA for DNA searching is motivated by the fact that queries on DNA data need to take into account various errors such as clinically irrelevant mutations, sequencing errors, incomplete specifications, etc. Such errors can be tolerated if the pattern is expressed using regular expressions, implemented as FA. We refer the reader to [3] for a detailed description of searching and alignment algorithms that can be implemented using FA. Then a service provider (such as, e.g., 23andMe [9]) can build a FA that implements a genomic test, and a customer who possess a private DNA sequence will use it as an input to the automaton. A DNA sequence is specified as a string of characters over the alphabet $\Sigma = \{A, C, T, G\}$ of length N, and a deterministic finite automaton (or a finite state machine (FSM)) corresponding to a DNA test is specified as a tuple $M = (Q, \Sigma, \Delta, q_0, F)$, where Q is a set of states, Σ is an alphabet, $\Delta : Q \times \Sigma \to Q$ is the transition function, $q_0 \in Q$ is the initial state, and $F \subseteq Q$ is the set of final states. W.l.o.g, the transition matrix is assumed to be complete, i.e., it specifies a transition from each state on each input, and is represented as a table of size $|Q| \times |\Sigma|$, where each value stores a state. The states are represented as integers in $\mathbb{Z}_{|Q|}$ and input characters are represented as integers in $\mathbb{Z}_{|\Sigma|}$. A FA M accepts a string $x = x_0 x_1 \ldots x_{N-1} \in \Sigma^N$ if on input x it transitions from q_0 to $q_N \in F$.

Contributions. Our contributions can be summarized as follows:

- We first show how the solution of [3] can be simplified to improve both the computation and communication for typical values of the parameters (i.e., when $|\Sigma|$ is small). We also provide a detailed (not just asymptotic) analysis of the original and modified solutions and show that the communication cost can be rather high and not suitable for all clients. Since most of the communication overhead of the solutions comes from the oblivious transfer (OT) protocol, we analyze the performance of the solutions using different OT realizations that allow us to achieve a computation-computation tradeoff.
- We give a protocol for outsourcing the computation of both the client and the FA owner (service provider) to two computational servers without increasing either the communication or computational complexity of the protocol. The communication complexity of the client and service provider becomes linear in the size of their data and involves virtually no computation.
- Next, we give a protocol that works for outsourcing the computation to any number of servers (i.e., the multi-party case). To minimize the overhead, we use a different structure from that used in the two-party outsourcing solution. To lower the communication complexity (and in part the computation overhead), we represent the transition matrix Δ as a square, so that the communication is decreased from $O(|\Sigma| + |Q|)$ to $O(\sqrt{|\Sigma||Q|})$.
- We also develop a threshold version of the multi-party outsourcing protocol which makes the solution suitable to work in unstable or dynamic environments such as grids. Due to space limitation, it could not be included in this article and can be found in the full version [10].

2   Related Work

There is a considerable number of publications on secure DNA comparison and matching (e.g., [1,8,11,3,5,12]). The majority of them (e.g., [1,7,8,2,6]) use dynamic programming (DP) to securely compute the edit distance between a pair of genomic sequences: There are two parties, each with its respective sequence, and the algorithms compute the edit distance between the sequences without revealing any information besides the output. Since the DP techniques involve computation quadratic in the input size, such solutions are computation and communication heavy. For that reason, consecutive work [7,8] considered outsourcing the edit distance computation to powerful helper servers, and another line of research [2,6] concentrated on making such solutions more efficient. Related to them, [13] gives secure computation of the longest common subsequence (LCS) using optimized techniques, and this research is continued in [14].

While these techniques are likely to improve the communication and/or computation complexity of the original DP solution, one might consider the edit distance computation to be a specific type of DNA comparison that might not be suitable when, e.g., error-resilient searching is necessary (handling sampling errors, incomplete specifications, etc.). For that reason, another line of research [3,4] uses FSMs to implement error-resilient searching over DNA data, and can support any searches that can be formulated as regular languages. These publications provide secure two-party protocols for OFAE, which can be used in any context and is not limited to DNA searching. We use the first publication in this domain [3] as a starting point for our outsourcing construction. A follow-up work [4] uses techniques similar to generic Boolean circuit evaluation to significantly lower the round complexity of the protocol (from $O(N)$ to $O(1)$) and lower the computation complexity as well. The circuit-based approach, however, does not generalize to the outsourcing scenario, since it assumes that the function to be evaluated (i.e., a FA in our case) is known to the participants. Other general secure function evaluation approaches are not suitable for the same reason.

Other work on privacy-preserving computing over DNA data includes [11], where the authors introduce a strategy for enhancing data privacy in a distributed network deploying the Smith-Waterman algorithm for sequence comparison. In [5], the authors build secure multi-party protocols for specific genetic tests such as parental tests; the approach can also handle a small number of errors, but the complexity of the protocol rapidly increases with the number of errors it can tolerate. Lastly, [12] presents a cryptographic framework for executing queries on databases of genomic data, where data privacy is achieved by relying on two non-colluding third parties.

3   Preliminaries

Homomorphic encryption. Prior and our work relies on a semantically secure homomorphic public-key encryption scheme. Let $\mathcal{E} = (\mathsf{Gen}, \mathsf{Enc}, \mathsf{Dec})$ be a public-key encryption scheme, where key generation algorithm Gen takes a security parameter 1^κ and produces a public-private key pair (pk, sk); encryption algorithm Enc takes pk and message m and produces a ciphertext c; and decryption algorithm Dec takes (pk, sk) and ciphertext c and produces m. For brevity, we use notation $\mathsf{Enc}_{pk}(m)$ and $\mathsf{Dec}_{sk}(c)$. Let n be the public modulus associated a public key pk; the message space is then $\mathbb{Z}_n^*$. We will assume that $|n| = \kappa$.

With homomorphic encryption, operations on ciphertexts translate into certain operations on the underlying plaintexts. For additively homomorphic schemes, $\mathsf{Enc}_{pk}(m_1) \cdot \mathsf{Enc}_{pk}(m_2) = \mathsf{Enc}_{pk}(m_1 + m_2)$, which implies $\mathsf{Enc}_{pk}(m)^a = \mathsf{Enc}_{pk}(ma)$ for known a. A ciphertext $\mathsf{Enc}_{pk}(m)$ can be re-randomized by multiplying it to $\mathsf{Enc}_{pk}(0)$; this makes it infeasible to link the new ciphertext to the original one.

Oblivious transfer. A 1-out-of-t oblivious transfer, OT_1^t, allows the receiver to retrieve one item from the t items at the sender in a way that the receiver does not learn anything besides that item and the sender learns nothing. It is a well studied cryptographic tool, with many available realizations. Different OT protocols from the literature allow one to achieve tradeoffs between sender and receiver computation and their communication. That is, OT_1^t from [15] has very efficient amortized cost (one modulo exponentiation per OT for the sender and the receiver) and linear communication cost $O(t)$. Other protocols (e.g., [16,17]) achieve sub-linear communication, but have larger computation requirements. Depending on the parameters used in OFAE (i.e., the number of states, input length, etc.) and resources available to the participants, one scheme might be preferred over another. We use different OT schemes in analysis in Section 5.

Oblivious evaluation of finite automata. Here we review the solution of [3], which is used as a starting point in this work. The service provider $\mathcal{S}$ holds Δ and the client $\mathcal{C}$ holds input x. The evaluation processes one input character at a time, and the current state is shared between $\mathcal{C}$ and $\mathcal{S}$ modulo $|Q|$. Throughout this paper, we will assume that the rows of the matrix are numbered 0 through $|Q| - 1$, and the columns of the matrix are numbered from 0 to $|\Sigma| - 1$. The solution consists of three sub-protocols: (i) a protocol for performing the first state transition, (ii) a protocol for executing a general kth state transition (for $k = 1, \ldots, N-1$), and (iii) a protocol for announcing the result to the client. Our description of the (main) kth state transition protocol here is slightly different from its original presentation in [3]: it is described for a transposed matrix to improve efficiency of the protocol (as was suggested in [3]). We use q_i to denote the current state in the execution after processing i input characters. Notation $a \overset{R}{\leftarrow} A$ means that a is chosen uniformly at random from the set A. The protocol uses a homomorphic encryption scheme $\mathcal{E}$ for which only $\mathcal{C}$ knows sk.

Protocol for 1st state transition. It allows $\mathcal{C}$ and $\mathcal{S}$ to evaluate the FA on the first input symbol, i.e., compute $q_1 = \Delta(q_0, x_0)$, and share it in an additively split form, i.e., $\mathcal{S}$ learns $q_1^{(1)}$ and $\mathcal{C}$ learns $q_1^{(2)}$ such that $q_1^{(1)} + q_2^{(2)} \bmod |Q| = q_1$.

1. $\mathcal{S}$ picks $r \overset{R}{\leftarrow} \mathbb{Z}_{|Q|}$ and blinds each value in row q_0 by adding r to it mod $|Q|$.
2. The parties engage in an $\mathrm{OT}_1^{|\Sigma|}$, where the sender $\mathcal{S}$ uses the blinded row q_0 as its database and receiver $\mathcal{C}$ retrieves the element at position x_0.

At the end, $\mathcal{S}$ has $q_1^{(1)} = -r \bmod |Q|$ and $\mathcal{C}$ has $q_1^{(2)} = q_1 + r \bmod |Q|$.

Protocol for kth state transition. Prior to the protocol, $\mathcal{C}$ and $\mathcal{S}$ additively share the kth state (i.e., $\mathcal{S}$ has $q_k^{(1)}$ and $\mathcal{C}$ has $q_k^{(2)}$ such that $q_k = q_k^{(1)} + q_k^{(2)}$ mod $|Q|$); $\mathcal{C}$ also holds the next input character x_k and $\mathcal{S}$ holds the transition matrix Δ. The output consists of $\mathcal{C}$ and $\mathcal{S}$ additively sharing the $(k+1)$st state q_{k+1}.

1. $\mathcal{S}$ chooses $r \xleftarrow{R} \mathbb{Z}_{|Q|}$ and blinds each element of Δ by adding r to the element modulo $|Q|$. $\mathcal{S}$ rotates the matrix $q_k^{(1)}$ rows up to obtain modified matrix Δ_k.
2. $\mathcal{C}$ generates a binary vector of length $|\Sigma|$ consisting of a 1 at position x_k and 0's in other positions. $\mathcal{C}$ encrypts the vector with pk and sends encrypted bits $e = (e_0, \ldots, e_{|\Sigma|-1})$ to $\mathcal{S}$, where each $e_i = \mathsf{Enc}_{pk}(b_i)$ and $b_i \in \{0, 1\}$.
3. $\mathcal{S}$ performs matrix multiplication of e and Δ_k using the homomorphic properties of the encryption. As a result, $\mathcal{S}$ obtains a new vector $v = (v_0, \ldots, v_{|Q|})$, that corresponds to an element-wise encryption of the column at position x_k.
4. Both parties engage in an $\mathrm{OT}_1^{|Q|}$, where the sender $\mathcal{S}$ holds vector v and receiver $\mathcal{C}$ retrieves the element at position $q_k^{(2)}$.
5. $\mathcal{C}$ decrypts the value and obtains $q_{k+1}^{(2)}$; $\mathcal{S}$ sets its share to $q_{k+1}^{(1)} = -r$.

Protocol for announcement of result. In the beginning of the protocol, $\mathcal{C}$ and $\mathcal{S}$ additively share state q_N modulo $|Q|$. As a result of this protocol, $\mathcal{C}$ learns whether the evaluation resulted in an accept state or not, i.e., it learns a bit.

1. $\mathcal{S}$ generates a random binary vector f of length $|Q|$ by setting its element at position $j + q_N^{(1)}$ to 1 if the state $j \in F$, and to 0 otherwise.
2. Both parties engage in an $\mathrm{OT}_1^{|Q|}$, where the sender $\mathcal{S}$ holds vector f and receiver $\mathcal{C}$ retrieves the element at position $q_N^{(2)}$.

4   Security Model

The requirements that a scheme for secure outsourcing of OFAE must meet are:

Correctness: The protocol should provide the client with correct evaluation of the service provider's finite state machine M on the client's input x.

Efficiency: Communication and computation complexity of $\mathcal{C}$ ($\mathcal{S}$) should be linear in the size of its input x (in the size of the automaton M (i.e., the size of Δ), respectively). Communication and computation complexity (including round complexity) of the servers should be minimized if possible.

Security: The servers should not learn any information throughout the protocol execution. We assume that the servers are trusted to perform their computation correctly, i.e., they are semi-honest or honest-but-curious in that that they will follow the protocol as prescribed, but might attempt to learn additional information from the intermediate values.

We now can formally define security using the standard definition in secure multi-party computation for semi-honest adversaries. Since the helper servers do not contribute any data to the computation, this should be interpreted as no private input to the function they are evaluating. Then for the purposes of the security definition, all data the servers receive before or during the computation (i.e., the transition matrix and client's input) are considered to be a part of the function and therefore must leak no information. We denote "no data" by $\perp$.

Definition 1. *Let parties $P_0, \ldots, P_{m-1}$ engage in a protocol π that computes function $f(\bot, \ldots, \bot) = (o_0, \ldots, o_{m-1})$, where o_i denotes output of party P_i. Let $\text{VIEW}_\pi(P_i)$ denote the view of participant P_i during the execution of protocol π. It is formed by P_i's input and any internal random coin tosses r_i, as well as messages $m_1, \ldots, m_t$ passed between the parties during protocol execution $\text{VIEW}_\pi(P_i) = (\bot, r_i, m_1, \ldots, m_t)$. We say that protocol π is secure against semi-honest adversaries if for each party P_i there exists a probabilistic polynomial time simulator S_i such that $\{S_i(f(\bot, \ldots, \bot))\} \equiv \{\text{VIEW}_\pi(P_i), \bot\}$, where $\equiv$ denotes computational indistinguishability.*

Note that this standard model allows the helper servers to collude (i.e., share the information) in the multi-party case. The security guarantees must hold as long as the coalition size does not exceed a specific threshold. The computational servers do not receive any output, but rather communicate the result to $\mathcal{C}$.

5   Secure FSM Evaluation

Before proceeding with outsourcing solutions, we give a simplification of the original approach that simultaneously improves its communication and computation overhead. Our simplification involves representing the matrix Δ as a one-dimensional list (instead of a two-dimensional table), and does not affect the functionality or security of the solution while allowing us to skip encryption and handling of encrypted data. When we represent the matrix as a list, we reference element (i, j) of the matrix as the element at index $|\Sigma| i + j$ in the list.

Protocol for 1st state transition. The same as before.

Protocol for kth state transition. Prior the protocol, $\mathcal{C}$ and $\mathcal{S}$ additively share the kth state modulo $|Q|$, and the output of the protocol consists of $\mathcal{C}$ and $\mathcal{S}$ additively sharing the $(k+1)$st state.

1. $\mathcal{S}$ chooses $r \xleftarrow{R} \mathbb{Z}_{|Q|}$ and blinds each element of Δ by adding r to it mod $|Q|$.
2. $\mathcal{S}$ rotates the matrix Δ $q_k^{(1)}$ rows up. Let Δ_k denote the modified matrix. $\mathcal{S}$ then represents Δ_k as a list of $|Q| \cdot |\Sigma|$ elements.
3. $\mathcal{C}$ and $\mathcal{S}$ engage in $\text{OT}_1^{|Q| \cdot |\Sigma|}$, at the end of which $\mathcal{C}$ obtains the element at position $|\Sigma| \cdot q_k^{(2)} + x_k$ from the list corresponding to Δ_k.

Protocol for announcement of result. The same as before.

We now can compare performance of the protocol above with the original solution from [3]. As suggested in [3], we assume that the efficient OT_1^t protocol with amortized single exponentiation per transfer [15] is used. Also, since in this application $|\Sigma| \ll |Q|$, we assume that the transition matrix is transposed (as presented in Section 3) to result in maximal savings from the OT protocol.

In the analysis, we include all modular exponentiations and also count modular multiplications if their number is large; the overall complexity is expressed in the number of modular exponentiations (1 mod exp = κ mod mult). The results for k executions of the kth state transition protocol are presented in

Table 1. Analysis of original and modified oblivious automata evaluation solutions

	Original [3]	Modified
$\mathcal{C}$'s exps	$(|\Sigma|+2)N$	N
$\mathcal{S}$'s exps	$|Q|+N(1+(\log(|Q|)|\Sigma|+|\Sigma|-1)|Q|/\kappa)$	$|Q||\Sigma|+N(1+|\Sigma||Q|/\kappa)$
Comm	$2\kappa N(|\Sigma|+|Q|)$	$\log(|Q|)N|\Sigma||Q|$

Table 1 (the rest of the work is much lower). In the original scheme, in each protocol round, $\mathcal{C}$ performs $|\Sigma|$ encryptions, 1 decryption, and 1 exponentiation (for the OT). $\mathcal{S}$'s work for N OT protocols involves $|Q|+1$ exponentiations and $N|Q|$ multiplications. To process the client's response in each round, it performs $|Q||\Sigma|$ exponentiations with small exponents (or length $\log|Q|$), which results in $N(\log(|Q|)|\Sigma|)/\kappa$ regular modular exponentiations overall. Since the client sends $|\Sigma|$ encrypted values and the OT protocol involves the transfer of $|Q|$ encrypted messages in each round, the overall communication is $2\kappa N(|\Sigma|+|Q|)$.

In the modified scheme, only OT is used, and thus $\mathcal{C}$'s work drops by a factor of $|\Sigma|+2$. $\mathcal{S}$'s work is also lowered, as the dominating term in the original solution is $|Q||\Sigma|N\log(|Q|)/\kappa$, while in the modified scheme it is $|Q||\Sigma|N/\kappa$. This means that the server's work drops by a factor of $\log|Q|$ (which is an improvement by at least an order of magnitude). Even though the communication complexity is now proportional to $N|\Sigma||Q|$ instead of $N(|\Sigma|+|Q|)$ in the original protocol, it can be two orders of magnitude lower due to the overhead caused by the security parameter κ in the original scheme (i.e., for any feasible finite automaton size, $\log|Q|\ll\kappa$; a typical setup can consist of $\log(|Q|)\leq 20$, $|\Sigma|=4$, and $\kappa=1024$).

One of our original motivations for this analysis was large communication overhead of the scheme. For instance, genome sequences can be billions of characters long, but even with the current ability to sample them, the sequences are in the thousands. A FSM that represents a search pattern can have significantly more states than the length of the pattern itself due to the need to handle errors. Thus, for a sample setup of $N=10,000$, $|Q|=50,000$, and $\kappa=1024$, the communication cost of the original solution is 10^{12} bits ≈ 0.125 TB (it is lowered to $\approx 3\cdot 10^{10}$ bits in the modified solution). Such overhead is prohibitively large for many clients (e.g., it can take several days or even months on a rather fast DSL link). Thus, we investigate the use of other OT protocols, which can lower the communication overhead of the protocol. Then depending on the computational power and the bandwidth one has, the most suitable choice can be used.

Besides existing OT protocols, the OT functionality can be achieved by utilizing a Private Information Retrieval (PIR) protocol, which differs from OT in that the receiver may learn additional information about the database besides the item or block it receives. Transferring a PIR protocol to a Symmetric PIR (in which privacy of the database is also preserved, and the receiver learns only its item) can be done at low cost using the techniques from [18] or [19], which will give us an OT protocol. We compare the performance of OFAE using three efficient PIR protocols of different nature. In particular, several PIR protocols (e.g., [20,21,16,17]) were studied in [22], and we select most communication

Table 2. Performance of the original OFAE protocol (except matrix multiplication) using different OT protocols

	Lipmaa OT	GR OT	AG OT
$\mathcal{C}$'s op.	$K_1 N \log(|Q|)(\log(|Q|)/2 - 1)$	$(4NK_e\sqrt{|Q|})$	$N(K_3^{\log 10} + 2K_3^{\log 5} + |Q|K_e)$
$\mathcal{S}$'s op.	$(2|Q| - \log(|Q|))K_1 N$	$2|Q|K_e N$	NK_3^2
Comm	$N((K_1/2)\log^2(|Q|)+$ $+3K_e\log(|Q|))$	$N(\log(|Q|) + K_e + 4$ $+ \log(\log(|Q|)))$	$N|Q|K_e K_3^2$

Table 3. Performance of the simplified OFAE protocol using different OT protocols

	Lipmaa OT	GR OT	AG OT
$\mathcal{C}$'s op.	$K_1 N \log(|Q||\Sigma|)\times$ $\times (\log(|Q||\Sigma|)/2 - 1)$	$(4N\log(|Q|)\sqrt{|Q||\Sigma|})$	$N(K_3^{\log 10} + 2K_3^{\log 5}$ $+|Q||\Sigma|\log(|Q|))$
$\mathcal{S}$'s op.	$(2|Q||\Sigma| - \log(|Q||\Sigma|))K_1 N$	$2|Q||\Sigma|\log(|Q|)N$	NK_3^2
Comm	$N((K_1/2)\log^2(|Q||\Sigma|)+$ $+3\log(|Q|)\log(|Q||\Sigma|))$	$N(\log(|Q||\Sigma|) + \log(|Q|)+$ $+4 + \log(\log(|Q||\Sigma|)))$	$N|Q||\Sigma|\log(|Q|)K_3^2$

efficient solutions of Lipmaa [16] and Gentry-Ramzan (GR) [17], as well as a recent lattice-based protocol of Aguilar Melchor-Gaborit (AG) [23] with very light computation overhead. We replace the original OT protocol [15] in both OFAE solutions of Sections 3 and 5 by an OT protocol based on these PIR schemes.

Before presenting our analysis, we need to point out the differences between these protocols because they are based on different setups, which will require the use of different security parameters and underlying operations. More precisely, the Lipmaa's protocol is based on the use of a length-flexible additively homomorphic encryption scheme (such as [24]), the GR protocol uses groups with special properties (in which Φ-hiding assumption holds), and the AG protocol is a lattice-based PIR scheme. Thus, to achieve as precise analysis as possible, we measure the computation overhead in the number of group operations, and describe what a group operation involves in each solution.

The complexity analysis of the original OFAE approach (except the matrix multiplication in step 3 of the kth state transition protocol in Section 3) is given in Table 2, where work is measured in group operations. The matrix multiplication cost (which is the same regardless of the OT scheme used) is given below:

	Matrix Multiplication
$\mathcal{C}$'s group op.	$(|\Sigma| + 2)K_e N$
$\mathcal{S}$'s group op.	$N|Q|K_e(\log(|Q|)|\Sigma| + |\Sigma| - 1)$
Comm	$NK_e(|Q| + |\Sigma|)$

Similarly, Table 3 presents analysis of our modified scheme. In the tables, K_1, K_2, and K_3 are security parameters for each scheme and K_e is the security parameter for the homomorphic encryption scheme (i.e., $K_e = \kappa$). In Lipmaa's solution, K_1 is the same as K_e, and thus is near 1024 ([25] also reports that in the Lipmaa's PIR the sender's computation could be reduced by almost 38% through optimization). In GR approach, K_2 is a parameter of a similar length, but it also depends on the configuration of the OT protocol for which it is used.

In particular, $K_2 = \max(\kappa, \ell, f(\log(t)))$ for OT_1^t, where ℓ is the size of an element in the OT protocol and $f(\cdot)$ is a polynomial function. K_2 is not used in the tables, but it determines the cost of the group operation (multiplication modulo K_2-bit numbers). Note that in the original solution, the OT protocol is called on blocks of size 2κ, and to reduce the overhead associated with high K_2, each block can be partitioned into several blocks of smaller size (which results in executing the OT more than once).

In the AG solution, the security parameter K_3 is suggested to be set to 50, but the group operations are performed using elements in $\mathbb{Z}_p$ for prime p of size $3(\lceil \log(tK_3) \rceil + 1)$ on the database of size t. Note that the value of t in OT_1^t is different in the original and modified solutions ($|Q|$ and $|Q||\Sigma|$, respectively), which will affect the overhead of group operations when they depend on t.

From these options, the AG solution has the highest communication cost (which can be further increased to lower the computation), but it is very computation efficient unlike other protocols (also see [26] for further discussion). Thus, it is ideally suited for parties with very fast communication links. The GR approach, on the other hand, has the lowest communication cost, although the amount of computation carried on the server side as well as the client side are more pronounced. Thus, the first two methods based on Lipmaa's and GR PIR schemes should be used when the bandwidth is an issue of consideration, while the third approach gives the fastest performance with respect to the execution time assuming a fast data link between the participants.

6   Secure Outsourcing of FSM Computation

Secure two-party outsourcing. The idea behind this solution is that the client $\mathcal{C}$ additively splits (modulo $|\Sigma|$) each character of its x between helper servers P_0 and P_1. Likewise, $\mathcal{S}$ splits (modulo $|Q|$) each element of its matrix Δ between P_0 and P_1. We refer to the P_i's share (for $i = 0, 1$) of string x as $x^{(i)}$ and its share of the kth character of x as $x_k^{(i)}$. Similarly, we refer to the P_i's share of Δ as $\Delta^{(i)}$ and its share of the element of Δ at position (j_1, j_2) as $\Delta^{(i)}(j_1, j_2)$. The helper servers are also given q_0, i.e., they know what row in the matrix is the start state (which gives no information about the automaton itself). Finally, P_0 and P_1 receive information about final states F in a split form. We represent F as a bit vector of length $|Q|$ that has jth bit set to 1 iff state $j \in F$. This vector is additively split modulo 2 (i.e., XOR-split) between P_0 and P_1.

During the kth state transition, P_0 acts as $\mathcal{S}$ in the previous solution and P_1 as $\mathcal{C}$, except that the share of the matrix P_0 possesses is rotated by both P_0's share of the next input character $x_k^{(0)}$ and its share of the current state $q_k^{(0)}$. At the end of this execution, P_0 and P_1 additively share some value q'. The same steps are also performed with the roles of P_0 and P_1 reversed (using P_1's share of the transition matrix), which results in P_0 and P_1 additively sharing another value q''. Finally, P_0 and P_1 each locally add their shares of q' and q'', which results in state q_{k+1} being split (modulo $|Q|$) between them.

Protocol for 1st state transition.

1. For $i = 0, 1$, P_i chooses value $r_i \xleftarrow{R} \mathbb{Z}_{|Q|}$, blinds each element of row q_0 by adding r_i to it modulo $|Q|$ and rotates the row $x_0^{(i)}$ elements left.
2. For $i = 0, 1$, P_i engages in $\mathrm{OT}_1^{|\Sigma|}$ with P_{1-i}, where the sender P_i holds the modified row q_0, and receiver P_{1-i} obtains the element at position $x_0^{(1-i)}$. Denote the element that P_{1-i} receives by s_i.
3. For $i = 0, 1$, P_i sets its share of state q_1 to $q_1^{(i)} = s_{1-i} - r_i \bmod |Q|$.

Protocol for kth state transition. Prior to the protocol, P_0 and P_1 additively share the kth state q_k (modulo $|Q|$), the kth input character x_k (modulo $|\Sigma|$), and each element $\Delta(i, j)$ of Δ for $0 \le i < |Q|$ and $0 \le j < |\Sigma|$ (modulo $|Q|$). The output consists of P_0 and P_1 additively sharing the state q_{k+1} modulo $|Q|$.

1. For $i = 0, 1$, P_i chooses $r_i \xleftarrow{R} \mathbb{Z}_{|Q|}$ and adds it to each $\Delta^{(i)}(j_1, j_2) \bmod |Q|$.
2. For $i = 0, 1$, P_i rotates the resulting matrix $\Delta^{(i)}$ $q_k^{(i)}$ rows up and $x_k^{(i)}$ elements left, and represents it as a list of $|Q| \cdot |\Sigma|$ elements, denoted by $\Delta_k^{(i)}$.
3. For $i = 0, 1$, P_i engages with P_{1-i} in $\mathrm{OT}_1^{|Q| \cdot |\Sigma|}$ (where P_i acts as the sender), at the end of which P_{1-i} obtains the element at position $|\Sigma| \cdot q_k^{(1-i)} + x_k^{(1-i)}$ from the database $\Delta_k^{(i)}$ prepared by P_i. Denote the retrieved element by s_i.
4. For $i = 0, 1$, P_i sets its share of state q_{k+1} to $q_{k+1}^{(i)} = s_{1-i} - r_i \bmod |Q|$.

In the above $q' = s_0 - r_0 \bmod |Q|$ and $q'' = s_1 - r_1 \bmod |Q|$, and also $q_{k+1}^{(0)} = s_1 - r_0 \bmod |Q|$ and $q_{k+1}^{(1)} = s_0 - r_1 \bmod |Q|$.

Protocol for announcement of result. In the beginning, P_0 and P_1 share XOR-split bit vector F, and at the end $\mathcal{C}$ learns the bit of F at position q_N.

1. For $i = 0, 1$, P_i generates a random bit b_i and blinds its vector $F^{(i)}$ by XORing it with b_i. P_i then rotates its $q_N^{(i)}$ bits left.
2. For $i = 0, 1$, P_i engages in $\mathrm{OT}_1^{|Q|}$ with P_{1-i}, where P_i uses it modified vector $F^{(i)}$ as the sender and P_{i-1} retrieves the bit c_i at position $q_N^{(1-i)}$.
3. For $i = 0, 1$, P_i sets it share of the result to $f^{(i)} = b_i \oplus c_{1-i}$.
4. P_0 and P_1 send $f^{(0)}$ and $f^{(1)}$ to $\mathcal{C}$, who XORs them and learns the result.

Secure multi-party outsourcing. To generalize the above solution to multiple parties $P_0, \ldots, P_{m-1}$, we first need to have $\mathcal{C}$ and $\mathcal{S}$ split their data among all parties. For a split item a, we use $a^{(i)}$ to denote the share party P_i has. Since now both the input characters and the current state will be split among m participants, any solution that involves data rotation by a share of the state or input character becomes more expensive. In particular, at least $m-1$ parties need to rotate the data in a predetermined order using their own shares. This means that the data to be rotated must be obfuscated from others (i.e., encrypted) when it leaves the owner and it also means that each party needs to re-randomize the data to hide the amount of rotation. With this (or any other secure) approach, the work performed by one party in a single execution of the state transition protocol is inevitably $O(|Q||\Sigma|)$ (and is also a function of κ), and we wish to minimize the amount of work other parties need to perform, as well as their communication complexity. Therefore, we reduce the overhead of most parties to $O(\sqrt{|Q||\Sigma|})$ by representing the transition matrix Δ as a two-dimensional array of size $\sqrt{|Q||\Sigma|} \times \sqrt{|Q||\Sigma|}$. The interaction is then similar at the high-level to the interaction in the original protocol and proceeds as follows: one party generates a vector of encrypted bits of size $\sqrt{|Q||\Sigma|}$, $m-2$ parties sequentially rotate and randomize it, and the last party performs matrix multiplication to create a new vector of the same size. This vector is also passed to $m-2$ parties for rotation and re-randomization, after which the last party obtains the decryption of one element of it. This process is repeated for each share of the matrix $\Delta^{(i)}$.

Our solution requires the parties to convert shares $v^{(i)}$ of value v additively split modulo n to additive shares of it modulo $|Q|$. To do so, the parties will need to compute the quotient $u = \lfloor \sum_{i=1}^{m} v^{(i)}/n \rfloor$ and use it to adjust the shares. To prevent the parties from learning u, we additively split it over integers. Since $0 \leq u < m$, we define $B > m2^{\kappa'}$, where κ' is a security parameter. Then if we choose shares of u from $[-B, B]$, the value of u will be statistically hidden.

Finally, the parties now use a threshold homomorphic encryption scheme, in which the public key pk is known to everyone, but the decryption key sk is split among them. Here we require all m parties to participate in decryption (i.e., use (m, m)-threshold encryption), and the threshold multi-party solution given in [10] will have the threshold set to t (i.e., (t, m)-threshold encryption).

Before presenting the main protocols, we describe a sub-protocol, RotateAndShare, that will be utilized in all of them, but will be called on different types of data. This sub-protocol assumes that one party, P_i, has a vector, which will be encrypted, and then rotated by a certain amount, re-randomized, and blinded by every party. P_i will be the data owner and plays a special role in the protocol. The amount of rotation is determined by some value additively split among all parties (e.g., the current state q_k). Blinding involves adding a random value r_i to the encrypted contents by each party. Then when the last party chooses an element of the vector, other parties jointly decrypt that value for it. At this point, all parties jointly hold additive shares of the result modulo n. As the last (and optional) step, they engage in the computation to convert the additive shares modulo n to additive shares modulo a different modulus n'.

RotateAndShare: The input consists of value i, $0 \leq i \leq m-1$, encryption $\mathcal{E}$ with public key pk, modulus n, and distributed secret key sk, final modulus n' (if no conversion is necessary, n' is set to $\perp$), party P_i inputs vector $v = (v_0, \ldots, v_{\ell-1})$ and its length ℓ, and each party P_j, $0 \leq j \leq m-1$ inputs amount of rotation $rt^{(j)}$. The output consists of the parties additively sharing value o modulo n' (or modulo n if $n' = \perp$), which corresponds to one of the values from vector v.

1. P_i chooses $r_i \xleftarrow{R} \mathbb{Z}_n$, adds it modulo n to each v_j, and encrypts each result with pk to obtain $e = (e_0, \ldots, e_{\ell-1})$, where $e_j = \mathsf{Enc}_{pk}(v_j + r_i)$ for $j = 0, \ldots, \ell - 1$. P_i circularly rotates the elements of e $rt^{(i)}$ positions left and sends the result to P_{i+1}.

2. P_{i+1} circularly rotates the vector it received $rt^{(i+1)}$ positions left. It also chooses $r_{i+1} \xleftarrow{R} \mathbb{Z}_n$ and multiplies each element of its resulting vector by different encryptions $\mathsf{Enc}_{pk}(r_{i+1})$ (or by the same encryption, but then

re-randomizes each element). This adds r_{i+1} to the encrypted values. P_{i+1} sends the result to P_{i+2}.

3. Each of $P_{i+2}, \ldots, P_{m-1}, P_0, \ldots, P_{i-2}$ sequentially perform the same steps at P_{i+1} using their respective values of randomness r and rotation amount rt.

4. Parties P_{i-2} and P_{i-1} engage in OT_1^ℓ, where the sender P_{i-2} has the final encrypted vector and receiver P_{i-1} uses index $rt^{(i-1)}$. This results in P_{i-1} obtaining an encrypted value at position $\left(\sum_{j=0}^{m-1} rt^{(j)}\right) \bmod \ell$ in v blinded with $\left(\sum_{j\in[0,m-1],j\neq i-1} r_j\right) \bmod n$. P_{i-1} re-randomizes that values asks the rest of participants to decrypt it, and sets r_{i-1} to the decrypted value.

5. Now, if $n' \neq \perp$, the parties re-share the result modulo n'. To do so, they compute the number of times the sum of the shares "wraps around" the modulus n and use it in their computation. The parties engage in secure multi-party computation, e.g., using a standard multi-party Boolean circuit [27]. Here each party inputs its share, they jointly compute $u = \lfloor(\sum_{j=0}^{m-1} r_j)/n\rfloor$ (e.g., by repeated subtraction of n from the sum) and the output is additively shared over the integers. That is, party P_j for $j = 0, \ldots, m-2$ receives a random $s_j \in [-B, B]$ and party P_{m-1} receives $s_{m-1} = u - \sum_{j=0}^{m-2} s_j$.

6. Party P_j, for $j = 0, \ldots, m-1$, sets its output $o^{(j)}$ to $(s_j \cdot n - r_j) \bmod n'$.

We are now ready to present the main protocols of the multi-party outsourcing.

Protocol for 1st state transition.

1. For $i = 0, \ldots, m-1$, execute in parallel: P_i sets v to be the q_0th row of its $\Delta^{(i)}$ and all parties execute $\mathsf{RotateAndShare}(i, \mathcal{E}, pk, sk, |Q|, v, |\Sigma|, x_0^{(0)}, \ldots, x_0^{(m-1)})$. Let $o_i^{(j)}$ denote the output P_j receives after such execution on P_i's data.

2. For $i = 0, \ldots, m-1$, party P_i sets its share of q_1 to $q_1^{(i)} = \sum_{j=0}^{m-1} o_j^{(i)} \bmod |Q|$.

Protocol for kth state transition. Prior to the protocol execution, the parties additively share the kth state q_k (modulo $|Q|$), the kth input character x_k (modulo $|\Sigma|$), and each element $\Delta(i,j)$ of Δ for $0 \le i < |Q|$ and $0 \le j < |\Sigma|$ (modulo $|Q|$). At the end, they additively share state q_{k+1} (modulo $|Q|$).

For $i = 0, \ldots, m-1$, perform in parallel using the share $\Delta^{(i)}$ of Δ:

1. P_i rotates the matrix $\Delta^{(i)}$ $q_k^{(i)}$ rows up and $x_k^{(i)}$ elements left. We denote the resulting matrix by $\Delta_k^{(i)}$. P_i represents $\Delta_k^{(i)}$ as a two-dimensional array of roughly square size as follows[1]: P_i computes the size of the first dimension of the matrix as $d_1 = \lceil\sqrt{|Q||\Sigma|}\rceil$ and the size of the second dimension as $d_2 = \lceil|Q|/d_1\rceil|\Sigma|$. P_i then creates columns 0 through $|\Sigma|-1$ of the modified matrix using rows 0 through $d_1 - 1$ of $\Delta_k^{(i)}$, columns $|\Sigma|$ through $2|\Sigma| - 1$ using rows d_1 through $2d_1 - 1$ of $\Delta_k^{(i)}$, etc. In other words, the modified square matrix, denoted $\tilde\Delta_k^{(i)}$, is filled in stripes of width $|\Sigma|$ until all of $|Q|$ rows are used (note that part of the square might be incomplete due to rounding in the computation). Empty cells are then filled with dummy entries to make it a full matrix of size $d_1 \times d_2$.

---

[1] In the current discussion we assume that $|\Sigma| < |Q|$, but the technique can be used when either $|\Sigma| < |Q|$ or $|Q| < |\Sigma|$.

2. Party P_{i+1} creates a vector of encrypted values $e = (e_0, \ldots, e_{d_1-1})$ using homomorphic encryption, where the value at position $q_k^{(i+1)} \bmod d_1$ corresponds to encryption of 1, and all other e_j's to encryption of 0.

3. Party P_{i+1} sends the vector to P_{i+2}, who performs a circular rotation of it $q_k^{(i+2)}$ values left and re-randomizes the encrypted values. The encrypted vector is sequentially processed by parties $P_{i+2}, \ldots, P_{m-1}, P_0, \ldots, P_{i-1}$ who perform the same operations as P_{i+2} using their respective shares of q_k.

4. P_{i-1} sends the final vector $\tilde{e} = (\tilde{e}_0, \ldots, \tilde{e}_{d_1-1})$ to P_i. P_i performs matrix multiplication using $\tilde{e}$ and $\tilde{\Delta}^{(i)}$ as follows: compute the jth element of the resulting vector v as $v_j = \prod_{\ell=0}^{d_1-1} \tilde{e}_\ell^{\tilde{\Delta}_k^{(i)}(\ell, j)}$. Now the vector v corresponds to the element-wise encryption of the row of the matrix $\tilde{\Delta}_k^{(i)}$ at index $q_k \bmod d_1$.

5. All parties execute a modified algorithm $\mathsf{RotateAndShare}(i, \mathcal{E}, pk, sk, |Q|, v, d_2,$ $(x_k^{(0)}, \lfloor q_k^{(0)}/d_1 \rfloor |\Sigma|), \ldots, (x_k^{(m-1)}, \lfloor q_k^{(m-1)}/d_1 \rfloor |\Sigma|))$ with the following changes:
   (a) The vector v is already in an encrypted form, so no encryption is performed in step 1 of $\mathsf{RotateAndShare}$.
   (b) Instead of each P_j rotating the vector by amount $rt^{(j)}$, $rt^{(j)}$ now consists of two parts, $rt_1^{(j)}$ and $rt_2^{(j)}$. Starting from $j = i$, P_j divides the vector v into blocks of size $|\Sigma|$ and circularly rotates each block $rt_1^{(j)}$ positions left, and then rotates the overall resulting vector $rt_2^{(j)}$ positions left.
   (c) Using two different values for the amount of rotation also affects the oblivious transfer in step 4 of the protocol. Now party P_{i-1} selects the element at position $rt_1^{(i-1)} + rt_2^{(i-1)} |\Sigma|$.

Let $o_j^{(i)}$ denote the output party P_j receives as a result of such execution. After executing these steps on all shares of the database $\Delta^{(i)}$, party P_j sets its share of q_{k+1}, $q_{k+1}^{(j)}$, to the sum of the values it received in step 5 of the protocol executions, i.e., $q_{k+1}^{(j)} = \sum_{i=0}^{m-1} o_i^{(j)} \bmod |Q|$.

Protocol for announcement of result. Prior to the protocol, $P_0, \ldots, P_{m-1}$ additively share the state q_N and also share vector F XOR-split between them.

1. For $i = 0, \ldots, m - 1$, execute in parallel: the parties call $\mathsf{RotateAndShare}(i, \mathcal{E}, pk, sk, \bot, F^{(i)}, |Q|, q_N^{(0)}, \ldots, q_N^{(m-1)})$. Let $o_j^{(i)}$ denote the output party P_j receives.

2. For $i = 0, \ldots, m - 1$, P_i computes $f^{(i)} = \sum_{j=0}^{m-1} o_j^{(i)} \bmod n$ and sends $f^{(i)}$ to $\mathcal{C}$.

$\mathcal{C}$ recovers the result by computing bit $b = \sum_{i=0}^{m-1} f^{(i)} \bmod n$.

The above protocol calls $\mathsf{RotateAndShare}$ without modulus conversion. The reason is that the client can easily recover the result by adding the shares it received modulo n. If the client is extremely weak, however, the above protocol can include modulus conversion from n to 2 at the cost of the increased work for the helper servers. In this case, the client performs only $m - 1$ bit XORs.

Also note that the protocol for announcement of the result can have a similar structure to the kth state transition protocol if the vector F is represented as a matrix of size $\sqrt{|Q|} \times \sqrt{|Q|}$. Then the computation and communication complexity of all parties will be reduced by a significant amount. But since this protocol is executed only once (as opposed to the kth state transition protocol), we leave it in the simple form above.

Remark. The above technique allow us to have communication associated with processing a square two-dimensional grid to be linear in the size of its one dimension. One might ask if it might be possible to further reduce the communication by represented the matrix as a high-dimensional hypercube and still have communication to be proportional to its single dimension. Such technique was employed in private information retrieval systems to dramatically decrease communication cost to $O(\ell^\epsilon)$ for any $\epsilon > 0$ [21] or $O(\log^2(\ell))$ [16] with stronger privacy guarantees for a database of size ℓ. Here we note that such a solution would not work in our setting because decreasing the dimension of the matrix (represented as a hypercube of any dimension) by one requires interaction of all of the participants, and thus would involve communication close to linear in the matrix size in our case (this technique worked for PIR systems when the entire database is stored at a single location).

7   Analysis

We now evaluate correctness and security properties and analyze complexity.

Correctness. Correctness of the protocols follows by examination. That is, during each round of the protocol, the parties additively share the value of the next state that can be found in matrix $\Delta^{(i)}$ for each participant P_i and add them all together to correctly share the next state. The same applies to the protocol for announcement of the result.

Security. The argument for achieving security in presence of semi-honest parties that we use here is very standard, and is based on the following components:

- The composition theorem due to Canetti [28] states that composition of secure protocols remains secure. This means that the security of the overall solution reduces to ensuring that sub-protocols or other tools used as a part of it are secure against semi-honest adversaries.
- Semantic security of homomorphic encryption ensures that no information about the underlying plaintext can be learned by observing its encryption. Threshold encryption ensures that participation of a predefined number of parties (including all parties) is necessary for decryption.
- Additive secret sharing ensures unconditional security as long as there is at least one honest party that does not collude with the rest of the participants.

Given the above, it is straightforward to build a simulator that will simulate the view of the computational parties without access to $\mathcal{C}$'s or $\mathcal{S}$'s data. That is, every time encryption is used, it can produce encryptions of random values that will be indistinguishable from real data due to the security property of encryption, and every time shares are used, it will also produce random shares that will be indistinguishable from the shares used in the real execution. Since only secure and composable components are used in the protocols, the overall solution is secure as well.

Complexity. We analyze computation and communication complexity of two-party and multi-party outsourcing protocols separately. The analysis corresponds to the N executions of the kth state transition protocol (as the rest of the overhead will be orders of magnitude lower).

Two-party outsourcing: The client C only splits its input between two servers, therefore the computation is near N (no cryptography is used) and communication is $2N \log(|\Sigma|)$. The service provider S splits the representation of its automaton M among two servers, with the computation being near $|M|$ and communication approximately twice the size of representing M (i.e., near $|Q||\Sigma| \log(|Q|)$). Each computational server incurs computation and communication overhead of both C and S in the solution with no outsourcing (as given in Table 1). That is, each server performs about $|Q||\Sigma| + N(2 + |\Sigma||Q|/\kappa)$ modulo exponentiations and communicates about $2 \log(|Q|) N |\Sigma||Q|$ bits.

Multi-party outsourcing: The work and communication of C and S remain similar to the two-party case, except that splitting of their data and communication needs to be done for m servers instead of two. This means that work becomes proportional to m (with no cryptographic operations, as before), which for C means mN and for S is $m|M|$, and their communication is $mN \log(|\Sigma|)$ and near $m|Q||\Sigma| \log(|Q|)$, respectively. The computation and communication requirements for the computational servers also now increase by a factor of m and are as follows. The main computation overhead comes from (i) $2\sqrt{|Q||\Sigma|}(m-1)$ modular exponentiations in each round due to re-randomization; (ii) $|Q||\Sigma| \log(|Q|)$ modular multiplications in each round for matrix multiplication; (iii) $\kappa \, \text{OT}_1^2$ executions for the Boolean circuit and one $\text{OT}_1^{\sqrt{|Q||\Sigma|}}$ in each round. We assume that the OT protocol with low amortized cost (one mod exp per transfer) is used. The communication complexity is dominated by the transmission of encrypted vectors and the OT protocol and is near $4\kappa(m-1)N\sqrt{|Q||\Sigma|}$.

Acknowledgments. Portions of this work were sponsored by grant AFOSR-FA9550-09-1-0223. The first author would like to thank Scott Emrich for useful discussions regarding DNA processing technology.

References

1. Atallah, M., Kerschbaum, F., Du, W.: Secure and private sequence comparisons. In: WPES, pp. 39–44 (2003)
2. Jha, S., Kruger, L., Shmatikov, V.: Towards practical privacy for genomic computation. In: IEEE Symposium on Security and Privacy, pp. 216–230 (2008)
3. Troncoso-Pastoriza, J., Katzenbeisser, S., Celik, M.: Privacy preserving error resilient DNA searching through oblivious automata. In: ACM CCS, pp. 519–528 (2007)
4. Frikken, K.: Practical private DNA string searching and matching through efficient oblivious automata evaluation. In: DBSec, pp. 81–94 (2009)
5. Bruekers, F., Katzenbeisser, S., Kursawe, K., Tuyls, P.: Privacy-preserving matching of DNA profiles. ePrint Cryptology Archive Report 2008/203 (2008)
6. Wang, R., Wang, X., Li, Z., Tang, H., Reiter, M., Dong, Z.: Privacy-preserving genomic computation through program specialization. In: ACM CCS, pp. 338–347 (2009)

7. Atallah, M., Li, J.: Secure outsourcing of sequence comparisons. In: PET, pp. 63–78 (2004)
8. Atallah, M., Li, J.: Secure outsourcing of sequence comparisons. International Journal of Information Security 4(4), 277–287 (2005)
9. Genetic Testing for Health, Disease & Ancestry; DNA Test – 23andMe, http://www.23andme.com
10. Blanton, M., Aliasgari, M.: Secure outsourcing of DNA searching via finite automata. Technical Report 2010–03, University of Notre Dame (2010)
11. Szajda, D., Pohl, M., Owen, J., Lawson, B.: Toward a practical data privacy scheme for a distributed implementation of the Smith-Waterman genome sequence comparison algorithm. In: NDSS (2006)
12. Kantarcioglu, M., Jiang, W., Liu, Y., Malin, B.: A cryptographic approach to securely share and query genomic sequences. IEEE Transactions on Information Technology in Biomedicine 12(5), 606–617 (2008)
13. Franklin, M., Gondree, M., Mohassel, P.: Communication-efficient private protocols for longest common subsequence. In: RSA, pp. 265–278 (2009)
14. Gondree, M., Mohassel, P.: Longest common subsequence as private search. In: WPES, pp. 81–90 (2009)
15. Naor, M., Pinkas, B.: Efficient oblivious transfer protocols. In: SODA, pp. 448–457 (2001)
16. Lipmaa, H.: An oblivious transfer protocol with log-squared communication. In: Zhou, J., López, J., Deng, R.H., Bao, F. (eds.) ISC 2005. LNCS, vol. 3650, pp. 314–328. Springer, Heidelberg (2005)
17. Gentry, C., Ramzan, Z.: Single-database private information retrieval with constant communication rate. In: ICALP, pp. 803–815 (2005)
18. Naor, M., Pinkas, B.: Oblivious transfer and polynomial evaluation. In: STOC (1999)
19. Crescenzo, G., Malkin, T., Ostrovsky, R.: Single database private information retrieval implies oblivious transfer. In: Preneel, B. (ed.) EUROCRYPT 2000. LNCS, vol. 1807, pp. 122–138. Springer, Heidelberg (2000)
20. Cachin, C., Micali, S., Stadler, M.: Computationally private information retrieval with polylogarithmic communication. In: Stern, J. (ed.) EUROCRYPT 1999. LNCS, vol. 1592, pp. 402–414. Springer, Heidelberg (1999)
21. Kushilevitz, E., Ostrovsky, R.: Replication is not needed: Single database, computationally-private information retrieval. In: IEEE FOCS, pp. 364–373 (1997)
22. Melchor, C.A., Deswarte, Y.: Single-database private information retrieval schemes: Overview, performance study, and usage with statistical databases. In: Privacy in Statistical Databases, pp. 257–265 (2006)
23. Aguilar-Melchor, C., Gaborit, P.: A lattice-based computationally-efficient private information retrieval protocol. In: WEWORC (2007)
24. Damgard, I., Jurik, M.: A length-flexible threshold cryptosystem with applications. In: Australasian Conference on Information Security and Privacy (2007)
25. Bae, H.: Design and analysis for log-squared and log private information retrieval (2008)
26. Melchor, C., Crespin, B., Gaborit, P., Jolivet, V.: High-speed private information retrieval computation on GPU. In: IEEE SECURWARE (2008)
27. Goldreich, O., Micali, S., Wigderson, A.: How to play any mental game. In: STOC, pp. 218–229 (1987)
28. Canetti, R.: Security and composition of multiparty cryptographic protocols. Journal of Cryptology 13(1), 143–202 (2000)

A Labelling System for Derived Data Control

Enrico Scalavino, Vaibhav Gowadia, and Emil C. Lupu

Department of Computing, Imperial College London
{escala,vgowadia,e.c.lupu}@imperial.ac.uk

Abstract. Existing ERM/DRM systems and more generally usage control systems aim to control who accesses data and the usage data is subject to even after the data has been disseminated to recipients. However, once the data has been used, no control or protection is applied to the information created as result of the usage. We propose a solution to derive protection requirements for *derived data* that makes use of Multi-Level Security (MLS) labels to associate data with its protection level and usage functions (*transformations*) with the protection requirements of the data they can derive. Users are also associated with clearance labels according to their roles. Clearance and data labels are used to determine whether a user can access data as in traditional Mandatory Access Control systems, while labels associated with transformations are used to derive labels for derived data. The solution assumes that the amount of sensitive information flowing from the input to the output of a transformation can be deduced from the input data and the transformation itself, so that adequate protection can be associated with the derived output.

1 Introduction

Controlling the usage of digital resources has been the focus of an intense research activity in recent years. Individuals and organisations share a vast amount of data often in an uncontrolled fashion. Fast and pervasive data sharing facilitates both social relationships and inter-organisational cooperation but also raises new issues that were partially neglected before. Most information flows freely without restrictions; the only controls are governance procedures with which employees in companies are expected to comply and *Data Sharing Agreements (DSAs)* between partners regarding the handling of shared data. However, data has often an intrinsic commercial or personal value and must therefore be protected from undesired accesses and usages, regardless of its physical location and thus even after it has been received by unknown remote parties. Further attention to this topic has been prompted by industrial interests in the development of Digital Rights Management (DRM) solutions and by public interests in the enforcement of an increasing amount of legislation regarding the handling of private data such as HIPAA in the US.

Approaches proposed by both academia and industry are sometimes referred to as *Enterprise Rights Management* (ERM) and rely on a client-side Virtual Machine (VM) that ensures data usage complies with the associated usage policies. Data is cryptographically protected before being disseminated so that only a central *trusted authority (TA)* (or *Control Centre*) can issue the decryption keys and access rights to the authorised

S. Foresti and S. Jajodia (Eds.): Data and Applications Security XXIV, LNCS 6166, pp. 65–80, 2010.

VMs on client devices. Solutions often rely on Trusted Computing (TC) architectures to guarantee trusted execution on VMs. Although the number of existing solutions covers different requirements and scenarios, they are generally based on a common perspective and only differ in their management of user authentication, policy and rights retrieval, audit of user actions and other tasks [1,2,3,4,5].

Despite the wide range of control policies that can be specified and deployed in current solutions, the important issue of catering for *derived data* has been generally ignored. In DRM derived data is defined as a resource that contains parts of an original work. Park and Sandhu [6] define derived data as an object created as a consequence of exercising rights on an original one (e.g. a log file). Stemming from this definition, we define derived data as *an object created as a consequence of performing a transformation on one or several original ones*. The concept of *transformation*, i.e. any function applicable to one or several data objects that either modifies them or returns a new one, is central to our solution. Here, we use the terms data, objects and (data) resources interchangeably.

Derivative works are protected in most jurisdictions amongst others by copyright law, such as the Copyright Act in the US. Protection of derived data is also a big concern for companies exchanging data under specific DSAs. Results, obtained through the usage of shared information, are an asset often more valuable than the original data and thus included in the sharing agreements. Existing DRM/ERM and Usage Control systems mostly neglect the problem. A user authorised to access protected data under certain constraints could use it to produce an unprotected derivative work, thus infringing the rights of the original owner. Legislations are purposely ambiguous in defining when a resource can be considered as "derived". However, when there is a significant economic interest at stake, relying on the recipients' interpretation of law may prove hazardous.

Similarly to other information flow solutions [7,8,9,10] we use a labelling system to label data under several sensitivity domains. When a new data item is derived (or simply modified), the amount of sensitive information for each sensitivity domain with respect to the original data can either increase, decrease or remain unchanged. With each derivation the data may therefore be declassified or classified, i.e. its applied protection may be decreased or increased respectively. Since the sensitivity of derived data does not solely depend on the sensitivity of the original data but also on the type of transformation that has been applied to it, we associate sensitivity domains with transformations as well as with the data itself. This ensures that the derived data is correctly protected on the basis of all the resources that contributed to its creation.

The remainder of this paper is organised as follows: related work is presented in Section 2 whilst Section 3 describes an application scenario providing a context for the examples; Section 4 introduces the concept of *data label*; Section 5 introduces the concept of *transformation* and shows how our work can be applied to XML data, whilst Section 6 shows how to integrate labels into an example ERM system; Section 7 describes the label derivation mechanism for derived data; Section 8 introduces a solution to create user-customised sensitivity domains. Finally, conclusions are drawn in Section 9, which also briefly discusses future work.

2   Related Work

Protecting data and controlling its usage when it is disseminated amongst unknown recipients has been gaining increasing attention in recent years, in particular because of the impulse given to the topic by DRM and ERM systems developed in industry. The architecture at the core of most existing systems such as Liquid Machines [11], Marlin [12], Authentica [1] or Microsoft RMS (Rights Management System) [2], is well-described by Park et al. [4] who identify different architectures for ERM design. A Virtual Machine running on recipients' devices enforces a Control Set, i.e. a list of usage control policies or rights received from a remote Control Centre. Control Centres are remote services evaluating recipients' requests and issuing policies, decryption keys and encryption keys when data originators need to *publish* new data. The solutions comprising these elements generally differ in the authorisation policy language they use, the authentication mechanisms employed, the policy deployment methods and the techniques used to store credentials.

Several languages for policy specification have also been proposed. Standard XML-based languages such as XACML [13], XrML [14], ODRL [15] and EPAL [16] specify access and usage control policies over data disseminated amongst cooperating companies and users exchanging resources. Despite being able to express several policies such as authorisations and obligations, the existing languages and enforcement platforms do not address the problem of derived data. Policies can express *who* can use the data and *under which conditions*, but cannot express what protection should be applied to the output of the usage.

A number of studies have been conducted in the database community on *data lineage* or *provenance* [17,18,19]. Data Lineage concerns tracing how the data aggregated into a data warehouse has been derived from the data sources. Although the proposed solutions allow to know the lineage of the queried data, they do not deal with data protection and with the derivation of the protection requirements for the derived data. Moreover, the solutions are tied to the relational model of the data and thus unusable in a general ERM system. Atluri and Gal [20] provide a definition for *derived authorisations* as authorisations for data derived through a reversible transformation on some original data. They also propose a method to verify whether a set of derived authorisations is *safe* with respect to the authorisations applied to the original data. A set of authorisations is safe if a user not authorised to access the original data cannot derive it back by applying a reversed transformation on the derived data that he can access. However, the authors propose a simplistic derivation method for authorisations based on the union of the sets of all original authorisations.

To address the challenge of derived data our solution is based on the core concepts of Multi-level security and information flow systems [7,8] and in particular on the approach adopted in the Asbestos operating system [10]. Information flow control systems aim to prevent the flow of sensitive data from secure processes to non-secure processes. This is achieved by associating sensitive data with security labels and processes with clearance labels and enforcing the *simple security property* and **-property*. A *label* is a set of $(tag, level)$ pairs where tags are identifiers for sensitivity domains and levels are discrete values that represent the current protection level applied to the data for each domain. In Asbestos, processes have two labels: a tracking label and a clearance label.

Tracking labels record the sensitivity of the most sensitive data received or observed so far, while the clearance label bounds the maximum tracking label a process can be associated with. Given the set of all labels LS and the set of all tags TS, a partial order is defined over the label dominance relation $\sqsubseteq$:

$$\forall L_a, L_b \in LS : L_a \sqsubseteq L_b \iff \forall t \in TS : L_a(t) \le L_b(t) \qquad (1)$$

where $L(t)$ indicates the current level for tag t in label L. Non secure information flows are prevented by forbidding processes from receiving data when the sender process' tracking label is not dominated by their clearance label. However, in data dissemination scenarios no check over the recipient clearance or rights can be performed before the dissemination as recipients are often not known in advance. Moreover, data senders other than the data originator may have little interest in checking the recipient's clearance label before sending the data. Controls cannot be introduced at programming language level either, e.g. by associating labels with variables and I/O channels, as in the Decentralized Label Model [21]. Instead data can be freely disseminated through any available channel since it is previously protected by encryption. An ERM system then guarantees that only authorised recipients will be able to decrypt the data. Our solution is based on the observation that as security labels flow from data to processes and from one process to the other, confidential content flows from data to its derivations through the transformations performed by the application accessing the data.

We propose a *floating labels system* to be integrated with traditional ERM architectures to control data derivation in dissemination environments. While in the Decentralized Label Model labels are not directly associated with data values but rather with I/O channels and variables, we consider labels as *sticky policies* [3] that are attached to the disseminated data. Our solution also allows data declassification (similar in concept to that allowed by Asbestos' discretionary labels). However, while in existing works [22] declassification is performed directly by data owners [21] or at programming language level [23] when needed by a process, we let declassification depend on the high-level transformations applied to the data when used. Moreover, information flow systems conservatively assume that any data produced by a process is the result of a *reversible transformation* of all the data received by the process in the past. Any received data contributes in fact to the increment of the recipient process's tracking label. This is not true in our system where the amount of information flowing strictly depends on the transformation used.

3   Scenario

We consider an application scenario where data is disseminated amongst several users working for cooperating organisations. Data is not only disseminated but also modified and new data is also created. As the data is transformed some information is lost and new information is created; the data protection requirements change accordingly. This implies that a different protection must be applied to the transformed data, depending on the original resources that contributed to its creation and the transformations applied. The scenario describes an accident that rapidly escalates into a threat to a larger surrounding area. Two civil protection agencies, namely the Police and the Red Cross, immediately intervene on the scene. While lending support and carrying on the rescue operations, rescuers gather information on the accident and its effects and share it to better organise their action and manage the crisis. In this context data confidentiality must be protected for several reasons: 1) victims' privacy is governed by legislation; 2) the surrounding buildings' and area plants, as well as information on the local service providers' facilities may be used by criminals for future crimes; 3) information on the accident may cause panic and if broadcast by media may actually hinder the rescue operations.

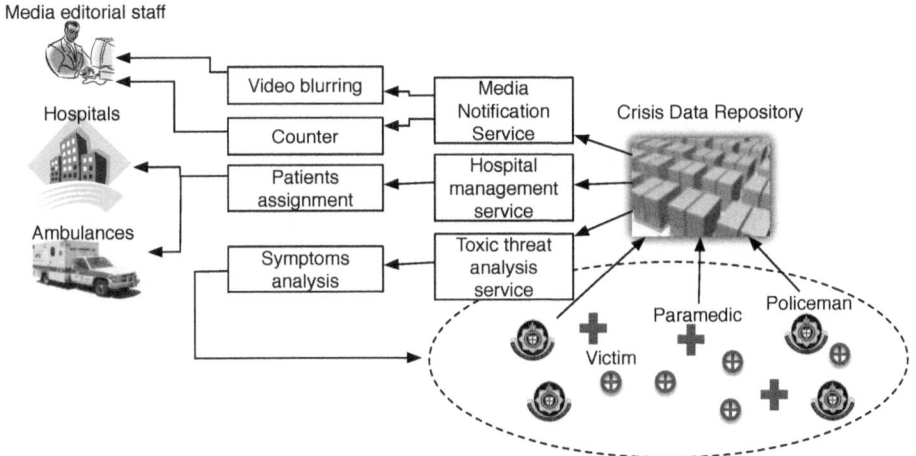

Fig. 1. Data sharing and elaboration scenario

Figure 1 shows a particular interaction in this scenario where information on the accident is sent to a central repository. The data we consider for the initial dissemination includes the victims' medical and personal information, a video of the accident and rescue scene obtained by a local CCTV system and information on the nearby hospitals and care centres. Three services located in the repository process the disseminated information and re-disseminate the results in the accident area: 1) a *media notification service* managed by police; 2) a *hospital management service* managed by Red Cross and 3) a *toxic threat analysis service* also managed by Red Cross. We will illustrate in our examples how our labelling system derives protection requirements for the output of the three services. In particular, the media notification service takes as input the victims' information and periodically updates a statement for the media with the currently known number of casualties. It also decreases the video's resolution so that faces cannot be recognised and gruesome details cannot be distinguished. The hospital management service combines the victims' information with the list of nearby care centres and generates a document specifying for each injured person the centre where he/she will be hospitalised. The document is periodically disseminated to all ambulances and paramedics. Finally, the toxic threat analysis service analyses the victims' conditions and calculates the risk of a chemical contamination in the area. The information is then disseminated among the rescuers so that they can react to a possible danger.

The information generated by the three services has different security requirements with respect to the original information gathered by the rescuers and stored in the central repository. On the one hand private information is removed and images of the scene can be accessed by a broader public since sensitive details are removed. On the other hand information on the hospital destination of the victims is considered sensitive while the information on the current threats the crisis is posing is highly confidential.

4   Sensitivity Domains and Data Labelling

Our solution stems from the idea that data can be protected under different domains and for different independent reasons. For example, data may be protected because it contains *private* or *commercially sensitive* information, or it may be related to *public safety* or *national security*. As in MLS systems, we identify each of such domains with a *security tag* and associate it with the data. When the data is modified, the amount of sensitive information it contains for each of the applied domains can either increase or decrease, as shown in Figure 2.

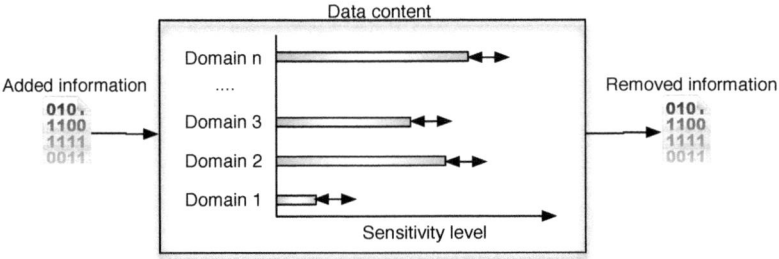

Fig. 2. The amount of sensitive information for each domain varies with changes to the data

We represent this situation by defining a tag for each domain and associating it to a range of discrete security levels. In traditional information flow systems such as Asbestos such ranges are fixed. In other words, $\forall t \in TS, L \in LS : 0 \leq L(t) \leq n$. In our solution we adopt flexible ranges so that each domain can be associated with a different number of security levels. Each data item is associated with a *data label* containing a discrete security level for each existing tag and representing the current protection applied to the data for each domain.

Whenever new data is created, the initial level for each tag in its data label is decided by several *Content Verification Procedures* (CVPs). CVPs are boolean functions that verify specific conditions on the data content. Each security level of each tag is associated with a CVP specifying whether the data label should contain that level for that specific tag. In our system a tag specification looks as follows:

$$t : * \rightarrow (0, CVP_{0,t}) \rightarrow (1, CVP_{1,t}) \rightarrow ... \rightarrow (i, CVP_{i,t}) \rightarrow ... \rightarrow (n, CVP_{n,t})$$

where the * level indicates that a security domain is not applicable to the data item, i.e. that the data must not be protected under that domain. Note that the * value is applied whenever no CVP returns true, otherwise the highest level whose CVP returns true is applied. CVPs are particularly useful whenever the initial security level for a given tag should not be decided manually by the data originator but on the basis of higher-level organisational policies.

5   Transformation and Data Model

In this setting, protecting derived data means deciding the security labels associated with it. To this end, we assume users and applications manipulate data through a series of *transformation functions*. These need to be known in advance by all partner organisation for two reasons. First, data originators or their organisations must be able to specify policies controlling how such transformations are used on the data they disseminate, even after the data crosses the organisational boundaries. Second, to specify how derived data must be protected, data originators must know how transformations actually process the original data.

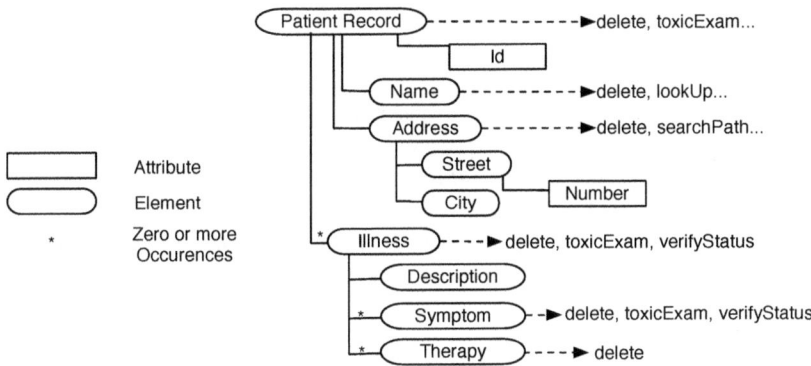

Fig. 3. Am example XML structure specifying transformations applicable to each element

We use here XML data as an example for data labelling, without any loss of generality for our approach. For the sake of simplicity, we consider an XML document as a collection of nested elements. Elements can be either *data containers* or *data items*, i.e. they can contain other elements or unstructured data. Both data containers and data items can be associated with attributes. We will not consider XML *entities* or *links* and consider only *valid* XML documents, i.e. documents that conform to a pre-defined document type definition (DTD) or XML schema. Consider the XML structure for a victim's medical record depicted in Figure 3. As described in works such as [24,25], any element and attribute of the XML structure can be associated with an access control policy. Similarly, elements and attributes can be associated with data labels and can be accessed and modified by a transformation. The set of transformations that can be performed on the data is specified at schema or DTD level. In this way, whenever an organisation or one of its members creates an XML document of a specific type, the set of transformations that can be applied is known, even when data is shared with external partner organisations. Using XML documents makes also easier to define CVPs, as they can leverage the document structure to analyse the data content.

6   Enforcement and Evaluation

In the following we will use role hierarchies in conjunction with our labelling solution. Consider the example role hierarchies for Police and Red Cross shown in Figure 4. Data must be protected under four different domains: privacy, video privacy (for video data), media (for police official statements) and confidentiality (for sensitive information on the rescue operations). We consider the sensitivity of private information and of police statements to vary across two levels, i.e. $0 \rightarrow 1$ and the sensitivity of confidential information to vary across three levels (see section 7.2 for further explanation on the example). Roles are assigned permissions in terms of clearance labels containing a security level for each existing tag. Permissions are inherited along the hierarchy, therefore, given the set of all roles RS, for each pair of roles (r_i, r_j) such that r_i dominates r_j in the hierarchy, r_i's label dominates r_j's. In other words:

$$\forall r_i, r_j \in RS, t \in TS | r_i \gg r_j : \ L_{r_i}(t) \geq L_{r_j}(t) \tag{2}$$

For example, the police commander is assigned the label $\{(\text{Privacy}, 1),(\text{VideoPrivacy},1),(\text{Media},1),(\text{Confidentiality},3)\}$. If not specified explicitly, roles are assigned to level 0 that also contains the special *public* group indicating every external subject who is not included in the role hierarchy.

Our labelling system is used to substitute the policy language or access control model of traditional ERM systems. For the sake of generality, we will not assume here any specific ERM platform. Clearance labels and tag definitions are kept on the system Control Centre. Whenever an XML document D is created and disseminated, each of

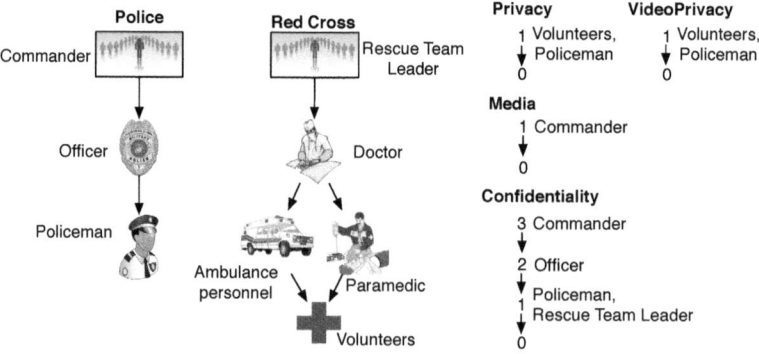

Fig. 4. Example of role hierarchy and sensitivity tags for the crisis management scenario

its elements is first associated with a label L_e (included in the XML structure as an attribute) and encrypted with a symmetric key k_e. The approach proposed in [24] can be used to use the same encryption key for elements with the same data label. The set of keys $\{k_1 \ldots k_n\}$ is then in turn encrypted for a specific Control Centre and attached to the data. Before accessing the data, a recipient *rec* must request permission and the decryption keys from the Control Centre, which verifies, for each data element in the document, the *Simple Security Property* (SSP):

$$\forall t \in TS \; \exists r \in RS | rec \; has \; role \; r \; and \; L_r(t) \geq L_D(t) \tag{3}$$

In other words, the Control Centre verifies that the data recipient requesting access belongs, for each tag, to a role associated with a clearance label whose level is either the same or higher than that in the data label. If the evaluation succeeds for some data elements, the Control Centre can send the corresponding decryption keys to the requesting recipient who can then access the data.

Note that since only recipients actually satisfying the SSP can decrypt the data, there is no need for a control on the dissemination channels as in traditional information flow systems. Security is in fact enforced by the Control Centre and Virtual Machine.

7   Transformation Labelling and Labels Flow

Each transformation function that can be applied on the data is associated with a *function label* containing a sensitivity level for each existing tag. Function labels represent the security level required by data derived by the corresponding transformation. The default level for tags in a function label, if not specified explicitly, is considered to be 0. As we will describe later this means that the function does not increase the security level of the input data. The range of security levels for function labels does not include the $*$ value. Intuitively, derived data may not be sensitive and thus be associated with sensitivity level 0. However, a security requirement specified at creation time for the original data cannot be completely removed from the derived one. Therefore derived data cannot be associated with the $*$ level, unless the original data is as well. Note that function labels are different from the Asbestos' tracking labels. Function labels are defined together with the transformation and do not change with usage.

Both function and data labels are partially ordered as in MLS systems according to dominance rule 1 introduced in section 2. Two labels L_a and L_b are incomparable, i.e. $L_a \not\sqsubseteq L_b$ and $L_b \not\sqsubseteq L_a$ if at least one tag in L_a has a greater level then in L_b and at least one tag in L_b has a greater level then in L_a. The labels form a lattice whose minimal element is label $\bot = [*]$, specifying that no security is applicable or necessary. The tags' level of the maximal element $\top$ depends instead on the width of the security ranges and contains for each tag the highest level possible. For each pair of labels L_a and L_b the greatest lower bound operator $L_a \sqcap L_b$ and least upper bound operator $L_a \sqcup L_b$ are defined as:

$$L_a \sqcap L_b(t) = \begin{cases} L_a(t) \; if \; L_a(t) \leq L_b(t) \\ L_b(t) \quad otherwise \end{cases} \tag{4}$$

$$L_a \sqcup L_b(t) = \begin{cases} L_a(t) \ if \ L_a(t) \geq L_b(t) \\ L_b(t) \quad otherwise \end{cases} \tag{5}$$

We must also consider the fact that when a specific security domain is not applicable for certain data (i.e. the level for the specific tag is equal to $*$), whatever transformation is applied to the data the $*$ value of the tag cannot be modified. We therefore introduce a further operator:

$$L_a \sqcup^* L_b(t) = \begin{cases} * \qquad\quad if \ L_a(t) = * \vee L_b(t) = * \\ L_a \sqcup L_b(t) \quad otherwise \end{cases} \tag{6}$$

7.1 Transformations and Policy Adaptation

As in existing ERM systems, once a decryption key has been obtained from a Control Centre the Virtual Machine installed on the client device locally enforces the usage control policies that are attached with the data. In our case, data is disseminated along with its applied data labels (one for each XML element or attribute). When the data is received by a recipient, the Virtual Machine ensures that any transformation applied to the data has an effect on the output data label as described below.

Whenever one or more data elements with data labels $L_{e_1} \ldots L_{e_n}$ are transformed through a transformation with function label L_f, the result d is assigned label:

$$L_d \longleftarrow (L_{e_1} \sqcup L_{e_2} \sqcup \ldots L_{e_n}) \sqcup^* L_f \tag{7}$$

For simplicity, in the following we will use the notation:

$$L_d \longleftarrow \bigsqcup L_{e_i} \sqcup^* L_f \tag{8}$$

This rule is very similar to the core rule of classic information flow systems. After the execution of a transformation function, the security level for each applicable tag is increased to be the least upper bound of the input data labels and function label. Note that the $*$ value is overridden if the labels of different input data elements have values higher than $*$ for the same tag. For simplicity and space reasons we consider here only transformations that return simple data items as output, i.e. unstructured data (and thus only one derived label is returned by rule 8). When a transformation is performed on one or more data containers, the label of the output data item is obtained considering the data labels of all the subelements as independent inputs.

The above rule only considers transformations that add value to the input data. However, transformations can also declassify data, e.g. by removing sensitive information. To address this case, we associate transformations with two further *declassification labels*, namely the *general declassification label* L_f^g and the *relative declassification label* L_f^-. Note that declassification and function labels can be applied at the same time.

Intuitively, while the function label represents the value added by the transformation to the input data, the general declassification label represents which part of the sensitive information is lost in the transformation process. If not specified explicitly, the default value for tags in general declassification labels is the highest possible level for that tag. With L_f^g the core label derivation rule now becomes:

$$L_d \longleftarrow \bigsqcup (L_{e_i} \sqcap L_f^g) \sqcup^* L_f \qquad (9)$$

The rule first considers the loss of information in the input data due to the declassification, and then increases the value of the declassified inputs according to the applied transformation. When for some tags' levels the input data does not contain enough sensitive information to be further declassified (i.e. $L_d(t) \leq L_f^g(t)$), the general declassification has no effect on such tags.

The relative declassification label represents the loss of information relative to the current sensitivity of the data. Consider for example an image data and a transformation that reduces its quality or resolution. The loss of information depends on the current resolution of the data, thus the security level required by the output data cannot be universally defined in a label. Relative declassification labels contain a real value in the range $[0 \ldots 1]$ for each tag. The default value for tags in relative declassification labels is 1. To apply relative declassification labels we introduce a further operator:

$$L_a - L_b(t) = \begin{cases} * & \text{if } L_a(t) = * \\ 0 & \text{if } L_a(t) \times L_b(t) < threshold \\ \lceil L_a(t) \times L_b(t) \rceil & otherwise \end{cases} \qquad (10)$$

The relative declassification label allows any discrete level to be decreased by a specific percentage and then rounded up to the next discrete level. With L_f^- the core policy derivation rule now becomes:

$$L_d \longleftarrow \bigsqcup ((L_{e_i} - L_f^-) \sqcap L_f^g) \sqcup^* L_f \qquad (11)$$

Note that a relative declassification label can cause a tag value to decrease to 0 depending on a specific threshold parameter defined with the function. The derivation rule described so far considers only transformations whose output, or at least its characteristics, are well-known. However, in many cases it is not possible to know in advance what the output of a transformation will look like. Examples are transformations performed by human users, such as text editing. A consequence of this impossibility is that a transformation may change one or more tags such that a wrong security level is applied to the output data. To address this problem we introduce the *decisional label* L^t. Decisional labels associate each tag to a boolean value indicating whether a content verification procedure is required (as for newly created data) to determine the security level of the output data. The default value for a tag in a decisional label is *false* (i.e. CVPs are not used by default). The final policy derivation rule can thus be expressed as:

$$L_d(t) \longleftarrow \begin{cases} max(i) \mid CVP_{i,t} = true \text{ if } L^t(t) = true \\ result \ of \ rule \ 11 & otherwise \end{cases} \qquad (12)$$

In other words, if the decisional label is set to true, the highest security level whose CVP is verified is applied to the data. If the decisional label is set to *true* for a tag but no CVP is satisfied after a transformation then the data modifications are considered not valid and the Virtual Machine provides to roll them back.

7.2 Examples

Consider the crisis management scenario described in section 3. Two distinct types of sensitive data are disseminated in the accident area: a video of the rescue operations and information on the victims. Information on nearby care centres is instead considered public. The tags agreed on by Police and Red Cross are defined as follows:

$$privacy : * \to (0, true) \to (1, NameAddressCheck());$$
$$videoPrivacy : * \to (0, true) \to (1, FaceCheck());$$
$$media : * \to (0, true) \to (1, VictimsCheck());$$
$$confidentiality : * \to (0, true) \to (1, Req(1)) \to (2, Req(2)) \to (3, Req(3));$$

where *NameAddressCheck()* is a procedure verifying whether the data contains personal names or addresses, *FaceCheck()* verifies whether a video shows identifiable faces and *VictimsCheck()* verifies whether the total number of casualties of the accident contained in a statement for the media is greater then zero. *Req(n)* CVPs simply verify whether the data originator explicitly requested an initial protection level for the data. When gathered, information on both victims and videos is labelled according to its content and the result of CVPs.

The video blurring transformation used by the media notification service decreases the video's resolution so that faces and gruesome details are made undistinguishable. It is thus associated with the general declassification label $L^g_{blur} = \{(videoPrivacy, 0)\}$ and with the relative declassification label $L^r_{blur} = \{(confidentiality, 0.5)\}$, with threshold parameter 0.5. L^r_{blur} ensures that every time a video is blurred, its confidentiality level decreases as more details are removed. The counter transformation used by the same service takes instead as input the information on victims and counts the total number of casualties, which is then inserted into an official statement for the media (updated every time the operation is run with new inputs). If the accident caused any casualties, the statement must be supervised by the Police commander before being publicly broadcast. Therefore, the counter transformation is associated with the general declassification label $L^g_{counter} = \{(privacy, 0)\}$ and the decisional label $L^t_{counter} = \{(media, true)\}$. The patient assignment transformation used by the hospital management service generates a document containing both personal information on the victims and confidential information on the hospitals they are assigned to. Therefore it is associated with the function label $L_{assign} = \{(privacy, 1), (confidentiality, 1)\}$. Finally, the symptoms analysis transformation used by the toxic threat analysis service generates, on the basis of the victims' medical conditions, an evaluation of the risk of toxic contamination in the area. All rescuers must be aware of the risk, but the information must not be publicly disclosed to avoid panic. Therefore, the transformation is associated with the function label $L_{tox} = \{(confidentiality, 1)\}$ and with the general declassification label $L^g_{tox} = \{(privacy, 0)\}$.

Given the above function and declassification labels, both Police and Red Cross are sure the data produced by their services will automatically be associated with an adequate level of protection. Videos where faces are unrecognisable are no longer protected for privacy reasons and everyone can access them, unless gruesome or confidential details on the rescue operations are still visible. In the latter case, the more the resolution is decreased, the wider is the set of recipients who can access the videos. In particular, with each iteration of the blurring transformation confidentiality is decreased of one level, until level zero is reached and the video is public. Access to any statement produced by the police service is forbidden to the media if the number of victims is not zero. This is reasonable as in this case the Police commander might wait for the operations to be concluded before releasing an official statement. Information on the hospital destinations of the victims and on the current risk of a toxic contamination of the environment is also automatically protected as private or confidential (or both) so that only rescuers that need to use that information can access it.

For the sake of simplicity we showed a scenario where gathered data is processed only once and derived data is not re-processed. Defining the transformation labels for this kind of scenario is therefore relatively easy. However, there are other cases were derived data is given as input to other transformations iteratively. Examples are complex research environments were large amounts of data are processed and the results are used again as input for new experiments and tests. In those cases our approach proves to be even more useful as data protection is ensured all over the cycle and each intermediate result is correctly labelled on the basis of its current content and the transformations applied to it so far.

8   Custom Domains

Security domains represent the scopes under which data must be protected. Our construction assumes that all possible recipients for the disseminated data know all transformations that could be applied to it. The assumption is necessary as Virtual Machines must be able to enforce the label derivation rule every time data is transformed, and this would not be possible without knowing the transformation's labels. This implies that both domains and transformations must be agreed upon at organisational level, and in a Data Sharing Agreement if several distinct organisations want to share data. However, this does not allow users to define their own domains. Consider for example an employee in an organisation sending a private email to a colleague. None of the tags defined by the agreement between the organisation and its partners would apply to the data (unless it contains sensitive data for the organisation). However the user still needs to protect his email. Defining a completely new tag and attaching its definition to the data is not a viable solution. The user should in fact know all the possible transformations his data could undergo and specify the new tag's values for the function and declassification labels.

To address this problem we allow users to define custom domains extending a *parent domain* defined at organisational level. Defining such a relationship with an existing domain allows the Virtual Machine on recipients' devices to know how transformations modify the custom tag's level. The same level derivation as for the parent domain's tag can in fact be used. However, users must be able to specify security requirements for their own domains that are different from those of the parent domains. To do so a user must first specify a mapping from the parent tag's to the custom tag's security levels. The custom tag may thus have the same number or fewer levels than its parent. In the latter case several levels in the parent tag are mapped to one level in the custom tag. If the user does not specify any CVP for the new domain, default ones are

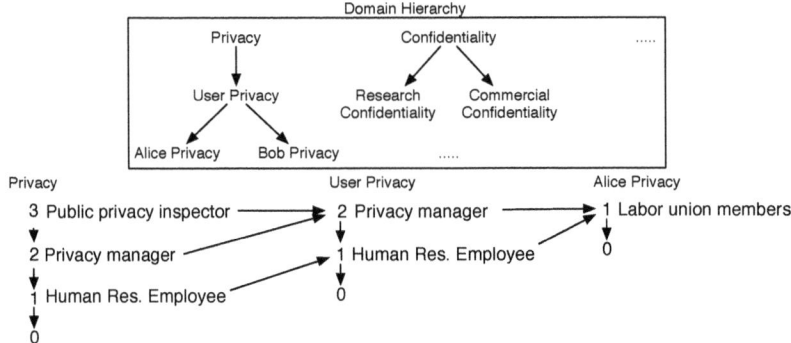

Fig. 5. Example of domain hierarchy and custom domains

applied that simply let the data originator decide (as the *Req(n)* procedures in section 7.2). The custom domain creator can then assign roles with different clearances even violating the permission inheritance rule 2 introduced in section 6. This is not a problem since custom tags are defined for users and thus are not subject to organisational constraints. In the example shown in figure 5 a custom *UserPrivacy* domain is specified by the organisation to allow employees to have personal data not subject to the control of a public privacy inspector. However Alice, the labor union representative, needs to disseminate messages amongst all the members of the union so that no one else can access them. The messages may contain names, dates, addresses for meetings and other information, therefore Alice decides to protect them as private data. Alice only needs two sensitivity levels (one for public data and one for data accessible only by members of the union) so she maps the two highest levels in the *UserPrivacy* tag to the only non-public level in her tag. Alice can then specify the clearance levels assigned to roles for her custom tag and that override those specified for the parent tag. The definition of the custom tag (level mappings and roles' clearances) is then attached to the data so that Control Centres and Virtual Machines can correctly handle authorisation requests and the data transformations. In other words the user modifies the roles' clearances by adding a new tag-value pair. In this example, Alice gives clearance 1 for the *Privacy/UserPrivacy/AlicePrivacy* tag to members of the union. Finally, the derived label for any transformation applied to such data is processed as if the data were protected by the privacy tag, with the exception that the derived levels are mapped to the custom tag's levels. Note that to avoid data leakage by rogue employees, tags at higher levels in the tag hierarchy always override tags at lower levels, if they both are applicable to the same data.

9   Conclusions and Future Work

Organisations often agree on sharing data in the expectation that systems and procedures are deployed to protect the disseminated data. However, no automatic protection is applied to the results of the data usages, for which the collaboration was initially set up. Our solution aims to offer a mechanism to control data that is derived through pre-defined transformations and whose content can vary according to a predefined scheme. We proposed our solution as an integration to existing ERM systems so that users do not have to bear the burden of defining further meta-policies for derived data control. However, such additional controls come at the cost of a restriction on the possible usages the data can be subject to and of a further effort for the organisations when stipulating their DSA. Note that we have only discussed data confidentiality aspects. Data integrity, i.e. the protection of data against unauthorised transformations, can be obtained with a simple extension to our model, where tags are specified for specific actions such as the *read* action (as by default in this work) and all the other applicable transformations.

We showed as an example the possible integration of our solution with role hierarchies. Future work will focus on investigating the integration with different policy languages to offer more flexibility in the specification of the security requirements. In particular we will study a *multi-level policy* system so that complex policies specified in languages such as XACML, ODRL and XrML can be merged into the label lattice presented in this work. The main challenge in doing this is the definition of a policy's *provided security level*, i.e. a measure to define whether a policy has stricter or looser requirements then another one. Such measure would allow us to create a policy lattice and thus to apply the label derivation mechanism shown above. We also aim to formally prove the information flow properties that can be achieved in our framework (e.g. the conformance to a defined DSA or other requirements) and to investigate possible criteria to be used when assigning labels to transformations so that desired properties can be obtained. Finally, we aim to further develop and integrate our solution with the XML data model, considering transformations returning complex data structures.

Acknowledgments. We acknowledge financial support from the EC Consequence project (Grant Agreement 214859).

References

1. Authentica: Enterprise rights management for document protection, White Paper (2005)
2. Microsoft: Technical overview of windows rights management services for windows server 2003 (2005), White Paper, http://www.safecomprogram.gov (accessed December 2009)
3. Mont, M.C., Pearson, S., Bramhall, P.: Towards accountable management of identity and privacy: Sticky policies and enforceable tracing services. In: 14th Int. Workshop on Database and Expert Systems Applications (DEXA), Prague, Czech Republic, September 2003, pp. 377–382 (2003)
4. Park, J., Sandhu, R.S., Schifalacqua, J.: Security architectures for controlled digital information dissemination. In: 16th An. Computer Security Applications Conf (ACSAC), p. 224. IEEE Computer Society, Los Alamitos (2000)
5. Pretschner, A., Hilty, M., Basin, D.A.: Distributed usage control. Commun. ACM 49(9), 39–44 (2006)
6. Park, J., Sandhu, R.S.: The $UCON_{ABC}$ usage control model. ACM Trans. Inf. Syst. Secur. 7(1), 128–174 (2004)
7. Bell, D.E., LaPadula, L.J.: Secure computer systems: Mathematical foundations. Technical Report M74-244, The Mitre Corp. (May 1973)

8. Dorothy, D.E.: A lattice model of secure information flow. Commun. ACM 19(5), 236–243 (1976)
9. Papagiannis, I., Migliavacca, M., Pietzuch, P.R., Shand, B., Eyers, D.M., Bacon, J.: Private-flow: decentralised information flow control in event based middleware. In: DEBS (2009)
10. Vandebogart, S., Efstathopoulos, P., Kohler, E., Krohn, M.N., Frey, C., Ziegler, D., Kaashoek, M.F., Morris, R., Mazières, D.: Labels and event processes in the Asbestos operating system. ACM Trans. Comput. Syst. 25(4) (2007)
11. Liquid Machines and Microsoft Windows Rights Management Services (RMS): End-to-end Rights Management for the Enterprise (2006),
    http://www.cmdsolutions.com/pdfs/LiquidMachines%20Windows
    %20RMS%20Business%20White%20Paper%20FINAL%20060213.pdf
    (accessed September 2009)
12. The Marlin Open Digital Content Sharing Platform (2009),
    http://www.marlin-community.com/ (accessed February 2010)
13. eXtensible Access Control markup language (xacml) version 2.0 (2005)
14. Content Guard: eXtensible rights Markup Language (XrML) 2.0, Specification (2001)
15. Iannella, R.: Open Digital Rights Language (ODRL), Version 1.1. W3c note, World Wide Web Consortium (2002)
16. Ashley, P., Hada, S.: Karjoth; G., Powers, C., Schunter, M.: The enterprise privacy authorization language (epal 1.1), Reader's Guide to the Documentation (2003)
17. Fan, H.: Tracing data lineage using automed schema transformation pathways. In: BNCOD, pp. 50–53 (2002)
18. Fan, H.: Data lineage tracing in data warehousing environments. In: BNCOD, pp. 25–36 (2007)
19. Fan, H., Poulovassilis, A.: Using schema transformation pathways for data lineage tracing. In: BNCOD, pp. 133–144 (2005)
20. Atluri, V., Gal, A.: An authorization model for temporal and derived data: securing information portals. ACM Trans. Inf. Syst. Secur. 5(1), 62–94 (2002)
21. Myers, A.C., Liskov, B.: Protecting privacy using the decentralized label model. ACM Trans. Softw. Eng. Methodol. 9(4), 410–442 (2000)
22. Sabelfeld, A., Sands, D.: Declassification: Dimensions and principles. In: Proceedings of the 18th IEEE Workshop on Computer Security Foundations (CSFW 2005), pp. 255–269 (2005)
23. Lux, A., Mantel, H.: Declassification with explicit reference points. In: Backes, M., Ning, P. (eds.) ESORICS 2009. LNCS, vol. 5789, pp. 69–85. Springer, Heidelberg (2009)
24. Bertino, E., Castano, S., Ferrari, E.: Securing XML documents with Author-X. Internet Computing, IEEE 5(3), 21–31 (2001)
25. Damiani, E., De Capitani di Vimercati, S., Paraboschi, S., Samarati, P.: A fine-grained access control system for xml documents. ACM Trans. Inf. Syst. Secur. 5(2), 169–202 (2002)

On the Identification of Property Based Generalizations in Microdata Anonymization

Rinku Dewri, Indrajit Ray, Indrakshi Ray, and Darrell Whitley

Colorado State University, Fort Collins, CO, USA
{rinku,indrajit,iray,whitley}@cs.colostate.edu

Abstract. Majority of the search algorithms in microdata anonymization restrict themselves to a single privacy property and a single criteria to optimize. The solutions obtained are therefore of limited application since adherence to multiple privacy models is required to impede different forms of privacy attacks. Towards this end, we propose the concept of a *property based generalization* (PBG) to capture the non-dominance relationships that appear when multiple objectives are to be met in an anonymization process. We propose an evolutionary algorithm that can identify a representative subset of the set of PBGs for the purpose of decision making.

1 Introduction

Anonymizing data is challenging because re-identifying the values in sanitized attributes is not impossible when other publicly available information or an adversary's background knowledge can be linked with the shared data. Matching shared attributes between different data sources can be made ambiguous by altering the released information to map to more number of individuals represented in the data set. Samarati and Sweeney enforce such mappings in the $k-anonymity$ model using *generalization* and *suppression* schemes [1,2,3].

An unavoidable consequence of performing data anonymization is the loss in information content of the data set. Researchers have therefore looked at different methods to obtain an optimal generalization [1,3,4,5,6] that maximizes the utility of the anonymized data while satisfying a pre-specified privacy property. The adoption of such an optimization framework brings forth pertinent practical issues that have been ignored for long.

First, data utility and respondent privacy are two equally important facets of data publishing. Proper anonymization thus involves weighing the risk of publicly disseminated information against the statistical utility of the content. In such a situation, it is imperative that the data publisher understands the implications of setting a parameter in a privacy model to a particular value. Second, the k-anonymity model is prone to other forms of attacks on privacy. As a result, a multitude of other privacy models have been proposed over time [7,8,9], quite often followed by newer forms of privacy attacks. The inclusion of multiple models in the anonymization process is desirable since a single comprehensive model

S. Foresti and S. Jajodia (Eds.): Data and Applications Security XXIV, LNCS 6166, pp. 81–96, 2010.

is yet to be developed. The third issue centers around the notion of biased privacy [10]. Consider the k−anonymity model where the measure of privacy (the value of k) is given by the minimum size of an equivalence class. Thus, two anonymizations inducing the same value of k will be considered equally good with respect to privacy protection. However, it is quite possible that for one of the anonymizations, a majority of the individual tuples have lesser probabilities of privacy breaches than their counterparts in the other anonymization. Individual privacy levels as depicted by such a model can therefore be misleading – higher for some, minimalistic for others.

In this paper, we propose resolutions to these issues using the notion of *property based generalizations*. First, inclusion of multiple objectives in the anonymization process is captured using *properties* as anonymization objectives. Second, evaluation of a generalization with respect to a privacy property is performed using both worst case and vector based measurements. The overall effectiveness of a generalization is then measured in terms of its achievement and trade-offs in the different properties. The concept of a single optimal solution is therefore discarded and a representative subset of the minimal solution set is sought. Towards this end, our third contribution is in terms of an evolutionary algorithm that can be used to efficiently search the domain generalization lattice to identify such representative solutions.

The remainder of the paper is organized as follows. Section 2 describes some of the related work in k-anonymization. Section 3 presents the preliminary concepts. Property based generalizations are introduced in section 4, followed by a description of the modified dominance operator in section 5. The evolutionary algorithm is presented in section 6. Section 7 discusses some empirical results. Finally, section 8 concludes the paper.

2   Related Work

Several algorithms have been proposed to find effective k-anonymization. The *μ-argus* algorithm is based on the greedy generalization of infrequently occurring combination of quasi-identifiers and suppresses outliers to meet the k-anonymity requirement [5]. The *Datafly* approach uses a heuristic method to first generalize the quasi-identifier containing the most number of distinct values [3]. Sequences of quasi-identifier values occurring less than k times are suppressed.

On the more theoretical side, Sweeney proposes the *MinGen* algorithm [3] that exhaustively examines all potential generalizations to identify the optimal generalization that minimally satisfies the anonymity requirement. However, the approach is impractical even on modest sized data sets. Meyerson and Williams have proposed an approximation algorithm that achieves an anonymization with $O(k \log k)$ of the optimal solution [11].

Samarati proposes an algorithm [1] that identifies all generalizations satisfying k-anonymity. The approach in *Incognito* [12] is also aimed towards finding all generalizations that satisfy k-anonymity for a given value of k.

A genetic algorithm based formulation is proposed by Iyengar to perform k-anonymization [6]. Bayardo and Agrawal propose a complete search method that iteratively constructs less generalized solutions starting from a completely generalized data set [4]. The idea of a *solution cut* is presented by Fung et al. in their approach to top down specialization [13]. LeFevre et al. extend the notion of generalization on attributes to generalization on tuples in the data set [14]. Dewri et al. [15] explore privacy and utility trade-offs using multi-objective optimization formulations involving an average case privacy measure. Huang and Du also explore multi-objective optimization in the problem of optimizing randomized response schemes for privacy protection [16].

3   Data Anonymization

A data set of size $\mathcal{N}$ is conceptually arranged as a table of rows (or *tuples*) and columns (or *attributes*). Each attribute denotes a semantic category of information that is a set of possible values. Attributes are unique within a table. Each row is a tuple of s values $\langle v_1, \ldots, v_s \rangle$, s being the number of attributes in the data set, such that the value v_j is in the domain of the jth attribute A_j, for $j = 1, \ldots, s$. The domain of attribute A_j is denoted by the singleton sets $A_j = \{a_{j1}\}, \ldots, \{a_{j|A_j|}\}$ where $|A_j|$ is the size of the domain of the attribute.

A *generalization* of attribute A_j is a union of its domain into supersets. Hence the generalized domain of A_j can be written as $H_j^1 = A_{j1}, \ldots, A_{jm}$ such that $\cup_i A_{ji} = \cup A_j$ and $A_{jp} \cap A_{jq} = \phi$ for $p \neq q$. We then say H_j^1 is a generalized domain of A_j, denoted as $H_j^1 <_G A_j$. The domain H_j^1 can be further generalized in a similar manner to the domain H_j^2. Generalization of an attribute's domain in this manner gives rise to a *domain generalization hierarchy* (DGH) $H_j^{N_j} <_G \ldots <_G H_j^1 <_G H_j^0$, where $H_j^0 = A_j$. N_j is called the *length* of the attribute's DGH. The DGH is a specification of how an attribute's values can be combined progressively to bigger sets. H_j^0 is a full specialization of attribute A_j, meaning that no two values belong to a single set. The other extreme of this is a full generalization $H_j^{N_j}$ where all values of the attribute belong to a single set. The *generalization level* of the attribute is signified by an integer between 0 and N_j. A generalization level of 0 signifies that all values are distinguishable from each other, while a level of N_j signifies that no two values can be distinguished from each other.

A *domain generalization lattice* is a graph with $\prod_i (N_i + 1)$ nodes. Every node $(n_1, \ldots, n_s); 0 \leq n_i \leq N_i$ is a vector of s dimensions where the ith element n_i specifies the generalization level for attribute A_i. An edge exists between two nodes $(n_1, \ldots, n_s)$ and $(m_1, \ldots, m_s)$ if and only if $\sum_i |n_i - m_i| = 1$.

Given a DGH for each quasi-identifier in the data set, a tuple is said to be in an *anonymized* form when a generalization is applied on the attribute values. The anonymized form is represented as follows. Let us assume a tuple $\langle v_1, \ldots, v_s \rangle$ in the data set. Let $(n_1, \ldots, n_s); 0 \leq n_i \leq N_i$ be the vector representing the generalization level for each attribute; n_i is the level to use in the

DGH for attribute A_i. To map the value v_1 to its generalized form we replace it by the index of the set to which it belongs in the generalized domain at level n_1. For example, if $H_1^{n_1} = A_{11}, \ldots, A_{1m}$ and $v_1 \in A_{1p_1}$, then v_1 is replaced by p_1. After performing similar operations for the other attribute values, the tuple is anonymized to the form $\langle p_1, \ldots, p_s \rangle$, p_i being the set index for value v_i in $H_i^{n_i}$. Transforming all tuples in the data set in this manner results in an anonymized data set.

The anonymized tuples of a data set can then be grouped together into equivalence classes. Two anonymized tuples $\langle p_1, \ldots, p_s \rangle$ and $\langle q_1, \ldots, q_s \rangle$ belong to the same equivalence class if $p_i = q_i; 1 \leq i \leq s$. The k-anonymity property requires that every such equivalence class should be of size at least k.

Attributes can be further divided into *sensitive* and *non-sensitive* ones. For example, values in the "Disease" attribute of a medical history data set is not sensitive in itself, but is considered so if a certain disease is linked to a certain patient. The ℓ-*diversity* property requires that every equivalence class resulting from anonymizing the quasi-identifiers should contain at least ℓ "well-represented" values for a sensitive attribute [8]. The property can be instantiated in different forms depending on the meaning of "well-represented". The instantiation we use here is called *distinct ℓ-diversity*. Distinct ℓ-diversity states that the number of distinct values for a sensitive attribute is at least ℓ in every equivalence class.

4   Property Based Generalization

Multiple objectives to meet during data anonymization are captured in the form of properties [10]. Formally, a property is defined as follows.

Definition 1. Property. *A property is a function $\mathcal{P}$ that maps a table T to a vector of size equal to the number of tuples in the table. The vector is called a property vector and denoted by $\mathcal{P}(\mathsf{T})$.*

A property refers to a privacy, utility or any other measurable feature of a tuple. It signifies the grounds under which a comparison is made between two nodes in the lattice. For example, applying the generalization levels corresponding to a node results in multiple equivalence classes. If we pick our property to be the *"size of the equivalence class to which a tuple belongs,"* then each tuple will have an associated integer. This results in a property vector $\mathcal{P}_{equiv}(\mathsf{T}) = (k_1, k_2, \ldots, k_\mathcal{N})$ for a data set of size $\mathcal{N}$, where k_i is the equivalence class size of the ith tuple. A property is therefore a vector based measurement. The motivation behind using such vector based measurements is two fold. First, it fits the conventional "worst case" method of measuring privacy. Second, it allows us to determine the efficiency of a node with respect to the distribution of privacy levels across the data set. These two methods of assessing a node are jointly represented through the use of *quality index functions*.

4.1   Quality Index Functions

Comparison between generalizations with respect to a single property can be done by defining an ordering operation on the co-domain of the property.

The ordering operator is a user-defined method of evaluating the superiority of a property vector. Typically, such operators are functions defined on the values of the property vectors.

Definition 2. Quality Index. *Let $\mathcal{T}$ be the collection of all possible generalized versions of a table T. Given a property $\mathcal{P}$, a quality index $\mathcal{I}_{\mathcal{P}}$ is a function $\mathcal{I}_{\mathcal{P}} : \mathcal{T} \times \mathcal{T} \rightarrow \mathbb{R}$ which assigns an ordered pair of two tables $\mathsf{T}_l, \mathsf{T}_m \in \mathcal{T}$ a real value $\mathcal{I}_{\mathcal{P}}(\mathsf{T}_l, \mathsf{T}_m)$.*

Quality index functions map a pair of nodes to the set of real numbers. The underlying idea is to quantify quality differences between generalizations by applying common metrics. The value $\mathcal{I}_{\mathcal{P}}(\mathsf{T}_l, \mathsf{T}_m)$ signifies the quality of table T_l relative to table T_m and with respect to the property $\mathcal{P}$. We would therefore say that T_l is preferable over T_m with respect to $\mathcal{P}$ if $\mathcal{I}_{\mathcal{P}}(\mathsf{T}_l, \mathsf{T}_m) > \mathcal{I}_{\mathcal{P}}(\mathsf{T}_m, \mathsf{T}_l)$, assuming that a higher value signifies better achievement of the property. Otherwise, the relationship is $\mathcal{I}_{\mathcal{P}}(\mathsf{T}_l, \mathsf{T}_m) < \mathcal{I}_{\mathcal{P}}(\mathsf{T}_m, \mathsf{T}_l)$.

Worst case measurements. A quality index function in the definition requires two tables as input. However, a commonly used method of evaluating a generalization is through *unary* quality index functions. Unary quality indices are functions applied independently on generalizations, i.e. they have a single table as input. For example, the k-anonymity property is a unary quality index based on the equivalence class size property $\mathcal{P}_{equiv}$, given as $\mathcal{I}_{\mathcal{P}_{equiv}}(\mathsf{T}) = \min_i(\mathcal{P}_{equiv}(\mathsf{T}))$.

Unary indices only allow the measurement of an aggregate property of a generalization. This prohibits any kind of comparison of individual property values maintained by tuples in a generalization with that maintained in another. Having said so, we do not specify any restriction on the formulation of a quality index function. This is because data utility functions are typically unary in nature, i.e. they are absolute estimates of the information content of the anonymized data. We keep the generic binary formulation since unary functions are a special case of binary functions. In other words, when using worst case privacy models or information loss measurements, we shall assume $\mathcal{I}_{\mathcal{P}}(\mathsf{T}_l, \mathsf{T}_m) \equiv \mathcal{I}_{\mathcal{P}}(\mathsf{T}_l)$.

Measuring quality with spread. Privacy of an anonymized table can also be quantified in terms of the differences in individual privacy levels when compared with another anonymized table. Characterizing privacy in this manner captures the changes brought forth in individual privacy levels when moving from one node to another in the generalization lattice. This helps distinguish the privacy preserving efficiency of the two nodes even when both generate the same worst case privacy. We use the *spread* based quality index function in this context. The function is based on the total amount of variation (or spread) present between tuples with respect to a property, given as

$$\mathcal{I}_{\mathcal{P}}^{spr}(\mathsf{T}_l, \mathsf{T}_m) = \sum_{i=1}^{\mathcal{N}} \max(p_i^l - p_i^m, 0)$$

where $(p_1^x, \ldots, p_{\mathcal{N}}^x) = \mathcal{P}(\mathsf{T}_x)$. Thus, T_l better preserves privacy than T_m if $\mathcal{I}_{\mathcal{P}}^{spr}(\mathsf{T}_l, \mathsf{T}_m) > \mathcal{I}_{\mathcal{P}}^{spr}(\mathsf{T}_m, \mathsf{T}_l)$. This characterization follows from the intuition

that a generalization better than another should be able to retain higher values
of the measured property for more individuals represented in the data set.

The spread quality index function provides a relative characterization of privacy. The function value is only representative of the quality of a node relative
to another. However, absolute estimates are more preferable since a node then
does not have to be evaluated repeatedly for the same property. Hence, a unary
function that can provide the same information as the binary spread function is
desired. Formulating such a function is not difficult as highlighted in the following observation.

Observation: *Let $S_{\mathcal{P}}(\mathsf{T}_x)$ denote the sum of the property values in the prop-
erty vector $\mathcal{P}(\mathsf{T}_x)$. Then $\mathcal{I}_{\mathcal{P}}^{spr}(\mathsf{T}_l, \mathsf{T}_m) > \mathcal{I}_{\mathcal{P}}^{spr}(\mathsf{T}_m, \mathsf{T}_l)$ if and only if $S_{\mathcal{P}}(\mathsf{T}_l) >
S_{\mathcal{P}}(\mathsf{T}_m)$.*

Comparing nodes under the light of the spread function can therefore be
performed using the sum of the property values, i.e. $\mathcal{I}_{\mathcal{P}}^{spr}(\mathsf{T}_l, \mathsf{T}_m) \equiv \mathcal{I}_{\mathcal{P}}(\mathsf{T}_l) =
S_{\mathcal{P}}(\mathsf{T}_l)$. Hence, in the subsequent sections, we shall use the notation $\mathcal{I}_{\mathcal{P}}(\mathsf{T}_l)$ to
denote the quality of T_l with respect to $\mathcal{P}$, keeping in mind that $\mathcal{I}_{\mathcal{P}}$ is either a
unary function (as used in worst case measurements and loss assessments) or the
sum function $S_{\mathcal{P}}$ (sufficient to infer the quality according to the binary spread
function).

4.2   Anonymizing with Multiple Properties

Ideally, any number of properties can be studied on a generalized table. Let us
consider an anonymization with respect to the set of properties $\mathbf{P} = \{\mathcal{P}_1, \ldots, \mathcal{P}_r\}$.
Assessing the quality of a generalization T_l with respect to the properties $\mathbf{P}$ will
result in a vector of values $\mathbf{I_P}(\mathsf{T}_l) = [\mathcal{I}_{\mathcal{P}_1}(\mathsf{T}_l), \ldots, \mathcal{I}_{\mathcal{P}_r}(\mathsf{T}_l)]$ where the ith element
represents the quality of T_l with respect to the property $\mathcal{P}_i$. A dominance rela-
tion $\succeq$ is then specified over the set of such vectors to characterize the efficiency
of a generalization, such that $\mathbf{I_P}(\mathsf{T}_l) \succeq \mathbf{I_P}(\mathsf{T}_m)$ if

1. $\forall i = 1 \ldots r : \mathcal{I}_{\mathcal{P}_i}(\mathsf{T}_l) \geq \mathcal{I}_{\mathcal{P}_i}(\mathsf{T}_m)$, and
2. $\exists j \in \{1, \ldots, r\} : \mathcal{I}_{\mathcal{P}_j}(\mathsf{T}_l) > \mathcal{I}_{\mathcal{P}_j}(\mathsf{T}_m)$.

This relation states that for a table to be better than another, it must not have
worse quality across all the properties while maintaining better quality with
respect to at least one property. Note that the dominance relation is transitive
in nature, i.e if $\mathbf{I_P}(\mathsf{T}_1) \succeq \mathbf{I_P}(\mathsf{T}_2)$ and $\mathbf{I_P}(\mathsf{T}_2) \succeq \mathbf{I_P}(\mathsf{T}_3)$, then $\mathbf{I_P}(\mathsf{T}_1) \succeq \mathbf{I_P}(\mathsf{T}_3)$.
Using dominance to evaluate a generalization introduces the concept of a *property
based generalization* (PBG).

Definition 3. Property Based Generalization. *Let $\mathcal{T}$ be the collection of
all possible generalized versions of a table T of size $\mathcal{N}$. Given the properties
$\mathbf{P} = \{\mathcal{P}_1, \ldots, \mathcal{P}_r\}$ and quality index functions $\mathbf{I} : \mathcal{I}_{\mathcal{P}_1}, \ldots, \mathcal{I}_{\mathcal{P}_r}$ (not necessarily
unique), $\mathsf{T}_l \in \mathcal{T}$ is a property based generalization of $\mathsf{T}_m \in \mathcal{T}$ with respect to $\mathbf{P}$,
denoted as $\mathsf{T}_l \vdash_{\mathbf{P}} \mathsf{T}_m$, if and only if $\mathbf{I_P}(\mathsf{T}_l) \succeq \mathbf{I_P}(\mathsf{T}_m)$.*

The following observations summarize the literary meaning of property based
generalizations.

- We consider T_l to be *better* than T_m if and only if $\mathsf{T}_l \vdash_\mathbf{P} \mathsf{T}_m$. Equivalently, T_m is *worse* than T_l.
- T_l and T_m are considered *incomparable* (or mutually non-dominated) if and only if $\mathsf{T}_l \nvdash_\mathbf{P} \mathsf{T}_m$, $\mathsf{T}_m \nvdash_\mathbf{P} \mathsf{T}_l$ and $\mathsf{T}_l \neq \mathsf{T}_m$.

Incomparable generalizations signify trade-offs across certain properties. Therefore, it is our objective to identify such generalizations for reporting. In addition, the chosen generalizations must also be minimal. Minimal property based generalizations are analogous to Pareto-optimal solutions in a multi-objective optimization problem.

Definition 4. Minimal Property Based Generalization. *Given a collection $\mathcal{T}$ of generalized versions of a table T and the properties $\mathbf{P} = \{\mathcal{P}_1, \dots, \mathcal{P}_r\}$, $\mathsf{T}_w \in \mathcal{T}$ is a minimal property based generalization of $\mathcal{T}$ if $\nexists \mathsf{T}_m \in \mathcal{T} : \mathsf{T}_m \vdash_\mathbf{P} \mathsf{T}_w$.*

5   Representative PBGs

One drawback of using the dominance relation $\succeq$ is the inability to control the number of minimal PBGs to report during the search process. We assume here a search process with a finite memory, called the *archive*, to store minimal PBGs. The search process iteratively tries to converge to the set of minimal PBGs. A *generator* component is responsible for creating a new candidate generalization, preferably using the current set of generalizations in the archive. An *updator* component performs a comparison of the candidate generalization with those maintained in the archive and removes all generalizations which cannot be minimal PBGs. The purpose behind maintaining such an archive is to guide the search process towards better regions of the search space, and at the same time maintain a list of the best solutions found so far.

The issue to address is the size of the archive. With no limitation on the size, it may become impossible to store additional prospective generalizations owing to restrictions on physical memory. The primary criteria to fulfill is that the archive maintain generalizations that are minimal PBGs and at the same time have enough diversity to represent the trade-off behavior across the multiple properties.

Let $\mathcal{M}$ denote the set of all minimal PBGs corresponding to a given data set. The objective is to obtain a polynomially bounded sized subset of $\mathcal{M}$. Let $(\epsilon_1, \dots, \epsilon_r); \epsilon_i > 0$ denote a *discretization vector*, r being the number of properties considered. The quality index space $\mathbb{R}^r$ is then discretized by placing a hypergrid with the co-ordinates $0, \epsilon_i, 2\epsilon_i, \dots$ along each of the r dimensions. This divides the space into boxes with side lengths same as the discretization vector. Assuming the quality index functions are bounded on both side, i.e. $0 < \mathcal{I}_{\mathcal{P}_i}(\mathsf{T}) \leq K_i$, the box of a generalization T_l is given by the vector

$$\mathcal{B}(\mathsf{T}_l) = \left[\left\lfloor \frac{\mathcal{I}_{\mathcal{P}_1}(\mathsf{T}_l)}{\epsilon_1} \right\rfloor, \dots, \left\lfloor \frac{\mathcal{I}_{\mathcal{P}_r}(\mathsf{T}_l)}{\epsilon_r} \right\rfloor \right].$$

Algorithm 1. Updator using $\succeq_{box}$

Input: Archive $\mathcal{A}$, candidate generalization T
Output: Updated archive $\mathcal{A}$

1. If $(\mathcal{A} = \phi)$ then $\mathcal{A} \leftarrow \{\mathsf{T}\}$; goto step 7
2. Let $\mathcal{S}_{dominate} = \{\mathsf{T}' \in \mathcal{A} | \mathbf{I_P}(\mathsf{T}) \succeq_{box} \mathbf{I_P}(\mathsf{T}')\}$
3. $\mathcal{A} \leftarrow \mathcal{A} - \mathcal{S}_{dominate}$
4. Let $\mathcal{S}_{dominated} = \{\mathsf{T}' \in \mathcal{A} | \mathbf{I_P}(\mathsf{T}') \succeq_{box} \mathbf{I_P}(\mathsf{T})\}$
5. Let $\mathcal{S}_{box} = \{\mathsf{T}' \in \mathcal{A} | \mathcal{B}(\mathsf{T}) = \mathcal{B}(\mathsf{T}')\}$
6. If $(\mathcal{S}_{dominated} = \phi$ and $\mathcal{S}_{box} = \phi)$ then $\mathcal{A} \leftarrow \mathcal{A} \cup \{\mathsf{T}\}$
7. Return $\mathcal{A}$

A modified dominance relation, called *box-dominance* and denoted by $\succeq_{box}$, is then formulated as

$$\mathbf{I_P}(\mathsf{T}_l) \succeq_{box} \mathbf{I_P}(\mathsf{T}_m) \iff \begin{cases} \mathcal{B}(\mathsf{T}_l) \succeq \mathcal{B}(\mathsf{T}_m) & \text{, if } \mathcal{B}(\mathsf{T}_l) \neq \mathcal{B}(\mathsf{T}_m) \\ \mathbf{I_P}(\mathsf{T}_l) \succeq \mathbf{I_P}(\mathsf{T}_m) & \text{, otherwise} \end{cases}.$$

The box-dominance relation first places the quality index value vectors ($\mathbf{I_P}(\mathsf{T}_l)$ and $\mathbf{I_P}(\mathsf{T}_m)$) in their boxes. If the vectors are on different boxes, then T_l cannot be a PBG of T_m if the box of T_l does not dominate the box of T_m. Otherwise, for the case when the boxes are same, the dominance is checked on the quality index values. Further, every box is allowed to hold only one generalization. Choice between two incomparable generalizations belonging to the same box is made arbitrarily.

Non-dominated boxes signify regions where a minimal PBG exists. By allowing the existence of a single generalization per non-dominated box, the modified dominance relationship maintains a representative subset of the minimal PBGs. The discretization vector determines the size of the boxes and hence impacts the size of the representative subset. If quality index values are in the integer domain, then using a discretization vector of all ones implies using the un-modified dominance relation.

An updator using $\succeq_{box}$: Algorithm 1 outlines an updator algorithm using box-dominance. The algorithm starts with an empty archive $\mathcal{A}$. The first candidate generalization from the generator is therefore automatically inserted into the archive. For subsequent candidates, use of $\succeq_{box}$ effectuates a two level dominance check as explained earlier. First, all generalizations for which the candidate T is a PBG are removed from the archive (Steps 2 and 3). Next, two sets are computed – (i) $\mathcal{S}_{dominated}$ as the set of all generalizations which are PBGs of T, and (ii) $\mathcal{S}_{box}$ as the set of all generalizations whose boxes are same as that of T. The candidate T should not be inserted into the archive if the set $\mathcal{S}_{dominated}$ is non-empty, i.e. there exists a generalization in the archive which is a PBG of T. Further, if $\mathcal{S}_{box}$ is not empty then inclusion of T in the archive will result in the presence of two different generalizations that are positioned in the same box. Step 6 checks for these two conditions, thereby guaranteeing that only non-dominated boxes contain a solution and only one solution is contained in a non-dominated box.

Theorem 1. *Let $\mathcal{M}_g$ denote the set of all generalizations produced by a generator until iteration t and $\mathcal{M}_g^*$ denote the set of minimal PBGs of $\mathcal{M}_g$. Then the archive $\mathcal{A}$ as maintained by Algorithm 1 contains only minimal PBGs of $\mathcal{M}_g$, i.e. $\mathcal{A} \subseteq \mathcal{M}_g^*$.*

Proof. We assume that Algorithm 1 is incorrect, implying $\mathcal{A} \not\subseteq \mathcal{M}_g^*$. Therefore there exists $\mathsf{T}_s \in \mathcal{A}$ generated at iteration s such that $\mathsf{T}_s \notin \mathcal{M}_g^*$.

If $\mathsf{T}_s \notin \mathcal{M}_g^*$ then there exists $\mathsf{T}_q \in \mathcal{M}_g$ discovered at iteration $q \neq s$ such that $\mathbf{I_P}(\mathsf{T}_q) \succeq \mathbf{I_P}(\mathsf{T}_s)$. Also, either $\mathcal{B}(\mathsf{T}_q) = \mathcal{B}(\mathsf{T}_s)$ or $\mathcal{B}(\mathsf{T}_q) \succeq \mathcal{B}(\mathsf{T}_s)$. We can merge these cases and say $\mathbf{I_P}(\mathsf{T}_q) \succeq_{box} \mathbf{I_P}(\mathsf{T}_s)$.

Case (i) $q < s$: If T_q is present in $\mathcal{A}$ at iteration s then T_s will not be included in the archive since $\mathcal{S}_{dominated}$ for T_s contains at least T_q. If T_q is not present in $\mathcal{A}$ at iteration s then it must have been removed by a generalization T_r in $\mathcal{A}$ such that $\mathbf{I_P}(\mathsf{T}_r) \succeq_{box} \mathbf{I_P}(\mathsf{T}_q)$. We therefore have $\mathbf{I_P}(\mathsf{T}_r) \succeq \mathbf{I_P}(\mathsf{T}_q)$ or $\mathcal{B}(\mathsf{T}_r) \succeq \mathcal{B}(\mathsf{T}_q)$. Using the transitivity of the $\succeq$ relation, we have $\mathbf{I_P}(\mathsf{T}_r) \succeq \mathbf{I_P}(\mathsf{T}_s)$ or $\mathcal{B}(\mathsf{T}_r) \succeq \mathcal{B}(\mathsf{T}_s)$, which implies $\mathbf{I_P}(\mathsf{T}_r) \succeq_{box} \mathbf{I_P}(\mathsf{T}_s)$. Hence in this case as well $\mathcal{S}_{dominated} \neq \phi$ for T_s. Note that T_r itself might have got removed from the archive between iteration r and iteration s. However, owing to the transitivity, the generalization which removes it will instead appear in $\mathcal{S}_{dominated}$ for T_s. Hence T_s will never appear in $\mathcal{A}$, i.e. $\mathsf{T}_s \notin \mathcal{A}$, which is a contradiction.

Case (ii) $q > s$: In this case, if T_s exists in $\mathcal{A}$ at iteration q then it would be removed from the archive as it belongs to the set $\mathcal{S}_{dominate}$ of T_q. Further, if T_q gets removed and T_s gets re-generated at a later iteration, the transitivity property would assure that T_s does not get re-inserted into the archive. Thus, $\mathsf{T}_s \notin \mathcal{A}$ which is again a contradiction.

Therefore, T_s can never be a member of the archive at iteration t if it is not a minimal PBG. We can therefore say Algorithm 1 is correct and the archive $\mathcal{A}$ contains only minimal PBGs of $\mathcal{M}_g$. $\qquad\square$

Theorem 2. *The archive $\mathcal{A}$ as maintained by Algorithm 1 is of bounded size, given as $|\mathcal{A}| \leq \prod_{i=1}^{r-1} b_i$ where b_i is the ith largest element of the vector $(\frac{K_1}{\epsilon_1}, \ldots, \frac{K_r}{\epsilon_r})$.*

Proof. Recall that $K_1, \ldots, K_r$ are the upper bounds of the quality index functions for r properties. These values can very well be equal. By using box coordinates at $0, \epsilon_i, 2\epsilon_i, \ldots$ along each dimension i, we have divided the quality index value space into $\prod_{i=1}^{r} \frac{K_i}{\epsilon_i}$ boxes and only one node in each box can be included in $\mathcal{A}$. We now cluster these boxes into groups of b_r boxes, giving us a total of $\prod_{i=1}^{r-1} b_i$ clusters. A cluster is formed by grouping together boxes that have the same co-ordinates in all but one dimension. Note that choosing b_r as the parameter to decide the number of boxes in a cluster gives us the smallest possible cluster size and hence the largest number of clusters. This is required if an upper bound on the archive size is to be computed. Next, in a cluster, the box having the maximum co-ordinate value in the differing dimension will dominate all other boxes in the cluster. Therefore, only such a box will contain a minimal PBG. Each cluster can therefore contribute only one minimal PBG, bounding the archive size to the number of such clusters, i.e. $|\mathcal{A}| \leq \prod_{i=1}^{r-1} b_i$. $\qquad\square$

Algorithm 2. PBG-EA

Output: Archive $\mathcal{A}$ of representative minimal PBGs

1. $\mathcal{A} \leftarrow \phi$; $t \leftarrow 0$
2. Initialize population P_t
3. Evaluate P_t
4. Update $\mathcal{A}$ with nodes in P_t
5. Assign fitness to nodes in P_t and $\mathcal{A}$
6. Perform selection in $P_t \cup \mathcal{A}$
7. Generate P_{t+1} by performing recombination on selected nodes
8. Update $\mathcal{A}$ with nodes in P_{t+1}
9. $t \leftarrow t + 1$; Repeat from Step 5 unless t=maximum number of iterations allowed
10. Return $\mathcal{A}$

---

6 An Evolutionary Generator

An efficient generator is required not only to find new candidate PBGs, but also to minimize the number of node evaluations performed during the search process. The generator evaluates each node that it explores and provides it to the updator. We propose here an evolutionary algorithm for this purpose, henceforth called *PBG-EA*. The algorithm follows the structure described in Algorithm 2. The update method from Algorithm 1 is used iteratively in steps 4 and 8. Specifics of the other steps are described next.

Population initialization. A population P_t is a collection of N_{pop} nodes in the lattice and undergoes changes as the algorithm progresses. Recall that every node is a vector of s dimensions where s is the number of quasi-identifiers. The population P_0 is created by randomly selecting nodes in the lattice. The fully generalized and fully specialized nodes are always inserted into this initial population as they are trivially minimal PBGs.

Node evaluation. Evaluation of a population means computing the quality index values for each node in the population. We focus on the strategy to handle outliers at this point. Outliers in a data set are uncommon combination of attribute values in a tuple. Enforcing a k-anonymity property in the presence of outliers may lead to excessive generalization in the attributes. The approach applied here is to use an upper bound on the number of suppressed tuples. Let η be the maximum number of tuples that is allowed for suppression and $\mathcal{N}$ be the total number of tuples in the data set. Consider the sets $E_1, \ldots, E_{\mathcal{N}}$ where E_i contains anonymized tuples that are indistinguishable from $i - 1$ other tuples. In other words, all tuples in the set E_i are i-anonymous. Note that some E_is may be empty sets. If the anonymized data set is to be made k-anonymous, then all tuples in the sets $E_1, \ldots, E_{k-1}$ must be suppressed. Given the hard limit on suppression, this will be possible only if the number of tuples in the union of these sets is less than or equal to η. The same strategy can be applied in a reverse manner. Tuples in all sets $E_1, \ldots, E_j$ are suppressed such that j is the smallest integer satisfying $\sum_{i=1}^{j+1} |E_i| > \eta$. The data set is then k-anonymous with $k = j + 1$. The number of tuples suppressed is $|E_1 \cup \ldots \cup E_j|$ and can be accounted for in the loss measurement.

Fitness assignment. Fitness signifies the potential of a node to be a minimal PBG relative to the current population and archive. The fitness assignment we use is adapted from the one used in the SPEA2 algorithm [17]. Let dom_P be the number of nodes in $P_t \cup \mathcal{A}$ dominated by $P \in P_t \cup \mathcal{A}$. The fitness of a node P is then computed as the sum of the dominance counts of the nodes which dominate P, or $Fitness_P = \sum_{P' \in P_t \cup \mathcal{A} \text{ and } P' \succeq P} dom_{P'}$. All non-dominated generalizations will therefore have a fitness of zero. Hence, lower fitness implies better generalizations.

Selection. Nodes are selected for recombination by using a binary tournament strategy in $P_t \cup \mathcal{A}$. Under this strategy, two nodes are randomly chosen from $P_t \cup \mathcal{A}$ and the one with the lower fitness is selected. The process is repeated for N_{pop} times, giving a selected population of size N_{pop}.

Recombination. The process of recombination involves the crossover and mutation operators, the resulting nodes from which are used as the next population P_{t+1}. A single point crossover is started by first choosing two nodes (without replacement) from the selected population. Parts of the vectors representing the two nodes are then swapped at a randomly chosen crossover point. The swapping procedure is performed with a probability of p_{cross}; otherwise chosen nodes move unchanged into the next population. Each crossover operation results in two nodes for the next population. Performing the operation on the entire selected population creates N_{pop} nodes for inclusion in P_{t+1}. An intermediate single-step mutation is performed on these nodes — with a probability p_{mut}, each attribute's generalization level is either increased or decreased by one using appropriate rounding so that generalization levels are between zero and the DGH lengths.

7   Performance Analysis

We applied our methodology to the "adult.data" benchmark data set available from the UCI machine learning database. The attributes used in this study along with their DGH lengths are listed in Table 1(a). The total number of nodes in the lattice is 17920. The suppression limit η is set at 1% of the data set size, i.e. $\eta = 301$.

k-anonymity and ℓ-diversity are used as the privacy objectives for experiments using worst case privacy. For experiments with spread based measurements, we consider the two properties $\mathcal{P}_1$: *size of equivalence class of a tuple* and $\mathcal{P}_2$: *count of sensitive attribute value of a tuple in its equivalence class*. Sum of the property values in the respective property vectors are denoted by S_k and S_ℓ respectively in the plots. We use the "Occupation" attribute as the sensitive attribute wherever required.

Information loss estimates are obtained using the general loss metric (GLM) and classification error (CM) [6]. The attribute "Salary Class" is used as the

Table 1. (a) Attributes and DGH lengths used from the *adult census* data set. (b) CE and RR values in PBG-EA anonymization with different sets of properties. Values are shown as $\frac{mean}{variance}$ from the 20 runs.

<table>
<tr><td align="center" colspan="3">(a)</td><td align="center" colspan="3">(b)</td></tr>
<tr><td>Attribute</td><td>No. of values</td><td>DGH length</td><td>Objectives</td><td>CE</td><td>RR</td></tr>
<tr><td align="center">Age</td><td align="center">74</td><td align="center">6</td><td align="center">k, GLM</td><td align="center">$\frac{3.7\times10^{-4}}{6.5\times10^{-9}}$</td><td align="center">$\frac{0.94}{8\times10^{-4}}$</td></tr>
<tr><td align="center">Work Class</td><td align="center">7</td><td align="center">3</td><td align="center">k, ℓ, GLM</td><td align="center">$\frac{3.3\times10^{-4}}{1.1\times10^{-7}}$</td><td align="center">$\frac{0.93}{1.1\times10^{-3}}$</td></tr>
<tr><td align="center">Education</td><td align="center">16</td><td align="center">3</td><td align="center">S_k, GLM</td><td align="center">$\frac{5.7\times10^{-4}}{2.5\times10^{-7}}$</td><td align="center">$\frac{0.84}{1.7\times10^{-3}}$</td></tr>
<tr><td align="center">Marital Status</td><td align="center">7</td><td align="center">3</td><td align="center">S_k, S_ℓ, GLM</td><td align="center">$\frac{6.6\times10^{-4}}{2.0\times10^{-7}}$</td><td align="center">$\frac{0.83}{1.4\times10^{-3}}$</td></tr>
<tr><td align="center">Race</td><td align="center">5</td><td align="center">1</td><td></td><td></td><td></td></tr>
<tr><td align="center">Gender</td><td align="center">2</td><td align="center">1</td><td></td><td></td><td></td></tr>
<tr><td align="center">Native Country</td><td align="center">41</td><td align="center">4</td><td></td><td></td><td></td></tr>
<tr><td align="center">Salary Class</td><td align="center">2</td><td align="center">1</td><td></td><td></td><td></td></tr>
<tr><td align="center">Occupation</td><td align="center">14</td><td align="center">sensitive</td><td></td><td></td><td></td></tr>
</table>

class label while performing experiments with the CM metric. The lattice size in this case is 8960. Solutions reported by PBG-EA are compared with those obtained by an exhaustive search of the entire generalization lattice. Note that the number of nodes evaluated in the exhaustive search is equal to the size of the lattice, while that used by PBG-EA is much less.

An instance of PBG-EA is run with a population size $N_{pop} = 25$ and for 100 iterations. Probability of crossover is set at $p_{cross} = 0.8$ and probability of mutation at $p_{mut} = 1/$number of quasi-identifiers $= 0.125$. Each experiment is run 20 times to compute the mean and variance of the performance metrics (discussed below). The discretization vector is set to all ones, unless otherwise indicated.

We use two metrics to quantify the efficiency of PBG-EA in terms of its ability to converge to the true minimal PBGs (as found by the exhaustive search) and how well the solutions represent the set of all minimal PBGs.

Let $\mathcal{M}$ be the set of all minimal PBGs for a data set and $\mathcal{M}'$ be the solutions in the archive at the end of the final iteration. Quality index values of all nodes in $\mathcal{M}$ and $\mathcal{M}'$ are normalized by dividing the values by the corresponding maximum in $\mathcal{M}$. The *convergence error* (CE) is then given as $CE = \sum_{M'\in\mathcal{M}'} \min_{M\in\mathcal{M}} [dist(\mathbf{I_P}(M), \mathbf{I_P}(M'))]$ where $dist$ is the euclidean distance between two vectors. A CE value of zero means all solutions in the archive have converged to some minimal PBG.

The *representation ratio* (RR) is the fraction of non-dominated boxes in $\mathcal{M}$ that are occupied by a solution in $\mathcal{M}'$. Given a discretization vector, solutions in $\mathcal{M}$ are assigned their respective boxes and the non-dominated boxes are marked. RR signifies how many of these marked boxes are occupied by a solution in the archive. A value of one signifies that a solution in each non-dominated box exists in the archive.

Figure 1 compares the PBG-EA solutions with those obtained from an exhaustive search for worst case privacy measurements as in k-anonymity and ℓ-diversity. Trade-offs between the k value and the loss are evident from the two

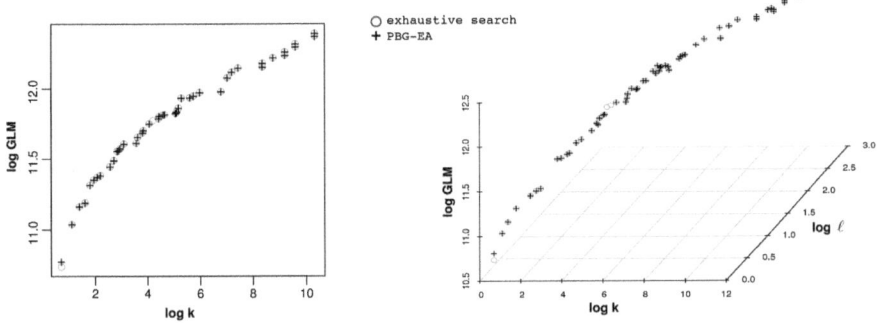

Fig. 1. PBG-EA solutions for the two property (k-GLM) and three property (k-ℓ-GLM) problems

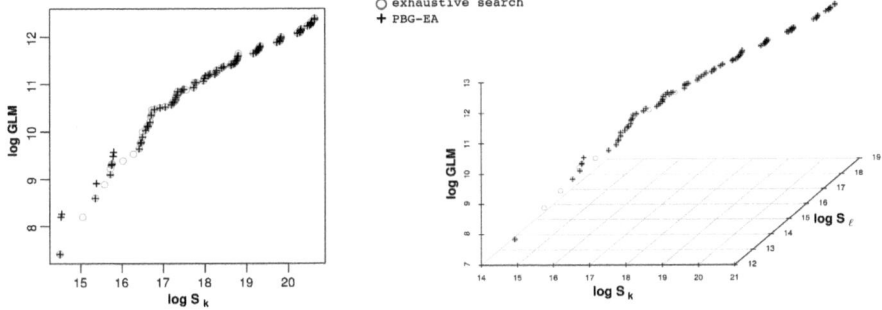

Fig. 2. PBG-EA solutions for the two property (S_k-GLM) and three property (S_k-S_ℓ-GLM) problems using spread based quality

property (k-GLM) solutions. The convergence efficiency of PBG-EA is worth mentioning as 94% of all minimal PBGs are discovered by the algorithm (Table 1(b)). Although the algorithm utilizes random numbers in a number of places, this performance of the algorithm is more or less persistent (low variance across the 20 runs). The trade-offs in the three property (k-ℓ-GLM) seem to be more in terms of loss, rather than between k and ℓ.

Figure 2 shows the PBG-EA solutions when the spread function is used to measure privacy. The RR is slightly lower in this case. Nonetheless, the convergence error is still low. Using the spread function induces a higher number of minimal PBGs whose discovery typically requires more number of iterations. We observe that increasing the number of properties from two to three has very little influence on the RR. A good fitness assignment strategy is required for early determination of solution efficiency. The dominance count based fitness assignment is ideally suited here. Typically, a solution is not worth exploring if it is dominated by a large fraction of the nodes in the lattice. The fitness scheme takes this a step further to also consider the quality of the solutions that dominate it.

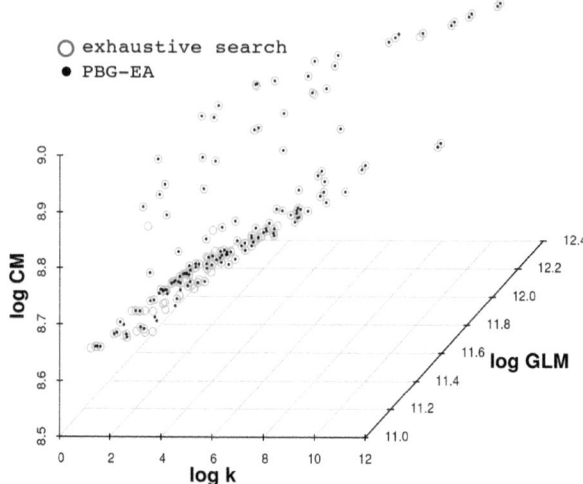

Fig. 3. PBG-EA solutions with a single privacy property (k-anonymity) and two loss metrics (GLM-CM)

PBGs can also be used to find generalizations that are acceptable in terms of more than one loss metric. Figure 3 shows the minimal PBGs obtained when the k-anonymity property is evaluated against two different loss metrics, namely GLM and CM. The heavily scattered points across the entire space signify the existence of reciprocal relationships between GLM and CM. Ideally, for a given k value, the convention is to choose the generalization with the lowest GLM. However, the multi-loss metric experiment indicates that choosing a generalization with a comparatively higher GLM can serve the dual purpose of making the anonymized data set also suitable for classification tasks.

Although the set of minimal PBGs for the data set used in the study is not unbounded in size, we experimented with several discretization vectors to demonstrate the efficiency of PBG-EA in finding a representative subset. Table 2(a) shows the performance measures for some vectors. The high representation ratio is indicative of the fact that PBG-EA solutions cover most of the non-dominated boxes generated by the use of the discretization vectors. For two property (k-GLM) anonymization, as higher ϵ values are used for the objectives, the efficiency of PBG-EA improves in terms of RR. However, using more number of properties tend to slightly affect the performance owing mostly to the limited number of iterations.

Efficiency of PBG-EA in converging quickly to a minimal PBG is evaluated by counting the number of unique nodes that are evaluated by it during the search process. Although the evolutionary algorithm can potentially explore 2500 (25 × 100) distinct nodes in the lattice, a much smaller number is actually evaluated. Table 2(b) lists the average (out of the 20 runs) number of unique node evaluations performed for different problem instances. We consider this low percentage of node evaluations to be a positive indication of the convergence efficiency of PBG-EA. This is particularly promising since the entire set of minimal PBGs (all one

Table 2. (a) CE and RR values in PBG-EA anonymization with different discretization vectors. (b) Average number of nodes evaluated in PBG-EA for different sets of properties. Total number of nodes in the first four sets is 17920 and that in the last set is 8960.

(a)

ϵ_k	ϵ_ℓ	ϵ_{GLM}	CE	RR
5	-	100	$\frac{4.3\times10^{-4}}{2.6\times10^{-7}}$	$\frac{0.95}{1.6\times10^{-3}}$
10	-	1000	$\frac{1.6\times10^{-4}}{8.0\times10^{-8}}$	$\frac{0.98}{8.2\times10^{-4}}$
50	-	10000	$\frac{1.7\times10^{-4}}{1.1\times10^{-8}}$	$\frac{1.0}{0.0}$
5	2	100	$\frac{4.9\times10^{-3}}{2.5\times10^{-7}}$	$\frac{0.92}{1.2\times10^{-3}}$
10	4	1000	$\frac{7.4\times10^{-3}}{9.3\times10^{-7}}$	$\frac{0.92}{7.0\times10^{-4}}$
50	6	10000	$\frac{1.8\times10^{-2}}{8.2\times10^{-6}}$	$\frac{0.88}{1.7\times10^{-3}}$

(b)

Objectives	Avg. node evaluations
k, GLM	916 (5.1%)
k, ℓ, GLM	946 (5.3%)
S_k, GLM	1136 (6.3%)
S_k, S_ℓ, GLM	1197 (6.7%)
k, GLM, CM	1073 (11.9%)

discretization vector) is found by exploring a small 5% of nodes in the lattice. The nodes evaluated is slightly higher for three property problems. This is not surprising since the number of minimal PBGs is also comparatively higher in such cases.

8   Conclusions

In this paper, we propose identifying the basic properties that provide the requisite protection from a privacy breach, and then measuring them for each underlying individual. This generates a property vector for every generalization. Comparison of generalizations with respect to a single property is performed using quality index functions that measure privacy using the variations in individual privacy levels. Optimality in such generalizations is signified by non-dominated generalizations (minimal PBGs) under a dominance relation. A representative subset of solutions is maintained by using a box-dominance operator in an evolutionary algorithm. Application on a benchmark data set shows that the algorithm can quickly discover a diverse set of minimal PBGs with a small number of node evaluations. Observations from our multi-loss experiment suggest that the problem of microdata anonymization to serve multiple usages needs to be explored in more details.

Acknowledgment

This work has been supported in part by a grant from the U.S. Air Force Office of Scientific Research (AFOSR) under contract FA9550-07-1-0042.

References

1. Samarati, P.: Protecting Respondents' Identities in Microdata Release. IEEE Transactions on Knowledge and Data Engineering 13(6), 1010–1027 (2001)
2. Samarati, P., Sweeney, L.: Generalizing Data to Provide Anonymity when Disclosing Information. In: Proceedings of the 17th ACM Symposium on Principles of Database Systems, vol. 188 (1998)

3. Sweeney, L.: Achieving k–Anonymity Privacy Protection Using Generalization and Suppression. International Journal on Uncertainty, Fuzziness and Knowledge-based Systems 10(5), 571–588 (2002)
4. Bayardo, R.J., Agrawal, R.: Data Privacy Through Optimal k-Anonymization. In: Proceedings of the 21st International Conference on Data Engineering, pp. 217–228 (2005)
5. Hundepool, A., Willenborg, L.: Mu and Tau Argus: Software for Statistical Disclosure Control. In: Proceedings of the Third International Seminar on Statistical Confidentiality (1996)
6. Iyengar, V.S.: Transforming Data to Satisfy Privacy Constraints. In: Proceedings of the 8th ACM SIGKDD International Conference on Knowledge Discovery and Data Mining, pp. 279–288 (2002)
7. Li, N., Li, T., Venkatasubramaniam, S.: t–Closeness: Privacy Beyond k–Anonymity and ℓ–Diversity. In: Proceedings of the 23rd International Conference on Data Engineering, pp. 106–115 (2007)
8. Machanavajjhala, A., Gehrke, J., Kifer, D., Venkitasubramaniam, M.: ℓ–Diversity: Privacy Beyond k–Anonymity. In: Proceedings of the 22nd International Conference on Data Engineering, p. 24 (2006)
9. Truta, T.M., Vinay, B.: Privacy Protection: p-Sensitive k-Anonymity Property. In: Proceedings of the 22nd International Conference on Data Engineering Workshops, p. 94 (2006)
10. Dewri, R., Ray, I., Ray, I., Whitley, D.: On the Comparison of Microdata Disclosure Control Algorithms. In: 12th International Conference on Extending Database Technology, pp. 240–251 (2009)
11. Meyerson, A., Williams, R.: On the Complexity of Optimal k-Anonymity. In: Proceedings of the 23rd ACM Symposium on the Principles of Database Systems, pp. 223–228 (2004)
12. LeFevre, K., DeWitt, D.J., Ramakrishnan, R.: Incognito: Efficient Full-Domain k-Anonymity. In: Proceedings of the 2005 ACM SIGMOD International Conference on Management of Data, pp. 49–60 (2005)
13. Fung, B.C.M., Wang, K., Yu, P.S.: Top-Down Specialization for Information and Privacy Preservation. In: Proceedings of the 21st International Conference in Data Engineering, pp. 205–216 (2005)
14. LeFevre, K., DeWitt, D.J., Ramakrishnan, R.: Mondrian Multidimensional K-Anonymity. In: Proceedings of the 22nd International Conference in Data Engineering, p. 25 (2006)
15. Dewri, R., Ray, I., Ray, I., Whitley, D.: On the Optimal Selection of k in the k-Anonymity Problem. In: Proceedings of the 24th International Conference on Data Engineering, pp. 1364–1366 (2008)
16. Huang, Z., Du, W.: OptRR: Optimizing Randomized Response Schemes for Privacy-Preserving Data Mining. In: Proceedings of the 24th International Conference on Data Engineering, pp. 705–714 (2008)
17. Zitzler, E., Laumanns, M., Thiele, L.: SPEA2: Improving the Strength Pareto Evolutionary Algorithm. In: Evolutionary Methods for Design, Optimization and Control with Applications to Industrial Problems, pp. 95–100 (2002)

Role Mining in the Presence of Noise

Jaideep Vaidya, Vijayalakshmi Atluri, Qi Guo, and Haibing Lu

MSIS Department and CIMIC, Rutgers University, USA
{jsvaidya,atluri,qiguo,haibing}@cimic.rutgers.edu

Abstract. The problem of role mining, a bottom-up process of discovering roles from the user-permission assignments (UPA), has drawn increasing attention in recent years. The role mining problem (RMP) and several of its variants have been proposed in the literature. While the basic RMP discovers roles that exactly represent the UPA, the *inexact* variants, such as the δ-approx RMP and MinNoise-RMP, allow for some inexactness in the sense that the discovered roles do not have to exactly cover the entire UPA. However, since data in real life is never completely clean, the role mining process is only effective if it is robust to noise. This paper takes the first step towards addressing this issue. Our goal in this paper is to examine if the effect of noise in the UPA could be ameliorated due to the inexactness in the role mining process, thus having little negative impact on the discovered roles. Specifically, we define a formal model of noise and experimentally evaluate the previously proposed algorithm for δ-approx RMP against its robustness to noise. Essentially, this would allow one to come up with strategies to minimize the effect of noise while discovering roles. Our experiments on real data indicate that the role mining process can preferentially cover a lot of the real assignments and leave potentially noisy assignments for further examination. We explore the ramifications of noisy data and discuss next steps towards coming up with more effective algorithms for handling such data.

1 Introduction

Today, Role Based Access Control (RBAC) is the de facto model used for advanced access control, and is widely deployed in diverse enterprises of all sizes. Under RBAC, roles represent organizational agents that perform certain job functions within the organization. Users, in turn, are assigned appropriate roles based on their responsibilities and qualifications [1,2]. Essentially, a role, can be viewed as a set of permissions. One main benefit of RBAC is simplified security administration as the role configuration need not be changed when users join or leave the organization.

Deploying RBAC requires first defining a complete and correct set of roles. This process, known as *role engineering* [3], has been identified as one of the costliest and most time consuming components in realizing RBAC [4]. The problem of role mining, a bottom-up process of discovering roles from the user-permission assignments (UPA), has drawn increasing attention in recent years.

S. Foresti and S. Jajodia (Eds.): Data and Applications Security XXIV, LNCS 6166, pp. 97–112, 2010.

Unlike the top-down approach where roles are defined by carefully analyzing and decomposing business processes into smaller units in a functionally independent manner, role mining has the advantage of automating the role engineering process. Role mining can be used as a tool, in conjunction with a top-down approach, to identify potential or candidate roles that can then be examined to determine if they are appropriate, given existing functions and business processes.

Work has been carried out on the top-down approach to role engineering[3,5,6], though it requires significant manpower effort to do correctly. To alleviate this, there have been several attempts to propose good bottom-up techniques to finding roles [7,8]. More recently, researchers [9,10,11,12,13,14,15] have begun formally defining the role mining problem (RMP) and proposed a number of RMP variants. There has also been some work on hybrid mining of roles[16,17]. The basic-RMP problem has been shown to be equivalent to a number of known problems including matrix decomposition and minimum biclique cover problem in graphs, among others. The basic-RMP as a matrix decomposition problem is as follows. Given m users, n permissions, then UPA can be represented as an $m \times n$ boolean matrix $M(UPA)$ where a 1 in cell $\{ij\}$ indicates the assignment of permission j to user i. If there are k roles, the user-to-role mapping (UA) can be represented as an $m \times k$ boolean matrix $M(UA)$ where a 1 in cell $\{ij\}$ indicates the assignment of role j to user i. Similarly, the role-to-permission mapping (PA) can be represented as a $k \times n$ boolean matrix $M(PA)$ where a 1 in cell $\{ij\}$ indicates the assignment of permission j to role i. The basic-RMP is to decompose $M(UPA)$ into a $m \times k$ matrix $M(UA)$ representing UA and a $k \times n$ matrix $M(PA)$ representing PA, such that k is minimal.

Apart from basic-RMP, other role mining problems have been defined with different minimization objectives. One objective is to discover roles in such a way that the total number of user-to-role assignments and role-to-permission assignments ($|UA| + |PA|$) is minimal. This, known as the Edge-RMP, has been studied by Vaidya et al. [9] and Ene et al. [12], among others. Other variants [14,10] focus on discovering optimal roles as well as role hierarchies.

While the above RMP problems attempt to discover roles that *exactly* describe the original UPA, this may be unnecessary. With this in mind, some *inexact* variants of RMP have been identified, which do not exactly describe the original UPA, but allow for some inexactness. This is justified since mistakes can always be made, and asking for roles to match those mistakes would actually worsen the situation. Moreover, in some sense, it may be possible to find more "fundamental roles" by only trying to match a certain percentage of the original UPA. To describe this. Vaidya et al. [18] have proposed two inexact variants of RMP, called the δ-consistent RMP and MinNoise RMP.

Any given UA, PA, and UPA are considered to be δ-consistent, if and only if the UPA derived from UA and PA matches the original UPA within δ. Now, the δ-approx RMP can be defined [18] as the problem of finding the minimal set of roles such that the discovered UA and PA and the original UPA are δ-*consistent*. As a problem formulation, the δ-approx Role Mining Problem is *always* better than the Basic Role Mining Problem when noise is present.

Table 1. User-Permission Assignment

(a) Without Noise   (b) With Noise

	p_1	p_2	p_3	p_4	p_5
u_1	1	1	1	0	0
u_2	0	0	1	0	1
u_3	1	1	1	0	1
u_4	1	1	1	0	0

	p_1	p_2	p_3	p_4	p_5
u_1	1	1	1	1	1
u_2	0	0	1	0	1
u_3	0	1	1	0	1
u_4	1	1	1	1	0

This is so, because, setting a nonzero value of δ gives the leeway to correct for the present noise errors. In this sense, any UPA divergent within δ from the original UPA satisfies the δ-approx definition. Obviously, all such formulations are not equally good. A good algorithm gives a UPA' that preferentially removes noise rather than making errors.

Another approach for inexactness could be by bounding the number of roles, and minimizing the approximation. This is the Minimal Noise Role Mining Problem (MinNoise RMP). This fixes the number of roles that one would like to find, but finds those roles that incur minimal difference with respect to the original user-permission matrix (UPA).

Since data in real life is never completely clean, the role mining process is only effective if it is robust to noise. By noise, we mean a permission being recorded as a denial or a denial being recorded as a permission. Our goal in this paper is to examine if the effect of noise in the UPA could be ameliorated due to the inexactness in the role mining process, thus having little negative impact on the discovered roles.

In the following, we provide a concrete example to justify our argument. Table 1(a) shows a sample user-permission assignment (UPA), for 4 users and 5 permissions. Table 1(b) shows the UPA with noise. Specifically, user u_1 has the extra permissions p_4, p_5, user u_3 has lost the permission p_1, while user u_4 gains the extra permission p_4 (i.e., cells (u_1, p_4), (u_1, p_5), and (u_4, p_4) are flipped from 0 to 1, while cell (u_3, p_1) is flipped from 1 to 0). This may happen due to the security administrator forgetting to remove old permissions that are no longer necessary (in the 0 to 1 case), or by mistake temporarily revoking a necessary permission (in the 1 to 0 case). Tables 2(a) and 2(b) depict a user-role assignment (UA) and role-permission assignment (PA) that completely describe the given (noisy) user-permission assignment (i.e., $M(UA) \otimes M(PA) = M(UPA)$). Indeed, the given UA, PA, and $ROLES$ are optimal. It is not possible to completely describe the given UPA with less than 3 roles. As one can see, Table 2, representing the basic-RMP approach, actually matches exactly reconstructs the input noisy UPA and in effect, matches all 4 noisy bits as well.

On the other hand, Tables 3(a) and 3(b) depict the optimal UA and PA, which cover none of the noisy bits and *accurately* cover (without introducing errors) all of the 1's. In fact, as one can see, this is actually the optimal decomposition of the original (clean) UPA, which unfortunately is never seen. This clearly shows that the optimal solution for basic-RMP is not always a better choice when noise is present.

In fact, noise can cause multiple problems in the process of role mining. First, as shown above, we may get a suboptimal (i.e., larger) number of roles. Worse, the

Table 2. Optimal role set for Basic-RMP over noisy data

(a) UA

	r_1	r_2	r_3
u_1	1	1	1
u_2	0	1	0
u_3	1	1	0
u_4	1	0	1

(b) PA

	p_1	p_2	p_3	p_4	p_5
r_1	0	1	1	0	0
r_2	0	0	1	0	1
r_3	1	0	0	1	0

Table 3. Optimal role set for Basic-RMP over Clean data

(a) UA

	r_1	r_2
u_1	1	0
u_2	0	1
u_3	1	1
u_4	1	0

(b) PA

	p_1	p_2	p_3	p_4	p_5
r_1	1	1	1	0	0
r_2	0	0	1	0	1

discovered role set reconstitutes noisy bits. Since the discovered roles are also con-taminated with noise, they perpetuate the existing errors. For example, in Table 2 role r_3 consists of $\{p_1, p_4\}$. Since bit p_4 is actually noisy, in effect any user who will now be assigned r_3 will also have the same error. Thus, due to the noise, not only is the wrong UPA reconstituted, but also, the error affects future users who may be mistakenly given over and underpermissions right from the start. This can create great problems and reduce the benefits of using RBAC in the first place.

In this paper, first we define a formal model of noise and then experimentally evaluate the previously proposed algorithm for the δ-approx RMP. Essentially, this would allow one to come up with strategies to minimize the effect of noise while discovering roles. Our experimental results indicate that if one sets the level of δ equal to the level of noise, the impact of noise is minimal in discovering roles. We evaluate the robustness of the algorithm using the standard F-score measure. Our results indicate that, under the presence of noise, the F-score for δ-approximate RMP is fairly uniform with increasing noise levels, whereas the F-score for basic-RMP deteriorates.

The rest of this paper is organized as follows. In Section 2, we review the RBAC model and the formal definitions of δ-approx RMP, and MinNoise RMP. In Section 3, we present an appropriate noise model, which include the definition of noise, degree of noise and the robustness measure. In Section 4, we illustrate the δ-approx RMP. In Section 5 we discuss our noise robustness evaluation ap-proach. In Section 6, we present the results of our experimental evaluation of the δ-approx RMP algorithm against noise robustness. In Section 7 we provide an insight into alternative strategies for reducing the effect of noise. Finally, Section 8 concludes the paper.

2   Preliminaries

In this section, we review the basic RBAC model and the formal role mining problem identified in [18].

2.1   Role Based Access Control Model

We adopt the NIST standard of the Role Based Access Control (RBAC) model [2]. For the sake of simplicity, we do not consider sessions, role hierarchies or separation of duties constraints in this paper.

Definition 1 (RBAC).

- $U, ROLES, OPS$, and OBJ are the set of users, roles, operations, and objects.
- $UA \subseteq U \times ROLES$, a many-to-many mapping user-to-role assignment relation.
- $PRMS$ (the set of permissions) $\subseteq \{(op, obj) | op \in OPS \bigwedge obj \in OBJ\}$
- $PA \subseteq ROLES \times PRMS$, a many-to-many mapping of role-to-permission assignments.[1]
- $UPA \subseteq U \times PRMS$, a many-to-many mapping of user-to-permission assignments.
- $assigned\_users(R) = \{u \in U | (u, R) \in UA\}$, the mapping of role R onto a set of users.
- $assigned\_permissions(R) = \{p \in PRMS | (p, R) \in PA\}$, the mapping of role R onto a set of permissions.

2.2   The Inexact RMP Variants

We review the formal definitions [18] of the δ-approx RMP and the MinNoise RMP as these inexact RMP variants are the focus of this paper.

Definition 2 (δ-approx RMP). *Given a set of users U, a set of permissions $PRMS$, a user-permission assignment UPA, and a threshold δ, find a set of roles, $ROLES$, a user-to-role assignment UA, and a role-to-permission assignment PA, δ-consistent with UPA and minimizing the number of roles, k.*

The basic-RMP is the case where $\delta = 0$ [18]. Given the user-permission matrix (UPA), the basic-RMP is to find a user-to-role assignment UA and a role-to-permission assignment PA such that UA and PA describe UPA while minimizing the number of roles. The notion of δ-consistency is useful, since it helps to bound the degree of approximation. The MinNoise RMP bounds the number of roles, which is defined as follows.

Definition 3 (MinNoise RMP). *Given a set of users U, a set of permissions $PRMS$, a user-permission assignment UPA, and the number of roles k, find a set of k roles, $ROLES$, a user-to-role assignment UA, and a role-to-permission assignment PA, minimizing $\| M(UA) \otimes M(PA) - M(UPA) \|_1$ where $M(UA), M(PA)$, and $M(UPA)$ denote the matrix representation of UA, PA and UPA.*

---

[1] Note that in the original NIST standard [2], PA was defined as $PA \subseteq PRMS \times ROLES$, a many-to-many mapping of permission-to-role assignments.

3   Noise

In reality, no data is clean, and the user-permission-assignment is no exception. Permissions are accidentally assigned to those who do not need them, or are not revoked once the permission is no longer needed. In addition, some users may not have all the permissions that others performing similar job functions have. Since noise in general is random in nature, we believe that using inexact variants of the RMP in discovering roles could use this noise to its benefit and may have little impact on the outcome of the role discovery process. In this section, we first present our noise model [19] that helps in evaluating the δ-approx RMP algorithms against their robustness to noise. Second, we present the degree of noise [19]. We now discuss each in detail.

3.1   Noise Model

The presence of noise essentially means that errors have occurred in the data – i.e., the actual data does not match the real data. In our case, the data consists of access permissions in the user-permission-assignment matrix (UPA). In this boolean matrix, a 1 signifies that the subject-object access is permissible (we denote this as allowed permission), and a 0 denotes lack/denial of permission (we denote this as disallowed permission). In this case, noise means that the actual boolean matrix is different from the desired boolean matrix with the following three types of errors occurring in the matrix:

1. **General noise:** Such noise results in bit-flipping errors. Thus, a 1 gets flipped to a 0 and vice-versa. Effectively, this means that either a permission is incorrectly revoked or a permission is incorrectly given by the security administrator.
2. **Additive noise:** In this case, a permission can only be incorrectly given, not incorrectly revoked. Thus, a 0 can incorrectly be changed to a 1 but not vice-versa. This could happen if an administrator had first given a permission to a user to accomplish some task, but then forgotten to revoke it after the task/duration is complete.
3. **Subtractive noise:** In this case, a permission could be incorrectly revoked, though not incorrectly given. Thus, a 1 is incorrectly changed to a 0, but not vice-versa. This could happen when a user is only given a subset of the overall permissions he may ultimately need. For example, when someone new starts in the organization, he may be given a set of permissions for some initial assignments but not the full set he will ultimately need because accurate assignment is time consuming.

It is clear that general noise actually includes both additive noise and subtractive noise. Thus, the presence of general noise implies the presence of both additive as well as subtractive noise. However, their percentages are not equal. In actuality, the degree of additive and subtractive noise depends on the number of 0s and 1s. All else being equal, any general noise will result in additive noise proportional to the number of 0s and subtractive noise proportional to the number of 1s.

Typically, the access control matrix will be sparse with fewer 1s and many more 0s. Therefore, additive noise will be more likely to occur. This corresponds to real situations where users are more likely to have more permissions than they need (additive noise) than less permissions than they need (subtractive noise) because otherwise they could not perform their job functions. For now, we explore the robustness of our algorithm to additive noise since we believe it is the type of noise we are most concerned.

One may argue that errors do not happen completely at random, and are predetermined based on actual usage. However, when there is no RBAC in place or preexisting policies (which could easily happen when you are freshly deploying RBAC), the random model of noise does accurately reflect reality.

3.2   Degree of Noise

To effectively take noise into account, one must consider the degree of noise along with the different types of noise discussed above. An obvious way to consider the degree of noise is computing it as a percentage of the amount of data. However, considering this percentage of noise for the entire number of bits in UPA may not be an accurate representation of noise. For example, consider a system with 2000 users and 500 permissions. This results in the UPA of 1,000,000 bits. 1% of this dataset equates to 10000 bits. However, it does not mean that 10000 bits should be flipped. This is because of the fact that the UPA is typically very sparse, i.e., the number of allowed permissions (1s) is significantly smaller than the number of disallowed permissions (0s). For example, only 4000 of the subject-object accesses might be allowed. In this case, flipping 10000 bits would completely obviate the true data. One must realize that unlike digital communications, in access control data, the signal is characterized only by the 1s, and not by the 0s. This implies that when considering the degree of noise, it should be a percentage of the number of 1s in the data. Thus, when considering noise percentages, we take noise to be a percentage of the number of 1s.

Finally, we need to consider how to add noise to the data. Again, assume 2000 users, 500 permissions and 4000 allowed subject-object pairs (4000 1s). If we wanted to introduce 10% general noise into this data set, how should we proceed? A simple way to add noise is to pick 400 bits at random from the 1,000,000 bits and flip them. But is this correct – should exactly *400* bits be flipped? The key issue is whether by 10% noise we mean that the noise is exactly 10% of the data or whether we mean that the probability of error in the data is 10%. The first case corresponds to flipping 400 bits. However, in the second case, we should go through all 1,000,000 bits and flip each bit with a probability of 0.04% (This is correct since 400 is actually 0.04% of 1000000). Though either way is fine, we argue that the second way of introducing noise more closely approximates real life.

In our experiments we considered 1%, 5%, 10%, 20% and 30% noise and introduced it into the datasets as described in the second method above. As a result of the discussion in the prior two sections, we define noise as follows:

Definition 4. *[19] p% General Noise: Given users U and permissions $PRMS$ and a user to permission assignment $UPA \subseteq U \times PRMS$, a noisy dataset with p% general noise consists of a modified permission assignment $UPA' \subseteq U \times PRMS$ such that: (i) if $x \in UPA$, $x \in UPA'$ with probability $1 - p$; (ii) if $x \notin UPA$, $x \in UPA'$ with probability p.*

4   Algorithm

As discussed earlier, Vaidya et al.[18] first formalized the Role Mining Problem and defined the δ-approx RMP. However, no solution was proposed for it. In [20], a heuristic solution has been proposed that can efficiently solve both the RMP as well as the δ-approx RMP. We now describe this solution.

The algorithm proceeds in two independent phases. In the first phase, a set of candidate roles is generated from the UPA. This is currently done using the FastMiner algorithm[19], though any other method could also be used instead. FastMiner generates candidate roles simply by intersecting all unique user pairs. Once the candidates are generated, the second phase greedily picks the best set of roles among them by picking the best candidate role from the remaining candidate roles until the original UPA can be reconstituted within the desired approximation factor (δ). Thus, in each iteration, for every remaining candidate role, the uncovered area of that role is computed by finding the number of 1s in $M(UPA)$ that are not already covered by any of the roles in $ROLES$ (the current minimum tiling). The best role is then selected and the algorithm reiterates until termination. Algorithm 1 gives the details.

Algorithm 1. δ-approx RMP(UPA, δ)

Require: User-Permission assignment, UPA
Require: the approximation threshold, δ
1: {Create candidate set of roles}
2: Create a candidate set of roles, $CROLES$, using the FastMiner [19] algorithm
3: $ROLES \leftarrow \phi$
4: **while** UPA is not covered within δ **do**
5:     $BestRole \leftarrow \phi$
6:     $BestArea \leftarrow 0$
7:     **for** each role C in $CROLES$ **do**
8:         $carea \leftarrow Uncovered\_Area(C, UPA, ROLES)$ {compute uncovered area of candidate role}
9:         **if** $carea > BestArea$ **then**
10:             $BestArea \leftarrow carea$
11:             $BestRole \leftarrow C$
12:         **end if**
13:     **end for**
14:     $ROLES \leftarrow ROLES \bigcup C$ {Add C to the set of roles, $ROLES$}
15:     Remove C from $CROLES$
16: **end while**
17: Return $ROLES$

It is important to note that the way in which candidate roles are generated (through subset enumeration), and the way the uncovered area is computed, plays a role in the kinds of the errors the algorithm can tolerate. Specifically, when reconstituting the UPA, the above algorithm can leave 1s uncovered though it does

not cover 0s with 1s. What this means is that the algorithm could potentially eliminate additive noise (by ignoring the added 1s), but cannot handle subtractive
noise (since a 1 that has been turned into a 0 is never reconstituted). In general,
since additive noise is much more of a vulnerability from the security standpoint,
and typically the UPA is sparse, this still may be acceptable in real life. However,
ideally one would prefer to have algorithms that are robust to both kinds of noise.

5   Noise Robustness Metric

Robustness, in essence, reflects the degree to which an algorithm is *not* affected
by noise. First, we define a *noisy* bit as a bit whose value has been erroneously
flipped. We also use the term non-noisy bit to describe those bits whose values are
not changed by mistake. A *completely robust* algorithm will somehow be able to
magically eliminate the effect of noise. Thus, the output of a "completely robust"
algorithm would be the same regardless of the presence of noise. In effect, a perfect algorithm would cover all of the original 1s and cover none of the original 0s,
regardless of their value after the introduction of noise. In order to compare noise
robustness of different algorithms, and to devise better algorithms, it is extremely
important to appropriately define a metric for noise robustness.

   A naïve approach to define the degree of robustness is to define it as ratio of
the number of appropriately reconstituted bits (noisy or non-noisy bits included)
to the total number of bits in UPA. For example, from Table 1(a) and Table
1(b), we can see the total number of bits in UPA are 20, among which, 4 bits
are noisy: (u_1, p_4), (u_1, p_5), (u_3, p_1), and (u_4, p_4). The solution in Tables 3(a)
and 3(b) reconstitutes the original values for all 4 noisy bits and all 16 non-noisy
bits. Therefore, the degree of robustness of the algorithm, as defined above, is
$20/20=100$ percent. On the contrary, the solution obtained for the Basic-RMP
(depicted in Tables 2(a) and 2(b)) does not reconstitute the original values of
any of the noisy bits, and therefore, has a degree of robustness of $16/20=0.8$. The
problem with this way of measurement is that it does not differentiate between
good performance on the original data versus good performance with respect to
noise. Thus, the solution for the Basic-RMP still has 0.8 robustness even though
it does not fix any of the errors associated with noise. In effect, it has 0 tolerance
to noise, though it reconstitutes the original non-noisy data perfectly.

   Another naïve approach to measure the degree of noise robustness is to define
it as the ratio of the number of noisy bits whose original (before-flipping) values
are reconstituted to the total number of noisy bits. In other words, it measures
the relative ratio of appropriately covered noisy bits. To use the same example
as above, the solution in Tables 3(a) and 3(b) reconstitutes the original values
for all 4 noisy bits. Therefore, the degree of robustness of the algorithm is 100
percent. On the contrary, The Basic-RMP algorithm in Tables 2(a) and 2(b),
does not reconstitute the original values of any noisy bit, therefore, having a
degree of robustness as 0.

   While this accurately measures how much noise is fixed, it does not take errors
made by the algorithm into consideration. For example, the algorithm may cover

a bit with 1 when its real value is 0 (though the value of the bit has not changed due to noise). Similarly, the algorithm may leave a bit uncovered as 0 when its real value is 1. Taking our original example into consideration, assume that a candidate algorithm almost reconstitutes the original UPA, but with only one error, say the value of a non-noisy bit (u_2, p_4) is 1 in the reassembled UPA. Under the above definition of degree of robustness, the algorithm would be considered to be 100 percent robust, which is clearly incorrect.

Indeed, the term *noise* can be used to describe the defect of the dataset, while the term *error* can be used to indicate the misjudgement made by the algorithm. A good definition of degree of noise robustness should measure both noise fixed as well as errors made by an algorithm. For this we must measure two sets of numbers – the percentage of correctly reconstituted noisy bits, as well as the percentage of errors made by the algorithm. We must also devise a way of integrating these into a unifying measure.

For this, work from the field of data mining and statistics comes to our aid. In a general classification problem, every data item must be classified to belong to a certain class. In a statistical classification task[21], the *Precision* for a class is the number of true positives divided by the total number of elements labeled as belonging to the class (i.e. the sum of true positives and false positives, which are items incorrectly labeled as belonging to the class). *Recall* is correspondingly defined as the number of true positives divided by the total number of elements that actually belong to the class (i.e. the sum of true positives and false negatives, which are items which were not labeled as belonging to that class but should have been). In this sense, Precision can be seen as a measure of exactness or fidelity, whereas Recall is a measure of completeness. The F-measure or balanced F-score is the harmonic mean of precision and recall: $F = 2 \cdot (\text{precision} \cdot \text{recall})/(\text{precision} + \text{recall})$.

Assuming only two classes, every instance originally belongs to one of these two classes and is classified into one of the two classes. From our perspective, the amount of noise fixed approximately corresponds to the notion of *Recall*, while the number of errors made approximately corresponds to the notion of *Precision*. Thus, we simply use the notion of F-score to check the overall degree of noise robustness of the algorithm.

6   Experimental Evaluation

The purpose of the experimental evaluation performed in this section is to compare the robustness of various role mining algorithms towards the noise. In Section 6.1, we discuss the design of the experiments and the their results are analyzed in Section 6.2.

6.1   Experimental Design

The experimental design consists of four steps: Data Creation, Noise Insertion, roles generation and UPA reconstitution, finally the computation of the degree of noise robustness. We will illustrate each step in separate sections.

Data Creation. The test data generator performs as follows: First a set of roles are created. For each role, a random number of permissions up to a certain maximum are chosen to form the role. The maximum number of permissions to be associated with a role is set as a parameter to the algorithm. Next, the users are created. For each user, a random number of roles are chosen. Again, the maximum number of concurrent roles a user can have is set as a parameter to the algorithm. finally, the user permissions are set according to the roles the user has been assigned. We will also consider certain cases where the number of roles randomly chosen is 0 indicating that the user has no roles and therefore no permissions.

Noise Insertion. Just as described in the Section 3.2, we take noise to be a percentage of the number of 1s. In our experiments we considered 1%, 5%, 10%, and 20% noise and introduced it into the datasets.

Reconstitution of UPA. To test noise robustness, we apply a role mining algorithm to the data contaminated with noise. As a result, a role set is generated followed by the reconstitution of the original UPA.

Computation of Robustness. The final step to consider is the computation of the noise robustness of the algorithm. We will use the way to do this based on Section 5.

Another way to do this is simply compute how many of the original roles are found in the results. This approach seems fine but actually suffer two serious weakness. (1) when we match roles, the matches are exact. While this is fine when there is no noise, in the presence of noise there is a good possibility that we may find approximate roles rather than the real roles. In this case, we should also calculate the pseudo-accuracy. This could be an important factor affecting the overall accuracy of the algorithm. However, for now, we restrict ourselves to exact matches and report the results obtained. In the future, we plan to see if approximate matching can lead to better results. (2) the percentage of common roles between original role set and newly generated role set is not a good indicator of robustness towards noise. There are various factors which could affect this value. For example, different algorithms may result in different way of matrix decomposition. They can be right at the same time and totally disjoint. This does not mean that the algorithm is not robust or at least not 0 percent robust.

6.2   Experimental Results

For an initial set of experiments, we created two datasets, the first with 100 users and 200 permissions, while the second was composed of 200 users and 200 permissions. Since the test data was randomly generated and the noise was also randomly inserted, we actually created three versions of the datasets with the same parameters. For each of these datasets, a corresponding noisy dataset was also created three times with the same set of noise parameters. The final results reported below were averaged over the 9 datasets generated for each set of parameters.

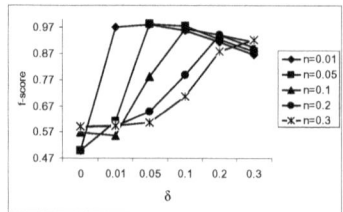

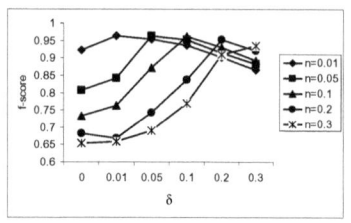

Fig. 1. Relative performance on dataset 1

Fig. 2. Relative performance on dataset 2

Figure 1 plots the f-score against different values of δ for different levels of noise for dataset 1. Figure 2 does the same for dataset 2. It can be observed that for every noise value, the f-score hits the peak at the corresponding value of δ. This implies that the δ-approx RMP algorithm does indeed perform very well with respect to noise. Furthermore, if the security administrator has some idea of the amount of noise present within the data, he can set the δ value to be that to provide great benefit during the role mining phase. Interestingly, when noise is present any $\delta > 0$ and up to that noise level is always beneficial. However, when the value of δ is set higher than the amount of noise present, the f-score decreases, since the algorithm starts making more errors without providing as much benefit.

Figures 3 and 4 plot the ratio of noise fixed / errors made by the algorithm for different δ values and different noise levels. For reasonable levels of noise, the fix/mistake ratio is always over 1, which implies that for any δ value more noise will be fixed as compared to the errors made. When the δ value is the same as the amount of noise, the fix/mistake ratio is very high, and using the inexact RMP has great benefit.

Finally, figure 5 plots the performance of the basic-RMP algorithm versus the δ-approx RMP algorithm for different levels of noise. This clearly shows the degradation of the basic-RMP w.r.t noise. However, the δ-approx RMP keeps its effectiveness even in the presence of noise. This supports our thesis that it makes great sense to use δ-approx RMP whenever noise may be present in the data. This works especially well when the degree of noise can be correctly estimated, but still gives some benefit when this cannot be reliably done. One of our future challenges is to come up with ways to estimate the degree of noise reliably which would greatly increase the effectiveness of noise-resistant algorithms.

6.3   Experiments with Real Data

We also carried out experiments with real data. For this, we utilized the 9 real datasets presented in [12]. Since it is impossible to find out whether any of the user-permission assignments was noisy, we instead simply ran δ-approx RMP algorithm on all of the datasets with different values of δ and counted the number of roles necessary to cover the UPA upto that threshold. We also measured the

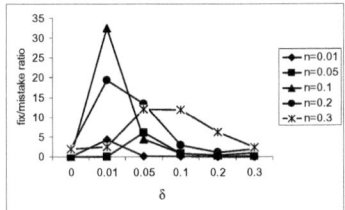

Fig. 3. Ratio of errors fixed to errors made for dataset 1

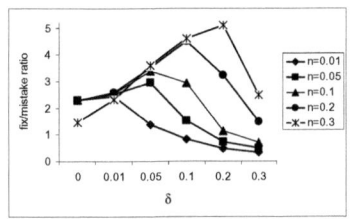

Fig. 4. Ratio of errors fixed to errors made for dataset 2

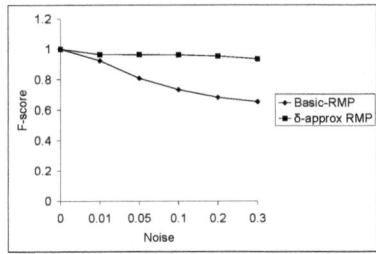

Fig. 5. Noise tolerance benefits of δ-approx RMP

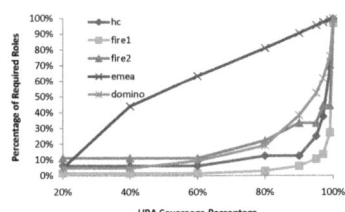

Fig. 6. Percentage of roles necessary to cover partial dataset

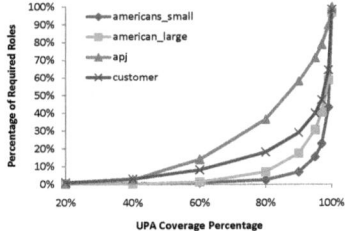

Fig. 7. Percentage of roles necessary to cover partial dataset

number of roles necessary to completely cover the entire UPA. Figures 6-7 plot the percentage of roles necessary to cover a certain percentage of the UPA. As can be seen, for almost all of the datasets (except *emea*), only 40% of the roles are necessary to cover 90% of the UPA. Indeed, the curve is non-linear, indicating that more roles are necessary to cover smaller parts of the UPA as the coverage increases. This can be clearly seen from Figures 8-9 which expand the portion depicting 80% to 100% coverage of the UPA. While we cannot confirm this, it is indeed an indication that the remaining UPA assignments are more likely to be noisy, or at the least, should be individually examined by the security administrator.

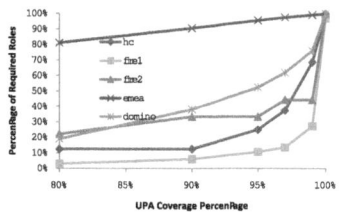
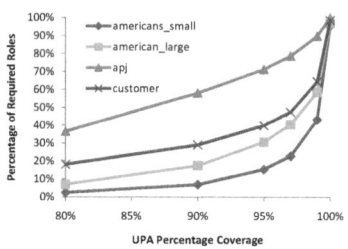

Fig. 8. Expanded part of Figure 6

Fig. 9. Expanded part of Figure 7

7 Discussion

So far, we have seen that using the inexact variants of the RMP problem can give signficantly better results in the presence of noise. Our experimental results show, that the δ-approx RMP algorithm of [20] can handle additive noise quite well, though it is unable to account for subtractive noise. Given the sparsity of the UPA in real life, this is still ok since noise is likely to be more additive than subtractive. Other solutions for δ-approx RMP may be able to give even better performance. In the following, we provide more insight into how to choose δ and discuss other noise removal strategies that we plan to explore in future work, which can further help in the role mining process.

7.1 Determining the Right Value for δ

So far, we have assumed that we could set the right value of δ for the δ-approx RMP algorithm. However, in reality, we may have little idea about this. Given that our δ-approx RMP uses a greedy strategy to pick roles, we could use that to adaptively define δ. Essentially, instead of setting δ from the start, the idea would be to iteratively pick the best role from among the candidates and then evaluate the quality of the role to determine whether to stop. Here, we use the role itself to help determine the right δ value. This is also possible because of the nature of access control data and the nature of noise. Access control data is tightly coupled whereas we assume that noise may occur at random. Thus, it is possible that later roles increasingly cover noisy bits as opposed to real data, and can be detected due to their heterogeneity. In any case, since using the inexact variant always does better in the presence of noise, an effective strategy could be to start with a fixed value for δ (say 0.7, since there is unlikely to be more than 30% noise in the data) and then incrementally increase the value of δ, while paying more attention to the roles obtained in latter phases. We will explore this further in the future.

7.2 Noise Removal by Prefiltering

An alternative strategy to handling noise is to somehow remove it to generate a "clean" UPA. Now, some Basic-RMP algorithm can be run over this cleaned

UPA to give the final roles. Then, the question is how can we detect and clean noise. An answer may come from the field of data mining. It is possible to model each permission as a class and then to build a classification model for it based on the values of the other permissions for all of the users. We can then use all of the created models to predict whether each individual bit is truly correct or noisy. The performance of this inherently depends upon the quality of the classification algorithm, and having some user input would significantly help. We will also further explore this in the future.

7.3   Noise Removal by Post-filtering

Another alternative strategy is to use the Basic-RMP algorithm on the given UPA. Now, we can use post-filtering strategies on the discovered UA and PA to somehow remove noise. This may again be done through use of classification strategies, or by evaluating how homogeneous each role is in terms of permissions or users. Domain semantics may vastly help to identify intelligent strategies to filter noise.

8   Conclusions

Given the noisy nature of data in the real world, deployment of role mining algorithms requires effective ways of addressing the problem of noise. In this paper, we take a first look at the problem of role mining in the presence of noise. We demonstrate the many problems noise can cause if it is not accounted for within the role mining process. We present a model for noise, devise metrics to evaluate noise robustness and investigate the effectiveness of inexact variants of the Role Mining Problem in terms of noise. Our preliminary experiments show that the algorithm developed for δ-approx RMP does indeed reduce the effect of noise. However, it is only able to handle additive noise. In the future, we plan to develop more complete noise aware algorithms that can effectively reduce or eliminate the problem of noise from the role engineering process. Algorithms for the MinNoise RMP can help with this. We will also examine whether approaches from data mining could be used to "clean" the noise from the user-permission data in the first place, thus allowing us to use any basic-RMP algorithm for discovering roles.

References

1. Sandhu, R.S., et al.: Role-based Access Control Models. IEEE Computer, 38–47 (February 1996)
2. Ferraiolo, D., Sandhu, R., Gavrila, S., Kuhn, D., Chandramouli, R.: Proposed NIST Standard for Role-Based Access Control. In: TISSEC (2001)
3. Coyne, E.J.: Role-engineering. In: 1st ACM Workshop on Role-Based Access Control (1995)
4. Gallagher, M.P., O'Connor, A., Kropp, B.: The economic impact of role-based access control. Planning report 02-1, National Institute of Standards and Technology (March 2002)

5. Roeckle, H., Schimpf, G., Weidinger, R.: Process-oriented approach for role-finding to implement role-based security administraiton in a large industrial organization. In: ACM (ed.) RBAC (2000)
6. Neumann, G., Strembeck, M.: A scenario-driven role engineering process for functional rbac roles. In: 7th ACM Symposium on Access Control Models and Technologies (June 2002)
7. Schlegelmilch, J., Steffens, U.: Role mining with orca. In: Symposium on Access Control Models and Technologies (SACMAT), June 2005, ACM, New York (2005)
8. Vaidya, J., Atluri, V., Warner, J.: Roleminer: mining roles using subset enumeration. In: CCS 2006: Proceedings of the 13th ACM conference on Computer and communications security, pp. 144–153 (2006)
9. Vaidya, J., Atluri, V., Guo, Q., Lu, H.: Edge-rmp: Minimizing administrative assignments for role-based access control. Journal of Computer Security 17, 211–235 (2009)
10. Molloy, I., Chen, H., Li, T., Wang, Q., Li, N., Bertino, E., Calo, S., Lobo, J.: Mining roles with semantic meanings. In: SACMAT 2008: Proceedings of the 13th ACM symposium on Access control models and technologies, pp. 21–30. ACM, New York (2008)
11. Zhang, D., Ramamohanarao, K., Ebringer, T.: Role engineering using graph optimisation. In: SACMAT 2007: Proceedings of the 12th ACM symposium on Access control models and technologies, pp. 139–144. ACM, New York (2007)
12. Ene, A., Horne, W., Milosavljevic, N., Rao, P., reiber, R.S., Tarjan, R.: Fast exact and heuristic methods for role minimization problems. In: The ACM Symposium on Access Control Models and Technologies (June 2008)
13. Vaidya, J., Atluri, V., Guo, Q., Adam, N.: Migrating to optimal rbac with minimal perturbation. In: The ACM Symposium on Access Control Models and Technologies (June 2008)
14. Guo, Q., Vaidya, J., Atluri, V.: The role hierachy mining problem: Discovery of optimal role hierarchies. In: Proceedings of the 24th Annual Computer Security Applications Conference, December 8-12, pp. 237–246 (2008)
15. Lu, H., Vaidya, J., Atluri, V.: Optimal boolean matrix decomposition: Application to role engineering. In: IEEE International Conference on Data Engineering (April 2008)
16. Frank, M., Streich, A.P., Basin, D., Buhmann, J.M.: A probabilistic approach to hybrid role mining. In: CCS 2009: Proceedings of the 16th ACM conference on Computer and communications security, pp. 101–111. ACM, New York (2009)
17. Fuchs, L., Pernul, G.: Hydro - hybrid development of roles. In: Sekar, R., Pujari, A.K. (eds.) ICISS 2008. LNCS, vol. 5352, pp. 287–302. Springer, Heidelberg (2008)
18. Vaidya, J., Atluri, V., Guo, Q.: The role mining problem: Finding a minimal descriptive set of roles. In: The Twelth ACM Symposium on Access Control Models and Technologies, Sophia Antipolis, France, June 20–22, pp. 175–184 (2007)
19. Vaidya, J., Atluri, V., Warner, J., Guo, Q.: Role engineering via prioritized subset enumeration. IEEE Transactions on Dependable and Secure Computing (to appear)
20. Vaidya, J., Atluri, V., Guo, Q.: The role mining problem: A formal perspective. ACM Transactions on Information Systems Security (to appear)
21. Duda, R.O., Hart, P.E., Stork, D.G.: Pattern Classification. Wiley-Interscience Publication, Hoboken (2000)

Distributed and Secure Access Control in P2P Databases

Angela Bonifati[1], Ruilin Liu[2], and Hui (Wendy) Wang[2]

[1] Italian National Research Council (CNR)
Via P. Bucci 41C, I-87036 Rende, Italy
bonifati@icar.cnr.it
[2] Stevens Institute of Technology
Dept. of CS, Castle Point on Hudson, Hoboken, NJ, USA, 07030
rliu3@cs.stevens.edu, hwang@cs.stevens.edu

Abstract. The intent of peer data management systems (PDMS) is to share as much data as possible. However, in many applications leveraging sensitive data, users demand adequate mechanisms to restrict the access to authorized parties. In this paper, we study a distributed access control model, where data items are stored, queried and authenticated in a totally decentralized fashion. Our contribution focuses on the design of a comprehensive framework for access control enforcement in PDMS sharing secure data, which blends policy rules defined in a declarative language with distributed key management schemes. The data owner peer decides *which data to share* and *whom to share with* by means of such policies, with the data encrypted accordingly. To defend against malicious attackers who can compromise the peers, the decryption keys are decomposed into pieces scattered amongst peers. We discuss the details of how to adapt distributed encryption schemes to PDMS to enforce robust and resilient access control, and demonstrate the efficiency and scalability of our approach by means of an extensive experimental study.

1 Introduction

Peer Data Management Systems (P2P databases or PDMS in short) introduce a revolutionary paradigm for distributed data management [1], [2], [3]. They provide fully decentralized and extensible data management architecture. In ordinary PDMS, data is freely shared in the network and peers unconditionally trust the other participants. However, since the data may contain sensitive information, flexible and effective access control on such data becomes crucial. A number of proposals consider the problem of enforcing access control in P2P networks [4,5,6,7]. They focus on the design of the architecture [4], the persistent storage [5], distributed file systems [6] and administrative distribution [7]. However, none of them considers flexible access control mechanisms that can effectively support multiple access policies as well as efficient and secure query access to PDMS.

In this paper, we design a robust distributed access control mechanism for large-scale PDMS. In particular, each peer is allowed to specify the access control

S. Foresti and S. Jajodia (Eds.): Data and Applications Security XXIV, LNCS 6166, pp. 113–129, 2010.

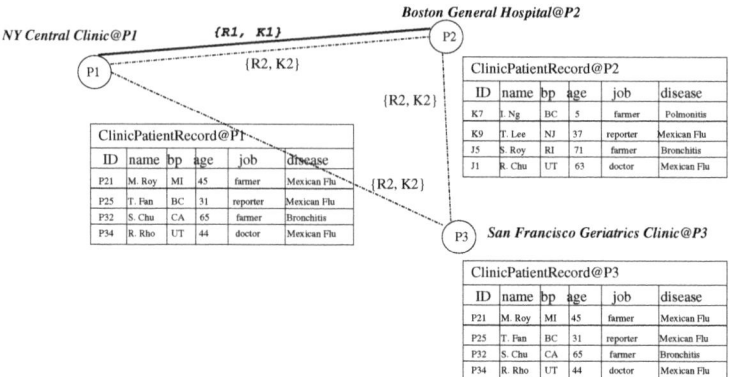

Fig. 1. Sharing Sensitive Information in a PDMS

requirements on its local data by means of policy rules; the other peers will attempt to retrieve its data by asking queries; however, only the peers who have appropriate data access can get the answer, if any. Due to the fact that the network lacks a centralized authentication module, one viable approach to enforce access control is by using encryption: the sensitive data within the peer databases is encrypted; only accessible peers can obtain appropriate keys to decrypt and access the data. Although it is an effective and popular approach in several contexts [8,9,10], adapting it to PDMS poses a few challenges.

Challenge #1: In our threat model, the malicious attackers can compromise any peer in the network and thus can learn all information, including the decryption keys, held by the compromised peers. It is straightforward that simply storing decryption keys in the network cannot effectively protect the data access. Thus, the first challenge is how to guard the decryption keys against malicious attackers that may enter the network.

Challenge #2: There may exist multiple access control policy rules that involve the same set of data values. Careless design of the encryption scheme, including the granularity and decryption keys, to enforce these rules, will lead to expensive overhead for data storage, communication, and query evaluation. For a better illustration of this challenge, we use the following example.

Example 1. Figure 1 illustrates a PDMS designed for the Health Care including hospitals, clinics, and research labs. For simplicity, assume that each peer holds a relational table ClinicPatientRecord, with the information about the patients' name, birthplace, age, job and disease. Assume one of the peers, the NY central clinic at peer P_1, denoted as NYCentralClinic@P1, has two sets of access control requirements. First, to help conduct the research on the 'Swine Flu' disease, it would like to share the *name*, *birthplace*, and *age* information of its patients who got 'Swine Flu' with the hospitals in the Eastern Coast of the U.S. (i.e. P_2). Second, for a different study of the correlation of birthplaces, jobs and diseases, it is willing to share the *birthplace, job*, and *disease* information of its patients with all other peers in the network (i.e. P_2 and P_3).

Assume that the enforcement of the first access control rule ($R1$), denoted in Figure 1 as a solid line, will result in that the `NYCentralClinic`, the owner of the `ClinicPatientRecord@P1` database, encrypts the *name, birthplace*, and *age* data and share the decryption keys with `BostonGeneralHospital@P2`. Furthermore, the enforcement of the second policy rule (`R2`) will lead to the encryption of the *birthplace, job*, and *disease* data, with the decryption keys shared with both `BostonGeneralHospital@P2` and `SanFrancescoClinic@P3` (highlighted with dashed lines in Figure 1). As the *birthplace* values for the same sets of tuples describing all patients are covered by both rules, if these two rules use different decryption keys, these *birthplace* values need to be replicated for separate encryptions by different peers, which may incur both data overhead and expensive network communication. Thus, a careful design of the encryption scheme is needed in order to identify the common values encrypted by multiple access control rules and thus overcome the above problem.   □

Challenge #3: In PDMS, network updates occur very frequently. Leave/join of peers can lead to the updates of access control configuration. For instance, new access control requirements may be introduced for the newly inserted peers. Efficient mechanisms that enforce the updates of access control on PDMS are vital to the security and performance of the system.

In this paper, we propose a comprehensive framework for access control enforcement in PDMS, using encryption, that provides the following important capabilities:

(i) Robust access guard against malicious attackers that can compromise all information of any peer in the network,

(ii) Fully decentralized authentication, as the network lacks centralized administration, and

(iii) Resilience to updates on the network as well as the access control policy.

We adopt a cryptographic approach that provides robust, decentralized, and resilient access control on PDMS. Our contributions include:

(1) We define a declarative distributed query language to specify access control policy in PDMS. Such language is based on SQL, yet powerful enough to allow expressive policies for access on various granularities.

(2) We enforce the access control policy rules by encryption; only authorized users can obtain the decryption key and consequently gain the access to the data. To support decentralized and resilient management of decryption keys, we adapt a classic cryptographic secret sharing protocol called (m, n) threshold scheme [11] to PDMS. In particular, a decryption key K is split into n pieces; only by collecting at least $m < n$ key pieces the peers can reconstruct K.

(3) We address the challenges of key management when multiple access control rules overlap the access on the same data values. These common data values are encrypted by using the same key. We show the relationship of this problem with query containment, restrict to the polynomial case [12], and identify a monotone property for key shares on common values. The monotone property

can significantly reduce the number of keys needed for the enforcement of access control rules.

(4) We further investigate how to manage keys when there exist updates on access control policies. We propose an effective scheme that preserves the monotone property of key shares when there are updates on access control policies.

(5) We demonstrate the efficiency and scalability of our approach by means of a comprehensive experimental study.

To the best of our knowledge, ours is the first attempt to address the challenges of enforcing SQL-based distributed access control policies on *dynamic* PDMS and efficiently handling *updates* on such policies.

The paper is organized as follows. Section 2 explains the model setup, including the access control framework and enforcement mechanism. Section 3 discusses the key management when there are multiple access control rules accessing the same data as well as updates on the rules. Section 4 presents our experimental study and Section 5 discusses the related work. Finally, Section 6 concludes the paper.

2   System Model

2.1   Network Model

A P2P network is an ad-hoc collection of peers willing to share their data. Each peer contributes its local storage to the global data store. Each peer is equipped with a relational database. In this paper, we assume that every peer in the network has the same database schema as the rest of the network; the extension to multiple heterogeneous schemas is orthogonal to the proposed techniques.

2.2   Threat Model

We assume every peer in the network can be compromised by the attacker. The attacker's intent is to access the data that he/she is not authorized to. He/she can learn all information held by the compromised peers, including the data and decryption keys, and can eavesdrop on the communication among all peers. However, he/she is assumed to be computationally bounded and thus cannot break the underlying cryptographic schemes without knowing the appropriate cryptographic keys.

2.3   Access Control Model

Access Control (AC) Policy. To specify which data is accessible to which peers, we define a declarative access control language. The access control policy is in the format of SQL queries with a *Peer* clause. In particular, an *access control* (AC) rule is in the form of:

```
SELECT target_List
FROM table_List
WHERE WhereExpr
PEER (peer_List | SELECT (peer_ID | *) FROM peer_List WHERE P_WhereExpr),
```

where *target_List* is the list of target attributes $A_1, \cdots, A_m$ in the AC rule, *table_List* is the list of relations $T_1, \cdots, T_k$, and *WhereExpr* is an arbitrary conjunctive predicate on *table_List*. The PEER clause may contain the *peer_List* as a list of peers $P_1, \cdots, P_n$ that have access to the data specified by the AC rules. In alternative, the PEER clause is expressed by means of an arbitrary query on the relation *peer_List*, with an arbitrary conjunctive predicate *P_WhereExpr* on *peer_List*. We use R^Q to denote the part of AC rule R without the PEER clause.

Example 2. The access control rules R_1 and R_2 below specify the access control requirement in Example 1:

R_1: SELECT name, birthplace, age
       FROM ClinicPatientRecord@P_1
       WHERE disease = 'Swine Flu'
       PEER (SELECT peer_ID FROM peer_List
          WHERE PeerLocation = 'United States East Coast')
R_2: SELECT birthplace, job, disease
       FROM ClinicPatientRecord@P_1
       PEER (SELECT * FROM peer_List)

We assume that all peers have access to all data *by default*. If a peer wants to limit the access to its own data, it defines one or more AC rules on its local peer database D; peers are not allowed to specify AC rules on data on other peers.

Overlap, Containment, and Equivalence of AC Rules. In the following, we use $\mathcal{R}$ and R to specify a set of access control rules and a specific access control rule. Let D be a database and R be a specific AC rule, we use $R^Q(D)$ to denote the set of tuples as result of evaluating R^Q on D. As customary, we assume that each tuple $t = \langle v_1, v_2, \cdots, v_n \rangle$ of the database D has values v_i, $1 \leq i \leq n$, where each v_i is an element of $dom(A_i)$, A_i being the name of an attribute in a relational schema. Moreover, each tuple t has a unique ID, given by its primary key. We denote the ID value of the tuple t as $t(ID)$, and the value v_i of the tuple t for attribute A_i as $t(A_i)$. Given two tuples t and t', we say that t and t' intersect $(t \cap t')$ if it exists at least one attribute A_i such that the values are the same, i.e. $t(A_i) = t'(A_i)$.

Definition 1. *Given a database D and two AC rules R_i and R_j on D, we define $R_i(D) \cap R_j(D) = \{t | t \in R_i^Q(D), \exists t' \in R_j^Q(D), t \cap t', t(ID) = t'(ID)\}$, and $R_i(D) - R_j(D) = R_i(D) - R_i(D) \cap R_j(D)$.*

As stated in Definition 1, the overlapping tuples of R_i and R_j *are exactly the same tuples*. In our context, AC rules are defined on the same peer database, thus the returned tuples have exactly the same identifier. We then define containment and equivalence of AC rules R_i and R_j. While the classical definition of query containment and equivalence [12] require that evaluating R_i and R_j on the database D returns compatible tuples (i.e. having the same schema), the definition below relaxes such requirement by identifying compatible tuples as those tuples having at least one attribute A_i in common, and the same ID value.

Definition 2. *Given two AC rules R_i and R_j, we say R_i overlaps R_j, denoted as $R_i \cap_{ac} R_j$ if $R_i(D) \cap R_j(D) \neq \oslash$. We say R_i is contained in $R_i(D)$, denoted as $R_i(D) \subseteq_{ac} R_j(D)$, if $\forall$ value $v \in R_i(D)$, $\exists v' \in R_i(D) \cap R_j(D)$ s.t. $v = v'$ and $v(ID) = v'(ID)$. We say the AC rule R_i is equivalent to the rule R_j, denoted as $R_i =_{ac} R_j$, if $R_j \subseteq_{ac} R_i$ and $R_i \subseteq_{ac} R_j$.*

Checking query containment in general is well-known to be NP-complete [13]. As shown by Saraiya [14] and Chekuri et al. [12], conjunctive query containment of acyclic queries can be solved in polynomial time. Since we only consider AC rules R whose R^Q are acyclic conjunctive queries, checking the containment of AC rules has polynomial time complexity, even though they may return the instances of different schemas. We have:

Lemma 1. *Given two AC rules R_i and R_j, checking whether $R_i \subseteq_{ac} R_j$ has polynomial time complexity.*

Cryptography-based Access Control Enforcement. P2P networks are characterized by the complete lack of centralized and trusted components, which brings difficulty to the design of access control mechanism. In view of this, we rely exclusively on cryptography to enforce the access control policy and provide access control to PDMS. In particular, each access control rule R corresponds to a set of encryption blocks; only peers who have access to the data in the encryption blocks can possess the corresponding decryption keys. The reason of using encryption is that cryptographic operations (such as keys) and authentication can be distributed among several peers.

To implement the cryptography-based access control mechanisms, we adopt a pioneering secret sharing protocol, namely the (m, n) threshold scheme [11], exhibiting an $O(n \, log^2(n))$ complexity, and considered fast enough for practical key management schemes. This secret sharing protocol is ideally suited to applications in which a group of mutually suspicious individuals must cooperate for a common goal. It is useful in distributed scenarios where secrecy and integrity of information needs to be protected, and make particular sense in a PDMS. Informally, the (m, n) threshold scheme [11] distributes a secret by a *dealer* to n *participants*, each of which is allocated a share of the secret. The secret can only be reconstructed when $m < n$ shares are combined together; individual shares are of no use on their own.

We adapt the above secret sharing protocol to PDMS, by considering every single decryption key as a secret. Every peer can be a participant. The dealer is the data owner who distributes the key pieces to the peers that he/she grants the access. In this way, discretionary access control (DAC) [15] is supported. We assume the *dealer* peers are *transiently honest*, i.e., they are considered honest when they split the decryption keys into key pieces, and destroy the decryption keys after the key pieces have been distributed. When there comes the need for data decryption, every peer, including the data owner, has to collect other key pieces to reconstruct the keys. This scheme supports fully decentralized authentication (as no single entity needs to be fully trusted), robust access control (as compromising any single peer will not enable the attacker to decrypt the data), and resilience of the system (as some of the peers may not be available or decide not to share their pieces of decryption key with other peers) to a number of up to $n - m$ simultaneously leaving/failing or compromised peers. Furthermore, this technique provides adjustable degree of attack protection and fault tolerance by controlling the value of m.

Encryption Granularity. Our access control policy allows access control specification at various granularities, including the individual values, attributes, tuples, and the whole database, as long as these are the output by the AC rules. The granularity at which data objects are encrypted is closely tied to the efficiency of handling decryption keys and processing queries on the decrypted data. There is a whole space of options here, leading to the observation that a finer encryption granularity (i.e. value-level or tuple-level granularity) would lead to excessive overhead, due to an unmanageable high number of keys in the network. By opposite, a database-level granularity would restrict the capability of sharing smaller data fragments in realistic distributed scenarios. We thus opted for a practical hybrid solution that associates a decryption key with the set of tuples covered by each AC rule. We denote such a set of tuples as an *encrypted block*. This rule-based encryption mechanism supports flexible encryption granularity that is decided by the AC rules. In particular, the enforcement of encryption will result in *one or multiple encrypted blocks*; any rule that does not overlap with other rules is enforced in the form of an individual encryption block, while the rules that overlap with the others lead to multiple blocks. Details of the construction of encryption blocks and decryption keys are given in Section 3.

Node Authentication. In our framework, only authorized nodes can collect the key pieces and reconstruct the key. We adopt a certificate-based approach, in which certification services, such as certificate issuing, renewal and revocation, are distributed by using threshold sharing of the certificate signing key. Our node authentication procedure is inspired by previous work on ad-hoc mobile networks [16,17]. Due to the lack of space, we do not discuss it further.

3   Key Maintenance with Multiple Rules and Updates

In this section, we first discuss how to encrypt the database when there exist overlapping AC rules (Section 3.1). Then, we investigate how to enforce the access control when there are updates on the network, which especially causes the updates of AC rules (Section 3.2).

3.1   Overlapping AC Rules

There may exist tuples that are accessible by multiple peers specified via different access control rules. For instance, the AC rules R_1 and R_2 in Example 2 overlap on *birthplace* data. One possible approach is to allow multiple keys, each corresponding to an AC rule, on the shared data. To support such mechanism without making chaos on access control (as Example 1 illustrates), a naive approach is to make as many replicas of the shared tuples as the number of overlapping AC rules, so that each replica is encrypted and accordingly decrypted by a unique key (according to one specific AC rule). However, such approach will introduce both key and data replication overhead and expensive network communication. In order to avoid such overhead, we devise a *blocking-based encryption* mechanism. The basic idea is that the overlapping AC rules will encrypt their shared data as a single block, and always use the same decryption key for that block. We formally define the mechanism as follows. We use R^{PL} to denote the peer list that is specified by the *PEER* clause of the AC rule R.

Definition 3. *For any pair of AC rules $\langle R_i, R_j \rangle$ such that $R_i \cap_{ac} R_j$:*
(1) $R_i(D) \cap R_j(D)$ is encrypted as a block B_{ij}. Each peer in R_i^{PL} and R_j^{PL} will have a piece of the decryption key K_{ij} of B_{ij}, and
(2) $R_i(D) - R_j(D)$ and $R_j(D) - R_i(D)$ are encrypted as two separate blocks B_i and B_j. Each peer in R_i^{PL} (R_j^{PL}, resp.) is assigned a key piece K_i (K_j, resp.) for decrypting B_i (B_j, resp.).
We say the AC rule R_i (R_j, resp.) is enforced by the encryption blocks B_{ij} and B_i (B_{ij} and B_j, resp.), and the keys needed for the enforcement of R_i (R_j, resp.) are K_{ij} and K_i (K_{ij} and K_j, resp.).

Intuitively, any rule that does not overlap with other rules is enforced in the form of an individual encryption block, while the rules that do overlap with the others lead to multiple blocks. In the remainder, we refer the keys needed for the enforcement of rule R as the *keys of R*.

We observe that the containment of AC rules naturally lead to the containment of keys of these rules, which is stated as following.

Property 1 (Monotonicity). Given two AC rules R_i and R_i such that $R_j \subseteq_{ac} R_i$, let K_i and K_j be the set of keys of R_i and R_j. Then $K_j \subseteq K_i$.

As an extension, if rule R_i is equivalent to rule R_j, the sets of keys K_i and K_j are the same. We call them *equivalent sets of keys*, if $K_i \subseteq K_j$ and $K_j \subseteq K_i$. Clearly, the monotonicity among keys can be used to reduce the number of the keys. We will show in Section 3.2 how to assign the keys while preserving the monotone property, especially in the presence of updates on access control rules.

3.2   Join/Leave of Nodes

Due to network churn, the peers may join and leave the network at will. This behavior may affect the AC rules as follows. First, join/leave of peers will not incur updates on AC rules, then such peers cause updates on AC rules and key pieces that need to be maintained. We discuss both cases in this section. We recall that we do not allow replication of key pieces to not compromise the security of the secret sharing protocol. By contrary, we allow key piece regeneration in order to avoid the key pieces exposed by security breaches and thus enhance security [11]. We discuss two possible scenarios, that the network updates lead to no updates on AC rules, and they do.

No Updates on AC Rules. When a new peer joins the network and is allowed by a data owner to share its data with the existing n peers by using some existing AC rules, the decryption keys are reconstructed by one of the existing peers, and the key pieces are regenerated in order to include the new peer. As shown in [11], since regenerating the key pieces is simply generating a new polynomial function, the cost is affordable. Furthermore, such key regeneration will actually enhance the security of the network, since the key pieces exposed to security breaches are replaced by new values. In Section 4, we study the effect of such regeneration on the network performance.

When a peer leaves, if the peer does not have any key piece, its disconnection does not affect the secret sharing protocol. If the leaving peer p has a key piece, it informs the data owner peer of its leave. The data owner peer checks the number of available key pieces (including the one that p holds). If the number of such key pieces is greater than m, the data owner informs the leaving peer to leave with no action; otherwise, if the number is equal to m, the data owner peer initiates the key reconstruction procedure. Notice that a set of peers may be leaving the network at the same time. In such a case, the above procedure is repeated if the number of participants left minus the number of such peers is equal or less than m. Finally, if the leaving peer is the data owner, it informs all peers that have the key pieces to destroy them.

Thus, deletion of existing key pieces, and leaves of peers would in the worst case lead to periodical refreshment on the key piece by reconstructing the secret and re-sharing it amongst the participants.

Updates on AC Rules. When the new peers join the network, existing peers may specify the access rights of their data to these peers. This may introduce new AC rules. Similarly, leave of the nodes will result in deletion of old AC rules. Inserting/deleting AC rules will introduce additional complexity on the key management. In what follows, we discuss various types of updates and the corresponding key management strategy.

Deletion of old AC rules. Assume the peer P deletes its AC rule R. Then P collects the key shares, re-constructs the key, and decrypts $R(D)$.

Insertion of new AC rules. Let $\mathcal{R}$ be the current set of AC rules on peer P. Assume the join of new peers requires that P defines a new AC rule R_{new}. There are five cases:

Case 1: there exists at least a rule $R \in \mathcal{R}$ s.t. $R \subseteq_{ac} R_{new}$. Let $R_1 \in \mathcal{R}$ be a rule that is maximally contained in R_{new}, i.e., $R_1 \subseteq_{ac} R_{new}$ and there is no other rule $R' \in \mathcal{R}$ s.t. $R_1 \subseteq_{ac} R'$. Let K_1 be the key of R_1. Then peer P encrypts $R_{new}(D) - R_1(D)$ as a block. Let K be the new key for decryption of this block. P distributes the key shares of both K and K_1 to the peers in R_{new}^{PL}.

Case 2: there exist the rules $R_1, \ldots, R_t \in \mathcal{R}$ such that $R_{new} \subseteq_{ac} R_1 \cdots \subseteq_{ac} R_t$. Peer P sorts them as $R_1, \ldots, R_t$. Then first, peer P reconstructs the decryption key of R_t, and decrypts $R_t(D)$. Note that, by this decryption, $R_{t-1}(D)$ will also be decrypted, and so on and so forth, until $R_1(D)$. Second,

- P encrypts $R_{new}(D)$ as a block, and distributes the key shares of the decryption key K to the peers in R_{new}^{PL}.
- For the i-th ($1 \leq i \leq t$) AC rule in the sorted list, if $i = 1$, P encrypts $R_1(D) - R_{new}(D)$ as a block, and distributes the key shares of K and K_1 to the peers in R_1^{PL}, where K_1 is a new key that decrypts $R_1(D) - R_{new}(D)$; otherwise, P encrypts $R_i(D) - R_{i-1}(D)$ as a block, and distributes the key shares of K_{i-1} and K_i to the peers in R_i^{PL}, where K_{i-1} is the key that decrypts $R_{i-1}(D)$ and K_i is a new key that decrypts $R_i(D) - R_{i-1}(D)$.

Case 3: there exists a rule $R \in \mathcal{R}$ s.t. $R_{new} =_{ac} R$. For this case, both R and R_{new} use the same keys.

Case 4: there exists a rule $R \in \mathcal{R}$ s.t. both Case 1 and 2 fail but $R(D) \cap_{ac} R_{new}(D)$. Then first, peer P reconstructs the key of R and uses it to decrypt $R(D)$. Second, P encrypts $R(D) \cap R_{new}(D)$ as a block, and distributes the key shares of the decryption key K to the peers in both R^{PL} and R_{new}^{PL}. Third, P encrypts $R(D) - R_{new}(D)$ and $R_{new}(D) - R(D)$ as two blocks, and distributes the key shares of K_1 to the peers in R^{PL}, and the key shares of K_2 to the peers in R_{new}^{PL}, where K_1 and K_2 are two new keys for decrypting $R(D) - R_{new}(D)$ and $R_{new}(D) - R(D)$.

Case 5: there does not exist any rule in $\mathcal{R}$ that satisfies any case above. Then P encrypts $R_{new}(D)$ as a block, and distributes the key shares of the decryption key K to the peers in R_{new}^{PL}.

These five cases may all apply to R_{new}. For instance, there may exist the rules R_1, R_2 that meet Case 1 and 2, as well as R_3 that meets Case 3, R_4 that meets Case 4 and R_5 that meets Case 5. Applying the five cases in a random order may result in wrong key assignment. For instance, in the above example, applying Case 2 before Case 1 will ruin the monotone property of the keys between R_1, R_2, and R_{new}. The failure to preserve the monotone property may result in incorrect encryption and thus inappropriate access control enforcement. Therefore, we propose the following construction procedure to assign keys to R_{new}, so that the monotone property of the keys is well preserved for contained AC rules. Initially the candidate rules is $\mathcal{R}$, the whole set of AC rules.

Superset rules (Step 1): For the rules such that $R_{new} \subseteq_{ac} R_1 \cdots \subseteq_{ac} R_m(D)$, sort them in their containment order, starting from R_{new}. Let S_1 be the sorted result, and $\mathcal{R}'$ be the result of $\mathcal{R} - S_1$.

Intersected rules (Step 2): for $k = n, n-1, n-2, \ldots, 2$, where n is the total number of AC rules in $\mathcal{R}'$, repeatedly check the intersection of k rules $R_1(D) \cap R_2(D) \cap \ldots R_k(D) \cap R_{new}(D)$ that is not empty. For the ith ($1 \leq i \leq n-1$) step in the loop, only the intersected rules that are not subsets of any that has been recorded in the previous steps are checked. For instance, $R_1 \cap R_2$ is not considered if $R_1 \cap R_2 \cap R_3 \neq \emptyset$. Note that the rules that intersect with R_{new} cover the rules that are contained in R_{new}.

Subset rules (Step 3): Let $\mathcal{I} = \{I_1, \ldots, I_t\}$ be intersection results from Step 2. Sort any I_i, I_j as $I_i < I_j$, if $I_i \subseteq I_j$. For those I_i and I_j s.t. they do not contain in each other but both satisfy that $I_i, I_j > I_i'$ and $I_i, I_j < I_{j'}$, they are put between

I_i' and I_j', but without any order within themselves. For example, the sorted order might be $\{R_1 \cap R_2 \cap R_{new}, R_1 \cap R_3 \cap R_{new}\} < R_2 \cap R_4 \cap R_{new} < R_5 \cap R_{new}$, in which the order between $R_1 \cap R_2 \cap R_{new}$ and $R_1 \cap R_3 \cap R_{new}$ is not decidable. Let the sorted result be S_2. It is straightforward that unlike S_1 (in Step 1) that has a total order, S_2 only has a partial order.

Final merge (Step 4): We merge S_1 and S_2 as $S = \{S_2, R_{new}, S_1\}$. Obviously all elements in S_2 is contained in R_{new} as well as all elements in S_1. Then starting from the first element in S, we apply Case 1 (if the intersection equals R_{new}), Case 2 (if the intersected rules are contained in R_{new}), and Case 4 (if the rules only intersect with R_{new} on each intersected result in S_2). For the rules with undecided orders, their key assignments are independent from each other. After finished S_2, we apply Case 3 on each rule in S_1, following their orders in S_1.

From the four construction steps, we have:

Lemma 2. *Given the original AC rules $\mathcal{R} = \{R_1, \dots, R_n\}$ and the new rule R_{new}, the construction procedure preserves the monotone property of the keys of $\mathcal{R} \cup \{R_{new}\}$, i.e., for any two rules $R_i, R_j \in \mathcal{R} \cup \{R_{new}\}$, let K_i and K_j be the keys of R_i and R_j, then if $R_i \sqsubseteq_{ac} R_j$, then $K_i \subseteq K_j$.*

Finally, we state the following theorem.

Theorem 1. *The above construction procedure is deterministic.*

4   Experiments

We conducted various experiments to gauge the effectiveness of our approach under various network configurations. We setup a P2P network by using FreeP-astry, a DHT-based P2P network simulation testbed. Our algorithms were implemented in *Java* and the experiments were run on an Intel Core 2 Duo, 2.4GHz, Windows machine equipped with $4GB$ main memory. Every result is the average of about 10 runs. Due to the space limit, more details about the experiments, including the AC rules and the queries used, can be found at the following URL [18].

4.1   Setup

We setup several networks, with size ranging from 100 to 1500 peers. For each network, we vary the percentage $p = 1\%, 5\%, 10\%, 25\%, 50\%, 100\%$ of nodes that share the key pieces. We employ the (m, n) threshold scheme by Shamir [11] in our experiments. For each setup of available key pieces, we vary the m values, i.e., the number of key pieces needed for reconstruction. To test the performance of our approach, we use three measurements of the time: (1) SST, the secret sharing time, which measures the time needed for generating and distributing the key pieces, (2) SRT, the secret reconstruction time, which measures the time needed for reconstructing the decryption key, and (3) NL, the network latency, indicating the communication cost due to the underlying network.

To measure the query evaluation performance over encrypted data, we use the TPC-H[1] benchmark dataset. We use MySQL 5.1 as the query engine. In our experiment, each node in the network stores locally a portion of the dataset. We design two schemes to vary the size of the local dataset, the *uniform distributed* scheme that evenly distributes the dataset to all nodes in the network, and the *randomly distributed* scheme that assigns local repositories of different sizes to the nodes. Furthermore, to measure the impact of the AC rule configuration, we setup five sets of AC rules (each set including 50 AC rules) that cover 20%, 40%, 60%, 80%, and 100% of nodes in the network. Typically, a query is asked locally on a node, and needs to be answered on all other nodes in the network. The query performance time has been considered as a composition of four times: the local query evaluation time, SRT, NL and the decryption time.

4.2 Overhead of Key Management

First, we vary the value of n, the number of key pieces, and use $m = [(n + 1)/2]$, which is the number of needed key pieces for key reconstruction for the worst case. Figure 2 (a) & (b) show the measurement of SST, SRT and NL. We observe that SST, SRT and NL time grow with larger n values. Moreover, the SST time is always orders of magnitude larger than SRT time. This shows that while the initial setup takes time, the later key reconstruction procedure incurs little overhead, thus showing that the enforcement of access control by using distributed encryption is indeed of practical use.

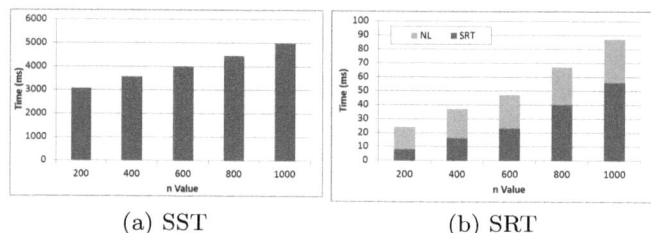

(a) SST   (b) SRT

Fig. 2. Various n values; $m = [(n + 1)/2]$; Network size: 1000 nodes

We also measure the impact of m values on SST, SRT and NL. We vary m values from the worst case $m = [(n + 1)/2]$ up to the total number of key pieces $m = n$. We observe that both SST and SRT time grow linearly with increasing m values, which is straightforward as more key shares are needed for key reconstruction. However, SST time increases with a more remarkable curve, as key distribution is a blind procedure that randomly chooses m peers, while key reconstruction is guided with index on the key distributee peers. We also observe that the NL time is not affected much by the variation of m values, as the keys have been distributed to a fixed number of peers; the communication time with these peers for key reconstruction is fixed. Due to the space limit, the results are omitted.

[1] http://www.tpc.org/tpch/

4.3 Network Churn

We simulate the join and leave of peers in our framework. Figure 3 shows the result of inserting new nodes. We consider two possible configurations, the newly inserted peers/old leaving peers are/are not among the participants of secret sharing. In the first case, when the new joining peers do not share the key pieces (Figure 3 (a)), SRT is not affected much, while the network latency slightly increases. Notice that SST time is not reported in this case since the distributed key pieces are not recomputed. In the second case, when the new joining peers participate in secret sharing (Figure 3 (b) & (c)), SST, SRT and network latency increase with larger number of such peers. In particular, the increase of SST is more significant than that of SRT and network latency, since the secret has to be recomputed. However, SST has still acceptable values for both schemes, thus confirming that the secret computation overhead is negligible.

We observe the similar results for leaving peers. First, when the leaving peers do not share the key pieces SRT does not change much, while the network latency slightly decreases, and SST stays the same for this configuration. Second, when the leaving peers participate in secret sharing, SST, SRT and network latency decrease with larger number of such peers. Finally, comparing the impact of leaving/joining peers to both SRT and NL, we observe that the former is less than the latter. The above trend is due to that fact that, in the case of leaving peers the number of participants sharing the secret is reduced, while, in the case of joining peers, such number is comparably increased. Due to space limit, the details of the results are omitted.

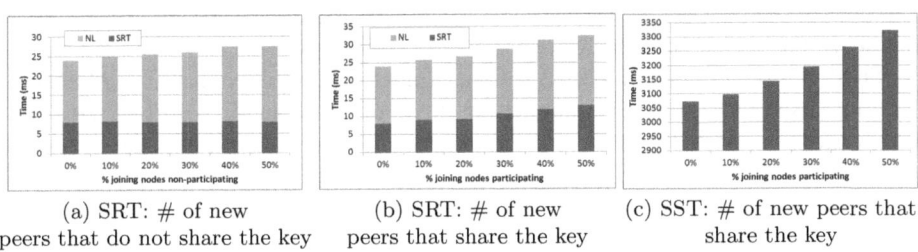

(a) SRT: # of new peers that do not share the key   (b) SRT: # of new peers that share the key   (c) SST: # of new peers that share the key

Fig. 3. Join of peers; $n = 200$; $m = [(n + 1]/2$; Network size: 1000 nodes

4.4 Query Evaluation

We start from the uniform distributed scheme, and measure the query performance in various cases. First, we vary the total number of tuples in the network from $100K$ to $500K$, while keeping the coverage of AC rules constant. Figure 4 (a) presents the results for TPC-H datasets. It can be observed that the SRT is relatively stable thus confirming that key reconstruction is independent of the underlying databases sizes; by opposite, local query evaluation time, NL, and decryption time increase for larger databases. Furthermore, local query evaluation

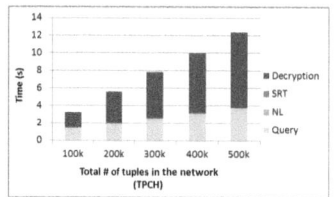
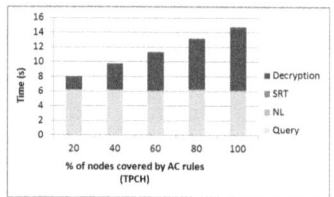

(a) Various total # of tuples; 100 nodes (b) Various coverage of AC rules; 500 nodes,
500k tuples

Fig. 4. Query performance on uniform distributed data

time and decryption time are dominant for all database sizes. Then, we vary
the coverage of AC rules in the network, while keeping the number of tuples
as $500K$. Figure 4 (b) shows that the query evaluation time does not change
much, as the queries are always evaluated on the whole network. However, the
decryption time increases when more nodes are covered by AC rules; the increase
is linear to the increase of number of nodes that are covered by AC rules. This
happens because the number of tuples that are encrypted is linear to the number
of AC rules (recall that each node has the same number of tuples). Nevertheless,
the increase is not overwhelming; even for the case that 100% nodes are covered,
the total time for query evaluation (including decryption, SRT and NL) is only
around 14 seconds. In other words, the overhead incurred by the AC rule configuration and enforcement is reasonably low. We also vary the network size from
100 nodes to 500 nodes and measure the query evaluation time. We observe that
query evaluation time and decryption time are relatively stable with regard to
the network size, since the queries are evaluated on the same size of data in the
network. For the sake of conciseness, we omit the results.

Then, we rerun the same experiments under a randomly distributed scheme.
The experiment results are similar to those of uniform distributed data. The
only difference we have observed is that when we vary the number of nodes that
are covered by AC rules, the increase of query evaluation time is not relatively
linear to the increase of number of nodes that are covered by AC rules, since the
data on these nodes are of different sizes. Due to the space limit, the results are
omitted. In Figures 5, we have compared the query performance for both cases
with and without access control (w/ AC and w/o AC, respectively; the latter
being the case in which no data is encrypted). We observe that the results are not
affected much by the increase of the network size (Figure 5 (a)). These results
show that the cost for applying our algorithms to protect the access to selected
items in a distributed scenario is affordable, thus confirming their utility and
efficiency. However, query performance grows with increase of AC rules coverage.
In particular, Figure 5 (b) shows that with small AC rules coverage (e.g., 20%),
access control enforcement only incurs the overhead as around 25% of the query
evaluation time needed for w/o AC case; with increasing AC rules coverage to
100%, the overhead of enforcing AC rules becomes around 150% of the query
evaluation time (TPC-H dataset, Figure 5 (b)) for the w/o AC rules case. This
is the price that we need to pay for the enforcement of access control policies.

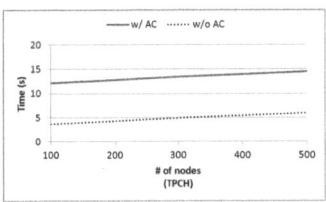
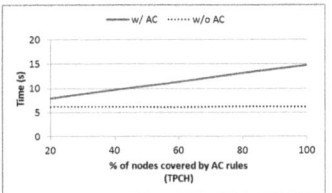

(a) Various # of nodes;   (b) Various coverage of AC rules;
AC rules Coverage: 100%.   500 nodes.

Fig. 5. Query performance comparison(w/ AC: with access control, w/o AC: without access control); total # of tuples: 500k

5   Related Work

Building distributed persistent storage has been the goal of previous file-sharing projects, such as OceanStore [5], Plutus [6] and Cryptree [19]. As opposed to our approach, all the above systems work in a client-server architecture, and do not scale for a large group of users. Even if with varied features, omitted for the sake of space, they rely on a common centralized authorization authority.

Access control over replicated databases is studied in [20], where a security mechanism based on secret sharing is enforced in the presence of quorum servers (pair-wise replicated servers with overlapping information). The underlying assumption is that the users might be untrusted, while the servers are all trustworthy.

Enforcing access control by using cryptography have been studied in various contexts (e.g., XML data publishing [8] and distributed file systems [10]). However, none of them would be applicable to PDMS, as they either do not need a distribution-aware policy language, or rather employ a one-to-one key assignment from the data owner to the user, as it is common in data publishing [8]. Furthermore, distributed key management has been studied in the network context (e.g., mobile ad-hoc networks [21] and ad-hoc wireless networks [16]). Such networks are characterized by peers with low bandwidth, intermittent network connectivity and scarcity of computational resources, which is not the case for PDMS [1], where each peer is a database. To the best of our knowledge, the problem of distributed and resilient access control in such databases has not been tackled before [3,2,1]. The literature on cryptographic access control to address the problem of cost effective key management has been studied in the context of the Web [22,23]. In our work, we focus on distributed access control in P2P networks, and discuss the extensions needed in such scenarios where previous key management approaches [22,23,24] are not directly applicable.

The most recent P2P algorithms realizing the efficient DHT (Distributed Hash Tables) abstraction [25,26] are vulnerable to misbehaving nodes, and the only measure adopted in [26] is to randomize the routing procedure in order to avoid the 'bad' nodes. However, this would not be tolerated in a PDMS, where robust database access control is of utmost importance. To the best of our knowledge, the only work that deals with the distribution of privilege enforcement in P2P networks is PACS [7]. However, they rely on role-based access control, where the access policy is determined by the system, not by the data owner. In this work, we focus on discretionary access control, and the capability of deciding the access granularity by using SQL-based policy rules. Bertino et al. [27] aimed at defining an extension of XACML access rules on resources located in large-scale distributed systems. They focus on the problems of integrating conflicting policies in such a setting. DTD secure views for XML data have been defined in [28]. The approach, based on DTD annotations and view-based, would not be applicable to our context.

6   Conclusions and Future Work

In this paper, we studied the problem of distributed and resilient access control in P2P databases. In particular, we adapted secret sharing to PDMS, devised a block-based encryption scheme that supports overlapping AC rules with shared access to the same data, and proposed a solution for the efficient enforcement of updates on AC rules. As a further goal, we plan to investigate the impact of heterogeneous schemas in PDMS, and the secure query reformulation strategies in such a distributed resilient paradigm.

References

1. Gribble, S.D., Halevy, A.Y., Ives, Z.G., Rodrigand, M., Suciu, D.: What Can Database Do for Peer-to-Peer?. In: Proc. of WebDB (2001)
2. Hose, K., Roth, A., Zeitz, A., Sattler, K.U., Naumann, F.: A research agenda for query processing in large-scale peer data management systems. Inf. Syst. 33(7–8), 597–610 (2008)
3. Bonifati, A., Chrysanthis, P.K., Ouksel, A.M., Sattler, K.U.: Distributed databases and peer-to-peer databases: past and present. SIGMOD Rec. 37(1), 5–11 (2008)
4. Sandhu, R., Zhang, X.: Peer to peer access control architecture using trusted computing technology. In: Proc. of ACMT (2005)
5. Kubiatowicz, J., Bindel, D., Chen, Y., Czerwinski, S., Eaton, P., Geels, D., Gummadi, R., Rhea, S., Weatherspoon, H., Weimer, W., Wells, C., Zhao, B.: Oceanstore: an architecture for global-scale persistent storage. SIGPLAN Not. 35(11), 190–201 (2000)
6. Kallahalla, M., Riedel, E., Swaminathan, R., Wang, Q., Fu, K.: Plutus: Scalable secure file sharing on untrusted storage. In: Proc. of FAST (2003)
7. Sturm, C., Hunt, E., Scholl, M.H.: Distributed privilege enforcement in pacs. In: DBSec, pp. 142–158 (2009)
8. Miklau, G., Suciu, D.: Controlling access to published data using cryptography. In: Proc. of VLDB (2003)
9. Damiani, E., di Vimercati, S.D.C., Paraboschi, S., Sarnarati, P.: Securing xml documents. In: Zaniolo, C., Grust, T., Scholl, M.H., Lockemann, P.C. (eds.) EDBT 2000. LNCS, vol. 1777, Springer, Heidelberg (2000)
10. Harrington, A., Jensen, C.: Cryptographic access control in a distributed file system. In: Proc. of ACMT (2003)
11. Shamir, A.: How to share a secret. Comm. of the ACM 22(11), 612–613 (1979)

12. Chekuri, C., Rajaraman, A.: Conjunctive query containment revisited. In: Proceedings of ICDT, pp. 56–70 (1998)
13. Chandra, A.K., Merlin, P.M.: Optimal implementation of conjunctive queries in relational databases. In: Proc. of STC (1977)
14. Saraiya, Y.P.: Subtree-elimination algorithms in deductive databases. In: Thesis, Stanford University (1991)
15. 5200.28-STD, D.S.: Trusted Computer System Evaluation Criteria. USA Dept. of Defense (1985)
16. Luo, H., Lu, S.: Ubiquitous and robust authentication services for ad hoc wireless networks. Technical report, University of California, Los Angeles (2000)
17. Joshi, D., Namuduri, K., Pendse, R.: Secure, redundant, and fully distributed key management scheme for mobile ad hoc networks: an analysis. EURASIP J. Wirel. Commun. Netw. (4), 579–589 (2005)
18. P2Pac Web Site, http://staff.icar.cnr.it/angela/p2pac/exp/exp.html
19. Grolimund, D., Meisser, L., Schmid, S., Wattenhofer, R.: Cryptree: A folder tree structure for cryptographic file systems. In: RDS, pp. 189–198 (2006)
20. Naor, M., Wool, A.: Access control and signatures via quorum secret sharing. IEEE TPDS 9(9), 909–922 (1998)
21. Merwe, J.V.D., Dawoud, D., McDonald, S.: A survey on peer-to-peer key management for mobile ad hoc networks. ACM Comp. Surveys (2007)
22. Kayem, A.V.D.M., Akl, S.G., Martin, P.: On replacing cryptographic keys in hierarchical key management systems. Journal of Computer Security 16(3), 289–309 (2008)
23. Sun, Y.L., Liu, K.J.R.: Analysis and protection of dynamic membership information for group key distribution schemes. IEEE Transactions on Information Forensics and Security 2(2), 213–226 (2007)
24. Blundo, C., Cimato, S., di Vimercati, S.D.C., Santis, A.D., Foresti, S., Paraboschi, S., Samarati, P.: Efficient key management for enforcing access control in outsourced scenarios. In: Proceedings of SEC (2009)
25. Stoica, I., Morris, R., Karger, D., Kaashoek, M.F., Balakrishnan, H.: Chord: A scalable peer-to-peer lookup service for internet applications. In: Proc. of SIGCOMM (2001)
26. Ratnasamy, S., Francis, P., Handley, M., Karp, R., Shenker, S.: A scalable content-addressable network. In: Proc. of SIGCOMM (2001)
27. Mazzoleni, P., Crispo, B., Sivasubramanian, S., Bertino, E.: XACML Policy Integration Algorithms. ACM TISS 11(1), 1–29 (2008)
28. Fan, W., Chee-Yong Chan, M.G.: Secure xml querying with security views. In: Proc. of SIGMOD 2004 (2004)

Constructing Key Assignment Schemes from Chain Partitions

Jason Crampton, Rosli Daud, and Keith M. Martin

Information Security Group, Royal Holloway, University of London

Abstract. In considering a problem in access control for scalable multimedia formats, we have developed new methods for constructing key assignment schemes. Our first contribution is to improve an existing cryptographic access control mechanism for scalable multimedia formats. We then show how our methods can be applied to a chain partition to develop alternative mechanisms for scalable multimedia formats and how these methods can themselves be extended to create a new type of key assignment scheme.

1 Introduction

Scalable multimedia formats, such as MPEG-4 [1] and JPEG2000 [2], consist of two components: a non-scalable base component and a scalable enhancement component. Decoding the base component will yield low quality results. The quality of the decoded data can be improved by decoding the enhancement component as well as the base component. The enhancement component may comprise multiple "orthogonal" layers, orthogonal in the sense that each layer controls a distinct aspect of the quality of the encoded content. The MPEG-4 FGS (fine granularity scalability) format [1], for example, has a bit-rate layer and a peak signal-to-noise ratio (PSNR) layer.

Zhu *et al* proposed a layered access control scheme for MPEG-4 FGS called SMLFE (scalable multi-layer FGS encryption) [3]. The purpose of SMLFE is to provide different end-users with access to the same content at different levels of quality (by controlling access to the enhancement component).

SMLFE assumes that each enhancement frame is decomposed into different *segments*, each of which is associated with some bit-rate level and some PSNR level. In other words, the *enhancement component stream* (a sequence of enhancement frames) is split into a number of distinct segment streams. Each of these segment streams is encrypted with a different key, and the ability of an end-user (or, more accurately, the decoder available to the end-user) to reconstruct the enhancement component is determined by the keys that are accessible to the user.

However, SMLFE had a number of inadequacies and subsequent research sought to address these deficiencies [4,5,6]. This later research uses a labeling technique, which associates each segment with a k-tuple and then uses iterative hashing to derive key components for each segment. Most of these labeling

S. Foresti and S. Jajodia (Eds.): Data and Applications Security XXIV, LNCS 6166, pp. 130–145, 2010.

schemes suffer from the distinct disadvantage that different users can combine their respective key components to derive keys for which no single user is authorized. The one exception [5] uses a very complicated labeling process that makes it very difficult to reason about the properties of the scheme (including whether it is secure against colluding users or not). Our first contribution is to construct a labeling scheme that can be proved to be secure against colluding users and has other significant advantages over existing schemes. We discuss labeling schemes in Sec. 3.

We then consider alternative approaches to the problem of layered access control for scalable multimedia formats. Our second contribution is to define several schemes in Sec. 4 that make use of chain partitions. One of our constructions makes use of the labeling scheme we introduce in Sec. 3. The constructions in Sec. 4 have demonstrable advantages, in the context of layered access control, over labeling schemes and existing approaches to cryptographic access control.

It can be shown that the enforcement of layered access control for scalable multimedia formats can be regarded as a instance of a *key assignment scheme*. Such schemes are used to enforce a no-read-up information flow policy using cryptographic techniques. A recent survey of such schemes proposed a classification into four generic types of scheme [8]. These schemes offer different trade-offs in terms of the amount of storage required and the complexity of key derivation. Our final contribution, presented in Sec. 5, is to show that the schemes in Sec. 4 can be generalized to create new types of generic key assignment schemes. These generic schemes offer different trade-offs from existing schemes, which may prove useful for certain applications.

We conclude the paper with some suggestions for future work. Before proceeding further, we introduce some relevant background material.

2   Background

In this section, we first recall some relevant concepts from mathematics and cryptography. The section concludes with a more formal statement of the problem of layered access control and a discussion of its relationship to work on key assignment schemes.

2.1   Definitions and Notation

A *partially ordered set* (or *poset*) is a pair $(X, \leqslant)$, where $\leqslant$ is a reflexive, antisymmetric, transitive binary relation on X. X is a *total order* (or *chain*) if for all $x, y \in X$, either $x \leqslant y$ or $y \leqslant x$. We say $A \subseteq X$ is an *antichain* if for all $x, y \in A$, $x \nleqslant y$ and $x \ngeqslant y$. We may write $y < x$ if $y \leqslant x$ and $y \neq x$, and we may write $x \geqslant y$ if $y \leqslant x$.

The (directed, acyclic) graph $(X, \leqslant)$ would include all "reflexive edges" and all "transitive edges", so it is customary to represent a poset using a smaller set of edges. We say x *covers* y, denoted $y \lessdot x$, if $y < x$ and there does not exist $z \in X$ such that $y < z < x$. Then the *Hasse diagram* of a poset $(X, \leqslant)$ is defined to be the (directed, acyclic) graph $(X, <)$ [9]. A simple Hasse diagram is shown in Fig. 1(a). Note that all edges in the diagram are assumed to be directed upwards.

A *partition* of a set X is a collection of sets $\{Y_1, \ldots, Y_k\}$ such that (i) $Y_i \subseteq X$ (ii) $Y_1 \cup \cdots \cup Y_k = X$, and (iii) $Y_i \cap Y_j \neq \emptyset$ if and only if $i = j$. The *greatest common divisor* of x and y is written $\gcd(x, y)$; we say x and y are *co-prime* if $\gcd(x, y) = 1$.

We assume the existence of an *RSA key generator* [10], a randomized algorithm that takes a security parameter k as input and outputs a triple (N, e, d) such that:

- $N = pq$, where p and q are distinct odd primes;
- $e \in \mathbb{Z}^*_{\phi(N)}$, where $\phi(N) = (p-1)(q-1)$, $e > 1$, and $\gcd(e, \phi(N)) = 1$;
- $d \in \mathbb{Z}^*_{\phi(N)}$, where $ed \equiv 1 \mod \phi(N)$.

Finally, let $h : \{0,1\}^* \rightarrow \{0,1\}^\ell$ be a hash function and let $k \geqslant 0$ be an integer. Then we define the *iterative hash function* $h^k : \{0,1\}^\ell \rightarrow \{0,1\}^\ell$ in the following way: $h^0(x) = x$ and $h^k(x) = h(h^{k-1}(x))$.

2.2   Key Assignment Schemes

We now rephrase the problem at hand in more formal terms and illustrate how this problem is related to existing work on *key assignment schemes*. Let us assume that we are concerned with a scalable multimedia format with two distinct layers (such as bit-rate and PSNR), containing m and n levels respectively.

Define $R_{m,n} = \{(x, y) : 1 \leqslant x \leqslant m,\ 1 \leqslant y \leqslant n\}$ and define $(x_1, y_1) \leqslant (x_2, y_2)$ if and only if $x_1 \leqslant x_2$ and $y_1 \leqslant y_2$. Then $(R_{m,n}, \leqslant)$ is a partially ordered set. Each segment (and segment stream) represents a distinct protected object and is labeled with a pair (i, j) indicating the corresponding levels in the bit-rate and PSNR layers, respectively. Each pair $(i, j) \in R_{m,n}$ is associated with an encryption key $\kappa_{i,j}$. Segment streams are encrypted with the corresponding key. Each user is authorized to access layered multimedia of some quality $q_{i,j}$, which implies that such a user must be able to compute $\kappa_{x,y}$ for all $x \leqslant i$ and all $y \leqslant j$ in order to decode the relevant segment streams. Figure 1(a) illustrates the poset $R_{3,4}$.

Clearly the access control requirements described above closely resemble the "no-read-up" component of an *information flow policy* [11,12]. There are many schemes in the literature for enforcing an information flow policy using cryptographic techniques (see the survey paper of Crampton *et al* [8], for example). Given a security lattice $(L, \leqslant)$, a set of subjects U, a set of protected objects O, and a security function $\lambda : U \cup O \rightarrow L$, we define a set of cryptographic keys $\{\kappa(x) : x \in L\}$. Then, adopting a cryptographic approach to policy enforcement, we encrypt object o with (symmetric) key $\kappa(\lambda(o))$. In order to correctly implement the information flow policy, a user u with security label should be given, or be able to derive, $\kappa(y)$ for all $y \leqslant x$. There are several generic solutions, the most obvious of which is to give u the set of keys $\{\kappa(y) : y \leqslant \lambda(u)\}$.

More commonly, we give u a single key $\kappa(\lambda(u))$ and publish additional information that enables the user to derive $\kappa(y)$ whenever $y < \lambda(u)$. The additional information "encrypts edges" in the graphical representation of L: that is, if $G = (L, E)$,

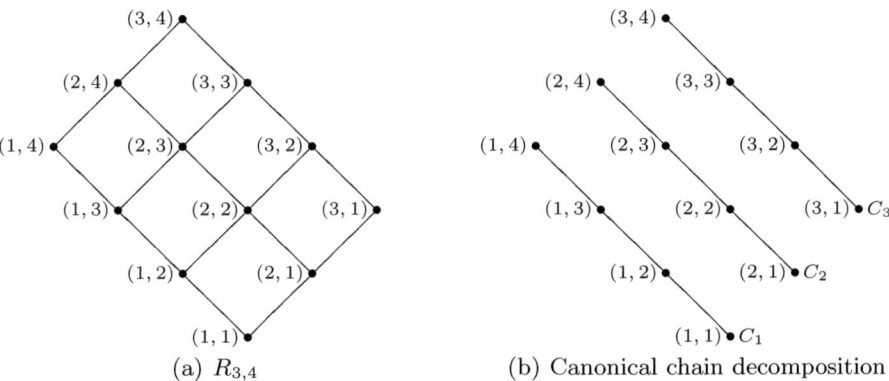

(a) $R_{3,4}$ (b) Canonical chain decomposition

Fig. 1. A typical poset used in layered access control for scalable multimedia formats

then we publish $\mathsf{Enc}_{\kappa(x)}(\kappa(y))$ for all $(x, y) \in E$. There are two obvious choices for E: the edge set corresponding to the full order relation $\leqslant$, in which case, key derivation can be performed in a single step; or the edge set corresponding to the cover relation $\lessdot$, in which case key derivation may take several steps. We call the former a *direct key encrypting* (DKE) key assignment scheme and the latter an *iterative key encrypting* (IKE) scheme [8]. Clearly, there is a trade-off between the amount of storage required and the number of steps required for key derivation.

Any key assignment scheme for enforcing an information flow policy should satisfy two criteria.

– The scheme is *correct* if for all y, $\kappa(x)$ can be derived from $\sigma(y)$ and the public information if $y \geqslant x$.[1]
– The scheme is *collusion secure* if, for all $x \in X$ and all $Y \subseteq X$ such that for all $y \in Y$, $y \ngeqslant x$, it is not possible to derive $\kappa(x)$ from $\{\sigma(y) : y \in Y\}$ and the public information. Note that this definition includes the case of a singleton subset Y, which corresponds to a single user "colluding" to recover a key for which she is not authorized.[2]

---

[1] It should be emphasized here that "derived from" means "derived from in a feasible amount of time". Very few cryptographic schemes provide unconditional security in an information-theoretic sense; rather, they guarantee with a high probability that a scheme is secure against an adversary with reasonable resources. The interested reader is referred to the literature for a more detailed discussion of these issues [10].

[2] Recent work has introduced the notions of *key recovery* and *key indistinguishability* [13]. A proof that a scheme is secure against key recovery is analogous to proving that a scheme is collusion secure. The main difference is that collusion security assumes that colluding users will try to compute a key using the particular methods of key derivation associated with the scheme, whereas a proof of security against key recovery establishes that the recovery of a key is as difficult as solving some known hard problem. While formal security proofs of this nature are certainly important in modern cryptographic research, space constraints mean they are out of scope for this paper.

Clearly, the problem of enforcing layered accessed control for scalable multimedia formats can be addressed by defining an appropriate key assignment scheme for the partially ordered set $(R_{m,n}, \leqslant)$. However, because of the particularly simple structure of $R_{m,n}$, in the next two sections we consider some key assignment schemes that are tailored to the problem of layered access control for scalable multimedia formats. In Sec. 3, we consider *labeling schemes*, in which each key is defined by a set of *key components*, each of which is obtained by iteratively hashing some secret value. In Sec. 4, we consider some alternative approaches using chain partitions of $R_{m,n}$.

3   A New Labeling Scheme for Layered Access Control

Apart from SMLFE [3], all existing schemes for layered access control (to our knowledge) associate a distinct k-tuple with each element of $R_{m,n}$ [4,5,6]. This k-tuple is used to construct k key components using iterative hashing. We write $\phi(x,y) \in \mathbb{Z}^k$ to denote the label assigned to $(x,y) \in R_{m,n}$ and we write $\phi_i(x,y)$ to denote the ith co-ordinate of $\phi(x,y)$. In this section, we first summarize the basic technique and then describe our new labeling scheme and compare it to existing work.

First we introduce some additional definitions. Let $a = (a_1, \ldots, a_k)$ and $b = (b_1, \ldots, b_k)$ be elements of $\mathbb{Z}^k$. Then we define $(a_1, \ldots, a_k) \leqslant (b_1, \ldots, b_k)$ (in $\mathbb{Z}^k$) if and only if $a_i \leqslant b_i$ for all i, and we define $a - b = (a_1 - b_1, \ldots, a_k - b_k)$. We say a is *positive* if $a_i \geqslant 0$ for all i.

Labeling schemes have the property that $(x,y) \geqslant (x',y')$ in $R_{m,n}$ if and only if $\phi(x',y') - \phi(x,y)$ is positive. It is this property that ensures the correctness of each scheme, since $\phi(x',y') - \phi(x,y)$ is used to construct k secrets per node using iterative hashing.

The content provider, hereafter called the *scheme administrator*, chooses a hash function $h : \{0,1\}^* \rightarrow \{0,1\}^\ell$ and k secrets $\sigma_1, \ldots, \sigma_k \in \mathbb{Z}^\ell$. Then the secret $\sigma_{x,y}$ assigned to $(x,y) \in R_{m,n}$ comprises k key components:

$$\sigma_{x,y} \overset{\text{def}}{=} (h^{\phi_1(x,y)}(\sigma_1), \ldots, h^{\phi_k(x,y)}(\sigma_k)).$$

For brevity, we may abuse notation and write $h^{\phi(x,y)}(\sigma)$ to denote $\sigma_{x,y}$. We define the key assigned to (x,y) to be

$$\kappa_{x,y} \overset{\text{def}}{=} h(h^{\phi_1(x,y)}(\sigma_1) \parallel \cdots \parallel h^{\phi_k(x,y)}(\sigma_k)),$$

where $s_1 \parallel s_2$ denotes the concatenation of s_1 and s_2.[3] Again, we may abuse notation and write $h(\sigma_{x,y})$ to denote $\kappa_{x,y}$.

---

[3] The schemes in the literature simply define the "key" associated with (x,y) to be the concatenation of the key components. We take the hash of the concatenation of those components to make the distinction between key and key components clearer. It also means that we have fixed-length, short symmetric keys, determined by the size of h's output.

Correctness. By construction $(x, y) \geqslant (x', y')$ if and only if $\phi_i(x', y') - \phi_i(x, y)$ is positive. Now the ith key component of $\kappa_{x,y}$ is $h^{\phi_i(x,y)}(\sigma_i)$ and the ith key component of $\kappa_{x',y'}$ is $h^{\phi_i(x',y')}(\sigma_i)$. Hence, if $(x, y) \geqslant (x', y')$, then we simply hash the ith component of $\kappa_{x,y}$ a total of $\phi_i(x', y') - \phi_i(x, y)$ times to obtain the ith key component of $\sigma_{x',y'}$. Conversely, if $(x, y) \not\geqslant (x', y')$, then for some i, $\phi_i(x', y') - \phi_i(x, y) < 0$, which implies that we can only obtain the ith component of $\kappa_{x,y}$ by inverting h, which is computationally infeasible provided h is chosen appropriately.

The IWFK-1 scheme [6, §3.1.1], for example, simply defines $\phi(x, y)$ for $(x, y) \in R_{m,n}$ to be $(m - x, n - y)$. So, for example, $\phi(2, 4) = (1, 0)$ and $\phi(1, 1) = (2, 3)$ in $R_{3,4}$. Then $\sigma_{2,4} = (h(\sigma_1), \sigma_2)$ and $\sigma_{1,1} = (h^2(\sigma_1), h^3(\sigma_2))$. Hence, $\sigma_{2,4}$ can be used to derive $\sigma_{1,1}$ by hashing the first component of $\sigma_{2,4}$ once and hashing the second component twice.

Collusion Security. It is known that all but one of the schemes in the literature are not collusion secure. Indeed, it is trivial to find examples that break each of the schemes: in the IWFK-1 scheme for $R_{3,4}$, for example, $\sigma_{2,4} = (h(\sigma_1), \sigma_2)$ and $\sigma_{3,3} = (\sigma_1, h(\sigma_2))$; clearly these keys can be combined to recover $(\sigma_1, \sigma_2) = \sigma_{3,4}$. The IFAK scheme is claimed to be collusion secure [5], although no proof of this claim is given.

3.1 The CDM Scheme

We now explain how our scheme works, which we call the CDM scheme for ease of reference.

Definition 1. *Let $(x, y) \in R_{m,n}$. Then we define the CDM label of (x, y) to be*

$$\phi_{\mathrm{CDM}}(x, y) \stackrel{\mathrm{def}}{=} (\underbrace{n - y, \ldots, n - y}_{x}, \underbrace{n, \ldots, n}_{m-x}).$$

Henceforth, we will simply write $\phi(x, y)$ to denote the CDM labeling of $(x, y) \in R_{m,n}$. Note the CDM labeling has m components. We now state several elementary results concerning the properties of the CDM labeling.[4]

Proposition 1. *Let $(x, y), (x', y') \in R_{m,n}$. Then $\phi(x', y') - \phi(x, y)$ is positive if and only if $(x, y) \geqslant (x', y')$.*

Proposition 2. *Let $(x, y), (x', y') \in R_{m,n}$ such that $(x, y) \geqslant (x', y')$. Then $\sigma_{x',y'}$ can be derived from $\sigma_{x,y}$ using precisely $xy - x'y'$ hash computations.*

---

[4] Lack of space precludes the inclusion of proofs in this version of the paper: the interested reader is referred to the extended version of the paper [7] for the relevant details.

Corollary 1. *The number of hash computations required is bounded by $mn - 1$.*

We now give some intuition behind the labeling and an example. The element $(x, y) \in R_{m,n}$ defines a sub-rectangle $R_{x,y}$. Removing $R_{x,y}$ truncates the first i chains and leaves the remaining chains intact. Our labeling simply records the lengths of the chains that are left following the removal of $R_{x,y}$. Hence, for example, $\phi(2, 4) = (0, 0, 4)$ and $\phi(1, 1) = (3, 4, 4)$. Note that $3 + 4 = 7$ operations are required to derive $\kappa_{1,1}$ from $\kappa_{2,4}$ (as we would expect from Proposition 2).

The geometric intuition behind the scheme also provides some understanding of why our scheme is collusion secure.

Proposition 3. *Let $(x_1, y_1), \ldots, (x_j, y_j) \in R_{m,n}$ such that $(x_i, y_i) \not\geq (x, y)$ for all i. Then there exists t, $1 \leqslant t \leqslant m$, such that $\phi_t(x, y) < \phi_t(x_i, y_i)$ for all i.*

Hence, no set of m colluding users can recover the tth component of $\sigma_{x,y}$. In other words, we have the following corollary.

Corollary 2. *The CDM scheme is collusion secure.*

3.2   Related Work

Table 1 provides a summary of the four schemes in the literature for layered access control (IWFK-1 [6, §3.1.1], IWFK-2 [6, §3.2.3], IFAK [5], and HIFK [4]), presented in chronological order and identified by the initial letters of the authors' surnames. Each component of $\sigma_{x,y} = h^{\phi(x,y)}(\sigma)$ is a distinct secret key component, as each component has to be hashed independently of the others. Hence, we believe it is appropriate to minimize the number of key components and the number of derivation steps that are required. The table reports precise storage requirements (given by the number of key components k) and worst case derivation (in terms of the number of hash computations required).

All of these schemes are correct, but only the IFAK scheme is claimed to be collusion secure, in the sense that a set of collaborating users cannot combine the secret components of their respective keys (and possibly use iterative hashing) to derive a key for which no one of them was authorized.

The characteristics of our scheme are shown in the last row of the table. Our scheme is collusion secure under the same assumptions that the IFAK scheme is

Table 1. A summary of labeling schemes for layered access control

Scheme	k	Key derivation	Collusion secure
IWFK-1	2	$m + n - 2$	N
IWFK-2	3	$m + 2n - 3$	N
IFAK	$m + n - 1$	$\frac{1}{2}(m + n - 2)(m + n - 1)$	Y
HIFK	3	$2m + 2n - 4$	N
CDM	m	$mn - 1$	Y

(claimed to be) secure. However, we use a smaller value of k and we require fewer derivation steps. Moreover, we have a systematic and easily implementable way of generating our labels (unlike the IFAK scheme); because of this we can also compute the number of derivation steps required for any $(x, y), (x', y') \in R_{m,n}$ and prove that our scheme is collusion secure. IFAK, in contrast, has an extremely complicated labeling scheme, which makes it difficult to reason about (i) the number of derivation steps required in the general case (ii) the collusion security of the scheme.

4   New Schemes for Layered Access Control

In this section, we propose a number of key assignment schemes for implementing layered access control for scalable multimedia formats. These schemes assume that the poset $(R_{m,n}, \leqslant)$ has been partitioned into chains. Dilworth's Theorem [14] asserts that every partially ordered set $(X, \leqslant)$ can be partitioned into w chains, where w is the *width* of X.[5]

Evidently, there are many different ways to partition the poset $R_{m,n}$ into chains, but we choose a particular partition that enables us to define two very simple schemes. We assume without loss of generality that $m \leqslant n$, and we define the *canonical* partition of $R_{m,n}$ into chains to be $\{C_1, \ldots, C_m\}$, where $C_i = \{(i, j) : 1 \leqslant j \leqslant n\}$. Figure 1(b) illustrates the canonical partition of $R_{3,4}$ into chains.

4.1   Schemes with No Public Information

Generally, key assignment schemes rely on public information for key derivation [8]. An interesting feature of the schemes in the previous section is that no public information is used. In this section we consider two different schemes that require no public information – one based on hash functions and one based on RSA – and have lower storage requirements than the CDM scheme.

A Scheme Based on Hash Functions. The scheme administrator first selects a family of m hash functions $h_i : \{0,1\}^* \rightarrow \{0,1\}^\ell$, $1 \leqslant i \leqslant m$. The scheme administrator also selects m secret values, $\sigma_1, \ldots, \sigma_m \in \{0,1\}^\ell$, where σ_i is associated with chain C_i. The scheme administrator then computes a secret key for each element in $R_{m,n}$, where $\kappa_{i,j}$ is defined to be $h_i^{n-j}(\sigma_i)$. Then a user authorized for content quality $q_{i,j}$ is given the keys $\{\kappa_{x,j} : 1 \leqslant x \leqslant i\}$. For reasons that will be apparent from the above description, we call this a *multiple-key iterated hash scheme*.

Correctness. We first show that a user can derive all keys for which she is authorized. Suppose that a user is authorized for quality $q_{i,j}$. (Equivalently, the user is associated with label $(i, j) \in R_{m,n}$.) Henceforth, we will simply write $u_{i,j}$

---

[5] The width of X is the cardinality of the largest antichain in X. Clearly, any partition into chains must contain at least w chains. It is harder to prove that no more than w are required.

for such a user. Then $u_{i,j}$ must be able to derive all keys in the rectangle $R_{i,j}$. Now, by construction, $u_{i,j}$ has $\kappa_{x,j}$ for all $x \leqslant i$. Moreover, $\kappa_{x,y} = h_x^{j-y}(\kappa_{x,j})$, $1 \leqslant y < j$. Hence, a user $u_{i,j}$ can derive any key in $R_{i,j}$ in no more than $j-1$ steps.

Collusion Security. Any "good" hash function will have the property that it is computationally hard to compute x given $y = h(x)$ (that is, *pre-image resistance*). Since keys are obtained by successively hashing elements in a chain, it is computationally hard to recover $\kappa_{i,j+1}$ from $\kappa_{i,j}$, as this would require the computation of the pre-image of $\kappa_{i,j}$. Hence, a user certainly cannot use a key from one key chain to derive a key higher up the same key chain (and hence for which she is not authorized), providing the scheme administrator chooses a suitable hash function. However, a user may have several keys: assuming that the key chains are independent – in the sense that knowledge of an element in C_i provides no information about any element in C_j, for all $j \neq i$ – then it is not possible for the user to derive any keys for which she is not authorized. We have chosen a different hash function for each chain in order to provide this key chain independence.

If two or more users collude – equivalently, if an adversary is able to obtain the keys of several users – then the set of keys available do not correspond to the nodes of a sub-rectangle (as they do for a single user). Suppose that an adversary (whether it is a group of colluding users or a single malicious entity) collectively has the keys $\kappa_{1,j_1}, \ldots, \kappa_{m,j_m}$. Then κ_{i,j_i} cannot be used to recover κ_{i,j_i+k} for any $k > 0$ if h_i has pre-image resistance. Hence, assuming the independence of key chains, as before, we see that such an adversary has no additional advantage over a single user.

A Scheme Based on RSA. In this scheme, we make use of a special case of the Akl-Taylor scheme [15], which can be applied to any poset. Specifically, we apply the scheme to each of the chains in the partition.

The scheme administrator first obtains m large compound integers $N_1, \ldots, N_m$ using an RSA key generator and makes these values public. For each chain C_i, the scheme administrator:

- chooses a secret $\sigma_i \in \mathbb{Z}_{N_i}^*$, such that for all σ_i and σ_j are co-prime if $i \neq j$;
- defines $\kappa_{i,j} = (\sigma_i)^{2^{n-j}} \bmod N_i$.

We call the sequence of keys

$$\kappa_{i,n} = (\sigma_i)^1, \ \kappa_{i,n-1} = (\sigma_i)^2 \bmod N_i, \ldots, \ \kappa_{i,1} = (\sigma_i)^{2^{n-1}} \bmod N_i$$

an *RSA key chain*. As before, user $u_{i,j}$ is given the keys $\{\kappa_{x,j} : 1 \leqslant x \leqslant i\}$. Henceforth, for reasons of clarity and brevity, we will write x rather than $x \bmod N_i$, when N_i is clear from context.

Correctness and Collusion Security. Key derivation is quite different using RSA key chains. To obtain $\kappa_{x,y}$, where $x < i$ and $y < j$, the user selects $\kappa_{x,j}$ and then computes

$$(\kappa_{x,j})^{2^{j-y}} = (\kappa_{x,j})^{\frac{2^{n-y}}{2^{n-j}}} = \left((\sigma_x)^{2^{n-j}}\right)^{\frac{2^{n-y}}{2^{n-j}}} = (\sigma_x)^{2^{n-y}} = \kappa_{x,y}$$

To illustrate, consider Fig. 1(b) and suppose that the keys for C_2 are

$$\kappa_{2,4} = \sigma_2, \ \ \kappa_{2,3} = \sigma_2^2, \ \ \kappa_{2,2} = \sigma_2^4, \ \ \kappa_{2,1} = \sigma_2^8.$$

Suppose we wish to derive $\kappa_{2,1}$ and we have $\kappa_{2,3}$. Then we compute

$$(\kappa_{2,3})^{2^{3-1}} = \kappa_{2,3}^4 = (\sigma_2^2)^4 = \sigma_2^8 = \kappa_{2,1}.$$

However, user with key $\kappa_{i,j}$ cannot derive $\kappa_{i,y}$ if $y > j$, since this would require the user to solve the *RSA problem*.[6] Similarly, no collection of keys that includes $\kappa_{i,j}$ (but no key higher up the ith chain) can be used to derive $\kappa_{i,y}$.

4.2 Schemes with Single Keys

Most key assignment schemes in the literature require the end-user to store a single key. The multiple-key schemes described above clearly do not satisfy this criterion.

In this section, we describe schemes that only require the end user to store a single key. The trade-off is that such schemes require a certain amount of public information.

A Scheme Based on Hash Functions. The scheme we now describe could be considered to be a hybrid of an iterative key encrypting (IKE) scheme [8] and a hash chain. Atallah *et al*, for example, define a concrete construction of an IKE scheme [13].

In our scheme, the content provider selects m hash functions $h_1, \ldots, h_m$ and m secrets $\sigma_1, \ldots, \sigma_m$, and defines key $\kappa_{i,j} = h_i^{n-j}(\sigma_i)$, as before. Now, however, the content provider publishes enough information to enable the computation of $\kappa_{x,j}$ from $\kappa_{i,j}$ for all $x < i$, by publishing $\left\{ \mathsf{Enc}_{\kappa_{i,j}}(\kappa_{i-1,j}) : 1 < i \leqslant m, 1 \leqslant j \leqslant n \right\}$. Hence, we require $(m-1)n$ items of public information.

Correctness and Collusion Security. Again, it is very easy to demonstrate that a user $u_{i,j}$ can derive the key for any node in $R_{i,j}$. First, $u_{i,j}$ is given $\kappa_{i,j}$ and this key, in conjunction with the public information, can be used to derive $\kappa_{x,j}$ for all $x < i$. Moreover, $\kappa_{x,y}$ can be obtained from $\kappa_{x,j}$ by $j - y$ applications of h. Hence, $u_{i,j}$ can obtain $\kappa_{x,y}$ in no more than $i - 1 + j - 1 = i + j - 2$ steps.

Collusion security follows from the fact that pre-image resistance of the hash function prevents the computation of $\kappa_{i,j+k}$ from $\kappa_{i,j}$ for any $k > 0$. The assumption that it is computationally hard to decrypt without knowledge of the secret key ensures that $\kappa_{i+k,j}$ cannot be derived from $\kappa_{i,j}$.

---

[6] That is, given N, $y \in \mathbb{Z}_N^*$ and an integer $e > 0$ that is co-prime to $\phi(N)$, compute $y^{1/e} \bmod N$.

A Scheme Based on RSA. Finally, we note that we can use the CDM labeling (Definition 1), in which modular exponentiation is used to recover keys. It is important to note that this scheme does not rely on the idea of encrypting edges, and is therefore quite different from the schemes described above. (It is, however, closely related to the Akl-Taylor scheme [15].)

Recall that we associate each $(x, y) \in R_{m,n}$ with a CDM label $\phi(x, y) \in \mathbb{Z}^m$. Moreover, $\phi(x', y') - \phi(x, y)$ is positive if and only if $(x, y) \geqslant (x', y')$. In this new scheme the scheme administrator

- obtains a large compound integer N using the RSA key generator;
- chooses small, distinct primes $p_1 = 2, p_2 = 3, \ldots, p_m \in \mathbb{Z}_N^*$ and makes them public;
- chooses a master secret $\sigma \in \mathbb{Z}_N^*$;
- defines

$$\pi(x, y) = \prod_{i=1}^{m} p_i^{\phi_i(x,y)};$$

- defines $\kappa_{x,y} = \sigma^{\pi(x,y)} \bmod N$.

Correctness and Collusion Security. Consider (x, y) and (x', y'), where $(x, y) \geqslant (x', y')$. Then $\phi(x', y') - \phi(x, y)$ is positive and

$$\frac{\pi(x', y')}{\pi(x, y)} = \prod_{i=1}^{m} p_i^{\phi_i(x',y') - \phi_i(x,y)} = \prod_{i=1}^{x'} p_i^{y-y'} \prod_{i=x'+1}^{x} p_i^{y}$$

Hence,

$$(\kappa_{x,y})^{\frac{\pi(x',y')}{\pi(x,y)}} = \left(\sigma^{\pi(x,y)}\right)^{\frac{\pi(x',y')}{\pi(x,y)}} = \sigma^{\pi(x',y')} = \kappa_{x',y'}$$

In other words, if $\phi(x', y') - \phi(x, y)$ is positive, we can compute $\kappa_{x',y'}$ from $\kappa_{x,y}$ since we can compute $\frac{\pi(x',y')}{\pi(x,y)}$. Specifically, given $\kappa_{x,y}$:

1. compute $\phi(x, y)$ and $\phi(x', y')$, which is trivial if m and n are known;
2. compute $\phi(x', y') - \phi(x, y)$ and hence $\pi(x', y')/\pi(x, y)$;
3. finally, compute $\kappa_{x',y'}$.

We cannot compute $\kappa_{x'',y''}$ from $\kappa_{x,y}$ if $(x, y) \not\geqslant (x'', y'')$ since this would imply that $\phi(x'', y'') - \phi(x, y)$ is not positive and we would have to compute integral roots modulo N to compute $\kappa_{x'',y''}$. (In other words, solve the RSA problem.) Moreover, Proposition 3 implies that any adversary with keys $\kappa_{x_1,y_1}, \ldots, \kappa_{x_j,y_j}$, such that $(x_i, y_i) \not\geqslant (x, y)$, would have to solve the RSA problem to compute $\kappa_{x,y}$.

4.3   Related Work

In Table 2, we summarize the properties of several schemes in the literature and compare them to the schemes we have introduced in this section. The table includes, for ease of reference, the best labeling scheme from Sec. 3. We also include IKE and DKE schemes for $R_{m,n}$. Atallah *et al* have demonstrated how an IKE scheme (and hence a DKE scheme) can be implemented using hash functions [13]; we will assume that this implementation is used for the purposes of our comparison. We write MKIH to denote the multiple-key iterative hash scheme and MKRSA to denote the multiple-key RSA scheme and replace 'M' with 'S' for the equivalent single-key schemes.

We write T_{Hsh} to denote the time taken to compute a hash function and T_{Mul} to denote the time taken to perform a modular multiplication. (Recall that the modular exponentiation a^n can be performed by a square-and-multiply algorithm using no more than $2\log_2 n$ modular multiplications.) We assume that our unit of storage is 128 bits. That is, all storage costs in Table 2 are expressed as multiples of 128 bits. We assume that the output of each hash function is 128 bits, and the RSA modulus is 1024 bits (that is, 8 units of storage). The table reports the worst case for storage costs and the number of key derivation steps.

Table 2. A summary of related work and a comparison with our schemes

Scheme	Private storage	Public storage	Key derivation
CDM	m	0	$(mn-1)T_{\text{Hsh}}$
IKE	1	$(m-1)n + m(n-1)$	$(m+n-2)T_{\text{Hsh}}$
DKE	1	$\frac{1}{4}mn((m+1)(n+1)-4)$	T_{Hsh}
MKIH	m	0	$(m-1)T_{\text{Hsh}}$
MKRSA	$8m$	0	$(m-1)T_{\text{Mul}}$
SKIH	1	$(m-1)n$	$(m+n-2)T_{\text{Hsh}}$
SKRSA	8	$8m$	$(2n\sum_{i=1}^{m}\log_2 p_i)T_{\text{Mul}}$

It is clear that even the best labeling scheme (CDM) does not compare well with either the generic schemes in the literature or the schemes we have introduced in this section. The main reason for this is that the key components in the labeling schemes do not provide as much information about keys as the other schemes do. In MKIH, for example, a single key is required to derive all the keys on any particular chain in the canonical decomposition, in contrast to the labeling schemes. We can see from the table that the RSA-based schemes, although attractive in principle, are unlikely to be as attractive in practice: the storage required per key is an order of magnitude greater than hash-based schemes and the key derivation method requires the comparatively expensive modular multiplication operation.

5   New Key Assignment Schemes

Our original motivation was to construct better schemes for layered access control. However, it became apparent that the schemes described in the preceding section could be generalized to create key assignment schemes that could be applied to any poset. Moreover, the resulting schemes do not fit into the taxonomy of generic key assignment schemes proposed by Crampton *et al* [8]. In this section, we describe briefly how two of our schemes for layered access control can be extended to create generic key assignment schemes.

Given a poset X, we first select a partition of X into chains $\{C_1, \ldots, C_w\}$, where w is the width of X.[7] We denote the length of C_i by ℓ_i, $1 \leqslant i \leqslant w$. We regard the maximum element of C_i as the first element in C_i and the minimum element as the last (or ℓ_ith) element.

Let $C = x_1 > x_2 > \cdots > x_m$ be any chain in X. Then we say any chain of the form $x_j > \cdots > x_m$, $1 < j \leqslant m$, is a *suffix* of C. Now, for any $x \in X$, the set $\downarrow x \stackrel{\text{def}}{=} \{y \in X : y \leqslant x\}$ has non-empty intersection with one or more chains $C_1, \ldots, C_w$. We now prove that the intersection of $\downarrow x$ and a chain C_i is a suffix of C_i. This result enables us to define the keys that should be given to a user with label x.

Proposition 4. *For all $x \in X$ and any chain $C \subseteq X$, either $\downarrow x \cap C$ is a suffix of C or $\downarrow x \cap C = \emptyset$.*

The above proposition indicates how we should allocate keys to users. Since $\{C_1, \ldots, C_w\}$ is a partition of X into chains, $\{\downarrow x \cap C_1, \ldots, \downarrow x \cap C_w\}$ is a disjoint collection of chain suffixes. Moreover, the keys for each element in X have been chosen so that the key for the jth element of a chain can be used to compute all lower elements in that chain. Hence, we can see that a user with label x must be given the keys for the maximal elements in the non-empty suffixes $\downarrow x \cap C_1, \ldots, \downarrow x \cap C_w$. Given $x \in X$, let $\hat{x}_1, \ldots, \hat{x}_w$ denote these maximal elements, with the convention that $\hat{x}_i = \bot$ if $\downarrow x \cap C_i = \emptyset$. Clearly the number of $\hat{x}_i$ such that $\hat{x}_i \neq \bot$ is no greater than w. The above result and observations provide the foundations of both the schemes that follow.

5.1   Multiple-Key Iterated Hash Scheme

We first consider the use of iterated hashing. The scheme administrator

- selects a chain partition of X into w chains $C_1, \ldots, C_w$;
- selects w secret values $\sigma_1, \ldots, \sigma_w$ and w hash functions $h_1, \ldots, h_w$;
- defines the key for the maximum element of chain C_i to be σ_i;
- for each pair $x, y \in C_i$ such that $x < y$, defines $\kappa(x) = h_i(\kappa(y))$;
- for each $x \in X$, defines the private information for x to be $\{\kappa(\hat{x}_i) : \hat{x}_i \neq \bot\}$.

We denote the key for the jth element of C_i by $\kappa_{i,j}$. Clearly (as in Sec. 4), a user in possession of $\kappa_{i,j}$ can compute $\kappa_{i,y}$, for any $y > j$, by $y - j$ iterative hash computations. Figure 2 illustrates a poset X of width 4 and one possible partition of X into 4 chains. If the chain $x_{11} > x_8 > x_4 > x_1$ is associated with the secret value σ, for example, then $\kappa(x_{11}) = \sigma$ and $\kappa(x_8) = h(\sigma)$, etc.

---

[7] Unlike $R_{m,n}$, there is no canonical partition for an arbitrary poset X. At this stage, we do not consider what features a "good" partition might have. We return to this question towards the end of the section.

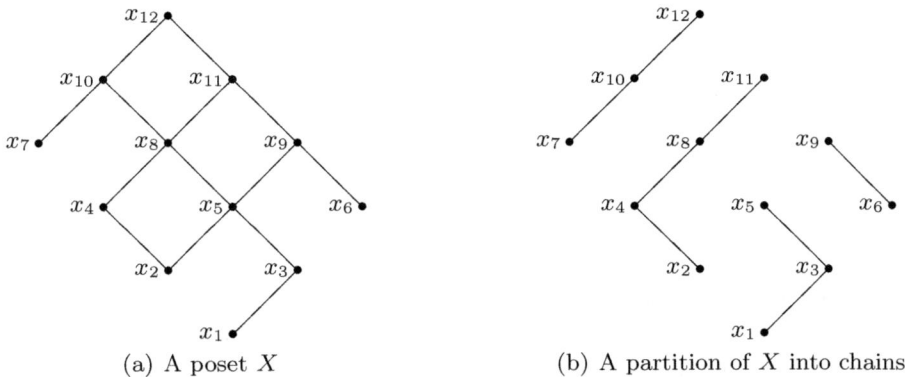

(a) A poset X (b) A partition of X into chains

Fig. 2. Partitioning an arbitrary poset into chains

Clearly, the number of steps required for key derivation is bounded by the length of the longest chain in the partition. With this is mind, it might be sensible to choose a chain partition in which the chains are as similar in length as possible. In terms of correctness and collusion security, the MKIH scheme for arbitrary posets is no different from the corresponding schemes for $R_{m,n}$.

5.2 Multi-key RSA Scheme

In the second scheme, we use RSA key chains. The scheme administrator generates and publishes $N_1, \ldots, N_w$ (as in Sec. 4.1). As in Sec. 5.1, the scheme administrator selects a chain partition of X and defines the key for the maximum element of the ith chain to be σ_i. Now, for each pair $x, y \in C_i$ such that $x < y$, the scheme administrator defines $\kappa(x) = (\kappa(y))^2 \bmod N_i$. Finally, the private information associated with $x \in X$ is defined to be $\{\kappa(\hat{x}_i) : \hat{x}_i \neq \bot\}$ (as in the preceding scheme).

5.3 Related Work

In Table 3, we summarize the differences between our schemes and existing generic key assignment schemes. We also compare the performance of these schemes for the poset and chain partition illustrated in Fig. 2. We write c for the cardinality of the cover relation $\lessdot$ and r for the cardinality of the order relation $\leqslant$. For example, DKE, in general, requires a single key, r items of public information, and one step to derive a key; the scheme requires 51 items of public information for the poset illustrated in Fig. 2. The table states the storage in terms of number of keys and number of operations. For simplicity we omit MKRSA from the comparison, enabling us to assume that all keys have the same length.

Table 3. A comparison of our schemes with existing generic key assignment schemes

Scheme	Private storage				Public storage		Key derivation			
	x	x_{12}	x_{10}	x_9			x	x_{12}	x_{10}	x_9
Trivial	$\|{\downarrow}x\|$	12	7	5	0		0			
DKE	1				r	51	1			
IKE	1				c	14	d	5	4	3
MKIH	$\leqslant w$	4	3	3	0		$\leqslant d$	3	2	2

The MKIH scheme provides a different trade-off from the three existing schemes: users may have multiple keys[8] but no public information is required and key derivation will generally be quicker than for an equivalent IKE scheme.[9]

6   Conclusion

We have shown how to construct a new type of generic key assignment scheme using chain partitions, the inspiration for the original constructions being provided by the problem of enforcing layered access control in scalable multimedia formats. Our schemes, both for layered access control and as generic key assignment schemes, compare favorably with those in the literature.

We have many ideas for future work. Of primary interest is whether we can prove that our schemes are secure against key recovery [13], a more exacting criterion than that of collusion security used in this paper. We also hope to gain some insight, either from a mathematical analysis or through experimental work, into what might be the best choice(s) of chain partition for an arbitrary poset. A third area for potential research is to generalize our constructions to more than two scalable components (most likely using a recursive construction with one of our schemes from Sections 3 and 4 as a base case). Finally, we would like to apply our schemes to access control for geo-spatial data [17], because the policies used are rather similar to those for scalable multimedia formats.

Acknowledgements. The authors would like to thank the anonymous referees for their valuable comments.

---

[8] Schemes with multiple keys were usually disregarded in the early literature [8], although several recent schemes have made use of multiple keys [13,17].

[9] Note that key derivation in our multi-key iterative hash scheme cannot be worse than key derivation in IKE and, in many cases, will be considerably better. As we observed earlier, it would be sensible to choose a chain partition in which all chains have approximately the same length. If this is possible, key derivation is approximately $|X|/w$. The poset in Fig. 2, for example, can be partitioned into 4 chains of length 3. Then any key can be derived in no more than 2 hops, whereas an IKE scheme would require 5 hops to derive $\kappa(x_1)$ from $\kappa(x_{12})$.

References

1. Li, W.: Overview of fine granularity scalability in MPEG-4 video standard. IEEE Transactions on Circuits and Systems for Video Technology 11(3), 301–317 (2001)
2. Christopoulos, C., Skodras, A., Ebrahimi, T.: The JPEG2000 still image coding system: An overview. IEEE Transactions on Consumer Electronics 46(4), 1103–1127 (2000)
3. Zhu, B., Feng, S., Li, S.: An efficient key scheme for layered access control of MPEG-4 FGS video. In: Proceedings of the 2004 IEEE International Conference on Multimedia and Expo., vol. 1, pp. 443–446 (2004)
4. Hashimoto, N., Imaizumi, S., Fujiyoshi, M., Kiya, H.: Hierarchical encryption using short encryption keys for scalable access control of JPEG 2000 coded images. In: Proceedings of the 2008 IEEE International Conference on Image Processing, pp. 3116–3119 (2008)
5. Imaizumi, S., Fujiyoshi, M., Abe, Y., Kiya, H.: Collusion attack-resilient hierarchical encryption of JPEG 2000 codestreams with scalable access control. In: Proceedings of the 2007 IEEE International Conference on Image Processing, vol. 2, pp. 137–140 (2007)
6. Imaizumi, S., Watanabe, O., Fujiyoshi, M., Kiya, H.: Generalized hierarchical encryption of JPEG 2000 codestreams for access control. In: Proceedings of the 2005 IEEE International Conference on Image Processing, vol. 2, pp. 1094–1097 (2005)
7. Crampton, J., Daud, R., Martin, K.: Constructing key assignment schemes from chain partitions. Technical Report RHUL-MA-2010-10, Royal Holloway, University of London (2010),
   http://www.ma.rhul.ac.uk/static/techrep/2010/RHUL-MA-2010-10.pdf
8. Crampton, J., Martin, K., Wild, P.: On key assignment for hierarchical access control. In: Proceedings of 19th Computer Security Foundations Workshop, pp. 98–111 (2006)
9. Davey, B., Priestley, H.: Introduction to Lattices and Order. Cambridge University Press, Cambridge (1990)
10. Katz, J., Lindell, Y.: Introduction to Modern Cryptography. Chapman & Hall/CRC (2007)
11. Bell, D., LaPadula, L.: Secure computer systems: Unified exposition and Multics interpretation. Technical Report MTR-2997, Mitre Corporation, Bedford, Massachusetts (1976)
12. Denning, D.: A lattice model of secure information flow. Communications of the ACM 19(5), 236–243 (1976)
13. Atallah, M., Blanton, M., Fazio, N., Frikken, K.: Dynamic and efficient key management for access hierarchies. ACM Transactions on Information and System Security 12(3), 1–43 (2009)
14. Dilworth, R.: A decomposition theorem for partially ordered sets. Annals of Mathematics 51, 161–166 (1950)
15. Akl, S., Taylor, P.: Cryptographic solution to a problem of access control in a hierarchy. ACM Transactions on Computer Systems 1(3), 239–248 (1983)
16. Atallah, M., Blanton, M., Frikken, K.: Key management for non-tree access hierarchies. In: Proceedings of 11th ACM Symposium on Access Control Models and Technologies, pp. 11–18 (2006)
17. Atallah, M., Blanton, M., Frikken, K.: Efficient techniques for realizing geo-spatial access control. In: Proceedings of the 2007 ACM Symposium on Information, Computer and Communications Security, pp. 82–92 (2007)

ƒQuery: SPARQL Query Rewriting to Enforce Data Confidentiality

Said Oulmakhzoune[1], Nora Cuppens-Boulahia[1],
Frédéric Cuppens[1], and Stephane Morucci[2]

[1] IT/Telecom-Bretagne, 2 Rue de la Chataigneraie, 35576 Cesson Sevigne, France
{said.oulmakhzoune,nora.cuppens,frederic.cuppens}@telecom-bretagne.eu
[2] Swid, 80 Avenue des Buttes de Coësmes, 35700 Rennes, France
stephane.morucci@swid.fr

Abstract. RDF is an increasingly used framework for describing Web resources, including sensitive and confidential resources. In this context, we need an expressive language to query RDF databases. SPARQL has been defined to easily localize and extract data in an RDF graph. Since confidential data are accessed, SPARQL queries must be filtered so that only authorized data are returned with respect to some confidentiality policy. In this paper, we model a confidentiality policy as a set of positive and negative filters (corresponding respectively to permissions and prohibitions) that apply to SPARQL queries. We then define rewriting algorithms that transform the queries so that the results returned by transformed queries are compliant with the confidentiality policy.

1 Introduction

The RDF [1](Resource Definition Framework) data model is based upon the idea of making statements about resources (in particular Web resources) in the form of subject-predicate-object expressions. These expressions are known as triples in RDF terminology. The subject denotes the resource, and the predicate denotes traits or aspects of the resource and expresses a relationship between the subject and the object. For example, one way to represent the proposition "Bob's salary is 60k" in RDF is as the triple: a subject denoting "Bob", a predicate denoting "has salary", and an object denoting "60k". A collection of RDF statements intrinsically represents a labeled, directed multi-graph. As such, an RDF-based data model is more naturally suited to certain kinds of knowledge representation than the relational model and other ontological models traditionally used in computing today.

However, in practice, as more data is being stored in RDF formats, a need has arisen for a simple way to locate specific information. SPARQL [2] (Simple Protocol And RDF Query Language) is a powerful query language which fills that space, making it easy to find the data you need in the RDF graphs. It was standardized by the RDF Data Access Working Group of the World Wide Web Consortium, and is considered a key semantic web technology. A SPARQL query consists of triple patterns, conjunctions, disjunctions, and optional patterns. SPARQL allows users to write globally unambiguous queries. For example,the following query returns names and salaries of all employees.

S. Foresti and S. Jajodia (Eds.): Data and Applications Security XXIV, LNCS 6166, pp. 146–161, 2010.
© IFIP International Federation for Information Processing 2010

```
PREFIX foaf:<http://xmlns.com/foaf/0.1/>
PREFIX emp:<http://tb.eu/employer/0.1/>
SELECT ?name ?salary
WHERE
{
     ?employee rdf:type    emp:Employee.
     ?employee foaf:name    ?name.
     ?employee emp:salary  ?salary.
}
```

Basically, the SPARQL syntax resembles SQL, but the advantage of SPARQL is that it enables queries spanning multiple disparate (local or remote) data sources containing heterogeneous semi-structured data. However, since a SPARQL query may access confidential data, it is necessary to design security mechanisms to control the evaluation of SPARQL queries and prevent these queries from illegally disclosing confidential data.

Our approach is to rewrite the user SPARQL query by adding some SPARQL filters to that query. When, the user sends his or her SPARQL query to the server, our system will intercept this query and checks the security rules corresponding to that user (Figure 1). Then it rewrites the query by adding the corresponding SPARQL filters. The execution result of the rewritten query is returned to the user. The figure 1 illustrates *f*Query, our approach.

In our approach, the answer to the rewritten may differ from the user's initial query. In that case and as suggested in [3], we can check the query validity of the rewritten query with respect to the initial query and notify the user when the query validity is not guaranteed.

The rest of this paper is organized as follows. Section 2 presents the basic principales of rewriting SPARQL query by introducing some examples. Section 3 presents some definition and theorems that are used in other sections. Section 4 defines the security policy model for SPARQL and some of its properties. In section 5, we specify the rewriting query algorithm. Section 6 presents some related works and finally section 7 concludes this paper.

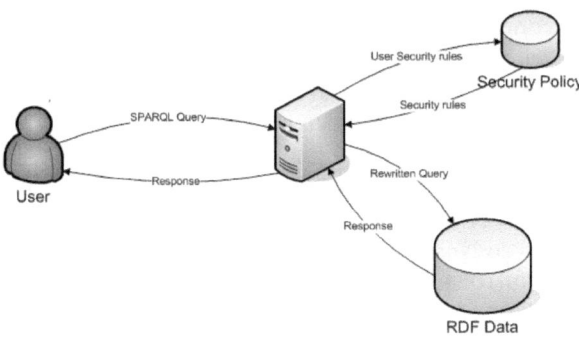

Fig. 1. *f*Query approach

2   Rewriting SPARQL Query: Basic Principles

Let us take an example of query transformation. We assume that the user Bob
tries to select the name and the salary of each employee. We assume also that
Bob is not permitted to see salaries of employees who earn more than 60K.
The table 1 shows Bobs SPARQL query before and after transformation. The
presence of the OPTIONAL construct in the transformed query makes it a non-
conjunctive (disjunctive) one. It means that: if the condition inside the OP-
TIONAL clause is False then the value of the salary variable is assigned to Null.

Table 1. Example of query transformation

Before transformation	After transformation

`SELECT ?name ?salary`
`WHERE`
`{`
`  ?employee rdf:type    emp:Employee.`
`  ?employee foaf:name   ?name.`
`  ?employee emp:salary ?salary.`
`}`
	`SELECT ?name ?salary`
	`WHERE`
	`{`
	`  ?employee rdf:type    emp:Employee.`
	`  ?employee foaf:name   ?name.`
	`  `*`Optional {`*
	`     `*`?employee emp:salary ?salary.`*
	`     `*`Filter(?salary<60000)`*
	`  `*`}`*
	`}`

The access control policy is based on filter definitions. For each user or group
of users, we assign a set of filters. Depending on the policy type, we consider two
different types of filter: (1) Positive filters corresponding to permission and (2)
Negative filters corresponding to prohibition.

Those filters may be associated with a simple condition or an involved condition. The example 5 (section 5.1) illustrates filter associated with a simple
condition. The example 6 (section 5.2) shows an example of filter associated
with an involved condition. Filters associated with involved condition provides
means to protect relationships, as illustrated in the example 6. In our approach
we assume that when a user asks a query, we can get additional information like
the user identity. This additional information may be used in the filter definition
(see the example 6).

Filters actually provide a generic approach to represent an access control
policy for RDF documents which does not rely on a specific language. However,
it would be also interesting to define a user friendly specification language to
express an access control policy for RDF documents. Due to space limitation,
this issue is not addressed in this paper but represent an extension of our work.

3   Notations, Definitions and Theorems

As mentioned in the introduction, an RDF database is represented by a set of triples. So, we denote E as the set of all RDF triples of our database. We denote $E_{subject}$ (respectively $E_{predicate}$,E_{object}) as the projection of E on subject (resp. predicate and object). $E_{subject}$ represents (resp. $E_{predicate}$, E_{object}) the set of all subjects (resp. predicates, objects) of the RDF triples of E.

Definition 1: We define a "condition of RDF triples" as the application ω : $E \rightarrow Boolean$ which associates each RDF triple $x = (s, p, o)$ of E to an element of set $Boolean = \{True, False\}$.

$$\omega : E \rightarrow Boolean, \ x \rightarrow \omega(x)$$

$\omega(x)$ is expressed in terms of s, p and o where $x = (s, p, o)$. We define also the negation of ω denoted $\bar{\omega}$ as follows:

$$\bar{\omega} : E \rightarrow Boolean, \ x \rightarrow \bar{\omega}(x) \text{ such that } (\forall x \in E)\bar{\omega}(x) = \overline{\omega(x)} = \neg(\omega(x))$$

For each element x of E, we say that $\omega(x)$ is satisfied if $\omega(x) = True$. Otherwise we say that $\omega(x)$ is not satisfied.

Definition 2: We define the "simple condition of RDF triples" as the condition of RDF triples that uses the same operators as the SPARQL filter ($regex, bound, =$, $<, > ...$) and constants (see [2] for a complete list of possible operators).

Example 1. $(\forall x = (s, p, o) \in E)\omega(x) = (s \neq$emp:Alice$) \vee ((p =$foaf:name$) \wedge (o \neq$'Alice'$))$

Definition 3: Let tp be a triple pattern of the where clause of a SPARQL query and ω be a condition on RDF triples. We define the projection of ω relative to tp as the condition $\omega(tp)$ expressed in terms of the tp SPARQL variables. We denote that projection as $\pi_{\omega/tp}$, $\pi_{\omega/tp} = \omega(tp)$.

Example 2. Let $x = (s, p, o) \in E$ such that
$\omega(x) = (s \neq$ emp:Alice$) \wedge (p =$foaf:name$) \wedge (s \neq o)$ and $tp = ($emp:Charlie,?m,?n$)$
$\pi_{\omega/tp} = \omega(tp)$
$\pi_{\omega/tp}(?m, ?n) = (?m =$foaf:name$) \wedge (?n \neq$emp:Charlie$)$

We denote constants of conditions of RDF triple Ω_{True} and Ω_{False} applications defined as follows:

$$\Omega_{True} : E \rightarrow Boolean \qquad \Omega_{False} : E \rightarrow Boolean$$
$$x \rightarrow True \qquad\qquad\quad x \rightarrow False$$

Definition 4: Let ω_1 and ω_2 be two conditions on RDF triples. We define the conditions $\omega_1 \wedge \omega_2$ and $\omega_1 \vee \omega_2$ as follows:

$$\omega_1 \wedge \omega_2 : E \rightarrow Boolean \qquad \omega_1 \vee \omega_2 : E \rightarrow Boolean$$
$$x \rightarrow \omega_1(x) \wedge \omega_2(x) \qquad\qquad x \rightarrow \omega_1(x) \vee \omega_2(x)$$

Definition 5: Let ω be a condition on RDF triples. We define the subset of E that satisfies the condition ω, denoted $I(\omega)$, as follows:

$$I(\omega) = \{x \in E| \quad \omega(x) = True\}$$

We define the complement of the set $I(\omega)$ in E, denoted $\overline{I(\omega)}$, as follows:

$$\overline{I(\omega)} = \{x \in E| \quad x \notin I(\omega)\} = E \backslash I(\omega)$$

Theorem 1: Let ω be a condition on RDF triples, $I(\bar{\omega}) = \overline{I(\omega)} = E \backslash I(\omega)$

Proof of theorem 1:
$$x \in I(\bar{\omega}) \iff \{x \in E| \quad \bar{\omega}(x) = True\} \iff \{x \in E| \quad \overline{\omega(x)} = True\}$$
$$\iff \{x \in E| \quad \omega(x) = False\} \iff \{x \in E| \quad x \notin I(\omega)\} \iff x \in \overline{I(\omega)}. \qquad \square$$

Theorem 2: Let ω_1 and ω_2 be two conditions on RDF triples. We have the following properties: $I(\omega_1 \wedge \omega_2) = I(\omega_1) \cap I(\omega_2)$ and $I(\omega_1 \vee \omega_2) = I(\omega_1) \cup I(\omega_2)$

Proof of theorem 2:
$$x \in I(\omega_1 \wedge \omega_2) \iff \omega_1(x) \wedge \omega_2(x) = True$$
$$\iff \omega_1(x) = True \text{ and } \omega_2(x) = True \iff x \in I(\omega_1) \text{ and } x \in I(\omega_2)$$
$$\iff x \in I(\omega_1) \cap I(\omega_2)$$
Then $I(\omega_1 \wedge \omega_2) = I(\omega_1) \cap I(\omega_2)$
With the same reasoning we can prove that $I(\omega_1 \vee \omega_2) = I(\omega_1) \cup I(\omega_2)$.
By induction (recurrence) we can prove the properties bellow. $\qquad \square$

Generalization of the theorem 2: Let $n \in \mathbf{N}^*$ and $\{\omega_i\}_{0 \leq i \leq n}$ be a set of conditions on RDF triples.

$$I(\wedge_{i=0}^n \omega_i) = \cap_{i=0}^n I(\omega_i)$$
$$I(\vee_{i=0}^n \omega_i) = \cup_{i=0}^n I(\omega_i)$$

4   Security Policy

In our proposal we define the security policy as a set of permissions or a set of prohibitions. We also assume that the policy is closed.

4.1   Permission

A security policy rule is defined as the permission for a user to select a set of RDF triples of E that satisfies a condition on RDF triples denoted ω. It means that the user is permitted to select only the RDF triples of the subset $I(\omega)$. We denote this permission as $Permission(\omega)$.

Example 3. Bob is permitted to see the name and email of all employees data stored in the RDF database. This rule can be expressed as the permission to select a set of RDF triples of E that satisfies the condition ω defined as follows:

$$(\forall x = (s, p, o) \in E) \quad \omega(x) = \begin{cases} True & \text{if } p \in P \\ False & \text{if } p \notin P \end{cases}$$

Such that $P = \{\text{foaf:name, foaf:mbox}\}$ is a set of predicates associated with the information name and email.

Let $\{Rule_i\}_{(1 \leq i \leq n)}$ be a set of security rules (permission rules) associated with a user and $\{\omega_i\}_{1 \leq i \leq n}$ be a set of conditions on RDF triples such that $n \in \mathbf{N}^*$ and $Rule_i = Permission(\omega_i)$. So the user could select the RDF triples of each set $I(\omega_i)$. It means that the user could select the RDF triples of the set $\cup_{i=1}^n I(\omega_i)$. According to the result of the theorem 2, the user is permitted to select the RDF triples of $I(\vee_{i=1}^n \omega_i)$. So the user is permitted to select RDF triples that satisfies the condition $\omega = \vee_{i=1}^n \omega_i$. We deduce that:

$$\bigcup_{i=1}^n Permission(\omega_i) = Permission(\bigvee_{i=1}^n \omega_i)$$

It means that a set of permission rules $\{Permission(\omega_i)\}_{1 \leq i \leq n}$ could be expressed as one permission rule defined as the permission to select RDF triples that satisfies the condition $\omega = \vee_{i=1}^n \omega_i$.

4.2   Prohibition

In the case of prohibition we define the security policy rule as the prohibition for a user to select a set of RDF triples of E that satisfies a condition on RDF triples denoted ω. It means that the user is prohibited to select any RDF triples of the subset $I(\omega)$. We denote this prohibition as $Prohibition(\omega)$.

Example 4. Bob is not permitted to select the salary and the birth day of all employees data stored in a RDF database. This rule can be expressed as $Prohibition(\omega)$ such that ω is defined as follows:

$$(\forall x = (s, p, o) \in E) \quad \omega(x) = \begin{cases} True & \text{if } p \in P \\ False & \text{if } p \notin P \end{cases}$$

Such that $P = \{\text{emp:salary, foaf:birthday}\}$ is a set of the predicates associated with the information salary and birth day. So ω could be written as:
$(\forall x = (s, p, o) \in E) \quad \omega(x) = (p =\text{emp:salary}) \vee (p =\text{foaf:birthday})$

With the same reasoning as on the previous section 4.1, we deduce that:

$$\bigcup_{i=1}^n Prohibition(\omega_i) = Prohibition(\bigvee_{i=1}^n \omega_i)$$

Assuming that $\{Prohibition(\omega_i)\}_{1 \leq i \leq n}$ are all security rules associated with a user, we can prove the following result:

$$\bigcup_{i=1}^n Prohibition(\omega_i) = Permission(\bigwedge_{i=1}^n \overline{\omega_i})$$

5 ƒQuery: Our Query Rewriting Model

We rewrite the user query by adding filters and/or removing triples of pattern from the where clause following the associated security policy (see section 5.1). Sometimes it is also necessary to add triples of pattern to the query in order to satisfy the security policy (see section 5.2).

Our query rewriting algorithm treats each BGP [2] (Basic Graph Pattern) of a SPARQL query. Each BGP is handled separately from the others.

5.1 Case of Simple Condition ω

Let Bgp be a basic graph pattern of the where clause of a SPARQL query. We check the security rule associated with the condition ω ($Permission(\omega)$ or $Prohibition(\omega)$) for each triple pattern $tp = (s, p, o)$ of Bgp by calculating the projection $\pi_{\omega/tp}$. There are three cases depending on the $\pi_{\omega/tp}$ value.

Permission case:

- $\pi_{\omega/tp} = \Omega_{True}$
  It means that $\pi_{\omega/tp}$ is always **true** for each SPARQL variable of the triple pattern tp. In this case the triple pattern tp matches with the security policy. So there is no action to do for tp. We check the security condition ω for the next triple pattern.
- $\pi_{\omega/tp} = \Omega_{False}$
  It means that $\pi_{\omega/tp}$ is always **false** for each SPARQL variable of the triple pattern tp. In this case the triple pattern tp does not match with the security policy. So we delete this triple pattern tp from Bgp. Then we check the security condition ω for the next triple pattern.
- Otherwise $\pi_{\omega/tp}$ is expressed in terms of tp variables. In this case, we put tp in an OPTIONAL construct and we add the positive filter φ to it. Then we add this optional construct to Bgp. The positive filter φ is defined as follows:

$$\varphi(tp) = FILTER(\pi_{\omega/tp}) = FILTER(\omega(tp))$$

This filter filters the RDF triples that satisfy the condition ω. The presence of the OPTIONAL construct in the transformed query makes it a non-conjunctive one.

Prohibition case:

- $\pi_{\omega/tp} = \Omega_{True}$
  It means that $\pi_{\omega/tp}$ is always **true** for each SPARQL variable of the triple pattern tp. In this case, RDF triples that match with the triple pattern tp are prohibited. So we delete this triple pattern tp from the basic graph pattern Bgp. Then we check the security condition ω for the next triple pattern.
- $\pi_{\omega/tp} = \Omega_{False}$
  It means that $\pi_{\omega/tp}$ is always **false** for each SPARQL variable of the triple pattern tp. In this case RDF triples that match with the triple pattern tp are allowed to be selected. So there is no action to do for tp. We check the security condition ω for the next triple pattern.

– Otherwise $\pi_{\omega/tp}$ is expressed in terms of tp variables. In this case, we put tp in an OPTIONAL construct and we add the filter φ to it. Then we add this optional construct to Bgp. The filter φ is defined as follows:

$$\varphi(tp) = FILTER(\overline{\pi_{\omega/tp}}) = FILTER(\overline{\omega(tp)})$$

This filter filters the RDF triples that do not satisfy the condition ω.

We define *Algo1*, the query rewriting algorithm for a simple condition and *handleBGP* the related algorithm that handles a basic graph pattern, in the case of a clause "where" with simple condition.

Algorithm 1. Algo1 (Query, ω, ruleType). Query rewriting Algorithm for a simple condition

---
Require: ω is simple condition
  for each basic graph pattern Bgp of Query **do**
    $handleBGP(Bgp, \omega, ruleType)$
  end for

Algorithm 2. handleBGP (Bgp, ω, ruleType)

Require: ω is simple condition
  for each triple pattern tp of Bgp **do**
    if $\pi_{\omega/tp}=\Omega_{True}$ **then**
      if $ruleType = $ PROHIBITION **then**
        delete tp from Bgp
      end if
    else if $\pi_{\omega/tp}=\Omega_{False}$ **then**
      if $ruleType = $ PERMISSION **then**
        delete tp from Bgp
      end if
    else
      create new optional element $opEl$
      move tp to $opEl$
      if $ruleType = $ PERMISSION **then**
        add the filter $FILTER(\pi_{\omega/tp})$ to $opEl$
      else if $ruleType = $ PROHIBITION **then**
        add the filter $FILTER(\overline{\pi_{\omega/tp}})$ to $opEl$
      end if
      add $opEl$ to Bgp
    end if
  end for

Example 5. Bob is not permitted to see salaries of employees who earn more than 50K and their premiums if it is greater than 9K. This prohibition could be expressed as $Prohibition(\omega)$ where ω is defined as: $(\forall x = (s, p, o) \in E)$

$$\omega(x) = ((p = \text{emp:salary}) \wedge (o \geq 50000)) \vee ((p = \text{emp:premium}) \wedge (o \geq 9000))$$

Bob tries to select the name, the salary of each employee and their premium if it is greater than 10K. He executes the following query:

```
SELECT ?name ?salary ?premium
WHERE
{
        ?s1 foaf:name   ?name,
            emp:salary ?salary.
        Optional{
                ?s1 emp:premium ?premium. Filter(?premium > 10000)
            }
}
```

Let $tp_1 = (?s1,\text{foaf:name}, ?name)$ and $tp_2 = (?s1,\text{emp:salary}, ?salary)$ and $tp_3 = (?s1,\text{emp:premium}, 10000)$ be triples of pattern of the where clause of Bob's query. The query has two basic graph patterns $Bgp_1 = \{tp_1, tp_2\}$ and $Bgp_2 = \{tp_3\}$.

We have $\pi_{\omega/tp_1} = \omega(tp_1) = False = \Omega_{False}$
$\pi_{\omega/tp_2} = \omega(tp_2) = (?salary \geq 50000)$
$\pi_{\omega/tp_3} = \omega(tp_3) = (?premium \geq 9000)$
$\pi_{\omega/tp_1} = \Omega_{False}$ so there is nothing to do with the triple pattern tp_1.
$\pi_{\omega/tp_2} = (?salary \geq 50000)$ so we add the filter FILTER($?salary < 50000$) =FILTER($\overline{\pi_{\omega/tp_2}}$) to the Bgp_1.
$\pi_{\omega/tp_3} = (?premium \geq 9000)$ so we add the filter FILTER($?premium < 9000$) to Bgp_2. The rewritten query will be as follows:

```
SELECT ?name ?salary ?premium
WHERE
{
 ?s1 foaf:name   ?name.
 Optional{
        ?s1 emp:salary ?salary.
        FILTER (?salary < 50000)
 }
 Optional{
        Optional{
             ?s1 emp:premium ?premium. Filter(?premium < 9000)
        }
        Filter(?premium > 10000)
 }
}
```

5.2   Case of Involved Condition ω

Definition 6. Before formally defining the concept of involved condition, let us first take an example. Bob is permitted to select the information of the network department employees. The condition ω associated with this rule could be expressed as follows:

$$(\forall x = (s,p,o) \in E)\ \omega(x) = \begin{cases} True & \text{if } (\exists y \in E)|y = (s,\text{emp:dept,'Network'}) \\ False & \text{Otherwise} \end{cases}$$

It means that Bob can select only the RDF triples where the subject has also the predicate emp:dept with the value 'Network'. $\omega(x)$ does not depend only on the RDF triple x but it also depends on another RDF triple y that shares the same subject of x and its predicate is $emp : dept$ with the value 'Network'.

Let $n \in \mathbf{N}^*$, $\{\omega_i\}_{1 \leq i \leq n}$ be a set of simple conditions on RDF triples and $\{p_i\}_{1 \leq i \leq n}$ a set of predicates of $E_{predicate}$. We can generalize the example above by defining the condition ω as follows: $(\forall x = (s, p, o) \in E)$

$$\omega(x) = \begin{cases} True & \text{if } (\exists(x_1, ..., x_n) \in E^n)|(\forall 1 \leq i \leq n)x_i = (s, p_i, o_i) \\ & \text{where } o_i \in E_{object} \text{ and } \omega_i(x_i) = True \\ False & \text{Otherwise} \end{cases}$$

$\omega(x)$ does not depend only on the RDF triple x but it also depends on other RDF triples $(x_1, \cdots, x_n)$ that share the same subject of x and satisfy respectively the simple conditions $(\omega_1, \cdots, \omega_n)$. The condition ω is called the involved condition. In other words, the involved condition for an element x of E is the existence of other properties $\{p_i\}_{1 \leq i \leq n}$ (predicates) of the subject of x and the value of each property p_i satisfies the simple condition ω_i.

In this section, we are interested in this kind of involved condition ω.

Algorithm 2. Let Bgp be a basic graph pattern, $\{s_i\}_{1 \leq i \leq m}$ the set of subjects of the Bgp triple patterns and $\{Gp_i\}_{1 \leq i \leq m}$ a set of group patterns [2] where Gp_i is a set of triple patterns of Bgp which has the same subject s_i. There are two cases to consider: $Permission(\omega)$ and $Prohibition(\omega)$.

Permission case: We handle each Gp_i separately from the others. For each $1 \leq j \leq n$, the subject s_i should have the property p_j such that its value should satisfy the simple condition ω_j. We verify if there exists a triple pattern $tp = (s, p, o)$ of Gp_i which has the property p_j $(p = p_j)$. If this triple exists, then it should satisfy the simple condition ω_j. For this purpose, we add a new SPARQL filter with the condition $\omega_j(tp)$. If there is no triple pattern with the property p_j on Gp_i then we create a new one $tp_{ij} = (s_i, p_j, ?\alpha_j)$ and we add it to Gp_i (where $?\alpha_j$ is a SPARQL variable). tp_{ij} should then satisfy the simple condition ω_j. So we add a new SPARQL filter with the condition $\omega_j(tp_{ij})$.

Prohibition case: In this case we verify for each $1 \leq j \leq n$ if there exists a triple pattern $tp = (s, p, o)$ of Gp_i with the property p_j $(p = p_j)$. If this pattern exists, then there are two cases. If its value 'o' is a SPARQL variable then it should not satisfy the condition ω_j or it should be unbound (i.e. s_i does not have the property p_j). In this case we add a new SPARQL filter with the condition $(\overline{\omega_j(tp)} \vee !bound(o))$. Otherwise, the value 'o' could not be unbound, then the triple pattern tp should not satisfy ω_j. In this case we add a new filter with the condition $\overline{\omega_j(tp)}$.

Now if there is no triple pattern with the property p_j on Gp_i, then we create a new one $tp_{ij} = (s_i, p_j, ?\alpha_j)$ and we add it to Gp_i. So tp_{ij} should not satisfy the condition ω_j or it should be unbound. In this case we add a new SPARQL filter with the condition $(\overline{\omega_j(tp_{ij})} \vee !bound(?\alpha_j)$. The expression $bound(variable)$ returns true if $'variable'$ is bound to a value. It returns false otherwise [2].

Algorithm 3. Algo2 (Query, ω, ruleType). Query rewriting Algorithm for an involved condition

---

Require: ω is an involved condition
  for each basic graph pattern Bgp of Query **do**
    Let $\{s_i\}_{1 \leq i \leq m}$ bea set of the subjects of the triples pattern of Bgp
    for each subject s_i **do**
      Let Gp_i be a set of triple pattern of Bgp with the same subject s_i
      $handle\,BGP(Bgp, Gp_i, \omega, ruleType)$
    end for
  end for

Example 6. Bob is a doctor and he can see only the information of his patients. The involved condition assigned (in the case of permission) to Bod could be expressed as:

$$(\forall x = (s,p,o) \in E) \; \omega(x) = \begin{cases} True & \text{if } (\exists y \in E)|y = (s,\text{pat:doctor},\$Bob\_id) \\ False & \text{Otherwise} \end{cases}$$

where \$Bob_id is the identifier of Bob. Bob tries to select names and locations of all patients. The table 2 shows Bob's query before and after transformation.

Table 2. Bob's query transformation

Before transformation	After transformation

`SELECT ?name ?location`
`WHERE`
`{`
    `?p rdf:type      pat:Patient.`
    `?p foaf:name     ?name.`
    `?p pat:location ?location.`
`}`
	`SELECT ?name ?location`
	`WHERE`
	`{`
	    `?p rdf:type      pat:Patient.`
	    `?p foaf:name     ?name.`
	    `?p pat:location ?location.`
	    `?p pat:doctor    ?doct.`
	    `Filter(?doct=Bob_id)`
	`}`

5.3   Composition of Simple and Involved Conditions

Let **Algo** be a rewriting query algorithm which takes a query Q as inputs, condition ω and type of security rule (permission, prohibition) and returns a new query Q'. In the case of a permission rule, the execution result of the query Q', denoted RQ', is composed of elements of $I(\omega)$, i.e. the execution result of Q' satisfies the condition ω. If we suppose that RQ is the execution result of Q, then $RQ' = RQ \cap I(\omega)$ (Figure 2-A). In the case of prohibition rule, the execution result of the query Q' is composed of elements of $\overline{I(\omega)} = E \backslash I(\omega)$, i.e. $RQ' = RQ \cap \overline{I(\omega)} = RQ \backslash I(\omega)$ (Figure 2-B).

Algorithm 4. handleBGP (Bgp, Gp, ω, ruleType)

Require: ω is an involved condition, Gp is set of triples pattern of Bgp with same
    subject s
    $\{\omega_j\}_{1 \leq i \leq n}$ a set of simple condition associated to ω
    $\{p_j\}_{1 \leq i \leq n}$ a set of predicates associated to ω
    for $j = 1$ to n **do**
      if $\exists tp = (s, p, o) \in Gp|\quad p = p_j$ **then**
        for each $tp = (s, p, o) \in Gp|\quad p = p_j$ **do**
          if *ruleType*= PERMISSION **then**
            add $FILTER(\pi_{\omega_j/tp})$ to Bgp
          else if *ruleType*= PROHIBITION **then**
            if o is SPARQL variable **then**
               add $FILTER(\overline{\pi_{\omega_j/tp}}\vee!bound(o))$ to Bgp
            else
               add $FILTER(\overline{\pi_{\omega_j/tp}})$ to Bgp
            end if
          end if
        end for
      else
        let $tp_j = (s, p_j, ?\alpha_j)$ be a triple of pattern
        add tp_j to Gp
        if *ruleType*= PERMISSION **then**
          add $FILTER(\pi_{\omega_j/tp_j})$ to Bgp
        else if *ruleType*= PROHIBITION **then**
          add $FILTER(\overline{\pi_{\omega_j/tp_j}}\vee!bound(?\alpha_j))$ to Bgp
        end if
      end if
    end for

Composition in the Case of Permission. Let ω_1 be a simple condition, ω_2 be an involved condition, ω the condition $\omega_1 \wedge \omega_2$ and ω' the condition $\omega_1 \vee \omega_2$. Let $Algo_1$ and $Algo_2$ be respectively the rewriting query algorithms of the simple conditions and involved conditions. Let Q, Q_1 and Q_2 be SPARQL queries, RQ, RQ_1 and RQ_2 be respectively the execution result of Q, Q_1 and Q_2 such that $Q_1 = Algo_1(Q, \omega_1, permission)$ and $Q_2 = Algo_2(Q_1, \omega_2, permission)$.

Logical AND: $\omega = \omega_1 \wedge \omega_2$ (Figure 3-A)
We have $RQ_2 = RQ_1 \cap I(\omega_2)$ and $RQ_1 = RQ \cap I(\omega_1)$ then $RQ_2 = RQ \cap I(\omega_1) \cap I(\omega_2)$. According to the result of theorem 2 we deduce that $RQ_2 = RQ \cap I(\omega_1 \wedge \omega_2) = RQ \cap I(\omega)$.

    Thus we can use $Algo_1$ and $Algo_2$ to rewrite the query Q in order to satisfy the security rule $Permission(\omega) = Permission(\omega_1 \vee \omega_2)$. The rewriting query algorithm corresponding to this case is defined as follows:

$$Algo(Q, \omega_1 \wedge \omega_2, permission) = Algo_2(Algo_1(Q, \omega_1, permission), \omega_2, permission)$$

Example 7. Bob is permitted to select salaries of the network department employees. This rule could be expressed as $Permission(\omega) = Permission(\omega_1 \vee \omega_2)$

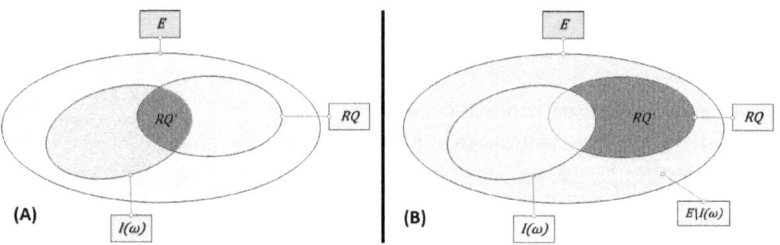

Fig. 2. (A) Permission case. (B) Prohibition case.

where: $\forall x = (s, p, o) \in E \ \omega_1(x) = (p = \text{emp:salary})$

$$\omega_2(x) = \begin{cases} True & \text{if } (\exists y \in E)|y = (s,\text{emp:dept}, \text{'Network'}) \\ False & \text{Otherwise} \end{cases}$$

Logical OR: $\omega = \omega_1 \vee \omega_2$ (Figure 3-B)
Let Q'_1 and Q'_2 be SPARQL queries, RQ'_1 and RQ'_2 be respectively the execution result of Q'_1 and Q'_2 such that $Q'_1 = Algo_1(Q, \omega_1, permission)$ and $Q'_2 = Algo_2(Q, \omega_2, permission)$.
We have $RQ'_2 = RQ \cap I(\omega_2)$ and $RQ'_1 = RQ \cap I(\omega_1)$ then $RQ'_1 \cup RQ'_2 = (RQ \cap I(\omega_1)) \cup (RQ \cap I(\omega_2)) = RQ \cap (RQ'_1 \cup RQ'_2)$.
So $RQ'_1 \cup RQ'_2 = RQ \cap I(\omega_1 \vee \omega_2)$.

We deduce that the rewriting query Q_{final} corresponding to $Permission(\omega')$ $= Permission(\omega_1 \vee \omega_2)$ is the union of the queries Q'_1 and Q'_2. So we can write $Q_{final} = Q'_1 \cup Q'_2$ as well as

$$Algo(Q, \omega_1 \vee \omega_2, permission) = Algo_1(Q, \omega_1, permission) \bigcup Algo_2(Q, \omega_2, permission)$$

Example 8. Bob is permitted to select the employees salaries. He is also permitted to select all the information of the network department employees. This rule could be expressed as $Permission(\omega) = Permission(\omega_1 \vee \omega_2)$ where: $\forall x = (s, p, o) \in E$, $\omega_1(x) = (p = \text{emp:salary})$

$$\omega_2(x) = \begin{cases} True & \text{if } (\exists y \in E)|y = (s,\text{emp:dept}, \text{'Network'}) \\ False & \text{Otherwise} \end{cases}$$

Composition in the Case of Prohibition. Let ω_1 be a simple condition, ω_2 be an involved condition. Let $Algo_1$ and $Algo_2$ be respectively the rewriting query algorithms of the simple condition and the involved condition. We use the same reasoning as in the previous section and by applying De Morgan's laws for sets, we obtain the following results:

Logical AND: $\omega = \omega_1 \wedge \omega_2$ (Figure 3-C)

$$Algo(Q, \omega_1 \wedge \omega_2, permission) = Algo_1(Q, \omega_1, permission) \bigcup Algo_2(Q, \omega_2, permission)$$

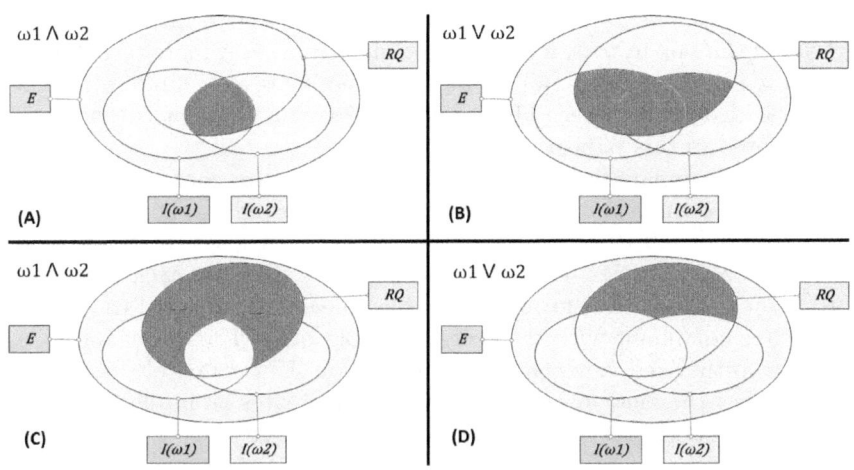

Fig. 3. (A) and (B) Permission case. (C) and (D) Prohibition case.

Logical OR: $\omega = \omega_1 \vee \omega_2$ (Figure 3-D)

$$Algo(Q, \omega_1 \vee \omega_2, permission) = Algo_2(Algo_1(Q, \omega_1, permission), \omega_2, permission)$$

6 Related Works

SPARQL is a recent query language. Even if there is a clear need to protect SPARQL queries, there is still no proposal to define an approach to evaluate SPARQL with respect to an access control policy.

If we now compare the approach suggested in this paper with SQL, we can observe that SQL security is based on view definitions. Using GRANT and RE-VOKE operators, one can specify which views a given user (or user role) is permitted to access. Transformation to apply security rules in SQL is based on a mechanism called view expansion. This mechanism is similar to macro expansion and consists in replacing a view by its definition when the query is evaluated. Thus, the initial query must only use authorized views, else the query is rejected.

An interesting variant to transform SQL queries was suggested by Oracle with its VPD [4] (Virtual Private Database) mechanism. In this case, the security policy is specified through the definition of predicates in PL-SQL that will apply as filters to transform the query. The general idea is similar to the one presented in this paper but the approach suggested by Oracle requires to know PL-SQL in order to implement the access control policy. This may lead to security policies complex to define and maintain.

Another interesting work was suggested by Stonebraker [5]. In this case, the query transformation is specified by adding conditions to qualification portion of the original query. The general idea is also similar to ours but the approach suggested by Stonebraker assumes that a similar mechanism would apply for *insert* and *update* operators, which is not generally true. A more recent approach was proposed by Wang et al. [6] where the objective is to securely maximize the answer provided to the user. This would represent a relevant extension to the work presented in this paper.

We can also compare our proposal with approaches to control access to XML documents. Two main approaches have been suggested in the literature: view materialization [7,8,9,10,11,12] and query transformation [13]. Most proposals are actually based on view materialization. In this case, for each user, the base of XML documents is transformed to extract the sub-part called the authorized view which is compliant with the access control policy. The query is then evaluated on the authorized view without modification. Unfortunately, it is generally considered that the view materialization process creates an intolerable overhead with respect to performance. Thus, more recent proposals suggest using query transformation, see for instance [13] that shows how to transform XPath queries.

However, there is a main difference between RDF and SPARQL: XML documents correspond to oriented graphs. As noticed in [12], this may lead to complication to protect some relationships in an XML document. This issue has been addressed using two different approaches: In [13], protection of XML relationships is embedded in document transformation whereas [12] suggests specifying access control policies using the concept of blocks in order to break some relationships that must be protected. We have no similar problems with RDF (or relational database). In our approach, every relationship may be protected using an involved condition filter.

7 Conclusion and Future Works

In this paper, we have defined an approach to protect SPARQL queries using query transformation. It is a generic approach to specify and apply an access control policy to protect RDF documents. An access control policy is modelled as a set of filters. A filter may be associated with a simple condition or an involved condition. Involved conditions provide means to protect relationships. In this paper, we consider two different types of filter: Positive filters corresponding to permission and negative filters corresponding to prohibition.

There are several possible extensions to this work. First, we only consider in this paper the case of *select* queries. There are some recent proposals to extend SPARQL to specify queries for updating RDF documents. Thus, an interesting extension of our work would be to also consider how to transform update queries with respect to an access control policy.

Second, in this paper, the access control policy is specified through a set of filters. This provides a generic approach to represent an access control policy for RDF documents which does not rely on a specific language. However and as suggested in section 2, a possible extension would be to define a user friendly specification language to express such an access control policy. For this purpose, a possible research direction would be to derive the filter definition from the specification of an access control policy based on RBAC [14] or OrBAC [15].

Finally, in the near future we intend to integrate other security related transformations in the policy specification, for instance anonymisation. Also we need to integrate our approach into service composition management.

References

1. Klyne, G., Carroll, J.: Resource description framework (rdf): Concepts and abstract syntax, http://www.w3.org/TR/2004/REC-rdf-concepts-20040210/
2. Prud Hommeaux, E., Seaborne, A.: Sparql query language for rdf (January 2008), http://www.w3.org/TR/rdf-sparql-query/
3. Rizvi, S., Mendelzon, A., Sudarshan, S., Roy, P.: Extending query rewriting techniques for fine-grained access control. In: Proc. ACM Sigmod Conf. (June 2004)
4. Huey, P.: Oracle database security guide: Ch. 7, using oracle virtual private database to control data access, http://download.oracle.com/docs/cd/E11882_01/network.112/e10574.pdf
5. Stonebraker, M., Wong, E.: Access control in a relational data base management system by query modification. In: Proceedings of the 1974 annual conference, June 1974, pp. 180–186 (1974)
6. Wang, Q., Yu, T., Li, N., Lobo, J., Bertino, E., Irwin, K., Byun, J.: On the correctness criteria of fine-grained access control in relational databases. In: Proceedings of the 33rd international conference on Very large data bases (September 2007)
7. Damiani, E., De Capitani di Vimercati, S., Paraboschi, S., Samarati, P.: A fine-grained access control system for xml documents. ACM Trans. Inf. Syst. Secur. 5(2), 169–202 (2002)
8. Gabillon, A.: A formal access control model for xml databases. In: Proc. Of the 2005 VLDB Workshop on Secure Data Management, SDM (2005)
9. Finance, B., Medjdoub, S., Pucheral, P.: The case for access control on xml relationships. In: Proc. of CIKM (2005)
10. Kudo, M., Hada, S.: Xml document security based on provisional authorization. In: Proc. of ACM CCS (2000)
11. Stoica, A., Farkas, C.: Secure xml views. In: Proc. of the 16th IFIP WG11.3 Working Conference on Database and Application Security (2002)
12. Cuppens, F., Cuppens-Boulahia, N., Sans, T.: Protection of relationships in xml documents with the xml-bb model. In: Jajodia, S., Mazumdar, C. (eds.) ICISS 2005. LNCS, vol. 3803, pp. 148–163. Springer, Heidelberg (2005)
13. Damiani, E., Fansi, M., Gabillon, A., Marrara, S.: A general approach to securely querying xml. In: Proc. of the 5th International Workshop on Security in Information Systems, WOSIS 2007 (2007)
14. Ferraiolo, D.F., Sandhu, R., Gavrila, S., Kuhn, D.R., Chandramouli, R.: Proposed NIST Standard for Role-Based Access Control. ACM Transactions on Information and Systems Security (TISSEC) 4(3) (2001)
15. Abou El Kalam, A., El Baida, R., Balbiani, P., Benferhat, S., Cuppens, F., Deswarte, Y., Miège, A., Saurel, C., Trouessin, G.: Organization Based Access Control. In: 8th IEEE International Workshop on Policies for Distributed Systems and Networks (POLICY 2003), Lake Como, Italy (June 2003)

Efficient Inference Control for Open Relational Queries

Joachim Biskup[1], Sven Hartmann[2], Sebastian Link[3],
and Jan-Hendrik Lochner[1]

[1] Fakultät für Informatik, TU Dortmund, D-44221 Dortmund, Germany
{biskup,lochner}@ls6.cs.tu-dortmund.de
[2] Institut für Informatik, Technische Universität Clausthal, Germany
sven.hartmann@tu-clausthal.de
[3] School of Information Management, Victoria University of Wellington, New Zealand
sebastian.link@vuw.ac.nz

Abstract. We present a control mechanism for preserving confidentiality in relational databases under open queries. This mechanism is based on a reduction of costly inference control to efficient access control that has recently been developed for closed database queries. Our approach guarantees that secrets being declared in form of a confidentiality policy are not disclosed to database users even if they utilize their a priori knowledge to draw inferences. It turns out that there is no straightforward transition from the approach for closed queries to open queries. We show, however, that hiding the confidentiality policy from database users is sufficient to preserve confidentiality. Moreover, we propose an algorithmic implementation of the control mechanism.

1 Introduction

In our modern information society, individuals disseminate personal information over various channels. In the sense of informational self-determination, one should be able to freely decide which information to reveal, but in fact it is hardly possible to foresee all consequences of a revealed piece of information. Thus it seems more appropriate for an individual to declare which information should *not* be disclosed to other individuals.

In the context of relational databases (potentially carrying lots of personal information), the goal of *confidentiality preservation* can be enforced by suitable mechanisms based on confidentiality policies declaring the information that should not be disclosed to other database users. Besides confidentiality, however, availability of information is another important security goal: a database can only be productively employed by a user if it delivers all information needed to complete the user's task. This apparently leads to a tradeoff between confidentiality and availability.

Another aspect to be pointed out is the notion of information. Where *data* are merely uninterpreted (not application-oriented) constants, *information* is usually gained by adding semantics to data. For instance, data from a relational

S. Foresti and S. Jajodia (Eds.): Data and Applications Security XXIV, LNCS 6166, pp. 162–176, 2010.

database can be combined with semantic constraints in order to deduce information. Consider a relational database system maintaining the account data of a bank; with the semantic constraint that account numbers are unique within the bank, a database user learns the balance of an account holder when first asking for the account number of this client and then asking for the balance of the account with the number returned. Here, the combination of account holder and balance is deduced information from the two query results and the semantic constraint.

Controlled Query Evaluation (CQE) is an effective inference control mechanism for protecting information as declared by a suitable confidentiality policy in logic-oriented information systems. Such a policy consists of logical sentences, called secrets, which the user must not know if they are true in the actual database instance. For closed database queries, CQE checks whether the true answer (or, in some cases, also the negated answer) to a query together with the a priori knowledge of the querying user allows for the disclosure of information being protected by the policy; if so, the answer is modified, either by lying (i. e., returning the negated answer) or by refusing the answer, or by a combination of both. CQE primarily aims at preserving confidentiality of the declared secrets but also ensures availability of information when confidentiality is guaranteed.

Regarding efficiency, CQE suffers from two problems. First, it relies on the implication decision in first-order logic (being undecidable in general): each decision whether a (closed) query may be answered correctly corresponds to the decision whether a set of logical sentences implies a secret. Second, CQE has to maintain a growing log file of the assumed user knowledge. This leads to high time and space complexity, respectively. To overcome these drawbacks, a static form of CQE has been developed reducing the expensive implication decision to a pattern matching problem and abandoning the log file while keeping up confidentiality preservation.

Being originally developed for closed database queries, in this work we extend static CQE to open queries. A closed query does not contain free variables and can thus be answered by either *true* or *false*. In contrast, an open query contains free variables and the evaluation is the set of variable substitutions making the query true in the database instance. Considering open queries is an important step in enhancing our query language since most practical database queries are open ones. Being confined to closed queries usually requires that a database user already has certain knowledge about the content of the database whereas open queries provide a higher degree of freedom in terms of expressiveness: Consider a database that maintains the names of the account holders of a bank and their balances. A user being confined to closed queries can only determine the balance of an account holder by asking for different balances until the correct value has been guessed. With open queries, however, this balance information can be retrieved in one simple step.

After an overview of related work in Sect. 2, in Sect. 3 we recall some database concepts and sketch previous results for static CQE for closed relational database queries. In Sect. 4 we show that these results cannot be extended straightforwardly to open queries; we propose a new control mechanism for open queries and prove it confidentiality preserving. In Sect. 5 we develop an algorithm for this control mechanism. Sect. 6 concludes the paper and gives perspectives for future research.

2   Related Work

Early approaches to security in relational databases mainly focused on discretionary access control (DAC), either by granting privileges to database users with data annotated by the respective access rights (see, e. g., [19]), or by modifying user queries in order to enforce a discretionarily declared security policy (see, e. g., [26]). Later, the concept of mandatory access control (MAC) was developed and deployed in various approaches. Instead of attaching access control information directly to the data (as DAC does), in MAC system-wide security policies are enforced on the basis of security models (see, e. g., [24]). (Relational) databases implementing MAC are also called "multilevel secure" (MLS) and make use of techniques like polyinstantiation; see, e. g., [22,21,14,23,18]. Moreover, e. g. in [22,2,13], comprehensive systems have been proposed that integrate DAC and/or MAC into the different stages of database design.

Beyond traditional access control, inference control mechanisms have been proposed to prevent unwanted flows of information. Information emerges from the answers to database queries by, e. g., additionally taking database constraints or common sense knowledge into account. An overview of the inference problem in different areas can be found, e. g., in [17]. Prevention of inferences in relational and MLS databases have been investigated, e. g., in [27,16,20,15,12].

Being initially proposed in [11,25] the ideas of protecting information in logical databases according to security policies by lying and/or refusing to answer have been elaborated in [6,4,7] under the notion of *Controlled Query Evaluation*. This technique was extended for relational databases in [5] and optimized for specific conditions in [8,10].

3   Preliminaries

3.1   Relational Databases and Open Queries

A *relation schema* $RS = \langle R, \mathcal{U}, \Sigma \rangle$ describes the structure of a relation in a relational database. R is the *relation symbol*, $\mathcal{U}$ is a finite set of *attributes* with $|\mathcal{U}| = n$, and Σ is a finite set of *semantic constraints* on $\mathcal{U}$ which we assume to be a minimal cover (see [1]) of functional dependencies – the most prevalent kind of local constraints in actual relational databases.

An *instance* r of a relation schema is a finite Herbrand interpretation of the schema satisfying Σ and considering R as a predicate. The values c_i of a *tuple* $\mu = R(c_1, \ldots, c_n)$ are elements of an infinite set of constants *Const* and the value of an attribute A in a tuple μ is referred to by $\mu[A]$. With $\models_M$ we denote the satisfaction relation between an interpretation and a formula, so if μ is element of r, we write $r \models_M \mu$.

Let $\mathcal{A}, \mathcal{B} \subseteq \mathcal{U}$, then r satisfies the *functional dependency (FD)* $\mathcal{A} \to \mathcal{B}$ if for any two tuples μ_1, μ_2 of r it holds that $\mu_1[B] = \mu_2[B]$ for every $B \in \mathcal{B}$ whenever $\mu_1[A] = \mu_2[A]$ for every $A \in \mathcal{A}$. $\mathcal{K} \subseteq \mathcal{U}$ is a *key* of RS if $\mathcal{K} \to \mathcal{U}$ is logically implied by Σ and $\mathcal{K}$ is minimal with this property. RS is in *Boyce-Codd normal form (BCNF)* if for each FD $\mathcal{A} \to \mathcal{B}$, logically implied by Σ and with $\mathcal{B} \not\subseteq \mathcal{A}$, $\mathcal{A}$ is a superset of a key. We assume single-relation databases (with schema $\langle R, \mathcal{U}, \Sigma \rangle$ and instance r unless otherwise stated), leaving inter-relational considerations for future research.

Database queries are expressed in a fragment of the relational calculus. Let *Var* be a set of variables, then the *query language* $\mathcal{L}_q$ is the set of formulas of the form $(\exists X_1) \ldots (\exists X_l) R(v_1, \ldots, v_n)$ with $0 \leq l \leq n$, $X_i \in Var$, $v_i \in Const \cup Var$, $\{X_1, \ldots, X_l\} \subseteq \{v_1, \ldots, v_n\}$, and $v_i \neq v_j$ if $v_i, v_j \in Var$ and $i \neq j$. If $\{v_1, \ldots, v_n\} \cap Var = \{X_1, \ldots, X_l\}$ for a query from $\mathcal{L}_q$, then it is *closed*; if there are free variables in the query, $(\{v_1, \ldots, v_n\} \cap Var) \backslash \{X_1, \ldots, X_l\} \neq \emptyset$, then it is *open*. We denote queries by $\Phi(V)$ where V is the vector of the free variables in Φ. When convenient we omit the variable vector V (if V is empty or not important in the context). With $\mathcal{L}_q^c$ we denote the language containing exactly the closed queries from $\mathcal{L}_q$.

With $sel(\Phi(V)) \subseteq \mathcal{U}$ we denote the set of attributes for which a constant appears in $\Phi(V)$. Since a closed query $\Phi(V) \in \mathcal{L}_q^c$ corresponds to a projection of a tuple to $sel(\Phi(V))$ we refer to formulas from $\mathcal{L}_q^c$ as *select-project-queries*. The assignment of attribute A in $\Phi(V)$ is denoted by $\Phi(V)[A]$ $(\in Const \cup Var)$. In the following we assume a single user sending queries to the database and call him "the user" for short.

3.2   Controlled Query Evaluation

The *ordinary evaluation* of a closed query Φ in an instance r is defined by $eval^*(\Phi)(r) := \mathtt{if}\ r \models_M \Phi\ \mathtt{then}\ \Phi\ \mathtt{else}\ \neg\Phi$. An open query $\Phi(V)$ is evaluated by replacing the free variables V with constants c such that the resulting (closed) sentence is true in r:

$$eval^*(\Phi(V))(r) = \{\Phi(c) \mid c \in Const \times \cdots \times Const \text{ and } r \models_M \Phi(c)\}.$$

Note that the evaluation of an open query always implies a negative part: a variable assignment c' makes $\Phi(V)$ *false* in the database instance if $\Phi(c')$ does *not* occur in $eval^*(\Phi(V))(r)$.

Controlled Query Evaluation (CQE) deviates from the ordinary evaluation if any of the previously declared potential secrets is going to be disclosed to the user. A *potential secret* Ψ is a sentence of a policy language $\mathcal{L}_{ps}$ being a fragment of a suitable logic as discussed in [4]. The user may learn that Ψ is false in the instance r; if, however, Ψ is true in r, then this information must be kept secret. The *confidentiality policy* (or "policy" for short) is a finite set *pol*, consisting of potential secrets. From a security perspective it is desirable to reach preservation of confidentiality even if the user knows the policy. However, this cannot always be guaranteed which justifies the option of hiding the policy, so it may be *known* or *unknown* to the user. We assume the policy language to be the set of (closed) select-project-queries over the relation R, i. e., $\mathscr{L}_{ps} = \mathscr{L}_q^c$. Finally, the user is supposed to be aware of the semantic constraints of the database being expressed by the set Σ of the relation schema RS.[1] We thus initially set the *user knowledge*, consisting of sentences that are true in r and that the user is supposed to be aware of, to $log_0 = \Sigma$.

For closed queries, CQE with potential secrets enforced by *refusal* has been defined, depending on the *user awareness a* regarding the policy ($a = known$ or $a = unknown$), by $cqe^a(Q, log_0)(r, pol) := \langle (ans_1, log_1), (ans_2, log_2), \ldots \rangle$ for a sequence $Q = \langle \Phi_1, \Phi_2, \ldots \rangle$ of closed queries. It uses a *censor function* to determine the returned answers ans_i (with mum denoting a refusal) and the updated user knowledges log_i. The censor inspects whether the true or the negated answer to a query would enable the user to infer a potential secret (in the case of an unknown policy only true potential secrets are considered).[2] If so, the answer is refused and the user knowledge does not change. Otherwise, the answer is given honestly and the user knowledge is updated with this answer. We recall the definitions from [4] amended by the "improved refusal"[3] result from [7]:

$$censor^{known}(pol, log, \Phi, r) := (\text{exists } \Psi)(\Psi \in pol \text{ and}$$
$$(log \cup \{eval^*(\Phi)(r)\} \models \Psi \text{ or } log \cup \{\neg eval^*(\Phi)(r)\} \models \Psi))$$
$$censor^{unknown}(pol, log, \Phi, r) := (\text{exists } \Psi)(\Psi \in pol \text{ and}$$
$$r \models_M \Psi \text{ and } log \cup \{eval^*(\Phi)(r)\} \models \Psi)$$
$$ans_i := \text{if } log_{i-1} \models eval^*(\Phi_i)(r) \text{ then } eval^*(\Phi_i)(r) \text{ else}$$
$$\quad \text{if } censor^a(pol, log_{i-1}, \Phi_i, r) \text{ then mum else } eval^*(\Phi_i)(r)$$
$$log_i := \text{if } log_{i-1} \models eval^*(\Phi_i)(r) \text{ or } censor^a(pol, log_{i-1}, \Phi_i, r)$$
$$\quad \text{then } log_{i-1} \text{ else } log_{i-1} \cup \{eval^*(\Phi_i)(r)\}$$

To model "correct" and "harmless" user knowledge we assume $r \models_M log_0$ and we require each instance-policy-pair (r, pol) to satisfy a precondition depending on the user awareness: if $a = known$ the precondition for (r, pol) is $log_0 \not\models \Psi$, for every $\Psi \in pol$; if $a = unknown$ the precondition is if $r \models_M \Psi$ then $log_0 \not\models \Psi$, for every $\Psi \in pol$. According to [4] the CQE cqe^a preserves confidentiality in the sense of the following definition:

Definition 1. *A CQE is* confidentiality preserving *for a policy pol if for every finite prefix Q' of a sequence Q of queries the following holds: For every $\Psi \in pol$ and for every instance r (with (r, pol) satisfying the precondition) there exists an instance r' and a policy pol' (with (r', pol') satisfying the precondition) with*
   (1) (r', pol') leads to the same answers for Q' as (r, pol);
   (2) $eval^*(\Psi)(r') = \neg\Psi$;
   (3) if $a = known$: $pol' = pol$.

---

[1] These semantic constraints may reflect business rules the user is aware of.
[2] Inspecting the negated answer is necessary to avoid meta-inferences [6].
[3] If the user already knows the answer to his query, the censor is bypassed.

A CQE is confidentiality preserving *if it is confidentiality preserving for all possible policies.*

Example 1. Consider the schema $\langle BANK, \mathcal{U}, \Sigma \rangle$ of a bank database with $\mathcal{U} = \{acc\_no, acc\_holder\}$, $\Sigma = \emptyset$, and the known policy $pol = \{\Psi\}$ with $\Psi \equiv (\exists X_N) BANK(X_N, \text{Smith})$, protecting that Smith has an account at the bank. The instance *bank* of *BANK* and a query Φ_1 are given by *bank* = $\{BANK(123, \text{Smith}), BANK(456, \text{Jones})\}$ and $\Phi_1 \equiv BANK(123, \text{Smith})$. Since $eval^*(\Phi_1)(bank) = \Phi_1$ and $\Phi_1 \models \Psi$ we get $censor^{known} = true$ and thus $cqe^{known}(\langle \Phi_1 \rangle, log_0)(bank, pol) = \langle (\text{mum}, log_0) \rangle$.

For convenience, we consider closed queries as specific open queries without free variables in the following. Consequently, the evaluation of a closed query Φ will be $\{\Phi\}$ (if $r \models_M \Phi$) or $\emptyset$ (if $r \not\models_M \Phi$), respectively.

3.3   Static CQE for Closed Queries

In previous work we investigated static forms of CQE for closed database queries. In this context "static" means that we proposed suitable restrictions regarding query and policy languages as well as schema constraints to avoid the costly inference control mechanism and the ever growing log file. In the following we shortly summarize our contributions.

In [9] we considered a simple query language only allowing for select-queries in combination with a policy language being equivalent to the query language $\mathscr{L}_q^c$ introduced in Subsect. 3.1. It turned out that no further schema restrictions are necessary when confining the user and the security administrator to these languages. We showed that the declarative goals of inference control (as in Def. 1) can be reached by applying a simple pattern matching algorithm to the single queries.

When relaxing the query language such that select-project-queries can be expressed we had to impose certain restrictions as elaborated in [8]. Basically, the relation schema must be in *object normal form (ONF)*, i.e., it must be in BCNF and have a unique key [3] (an assumption that occurs frequently in practice), and potential secrets must adhere to a syntactic constraint to still guarantee preservation of confidentiality.

In [10] we refined the results of [8]. We found conditions for using logical connectives in query and policy languages and we relaxed the syntactic constraint for potential secrets. Since we refer to this constraint in the following section we recall the definition from [10]:

Definition 2. *Let $RS = \langle R, \mathcal{U}, \Sigma \rangle$ be a relation schema in ONF with Σ being a minimal cover of FDs. The left-hand side of an FD $\sigma \in \Sigma$ is denoted by $lhs(\sigma)$. The set of fact schemas of RS is then defined by*

$$fs(RS) = \{\mathcal{A} \mid \mathcal{A} \in \mathcal{U}\} \cup \{\mathcal{A} \mid \text{exists } \sigma \in \Sigma : \mathcal{A} \subseteq lhs(\sigma)\} \cup$$
$$\{\mathcal{AB} \mid \text{exists } \sigma \in \Sigma \text{ with } \mathcal{A} \subseteq lhs(\sigma) \text{ and } \mathcal{B} \in \mathcal{U} \backslash lhs(\sigma)\}.$$

4   Static Controlled Evaluation of Open Queries

Several CQE approaches to open queries have been proposed by Biskup and Bonatti [5] for the enforcement methods of lying and refusal. Although being effectively computable due to suitable syntactic restrictions, these approaches still suffer from high computational complexity and the need of a log file. Our goal is the development of a static CQE for open queries with refusal as enforcement method. We only consider policies $pol \subseteq \mathscr{L}_{ps}$ satisfying $sel(\Psi) \in fs(RS)$ for each $\Psi \in pol$ and assume for Subsect. 4.1 and 4.2 that pol is known to the user.

4.1   A First Approach

As described in Subsect. 3.2, the ordinary evaluation of an open query yields a set of sentences being true in the database instance. Consequently, the original form of static CQE cannot be applied to open queries, since the censor was constructed with singleton answer sets in mind. Moreover, it does not seem appropriate to either allow or refuse entire queries; regarding an open query, some assignments of the free variables may compromise confidentiality whereas others may not. Thus, evaluating open queries in a controlled way should basically determine which variable assignments will lead to a disclosure of secrets and exclude them from the answer. A variable assignment not being returned as part of the answer to a query then can be interpreted in two different ways: it may make the query false in the database instance; or it may lead to the disclosure of a potential secret. The user is able to distinguish these two cases since he is supposed to be aware of the policy.

The positive part ans of the controlled answer to an open query $\Phi(V)$ is determined by means of the ordinary query evaluation $eval^*$ and the set $ref(used)$ possibly being infinite and containing every "harmful" $\Phi(c)$:

$$ref(\Phi(V), pol) = \{\Phi(c) \mid c \in Const \times \cdots \times Const \qquad (1)$$
$$\text{and exists } \Psi \in pol : \Phi(c) \models \Psi\}$$

$$ans(\Phi(V), pol, r) = eval^*(\Phi(V))(r) \backslash ref(\Phi(V), pol) \qquad (2)$$

Besides this positive part, the user is aware of a completeness information, as introduced in [5], basically saying that each substitution of the variables in V is either false in the instance r or true in r and part of the answer or true in r and not part of the answer. This is expressed by the following *completeness sentence* (with ans denoting the positive part (2) of the controlled answer, i.e., a finite set of ground substitutions of $\Phi(V)$):

$$comp(\Phi(V), ans) \equiv \qquad (3)$$
$$(\forall V)[\neg\Phi(V) \vee (\Phi(V) \wedge \bigvee_{\Phi(c) \in ans} V = c) \vee (\Phi(V) \wedge \bigwedge_{\Phi(c) \in ans} V \neq c)]$$

Observe that this completeness sentence is actually a tautology because it is equivalent to $(\forall V)[\neg\Phi(V) \vee \Phi(V)]$; therefore the user can construct it by himself and it needs not to be added to the user knowledge explicitly.

Having sent an open query $\Phi(V)$ to the database, the answer according to (2) will be returned to the user and the assumed user knowledge log will be updated, i.e., if log_i denotes the user knowledge before answering $\Phi(V)$, then the user knowledge log_{i+1} after having answered $\Phi(V)$ is determined by $log_{i+1} = log_i \cup ans(\Phi(V), pol, r)$.

4.2 The "Known Policy Problem"

At first glance, a known policy does not give the user any useful information with respect to the disclosure of secrets: each element of the policy is a *potential secret*, i.e., it has to be kept secret if it is true in the database. However, the user is not able to gain information about the actual truth value of a potential secret when only considering the policy. Nevertheless, a problem might emerge from the user awareness regarding the policy in combination with the completeness sentence which can be rewritten as an implication and then be exploited for disclosing a potential secret. We first illustrate this problem by an example and then analyze it more generally.

Example 2. Consider schema, policy and instance from Example 1, but assume that $\Sigma = \{acc\_no \rightarrow acc\_holder\}$. Observe that $BANK$ is in ONF. Two queries are given by $\Phi_1(X_N, X_H) \equiv BANK(X_N, X_H)$ and $\Phi_2 \equiv (\exists X_H)BANK(123, X_H)$. Φ_1 is an open query, asking for all tuples in *bank*. According to the (tentative) mechanism from Subsect. 4.1 we get:

$$eval^*(\Phi_1)(bank) = \{BANK(123, \mathrm{Smith}), BANK(456, \mathrm{Jones})\} \tag{4}$$

$$ref(\Phi_1, pol) = \{BANK(123, \mathrm{Smith})\} \tag{5}$$

$$ans(\Phi_1, pol, bank) = \{BANK(456, \mathrm{Jones})\} = ans_1 \tag{6}$$

$$comp(\Phi_1, ans_1) \equiv (\forall X_N)(\forall X_H)[\ \neg BANK(X_N, X_H) \tag{7}$$
$$\vee\, (BANK(X_N, X_H) \wedge (X_N = 456 \wedge X_H = \mathrm{Jones}))$$
$$\vee\, (BANK(X_N, X_H) \wedge (X_N \neq 456 \vee X_H \neq \mathrm{Jones}))\ \ ]$$

Φ_2 is a closed query (since it does not contain free variables) and asks whether there is an account with the number 123. Confidentiality is not compromised since $\Phi_2 \not\models \Psi$. Therefore, Φ_2 is answered as follows:

$$ans(\Phi_2, pol, bank) = \{(\exists X_H)BANK(123, X_H)\} \tag{8}$$

The user knowledge now consists of $log_0(= \Sigma)$, the answers to Φ_1 (6) and Φ_2 (8), and the completeness sentence (7). From (8) the user knows that $BANK(123, c)$ holds in *bank* for some suitable constant $c \in Const$. The variable assignment $(123, c)$ belongs to the third part of the disjunction in (7): it makes Φ_1 true in *bank* but is not part of the answer to Φ_1. Thus, $BANK(123, c)$ must be a secret. Since the only secret is $(\exists X_N)BANK(X_N, \mathrm{Smith})$, the constant c must be identified with Smith. As a result the user knows that the secret is true in *bank*: $bank \models_M BANK(123, \mathrm{Smith})$ and $BANK(123, \mathrm{Smith}) \models \Psi$ and thus $bank \models_M \Psi$.

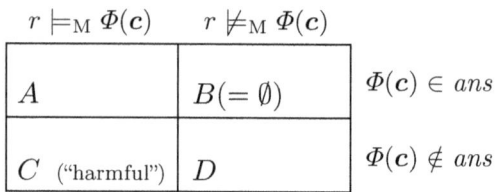

Fig. 1. Classification of variable assignments

For a more general analysis first reconsider the completeness sentence (3) and its visualization in Fig. 1: The box depicts the (infinite) set of all possible variable assignments c for the free variables V of an open query $\Phi(V)$ and is partitioned into four disjoint subsets. The horizontal partition differentiates between c being part of the explicitly returned controlled answer or not whereas the vertical partition differentiates between c making $\Phi(V)$ true or false in r. Variable assignments being covered by the first part of the disjunction in (3) belong to either subset B or subset D of the figure; variable assignments being covered by the second part of the disjunction belong to subset A; and variable assignments being covered by the third part of the disjunction belong to subset C. B is empty (variable assignments not making $\Phi(V)$ true are not part of the answer) and C contains exactly the "harmful" variable assignments that are true in r but not part of the answer (because they imply a secret). Thus, a variable assignment neither belonging to A nor to D belongs to C. Second, a known policy carries additional information: the variable substitutions not belonging to A and D in Fig. 1 may be identified by inspecting the policy: if $\Phi(c) \models \Psi$ for a $\Psi \in pol$ then c belongs to C. Assuming a unary relation[4] we formalize this information for $pol = \{R(c_1), \ldots, R(c_m)\}$:

$$pol\_inf_i \equiv (\forall X)[(\Phi_i(X) \land \bigwedge_{\Phi_i(c) \in ans_i} X \neq c) \implies \bigvee_{j=1}^{m} X = c_j] \qquad (9)$$

If $(\exists X)R(X) \in pol$, each query would be refused since pol would protect the existence of any tuple in the instance. The system would thus be useless in some sense and therefore we neglect this case in the following.

Now consider a more formal variant of Example 2 for a unary relation with instance $r = \{R(c_1)\}$. The policy and the two queries are given by $pol = \{R(c_1)\}$ with $c_1 \in Const$, $\Phi_1(X) \equiv R(X)$ (asking for all tuples in r), and $\Phi_2(X) \equiv (\exists X)R(X)$ (asking for the existence of a tuple in r). According to the (tentative) control mechanism described above we get the following answers, completeness information, and policy information:

---

[4] Our considerations can easily be adapted to general n-ary relations.

$$ans_1 = \emptyset, \quad ans_2 = (\exists X)R(X)$$

$$comp_1 = (\forall X)[\,\neg R(X)\vee$$
$$(R(X) \wedge \bigvee_{R(c)\in ans_1} X = c) \vee (R(X) \wedge \bigwedge_{R(c)\in ans_1} X \neq c)]$$
$$\equiv (\forall X)[\,R(X) \implies (\bigvee_{R(c)\in ans_1} X = c \vee \bigwedge_{R(c)\in ans_1} X \neq c)]$$

$$pol\_inf_1 \equiv (\forall X)[(R(X) \wedge \bigwedge_{R(c)\in ans_1} X \neq c) \implies X = c_1]$$

Combining ans_2 and $comp_1$ then yields[5]

$$(\exists X)[R(X) \wedge (\bigvee_{R(c)\in ans_1} X = c \vee \bigwedge_{R(c)\in ans_1} X \neq c)]$$
$$\equiv (\exists X)[R(X) \wedge \bigwedge_{R(c)\in ans_1} X \neq c]$$

which, together with pol_inf_1, leads to $X = c_1$. It follows that $r \models_M R(c_1)$ resulting in the user being able to disclose a potential secret.

4.3   Inference Control with Unknown Policies

One possibility to avoid the problem sketched in the previous subsection is to reconsider the query language and the policy language. Confining the user or the security administrator in expressing queries or policies, respectively, might help to avoid the harmful inference problem. We, however, refrain from adjusting the query and policy languages since we consider this a step backwards in our attempt to develop a system being convenient from the perspective of database users and security administrators.

A more promising approach is a reconsideration of the user's knowledge about the policy which is a crucial part of the harmful inference in Example 2. The completeness information together with the information from the policy may be exploited to infer a secret; consequently, if we hide the potential secrets from the user, we might be able to preserve confidentiality again. The completeness sentence (3) is independent of the user awareness since it does not refer to specific policy elements. We may thus assume the policy to be unknown to the user without having to change the control mechanism as sketched in Subsect. 4.1. This mechanism is secure in the sense of Def. 1 when assuming an unknown policy.

Theorem 1. *Static CQE for open queries with unknown policies preserves confidentiality in the sense of Def. 1.*

Remark. Since static CQE does not need a user log, queries from a sequence may be evaluated separately without compromising confidentiality.

To prepare for a proof sketch for Theorem 1 we now explain our notion of the chase for elements from $\mathscr{L}_q^c$ and present three technical lemmas.

---

[5] The equivalence holds since $\bigvee_{R(c)\in ans_1} X = c$ is empty being equivalent with *false*.

The Chase for Generalized Tuples. Originally, the chase is defined for sets of (full) tuples[6], whereas we consider subsets of the language $\mathscr{L}_q^c$. Because of the structure of these formulas, however, we are able to interpret them as generalized tuples, i.e., tuples possibly containing null values, by (temporarily) neglecting the existential quantifiers and interpreting the variables as null values of the type "existing but unknown". Considering elements from *Const* as distinguished and elements from *Var* as non-distinguished variables the notion of chasing can be applied to subsets of $\mathscr{L}_q^c$ as well. We will use this mechanism in the proof of Theorem 1.

Proof of Confidentiality. For each formula being true in a database instance there must be a ground atom, i.e., a sentence not containing any variables, implying this formula and also being true in the instance:

Lemma 1. *Consider an instance r and a $\chi \in \mathscr{L}_q^c$. It holds that $r \models_M \chi$ iff there exists a ground atom $\chi_g \in \mathscr{L}_q^c$ with $r \models_M \chi_g$ and $\chi_g \models \chi$.*[7]

When we chase a set $\mathcal{S}$ of closed select-project-queries (considered as generalized tuples by neglecting the existential quantifiers) with FDs Σ to construct a database instance (represented by a set of ground atoms) then each formula being true in this instance and containing only existentially bound variables or constants that already occur in $\mathcal{S}$ is implied by $\mathcal{S} \cup \Sigma$:

Lemma 2. *Consider a disjoint partition of the set of constants, $Const = Const_A \uplus Const_B$, and let $\mathcal{S} \subset \mathscr{L}_q^c$ such that each constant occurring in an element of $\mathcal{S}$ is from $Const_A$; Σ a set of FDs; $\chi_c \in \mathscr{L}_q^c$ a generalized tuple from the result of chasing $\mathcal{S}$ with Σ; $\chi_g \in \mathscr{L}_q^c$ a ground atom resulting from replacing all (existentially quantified) variables in χ_c with constants from $Const_B$; and $\chi \in \mathscr{L}_q^c$ with $\chi_g \models \chi$ and $\chi[A] \in Var$ or $\chi[A] \in Const_A$ for every attribute A. Then it holds that $\mathcal{S} \cup \Sigma \models \chi$.*

By Lemma 3, a potential secret being implied by a set $\mathcal{S}$ of closed select-project-queries and a set of FDs is already implied by a single formula from $\mathcal{S}$ under the assumption of ONF.

Lemma 3. *Consider a relation schema $RS = \langle R, \mathcal{U}, \Sigma \rangle$ being in ONF, a set $\mathcal{S} \subset \mathscr{L}_q^c$, and a potential secret $\Psi \in \mathscr{L}_q^c$ with $sel(\Psi) \in fs(RS)$. It holds that $\mathcal{S} \cup \Sigma \models \Psi$ iff $\chi' \models \Psi$ for a $\chi' \in \mathcal{S}$.*

We are now well prepared for providing a proof sketch for Theorem 1.

Sketch of Proof. By Def. 1, considering an instance-policy-pair (r, pol), for each potential secret Ψ and each (prefix of a) query sequence Q we have to find an alternative instance-policy-pair (r', pol') (satisfying the precondition) with these properties: (1) (r', pol') leads to the same answers for Q as (r, pol); (2)

---

[6] Refer to [1] for an explanation of the original chase.
[7] The symbol $\models$ denotes logical implication.

r' makes Ψ false. There is no additional requirement regarding pol' since we consider unknown policies. For constructing r' we basically chase the answers to Q regarding r with Σ and replace the remaining variables with new constants. Then, pol' is constructed by adding a potential secret for each constant being newly introduced during the chase. Property (1) follows from this construction and Lemmas 1–3, and property (2) is proven indirectly by assuming that $eval^*(\Psi)(r') = \Psi$ and applying Lemmas 1–3, leading to the disclosure of Ψ by the answers to Q regarding r and pol which contradicts the definition of the CQE mechanism. $\square$

The transition from known to unknown policies slightly changes the semantics of the refusal method. If pol is known to the user, he is able to determine for every variable assignment $\boldsymbol{c}$ not being returned as part of the answer to $\Phi(\boldsymbol{V})$ whether $\boldsymbol{c}$ makes $\Phi(\boldsymbol{V})$ false in r or $\boldsymbol{c}$ leads to the disclosure of a potential secret (i.e., belongs to the *ref*-part of the answer). Refusals are not returned explicitly because the user is able to figure them out himself. If, however, pol is unknown, the *ref*-part of the answer cannot be determined by the user since hiding the policies from the user aims at making the subsets C and D of Fig. 1 indistinguishable. We must still not return explicit refusals in order to keep up this indistinguishability. Therefore, with unknown policies static CQE is enforced rather by filtering than by refusing the answer. Summing up we regain the goal of confidentiality-preservation at the price of leaving the user uncertain about the *ref*-part of the answer to his query.

5 A Control Mechanism for Open Queries

We now sketch an algorithmic implementation of static CQE for open queries. We assume a single query rather than a query sequence which is justified by the remark to Theorem 1. Our implementation makes use of "classification instances", introduced in [9]. A classification instance is a relational representation of a policy: each secret from pol is represented by a tuple where existentially bound variables are replaced by the symbol #.

Static CQE for open queries

---

input : database instance r, policy $pol = \{\Psi_1, \Psi_2, \ldots, \Psi_m\}$, query Φ
output : controlled answer *ans*

1. PREPROCESSING
   For each potential secret[8] $\Psi_i \equiv (\exists X_1) \ldots (\exists X_{l_1}) R(\underbrace{X_1, \ldots, X_{l_1}}_{\text{bound variables}}, c_1, \ldots, c_{l_2})$:

   Add a tuple $\mu = R^c(\underbrace{\#, \ldots, \#}_{l_1 \text{ times}}, c_1, \ldots, c_{l_2})$ to the classification instance r^c.

2. ANSWERING QUERIES
   (a) If Φ is a *closed* query:

---

[8] The positions of variables and constants are w.l.o.g.

If exists $\mu \in r^c$ such that for all attributes A:
- if $\Phi[A] \in Const$ then $\mu[A] \in \{\Phi[A], \#\}$ (*)
- if $\Phi[A] \in Var$ then $\mu[A] = \#$ (**)

then return mum,

else set $ans := eval^*(\Phi)(r)$.

(b) If $\Phi(V)$ is an *open* query:

    i. Compute the ordinary query evaluation $eval^*(\Phi(V))(r)$.

    ii. Set $ref(\Phi(V), pol) := \emptyset$.

    iii. For each $\Phi(c) \in eval^*(\Phi(V))(r)$:

        If exists $\mu \in r^c$ satisfying (*) and (**) for all attributes A,
        then set $ref(\Phi(V), pol) := ref(\Phi(V), pol) \cup \{\Phi(c)\}$.

    iv. Set $ans := eval^*(\Phi(V))(r) \backslash ref(\Phi(V), pol)$.

(c) Return ans.

In the first step the policy is converted into the classification instance which can be done in linear time (in the size of the policy). The second step differs depending on Φ being a closed query or an open query. If Φ is closed, r^c is searched for a tuple satisfying (*) and (**) ($\Phi \models \Psi$ for a $\Psi \in pol$ iff there exists such a tuple). This can be done by constructing a set P_Φ that contains *all* tuples satisfying (*) and (**) and then checking whether $r^c \cap P_\Phi$ is non-empty. With n denoting the number of attributes in R, we get $|P_\Phi| \leq 2^n$ and when storing r^c in a suitable data structure like a B-tree the control mechanism has a runtime of $O(2^n \cdot log(m))$ or $O(log(m))$ if we consider the number of attributes in R fixed and reasonably small (cf. [9]). If Φ is open, a set $P_{\Phi(c)}$ can be constructed analogously for each c with $\Phi(c) \in eval^*(\Phi(V))(r)$. The runtime can then be estimated by $O(k \cdot log(m))$ with k denoting the number of tuples in $eval^*(\Phi(V))(r)$.

6   Conclusion and Future Work

We presented an inference control approach for open relational database queries which is static in the sense that the goals of computationally expensive inference control can be reached at runtime by actually performing an efficient filtering mechanism. We developed our approach in the framework of CQE. It turned out that assuming the user to be aware of the confidentiality policy is incompatible with open queries but we formally showed that hiding the policy is sufficient to preserve confidentiality. We also proposed an implementation of our mechanism with a linear preprocessing time (in the size of the policy) and a runtime of $O(k \cdot log(m))$ per query (with k denoting the answer size and m denoting the policy size).

Future research should address several enhancements. For example, more expressive query and policy languages could be investigated, allowing for conjunction, disjunction and negation. Also further kinds of constraints like (intra-relational) multivalued dependencies or (inter-relational) inclusion dependencies could be taken into account. Finally, an implementation of our approach with actually employed access control mechanisms like Oracle's virtual private databases would be desirable.

References

1. Abiteboul, S., Hull, R., Vianu, V.: Foundations of Databases. Addison-Wesley, Reading (1995)
2. Bertino, E., Sandhu, R.: Database security – concepts, approaches, and challenges. IEEE Trans. Dependable Sec. Comput. 2(1), 2–18 (2005)
3. Biskup, J.: Boyce-Codd normal form and object normal forms. Inf. Process. Lett. 32(1), 29–33 (1989)
4. Biskup, J., Bonatti, P.: Controlled query evaluation for enforcing confidentiality in complete information systems. Int. J. Inf. Sec. 3(1), 14–27 (2004)
5. Biskup, J., Bonatti, P.: Controlled query evaluation with open queries for a decidable relational submodel. Ann. Math. Artif. Intell. 50, 39–77 (2007)
6. Biskup, J., Bonatti, P.A.: Lying versus refusal for known potential secrets. Data Knowl. Eng. 38(2), 199–222 (2001)
7. Biskup, J., Bonatti, P.A.: Controlled query evaluation for known policies by combining lying and refusal. Ann. Math. Artif. Intell. 40, 37–62 (2004)
8. Biskup, J., Embley, D.W., Lochner, J.-H.: Reducing inference control to access control for normalized database schemas. Inf. Process. Lett. 106(1), 8–12 (2008)
9. Biskup, J., Lochner, J.-H.: Enforcing confidentiality in relational databases by reducing inference control to access control. In: Garay, J.A., Lenstra, A.K., Mambo, M., Peralta, R. (eds.) ISC 2007. LNCS, vol. 4779, pp. 407–422. Springer, Heidelberg (2007)
10. Biskup, J., Lochner, J.-H., Sonntag, S.: Optimization of the controlled evaluation of closed relational queries. In: Gritzalis, D., Lopez, J. (eds.) Proc. IFIP SEC. IFIP AICT, vol. 297, pp. 214–225. Springer, Heidelberg (2009)
11. Bonatti, P., Kraus, S., Subrahmanian, V.S.: Foundations of secure deductive databases. IEEE Trans. Knowl. Data Eng. 7(3), 406–422 (1995)
12. Brodsky, A., Farkas, C., Jajodia, S.: Secure databases: constraints, inference channels, and monitoring disclosures. IEEE Trans. Knowl. Data Eng. 12(6), 900–919 (2000)
13. Byun, J.-W., Bertino, E.: Micro-views, or on how to protect privacy while enhancing data usability—concepts and challenges. ACM SIGMOD Record 35(1), 9–13 (2006)
14. Cuppens, F., Gabillon, A.: Cover story management. Data Knowl. Eng. 37(2), 177–201 (2001)
15. Dawson, S., De Capitani di Vimercati, S., Samarati, P.: Specification and enforcement of classification and inference constraints. In: IEEE Symposium on Security and Privacy, pp. 181–195 (1999)
16. Delugach, H.S., Hinke, T.H.: Wizard: A database inference analysis and detection system. IEEE Trans. Knowl. Data Eng. 8(1), 56–66 (1996)
17. Farkas, C., Jajodia, S.: The inference problem: a survey. SIGKDD Explorations 4(2), 6–11 (2002)
18. Galinovic, A., Antoncic, V.: Polyinstantiation in relational databases with multi-level security. In: Proc. ITI, pp. 127–132. IEEE, Los Alamitos (2007)
19. Griffiths, P.P., Wade, B.W.: An authorization mechanism for a relational database system. ACM Trans. Database Syst. 1(3), 242–255 (1976)
20. Hale, J., Shenoi, S.: Analyzing FD inference in relational databases. Data Knowl. Eng. 18(2), 167–183 (1996)
21. Jajodia, S., Sandhu, R.S.: Toward a multilevel secure relational data model. In: Clifford, J., King, R. (eds.) SIGMOD Conference, pp. 50–59. ACM Press, New York (1991)

22. Lunt, T.F., Denning, D.E., Schell, R.R., Heckman, M., Shockley, W.R.: The Sea-
    View security model. IEEE Trans. Software Eng. 16(6), 593–607 (1990)
23. Rjaibi, W., Bird, P.: A multi-purpose implementation of mandatory access control
    in relational database management systems. In: Nascimento, M.A., Özsu, M.T.,
    Kossmann, D., Miller, R.J., Blakeley, J.A., Schiefer, K.B. (eds.) Proc. VLDB, pp.
    1010–1020 (2004)
24. Sandhu, R.: Lattice-based access control models. Computer 26(11), 9–19 (1993)
25. Sicherman, G.L., de Jonge, W., van de Riet, R.P.: Answering queries without re-
    vealing secrets. ACM Trans. Database Syst. 8(1), 41–59 (1983)
26. Stonebraker, M., Wong, E.: Access control in a relational data base management
    system by query modification. In: Proc. ACM/CSC-ER Annual Conference, pp.
    180–186. ACM Press, New York (1974)
27. Su, T.-A., Özsoyoglu, G.: Controlling FD and MVD inferences in multilevel rela-
    tional database systems. IEEE Trans. Knowl. Data Eng. 3(4), 474–485 (1991)

Query Racing: Fast Completeness Certification of Query Results*

Bernardo Palazzi[1,2], Maurizio Pizzonia[1], and Stefano Pucacco[1]

[1] Roma TRE University, Rome Italy
{palazzi,pizzonia,pucacco}@dia.uniroma3.it
[2] Brown University, Department of Computer Science, Providence, RI USA

Abstract. We present a general and effective method to certify completeness of query results on relational tables stored in an untrusted DBMS. Our main contribution is the concept of "Query Race": we split up a general query into several single attribute queries, and exploit concurrency and speed to bind the complexity to the fastest of them. Our method supports selection queries with general composition of conjunctive and disjunctive order-based conditions on different attributes at the same time. To achieve our results, we require neither previous knowledge of queries nor specific support by the DBMS.

We validate our approach with experimental results performed on a prototypical implementation.

1 Introduction

Advances in networking technologies and continued spread of the Internet, jointly with cost-effective offers, have triggered a trend towards outsourcing data management to external service providers, often on the Cloud. Database outsourcing is a known evidence of this trend. The outsourced database users rely on provider infrastructure, which include hardware, software and manpower, for the storage, maintenance, and retrieval of their data. That is, a company stores all its data, and possibly business-critical information, at an external service provider, that is generally not fully trusted. Actually, this approach involves several security issues that range from confidentiality preservation to integrity verification. Special attention has been posed to the problem of checking completeness of results. In fact, tuple-level integrity is easy to ensure by adopting some sort of tuple-level signature, but assessing that no malicious tuples deletion or insertion has been performed is a much harder task, if we intend to maintain DBMS-level efficiency.

Many proposal can be found in literature, some are based on *authenticated data structures* [1,2,3,4,5], some on the insertion of spurious data [6,7], some on signatures aggregation [8]. Each of them has strengths and weaknesses with respect to efficiency, privacy, kind of queries supported, etc.

---

* This work is partially supported by the Italian Ministry of Research, Grant number RBIP06BZW8, FIRB project "Advanced tracking system in intermodal freight transportation" and under Project "ALGODEEP: Sfide algoritmiche per elaborazioni data-intensive su piattaforme di calcolo emergenti", MIUR PRIN.

S. Foresti and S. Jajodia (Eds.): Data and Applications Security XXIV, LNCS 6166, pp. 177–192, 2010.
© IFIP International Federation for Information Processing 2010

This paper proposes a novel technique that achieves high efficiency level in practice. We decompose the query in many simpler queries, to be concurrently run, and bind the overall efficiency to the fastest of them. We experimentally verified on a common DBMS implementation, that, in the vast majority of cases, the fastest query is also the most selective.

Many of the techniques known in literature restrict the kind of conditions supported or need to know the queries in advance to optimize data structures. Our proposal supports all conjunctive and disjunctive combination of order-based conditions on any subset of attributes.

By using *authenticated skip lists* represented into regular tables [2], our technique is easy to implement on any DBMS without need for specific support on the server. Also, if our technique should be applied to a pre-existing database, no change to its schema is needed and tables storing authenticated skip lists can also be stored on a different and independent server.

The paper is organized as follows. Section 2 briefly review the state of the art. Section 3 introduces basic background about authenticated skip lists. In Section 4 we describe query racing technique and possible optimizations. In Section 5 we comment about efficiency of our method. Section 7 presents experiments that show feasibility and scalability of our approach. In Section 6 we discuss strengths and weaknesses of our approach with respect to the state of the art.

2   State of the Art

The problem of providing provably authentic results using untrusted DBMS has been largely studied.

Some techniques known in literature provide solutions that rely on hashes and signatures or on inserting spurious data into the database, however, most of the works, rely on *authenticated data structures* [9] (*ADS*).

An ADS represents a collection of elements from an ordered domain. Supported operations are insertion, deletion, and query (equality and range). Usually, all operations require $O(\log n)$ time where n is the number of elements in the ADS. A cumulative hash (*root* or *basis*) of the whole data structure is known to the user. Query operations return a proof of correctness, of size $O(\log n)$, that basically allows the verifier to construct a hash chain from the result to the basis. Insertion and deletion update the basis which is a fingerprint of the collection stored into the ADS. The most common ADSes are Merkle hash trees [10] and authenticated skip lists [11]. Improvements to basic techniques are in [12,13].

The first use of an ADS to authenticate relational database operations is presented in [1] and later improved in [14]. The latter introduces the use of authenticated multidimensional *range trees* in order to support conjunctive queries involving multiple attributes. Usually, adoption of ADS introduces privacy problems because, to check correctness, all attributes involved in the selection condition have to be unveiled, even if some of them are supposed to be filtered out through projection. An interesting approach to solve this problem is presented by Pang et al. [5]. They propose a method to authenticate projection queries using ADSes. An improvement of this work is presented in [4] where they also exploit condensed RSA signatures aggregation scheme introduced in [8]. A recent work that allows to preserve privacy is presented in [15].

Yang et al. [16] provide techniques for authenticated join operation. In [17] a scalable technique for verification of queries, in particular for the equi-join operation, is presented. That approach is based on Bloom filters [18].

Xie et al. [6] show a method for integrity auditing of outsourced data that uses a probabilistic approach. The proposed technique scatters some control values that are indistinguishable from real values inside the relational table.

In [19] a method to authenticate k nearest neighbors queries is introduced.

Li et al. [20] propose to transform B-trees, used by DBMS for indexes, into an ADS, hence requiring support from the DBMS itself. The problem of efficiently storing ADSes into a regular DBMS has been studied by Miklau and Suciu [3] for Merkle trees and by Di Battista and Palazzi [2] for authenticated skip lists.

Users may need to be sure that queries are performed on the latest version of the database. Some results on this topic are provided in [21,7].

Another work [22] focuses on authenticity and completeness guarantees of query replies, analyzes an approach for various query types, and compares it with straightforward solutions that adopt ADSes.

A technique that reduces the size of the additional information sent to users or to the client for verification purpose is presented in [23].

The authentication of outsourced data through web services and XML signatures is investigated in [24].

3   Background

In this section we provide some details on authenticated skip lists that will be used in the rest of the paper.

A *skip list* [25] is a probabilistic data structure that maintains a subset of elements of an ordered set, allowing searches and updates in $O(\log n)$ time with high probability (w.h.p.), where n is the current number of elements. A skip list for n elements has $O(\log n)$ levels w.h.p., the base level is a sorted list of all elements; a subset of these elements also appears on the second level; for each node in a given level of the skip list, a coin flip determines whether or not it will exist in the next higher level.

We call the set of nodes associated with an element a *tower*. The *height* of the tower is the level of the highest node in that tower. Each node in the structure contains pointers to the node to its right (R) and to the node below it (B). In the following, the notation $V.element$ denotes the element of node V. A search in the structure for a target element e is performed in the following way. We begin at the top left node. If $R.element > e$, then we move to B. Otherwise, we move to R. We continue this process until we are pointing to a node whose element is e (we have found the target), or we are pointing to a node on the base level whose element is greater than e (e is not contained). The nodes involved in the search identify a *search path*.

An *authenticated skip list* [11] supports authenticated versions of the skip list operations. Namely, the nodes on the base level correspond to data elements whose integrity and completeness we would like to certify in query results. Each node in the structure contains a hash value which is the *commutative crypto-graphic hash* (a cryptographic hash of a pair of data, whose value is independent of the ordering of the pair) of the hash values of a pair of adjacent nodes. In this way the authenticated skip list is similar to the Merkle hash tree structure. For a node V, we denote $V.hash$ the hash value stored in V, $V.level$ the level of V, and $V.height$ the height of the tower of V. The notation $h(A, B)$ indicates a commutative cryptographic hash of the values A and B.

The hash value of a particular node V in the structure is given as follows. We have two rules

Rule 1 (*V.level* = 0): If $R.height = 0$ (it has only a base level node) then $V.hash = h(V.element, R.hash)$, else $V.hash = h(V.element, R.element)$.

Rule 2 (*V.level* > 0): If $R.height = V.level$ then $V.hash = h(B.hash, R.hash)$, else $V.hash = B.hash$.

Application of the above rules leads to a computation of hashes that flow from bottom-right to top-left, like in the example for the element 9 (see Fig. 1). Top left node of the skip list is particularly important since its hash value, called *basis*, is an accumulation of all hashes in the whole structure. If any element in authenticated skip list changes, basis changes. Each authenticated skip list includes additional elements, minimum and maximum, and their corresponding towers ensuring that a basis exists even if our data set is empty.

Queries, for an authenticated skip list, return zero or more elements and a *proof of integrity* (also called *verification object*). Consider an element e stored in its level zero node V and its search path p. The proof of integrity of e is constituted by the hashes stored in the nodes that are on the right and below of each node in p (see Fig. 1).

If the result is empty, queried element b is not in the collection, the proof is composed by proof of two elements nearest to b in the collection according to the

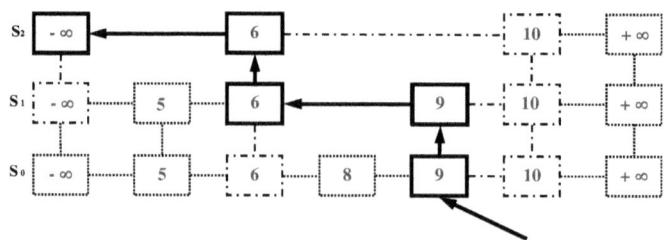

Fig. 1. In a skip list, for each element, there is a search path. For element 9 the search path is made of nodes with thick border. In an authenticated skip list, given the search path p, the proof of integrity is made of the hashes of the nodes that are on the right of p and below p. For element 9 the proof is made of hashes stored in nodes with dash-dotted border.

order. For range queries, the simplest method to provide the proof of integrity of all elements is inefficient. We provide an efficient solution in Section 4.3.

4   Completeness Certification by Query Racing

In this section we describe how to perform certified selection queries by using the query racing technique. We first describe the technique for a restricted class of selections, then we extend our techniques to general selections.

4.1   Basic Queries

Suppose to have a relational table T with attributes $a_1, \ldots, a_m$. We always assume that attribute types have orders and comparison operators which is the case in the vast majority of practical situations.

Basic Query. We call *basic query* a selection query in the following form $\sigma_{f(a_1,\ldots,a_m)}(T)$ where $f(a_1,\ldots,a_m) = \bigwedge_{i=1}^{n}(\alpha_i \star c_i)$ and $\alpha_i \in \{a_1,\ldots,a_m\}$ is an attribute of T, c_i is a constant of the the same type of α_i, and $\star$ is one of the following operators: $=, >, \geq, <, \leq$. Expressions $\alpha_i \star c_i$ are called *atoms*.

In other words, a basic query is a selection on a single table whose condition is a conjunction of equality based and order based atoms on single attributes.

In a basic query Q, if cardinality of referred attributes set $\mathrm{attr}(Q) = \bigcup_{i=0}^{n}\{\alpha_i\}$ is equal to one, we say that Q is *monodimensional* and if $\mathrm{attr}(Q) = \{a\}$ we say that Q is on a. Otherwise we say that Q is *multidimensional*.

Consider a monodimensional basic query Q on attribute a, formally $\sigma_f(T)$ where $f = \bigwedge_{i=0}^{n} a \star c_i$. There exist an expression f', logically equivalent to f, in one of the following *canonical* forms where operators $\lesssim$ ($\gtrsim$) must be intended to be either $<$ or $\leq$ ($>$ or $\geq$).

$$\texttt{true, false, } a = c, \ a \lesssim c, \ a \gtrsim c, \ (a \gtrsim c_1) \wedge (a \lesssim c_2) \tag{1}$$

where c, c_1, and c_2 are constants of the same type of a. By extension, basic query Q' which is equivalent to Q, where f is replaced by f', is said to be *canonical*.

A multidimensional basic query $\sigma_{f(a_1,\ldots,a_m)}(T)$ can be decomposed in several canonical monodimensional basic queries, by a simple syntactic processing on f, such that $\sigma_{f(a_1,\ldots,a_m)}(T) = \sigma_{f(a_1)}(T) \bigcap \cdots \bigcap \sigma_{f(a_m)}(T)$.

4.2   Completeness Certification for Multidimensional Basic Queries

Consider a table T on which basic queries should be performed. To support completeness certification of basic query results we introduce two new concepts.

Per Column Security Table. We introduce, for each attribute a of T, a *security table* S_a. Each security table represents an authenticated skip list (see Section 3) that allows the client to easily certify completeness and integrity of the result of monodimensional basic queries in canonical form on a using the techniques described in [2]. Given a monodimensional canonical basic

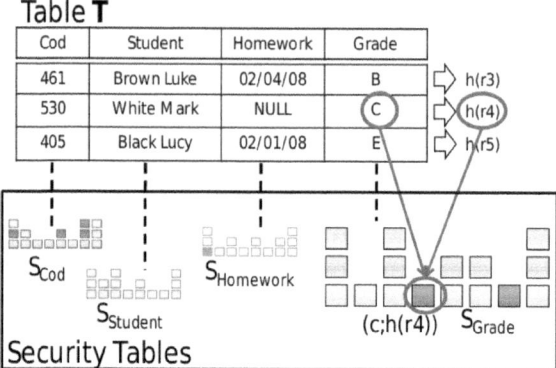

Fig. 2. Each attribute of a table is associated with a security table. Each security table represents an authenticated skip list containing all the values of that attribute with the hash of the corresponding rows.

query Q on a, we call *security query* the corresponding query $\overline{Q}$ on security table S_a whose result provides a *proof of completeness*, or *verification object*, for the result of Q. To exploit such verification object the user also needs to know a basis for table S_a. Section 4.3 shows, for any basic query, how it is possible to obtain the verification object with a single security query. For every monodimensional basic query on a, the corresponding security query on S_a can be easily built [2].

Row-Hashing. For each tuple r of T, a hash value $h(r)$ of r is computed, by hashing the concatenation of all the values of the attributes of the row. Suppose that a tuple r has value v for attribute a. The value stored into security table S_a is the pair $\langle v, h(r) \rangle$. Concerning the order of the value within the skip list represented by table S_a, pairs $\langle v, h(r) \rangle$ are ordered according to the order defined for the types of a and $h(r)$ considering v as the most significant part. This also avoids any problem about duplicate value on that attribute provided that there are no duplicated tuples in T.

We are now ready to introduce the query race technique.

Query Race. A multidimensional basic query Q is decomposed in several canonical monodimensional queries (see Section 4.1) that are concurrently executed along with their corresponding security query. The result of the fastest query is taken as a reference for computing the result of Q, other queries are aborted. The result of the fastest query is certified and processed on the client, in trusted environment, to obtain the final result.

Consider a relational table T with attributes $a_1, \ldots, a_m$ and the basic query Q on T. Without loss of generality, we suppose that all attributes $a_1, \ldots, a_m$ are involved in the condition of Q.

For each attribute a_i, consider the atoms $g_1, \ldots, g_{k_i}$ of the condition of Q that refer to attribute a_i, and let Q_i be a canonical basic query on T whose condition is $g_1 \wedge \cdots \wedge g_{k_i}$.

We now provide algorithmic details to certify completeness of result R of multidimensional basic query Q on relational table T. The following algorithm is intended to be run on the (trusted) client, for a two-party model, or on the users for a three-party model. We assume the client knows, for each security table the corresponding basis.

Algorithm 1

1. Decompose basic query Q into several canonical monodimensional basic queries $Q_1, \ldots, Q_m$ on attributes $a_1, \ldots, a_m$ respectively such that for their results $R_1, \ldots, R_m$ it holds $R = R_1 \cap \cdots \cap R_m$ (see Section 4.1).
2. If among $Q_1, \ldots, Q_m$ there is one query whose condition is `false`, then result of Q is empty and complete.
3. Queries $Q_1, \ldots, Q_m$ and their corresponding security queries $\overline{Q}_1, \ldots, \overline{Q}_m$ are all concurrently executed.
4. Consider the *query pairs* $(Q_i, \overline{Q}_i)$. A query pair is considered finished when both queries are finished. Let a_j be the attribute whose query pair finishes first. As soon as query pair for a_j finishes, all other running queries are aborted. Let R_j be the result of Q_j and $\overline{R}_j$ be the result of $\overline{Q}_j$. $\overline{R}_j$ provides the verification object of R_j.
5. Certify correctness and completeness of $\overline{R}_j$ using the basis for S_{a_j} as described in Section 3 or with the optimized procedure described in Section 4.3. If check fails $\overline{R}_j$ is not genuine and it is impossible to certify R_j.
6. We consider R_j ordered according to a_j and $\overline{R}_j$ as defined before for the authenticated skip list represented in S_{a_j}. For each element $\langle v, h \rangle$ of $\overline{R}_j$ perform the following three steps.
   (a) Consider the tuple r of R_j corresponding to element $\langle v, h \rangle$ of $\overline{R}_j$ in the given orders.
   (b) Certify integrity of r by checking if $h(r) = h$. If check fails R_j is not genuine.
   (c) Evaluate condition of Q on r, if condition is true then r is in the result R of Q.
7. If all previous checks are successful R is the certified result of Q.

Theorem 1. *Algorithm 1 correctly certifies completeness and integrity of a basic query in one query round.*

Proof. (sketch) Consider query Q with result R and queries $Q_1, \ldots, Q_m$, as computed in Step 1, and their results $R_1, \ldots, R_m$. For all $i = 1 \ldots m$, $R \subseteq R_i$ holds. This implies that R can be computed starting from an arbitrary R_j, also the one that is the result of the fastest query as selected in Step 4.

From results summarized in Section 3, we assume results $\overline{R}_1, \ldots, \overline{R}_m$ of the corresponding security queries to be correctly certified as complete by Step 5.

By matching each tuple of R_j with the corresponding tuple of $\overline{R}_j$ (Step 6.a) and exploiting the row-hashing technique (Step 6.b), we certify that R_j is correct and complete. Step 6.c selects from R_j only the rows that belongs to R. Completeness and correctness of R derives from completeness and correctness of R_j and from the fact that final selection is performing in a trusted environment.

The presented algorithm provides certification of completeness of result of Q with only one query round. In this query round all queries $Q_1, \ldots, Q_m, \overline{Q}_1, \ldots, \overline{Q}_m$ are concurrently performed.

Alternatively, if we admit two query rounds it is possible to obtain the same result performing much less queries and transferring much less data. Step 3 (first query round) only perform security queries $\overline{Q}_1, \ldots, \overline{Q}_m$ thus avoiding to transfer potentially big tuples in results for $Q_1, \ldots, Q_m$. Step 4a select the fastest, say $\overline{Q}_j$ and abort the others. Step 4b (second query round) performs query Q_j. The rest of the algorithm is unchanged. Also, in certain circumstances, might be convenient to choose one of the security queries $\overline{Q}_1, \ldots, \overline{Q}_m$ that is expected to be the fastest.

4.3   Optimized Security Queries

Suppose to have a table T and a security table S_a on attribute a of T. Suppose to have a monodimensional canonical basic query, asking for all elements in the range $[x, y]$ (extremes may or may not be included), and its result R. We need verification object $\overline{R}$ for R. The simplest way to proceed leads to obtain a verification object for each value in the interval requiring $O(|R|)$ queries, and $O(|R| \log |T|)$ size overall for the verification object of R. However, when considering elements of a range, verification objects of consecutive elements largely overlap, as shown in Fig. 3.

In this section, we describe a procedure for getting a verification object of size $O(|R| + \log |T|)$ with $O(1)$ queries and a procedure to certify the completeness and integrity of the result $\overline{R}$ of the security query $\overline{Q}$ for range $[x, y]$.

Di Battista and Palazzi [2] show two ways to represent an authenticated skip list in a relational table: (i) a coarse-grained representation, in which each tuple stores an entire tower, and (ii) a fine-grained representation, in which each tuple stores only one level of a tower. For canonical monodimensional basic queries whose conditions contain only equalities, they show how to retrieve the verification object using $O(\log |T|)$ queries, in the coarse-grained approach, and using only one query, in the fine-grained approach.

We adopt the fine-grained representation. Let x' (y') be the first element less (greater) than or equal to x (y). The verification object $\overline{R}$ contains verification objects $V_{x'}$ and $V_{y'}$ for elements x' and y', the elements within that range (x' and y' included), and corresponding height of the tower for each of that elements. Adopting a fine-grained representation this can be done using only three queries that can be concurrently executed, namely, one query for the elements and the corresponding heights of the towers, and two queries for the verification objects of interval bounds x' and y'. Note that, in the above queries, x' and y' are not

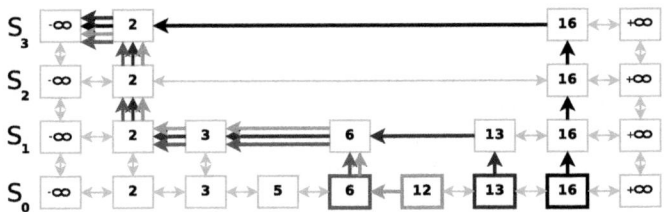

Fig. 3. Overlapping of verification objects for elements in a range

mentioned, x and y are specified instead, so that no further queries to obtain x' and y' are needed.

On the client, that is, in a trusted environment, the portion of the authenticated skip list for elements of $\overline{R}$, and hence their verification objects, can be computed starting from $\overline{R}$, $V_{x'}$, $V_{y'}$ and the height of the towers. The complete certification algorithm follows.

Algorithm 2

1. Certify verification objects $V_{x'}$, $V_{y'}$ as explained in Section 3.
2. Consider the values of elements e in $\overline{R}$, from the greatest value to the lowest, and for each of them perform the following steps.
   (a) Re-construct tower for element e computing hashes of each level according to the rules of the skip list data structure (see Section 3).
   (b) When a level of a tower is also present in either $V_{x'}$ or $V_{y'}$ compare the value of the hash previously known with that computed. If this check fails $\overline{R}$ is not genuine.
3. If all previous checks are successful $\overline{R}$ is correct and complete.

Theorem 2. *Algorithm 2 correctly certifies completeness of a security query asking for a range of values.*

Proof. (sketch) If Step 1 fails, at least one of the extremes of the result is not correct, as recalled in Section 3. So, suppose $V_{x'}$, $V_{y'}$ have been correctly certified and the result returned by the query within the range $[x', y']$ is not correct or is not complete, we prove that Step 2.b must fail. Let $w \in [x, y]$ be an element contained in the original skip list that is not present in the result. Let w' the greatest element belonging to the result that is lesser than w, possibly coinciding with x'. Consider the reconstruction of the original skip list as performed in Step 2.a and consider the search path for w' connecting the bottom nodes of the tower of w' and the top node of the tower for $-\infty$. According to the skip list rules (see Section 3), in the original skip list, the hash values in this path accumulates also hash values coming from w. This path must overlap the search paths for x' and y' (they overlap at least at the top node of the tower for $-\infty$). If Step 2.b does not fail on the overlapping, either the result is correct and complete or a collision for the hash function can be found comparing the reconstruction of the partial skip list and the original one.

When this algorithm is used within Algorithm 1, a further optimization can be performed. It is not needed, for the verification object $\overline{R}$, to report values contained in the authenticated skip list. Such values, as well as, row-hash values can be computed from the result of the query on the regular table (that is, from R). Note that, this can be relevant in practice, even if it does not bring any asymptotic improvement for the size of the verification object since height of towers are still needed and contribute $O(|R|)$ to it.

4.4   General Selection Queries

In this section we define a larger class of queries that we handle in Section 4.5.
    Let T be a relational table with attributes $a_1, \ldots, a_m$.

General Selection Query. We call *general selection query* a query in the following form $\sigma_{f(a_1,\ldots,a_m)}(T)$ where $f(a_1, \ldots, a_m)$ is a generic boolean expression arbitrarily composed using operators $\wedge$, $\vee$, and $\neg$. Sub-expressions that do not contain those operators are called *atoms* and are in the form $\alpha \star c$ where $\alpha \in \{a_1, \ldots, a_m\}$ is an attribute of T, c is a constant of the the same type of α, and $\star$ is one of the following operators: $=, >, \geq, <, \leq$.
    For any boolean formula, an equivalent boolean formula in disjunctive normal form can be obtained using elementary boolean algebra. Also, using the following elementary equivalence rules, it is possible to obtain equivalent expressions in disjunctive normal form that does not contain negation.

$$\neg(a = c) \equiv a > c \vee a < c, \; \neg(a > c) \equiv a \leq c, \; \neg(a \geq c) \equiv a < c,$$
$$\neg(a < c) \equiv a \geq c, \; \neg(a \leq c) \equiv a > c$$

A general selection query is said *canonical* if its condition is in disjunctive normal form and does not contain negation.

4.5   Completeness Certification for General Selection Queries

Consider a relational table T with attributes $a_1, \ldots, a_m$ and a general selection query Q on T. Without loss of generality, we assume Q to be canonical and having condition $\bigvee_{j=1}^{q} g_i$, where g_i is in the form $g_i = \bigwedge_{j=1}^{n_q} f_{ij}$ and each f_{ij} is an atom. To execute Q on a table T client performs the following algorithm.

Algorithm 3

1. Construct q basic queries Q_i $(i = 1, \ldots, q)$, in the form $\sigma_{g_i}(T)$
2. Basic queries $Q_1, \ldots, Q_q$ are all concurrently executed using Algorithm 1 obtaining certified results $R_1, \ldots, R_q$.
3. The result of Q is $R_1 \cup \cdots \cup R_q$.

5   Remarks on the Execution of Query Racing

Algorithms described in Section 4 assume that smaller the result of a query, shorter the time a user/client has to wait for it. Even if this assumption sounds reasonable, several aspects affect the waiting time of a user. In Section 4, we implicitly assumed that concurrent queries either are run on distinct processor or are fairly scheduled such that at each query is given roughly the same amount of CPU/Disk time. Also, current systems are rather complex. The DBMS server interacts with network, and operating systems in ways that are hard to predict, also, indexes can greatly speed up some queries with respect to others.

Even if in this context it is impossible to provide any theoretical statement about the time a query takes to complete, we experimentally verified that the time increases with the size of the result in most of the common cases. In certain particular cases, the results of monodimensional queries might turn out to be much bigger of the result of the main query (for example, selecting a particular date when day, month, and year are stored in distinct attributes). In these cases, concerning security queries, the set of attributes that are responsible for the problem can be treated like a single attribute, solving the efficiency problem.

The main contributions to the waiting time are the time taken by the DBMS to compute the result and the time taken by the network to transfer it.

If network is a bottleneck, our assumption is reasonable: supposing that all queries traverse same network, transferring more data implies longer wait time.

Suppose the DBMS server is the bottleneck. If the system is highly parallel with respect to CPU and disks, which is the case for large clouds, we can assume each query does not have to compete with the others for CPU and Disk, hence concerning waiting time we can assume it runs alone. If the system is not highly parallel, we can always suppose that they get the same share of CPU and disk. In both cases, the important thing to understand is if the time taken by a DBMS to complete a query, behave monotonically with respect to query size result. This is investigated experimentally in Section 7.

6   Comparison with the State of the Art

In this section we briefly discuss our results with respect to the state of the art according to criteria expressed in Section 2.

We provide completeness certification for general multidimensional selection queries on dynamic databases, having as condition any boolean expression with any order-based operator on any set of attributes.

This result is also achieved in other papers [14,20,4,6,16,17] but with different trade offs. We now briefly compare our work with each of them.

Our approach allows us to answer any selection query with the same efficiency, while Devanbu et al. [14] adopt range trees optimized for a specific set of queries to be decided when the authenticated database is created.

Concerning efficiency, we require only one query-round, do not mandate any (symmetric or asymmetric) encryption, except for the basis, and complexity verification is bounded to the fastest query which is very often the most selective (see Section 7. Pang et al. [4,17] require to sign each tuple and/or to compute complicated hashes which may be a burden for client and users.

The technique described by Yang et al. [16] provide verification objects of unpractical size and uses many query-rounds.

Xie et al. [6] describe an efficient and flexible probabilistic method, however, they do not assure to detect all malicious changes, in particular for punctual ones.

The solution provided by Li et al. [20] requires a customized DBMS while our approach can use a plain DBMS.

Our method does not hinder the possibility to adopt other complementary techniques known in literature. In particular, concerning privacy, results described in [5] and also order preserving encryption can be adopted. Concerning freshness, results from [7] can be used.

7 Experimental Evaluation

This section shows experimental results that aim to validate techniques and discussions presented in Sections 4 and 5, and to report the performance of our prototypical implementation. We based our experiments on two data sets. The first data set, called *artificial*, is randomly built. We created tables with number of tuples ranging from $10,000$ to $1,000,000$ and with number of attributes ranging from 1 to 100. All attributes have type string (MySql type `varchar`). The second is the *Adult Data Set* publicly available from Machine Learning Repository [26]. It has 14 attributes and 32,561 tuples.

7.1 Validation of Monotonicity

Our first aim is to provide a first empirical validation to the hypothesis that the time taken by a DBMS server to execute a query monotonically increases with result set size (see Section 5).

We considered 13 different queries on Adult Data Set, the result set size is recorded for each of them. We run each query ten times and we recorded execution time for each run. We performed our experiments on a MySQL DBMS server (ver. 5.0) running on a Linux system (kernel version 2.6.24 with cfq disk scheduler), on a small laptop with 2GB of ram and no other significant load on the machine. Time measures were taken by the MySQL profiling system (using `SHOW PROFILES`).

We performed the whole experiment in four possible situations that encompass having or not having indexes on the (six) attributes involved by the queries, and exploiting or not exploiting caches in MySQL (cache disabled by issuing `SET GLOBAL query_cache_type=OFF`) and Linux (cache cleaned before each query by issuing `sync; echo 3 > /proc/sys/vm/drop_caches`).

Results are summarized in Fig. 4. It is possible to see that, in our experiments, monotonicity is roughly respected in all situations. We can see that when caches are available, performances are more predictable (smaller min-max ranges), see Figs. 4(b) and 4(d). In our experiments, indexes do not provide very much improvement while augmenting the possibility of non-monotonic behavior,

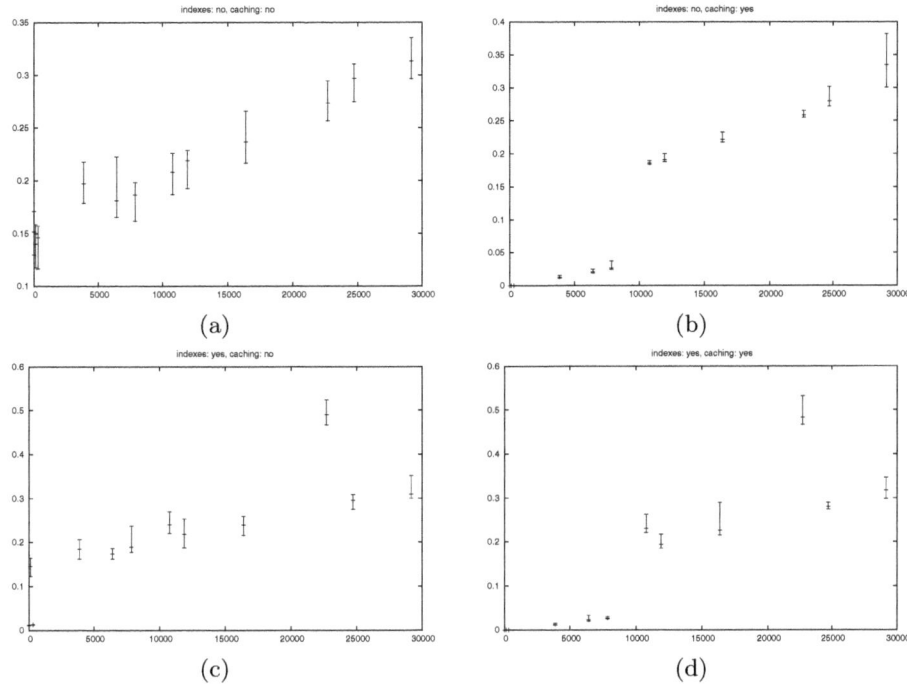

Fig. 4. Results of experiments performed on Adult Data Set to validate monotonicity of query execution time vs. size of the result. Abscissae report the size of the result set of the query, ordinates report average, minimum, and maximum time taken by the DBMS server to execute the query. The four charts show measure in the following four situations: (a) neither indexes nor caches, (b) no index and caching activated, (c) indexes available and caching not active, (d) indexes available and caching active.

see Figs. 4(c) and 4(d). The most evident misbehavior is the query with whose result set size is 22,696 which is much slower than the others and whose behavior can be hardly explained considering the cardinality (nine) of the values of the single attribute on which the query performs selection.

7.2 Performance

We now intend to show the performance of certified queries using our prototypical implementation.

The following experiments were performed on a dual core CPU 2.10GHz with 3 Gb of RAM and one hard disk (5,400 rpm Serial ATA) running Linux 2.6.24 (Ubuntu™8.04, 32 bit). We used the MySQL DBMS (version 5.0.45). The prototypical software is written in Java™and uses MySql JDBC Connector Java-bean 5.1.15 to connect to the DBMS.

Our prototypical implementation, adopts the algorithm described in Section 4.1 using the coarse-grained representation. This means that optimizations described

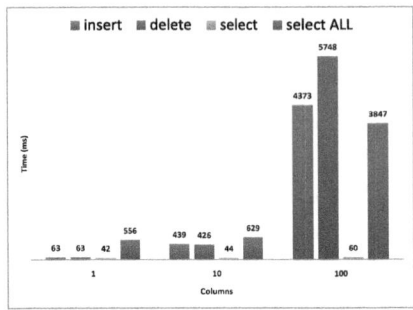
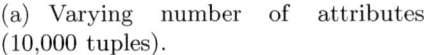
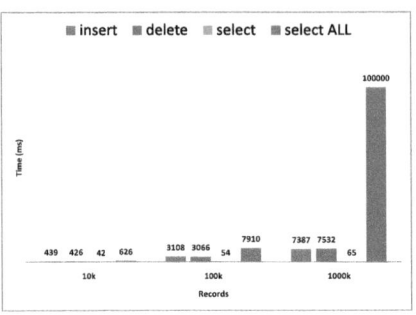

(a) Varying number of attributes (10,000 tuples).

(b) Varying number of tuples (10 attributes).

Fig. 5. Scalability analysis for operation insert, delete, select, and select-all. (a) Variation of performace while increasing the number of attributes. (b) Variation of performances while increasing the number of tuples.

in Section 4.3 are only partially implemented, hence, data presented in this section are pessimistic with respect to potential performance of the proposed technique. Namely, the number of query rounds to obtain a verification object for a (range) query is $O(\log |T|)$, where $|T|$ is the number of tuples in the table. After the verification object is received, verification is performed as described in Section 4.3. Select-all queries are more optimized in the sense that even if the skip list representation is coarse-grained, the verification object is obtained using a single query.

We first report tests about scalability performed on Artificial data set and then report performances on Adult Data Set taken from real life.

Scalability. We analyze performances of our prototype for the following four operations: insertion (*insert*), deletion (*delete*), single value selection (*select*), and full table selection (*select-all*).

For each operation and for each size of the artificial data set, we performed the operation 10 times. Time measurements have been performed within the software, and hence it accounts for transmission time to obtain data and verification object and computation time get certification of completeness and integrity.

Results in Fig. 5(a) show scalability with respect to number of attributes and in Fig. 5(b) show scalability with respect to number of tuples.

As figures show, our techniques perform very well for selections, since verification object is obtained with a few query rounds in our implementation. Also select-all queries scale well considering the amount of data involved. Theoretically, augmenting the number of attributes, the cost of computing row-hash increases linearly with the number of attributes. However, the time taken for computing row-hash is negligible with respect to query execution time.

Insertion and deletion scale poorly with respect to the number of attributes, see Fig. 5(a), since each change has to be performed on each security table. On the contrary, scalability, with respect to the number of tuples, is fairly good

Query Condition	Result Size (tuples)	Result Size (bytes)	Plain Execut. (ms)	Certified Execut. (ms)	Verifi-cation (ms)
makemoney = '>50K' AND age BETWEEN '17' AND '25'	114	14029	323	1363	203
makemoney = '>50K' AND age BETWEEN '17' AND '25' AND race = 'Amer-Indian-Eskimo'	2	276	254	392	14
makemoney = '>50K' AND workclass = 'Private' AND nativecountry = 'United-States' AND sex = 'Male'	3879	470016	1852	14543	1877

Fig. 6. Execution time for some example queries on the Adult Data Set

since authenticated skip lists are quite efficient. Also note that, these kind of operations might greatly benefit of a more parallel platform in which changes to the security tables can be concurrently performed. In our experiment, the time taken to perform insertion or deletion is basically the sum of the time taken to perfrom the operation on each security table.

Performances on real data. We consider some queries on Adult Data Set. Table 6 reports, for each query, result set size (tuples and bytes as reported by MySQL), time taken by a plain execution, total time taken by an execution with certified completeness and integrity, and time spent by client for result certification. For this experiments, we used the same non-optimized prototype that may perform several query rounds for each security query.

8 Conclusion

We presented a method that largely improves, with respect of the state of the art, the class of queries that can be authenticated using a conventional DBMS, without modifying pre-existing schemas and data, and without knowing the structure of the queries in advance. As future work we intend to exploit the same ideas in the context of queries involving join operations.

References

1. Devanbu, P.T., Gertz, M., Martel, C.U., Stubblebine, S.G.: Authentic third-party data publication. In: DBSEC, pp. 101–112 (2001)
2. Di Battista, G., Palazzi, B.: Authenticated relational tables and authenticated skip lists. In: DBSEC, pp. 31–46 (2007)
3. Miklau, G., Suciu, D.: Implementing a tamper-evident database system. In: ASIAN: 10th Asian Computing Science Conference, pp. 28–48 (2005)
4. Pang, H., Jain, A., Ramamritham, K., Tan, K.: Verifying completeness of relational query results in data publishing. In: SIGMOD Conf., pp. 407–418 (2005)

5. Pang, H., Tan, K.L.: Authenticating query results in edge computing. In: Proc. of the 20th Int. Conference on Data Engineering, pp. 560–571 (2004)
6. Xie, M., Wang, H., Yin, J., Meng, X.: Integrity auditing of outsourced data. In: VLDB, pp. 782–793 (2007)
7. Xie, M., Wang, H., Yin, J., Meng, X.: Providing freshness guarantees for outsourced databases. In: EDBT, pp. 323–332. ACM, New York (2008)
8. Mykletun, E., Narasimha, M., Tsudik, G.: Authentication and integrity in outsourced databases. Trans. Storage 2(2), 107–138 (2006)
9. Tamassia, R.: Authenticated data structures. In: Di Battista, G., Zwick, U. (eds.) ESA 2003. LNCS, vol. 2832, pp. 2–5. Springer, Heidelberg (2003)
10. Merkle, R.C.: A certified digital signature. In: Brassard, G. (ed.) CRYPTO 1989. LNCS, vol. 435, pp. 218–238. Springer, Heidelberg (1990)
11. Goodrich, M.T., Tamassia, R., Schwerin, A.: Implementation of an authenticated dictionary with skip lists and commutative hashing. In: Proc. DISCEX II, pp. 68–82 (2001)
12. Buldas, A., Roos, M., Willemson, J.: Undeniable replies for database queries. In: Proc. Intern. Baltic Conf. on DB and IS, vol. 2, pp. 215–226 (2002)
13. Goodrich, M.T., Tamassia, R., Triandopoulos, N.: Super-efficient verification of dynamic outsourced databases. In: Malkin, T.G. (ed.) CT-RSA 2008. LNCS, vol. 4964, pp. 407–424. Springer, Heidelberg (2008)
14. Devanbu, P., Gertz, M., Martel, C., Stubblebine, S.G.: Authentic data publication over the Internet. Journal of Computer Security 11(3), 291–314 (2003)
15. Singh, S., Prabhakar, S.: Ensuring correctness over untrusted private database. In: EDBT 2008, pp. 476–486. ACM, New York (2008)
16. Yang, Y., Papadias, D., Papadopoulos, S., Kalnis, P.: Authenticated join processing in outsourced databases. In: SIGMOD 2009, pp. 5–18. ACM, New York (2009)
17. Zhou, Y., Salehi, A., Aberer, K.: Scalable delivery of stream query results. PVLDB 2(1), 49–60 (2009)
18. Bloom, B.H.: Space/time trade-offs in hash coding with allowable errors. Communications of the ACM 13, 422–426 (1970)
19. Cheng, W., Tan, K.: Authenticating knn query results in data publishing. In: Proc. 4th Int. Workshop on Secure Data Management, pp. 47–63 (2007)
20. Li, F., Hadjieleftheriou, M., Kollios, G., Reyzin, L.: Dynamic authenticated index structures for outsourced databases. In: ACM SIGMOD, pp. 121–132 (2006)
21. Dang, T.K.: Ensuring correctness, completeness, and freshness for outsourced tree-indexed data. Information Resources Management Jrnl., 59–76 (2008)
22. Narasimha, M., Tsudik, G.: Authentication of outsourced databases using signature aggregation and chaining. In: Li Lee, M., Tan, K.-L., Wuwongse, V. (eds.) DASFAA 2006. LNCS, vol. 3882, pp. 420–436. Springer, Heidelberg (2006)
23. Yang, Y., Papadopoulos, S., Papadias, D., Kollios, G.: Spatial outsourcing for location-based services. In: ICDE, pp. 1082–1091 (2008)
24. Polivy, D.J., Tamassia, R.: Authenticating distributed data using Web services and XML signatures. In: Proc. ACM Workshop on XML Security (2002)
25. Pugh, W.: Skip lists: A probabilistic alternative to balanced trees. In: Workshop on Algorithms and Data Structures, pp. 437–449 (1989)
26. UCI Machine Learning Repository, University of California, Irvine, School of Information and Computer Sciences (2007),
http://www.ics.uci.edu/~mlearn/MLRepository.html

Mining Likely Properties of Access Control Policies via Association Rule Mining

JeeHyun Hwang[1], Tao Xie[1], Vincent Hu[2], and Mine Altunay[3]

[1] Department of Computer Science, North Carolina State University, Raleigh
jhwang4@ncsu.edu, xie@csc.ncsu.edu
[2] Computer Security Division, National Institute of Standards and Technology,
Gaithersburg
vincent.hu@nist.gov
[3] Computing Division, Fermi National Laboratory, Batavia
maltunay@fnal.gov

Abstract. Access control mechanisms are used to control which principals (such as users or processes) have access to which resources based on access control policies. To ensure the correctness of access control policies, policy authors conduct policy verification to check whether certain properties are satisfied by a policy. However, these properties are often not written in practice. To facilitate property verification, we present an approach that automatically mines likely properties from a policy via the technique of association rule mining. In our approach, mined likely properties may not be true for all the policy behaviors but are true for most of the policy behaviors. The policy behaviors that do not satisfy likely properties could be faulty. Therefore, our approach then conducts likely-property verification to produce counterexamples, which are used to help policy authors identify faulty rules in the policy. To show the effectiveness of our approach, we conduct evaluation on four XACML policies. Our evaluation results show that our approach achieves more than 30% higher fault-detection capability than that of an existing approach. Our approach includes additional techniques such as basic and prioritization techniques that help reduce a significant percentage of counterexamples for inspection compared to the existing approach.

1 Introduction

Access control mechanisms are used to control which principals (such as users or processes) have access to which resources in a system. Database management systems often adopt access control mechanisms to offer fine-grained access control to sensitive resources based on access control policies (in short as policies). In such a situation, identifying discrepancies between polices and their intended function is crucial because correct policy behaviors are based on the premise that the policies are correctly specified. These discrepancies may result in unexpected policy behaviors such as allowing malicious users to access sensitive resources. To increase our confidence on the correctness of policy behaviors, policies must undergo rigorous verification.

S. Foresti and S. Jajodia (Eds.): Data and Applications Security XXIV, LNCS 6166, pp. 193–208, 2010.
© IFIP International Federation for Information Processing 2010

There are property verification tools [1, 2] available for policies specified in specification languages such as XACML (eXtensible Access Control Markup Language) [3] and Ponder [4]. Given a policy and its properties, property verification is to verify whether the policy satisfies the properties. If a property is not satisfied, a property verification tool produces counterexamples that violate properties. An example property for a policy in a grading system used by Fisher et al. [1] is that a student cannot assign grades. Any violations (that allow a student to assign grades) against the property expose faults in the policy. In addition, the quality of the properties can be measured based on their fault-detection capability. Our previous work [5] showed that the confidence on policy correctness based on property verification is dependent on the quality of the specified properties. In other words, policy authors require properties of high quality (which have a high chance to detect faults in the policy) to increase the confidence on policy correctness sufficiently.

While property verification is useful to detect faults, in practice, most policies are not equipped with properties. In addition, manually writing properties is not a trivial task for two reasons. First, the policy authors must have sufficient domain knowledge of a given policy to identify properties for the policy. Second, as the size of a policy increases and the structure of a policy becomes complex, identifying properties is more challenging.

To address these issues, we present an approach that automatically mines likely properties (from a policy) via association rule mining [6]. Association rule mining is used to discover correlations among data in a large database. When a policy includes many rules in a sophisticated structure, manually inspecting each policy behavior for fault detection is not trivial and error-prone. In such a situation, mined patterns of policy behaviors can be used to detect a fault in a policy [7].

In the policy context, we apply association rule mining to mine patterns of interest, called *likely properties* characterizing correlations of policy behaviors with regards to attribute values. For example, in the policy for a grading system, based on similar policy behaviors of a lecturer and a faculty member, our approach mines a property: if a lecturer is permitted to conduct actions (e.g., assign/modify) on grades, a faculty member is likely to be permitted to conduct the same actions on grades. We call these properties as *likely properties* because our approach mines properties that may not be true for all the policy behaviors but are true for most of the policy behaviors. In such a situation, *likely properties* may lead to a small number of violations. As these violations are deviations from the policy's normal behavior, these violations are special cases for inspection to determine whether these violations expose faults.

This paper makes the following three main contributions:

- We develop an approach that analyzes a policy under verification and mines *likely properties* characterizing correlations of policy behaviors with regards to attribute values.
- We verify a policy under verification with likely properties to check whether a policy includes a fault. Our fault-detection approach includes two techniques:

the basic technique is to inspect counterexamples in no particular order, and the prioritization technique is to inspect counterexamples by the order of their fault-detection likelihood.
- We compare our approach with a previous related approach [8] in terms of cost and effectiveness. Our approach achieves more than 30% higher fault-detection capability than that of the previous related approach. Our approach such as the basic and prioritization techniques helps reduce a significant percentage of counterexamples for inspection compared to the existing approach.

The rest of the paper is organized as follows. Section 2 presents an illustrative example. Section 3 presents definitions of our proposed likely properties. Section 4 presents our fault-detection approach. Section 5 presents evaluation of our approach. Sections 6 and 7 discuss related work and issues. Section 8 concludes the paper.

2 Example

Figure 1 illustrates an example access control policy for a grading system in a university as if-else statements in code. Lines 1-3 include rules that allow a faculty member to assign or view ExternalGrade or InternalGrade. Lines 4-6 include rules that allow a Teaching Assistant (TA) to assign or receive InternalGrade. Lines 7-9 include rules that allow a student to receive ExternalGrade. Lines 10-12 include rules that allow a family member to receive ExternalGrade. Lines 13-15 include rules that allow a lecturer to assign or view ExternalGrade or InternalGrade. Line 16 is a tautology rule to deny requests that are not applicable in the preceding rules.

Figure 1 is a faulty version of the policy used by Fisher et al. [1]. The faulty version includes a fault at Line 6, where action attribute "Receive" is used instead of "View". Due to this fault, we observe two incorrect policy behaviors. First, a TA is *Denied* to *View* InternalGrade while a correct behavior is that a TA is *Permitted* to *View* InternalGrade. Second, a TA is *Permitted* to *Receive* InternalGrade while a correct behavior is that a TA is *Denied* to *Receive* InternalGrade.

We observe that actions over different roles may have similar policy behaviors. Figure 1 is a Role-Based Access Control policy (RBAC) [9]. In RBAC policies, one role'permissions may inherit another role's permissions based on role inheritance such as that a faculty member inherits all permissions of a TA in a policy. In such a situation, one's (e.g., a faculty member's) permissions may be dependent on another's (e.g., TA's) permissions. Based on this implication, we discover correlation of subjects with regards to their corresponding decisions. We can also discover correlation of actions with regards to their corresponding decisions. For example, in Figure 1, regardless of any roles or resources, if one role (e.g., Faculty) is *Permitted* to *Assign* a resource (e.g., InternalGrade), the role is likely to be *Permitted* to *View* the resource. In the paper, we denote such a correlation as implication relation (based on action attributes). Formally, an attribute item *Item* $(v,$

```
 1 If role = Faculty
 2   and resource = (ExternalGrade or InternalGrade)
 3   and action = (View or Assign) then Permit
 4 If role = TA
 5   and resource = (InternalGrade)
 6   and action = (Assign or Receive) then Permit // Faulty Line
 7 If role = Student
 8   and resource = (ExternalGrade)
 9   and action = (Receive) then Permit
10 If role = Family
11   and resource = (ExternalGrade)
12   and action = (Receive) then Permit
13 If role = Lecturer
14   and resource = (ExternalGrade or InternalGrade))
15   and action = (Assign or View) then Permit
16 Deny
```

Fig. 1. An example policy including a fault (in Line 6); "Receive" (instead of "View", which is correct) is specified

		Assign	View	Receive
External Grade	Faculty	Permit	Permit	Deny
	TA	Deny	Deny	Deny
	Student	Deny	Deny	Permit
	Family	Deny	Deny	Permit
	Lecturer	Permit	Permit	Deny
Internal Grade	Faculty	Permit	Permit	Deny
	TA	Permit	Deny	Permit
	Student	Deny	Deny	Deny
	Family	Deny	Deny	Deny
	Lecturer	Permit	Permit	Deny

Fig. 2. Decision table for the policy in Figure 1 based on action relations

dec) represents any request that includes v is evaluated to dec. For example, $Item$ ({Assign}, Permit) represents that any request that includes an "Assign" action is evaluated to be *Permitted*. We represent the example correlation as $\{Item$ (Assign, Permit)$\} \Rightarrow \{Item$ (View, Permit)$\}$ described in Section 3.

We next describe how to mine such implication relations. To mine implication relations (based on action attributes), we describes all possible request-decision pairs in a table in Figure 2. Each request requires three attribute values (such as subject, resource, and action attributes). Columns 1 and 2 show all possible combinations of resource and subject (role) attributes, respectively. Columns 3-5 describe the decisions (e.g., Permit or Deny) of a combination of a subject and a resource (in Columns 1 and 2) associated with an action "Assign", "View", or "Receive", respectively. For example, in the second row, given a role (Faculty) and a resource (ExternalGrade), the table describes decisions associated with action attributes such as "Assign", "View", or "Receive". Three requests, r_1 (Faculty, Assign, ExternalGrade), r_2 (Faculty, View, ExternalGrade), and r_3 (Faculty, Receive, ExternalGrade) are evaluated to "Permit", "Permit", and "Deny" (which are described in the second row), respectively.

Relation	Frequency	Confidence (%)
({Receive}, Permit) → ({View}, Deny)	3	100
({View}, Permit) → ({Assign}, Permit)	4	100
({View}, Permit) → ({Receive}, Deny)	4	100

Fig. 3. Implication relations $R1$ with 100% confidence

Relation	Frequency	Confidence (%)
({Receive}, Permit) → ({Assign}, Deny)	2	66
({Assign}, Permit) → ({View}, Permit)	4	80
({Assign}, Permit) → ({Receive}, Deny)	4	80

Fig. 4. Implication relations $R2$ with at least 65% but less than 100% confidence

Counterexamples	Fault Detection
TA is Permitted to Assign InternalGrades	
TA is Denied to View InternalGrades	detected
TA is Permitted to Receive InternalGrades	detected

Fig. 5. Counterexamples and their fault-detection capability

Then, we feed these request-decision pairs into an association mining tool to mine implication relations. We set the confidence threshold as 65%, which is derived based on our preliminary experience. The confidence (described in Section 4) reflects likelihood of an implication relation. Figures 3 and 4 show mined implication relations $R1$ with 100%, and relations $R2$ with at least 65% but less than 100% confidence. For example, in $R1$, the relation $\{Item$ (Receive, Permit)$\}$ $\Rightarrow \{Item$ (View, Deny)$\}$ in Figure 3 indicates that if a subject is *Permitted* to *Receive* a resource r, the subject is *Denied* to *View* r with 100% confidence. An example case is that if a Student is *Permitted* to *Receive* ExternalGrades, then, a Student is *Denied* to *View* ExternalGrade (as described at fourth row in Figure 2). Column "Frequency" denotes the number of occurrences of such cases.

As implication relations in $R2$ cannot achieve 100% confidence, we find counterexamples violating the implication relations. If a counterexample is evaluated to be an unexpected decision, we say that the counterexample exposes a fault. The relation $\{Item$ (Assign, Permit)$\} \Rightarrow \{Item$ (Receive, Deny)$\}$ in Figure 4 indicates that if a subject is *Permitted* to *Assign* a resource r, the subject is *Denied* to *Receive* r with 80% confidence. As this relation cannot achieve 100% confidence, we can find a counterexample satisfying $\{Item$ (Assign, Permit)$\} \Rightarrow \{\neg$ $Item$ (Receive, Deny)$\}$. A counterexample against the implication relation is that a TA is *Permitted* to *Receive* InternalGrade (while the TA is *Permitted* to *Assign* InternalGrade). Note that the correct policy behavior is that a TA is *Denied* to *Receive* InternalGrade. Therefore, we inspect the counterexample and determine that the counterexample exposes the fault in the example policy. Figure 5 describes counterexamples, which do not satisfy the implication relations in $R2$. In Figure 5, two counterexamples are determined to expose the fault.

3 Definitions

This section presents definitions for attribute item set and implication relations. Let $\mathcal{S}$, $\mathcal{O}$, and $\mathcal{A}$, respectively, denote the set of all the subjects (e.g., user's role or rank), resources (e.g., file) and actions (e.g., write or read) in an access control system.

3.1 Attribute Item Set

An attribute item set is used to represent a policy behavior with regards to a specific set of attribute values v (e.g., faculty and file) and a decision dec (e.g., Permit). An attribute item $Item$ (v, dec) represents that any request that includes v is evaluated to dec. For example, $Item$ ({Faculty}, Permit) represents that any request that includes a faculty role is evaluated to be *Permitted*. Note that v may include multiple attribute values.

3.2 Implication Relations

An implication relation $\{Item_1 \ (v_1, \ dec_1)\} \Rightarrow \{Item_2 \ (v_2, \ dec_2)\}$ represents that, if a request r_1 including v_1 and values V of other attributes is evaluated to dec_1, then a request r_2 including v_2 and the same values V of other attributes is likely to be evaluated to dec_2.

In this paper, we propose implication relations based on subjects, actions, and subject-action relations, as presented next. Based on selection of attributes, other types of relations can be mined from a policy. We discuss these other implication relations in Section 7.

Implication relation of subject attribute item sets. We denote this implication relation as $\{Item_1 \ (s_1, \ dec_1)\} \Rightarrow \{Item_2 \ (s_2, \ dec_2)\}$ where s_1 and s_2 are subjects (i.e., $s_1 \in \mathcal{S}$ and $s_2 \in \mathcal{S}$). This implication relation indicates that dec_1 of a request including s_1 and values V of other attributes implies dec_2 of a request including s_2 and the same values V of other attributes. In a Role-Based Access Control (RBAC) policy [9], one role'permissions may inherit another role's permissions according to role inheritance. In such a situation, one role's permissions may be associated with another role's permissions. For example, Faculty inherits permissions of TA in a grading policy. We represent this role inheritance as $\{Item_1 \ (\{TA\}, Permit)\} \Rightarrow \{Item_2 \ (\{Faculty\}, Permit)\}$.

Implication relation of action attribute item sets. We denote this implication relation as $\{Item_1 \ (a_1, \ dec_1)\} \Rightarrow \{Item_2 \ (a_2, \ dec_2)\}$ where a_1 and a_2 are actions (i.e., $a_1 \in \mathcal{A}$ and $a_2 \in \mathcal{A}$). This implication relation indicates that dec_1 of a request including a_1 and values V of other attributes implies dec_2 of a request including a_2 and the same values V of other attributes. For example, in a grading policy, if a user is *Permitted* to *Assign* grades, the user is likely to be *Permitted* to *View* grades. In such a case, the "Assign" action is likely to be correlated with "View". We represent this case as $\{Item_1 \ (\{Assign\}, Permit)\} \Rightarrow \{Item_2 \ (\{View\}, Permit)\}$.

Implication relation of subject-action attribute item sets. We denote this implication relation as $\{Item_1 \ (\{s_1,\ a\},\ dec_1)\} \Rightarrow \{Item_2 \ (\{s_2,\ a\},\ dec_2)\}$ where s_1 and s_2 are subjects, and a is an action (i.e., $s_1 \in \mathcal{S}$, $s_2 \in \mathcal{S}$, and $a \in \mathcal{A}$). This implication relation indicates that dec_1 of a request including s_1, a, and values V of other attributes implies dec_2 of a request including s_2, a, and the same values V of other attributes. For example, in a grading policy, if a TA is *Permitted* to *Assign* grades, *Faculty* is likely to be *Permitted* to *Assign* grades. We represent this role inheritance with specific action *assign* as $\{Item_1 \ (\{$TA, *Assign*$\},$ Permit$)\} \Rightarrow \{Item_2 \ (\{$Faculty, *Assign*$\},$ Permit$)\}$. This implication relation considers both subjects and actions together.

Based on the preceding definitions, we mine relations of various attribute item sets. Each of implication relations focuses on mining relations of specific attribute items.

4   Approach

This section presents our approach for detecting faults in a policy using our likely-property verification techniques. Our approach includes three components: relation-table generation, association rule mining, and likely-property verification. The relation-table generation component takes a policy p as an input and generates tables based on attribute items in the policy p. The association rule mining component takes attribute items (from the table produced by the previous component) and mines our proposed implication relations r of attribute item sets. The likely-property verification component takes p and r as inputs and verifies p against r. The component produces verification reports based on whether the given likely properties p are satisfied; when a property is violated, counterexamples are generated accordingly. The policy authors inspect counterexamples to determine whether they expose faults. To detect faults effectively, we propose a prioritization technique to recommend the policy authors to inspect counterexamples by the order of their fault-detection likelihood.

4.1   Relation-Table Generation

Our approach first analyzes a policy p and generates a policy behavior report charactering all possible request-response pairs in the policy p. Our approach next analyzes the policy behavior report, and then generates relation tables (including all request-response pairs) that can be used as input for an association rule mining tool. For example, to mine implication relations of action attribute items (as shown in Figure 2), we generate a relation table that organizes all possible request-decision pairs. Based on this table, we generate our proposed attribute item sets used to mine implication relations.

4.2   Implication Relations of Attribute Items

Given attribute items, we use association rule mining [6] to mine relations of attribute items. We focus on mining implication relations, which are of the form

$\{Item\ (v_1,\ dec_1)\} \Rightarrow \{Item\ (v_2,\ dec_2)\}$ described in Section 3. We use an association rule mining tool, called Apriori [10], that takes attribute items in a relation table as an input and generates implication relations of attribute item sets.

In association rule mining, thresholds such as *support* and *confidence* are used to constrain generating association relations. Let t denote the total number of transactions that corresponds to the number of rows in a relation table. For example, Figure 2 includes 10 transactions. Let d denote the number of transactions including an attribute item X. The support supp(X) of X is $\frac{d}{t}$. We measure *confidence*, which is likelihood of an implication relation: confidence($X \Rightarrow Y$) = $\frac{\text{supp}(X \cup Y)}{\text{supp}(X)}$. These implication relations are *likely proper-ties*, which are true for most of the policy behaviors and may lead to a small number of violations. Our rationale is that violations produced by likely-property verification deviate from the policy's normal behaviors and are special cases for inspection to determine whether these violations expose faults.

As mined implication relations can be many, our approach filters out mined implication relations with two mechanisms. First, we report only implication relations with confidence values over a pre-defined confidence threshold. As a confidence value measures likelihood of likely properties, likely properties with high confidence values are true for most of the policy behaviors. We set a confidence threshold based on our preliminary experience. Second, we report only implication relations each of which has fewer than n counterexamples where n is a pre-defined number. Consider a policy that is mostly correct and faults in the policy are not many. If the number of counterexamples (produced by verification of a likely property) is small, this property may deviate from normal policy behaviors. Therefore, we constrain the number of counterexamples produced for likely properties as less than n, i.e., mined likely properties with more than n counterexamples are filtered out and not reported. Based on these filtering mechanisms, we can reduce a large number of implication relations and report only reduced implication relations as likely properties.

4.3   Likely-Property Verification

Our approach next verifies the policy with the likely properties to check whether the policy includes a fault. Our rationale is that, as likely properties are true for most of the policy behaviors, counterexamples (which do not satisfy the likely properties) deviate from the policy's normal behaviors and are special cases for inspection.

Basic and Prioritization Techniques. A basic technique is to inspect counterexamples without any inspection order among the counterexamples. Since the number of generated counterexamples can be large, manual inspection of the counterexamples can be tedious. To address the preceding issue, we propose a prioritization technique that classifies counterexamples into various counterexample sets based on their fault-detection likelihood. The technique evaluates

Algorithm 1. Counterexample classification

Input: $c_1, c_2, \cdots, c_n$ where each c_i is a counterexample, m, which is the largest
number of counterexamples generated for a likely properties.
Output: $CS_{du}, CS_1, \cdots, CS_m$ where each CS_j is a set of counterexamples.

```
1  CS_du := ∅; CS_1 := ∅; ···; CS_m := ∅;  for i := 1 to n do
2     if c_i ∉ CS_du then
3        Flag := false ;
4        for j := 1 to m do
5           if c_i ∈ CS_j then
6              CS_j = CS_j − {c_i} ;
7              CS_du = CS_du ∪ {c_i} ;
8              Flag := true ;

9        if Flag = false then
10          Prop := the property for which counterexample c_i is generated;
11          w := the number of counterexamples generated for Prop;
12          CS_w = CS_w ∪ {c_i} ;

13 return CS_du, CS_1, ···, CS_m;
```

counterexamples in each of the counterexample sets by the order of their fault-detection likelihood until a fault is detected. The prioritization technique maintains the same level of fault-detection capability of the basic technique when the policy contains a single fault.

We next describe how we classify counterexamples into counterexample sets CS_{du}, CS_1, ..., CS_n, based on their fault-detection likelihood. First, we give the highest priority to duplicate counterexamples, which are classified to CS_{du}. Duplicate counterexamples produced from different likely properties can be more suspicious to expose fault. Second, we investigate the number of counterexamples produced by likely properties to set priorities among counterexamples. As a likely property may lead to less number of counterexamples, the policy authors are required to verify less number of counterexamples to ensure the correctness of likely properties to be true for all policy behaviors. Given a property that has w counterexamples, we classify these counterexamples to CS_w ($1 \leq w \leq m$ where m is the largest number of counterexamples generated for a likely property). The pseudocode of the classification algorithm is in Algorithm 1. The policy authors first inspect counterexamples in CS_{du}. The policy authors then inspect counterexamples in CS_i by the order of CS_1, ..., CS_m ($1 \leq i \leq m$) until a fault is detected.

5   Evaluation

We next describe the evaluation results to show the effectiveness of our approach with four real-world access control policies as subjects.

5.1   Research Questions and Metrics

In our evaluation, we try to address the following research questions:

- RQ1: How higher percentage of faults are detected by our approach compared to an existing related approach [8]? This question helps to show that our approach can perform better than the existing approach in terms of fault-detection capability.
- RQ2: How lower percentage of distinct counterexamples are generated by our approach compared to the existing approach [8]? This question helps to show that our approach can perform better than the existing approach in terms of cost (i.e., the number of distinct counterexamples for inspection) for detecting faults.
- RQ3: For cases where a fault in a faulty policy is detected by our approach, how high percentage of distinct counterexamples (for inspection) are reduced by our prioritization technique (in terms of detecting the first-detected fault) over our basic technique? This question helps to show that our prioritization technique can perform better than the basic technique in terms of cost (i.e., the number of distinct counterexamples for inspection) for detecting the first fault.

To measure fault-detection capability in our evaluation, we synthesize faulty policies, $f_1, f_2, ..., f_n$ by seeding faults into a subject policy f_o, with only one fault in each faulty policy for ease of evaluation. Then, the chosen approach generates counterexamples for each faulty policy to detect the seeded fault. Note that we seed a single fault for f_i. For n faulty policies, n faults exist. Let $CP(f_i)$ be distinct counterexamples generated by the chosen approach for f_i. Let $Count(f_i)$ be the number of distinct counterexamples in $CP(f_i)$ for f_i. Let $DE(f_i)$ be the reduced number of distinct counterexamples by the prioritization technique to detect the fault in f_i for cases where the fault in f_i is detected by our approach.

- **Fault-detection ratio (FR)**. Let p be the number of faults detected by counterexamples (generated by the chosen approach) for $f_1, f_2, ..., f_n$. The FR is $\frac{p}{n}$. The FR is measured to address RQ1.
- **Counterexample count (CC)**. The counterexample count is the average number of distinct counterexamples generated by the chosen approach for each faulty policy. The counterexample count is $\frac{\sum_{i=1}^{n} Count(f_i)}{n}$. Note that a counterexample is synonymous to a request. The CC is measured to address RQ2. The CC is used to define the CRB metric below.
- **Counterexample-reduction ratio (CRB) for our approach over the existing approach**. Let CC_1 and CC_2 be counterexample counts (CCs) by our approach and the existing approach, respectively. The CRB is $(\frac{CC_2 - CC_1}{CC_2})$. The CRB is measured to address RQ2.
- **Counterexample-reduction ratio (CRP) for the prioritization technique over the basic technique**. Let $f'_1, f'_2, ..., f'_m$ be faulty policies that are detected by our generated counterexamples. The CRB is a percentage that measures the reduction ratio in terms of the number of the counterexamples for inspection to detect the first fault by the prioritization technique

over the basic technique. The CRP is ($\frac{\sum_{i=1}^{m} Count(f'_i) - \sum_{i=1}^{m} DE(f'_i)}{\sum_{i=1}^{m} Count(f'_i)}$). The CRP is measured to address RQ3.

5.2 Evaluation Setup

We use fault types defined in a policy fault model [11] to automatically seed a policy with faults for synthesizing faulty policies, with only one fault in each faulty policy for ease of evaluation. We use four fault types: Change-Rule Effect (CRE), Rule-Target True (RTT), Rule-Target False (RTF), and Removal Rule (RMR). A CRE fault inverts a decision (e.g., change `Permit` to `Deny`) in a rule. An RTT fault indicates changing a rule to be applicable for any request. An RTF fault indicates changing a rule to be applicable for no request. An RMR fault indicates that a rule is missing. We seed one fault to form each of faulty policies, i.e., each synthesized faulty policy includes only a single fault.

For the inspection for our approach, we use a tool, called Margrave [1], that is verification tool for XACML policies. Margrave also has a feature that statically analyzes an XACML policy and produces all possible request-decision pairs in a summarized format. Given a faulty policy, Margrave generates all possible request-decision pairs to be used for generating relation tables. We next mine implication relations from the relation tables using an association rule mining tool [10]. Our approach filters out implication relations each of which produces at most five counterexamples.

We compare the results of our approach with those of a previous related approach [8]. Let a decision tree (DT) denotes the related approach that uses a decision tree to infer properties. Given request-decision pairs, DT learns policy behaviors and generates request-classification rules. Therefore, incorrectly classified requests (i.e., counterexamples) deviate from normal policy behaviors, and are required to be inspected. We specify a confidence threshold as 0.4% based on our tuning of evaluation setup for DT to generate similar counterexamples as our approach for the small sample of faulty policies used in the tuning of evaluation setup. In our evaluation, inspection of counterexamples (to determine whether the counterexamples expose faults) is automatically conducted by comparing the two decisions evaluated by a faulty policy and its corresponding original policy (that is assumed to be correct). However, in general, this inspection is often a manual process conducted by the policy authors.

5.3 Evaluation Subjects

In our evaluation, we use four policies specified in XACML [3]. XACML is an access control policy specification language. Figure 6 summarizes the characteristics of each policy. Columns 1-5 show the evaluation subject name, the number of rules, and distinct attribute values in the subject, resource, and action attributes in the policy, respectively. A subject attribute corresponds a role attribute since the policies are based on the Role-Based Access Control (RBAC) model [9]. We denote the number of roles, actions, and resources as # roles, # actions, and

Policy	# Rules	# roles	# actions	# resource
codeD2	12	5	3	2
continue-a	298	5	5	26
continue-b	306	5	5	26
univ.	27	7	7	8

Fig. 6. Subjects used in our evaluation

resource, respectively. Policies such as `continue-a` include attributes to describe constraints (e.g., checking whether a role has conflicts with another role). Our approach does not use these attributes for mining implication relations. The largest policy consists of 306 rules. The `codeD2` is a modified version of the `codeD`[1] by adding rules for a Lecturer role. For grading, a Lecturer role has the same privileges as a Faculty role. Two of the policies, namely `continue-a` and `continue-b`, are examples used by Fisler et al. [1] to specify access control policies for a conference review system. The `univ` policy is an RBAC policy used by Stoller et al. [12]. As its original policy is not written in XACML, we specified its policy behaviors in XACML.

5.4   Results

We conducted our evaluation on a laptop PC running Windows XP SP2 with 1G memory and dual 1.86GHz Intel Pentium processor. In our evaluation, for a faulty policy, we also measure the total processing time of request-response-pair generation, likely-property generation, counterexample generation, and automated inspection for correctness of given counterexamples. For each faulty policy (with at most 306 rules), our results show that the total processing time is less than 10 seconds.

We first show our detailed evaluation results for only Change-Rule-Effect faulty policies due to space limit. We then show our summarized evaluation results in Figure 8 for Rule-Target-True, Rule-Target-False, and Removal-Rule faulty policies. Figure 7 summarizes the detailed results for Change-Rule-Effect (CRE) faulty policies of each policy. Columns 1-2 show the evaluation subject name and the number of CRE faulty policies. Columns 3-11 show fault-detection ratio (denoted as "% FR"), counterexample count (denoted as "# CC"), CRB (for only the basic and prioritization techniques), and CRP (for only the prioritization technique) for each technique/approach, respectively. Let *Basic* and *Prioritization* denote our basic and prioritization techniques, respectively.

Results to address *RQ1*. In Figure 7, we observe that *DT*, *Basic* and *Prioritization* detect averagely 25.9%, 62.3%, and 62.3% (in Column "% FR") of CRE faulty policies, respectively. Our approach (including *Basic* and *Prioritization* techniques) outperform *DT* in terms of fault-detection capability. Our approach uses implication relations based on similar policy behaviors

---

[1] http://www.cs.brown.edu/research/plt/software/margrave/versions/01-01/
examples/college

Policy	# Pol	DT Approach		Basic Technique			Prioritization Technique			
		% FR	# CC	% FR	# CC	% CRB	% FR	# CC	% CRB	% CRP
code2D	12	66.6	4.0	83.3	1.1	72.5	83.3	1.1	72.5	27.3
univ	27	0.0	26.0	51.8	7.1	72.7	51.8	7.1	72.7	46.5
continue-a	33	21.2	85.4	66.6	39.8	53.4	66.6	39.8	53.4	44.5
continue-b	38	15.8	81.1	47.3	39.5	51.3	47.3	39.5	51.3	31.4
AVERAGE	27.5	25.9	49.1	62.3	21.9	55.5	62.3	21.9	55.5	38.5

FR : fault-detection ratio   CC : counterexample count
CRB : counterexample reduction ratio for our approach over the existing approach [8]
CRP : counterexample reduction ratio for the prioritization technique over the basic technique

Fig. 7. Fault-detection capability results of Change-Rule Effect (CRE) faulty policies for each policy and each technique

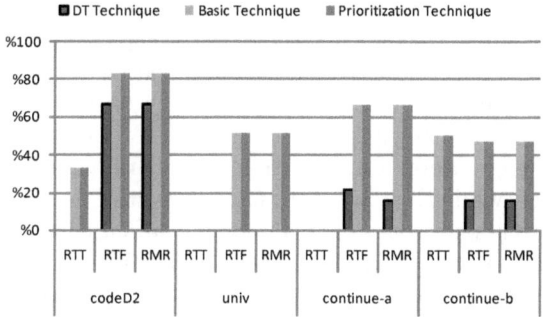

Fig. 8. Fault-detection ratios of faulty policies for each policy, each fault type, and each technique/approach

of different attributes values (e.g., Faculty and Lecturer). Therefore, if a faulty rule violates certain implication relations of attribute items, our techniques have better fault-detection capability than that of DT. However, DT constructs classification rules based on the number of the same decisions without taking into how different attribute values interact. Therefore, generated rules are rigid and often may easily miss certain correct policy behaviors. For example, in Figure 1, most requests that include a Faculty are evaluated to be *Permitted*. DT generates a classification rule that classifies requests including a Faculty to be *Permitted*. The rule is rigid since the rule's counterexamples reflects cases where a Faculty is *Denied* to take certain actions (e.g., a Faculty is *Denied* to *Receive* InternalGrades in Figure 1).

Results to address $RQ2$. Our goal is to detect a fault with as fewer counterexamples for inspection as possible. Intuitively, with more counterexamples to be inspected, fault-detection capability is likely to be improved. Our results show that our approach reduced the number of counterexamples by 55.5% (in Column "% CRB") over DT. As a result, we observe that our approach significantly reduced the number of counterexamples while our approach detected a higher percentage of faults (addressed in $RQ1$). In addition, our approach requires a small number of counterexamples for inspection compared with the number of all possible counterexamples. Given N_s subject, N_a action, and N_r resource values, the maximum number MAX_c of possible counterexamples is $N_s \times N_a \times N_r$. For example, for the continue-b policy, MAX_c is $5(N_s) \times 5(N_a) \times 26(N_r) = 650$ counterexamples. However, our approach generated only averagely 39.5 counterexamples (in Column "# CC") for inspection.

Results to address $RQ3$. *Prioritization* is a technique that enables to inspect counterexamples by the order of their fault-detection likelihood while keeping the same level of fault-detection capability of the *Basic* technique. Figure 7 shows that *Prioritization* reduced averagely 38.5% of counterexamples (for inspection) (in Column "% CRP") over *Basic*.

Note that inspecting counterexamples could not always detect faults. The continue-a policy consists of 298 rules and is complex enough to handle corner cases for granting correct decisions to different roles (e.g., an Administrator and a Member for paper review). Consider that rel_3 {*Item* ({Write}, Permit)} $\Rightarrow$ {*Item* ({Read}, Permit)} represents an implication relation of "Write" and "Read" attribute items. For the continue-a policy (without any seeded fault), there exist 41 requests satisfying rel_3. There are 3 requests (counterexamples) violating rel_3. One counterexample is that Members are *Denied* to read their Password resources, while they are *Permitted* to write Password resources. Considering a Password resource as a critical resource and are *Denied* to be read, this counterexample does not reveal a fault in the policy. In our evaluation, assuming that an original policy is correct, such counterexamples could not detect faults. However, we suspect that inspecting these special cases of policy behaviors would still provide value in gaining high confidence on the policy correctness, reflected by the preceding password example.

In addition, Figure 8 illustrates the average fault-detection ratios for each policy, each other fault type, and each technique/approach. For other fault types, our results show that *Prioritization* and *Basic* achieve the highest faulty-detection capability.

6   Related Work

Prior work that is closest to ours is Bauer et al.'s approach [7]. They proposed an approach to mine association rules, which are used to detect misconfiguration in a policy. Our proposed approach is different from their approach in three aspects. First, given subject, action, and resource attributes, our approach mines various implication relations such as relations of subject, action, and subject-action attribute item sets. In contrast, their mined implication relations are limited since their approach does not consider action attributes separately. Second, our approach includes a technique to prioritize which counterexamples should be inspected first based on their fault-detection likelihood while their approach does not include such a prioritization technique. Third, our approach exploits of characteristics of RBAC policies to mine implication relations whereas their approach uses historical access data to mine implication relations.

Our previous work [5] developed an approach for measuring the quality of policy properties in policy verification. Given user-specified properties, our previous approach measures the quality of the properties based on fault-detection capability. Our previous work [8] developed an approach to use machine learning algorithms (e.g., a classification algorithm) to mine policy properties automatically. Given request-decision pairs, this previous approach mines request-classification rules that classify requests to certain decisions. The rules there are based on a statistical policy-behavior model, which is statistically true. Therefore, faults can be likely to be detected when the policy violates this model. While this previous approach relies on classification rules, in this paper, we propose a new approach to mine likely properties based on implication relations (via association rule mining) and our evaluation shows that our new approach performs better than this previous approach.

7   Discussion

Our approach could be practical and effective to detect real faults in policies. Real faults may consist of one or several simple faults as described in our evaluation, and may cause a policy's behaviors to deviate from the policy's normal behaviors. Detecting real faults often depend on detecting such simple faults, which are shown to be effectively detected by our proposed approach. Our approach relies on attribute items (generated from a policy) for mining likely properties and thus could be applied to other types of access control policy beyond XACML policies.

In this paper, we do not consider implication relations based on resource, subject-resource, or action-resource attribute item sets. These implication relations can be used to derive valuable information indicating how resource attributes (with subject or action attributes) are correlated. Therefore, these relations may be useful for a policy with resource hierarchy (e.g., classified, unclassified, and shared resources) in a system. We plan to mine these implication relations to empirically investigate their effectiveness in terms of fault-detection capability.

8   Conclusions

We have developed an approach that analyzes a policy under verification and mines likely properties based on implication relations of subject, action, and subject-action attributes via association rule mining. Our approach also conducts likely-property verification to produce counterexamples, which are used to help policy authors detect faults in a policy. We compared our two techniques in our approach with a previous related approach [8] in terms of fault-detection capabilities in four different XACML policies. Our results showed that our approach has more than 30% higher fault-detection capability than that of the previous related approach, which mines properties based on a classification algorithm. Our results showed that our basic and prioritization techniques reduce a significant percentage of counterexamples for inspection compared to the related technique. Moreover, the prioritization technique further reduced a number of counterexamples (for inspection) to detect a first fault over the basic technique.

Acknowledgment

This work is supported in part by NSF grant CNS-0716579 and a NIST contract.

References

1. Fisler, K., Krishnamurthi, S., Meyerovich, L.A., Tschantz, M.C.: Verification and change-impact analysis of access-control policies. In: Proc. 27th International Conference on Software Engineering, pp. 196–205 (2005)
2. Hughes, G., Bultan, T.: Automated verification of access control policies. Technical Report 2004-22, Department of Computer Science, University of California, Santa Barbara (2004)
3. OASIS eXtensible Access Control Markup Language, XACML (2009), http://www.oasis-open.org/committees/xacml/
4. Damianou, N., Dulay, N., Lupu, E., Sloman, M.: The Ponder policy specification language. In: Proc. International Workshop on Policies for Distributed Systems and Networks, pp. 18–38 (2001)
5. Martin, E., Hwang, J., Xie, T., Hu, V.: Assessing quality of policy properties in verification of access control policies. In: Proc. Annual Computer Security Applications Conference, pp. 163–172 (2008)
6. Agrawal, R., Srikant, R.: Fast algorithms for mining association rules in large databases. In: Proc. 20th International Conference on Very Large Data Bases, pp. 487–499 (1994)
7. Bauer, L., Garriss, S., Reiter, M.K.: Detecting and resolving policy misconfigurations in access-control systems. In: Proc. 13th ACM Symposium on Access control Models and Technologies, pp. 185–194 (2008)
8. Martin, E., Xie, T.: Inferring access-control policy properties via machine learning. In: Proc. 7th IEEE Workshop on Policies for Distributed Systems and Networks, pp. 235–238 (2006)
9. Ferraiolo, D.F., Sandhu, R., Gavrila, S., Kuhn, D.R., Chandramouli, R.: Proposed NIST standard for role-based access control. ACM Trans. Inf. Syst. Secur. 4(3), 224–274 (2001)
10. Borgelt, C.: Apriori - Association Rule Induction/Frequent Item Set Mining (2009), http://www.borgelt.net/apriori.html/
11. Martin, E., Xie, T.: A fault model and mutation testing of access control policies. In: Proc. 16th International Conference on World Wide Web, pp. 667–676 (2007)
12. Stoller, S.D., Yang, P., Ramakrishnan, C., Gofman, M.I.: Efficient policy analysis for administrative role based access control. In: Proc. 14th ACM Conference on Computer and Communications Security, pp. 445–455 (2007)

Scalable and Efficient Reasoning for Enforcing Role-Based Access Control

Tyrone Cadenhead*, Murat Kantarcioglu, and Bhavani Thuraisingham

Department of Computer Science,
The University of Texas at Dallas, Richardson, TX 75083
{thc071000,muratk,bxt043000}@utdallas.edu
http://www.utdallas.com

Abstract. Today, many organizations generate large amount of data and have many users that need only partial access to resources at any time to collaborate in making critical decisions. Thus, there is a need for a scalable access control model that simplifies the management of security policies and handles the heterogeneity inherent in the information system. This paper proposes an ontology-based distributed solution to this problem, with the benefits of being scalable and producing acceptable response times.

1 Introduction

Organizations have large or varied access policies that suggest a need for more scalable and interoperable systems. There is still work to be done in addressing these two issues, in particular to build integrated access control systems that are simple to manage and require little changes as growth occurs within the organization. The semantic web offers benefits to organizations that wish to migrate to take advantage of the interoperability, reuse and the semantics it offers. However, access control is still a concern with this migration. This web environment must respect the privacy of sensitive information that it stores, and also support the implementation of models that grant privileges to the data. The Health Insurance Portability and Accountability Act, HIPAA [11], require that we prevent unintended disclosure of any part of the patient's record, thus requiring careful coordination and rules that associate users to the various segments of patients' records. To model such constraints, we utilize an existing security model, role-based access control (RBAC) [5,7], which already simplifies the security management of resources. In this paper, we leverage this feature of RBAC with existing semantic web technologies to allow for flexible integration and easily extensible semantic rules to automatically enforce access policies and ensure consistency of policies. In RBAC, the administrator statically defines privileges for users based on the user's role by associating permissions with the roles. This,

---

* This work is partially supported by Air Force Office of Scientific Research MURI Grant FA9550-08-1-0265, National Science Foundation Grant Career-0845803 and National Institutes of Health Grant 1R01LM009989.

S. Foresti and S. Jajodia (Eds.): Data and Applications Security XXIV, LNCS 6166, pp. 209–224, 2010.
© IFIP International Federation for Information Processing 2010

however, does not consider the case when a patient visits the emergency room for immediate treatment and the user is not preassigned to a role with access to the record. Although in this paper we use the healthcare domain as an illustration, our approach is applicable to other domains as well.

To make RBAC more dynamic, we extend our solution to the temporal RBAC (TRBAC) [2,13] model to allow roles to be enabled for a duration of time, which will allow temporary privileges to users for various reasons. Organizations, however, have different structures and disparate platforms supporting their security guidelines, and so the extended model must be able to support existing systems that may already have their own access control mechanisms. In addition, such a model must address the scalability and manageability issues that may arise as more systems are integrated. Therefore, we need an access control model that is not only temporally flexible, but also provides interoperability between platforms without sacrificing the simplicity of the model. In general, ontologies enable reconciliation and translation between different standards and so our extended model could incorporate both the properties of ontologies and RBAC. For example, hospital operational environments require collaboration between different specialists and the exchange of their expertise and knowledge [26,14], together with flexible access to records and resources. Ontologies also adhere to a description logic (DL) modeling formalism, thus adding the benefits of a DL knowledge base and an inference service, which we can use to check the consistency of policies. Also, we can extend the expressiveness of an ontology knowledge base with semantic rules. Moreover, using ontologies would provide the added benefits to build a scalable and efficient semantic web implementation of TRBAC that could provide accurate reasoning about what privileges the user should have on a resource.

The main contributions of this paper are the following: (i) to implement TRBAC using existing semantic technologies; (ii) to reason about particular users over a large number of instances in a DL knowledge base (KB); and (iii) to offer the ability to efficiently and accurately reason about access rights under any situation.

To achieve the first objective, we transform the access control policies into the semantic web rule language (SWRL) [12], which is more consistent with the web ontology language (OWL) specification (the W3C Recommendation for ontologies [18]). Second, various organizations, like hospitals, can integrate our semantic TRBAC model with their existing policies. Finally, using our solution allows the storing of data in a standard data interchange format, the querying and the reasoning to be done by a semantic query language and a description logic reasoner.

We realize the second objective by partitioning our knowledge base (which has a terminology box (TBox) and a assertion box (ABox)) into a set of smaller knowledge bases, which have the same TBox but a subset of the original ABox. A TBox consists of a set of classes and properties that model a domain, and the ABox contains the instances created based on the TBox. In addition, the underlying knowledge base data is expressed in the Resource Description Framework

(RDF) [22], the standard language for storing metadata about web resources. A global knowledge base normally resides in memory and offers real-time reasoning and querying, but is not scalable as we stream more data to it. The main reason is that the instances in the ABox grow as we scale our implementation, while the size of the TBox remains relatively the same. We propose a solution that only perform reasoning with a subset of instances (from the smaller ABoxes) in memory for a given RBAC session.

Finally, our proposed solution attempts to address two key objectives. First, efficiency determines the response time to make a decision; and second, correct reasoning ensures that all the data assertions (facts) are available when applying the security policies. To illustrate, we consider the healthcare domain, where making decisions in emergencies for a patient are critical and must be made in short periods of time.

This paper is organized as follows. Section 2 reviews previous work. Section 3 provides a theoretical background for the reader. Section 4 describes our architecture. Section 5 details our approach and techniques used to realize the scalability and efficiency of our implementation. Section 6 presents our experimental results. Section 7 provides a discussion of future research directions.

2   Related Work

Research has been active in the area of access control dealing with reasoning and scalability [4,27,6,15,17]. Previous approaches to modeling RBAC with description logic include the work by Cirio et. al. [4]. Their approach extends RBAC with contextual attributes and use a DL reasoner to classify users and resources and also verify the consistency of the access control policies. Moreover, they allow roles to be determined based on the users' attributes, which is unlike our approach where roles are temporally determined. Another approach is that done by Zhao et. al.[27]. They describe a formalism of RBAC using the DL language $\mathcal{ALCQ}$. In their work, they show how to use DL to model policy constraints (separation of duty, security role hierarchies). Furthermore, Finin et. al. [6] show different approaches to support RBAC in OWL. They investigate the use of OWL to unify parallel approaches to policy needs in real world domains. They discuss the use of rules and attributes in enforcing policies in SWRL and N3 logic with respect to examples with separation of duty. However, they did not show any experimental results for their domain. Our approach adds one more facet to the RBAC model, by addressing the scalability and efficiency aspects of RBAC reasoning with a temporal extension. There is also work on access control in the policy language XACML (the AOSIS standard for access control), where [15] addresses reasoning aspects and [17] focuses on the scalability aspects. Some other approaches address the scalability or the efficiency issues [20,23,9]. For example, Levandoski and Mokbel [16] store RDF data into relational databases, and use clustering and partitioning to reduce the number of joins and improve querying time. Database approaches to reasoning, however, require all instances of the data in the entire knowledge base (KB). To the best of our knowledge, this is the first work that implements TRBAC in a semantic web environment, with an emphasis on the healthcare domain, using a distributed modular approach.

3   Theoretical Background

We first present a description of the standard RBAC and the extended features in TRBAC . Next, we provide a brief background of description logics and rules.

3.1   RBAC

This model [5,7] generally comprises of loosely coupled components: (i) a *user* is usually a human or an autonomous agent; (ii) a *role* is a collection of permissions needed to perform a certain job function; (iii) a *permission* is an access mode that can be exercised on an *object*; and (iv) a *session* relates a user to roles.

- $PA : Roles \rightarrow Permissions$ the permission assignment function, that assigns to roles the permissions needed to complete their jobs;
- $UA : Users \rightarrow Roles$ the user assignment function, that assigns users to roles;
- $user : Sessions \rightarrow Users$, that assigns each session to a single user;
- $role : Sessions \rightarrow 2^{Roles}$, that assigns each session to a set of roles; and
- $RH \subseteq Roles \times Roles$, a partially ordered role hierarchy (written $\geq$).

To avoid confusion of the term role, we will use the term "role" when we are referring to the roles in the RBAC model, and instead use the term "property" when we are referring to the binary relations in DL.

3.2   TRBAC

The Temporal-RBAC (TRBAC) model as described in [2] is an extension of RBAC models that supports temporal constraints on the enabling/disabling of roles. TRBAC also supports periodic role enabling and disabling, and temporal dependencies among such actions. Such dependencies are expressed by means of role triggers that can also be used to constrain the set of roles that a particular user can activate at a given time instant. The firing of a trigger may cause a role to be enabled/disabled either immediately, or after an explicitly specified amount of time. The enabling/disabling actions may be given a priority that may help in solving conflicts, such as the simultaneous enabling and disabling of a role. We now formally introduce TRBAC extensions as presented in [2].

A periodic time is represented as the pair $\langle [begin, end], P \rangle$, where P is a periodic expression denoting an infinite set of periodic time instants, and $[begin, end]$ is a time interval denoting the lower and upper bounds that are imposed on instants in P. Two event expressions $enableR_1$ and $disableR_2$ are conflicting if $R_1 = R_2$. $(Prios, \preceq)$ is a totally ordered set of priorities, such that for all $x \in Prios$, $begin \preceq x \preceq end$ and we write $x \prec y$ if $x \preceq y$ and $x \neq y$. Periodic events are of the form $(I, P, p : E)$, where I is a time interval; P is a periodic expression; and $p : E$ is a prioritized event expression with $p \prec end$. Also, the role triggers are of the form: $E_1, \ldots, E_n, C_1, \ldots, C_k \rightarrow p : E$ after Δt, where the $E_i s$ are simple event expressions, the $C_i s$ are role status expressions, $p : E$ is a prioritized event expression with $p \prec end$, and Δt is a duration expression.

3.3   Description Logics

Just for this section, we will adopt the normal meaning of roles to formally describe the language $\mathcal{ALCQ}$. This language like other DL languages are decidable fragments of first order logic (FOL).

$\mathcal{ALCQ}$ consists of a countable set of individuals Ind, a countable set of atomic concepts CS, a countable set of roles RS and the concepts built on CS and RS as follows:

$C, D := A|\neg A|C \sqcap D|C \sqcup D|\exists R.C|\forall R.C|(\leq nR.C)|(\geq nR.C)$,

where $A \in CS, R \in RS, C$ and D are concepts and n is a natural number. Also, individuals are denoted by $a, b, c, \ldots$.

This language includes only concepts in negation normal form. The complement of a concept $\neg(C)$ is inductively defined, as usual, by using the law of double negation, de Morgan laws and the dualities for quantifiers. Moreover, the constants $\top$ and $\bot$ abbreviate $A \sqcup \neg A$ and $A \sqcap \neg A$, respectively, for some $A \in CS$. An interpretation $\mathcal{I}$ consists of a non-empty domain, $\Delta^{\mathcal{I}}$, and a mapping, $.^{\mathcal{I}}$, that assigns

- to each individual $a \in Ind$ an element $a^{\mathcal{I}} \in \Delta^{\mathcal{I}}$
- to each atomic concept $A \in CS$ a set $A^{\mathcal{I}} \subseteq \Delta^{\mathcal{I}}$
- to each role $R \in RS$ a relation $R^{\mathcal{I}} \subseteq \Delta^{\mathcal{I}} \times \Delta^{\mathcal{I}}$

The interpretation I extends then on concepts as follows:

$\neg A^{\mathcal{I}} = \Delta^{\mathcal{I}} \backslash A^{\mathcal{I}}$
$(C \sqcup D)^{\mathcal{I}} = C^{\mathcal{I}} \cup D^{\mathcal{I}}$
$(C \sqcap D)^{\mathcal{I}} = C^{\mathcal{I}} \cap D^{\mathcal{I}}$
$(\exists R.C)^{\mathcal{I}} = \{x \in \Delta^{\mathcal{I}} | \exists y((x, y) \in R^{\mathcal{I}} \wedge y \in C^{\mathcal{I}})\}$
$(\forall R.C)^{\mathcal{I}} = \{x \in \Delta^{\mathcal{I}} | \forall y((x, y) \in R^{\mathcal{I}} \Longrightarrow y \in C^{\mathcal{I}})\}$
$(\leq nR.C)^{\mathcal{I}} = \{x \in \Delta^{\mathcal{I}} | \#\{y|((x, y) \in R^{\mathcal{I}} \wedge y \in C^{\mathcal{I}})\} \leq n\}$
$(\geq nR.C)^{\mathcal{I}} = \{x \in \Delta^{\mathcal{I}} | \#\{y|((x, y) \in R^{\mathcal{I}} \wedge y \in C^{\mathcal{I}})\} \geq n\}$

We can now define the notion of a knowledge base and its models. An $\mathcal{ALCQ}$ knowledge base KB is the union of

1. a finite terminological set (TBox) of inclusion axioms that have the form $\top \sqsubseteq C$, where C is called inclusion concept, and
2. a finite assertional set (ABox) of assertions of the form $a : C$ (concept assertion) or $(a, b) : R$ (role assertion) where R is called assertional role and C is called assertional concept.

We denote the set of individuals that appear in KB by $Ind(KB)$. An interpretation I is a model of

- an inclusion axiom $\top \sqsubseteq C$ $(I \models \top \sqsubseteq C)$ if $C^{\mathcal{I}} = \Delta^{\mathcal{I}}$
- a concept assertion $a : C$ $(I \models a : C)$ if $a^{\mathcal{I}} \in C^{\mathcal{I}}$
- a role assertion $a, b : R$ $(I \models (a, b) : R)$ if $(a^{\mathcal{I}}, b^{\mathcal{I}}) \in R^{\mathcal{I}}$

Let KB be the $\mathcal{ALCQ}$-knowledge base of a TBox $\mathcal{T}$ and an ABox $\mathcal{A}$. An interpretation I is a model of KB if $I \models \phi$, for every $\phi \in \mathcal{T} \cup \mathcal{A}$. A knowledge base KB is consistent if it has a model. Moreover, for φ an inclusion axiom or an assertion, we say that $KB \models \varphi$ (in words, K entails φ) if for every model I of K, $I \models \varphi$ also holds.

The consistency problem for $\mathcal{ALCQ}$ is ExpTime-complete. The entailment problem is reducible to the consistency problem as follows: Let KB be an $\mathcal{ALCQ}$ knowledge base and d be an individual not belonging to $Ind(KB)$. Then,

- $KB \models \top \sqsubseteq C$ iff $KB \cup \{d : \neg C\}$ is inconsistent and
- $KB \models a : C$ iff $KB \cup \{a : \neg C\}$ is inconsistent.

This shows that an entailment can be decided in ExpTime. Moreover, the inconsistency problem is reducible to the entailment problem and so, deciding an entailment is an ExpTime-complete problem too.

3.4 SWRL Rules

A SWRL rule has a function-free Horn-like syntax that share the common unary and binary predicates with its OWL counterpart. The antecedent of a SWRL rule is referred to as the rule body and the consequent as the head. The head and the body are composed of a conjunction of one or more atoms. SWRL rules reason about OWL individuals. Atoms can be of the form $C(x)$, $P(x, y)$, $sameAs(x, y)$ or $differentFrom(x, y)$, where C is an OWL DL description, P is an OWL property, and x, y are either variables, OWL individuals or OWL data values. The model-theoretic semantics for SWRL is a straightforward extension of the semantics for OWL. Extensions of OWL interpretations are bindings that map variables to elements of the domain [12]. Horn rules and DL languages such as $\mathcal{ALCQ}$ and OWL-DL ($\mathcal{SHOIN}(\mathcal{D})$) are decidable, but when the latter is combined with SWRL, the language may no longer be decidable. However, [19] proposes a combination of both languages that is decidable, where each variable of a rule is required to occur in the body (i.e. the DL-safe rules).

4   Overview of Our Approach

Our architecture is composed of three stages:

1. We partition the global KB, KB_{global}, into n smaller KBs, as shown in Figure 1(a). Then, we store each partition to disk by indexing each assertion (or asserted statement) subparts, namely the subject, predicate and object (s p o), referred to as a RDF triple [22,3]. This facilitates faster retrieval at run-time once we identify the target KB for the assertion. In addition, we build this step offline and we restrict each partition size to ensure that it fits into the memory on the machine.

$$KB_{global} \xrightarrow{\quad partition \quad} KB_i \dots KB_n \xrightarrow{\quad store \quad} Disk$$

(a) Stage 1

$$KB_{inf} \xrightarrow{\quad add\ rules \quad} KB_{inf}$$

(b) Stage 2

$$Disk \xrightarrow{\ Load\ } KB_i \xrightarrow{\ query\ } KB_{inf} \xrightarrow{\ add\ } New\ Facts$$

(c) Stage 3

Fig. 1. Architecture

2. Then, we load the SWRL rules into a new KB, KB_{inf} (see Figure 1(b)). These rules are a finite set of authorizations defined by the organization's security policies, and therefore they are used to determine which assertions are relevant to determine any policy objective. Adding SWRL rules to KB_{inf} does not have a huge impact on the reasoning time as indicated by our experimental results. This is due to the fact that we are only retrieving a small subset of triples which reduces the number of symbols in the ABox when the rules are applied.

3. Finally, starting with one patient, we retrieve the relevant assertions from disk, one step at a time, and update our inference KB (see Figure 1(c)). Once this is done, the rules in KB_{inf} could also cause new facts to be added to KB_{inf}. Some of these facts could be special assertions to indicate what rules were fired. These special assertions could then provide a feedback as to whether the inference was consistent with the organization policies.

When there is an access request for a specific patient, we start executing stages two and three. Moreover, these two are our inferencing stages where we enforce the security policies. These can also be executed concurrently for many patients.

Moreover, this architecture improves performance. Firstly, the partitions, $KB_1, \dots, KB_n$, function as materialized owl knowledge bases that perform inferencing when the data is loaded into them. In particular, performing consistency tests in the preprocessing stage avoids the delays in querying at run-time, since these tests are usually expensive [23] and OWL reasoning is exponential in time and memory in the worst case [1]. Secondly, KB_{inf} stores SWRL rules to do RBAC policy inferencing at run-time on a very small subset of assertions.

4.1   Defining KB Partitions

We believe that performing reasoning in KB_{inf} instead of KB_{global} will scale our approach. We never directly apply the SWRL rules to KB_{global}, but instead we apply them to KB_{inf}, which has a smaller subset of instances. We believe that if we do not restrict the number of individuals in a KB, then all the satisfied SWRL rules will fire and add many irrelevant assertions (which could be recursive). Each partition has a local reasoner, so by restricting the number of symbols in a KB, we can perform distributed local reasoning instead of full-scale reasoning. We think this is more efficient in a RBAC setting.

Definition 1. *(Domain Modules). The set $\mathfrak{D}$ consists of disjoint modules, where*

- *RBAC defines Users, Roles, Sessions, Permissions, and Objects;*
- *the hospital extends Users to employees; Roles to the organizational structure; Objects to Records (plus other resources like equipments, etc.); and*
- *the hospital defines Patients (plus other stakeholders like suppliers, etc.).*

In order to ensure that the TBox, $\mathcal{T}$, is the same in all our KBs but the ABox, $\mathcal{A}$, is different, we define $KB_i = \{\mathcal{T}, \mathcal{A}_i\}$. Also, we allow arbitrary partitioning. For example, $KB_{patient}$ is further partitioned into $KB_{patient_1}, KB_{patient_2} \dots$. Furthermore, $KB_{global} = (\mathcal{T}, \mathcal{A}_{global})$ and we distribute the ABox, $\mathcal{A}_{global}$, over each KB_i, such that $\mathcal{A}_{global} = \mathcal{A}_1 \cup \mathcal{A}_2 \cup \dots \cup \mathcal{A}_n$.

4.2   Mapping RBAC to Description Logic

We use $\mathcal{ALCQ}$ Knowledge Bases to represent the concepts in the TRBAC model. For example, the underlying core RBAC concepts are represented in the TBox terminology. In addition, Role hierarchy is supported by concept hierarchy in the TBox. For example, since *Roles* is a finite set of job descriptions, they are organized so that family physicians and emergency physicians are both physicians. In this paper, we focus on scalability, but a more detail work of mapping RBAC to $\mathcal{ALCQ}$ can be found in [27].

5   Our Approach

Performing reasoning with large ABoxes must be efficient and scalable. Already, there are reasoners that implement an optimized version of the tableaux algorithm. For example, Pellet, a complete DL reasoner [24], performs well with moderate TBox and ABox sizes in memory. There are also some approaches to perform scalable [9] and optimized reasoning in a modular fashion. Other approaches intend to use secondary storage by partitioning the ontology [24].

Table 1 shows the performance of scaling the ABox, when all assertions and rules are in one knowledge base (which causes memory exception). This prompts us to divide the global KB into autonomous KBs so we could take advantage of the loosely coupled RBAC components. We use SPARQL [25] [21] , a query

Table 1. Memory Exception after adding 1000 individuals + 16(Rules)

Inference Statistics					
Individuals	112	336	560	784	1008
Time(ms)	152	211	276	448	552

language for RDF data, to retrieve both new and existing knowledge from our knowledge bases. When we need to make a policy decision, we issue SPARQL queries over the relevant partitions and then combine each partition result with the ones already in KB_{inf}, so that we can perform further reasoning tasks. Such technique is also called conjunctive query [24,8], and is suitable for reasoning and retrieving instances over large ABoxes.

5.1   Partitioning

We first define terminologies for special properties (or mappings) that restrict how the domain modules communicate with each other, then we define how an assertion is placed into a partition, and finally, we give special names for a mapping that physically connect two KBs.

Definition 2. *(Mapping Function). The set $\mathfrak{M}$ consists of unique atomic properties (binary relations) connecting two domain modules in $\mathfrak{D}$ so that we have:*

- *RBAC assignments: the mappings user-role, role-user, role-permission, permission-role, user-session, role-role and role-session;*
- *Hospital extensions: the mappings patient-user, user-patient and patient-session; and*
- *Patient-Record constraint: the one-to-one mappings patient-record and record-patient,*
  where user $\in$ Users, role $\in$ Roles, permission $\in$ Permissions, session $\in$ Sessions, patient $\in$ Patients and record $\in$ Records.

Definition 3. *(Home Partition). We define a home partition KB_i for all the triples, where $i = 1, 2, \ldots n$, such that*

- *the TBox, T, is in KB_i; and*
- *for all assertions of form $C(x)$ and $R(x, Y)$, both have the same home, KB_i, and C is a concept, R is an atomic property, x is restricted to individuals in $\mathfrak{D}$ and Y is either an individual or a literal (for object or dataType property respectively). In particular, the home is determined by x, the domain of R.*

Definition 4. *(P-link). A P-link is a directed arc that allows navigation from one materialized KB to the next. An atomic property $\rho \in RS$, the set of properties in $\mathcal{ALCQ}$, is a P-link if $\rho \in \mathfrak{M}$. Also, a P-link has a home partition.*

The representation of the RDF triples on disk must be able to facilitate scalable reasoning, as well as answer TRBAC queries. The basic intuition is that we do not need global knowledge to answer TRBAC queries. To facilitate this, we connect triples from one partition to the next by using partition links (*P-links*). This allows the combining of local knowledge bases without physically joining the partitions. Also, the number of *P-links* is finite: (i) the basic RBAC modules are fixed, (ii) we only have a finite set of *P-links* definitions in the TBox (since there is a finite set of property definitions); and (iii) our ABox is distributed over a finite set of partitions of finite sizes. Another benefit of these links is that they allow arbitrary partitioning.

5.2   A Query-Retrieval Process

Definition 5. *(Policy Query). Given a set of partitions KS, a policy (or access) query q against KS is a tuple (s, α, K, Ψ, o), where s is of the form $[t_1, t_2]$, α is an individual, K is an ordered set of partitions, Ψ is a set of access policy rules and o is the output of a positive query. Furthermore, K represents a flow and is of the form $\langle KB_1 \prec \ldots \prec KB_m \rangle$ such that $KB_1 \prec KB_2$ means KB_1 precedes KB_2, and the query process starts from KB_1 and ends in KB_m. Also, KB_k and KB_{k+1} are connected by a P-link, where $k < m$. In addition, Ψ are SWRL rules of the form : $H_1 \wedge \ldots \wedge H_{m'} \longleftarrow B_1 \wedge \ldots \wedge B_{n'}$ where $B_i, H_j, 1 \le i \le n', 1 \le j \le m'$ are atoms of the following form $C(i)$ or $P(i, j)$.*

A policy query for a patient *Bob* in session $[t_1, t_2]$ would be $([t_1, t_2], Bob, \langle KB_{patient} \prec KB_{user} \prec KB_{role} \rangle, \Psi, o)$.

A rule in Ψ would be: $Patient(?x1) \wedge patUser(?x1, ?x2) \wedge patSess(?x1, ?x4) \wedge patRec(?x1, ?x3) \wedge userRole(?x2, ?x5) \wedge userSess(?x2, ?x4) \wedge roleSess(?x5, ?x4) \wedge rolePerm(?x5, ?x6) \longrightarrow canAccess(?x2, ?x3) \wedge grantPerm(?x2, ?x6)$,

which means that a *user* on duty, who plays the appropriate *role* (e.g. patient's physician) will be granted access to the patient's *record* within the specified *session* (e.g. the patient's session).

Figure 2 outlines a trace of a policy query for a patient *Bob* entering the hospital at interval $[t_1, t_2]$. At each stage of the query, we are retrieving a set of

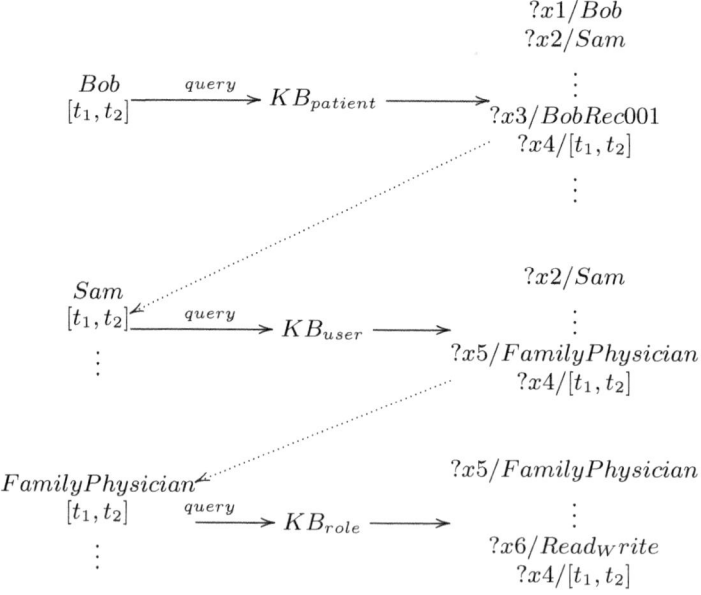

Fig. 2. A trace for a patient *Bob*

results (on the right) for the individual (possibly many) and session on the left. In the diagram, we assume *Sam* is *Bob*'s physician.

To determine the first output, o_1, we issue the first query against $KB_{patient}$. We then execute the other queries against KB_{doctor} and KB_{role}, so that at each step the results are added to KB_{inf}, until we have $o = o_1 \cup \ldots \cup o_3$.

Queries are also used to retrieve facts from a KB, including those inferred as a result of the SWRL rules in KB_{inf}. However, under the open world assumption of OWL and SWRL, a negative response to a query is not treated as failure to prove the query (a KB is assumed incomplete). Furthermore, OWL assumes monotonic reasoning. This is unlike the database approach, which uses default reasoning, where the assumption is that what is not known to be true is believed to be false. Nevertheless, in the partitioned approach we presented for RBAC, a policy query is positive if $o_i \neq \varnothing \ \forall i$. This avoids the problem of a user having the ability to perform unnecessary and potentially harmful actions merely as a side effect of granting access using incomplete knowledge from a set of KBs.

5.3   Optimization and Heuristics

We use two types of indexing to improve the efficiency of our approach by (i) indexing the assertions; and (ii) creating a high level index. In the first case, we index the subparts ($s\ p\ o$) of a triple to facilitate faster retrieval at query time. We do this with LARQ[1], which is a text indexing API for SPARQL. This allows us to find a triple by a subject (s), a predicate (p) or an object (o), without the cost of a linear search over all the triples in a partition. In the second case, we keep another level of index structure that points to the location of the partitions on disk (by using a Lucene index [10]). At retrieval time, we use the index to locate a partition for an assertion. Thus, retrieving the relevant assertions is at most linear with respect to the number of partitions.

We limit n for concepts $C \sqsubseteq\ \geq nR.C$ and $C \sqsubseteq\ \leq nR.C$. For instance, with n_u users and n_r roles, the combination of users and roles is at most $n_u \times n_r$. Also, a given user, a, could theoretically have n_r assertions of form $R(a, r_i), i = 1 \ldots n_r$, and this could cause the home partition of a to not fit into memory for local reasoning. In our domain, however, this is less likely to be the case; for example, there are different competences among users and roles are based on the user's ability. Moreover, an added benefit of TRBAC is the temporal constraints on roles; during an interval, the number of enabled roles may not be that large.

5.4   Correctness

As stated in Section 3.3, complex concepts are built from atomic concepts in CS, and properties in RS of the language $\mathcal{ALCQ}$. Table 2 displays the predicate logic translation of these concepts [1, sec. 2.2].

Let F infer assertions from KB_i, such that $F(\mathcal{T}, \mathcal{A}_i) = Inf_i$, Q be a query over a set of triples and S be a subset of KBs. For *RBAC system* discussed in this

---

[1] http://jena.sourceforge.net/ARQ/lucene-arq.html

Table 2. $\mathcal{ALCQ}$ rule engine

Group 1	
$D(x) \longleftarrow C(x)$	$C \sqsubseteq D$
$C(x) \longleftarrow R(x,y), D(y)$	$\exists R.D \sqsubseteq C$
$D(y) \longleftarrow R(x,y), C(x)$	$C \sqsubseteq \forall R.D$
$\neg A(x)$	$\neg A$
Group 2	
$C(x) \longleftarrow \exists y_1 \ldots y_n.R(x,y_1) \wedge \ldots \wedge R(x,y_n) \wedge \bigwedge_{i<j} y_i \neq y_j$	$C \sqsubseteq \ \geq nR.D$
$\bigvee_{i<j} y_i = y_j \longleftarrow \forall y_1 \ldots y_{n+1}.R(x,y_1) \wedge \ldots \wedge R(x,y_{n+1}),\ C(x)$	$C \sqsubseteq \ \leq nR.D$
Group 3	
$C(x) \longleftarrow D_1(x) \wedge \ldots \wedge D_n(x)$	$D_1 \sqcap \ldots \sqcap D_n \sqsubseteq C$
$C(x) \longleftarrow D_1(x) \vee \ldots \vee D_n(x)$	$D_1 \sqcup \ldots \sqcup D_n \sqsubseteq C$

paper, our partitioning based reasoning scheme correctly infers all the necessary triples needed for enforcing security policy.

Theorem 1. $Q(F(KB_{global})) \equiv F(\bigcup_{i \in S} Q_{S_i}(F(KB_i)))$

Proof Sketch. Our goal is to prove that our partitioning scheme correctly infers all the relevant triples associated with a given session, user, role and permission. Basically, we argue that in order to correctly infer all the triples associated with the KB_{global}, we can just do reasoning using each partition and combine the selected results of the local reasoners.[2]

To prove this claim, we will use the rule engine given in Table 2. First, we argue that the information needed to use the rules given in Table 2 is already captured by the TBox and the local ABox instances. To prove this we will examine all the rules given above and argue that correct application of those rules could be done without combining instances in different partitions.

Please note that the first rule in group 1 could be correctly applied by just using the TBox. The second and third rules in group 1 could be correctly applied by using the triple $(x\ R\ y)$ given in some local partition and TBox since the definition of R in TBox precisely specifies the domain and the range of the relation. The fourth rule in group 1 is just the negation of an atomic concept.

For rules in group 2, for correct reasoning, we need to find out triples of the form $(x\ R\ y_i), \forall i$. Since our partitioning puts all the triples with subject x to the same partition, all needed triples for correct inference will be in the same partition.

For the rules in group 3, we need to have all concepts D_i to be present at the time of reasoning. Clearly some of the concepts could be in different partitions. The way our system works is we query all the materialized results for each partition (i.e., $F(KB_i)$) related to RBAC query and get the D_i concepts needed.

---

[2] Please note that, all the local reasoners share the same TBox.

Using these D_i concepts and a TBox, we infer all $C(x)$ and associated triples in memory (i.e., in KB_{inf}).   □

In our partition approach, we evaluate each policy query (s, α, K, Ψ, o), against the ordered set K of materialized KBs.

Therefore, $Q(K) = Q(\langle KB_1 \prec \ldots \prec KB_m \rangle) \equiv Q(\langle KB_{global} \rangle)$.

6   Experiments and Results

We perform experiments with synthetic data supporting large number of users, patients, rules, and other RBAC assertions (like sessions and role instances) on a Dell Inspiron 2.4GHz with 8GB RAM. Each user and patient has on average 30 object and data type properties. We then collect the time for inferencing the action to be taken for each patient. In particular, we scale one variable in the set {(D)octors, (N)urses, (P)atients (R)ules, TBox} at a time, while keeping the other variables constant. We use Protégé to build our TBox, and Jena[3][3] to build our ABoxes and programmatically extend the TBox. We use Lucene [10] for indexing the partitions and LARQ with SPARQL for the sequential and incremental extraction of triples from each materialized partition. We use Java as a programming language and we plug in pellet[24] as a reasoner for Jena. Also, these technologies are all open source. In addition, we follow the $\mathcal{ALCQ}$ specifications, where we only support atomic properties in our TBox, i.e. no transitive, inverse properties, etc. The time to build a set of materialized KBs range from one to three hours, while the time to retrieve the assertions and check the policies in KB_{inf} are presented in Figure 3 and Figure 4. We use various sources, such as WebMD[4], pubmed[5], and related literature to investigate the healthcare domain, in order to implement healthcare-specific data. For the TRBAC domain, we use the reference literature to design the data and rules for the security aspects. Also, we create individuals and their properties randomly in Jena, using the appropriate set of resources and data types.

Performance of our inference KB, KB_{inf}, displays fluctuations as we simulate various activities in our experiment. This is due to the fact that the index of any of the most accessed KBs will cache previous results, and this has unpredictable behavior. Also, for our base-line, we compare our performances to those in [15], which evaluates reasoning for a similar policy language, XACML. In addition, we use a naive approach to generate assertions for an in memory KB (see Table 1). We perform various runs, each time with different combination of individuals from our hospital domain.

The results in Figure 3(a) and 3(b) show that we achieve almost constant time for determining a policy decision as we scale the instances in our application. These results are consistent with (i) initiating the flow with one patient and (ii) using an index for locating both a partition and an assertion.

---

[3] http://jena.sourceforge.net/
[4] http://www.webmd.com/
[5] pubmed.gov

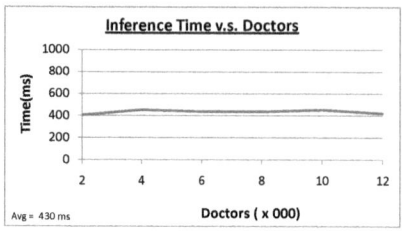
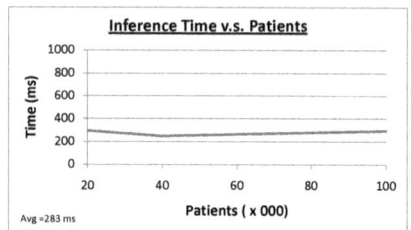
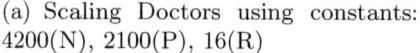

(a) Scaling Doctors using constants: 4200(N), 2100(P), 16(R)

(b) Scaling Patients using constants: 3862(D), 3940(N), 16(R)

Fig. 3. Scaling Individuals

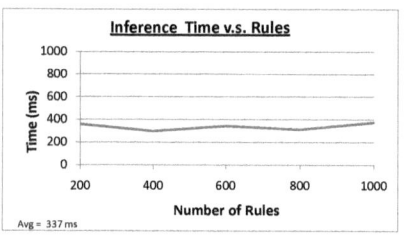
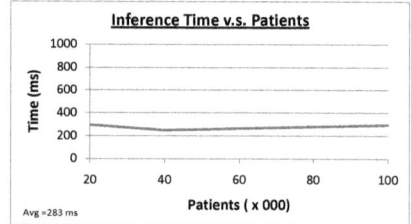

(a) Scaling Rules using constants: 320(D), 640(N), 1280(P)

(b) Scaling TBox using constants: 320(D), 640(N), 1280(P), 16(R)

Fig. 4. Scaling TBox and Rules

The results in Figure 4(a) also show that even though we scale the number of rules, our run-time is fairly constant. This is because the rules only fire for one patient. The results in Figure 4(b), on the other hand, show that scaling our TBox terms does have some performance limitations. This could be that the DL reasoner must perform more expensive tests each time the TBox size increases. Our implementation is therefore quite scalable with respect to ABox and SWRL rules, but not so with TBox. Nevertheless, we expect the TBox size to be fairly constant for our chosen domain. Furthermore, when we compare our inference times to the verification times in [15] for policies using pellet reasoner, our approach gives similar performances for Figure 3(a), Figure 3(b) and Figure 4(a), where we use a small TBox.

7   Conclusions

We presented an implementation of a scalable TRBAC application, with particular reference to the healthcare domain. We addressed the problem of having a successful and scalable application in the semantic web, as well as highlighted the limitations of performing reasoning with very large ABoxes. We provided our solution to this problem by partitioning the ABoxes. We advocated that by retrieving only the relevant assertions, our reasoning task can be reduced from being global to being local and still correctly and efficiently determine the policy-decisions with respect to a patient. In the future, we would like to use data from other domains besides healthcare. In addition, we plan to use TBox-partitioning techniques to allow the scaling of concepts.

References

1. Baader, F., McGuinness, D.L., Nardi, D., Patel-Schneider, P.F.: The Description Logic Handbook: Theory, Implementation and Applications. Cambridge University Press, Cambridge (2007)
2. Bertino, E., Bottati, P.A., Ferrari, E.: TRBAC: A Temporal Role-Based Access Control Model. ACM Transactions on Information and System Security 3(3), 191–223 (2001)
3. Carroll, J.J., Dickinson, I., Dollin, C., Reynolds, D., Seaborne, A., Wilkinson, K.: Jena: Implementing the Semantic Web Recommendations: HP Laboratories Bristol HPL-2003-146 (2003)
4. Cirio, L., Cruz, I.F., Tamassia, R.: A Role and Attribute Based Access Control System Using Semantic Web Technologies: On the Move to Meaningful Internet Systems 2007. In: OTM 2007 Workshops (2007)
5. Ferraiolo, D.F., Sandhu, R., Gavrila, S.: Proposed NIST Standard for Role-Based Access Control. ACM Transactions on Information and System Security, 224–274 (August 2001)
6. Finin, T.W., Joshi, A., Kagal, L., Niu, J., Sandhu, R.S., Winsborough, W.H., Thuraisingham, B.M.: ROWLBAC-Representing Role Based Access Control in OWL. In: Proceedings of the 13th ACM symposium on Access control models and technologies, pp. 73–82 (2008)
7. Ferraiolo, D.F., Kuhn, D.R., Chandramouli, R.: Role-Based Access Control. Artech House, Inc. (2003)
8. Glimm, B., Horrocks, I., Lutz, C., Sattler, U.: Conjunctive Query Answering for the Description Logic SHIQ. Journal of Artificial Intelligence Research 31, 157–204 (2008)
9. Guo, Y., Heflin, J.: A Scalable Approach for Partitioning OWL Knowledge Bases. In: International Workshop on Scalable Semantic Web Knowledge Bases (2006)
10. Hatcher, E., Gospodnetic, O., McCandless, M.: Lucene in Action, 2nd edn. Manning (2004)
11. HIPAA: U.S. Department of Health and Human Services, http://www.hhs.gov/ocr/privacy/
12. Horrocks, I., Patel-Schneider, P.F., Boley, H., Tabet, S., Grosof, B., Dean, M.: SWRL: A Semantic Web Rule Language Combining OWL and RuleML: W3C Member Submission May 21 (2004), Latest version is available at http://www.w3.org/Submission/SWRL/
13. Joshi, J.B.D., Bertino, E., Ghafoor, A.: A Generalized Temporal Role-Based Access Control Model. IEEE Transactions on Knowledge and Data Engineering 17 (January 2005)
14. Kataria, P., Juric, R., Paurobally, S., Madani, K.: Implementation of Ontology for Intelligent Hospital Wards. In: Proceedings of the 41st Annual Hawaii International Conference on System Sciences, HICSS 2008 (2008)

15. Kolovski, V., Hendler, J., Parsia, B.: Analyzing web access control policies. In: Proceedings of the 16th international conference on World Wide Web, Banff, Alberta, Canada, May 08–12 (2007)
16. Levandoski, J.J., Mokbel, M.F.: RDF Data-Centric Storage. In: ICWS (2009)
17. Liu, A.X., Chen, F., Hwang, J., Xie, T.: Xengine: a fast and scalable XACML policy evaluation engine. In: ACM Sigmetrics Performance Evaluation Review, SIGMETRICS 2008 (2008)
18. McGuinness, D.L., Harmelen, F.: OWL Web Ontology Language Overview. World Wide Web Consortium W3C Recommendation February 10 (2004), http://www.w3.org/TR/owl-features/
19. Motik, B., Sattler, U., Studer, R.: Query Answering for OWL-DL with Rules. Web Semantics: Science, Services and Agents on the World Wide Web 3(1), 41–60 (2005)
20. Owens, A., Seaborne, A., Gibbins, N.: Clustered TDB: A Clustered Triple Store for Jena. In: WWW 2009 (2009)
21. Perez, J., Arenas, M., Gutierrez, C.: Semantics and complexity of SPARQL. ACM Transactions on Database Systems, TODS (2009)
22. Resource Description Framework (RDF): Concepts and Abstract Syntax. W3C Recommendation (2004), http://www.w3.org/RDF/
23. Sirin, E., Parsia, E.: Optimizations for Answering Conjunctive ABox Queries: First Results. In: Proceedings of the 2006 International Workshop on Description Logics (2006)
24. Sirin, E., Parsia, B., Grau, B.C., Kalyanpur, A., Katz, Y.: Pellet: A Practical OWL-DL Reasoner. Journal of Web Semantics (2007)
25. SPARQL Query Language for RDF, W3C Recommendation January 15 (2008), http://www.w3.org/TR/rdf-sparql-query/
26. Winter, A., Brigl, B., Wendt, T.: A UML-based Ontology for Describing Hospital Information System Architectures. Studies in health technology and informatics 2001, pp. 778–782 (2005)
27. Zhao, C., Heilili, N., Liu, S., Lin, Z.: Representation and Reasoning on RBAC: A Description Logic Approach. In: Van Hung, D., Wirsing, M. (eds.) ICTAC 2005. LNCS, vol. 3722, pp. 381–393. Springer, Heidelberg (2005)

Enforcing Request Integrity in Web Applications

Karthick Jayaraman, Grzegorz Lewandowski,
Paul G. Talaga, and Steve J. Chapin

Department of EECS, Syracuse University
{kjayaram,grlewand,pgtalaga,chapin}@syr.edu

Abstract. A web application is constructed to process an intended sequence of requests. Failing to enforce the intended sequences can lead
to request integrity (RI) attacks, wherein an attacker forces an application into processing an unintended request sequence. Cross-site-request
forgeries (CSRF) and workflow violations are two classes of RI attacks.
Enforcing the intended request sequences is essential for ensuring the
integrity of the application. We describe a new approach for enforcing
request integrity in a web application, and its implementation in a tool
called BAYAWAK. Under our approach, the intended request sequences of
an application are specified as a security policy, and a framework-level
method enforces the security policy strictly and transparently without
requiring changes in the application's source code. Our approach can be
compared to operating system (OS) support for access control—access
control is not built into the application, but based on OS level policy
settings. We evaluated BAYAWAK using nine open source web applications. Our results indicate that our approach is effective against request
integrity attacks and incurs negligible overhead.

1   Introduction

An upsurge of vulnerabilities that affect web applications has paralleled the
trend toward their widespread deployment and use. Several web applications,
particularly those comprising an office suite, have supplanted desktop applications. Furthermore, web applications such as web-mail systems, online retailing
applications, and group-ware applications affect everyday life. However, existing
methods for ensuring the integrity of these applications are inadequate and, as
a result, web applications continue to be attractive targets of exploitation.

One aspect of web application integrity protection that remains inadequately
addressed is enforcing request integrity. A web application is constructed to
process certain intended request sequences. Violation of these sequences can
lead to a compromise of application integrity or user privacy. Request integrity
(RI) attacks are attacks wherein an external attacker or a malicious user tricks
a web application into processing an unintended request sequence. There are
two classes of attacks, namely cross-site-request forgeries (CSRF) and workflow
attacks (WF), which until now have been treated as unrelated attacks, but which
are actually subclasses of RI attacks.

S. Foresti and S. Jajodia (Eds.): Data and Applications Security XXIV, LNCS 6166, pp. 225–240, 2010.

Currently the task of enforcing request integrity is considered as belonging to the application developer. The proliferation of web application vulnerabilities rooted at developers' mistakes clearly shows that this approach did not succeed. There are several reasons for this failure. First, developers are not security experts. As a result, they may not be aware of the vulnerabilities and appropriate secure coding methods. Second, developers are prone to making mistakes. Consider the fact that all of the top 10 web application vulnerabilities can be traced to programming errors [1]. Finally, the weaknesses that make RI attacks possible are rooted at the very nature of web applications and web browsers. For example, the structure of a web application does not significantly change over time. As we explain later, this lack of diversity can be abused to gather knowledge about application's structure and then construct seemingly valid request sequences. Also, the way browsers and web applications manage user sessions is vulnerable to an attacker injecting request into existing request sequences.

Depending on developers to enforce request integrity will not only result in rapidly increasing application complexity, but also force developers to implement similar countermeasures time and again. Moreover, this approach will not work for application vulnerabilities discovered in legacy code, where modifying the source code is difficult or perhaps impossible. To avoid these problems, the task of enforcing request integrity should be performed by a security framework, not by the application developers. This is similar to the approach in operating systems, where access control is not built into individual applications, but controlled by OS level policy settings. Such an approach can also provide an assurance to the publisher that request integrity is strictly enforced.

In this paper, we describe a new approach for enforcing request integrity and its implementation in a tool called BAYAWAK that moves the enforcement mechanism into a security framework. In BAYAWAK, the valid request sequences for a web application are specified as a security policy, and a server-side method transparently enforces the valid request sequences, eliminating attacks that trick the application into processing an invalid request sequence. BAYAWAK does not require any changes in the web application. The valid request sequences can be abstractly specified using a request-flow graph (RFG)[1]. For example, Figure 1 contains the RFG of an online message board application. The RFG is enforced using three steps. First, BAYAWAK performs a behavior-preserving diversification of the RFG for each session. Second, BAYAWAK modifies the web pages produced by the application to be compatible with the varied per-session RFG. Third, BAYAWAK validates each incoming request against the per session RFG before forwarding to the application for further processing. We argue that these three steps eliminate the underlying root causes that facilitate RI attacks.

The effectiveness of our approach depends on the correctness of the RFG. There are several methods for obtaining the RFG for a web application. The RFG could be derived from the specification of the application. In the case of legacy web applications, the RFG could be derived from the source code using reverse engineering. The reverse engineering methods vary in their sophistication

---

[1] We will define the term in section 2.

ranging from simple web spiders to advanced program analysis methods such as
WAMse [2] and Tansuo [3]. In our evaluation, we used a web spider for simple
web applications and WAMse for relatively more complex web applications.

We evaluated BAYAWAK using nine open source web applications. We identified several RI attacks in each of the applications. After configuring BAYAWAK
instances for each of the application, all the attacks were eliminated. Furthermore, the BAYAWAK instances incurred negligible overhead.

The key contributions of the paper can be summarized as follows:

1. An approach for enforcing request integrity in web applications that moves
   the enforcement from the application into a security framework.
2. Our approach eliminates both classes of RI attacks, namely CSRF and workflow violations, which were previously considered unrelated attacks.
3. Implementation of our approach for the Apache web server in a tool called
   BAYAWAK, and evaluation using nine open-source web applications.

Organization. The remainder of the paper is structured as follows. In Section
2, we provide background information on web applications. In Section 3, we describe RI attacks. In Section 4, we describe our approach and its implementation.
In Section 5, we describe our experimental evaluation and results. We compare
our work with related work in Section 6 and conclude in Section 7.

2 Anatomy of Web Applications

This section will provide background information on web applications and define
the terminology we will use in the remainder of the paper. A web application
comprises components such as server-side scripts, databases, and resources such
as images and JavaScript programs, and is accessed over the Internet using the
HTTP protocol. Typically, a user accesses a web application using a web browser.
The web browser constructs HTTP requests in response to the user interacting
with hyperlinks and forms in a web page, forwards them to the application,
and displays the web page received in the response. Web applications receive
and process incoming requests using their *interfaces* [2]. An interface receives
an HTTP request and returns a web page in the response. Each HTTP request
contains a target URL and several arguments in the form of name-value pairs
that are either part of the URL (known as a query string) or the message body.
The target URL and the name-value pairs in the request identify the target
interface and we will refer to them as *interface names.*

Usually, web applications need to group incoming requests into sessions. For
example, in an online shopping application, a user may add products to his
shopping cart in one request, and then initiate a purchase transaction in another
request. The shopping cart application should be able to group these requests
into a single session and also associate the contents of the shopping cart with the
correct user's session. However, the HTTP protocol was designed to be stateless
so that hosts do not have to retain information about users between requests [4].

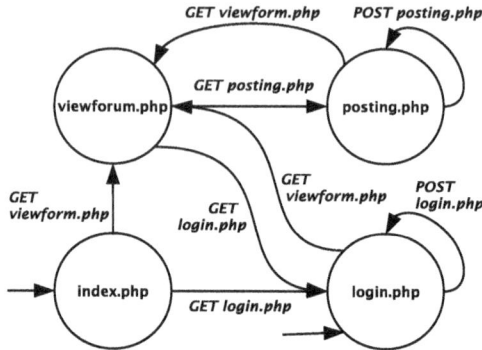

Fig. 1. RFG for an online message board

Therefore, web applications use cookies to group requests into sessions. Whenever a new session is created, web applications create a cookie in the web browser
using the *set-cookie* HTTP header in the response. Web browsers attach all the
cookies created by the application to all subsequent requests, helping the application associate each incoming request with its session.

Enforcing Intended Request Sequences: Each web application is designed to process certain intended sequences of requests. For example, in an online-shopping
application, a request to initiate a purchase transaction is expected only after
a user is signed in, and a request to finalize the purchase is expected only after a user provides valid payment information. Similarly, some web applications
display the URL for the administrative interface in a web page only if the user
is logged in as an administrator. These rules reflecting the intended request sequence can be abstractly represented using a graph; each node corresponds to
an interface and edges correspond to HTTP requests. Two nodes are connected
by a directed edge, if the web page created by an interface contains a hyperlink
or form targeted to the other node. We refer to this graph as the *request flow
graph (RFG)* of a web application.

In a typical intended access model, users access the web application starting
from a *session-initializing* interface (SII), which creates a new user session that
will be shared by all subsequent requests from the user until the session ter-
minates. In most applications, all requests targeted to the domain name of the
application are redirected to a SII. Also, in the absence of a session, all requests
to non-SII are redirected to a SII. After the session is initialized, the browser
issues all subsequent requests based on the user interaction with the hyperlinks
and forms in the web page.

Example. The online message board application in Figure 1 has four interfaces
and 10 interlinks between the interfaces. For the sake of illustration, we explain
one node and its edges in the RFG. The message board application contains
two SII, namely *index.php* and *login.php*. The node *login.php* has two outgoing
edges. The edge to itself corresponds to a form in the web page that constructs an

HTTP POST request for *login.php* using the username and password supplied by the user. The other edge corresponds to a hyperlink in the web page for *viewforum.php*.

Developers typically enforce the intended request sequence using a combination of *interface hiding* and *validation*. Interface hiding aims to prevent users from performing an illegal action by not providing GUI that would be used to initiate the action. Web pages created by the application typically display only the necessary hyperlinks and forms in web pages that are required in the next interaction step. For example, the hyperlink or form for the next step in a transaction is displayed only if a prior step completed successfully. Similarly, the hyperlink for the administrative interface is only displayed if a user is logged in as an administrator. Validation refers to the process of embedding checks in the application in order to verify that the request in the previous step completed successfully by checking the application's state before processing the current request.

3   Request Integrity (RI) Attacks

Request integrity (RI) attacks violate the intended RFG of a web application by tricking interfaces into accepting and processing unintended requests[2]. RI attacks take advantage of the very nature of web applications and browsers and attack the underlying assumptions or weaknesses of prevailing methods used to enforce the intended request sequences. The root causes of RI attacks can be traced to three weaknesses. We will explain the three weaknesses and then present two classes of existing RI attacks.

First, the web pages created by a web application do not significantly vary between sessions because the interface names do not change. An attacker who understands the application and interface names can forge requests for the application. There are several opportunities for understanding an application. Because web applications are easily accessible to both users and attackers, attackers can understand the application by using it. Furthermore, the source code of some widely used web applications such as phpBB are publicly available.

Second, methods such as interface hiding and validation used by web applications do not strictly enforce intended request sequences. Interface hiding enforces request sequences only if the application is accessed using its web pages. For example, many web applications send web pages containing login forms to users, and expect an HTTP POST request in response. However, those applications will often process a similar HTTP POST request containing login information even if the user has not retrieved a web page containing a login form. In this case, the applications naively assume that they are accessed only via their web pages and do not strictly enforce their implicit access restrictions. In the case of validation, the checks embedded inside the application have to be complete and there should be no way to bypass the checks in order to strictly enforce the request sequence.

---

[2] Unintended by the application designer; clearly these requests are intentional on the part of the attacker.

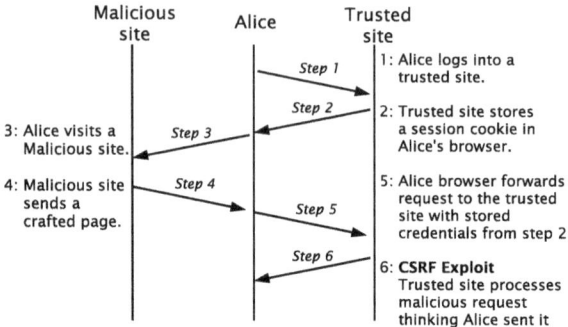

Fig. 2. Cross-site-request forgeries

Attackers attack these underlying assumptions to identify a vulnerability in the application. Furthermore, both these methods are implemented by a developer. Therefore, the efficacy of the enforcement is dependent on the security knowledge of the developer.

Third, the prevailing access policy used by web browsers for managing cookies can be abused by malicious web sites to inject session requests—web browsers attach all the cookies associated with a web application to all requests targeting the application irrespective of the origin of a request. Therefore, if a web site A embeds a HTML form or hyperlink that invokes an interface of web site B, the browser automatically attaches all the cookies (which may include a session cookie) of web site B (if any) to the requests created by web site A. As a result, web site A can inject requests into a session that the user has with web site B without the user's knowledge or consent.

Cross-site-request forgeries (CSRF): In a CSRF attack [5], an attacker uses a malicious web site to forge a request for a trusted site as though it is coming from the victim user. In a typical scenario, a user unknowingly visits a malicious site while having an active session with a trusted site. Figure 2 contains an example. Alice visits a trusted site and creates a new session (steps 1 and 2). Simultaneously, Alice also visits a malicious site (step 3), which sends a crafted page to Alice (step 4). Browsers do not have any restrictions on the URL that can be used in HTML tags such as *img, form, iframe*, etc. Using a crafted page, a malicious site can trick either the user or the browser into making a malicious request to the trusted site. When the web browser renders the crafted page, it forwards a request to the trusted site and also attaches all the cookies of the trusted site to the request (step 5). The trusted site processes the malicious request thinking it was created by Alice.

The *login CSRF* attack [6] is an interesting variation of CSRF that does not affect a user's active session. Rather, login CSRF creates a new session using the attacker's username and password. The attacker hosts a crafted page in his site that, when visited by the user, sends a login request for a trusted site using the attacker's credentials. This results in a session cookie associated

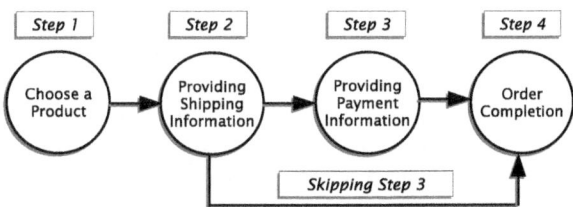

Fig. 3. A workflow violation in a purchase transaction: Using a workflow attack, an attacker skips the third step and completes the order without paying

with the attacker's credentials being stored in the user's browser. The attacker hopes that the user will later visit the trusted site; in such an event, all user activity will be attached to the attacker's session. An attacker could use this to monitor the activity of the user on a trusted site or for other malicious purposes. For instance, an attacker may be able to track all the videos that a user views on http://www.youtube.com.

Workflow Attacks: A workflow is a specific sequence of interactions that a web application expects a user to perform to complete a transaction. Workflows range from simple two-step workflows to highly complicated workflows. An example of a simple workflow is a web application expecting an admin user to be signed in before accessing an administrative interface. An example of a slightly more complex workflow is a purchase transaction consisting of choosing a product, providing shipping information, providing payment information, and reviewing the order before final submission (Figure 3). Recall that interface hiding and validation are typically used to enforce the workflow. Workflow attackers exploit errors in these checks, or the lack of such checks, to bypass certain steps. In the simple workflow example, an attacker could directly visit the administrative interface using its URL while being logged in as a normal user. Similarly, in the a purchase workflow, an attacker may directly visit the page associated with the final step after submitting the shipping information, thereby submitting an order without payment.

4   Bayawak

In this section, we describe the architecture of BAYAWAK, explain how it avoids the RI attacks, and describe BAYAWAK's implementation.

4.1   Architecture

The input to BAYAWAK is a configuration file that specifies the list of interface names in the web application, the sequences of workflows, and the name of the session cookie. Methods for obtaining the interface names vary with respect to the complexity of the application. In the case of simple applications, where each interface corresponds to a single server-side script, the list of interfaces is essentially the list of server-side scripts in the deployment directory. Web spiders could also be used for the purpose. In more complex applications, each server-side script may implement several interfaces, each of which are distinguished by the parameters in the URL. For such applications, we need more sophisticated program analysis methods such as WAMse [2] or Tansuo [3]. WAMse uses an analysis technique based on symbolic execution for precisely identifying the interfaces in web applications.

BAYAWAK instantiates a run-time monitor for the web application based on the configuration file. The run-time monitor protects the application using the following three steps:

1. Diversify the interface names in the application for each session.
2. Modify the web pages created by the application to reference the correct interface names for the session.
3. Verify whether each incoming request references the correct interfaces names and only forward conforming requests to the application.

Step 1: Behavior-preserving Diversification: BAYAWAK creates a session-specific RFG whenever the web application creates a new session. BAYAWAK tracks the *set-cookie* header in the responses to detect the creation of a new session. A web application creates a new session in two steps. First, the application initializes a new session and assigns an identifier. Second, the application instructs the web browser to create a session cookie using the *set-cookie* header in the response. BAYAWAK intercepts each response created by the application and detects for the presence of the *set-cookie* header. On detecting a new session, BAYAWAK labels all the interfaces using a set of random numbers. We will refer to the labels identifying each node as interface identifiers (IID). In the session RFG, the interface names additionally include the IID.

The IID for the interfaces is a server-side secret associated with each session. BAYAWAK stores the mapping between the interfaces and IID for each session

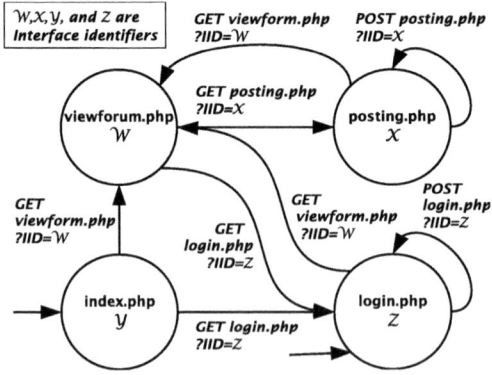

Fig. 4. Diversified session RFG

in an in-memory map. The IID should be sufficiently long, so that it is nearly impossible to guess them. By default, the IID are 256 bit numbers, but can be configured to be larger numbers. Figure 4 contains a session RFG for the online message board we described in section 2. There are no changes to the edges, which determine the request-response behavior of the application. Essentially, the RFG of each session vary only in the IID, so the RFG of various sessions can be considered isomorphic to each other. Therefore, the behavior of the application does not vary with the sessions.

BAYAWAK refreshes the IID for workflow interfaces on a per-transaction basis. Therefore, the set of IID that identify the interfaces involved in a workflow are unique to each transaction. All other interfaces are issued a per-session IID, which expires only at the end of the session.

Step 2: Modifying the web pages: Because the interfaces names vary with the session, the web pages created by the application do not have the correct IID and are no longer compatible with the session RFG. Therefore, the web pages are also varied for each session to incorporate the correct IID in all the URL, each time a web page is created by the application. The IID can be incorporated in the URL as a parameter; Figure 4 describes how the IID can be added to the URL as a parameter. The following HTML tags can specify a URL as an attribute and instruct the browser to create an HTTP request for the application:

1. *href* attribute of *a, style,* and *link* tags.
2. *action* attribute of *form* tags.
3. *src* attribute of *frame, iframe.*
4. *onclick* attributes of *button* tags.
5. *refresh* attribute of *button* and *meta* tags.
6. *url* attribute of *refresh* meta tags.

BAYAWAK modifies the URL in all these tags to incorporate the IID. HTTP redirects are a special case of responses that should be handled separately. Sometimes web applications may redirect users to URL2 in response to requests for URL1. The target for redirection, URL2, is specified using the *Location* header in an HTTP 302 response. The browser issues a request for the target URL2 when it receives the redirect response. BAYAWAK intercepts redirect responses and adds the IID to the URL specified in the *Location* header.

Because the IID are specific for each session and are only contained in the web pages, users can access the application only using the web pages. Essentially, the web pages become a capability required to access the application. Without the capability, users cannot access the application.

Step 3: Validating requests: BAYAWAK validates each incoming request before allowing the web application to process the request. There are two type of requests, namely session and non-session requests. Session requests are part of an on-going session and carry a session identifier. Non-session requests are not part of a session and typically target a SII and the application creates a new session when processing the requests. Non-session requests are directly forwarded to the application. All session requests are expected to carry the correct IID required to invoke the interface. If a session request does not contain the correct IID, the request is treated as a non-session request and redirected to an SII, after invalidating the session. Whenever a request carries the correct IID, it is evidence that the request was created as a result of the user interacting with the web page created by the application.

4.2   Avoiding RI Attacks

BAYAWAK addresses the root causes of RI attacks as follows:

1. The web pages and the RFG are varied per session, so any information obtained from using one application instance or reading the source code is not adequate for forging requests to the application. This is because the IID required for making a request vary with session and are sufficiently long to thwart brute-force attacks.
2. Users are forced to access the application using the web pages because only the web pages carry the correct IID required to invoke the interfaces. The web pages force users to access the application in the intended way and all the intended request sequences are strictly enforced irrespective of the completeness of the validation checks or the integrity of the session variables used in the interfaces.
3. Malicious web sites cannot access the IID necessary to invoke an interface. The IID are only embedded inside the web pages of the application. The *same-origin policy* prohibits web applications belonging to one domain from accessing the contents of the web page belonging to other domains [7].

We now describe how our approach avoids the two RI attacks we described in section 3.

Cross-site-request Forgeries (CSRF): A malicious site cannot access the IID required to invoke an interface. Therefore, the malicious site can only create a request without the IID. Such requests are treated as non-session requests and are redirected to an SII, thwarting the attacks. A Login CSRF attack forges a login request for the application. Depending on how an application creates a new session, a login request may or may not be a session request, but our approach avoids the attack in either case. In general, applications use one of two methods for creating new sessions. First, applications may create a new session in response to a non-session request. In this case, the user is not authenticated when the session is created and is expected to login only after the session is created. As a result, all login requests are session requests and are expected to have the IID that the attacker cannot access. Hence, the attack is thwarted. Second, applications may create a new session only after user authentication. In this case, the login request is a non-session request, which is forwarded to the application. Therefore, an attacker may be able to forge a login request for the application using the attacker's credentials. However, the session initializing processes creates a new session and a session RFG and the victim user does not have access to the IID compatible with session RFG. Therefore, when the user initiates a new request to the application independently using the browser, it will be associated with the session but will not have the appropriate IID. Recall that such requests invalidate the session, and are redirected to a SII, forcing the user to authenticate.

Workflow Attacks: Workflow attacks are eliminated in two ways. First, the web pages would only carry the IID for the interfaces they reference. Therefore, users cannot access interfaces that are not referenced by the web pages, thwarting arbitrary URL accesses. Second, the IID for the workflow interfaces are unique for each transaction. Typically, the web pages display the hyperlinks for the workflow steps in the intended sequence. The hyperlink for a step is displayed only on successful completion of the previous step. Therefore, the user is forced to step through the workflow only in the intended way. Moreover, because the IID for workflow interfaces expire at the end of each transaction, IID collected from completing a prior transaction in the session cannot be used to directly invoke the interface associated with the final step in a subsequent transaction.

4.3   Implementation

BAYAWAK is available in two forms—an Apache module written using mod_perl and a Java class implementing a Servlet API filter. The Apache module extends the request-response processing pipeline to implement BAYAWAK. The Java filter is essentially a hook into the Servlet interpreter for manipulating the requests and responses processed by the application. Both of our implementations are functionally equivalent.

5   Experimental Evaluation

We evaluated BAYAWAK using open source web applications to ascertain the following:

1. Resistance to RI Attacks.
2. Run-time overhead of using BAYAWAK instances for protecting applications.

Experimental Setup. We installed and configured nine web applications, namely phpBB [8], punBB [9], Scarf [10], osCommerce [11], WebCalendar [12], Bookstore [13], Classifieds [14], Employees [15], and Events [16] on a web server configured with Intel Pentium-4 933MHz processor, 1GB RAM, Ubuntu Linux 8.04, MySQL 5.0, and the Apache 2 web server. phpBB and punBB are discussion board applications, Scarf is a conference management system, WebCalendar is a multi-user calendar application, osCommerce is an e-retailer application complete with a shopping cart, Bookstore is an online bookstore application, Events is a multi-user group-ware application, Classifieds is an online classifieds management application, and Employees is an online employee directory. Each application was installed as specified for use with a MySQL database. Web clients accessed the applications over a 100Mb Ethernet connection to measure their performance. phpBB, punBB, Scarf, osCommerce, and WebCalendar are built using PHP, so we used BAYAWAK available in the form of a mod_perl module. Bookstore, Classifieds, Employees, and Events are built using JSP, so we used BAYAWAK available in the form of a Servlet API filter.

Collecting Interface Names. We collected interface names for the various web application using two methods. For phpBB, punBB, Scarf, osCommerce, and WebCalendar, we used a simple web spider. For Bookstore, Classifieds, Employees, and Events, we used the WAMse tool to extract the list of interface names.

5.1   Resistance to RI Attacks

We identified several RI attacks for all the nine web applications. Table 1 provides a summary of attacks.

We found several CSRF vulnerabilities in all the applications. In the discussion board applications, phpBB and punBB, the vulnerabilities allow an attacker to forge new messages or delete existing ones. In osCommerce, we identified attacks that can add, modify, or delete products in the shopping cart and submit forged product reviews. In Scarf, the identified attacks can add or delete papers to sessions in a conference. In WebCalendar, the attacker can add or delete entries in the calendar and add or delete users from the calendar. In Classifieds, an attacker may add add, update, or delete the classified category headings or advertisements. In Events, an attacker may add, update, or delete events, user records, or category headings for events. In Employees, an attacker may add, update, or delete employee records or department names. In Bookstore, an attacker may add items to the shopping cart or add artificially high or low ratings for a book.

Table 1. RI attacks on example applications

Web Application	Attack Type	Attacks	Attacks Eliminated
osCommerce	CSRF	7	7
phpBB	CSRF	5	5
	Workflow attacks	1	1
punBB	CSRF	6	6
Scarf	CSRF	5	5
	Workflow attacks	1	1
WebCalendar	CSRF	5	5
Bookstore	CSRF	4	4
Employees	CSRF	3	3
	Workflow attacks	1	1
Classifieds	CSRF	6	6
	Workflow attacks	1	1
Events	CSRF	3	3

Scarf and Classified applications contained illegal URL access attacks. In Scarf, a server-side script that processes the site-wide configuration settings does not check whether the user has administrator privileges before making changes. The URL for the configuration page is only displayed in the web page if an administrator logs in. However, users can directly visit the URL associated with the configuration page and make changes. Similarly, in Classifieds, a server-side script that updates or deletes the category headings does not check whether the user has administrative privileges before making changes. Therefore, normal users can directly visit the URL associated with the server-side script and make changes. We created a illegal URL access vulnerability in phpBB. By default, the application displays the URL for the administrative interface only when the administrator logs in and the administrative script additionally checks the permission of the user. We disabled the permission checks to create an illegal URL access vulnerability.

For the purpose of evaluation, we created a workflow vulnerability in the osCommerce application. The checkout workflow comprises adding items to the shopping cart, entering shipping information, payment information, and final submission of the order. We created a vulnerability so that users could skip the payment step and directly proceed to the final submission step by visiting the URL directly.

All the attacks failed when we configured BAYAWAK instances for the web applications.

5.2 Performance Overhead

We measured the performance overhead of BAYAWAK by comparing the average response times for typical use cases of the applications with and without BAYAWAK instances. For each application multiple use cases were repeated with different users and content, providing at least 100 request-response pairs per application. Table 2 summarizes the average overhead of using BAYAWAK for all nine applications. The performance overhead significantly varied between the two forms of BAYAWAK. While the Apache mod_perl module incurred an

Table 2. Performance overhead from using BAYAWAK instances

Web Application	Application Response (msec)	Avg. Bayawak Overhead (msec)	Percent Overhead (%)
phpBB	278	55	19%
punBB	106	29	27%
Scarf	65	62	94%
WebCalendar	295	31	10%
osCommerce	325	96	29%
Bookstore	136	7	5%
Employees	121	4	3.5%
Classifieds	165	15	9%
Events	119	6	5%

overhead of 55ms, the Java-based Servlet API filter incurred an overhead of 8ms. The overhead of the Apache module could be reduced by implementing using C instead of Perl.

BAYAWAK's absolute overhead is related to the HTML document length, not application complexity. BAYAWAK detects the *set-cookie* header, creates a new RFG if necessary, but then must parse the HTML and rewrite URL. Therefore, the relative slowdown incurred by BAYAWAK will be the smallest for applications with non-trivial logic and relatively simple output. Conversely, simple applications with verbose output will have a higher relative overhead. Scarf is an example of a simple application with minimal server-side processing. Hence, its relative slowdown was the highest of all tested applications and is misleading as it represents the worst-case scenario for BAYAWAK deployment. All the other tested applications feature non-trivial logic and had significantly smaller relative overhead. In all cases BAYAWAK's overhead was imperceptible to end users. Moreover, our relative overhead estimates are conservative because the network latency in our test environment is likely to be much smaller compared to real deployments.

6   Related Work

In this section, we provide a comparison of our approach to current work.

Intrusion detection. BAYAWAK is related to intrusion detection approaches that enforce a security policy derived from a program's implementation. For example, there is work on constraining the execution of a program based on the model of system-call invocation derived from the program [17,18]. In these approaches, a run-time monitor tracks the current state/context of the program and detects malicious system-call sequences. Guha et al. [19] proposes a similar method for detecting malicious client-side behavior in AJAX-based applications. These approaches are broadly not applicable to web applications for two reasons. First, in web applications, unlike desktop applications, a single application instance is shared by multiple users. Second, a user may be simultaneously viewing several web pages. Both these aspects of web applications can confuse these state-tracking methods, leading to a lot of false positives.

BAYAWAK is related to control flow integrity (CFI) enforcement, in which a control-flow graph derived from a program is enforced by inserting run-time checks into the program binary [20]. Our approach can be considered a variant of this technique for web applications for the purpose of avoiding RI attacks. The enforcement mechanism under our setting is more complex compared to CFI, because we vary the RFG for each session.

BAYAWAK is related to work on using probabilistic models for detecting web-based attacks [21,22,23,24]. In particular, Swaddler [21] uses probabilistic models to characterize the internal session variables and associate invariants with blocks of code for the purpose of detecting workflow attacks. BAYAWAK avoids all RI attacks as opposed to just workflow attacks. Moreover, BAYAWAK does not require any training.

Mitigation Techniques. Current work has proposed several mitigation methods for preventing CSRF attacks such as purely client-side methods [25, 26], HTTP referrer header validation [27], proposals for new headers [6], and secret-token validation techniques [5]. A key difference of our approach from this body of work is that our approach more generally avoids RI attacks. In particular, BAYAWAK avoids workflow violations, which are outside the scope of these techniques.

Ripley [28] uses redundant execution of client-side code at the server-side to detect malicious JavaScript clients that subvert the client-side computation in AJAX-based applications. This is different from our problem setting, which is RI attacks.

Secure construction frameworks. SIF [29] uses language-based information flow control to enforce confidentiality and integrity policies on data. Robertson and Vigna [30] propose the use of strong typing to statically enforce strict separation of structure and content in web pages for avoiding cross-site scripting attacks. In contrast to both these approaches, our approach is focused on RI attacks and does not require any changes in the web application. At the same time, our approach is complimentary and can be implemented in these frameworks for avoiding RI attacks.

7 Conclusion

We described an approach for enforcing request integrity in web applications, and its implementation in a tool called BAYAWAK. BAYAWAK moves the request integrity enforcement mechanism from the application code into a security framework. Under our approach, the application's intended request sequences, or the request-flow graph (RFG), are specified as security policy and a server-side component transparently enforces the intended request sequences, without requiring any changes in the application's source code. Our approach is based on applying a form of behavior-preserving diversification on the RFG. We evaluated BAYAWAK using nine open source web applications. We identified several RI attacks in these applications. All the attacks were eliminated, when we configured BAYAWAK instances for the application. Moreover, BAYAWAK instances incurred negligible performance overhead.

References

1. Williams, J., Wichers, D.: OWASP Top 10 2010 rc1,
   http://www.owasp.org/images/0/0f/OWASP_T10_-_2010_rc1.pdf
2. Halfond, W.G., Anand, S., Orso, A.: Precise interface identification to improve testing and analysis of web applications. In: ISSTA (2009)
3. Wang, W., Lei, Y., Sampath, S., Kacker, R., Kuhn, R., Lawrence, J.: A combinatorial approach to building navigation graphs for dynamic web applications. In: ICSM (2009)
4. Fielding, R., Gettys, J., Mogul, J., Frystyk, H., Masinter, L., Leach, P., Berners-Lee, T.: Hypertext Transfer Protocol – HTTP/1.1. RFC 2616, Draft Standard (1999)

5. Jovanovic, N., Kirda, E., Kruegel, C.: Preventing Cross Site Request Forgery Attacks. In: IEEE Secure Comm. (2006)
6. Barth, A., Jackson, C., Mitchell, J.C.: Robust Defenses for Cross-Site Request Forgery. In: ACM CCS (2008)
7. Ruderman, J.: The Same origin policy,
   https://developer.mozilla.org/En/Same_origin_policy_for_JavaScript
8. phpBB Group: phpbb, http://www.phpbb.com/
9. PunBB: Punbb, http://punbb.informer.com/
10. SCARF, http://scarf.sourceforge.net/
11. osCommerce, http://www.oscommerce.com/
12. WebCalendar, http://sourceforge.net/projects/webcalendar/
13. Bookstore, http://www.gotocode.com/apps.asp?app_id=3&/
14. Classifieds, http://www.gotocode.com/apps.asp?app_id=5&/
15. Employee, http://www.gotocode.com/apps.asp?app_id=6&/
16. Events, http://www.gotocode.com/apps.asp?app_id=7&/
17. Wagner, D., Dean, D.: Intrusion Detection via Static Analysis. In: IEEE SP (2001)
18. Xu, H., Du, W., Chapin, S.J.: Context Sensitive Anomaly Monitoring of Process Control Flow To Detect Mimicry Attacks and Impossible Paths. In: RAID (2004)
19. Guha, A., Krishnamurthu, S., Jim, T.: Using Static Analysis for Ajax Intrusion Detection. In: WWW (2009)
20. Abadi, M., Budiu, M., Erlingsson, U., Ligatti, J.: Control-flow integrity. In: ACM CCS (2005)
21. Cova, M., Balzarotti, D., Felmetsger, V., Vigna, G.: Swaddler: An Approach for the Anomaly-based Detection of State Violations in Web Applications. In: RAID (2007)
22. Ingham, K.L., Somayaji, A., Burge, J., Forrest, S.: Learning DFA representations of HTTP for protecting web applications. Computer Networks 51(5) (2007)
23. Kruegel, C., Vigna, G.: Anomaly detection of web-based attacks. In: ACM CCS (2003)
24. Valeur, F., Vigna, G., Kruegel, C., Kirda, E.: An anomaly-driven reverse proxy for web applications. In: ACM SAC (2006)
25. Johns, M., Winter, J.: RequestRodeo: Client-side Protection Against Session Riding. In: OWASP Europe (2006)
26. Mao, Z., Li, N., Molloy, I.: Defeating Cross-Site Request Forgery Attacks with Browser-Enforced Authenticity Protection. In: Financial Cryptography and Data Security (2009)
27. Kerschbaum, F.: Simple cross-site attack prevention. In: Secure Comm. (2007)
28. Vikram, K., Prateek, A., Livshits, B.: Ripley: Automatically securing web 2.0 applications through replicated execution. In: ACM CCS (2009)
29. Chong, S., Vikram, K., Myers, A.C.: SIF: Enforcing confidentiality and integrity in web applications. In: USENIX-SS (2007)
30. Robertson, W., Vigna, G.: Static Enforcement of Web Application Integrity Through Strong Typing. In: USENIX-SS (2009)

Using Trust-Based Information Aggregation for Predicting Security Level of Systems[*]

Siv Hilde Houmb[1], Sudip Chakraborty[2], Indrakshi Ray[3], and Indrajit Ray[3]

[1] Telenor GBD&R
siv-hilde.houmb@telenor.com
[2] Valdosta State University
schakraborty@valdosta.edu
[3] Colorado State University
{iray,indrajit}@cs.colostate.edu

Abstract. Sometimes developers must design innovative security solutions that have a rapid development cycle, short life-time, short time-to-market, and small budget. Security evaluation standards, such as Common Criteria and ISO/IEC 17799, cannot be used due to resource limitations, time-to-market, and other constraints. We propose an alternative time and cost effective approach for predicting the security level of a security solution using information sources who are trusted to varying degrees. We show how to assess the trustworthiness of each information source and demonstrate how to aggregate the information obtained from them. We illustrate our approach by showing the security level prediction for two Denial of Service (DoS) solutions.

1 Introduction

Often times there is a need to build a security solution, that has a rapid development cycle, short life-time, and short time-to-market. It is important to predict the security level of such a solution before it can be deployed. Predicting the security level of a solution using standards, such as the Common Criteria [1] has drawbacks. First, the result of a Common Criteria evaluation is not given as a statement of the security level of a system, but rather as the level of assurance that the evaluator has based on whether the set of security features present provide adequate security. Second, Common Criteria evaluations are time and resource intensive. Third, the documentation and tests required by Common Criteria may not be suitable for the required system [2].

Such shortcomings motivated us to propose an alternative approach for predicting the security level of a system using information collected from different sources, not all of whom are equally trustworthy. We propose a model of trust to capture the trustworthiness of information sources, specifically that of domain experts. Trust is a relationship between a truster and a trustee with respect to some given context. Here, the entity trying to obtain information from the sources is the truster, the information source is the trustee, and the problem for which the information is requested is the trust context. The trustworthiness of an information source depends on two factors, namely, its *knowledge*

---

[*] This work was supported in part by AFOSR under contract number FA9550-07-1-0042.

S. Foresti and S. Jajodia (Eds.): Data and Applications Security XXIV, LNCS 6166, pp. 241–256, 2010.

level and *expertise level*. Knowledge level captures the level of knowledge possessed by the information source with respect to the problem being addressed. Expertise level captures the experience and qualifications of the information source. We show how to evaluate these factors and quantify the trustworthiness of sources which are later used for security level prediction.

The rest of the article is organized as follows. Section 2 presents the approach for predicting the security level of a solution. Section 3 illustrates our approach by predicting the security level of two DoS solutions. Section 4 summarizes the related work in this area. Section 5 concludes the paper with pointers to future directions.

2   Predicting the Security Level of Security Solutions

The first step in security level prediction is assessing the trustworthiness of an information source. The trustworthiness of a source depends on the *knowledge level* and *expertise level* of an information source. *Knowledge level* of an information source is defined as a measure of awareness of the information source about the knowledge domains related to the security level prediction of the security solution. It is represented in terms of a number called *knowledge score*. *Expertise level* of an information source is defined as a measure of degree of ability of the information source to assess the security level of a security solution. It is represented in terms of a number called *expertise score*. *Trustworthiness* of an information source is defined as a measure of the competence of the information source to act desirably and to provide information to the best of its abilities. It is represented in terms of a number called *trustworthiness score*. Trustworthiness score is derived from knowledge score and expertise score.

2.1   Evaluating Knowledge Score of an Information Source

The knowledge score of an information source gives a measure of how closely his/her knowledge is related to the desired knowledge in the problem context. It is calculated from two scores – *reference knowledge domain score* and *information source knowledge domain score* which are derived from the *reference knowledge domain model* and *information source knowledge domain model* respectively. The reference knowledge domain model provides the relative importance of different knowledge domains regarding the problem context. The information source knowledge domain model gives an assessment, by a third party, of the relative importance of knowledge level of an information source corresponding to the knowledge domains identified in reference knowledge domain model.

Reference Knowledge Domain Model
Prediction of security level of a security solution typically involves knowledge in several domains, not all of which are equally important. Knowledge level of an information source measures his/her awareness about these knowledge domains. We develop a reference knowledge domain model that captures the domains that are of interest and their relative importance with respect to the problem context. The relative importance of a domain is measured in terms of *importance weight* which is defined to be the percentage of the whole reference knowledge domain covered by that particular knowledge

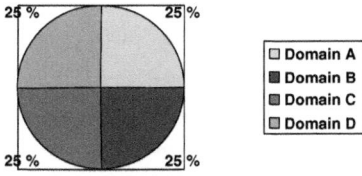

Fig. 1. Reference knowledge domain model

domain. Figure 1 shows a reference knowledge domain model for a security solution consisting of four domains: domain A (network security) domain B (Internet Protocol), domain C (authentication) and domain D (access control). All these domains cover the whole knowledge domain equally (25%), and hence have equal importance. Thus the importance weight of each domain is 0.25.

In the computation of reference knowledge domain score, we find out the knowledge domains that are of interest for the particular security level case prediction, arrange the knowledge domains in some order, and find their respective importance weight. A vector, called *reference knowledge domain scores*, represents the relative importance of all knowledge domains pertinent to the security level prediction of the target security solution. Each element of the vector indicates the importance weight of the corresponding domain.

Calculating Reference Knowledge Domain Score
Each knowledge domain in the reference model has a particular importance weight associated to it. Since multiple stakeholders are often involved in formalizing the problem context, the different stakeholders may assign different weights to it. Suppose the stakeholders are denoted by the set X and the cardinality of the set is q. We use x to denote an individual stakeholder. Suppose m is the number of knowledge domains in the problem context. The importance of knowledge domains, from the point of view of a stakeholder x, are represented as an m-element vector. This vector is denoted by $W_{Kimp}(x)$ where $W_{Kimp}(x) = [w_{Kimp}(x(j))]_{j=1}^{m}$ (Equation 1). Here, $w_{Kimp}(x(j)) \in [0, 1] \ \forall j = 1, \ldots, m$ and $\sum_{j=1}^{m} w_{Kimp}(x(j)) = 1$. Note, we obtain such vector for each of the q stakeholders in the set X. The importance of the m different domains given by q stakeholders is presented in a $q \times m$ matrix denoted by $W_{allKimp}(X)$ (Equation 2). The next step is to aggregate the information obtained from q stakeholders using an aggregation function, denoted by $f_{aggregation1}$, on the $q \times m$ matrix $W_{allKimp}(X)$ to merge the rows, resulting in a vector of size m. Equation 3 indicates the result of this aggregation. Here we do the aggregation by taking the arithmetic average for each m elements from all q number of vectors and put them into a single vector (for X), $W_{aggregatedKimp}(X)$, which is given by $[w_{aggregatedKimp}(X(j))]_{j=1}^{m}$. To normalize this vector, the normalization factor is obtained using Equation 4. Finally, the weight of each domain in the problem context is obtained by normalizing each element in the vector $W_{aggregatedKimp}(X)$ by the above normalization factor to obtain the vector $W_{refKnowledgeDomainScore}(X)$ (Equation 5). This vector derives the relative importance for each knowledge domain in the reference knowledge domain model.

$$W_{Kimp}(x) = [w_{Kimp}(x(j))]_{j=1}^{m} \qquad (1)$$

$$W_{allKimp}(X) = [W_{Kimp}(x)]_{x=1}^{q} \qquad (2)$$

$$W_{aggregatedKimp}(X) = f_{aggregation1}(W_{allKimp}(X))$$
$$= [w_{aggregatedKimp}(X(j))]_{j=1}^{m} \qquad (3)$$

$$f_{refKnorm} = \frac{1}{\sum_{j=1}^{m} w_{aggregatedKimp}(X(j))} \qquad (4)$$

$$W_{refKnowledgeDomainScore}(X) = f_{refKnorm} \times W_{aggregatedKimp}(X)$$
$$= [w_{refKnowledgeDomainScore}(X(j))]_{j=1}^{m} \qquad (5)$$

If simple average is used as an aggregation technique then we do not need to normalize the vector $W_{aggregatedKimp}(X)$ as each element of the vector will be in $[0, 1]$ and sum of all elements will be 1. In that case, we can ignore Equation 4 and we will have $W_{aggregatedKimp}(X) = W_{refKnowledgeDomainScore}(X)$.

Information Source Knowledge Domain Model
An information source may not have knowledge in all the knowledge domains represented in the reference domain model. The information source knowledge domain model provides the relative importance of the knowledge level of the source corresponding to the knowledge domains in reference knowledge domain model. This relative importance is assessed by a third party to reduce the bias involved in self-assessment.

Consider the reference knowledge domain example shown in Figure 1. Now, for an information source, say b, a third party assessor assesses the relative importance of knowledge level of b on the identified knowledge domains as 30% on domain A, 30% on domain B, and 40% on domain D. Thus, the relative importance of b's knowledge level on the domains, as assessed by a third party, is $[0.3, 0.3, 0.0, 0.4]$.

Suppose we have n information sources, denoted by $b_1, b_2, \ldots, b_n$, in a security level prediction. Suppose Y is the set of third parties assessing the knowledge of these n information sources. Suppose, cardinality of Y is z and an individual third party in the set Y is denoted by y. Then, information source knowledge domain score is represented as an m-element vector where each element corresponds to some knowledge domain of the information source. Each element indicates the relative weight of that domain and has a weight between 0 and 1. Equations 6–10 show how to compute the information source knowledge domain score for a source b_i.

$$W_{Kis}(y(b_i)) = [w_{Kis}(y(b_i(j)))]_{j=1}^{m} \qquad (6)$$

$$W_{allKis}(Y(b_i)) = [W_{Kis}(y(b_i))]_{y=1}^{z} \qquad (7)$$

$$W_{aggregatedKis}(Y(b_i)) = f_{aggregation2}(W_{allKis}(Y(b_i)))$$
$$= [w_{aggregatedKis}(Y(b_i(j)))]_{j=1}^{m} \qquad (8)$$

$$f_{isKnorm} = \frac{1}{\sum_{j=1}^{m} w_{aggregatedKis}(Y(b_i(j)))} \qquad (9)$$

$$W_{isKnowledgeDomainScore}(Y(b_i)) = f_{isKnorm} \times W_{aggregatedKis}(Y(b_i))$$
$$= [w_{isKnowledgeDomainScore}(Y(b_i(j)))]_{j=1}^{m} \qquad (10)$$

Each third party $y \in Y$ provides a vector, denoted by $W_{Kis}(y(b_i))$, of m-elements. Each element represents the assessed weight of knowledge level of the information source b_i corresponding to the domain represented by that element as shown in Equation 6. This step is repeated for each y in the set Y and results in z such vectors. To aggregate information from all y for the information source b_i, these z vectors are first combined in a $z \times m$ matrix in Equation 7 and then aggregated using some aggregation function in Equation 8. The aggregation function is denoted as $f_{aggregation2}$ in the equation. The aggregation technique used here is arithmetic average. We normalize this vector using the normalization factor obtained in Equation 9. Finally, the weight of each domain in the problem context is obtained by normalizing each element in the vector $W_{aggregatedKis}$ by the above normalization factor to obtain the vector $W_{isKnowledgeDomainScore}$ (Equation 10). The result gives one vector for the set Y holding the relative knowledge domain scores for the information source b_i. All these steps are then repeated n times (as we have n number of information sources in the security level prediction).

Calculating Knowledge Score of Information Sources
The knowledge score of an information source b_i, denoted by $K_{score}(b_i)$, gives a measure of the source's knowledge level and is calculated using the reference knowledge domain score and the information source knowledge domain score of b_i. For an information source b_i, this score is calculated as follows.

$$K_{score}(b_i) = \sum_{j=1}^{m} \{ w_{refKnowledgedomainScore}(X(j)) \times w_{isKnowledgeDomainScore}(Y(b_i(j))) \}$$

(11)

The result of the above equation is a real number derived by component-wise multiplication of the two vectors $W_{refKnowledgeDomainScore}(X)$ and $W_{isKnowledgeDomainScore}(Y(b_i))$ and then adding all the product values.

2.2   Evaluating Expertise Score of an Information Source

Expertise level of an information source with respect to assessing the security level of a security solution is represented by the *expertise score*. We propose to evaluate the expertise score using questionnaires to reduce the bias of subjective assessment. Each questionnaire consists of a set of *calibration variables* which are further divided into *categories*. Table 1 provides an example questionnaire.

Each information source is assessed on each calibration variable according to the information source's category for that variable. The importance value for each calibration variable and the value associated with each category is determined by some external source, such as an expert[1]. To derive expertise score of an information source, we develop *calibration variable importance weight model* and *calibration variable category importance weight model*.

---

[1] Interested readers are referred to Cooke [3] and Goossens et al. [4] for an overview of the general challenges and benefits related to expert judgments.

Table 1. Example calibration variables for determining expertise level of information sources

Variables	Categories
level of expertise	low, medium and high
age	under 20, [20-25), [25-30), [30-40), [40-50), over 50
years of relevant education	1 year, 2 years, Bsc, Msc, PhD, other
years of education others	1 year, 2 years, Bsc, Msc, PhD, other
years of experience from industry	[1-3) years, [3-5) years, [5-10) years, [10-15) years, over 15 years
years of experience from academia	[1-3) years, [3-5) years, [5-10) years, [10-15) years, over 15 years
role experience	database, network management, developer, designer, security management and decision maker

Calibration Variable Importance Weight Model

The relative importance of a calibration variable is assessed by external sources. Suppose the set of such external sources is denoted by X' and the cardinality of the set is u. Each calibration variable that is pertinent to the problem context is associated with an importance value. A member x' of the set X' assigns an importance value from the range $(0, 1]$ to a calibration variable such that the sum of the importance value of all the calibration variables used is 1. Let there be p calibration variables denoted by $l_1, l_2, \ldots, l_p$ and $W_{l_1}, W_{l_2}, \ldots, W_{l_p}$ be their relative importance value assigned by the external source x'. This is represented by a vector $W_l(x') = [w_{l_j}(x')]_{j=1}^p$ and shown in Equation 12. All u members of X' will assign such values. For each calibration variable, the final importance value is derived by applying an aggregation function, $f_{aggregation3}$, on $W_l(X')$ (Equation 14). Since, $w_{l_j}(x') \in (0, 1]$ for all $j = 1, \ldots, p$ and for each $x' \in X'$, the aggregation function is so chosen that each element of $W_l(X')$ is in $(0, 1]$ and $\sum_{j=1}^p W_{l_j}(X') = 1$.

$$W_l(x') = [w_{l_j}(x')]_{j=1}^p \tag{12}$$

$$W_l(X') = [W_l(x')]_{x'=1}^u \tag{13}$$

$$W_{aggregatedCalwt}(X') = f_{aggregation3}(W_l(X')) \tag{14}$$

Calibration Variable Category Importance Weight Model

Each category in a calibration variable is also associated with a value that denotes the importance weight of the category of that calibration variable. These values are assigned by the external sources in X'. Let the calibration variable l_j have s categories denoted by $l_{j_1}, l_{j_2}, \ldots, l_{j_s}$ where $l_{j_k} \in [0, 1]$ for all $k = 1, \ldots, s$ (Equation 15). All u members of X' assign weights and then an aggregation function is used to derive the category weights for calibration variable l_j (Equations 16 and 17 respectively).

$$W_c(x'(l_j)) = [w_c(x'(l_j(i)))]_{i=1}^s \tag{15}$$

$$W_c(X'(l_j)) = [W_c(x'(l_j))]_{x'=1}^u \tag{16}$$

$$W_{aggregatedC}(X'(l_j)) = f_{aggregation4}(W_c(X'(l_j))) \tag{17}$$

Therefore, $W_{aggregatedC}(X'(l_j))$ holds the importance weight (as derived by all external sources in X') of each category of the calibration variable l_j. The above is done for all the calibration variables $(j = 1, \ldots, p)$. Here, note that all the p calibration variables may not have s categories.

Information Source Calibration Variable Category Score Model
An information source (b_i) receives scores for applicable categories within each calibration variable by a set Y' of external sources where cardinality of y' is v. This score is computed as follows. Each information source b_i is required to fill the questionnaire. Each member of Y' assesses the filled questionnaire and assigns a score in the range $[0, 1]$ for applicable categories within each calibration variable. Equation 18 shows such scores, assigned by an $y' \in Y'$, for the calibration variable l_j. All v members of Y' assigns such scores and then an aggregation is used to reduce it to single set of values (Equations 19 and 20). Hence, information source calibration variable category score model is designed as

$$W_{isCat}(y'(b_i(l_j))) = [w_{isCat}(y'(b_i(l_j(m))))]^s_{m=1} \tag{18}$$

$$W_{isCatAll}(Y'(b_i(l_j))) = [W_{isCat}(y'(b_i(l_j)))]^v_{y'=1} \tag{19}$$

$$W_{isCatAggregated}(Y'(b_i(l_j))) = f_{aggregation5}(W_{isCatAll}(Y'(b_i(l_j)))) \tag{20}$$

The above is done for all calibration variables considered for the problem. Note, for some calibration variable, the members of Y' may not need to assign any score. For example, for the calibration variable *level of expertise*, the importance weight of the applicable category (according to filled questionnaire) can work as the score. Hence, members of Y' can assign simply 1.0 to the category.

Calculating Expertise Score of Information Sources
The set X' of external experts assigns importance weights of each category within each calibration variable. Also the information source b_i receives scores for applicable categories within each calibration variable by another set of experts Y'. These two are combined to derive the information source's score for each calibration variable. Equation 21 gives the value obtained by b_i for calibration variable l_j. The weighted sum of all these calibration variable scores, where the weight is the importance weight of the corresponding calibration variable, gives the expertise score of b_i, denoted by $E_{score}(b_i)$ as demonstrated by Equation 22.

$$W_{calScore}(b_i(l_j)) = \sum_{m=1}^s W_{aggregatedC}(X'(l_j(m))) \times W_{isCatAggregated}(Y'(b_i(l_j(m)))) \tag{21}$$

$$E_{score}(b_i) = \sum_{j=1}^p W_{aggregatedCalwt}(X'(j)) \times W_{calScore}(b_i(l_j)) \tag{22}$$

2.3 Computing Information Source Trustworthiness

The information sources involved in the security level prediction have varying degrees of trustworthiness, which depends on their knowledge levels and expertise levels.

Therefore, the knowledge score and the expertise score must be combined to compute the trustworthiness of an information source. Here again, the problem context will determine the relative importance of each score. Let k and e be the relative importance of the knowledge and expertise score. The following relations hold: $0 \leq k, e \leq 1$ and $k + e = 1$. The values of k and e can be set by the evaluator (or, truster). The trustworthiness score for information source b_i, denoted by $T_{score}(b_i)$, is computed as follows.

$$T_{score}(b_i) = k \times K_{score}(b_i) + e \times E_{score}(b_i) \tag{23}$$

2.4 Computing Security Level of a Security Solution

The trustworthiness score of an information source is used to compare the security level of different security solutions. The information obtained from each source b_i (in the form of a number $\in [0, 1]$), denoted by $b_i(I)$, is multiplied by the trustworthiness score of that source. This is done for all the sources. The results are then added and divided by n. This gives the initial security level for the security solution s_j as shown by Equation 24. This is done for all s_j in the set of security solutions S. Since the r security solutions are compared against each other, we must obtain a relative security level for each solution. The relative security level of s_j is computed using Equation 25.

$$F_{initialSL}(s_j) = \frac{\sum_{i=1}^{n} \{b_i(I) \times T_{score}(b_i)\}}{n} \tag{24}$$

$$F_{SL}(s_j) = \frac{F_{initialSL}(s_j)}{\sum_{j=1}^{r} F_{initialSL}(s_j)} \tag{25}$$

3   Example Application: Evaluating DoS Solutions

We now describe how to use our approach to predict the security level of two solutions for protecting against Denial of Service (DoS) attacks that can be launched at the user authentication mechanism of ACTIVE, an e-Commerce platform that was developed by the EU EP-27046-ACTIVE project [5]. Here we evaluate two such solutions – a cookie solution and a filtering mechanism. The cookie solution adds a patch to the network stack software that keeps track of sessions and their states. It begins by sending a cookie to the client. If the client does not respond within a short period of time, the cookie expires and the client must re-start the request for a connection. If the client responds in time, the SYN-ACK message is sent and the connection is set up. Adding the cookie message makes it unlikely that an attacker can respond in time to continue setting up the connection. If the client address has been spoofed, the client will not respond in any event. The filtering mechanism works a bit differently. The filtering mechanism has an outbound and an inbound part (Figures 2(a) and 2(b)) that checks the source address (srcAddr) against a set of accepted source IP addresses stored in internalNetAddr. The filtering mechanism is implemented on the server side (usually on a firewall or an Internet router) and configured to block unauthorized connection attempts.

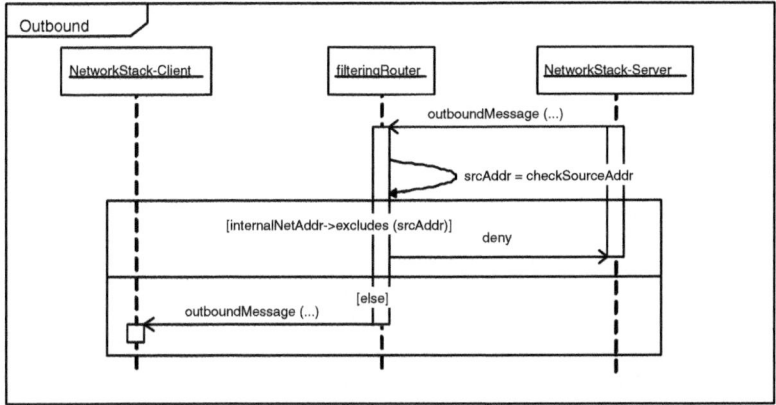

(a) Outbound

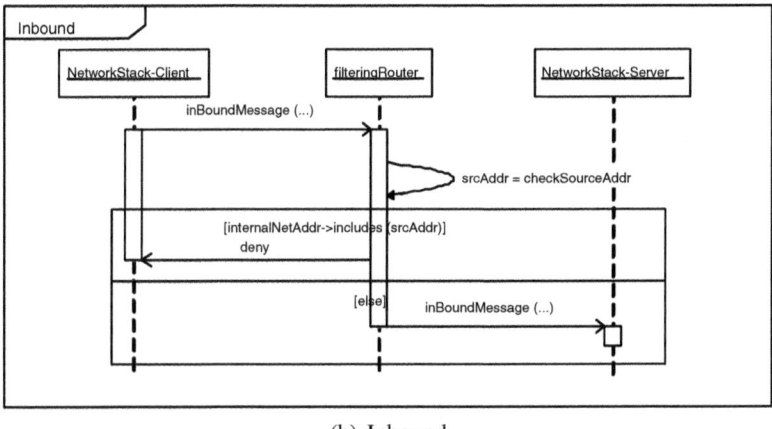

(b) Inbound

Fig. 2. Filter mechanism

A decision maker (truster) A needs help to choose between the two security solutions. For this purpose A seeks help of information sources regarding anticipated number of DoS attacks for the two solutions. In our example, we have five information sources; one honeypot [6] and four domain experts from a pool of 18 domain experts. The four chosen domain experts are denoted as b_4, b_6, b_{15}, b_{18} and the honeypot is denoted by $b_{honeypot}$. These five information sources provide information on the anticipated number of DoS attacks for the two involved solutions to A. The truster A has complete trust in the abilities of honeypot to provide accurate and correct information on the potential number of successful DoS attacks and therefore $T_{score}(b_{honeypot}) = 1$. Elicitation of expert judgments are done using a combined knowledge level and expertise level questionnaire as shown in Table 2.

The reference knowledge domain model was created by a third party who has experience with secure systems; thus, the set of external sources X has only one member x_1.

Table 2. The combined knowledge and expertise level questionnaire and the information provided

Expert no.	Calibration variable	Information provided
4	level of expertise	medium
	years of relevant of education	Bsc
	years of experience from industry	0
	role experience	database, security management
6	level of expertise	low
	years of relevant of education	Bsc
	years of experience from industry	0
	role experience	database
15	level of expertise	high
	years of relevant of education	Bsc
	years of experience from industry	0
	role experience	designer, developer, security management
18	level of expertise	low
	years of relevant of education	Bsc
	years of experience from industry	0.5
	role experience	developer

Here the relevant knowledge domains are *security management (50%)*, *design (10%)*, *network management (20%)*, *database (15%)*, and *developer (5%)*. The importance vector, obtained using Equation 1, is $W_{Kimp}(x_1) = [0.5, 0.2, 0.15, 0.1, 0.05]$. Since we have only one external source x_1, we obtain, $W_{aggrgatedKimp}(X) = W_{allKimp}(X) = W_{Kimp}(x_1)$. The knowledge domains are already normalized and we do not need to normalize the elements in the vector $W_{aggrgatedKimp}(X)$. Hence, $(W_{refKnowledgeDomainScore}(X) = W_{aggrgatedKimp}(X) = [0.5, 0.2, 0.15, 0.1, 0.05]$.

An external source y_1 assesses relative weights for each knowledge domain for each information source. Here y_1 is same as x_1 who assessed the importance weights in reference knowledge domain model. The weights that each of the experts has for the knowledge domains are: for b_4, 85% on security management and 15% on database; for b_6, 100% on database; for b_{15}, 60% on design, 30% on developer, and 10% on security management; for b_{18}, 100% on developer. Equation 6 gives the information source knowledge domain vectors for the sources as follows.

- $W_{Kis}(y_1(b_4)) = [0.85, 0.0, 0.15, 0.0, 0.0]$
- $W_{Kis}(y_1(b_6)) = [0.0, 0.0, 1.0, 0.0, 0.0]$
- $W_{Kis}(y_1(b_{15})) = [0.1, 0.0, 0.0, 0.6, 0.3]$
- $W_{Kis}(y_1(b_{18})) = [0.0, 0.0, 0.0, 0.0, 1.0]$

Since there is only one external source $y_1 (= x_1)$ in the set Y of external sources providing assessment on the information sources, we have $W_{isKnowledgeDomainScore}(Y(b_i)) = W_{aggregatedKis}(Y(b_i)) = W_{Kis}(y_1(b_i))$, for $i = 4, 6, 15, 18$.

The knowledge score for each information source is derived using Equation 11:

- $K_{score}(b_4) = 0.85 * 0.5 + 0 * 0.2 + 0.15 * 0.15 + 0 * 0.1 + 0 * 0.05 \approx 0.45$
- $K_{score}(b_6) = 0 * 0.5 + 0 * 0.2 + 1 * 0.15 + 0 * 0.1 + 0 * 0.05 = 0.15$

- $K_{score}(b_{15}) = 0.1 * 0.5 + 0 * 0.2 + 0 * 0.15 + 0.6 * 0.1 + 0.3 * 0.05 \approx 0.13$
- $K_{score}(b_{18}) = 0 * 0.5 + 0 * 0.2 + 0 * 0.15 + 0 * 0.1 + 1.0 * 0.05 = 0.05$

The level of expertise of an information source is derived using the calibration variables described in Table 2. The external expert x_1 gives the relative importance values for calibration variables and the weights of categories for each calibration variable. Hence, $X' = Y = X = \{x_1\}$. We use three calibration variables to determine level of expertise – *level of experience* denoted by l_1, *years of relevant education* denoted by l_2, and *years of experience from industry* denoted by l_3. This gives the following vectors of categories for the three calibration variables: (i) $l_1 = [low, medium, high]$, (ii) $l_2 = [Bsc]$, (iii) $l_3 = [no\_of\_year]$ Suppose the expert x_1 assigns the following weights for the categories of calibration variables: $w_c(l_1(low)) = 0.2$, $w_c(l_1(medium)) = 0.5$, $w_c(l_1(high)) = 1.0$, $w_c(l_2(Bsc)) = 0.2$ and $w_c(l_3(no\_of\_year)) = 0.2$ for each year of industrial experience. Therefore,

- $W_{aggregatedC}(x_1(l_1)) = [0.2, 0.5, 1.0]$
- $W_{aggregatedC}(x_1(l_2)) = [0.2]$
- $W_{aggregatedC}(x_1(l_3)) = [0.2]$

Suppose the importance value given to the calibration variables by the external expert are 0.3 for *level of experience*, 0.2 for *years of relevant education*, and 0.5 for *years of experience from industry*. Therefore, $W_{l_1} = 0.3$, $W_{l_2} = 0.2$ and $W_{l_3} = 0.5$.

We then look at the information about categories of calibration variables provided by the information sources b_4, b_6, b_{15}, b_{18} in the questionnaire. We do not need to aggregate these scores as we are considering assessment from only one external expert. The scores for the four sources are as follows:

- $W_{isCat}(b_4(l_1)) = [0, 1, 0]$, $W_{isCat}(b_4(l_2)) = [0, 0, 1, 0, 0, 0]$, $W_{isCat}(b_4(l_3)) = [0]$.
- $W_{isCat}(b_6(l_1)) = [1, 0, 0]$, $W_{isCat}(b_6(l_2)) = [0, 0, 1, 0, 0, 0]$, $W_{isCat}(b_6(l_3)) = [0]$.
- $W_{isCat}(b_{15}(l_1)) = [0, 0, 1]$, $W_{isCat}(b_{15}(l_2)) = [0, 0, 1, 0, 0, 0]$, $W_{isCat}(b_{15}(l_3)) = [0]$.
- $W_{isCat}(b_{18}(l_1)) = [0, 0, 1]$, $W_{isCat}(b_{18}(l_2)) = [0, 0, 1, 0, 0, 0]$, $W_{isCat}(b_{18}(l_3)) = [0.5]$.

Using the above information, the evaluator calculates the expertise score of the information sources using Equations 21 and 22.

- $E_{score}(b_4) = 0.3 * 0.5 + 0.2 * 0.2 + 0.5 * 0 = 0.15 + 0.04 + 0 = 0.19$
- $E_{score}(b_6) = 0.3 * 0.2 + 0.2 * 0.2 + 0.5 * 0 = 0.06 + 0.04 + 0 = 0.10$
- $E_{score}(b_{15}) = 0.3 * 1.0 + 0.2 * 0.2 + 0.5 * 0 = 0.3 + 0.04 + 0 = 0.34$
- $E_{score}(b_{18}) = 0.3 * 1.0 + 0.2 * 0.2 + 0.5 * (0.5 * 0.2) = 0.3 + 0.04 + 0.5 = 0.84$

The knowledge and expertise scores are combined into an information source trustworthiness weight using Equation 23. The truster A has assigned relative importance of the knowledge and expertise score as 0.6 and 0.4 respectively. Recall that $T_{score}(b_{honeypot}) = 1.0$. Thus, the trustworthiness score for the experts $b_{honeypot}$, b_4, b_6, b_{15}, b_{18} are derived as,

- $T_{score}(b_{honeypot}) = 1.0$.
- $T_{score}(b_4) = 0.6 * 0.45 + 0.4 * 0.19 = 0.27 + 0.076 = 0.346$.
- $T_{score}(b_6) = 0.6 * 0.15 + 0.4 * 0.1 = 0.09 + 0.04 = 0.130$.

- $T_{score}(b_{15}) = 0.6 * 0.13 + 0.4 * 0.34 = 0.078 + 0.136 = 0.214.$
- $T_{score}(b_{18}) = 0.6 * 0.05 + 0.4 * 0.84 = 0.03 + 0.336 = 0.366.$

Now we predict the security level of the two solutions of the DoS problem. Let us denote the *cookie solution* by s_1 and *filter mechanism* by s_2. To derive the security level for s_1 and s_2, the information provided by the different information sources are interpreted and combined with their trustworthiness score using the Equations 24 and 25 mentioned in Section 2.4. The honeypot reports 1.5 average monthly successful attack for cookie solution (s_1) and 4.0 average monthly successful attack for filter mechanism (s_2). The information provided by the experts are as follows:

- $b_4(s_1) = medium, \ b_4(s_2) = low$
- $b_6(s_1) = medium, \ b_6(s_2) = medium$
- $b_{15}(s_1) = medium, \ b_{15}(s_2) = low$
- $b_{18}(s_1) = high, \ b_{18}(s_2) = low$

In order to calculate the security level from these pieces of information, the information must be at the same level of abstraction and comparable. The honeypot reports less number of average monthly successful attack for cookie solution than filter mechanism. This shows that according to the information source $b_{honeypot}$, the cookie solution s_1 has higher security level. To measure this level, we transform the average monthly successful attack inversely and the reciprocal of this average value is used to calculate the security level. This gives: $b_{honeypot}(s_1) = 1/1.5 = 0.667$ and $b_{honeypot}(s_2) = 1/4.0 = 0.25$. For the other information sources, we assign 0.2 for the level *low*, 0.5 for the level *medium* and 1.0 for the level *high*. Hence, the initial security level of the security solutions are evaluated as

- $F_{initialSL}(s_1) = (0.667 * 1.0 + 0.5 * 0.346 + 0.5 * 0.130 + 0.5 * 0.214 + 1.0 * 0.366)/5 = 0.2756$
- $F_{initialSL}(s_2) = (0.25 * 1.0 + 0.2 * 0.346 + 0.5 * 0.130 + 0.2 * 0.214 + 0.2 * 0.366)/5 = 0.10004$

Using Equation 25 the initial security level is updated to relative security level for each solution, which gives

- $F_{SL}(s_1) = 0.2756/(0.2756 + 0.10004) \approx 0.734$
- $F_{SL}(s_2) = 0.10004/(0.2756 + 0.10004) \approx 0.266.$

This relative security level is a prediction and should not be considered as the actual security level, but rather an expression of the difference in security level between the two DoS solutions. The actual security level depends on many uncertain factors, such as future attacks, changes in the security environment, relevant operational procedures, maintenance strategy, the resources available etc. What we can infer from the result is that the cookie solution is a much better choice when it comes to security solutions of DoS attacks than the filter mechanism. The relative difference between the two solutions is 2.76 ($\frac{F_{SL}(s_1)}{F_{SL}(s_2)} = \frac{0.734}{0.266} \approx 2.759$), which means that the cookie solution is almost three times a better choice than the filter mechanism.

3.1 Validation of Example Application Results

DoS attacks are often performed using legitimate protocols and services; the malicious activities differ from legitimate ones only by intent and not by content. Since it is hard to measure intent, many of the existing DoS solutions do not offer a proper defense. In [7] Karig and Lee gives an overview of common DoS attacks and potential countermeasures for DoS attacks. In this context, the filtering mechanism is categorized as a network device level countermeasure while the cookie solution is categorized as an OS level countermeasure. A network device level DoS solution provides measures to protect against potential misuse of a communication protocol. Thus, the protection is often on the IP or transport layer and hence there are possible ways around the mechanism, such as those discussed in [7]. The main shortage of filtering mechanisms are their inability to filter out spoofed packets [7]. There are, however, more efficient filtering mechanisms available, such as the one discussed in [8]. The other DoS solution discussed in this paper, the cookie solution, operates on the OS level. An OS level DoS solution integrates protection into the way a protocol is implemented in a particular operating system. Thus, the measure is deployed on the source (target) and refers to a host-based protection solution. Hence, the cookie solution represents a more defense-in-depth DoS solution than the filtering mechanism. Furthermore, the cookie solution discussed in this paper is a SYN cookie, which has been well tested and is well understood. SYN cookies have also been incorporated as a standard part of Linux and Free BSD and are recognized as one of the most effective DoS mechanisms [9].

In general, a DoS solution should be effective, transparent to existing Internet infrastructure, have low performance overhead, be invulnerable to attacks aimed at the defense system, be incrementally deployable and have no impact on the legitimate traffic [10]. The filtering mechanism is somewhat effective in stopping attacks on the spot. It is not transparent to existing Internet infrastructure and results in some performance overhead. The filter mechanism can also be vulnerable to attacks due to its scanning of each packet and hence may have impact on legitimate traffic. However, the mechanism can be incrementally deployed. The cookie solution is documented to be effective against DoS attacks, but has been demonstrated to be somewhat unable to detect and prevent against zombie attacks. The mechanism is transparent to the network infrastructure, but leads to some performance overhead, but in practice no impact on legitimate traffic. The cookie solution is already included in some operating systems and is easy to deploy. Thus, we can conclude that the cookie solution is a better choice than filtering mechanism for DoS attacks. Our trust-based information aggregation approach also shows that the cookie solution is approximately 2.76 times better than the filtering mechanism.

4 Related Work

Jøsang [11,12] proposed a model for trust based on a general model for expressing relatively uncertain beliefs about the truth of statements. Cohen et al. [13] proposed an alternative, more differentiated concept of trust called Argument-based Probabilistic Trust model (APT). Yahalom et al. [14,15] proposed a formal model for deriving new trust relationships from existing ones. Beth et al. [16] extended the ideas presented by Yahalom et al. to include relative trust. Xiong and Liu [17] presented a coherent adaptive trust model for quantifying and comparing the trustworthiness of peers based on a transaction-based feedback system. Bacharach and Gambetta [18] defined trust as a particular belief, which arises in games with a certain payoff structure. Purser [19] presented a simple, graphical approach to model trust and discussed the relationship between trust and risk. Ray and Chakraborty [20] and Ray et al. [21] described the factors on which trust depends, showed how to quantify these factors and obtain a quantitative value for trust. Other works include logic-based formalisms of trust [22,23,24,25].

Littlewood et al. [26] was one of the earliest works on measuring operational security. Subsequently, Ortalo et al. in [27] proposed a quantitative model for known Unix security vulnerabilities using a privilege graph. Madan et al. [28] discussed how to quantify security attributes of software systems using traditional reliability theory for modeling random processes, such as stochastic modeling and Markov analysis. Jonsson and Olovsson [29] looked at the problem in a more practical way by analyzing attacker behavior through controlled experiments.

Several efforts have been devoted to developing structured and systematic security risk assessment approaches. The three main approaches are the OCTAVE [30], CRAMM [31] and the CORAS frameworks [32]. Security management standards aid in the overall and detailed management of security in an organization. The most important standards in this area are the ISO/IEC 27002:2005 Information technology – Code of Practice for information security management [33], ISO/IEC TR 13335:2004 Information technology – Guidelines for management of IT Security [34] and the Australian/New Zealand standard for risk management AS/NZS 4360:2007 [35].

TCSEC is the oldest known standard developed in the U.S. for evaluation and certification of information security in IT products. Subsequently, the European countries collaborated and produced their own standard ITSEC. The International Organization for Standardization (ISO) developed the Common Criteria, as a response to the various types of evaluation criteria that were developed by different nations, which has replaced TCSEC and ITSEC.

Our work refines that proposed by Houmb et al. [36] by (i) extending the sophistication with which knowledge score, experience score, and relative trustworthiness is calculated and (ii) allowing for the direct evaluation and comparison of security solutions using whatever security-related information that is available.

5   Conclusion

In this article we present a trust-based information aggregation approach to predict security level of security solutions. We have proposed a quantitative approach for evaluating the trustworthiness of sources and using this information to predict the security level of a solution. We have demonstrated our approach for predicting the security level of two solutions used for preventing DoS attacks on an example .NET e-commerce system. Our results help validate that one solution is superior than the other for preventing DoS attacks. Future work includes controlled experiments, and eventually a case study, to gain realistic experience with the current version of the trust-based information aggregation approach. Investigating how to reduce the subjectivity of the approach also needs to be investigated. Future work also involves transitioning from the deterministic trust model to a probabilistic one which will allow reasoning with uncertainty and implementing such a model using existing Bayesian Belief Network tools, such as HUGIN. Incorporating such a trust model in other applications, such as social networks, is also planned for the future.

References

1. ISO 15408:1999 Common Criteria for Information Technology Security Evaluation. Version 2.1, CCIMB–99–031, CCIMB-99-032, CCIMB-99-033 (August 1999)
2. Common Criteria for Information Technology Security Evaluation (2010), http://en.wikipedia.org/wiki/Common_Criteria
3. Cooke, R.: Experts in Uncertainty: Opinion and Subjective Probability in Science. Oxford University Press, Oxford (1991)
4. Goossens, L., Harper, F., Kraan, B., Meacutetivier, H.: Expert Judgement for a Probabilistic Accident Consequence Uncertainty Analysis. Radiation Protection and Dosimetry 90(3), 295–303 (2000)
5. EU Project EP-27046-ACTIVE: EP-27046-ACTIVE, Final Prototype and User Manual, D4.2.2, Ver. 2.0, 2001-02-22 (2001)
6. Østvang, M.E.: The Honeynet Project, Phase 1: Installing and Tuning Honeyd using LIDS, Project assignment, Norwegian University of Science and Technology (2003)
7. Karig, D., Lee, R.: Remote Denial of Service Attacks and Countermeasures. Technical report CE-L2001-002, Department of Electrical Engineering, Princeton University (October 2001)
8. Barkley, A., Liu, S., Gia, Q., Dingfield, M., Gokhale, Y.: A Testbed for Study of Distributed Denial of Service Attacks (WA 2.4). In: Proceedings of the IEEE Workshop on Information Assurance and Security, June 2000, pp. 218–223 (2000)
9. Bernstein, D.: SYN Cookies, http://crypto/syncookies.html (accessed November 2006)
10. Lin, S., Chiueh, T.: A Survey on Solutions to Distributed Denial of Service Attacks. Technical report RPE TR-201, Department of Computer Science, Stony Brook University (September 2006)
11. Jøsang, A.: A Subjective Metric of Authentication. In: Proceedings of the 5th European Symposium on Research in Computer Security, September 1998, pp. 329–344 (1998)
12. Jøsang, A.: An Algebra for Assessing Trust in Certification Chains. In: Proceedings of the 1999 Network and Distributed Systems Security Symposium (February 1999)
13. Cohen, M., Parasuraman, R., Freeman, J.: Trust in Decision Aids: A Model and a Training Strategy. Technical Report USAATCOM TR 97-D-4, Cognitive Technologies Inc (1997)
14. Yahalom, R., Klein, B., Beth, T.: Trust Relationship in Secure Systems: A Distributed Authentication Perspective. In: Proceedings of the IEEE Symposium on Security and Privacy, May 1993, pp. 150–164 (1993)
15. Yahalom, R., Klein, B., Beth, T.: Trust-based Navigation in Distributed Systems. Computing Systems 7(1), 45–73 (1994)
16. Beth, T., Borcherding, M., Klein, B.: Valuation of Trust in Open Networks. In: Proceedings of the 3rd European Symposium on Research in Computer Security, November 1994, pp. 3–18 (1994)
17. Xiong, L., Liu, L.: A Reputation-Based Trust Model For Peer-To-Peer Ecommerce Communities. In: Proceedings of the IEEE Conference on E-Commerce, June 2003, pp. 275–284 (2003)

18. Bacharach, M., Gambetta, D.: Trust as Type Identification. In: Trust and Deception in Virtual Societies, pp. 1–26. Kluwer Academic Publishers, Dordrecht (2000)
19. Purser, S.: A Simple Graphical Tool For Modelling Trust. Computers & Security 20(6), 479–484 (2001)
20. Ray, I., Chakraborty, S.: A Vector Model of Trust for Developing Trustworthy Systems. In: Proceedings of the 9th European Symposium on Research in Computer Security, September 2004, pp. 260–275 (2004)
21. Ray, I., Ray, I., Chakraborty, S.: An Interoperable Context Sensitive Model of Trust. Journal of Intelligent Information Systems 32(1), 75–104 (2009)
22. Abdul-Rahman, A., Hailes, S.: Supporting Trust in Virtual Communities. In: Proceedings of the 33rd Annual Hawaii International Conference on System Sciences, January 2000, pp. 4–7 (2000)
23. Burrows, M., Abadi, M., Needham, R.: A Logic of Authentication. ACM Transactions on Computer Systems 8(1), 18–36 (1990)
24. Jones, A., Firozabadi, B.: On the Characterization of a Trusting Agent – Aspects of a Formal Approach. In: Trust and Deception in Virtual Societies, pp. 157–168. Kluwer Academic Publishers, Dordrecht (2000)
25. Jajodia, S., Samarati, P., Subrahmanian, V.: A Logical Language for Expressing Authorizations. In: Proceedings of the IEEE Symposium on Security and Privacy, May 1997, pp. 31–42 (1997)
26. Littlewood, B., Brocklehurst, S., Fenton, N., Mellor, P., Page, S., Wright, D., Dobson, J., McDermid, J., Gollmann, D.: Towards Operational Measures of Computer Security. Journal of Computer Security 2, 211–229 (1993)
27. Ortalo, R., Deswarte, Y.: Experiments with Quantitative Evaluation Tools for Monitoring Operational Security. IEEE Transaction on Software Engineering 5(25), 633–650 (1999)
28. Madan, B., Popstojanova, K.G., Vaidyanathan, K., Trivedi, K.: Modeling and Quantification of Security Attributes of Software Systems. In: Proceedings of the International Conference on Dependable Systems and Networks, June 2002, pp. 505–514 (2002)
29. Jonsson, E., Olovsson, T.: A Quantitative Model of the Security Intrusion Process based on Attacker Behavior. IEEE Transaction on Software Engineering 4(25), 235–246 (1997)
30. Alberts, C., Behrens, S., Pethia, R., Wilson, W.: Operationally Critical Threat, Asset, and Vulnerability Evaluation (OCTAVE) Framework, Version 1.0. Technical report, Software Engineering Institute, Carnegie Mellon University (June 1999)
31. Barber, B., Davey, J.: The Use of the CCTA Risk Analysis and Management Methodology CRAMM in Health Information Systems. In: Proceedings of the International Medical Informatics Conference, September 1992, pp. 1589–1593 (1992)
32. CORAS (2000–2003): IST-2000-25031 CORAS: A Platform for Risk Analysis of Security Critical Systems (accessed February 2006)
33. International Organization for Standardization (ISO/IEC): ISO/IEC 27002:2005 Information Technology – Security Techniques – Code of Practice for Information Security Management (2000)
34. International Organization for Standardization (ISO/IEC): ISO/IEC TR 13335:2004 Information Technology – Guidelines for Management of IT Security (2001)
35. Australian/New Zealand Standards: AS/NZS 4360:2007 Risk Management (2004)
36. Houmb, S., Ray, I., Ray, I.: Estimating the Relative Trustworthiness of Information Sources in Security Solution Evaluation. In: Proceedings of the 4th International Conference on Trust Management, May 2006, pp. 135–149 (2006)

Modelling Dynamic Trust with Property Based Attestation in Trusted Platforms

Aarthi Nagarajan and Vijay Varadharajan

Macquarie University, Sydney, Australia
{aarthi,vijay}@ics.mq.edu.au

Abstract. Binary attestation in trusted computing provides the ability to reason about the state of a platform using integrity measurements. Property based attestation, an extension of binary attestation enables more meaningful attestation by abstracting low level binary values to high level security properties or functions of platforms. We believe that despite having trusted processes for integrity measurement, binary and property based attestation may still lead to ambiguities. These ambiguities may reduce the overall trust that can be placed on the measurements and properties that are attested by a platform. To address this issue, we propose TESM: a Trust Enhanced Security Model for trusted computing platforms. The overall aim of the model is to reduce the ambiguities and thereby enable better reasoning of properties that are satisfied by a platform with improved clarity.

1 Introduction

Trusted computing, standardised by the Trusted Computing Group (TCG) [1] provides techniques for achieving security using hardware in computing platforms. The core of the trusted computing technology is the Trusted Platform Module (TPM) chip that enables special functions in the platform. These functions include platform authentication that is used to ensure that the host platform is identifiable and genuine, secure storage for data and secrets, and platform attestation. Attestation, perhaps the key function of a trusted platform [1] provides the ability to reason about the state of a trusted platform in the form of hash measurements. A trusted platform consists of special measurement processes that measure every component installed on the platform at the time of boot and securely stores the measurements in the TPM chip. These measurements can then be reported to a third party who wishes to learn about the platform state. Based on the reported measurements, the third party may make judgements if the platform is in an acceptable and trustworthy state.

Recently, many researchers have proposed that it is more useful to reason about the state of a platform based on the security properties of the platform rather than plain hash measurement values [2,3]. Several reasons for this have been put forth [2,3,4]. For example binary measurements change each time a component is updated and it is difficult to keep a record of all possible correct measurements while properties are more stable and do not change often

S. Foresti and S. Jajodia (Eds.): Data and Applications Security XXIV, LNCS 6166, pp. 257–272, 2010.
© IFIP International Federation for Information Processing 2010

for trivial updates. To address this issue, an alternate form of attestation called property based attestation has been proposed. Property attestation leverages binary attestation to abstract low level binary hash values to high level security properties of platforms. The main aim of property attestation is to be able to prove that the availability of a certain hash measurement guarantees the availability of a certain security property. Several techniques for property attestation have been proposed recently and a comparison of these techniques can be found in [4]. In this paper, we adopt the certification based property attestation mechanism proposed in [3]. In this approach, a property certification authority (CA) evaluates the properties satisfied by a platform (or platform component) and issues a mapping between the expected hash of the platform to the properties satisfied in the form of a property certificate. If a platform measures up to the expected hash, then using the platform certificate it can prove that it satisfies the properties that are attested by the CA.

In this paper, we focus on the reliability of property based attestation. We believe that given the nature of the property attestation mechanism, certain ambiguities are introduced, which raises some fundamental questions on trusting the properties attested. We propose TESM: A Trust Enhanced Secure Model for trusted computing platforms. The overall aim of the model is to reduce ambiguities that arise in property based attestation; it takes into account the uncertainties and help reason about the properties of a system with better confidence. This is the important contribution of this paper. The rest of the paper is organised as follows. Section 2 outlines the motivation for the TESM model. Section 3 gives a basic introduction on subjective logic, which is used in the development of our trust model. Section 4 explains the Trust Enhanced Security Model (TESM) in detail. Section 5 describes how the trust model is being used in authorisation evaluation and we demonstrate this using an example scenario. Concluding remarks are given in section 6. A full description of the proposed model along with the architecture and implementation can be found in [5].

2   Motivation

The main aim of property based attestation is to abstract out binary measurements to more meaningful properties of systems. Once an attestation requester is able to reason about the properties of an attesting platform in a trustworthy manner, then these properties can be used in various security decision making processes. Currently, trust on property based attestation is derived from trust on binary attestation process which in turn is dependent on the trust on the measurement processes and the TPM that stores these measurements.

A fundamental question that arises then is - given that the process of property based attestation is significantly different from binary attestation and that the chain of trust is extended, how much can an Attestation Requester (AR) trust the properties that are presented by an Attesting Platform (AP)? In other words, when AP reports its system state with a set of properties to AR, how certain can AR be that these reported values are true and that AP actually satisfies these claims. We belive that given the nature of property based attestation, uncertainties are introduced in the attestation process. This reduces trust on the property attestation process and leads to situations where AR cannot be completely certain if AP truly satisfies the properties presented to it. The reasons for such uncertainties in property based attestation have been listed below.

- In binary attestation, when AR requests AP for an attestation report, AR receives the measured values, reference values and the measurement list in response. These measurements that indicate the state of the components at the time of boot and not at the time of challenge. Today's systems are highly dynamic in nature and system components are constantly upgraded with updates from manufacturers. Furthermore, systems are also reasonably stable and they can go on without being rebooted for a very long time. This combination of a dynamic system that is not rebooted often means that values measured at boot time do not necessarily represent the state of the system at the time of attestation. This design admits potential for time-of-check time-of-use vulnerabilities: values reflect the state of the system when it was measured and not when it is reported. This makes the attestation report less useful. As the time between boot and attestation increases, AR is uncertain about how much it can trust the attestation report.
- In property attestation, AP proves that it satisfies a required set of properties using binary measurements and corresponding property certificates. These property certificates are issued by third party property certification authorities (CA). The process of property assessment and property certification by a CA does not happen on the run but much in advance before an attestation challenge is issued to AP. Also, property certificates are generated for each standalone component and not for the AP system as a whole. The reason being, with respect to security, it is easier to verify properties of individual components(which are smaller in size) than attempting to verify one large monolithic system.

  It is also possible that the environment under which the component is verified by CA could be different to the environment in which the component is measured during attestation. For example, a CA may install a component in its own system, verify it and certify it. When the component is later installed on a trusted platform, the component might not satisfy the property anymore because the state of the attesting platform is different from the state in which it was evaluated and certified. In some sense, this leads to the age old problem of secure composition of systems. Researchers have spent almost three decades trying to understand the composition of security properties in systems. The goal of secure composition process is to ensure that a composed system preserves the security properties of the individual constituent components. Two components may be individually evaluated for a property and certified. However, when the components are integrated in the same platform, it is often difficult to guarantee that they will preserve their properties under the influence of each other or other components that are already installed in the platform. The effects of composition might not even be reflected in the measurement values of the component.

This means that, even though the measured value and the certified value (in the property certificate) match, a property may still not be 'actually' satisfied.

– Like in any system that involves third party certification authorities, trust on the property certification authority is subjective and can vary depending on the context. The trustworthiness on the properties depends on the trustworthiness of the CA and verification mechanisms used by the CA to evaluate a component for a property. Therefore, trust on property attestation and the properties certified are directly dependent on AR's trust on the CA that certifies that property. If AR does not trust the honesty and the competency of the CA to verify and attest properties, AR may not trust the property certificates certified by that CA. Also, AR may trust a CA to certify one type of property but not other types. In some cases, AR may not even know if the CA is trustworthy or not. Such information must also be taken into consideration at the time of attestation verification.

In the next section, we take these uncertainties into consideration and design an automated trust model for property based attestation. The main aim of the model is provide a way of determining whether a platform can be trusted to satisfy a property given these uncertainties and how they can be factored into security decision making such as authorisation evaluation.

3   Context of the Model

This model is set in the context of subjective logic based belief modelling. Subjective logic proposed by Jøsang [6] is used to model trust that include uncertain outcomes. In this logic, trust is represented using an opinion metric which is denoted as ω where $\omega = (b, d, u)$ and b, d and u are belief, disbelief and uncertainty respectively. Values of $b, d, u \in [0, 1]$ and $b + d + u = 1$. Our model is based on subjective logic and some operations in this logic that are relevant to this paper are given below. We refer the reader to [6] for more details on subjective logic.

Evidence to Opinion mapping - Let pos, neg, unc denote the total number of positive, negative and uncertain experiences of A on B regarding the property x. Then A's opinion about property x in B is given by $^A\omega_B^x$ where $^Ab_B^x$ is A's belief on B about x, $^Ad_B^x$ is A's disbelief on B about x and $^Au_B^x$ is A's ignorance on B about x.

$$^A\omega_B^x = {}^Ab_B^x, {}^Ad_B^x, {}^Au_B^x$$
$$^Ab_B^x = {}^Apos_B^x/({}^Apos_B^x + {}^Aneg_B^x + {}^Aunc_B^x)$$
$$^Ad_B^x = {}^Aneg_B^x/({}^Apos_B^x + {}^Aneg_B^x + {}^Aunc_B^x)$$
$$^Au_B^x = {}^Aunc_B^x/({}^Apos_B^x + {}^Aneg_B^x + {}^Aunc_B^x)$$

Conjunction of Opinions - Let A define two opinions $^A\omega_B^x$ and $^A\omega_B^y$ about two different properties x and y in the same platform B. Then $^A\omega_B^{x,y}$ is called the conjunction ($\odot$) of the opinions $^A\omega_B^x$ and $^A\omega_B^y$ representing A's opinion about both x and y in B.

$$^A\omega_B^{x,y} = {}^A\omega_B^x \odot {}^A\omega_B^y$$
$$^Ab_B^{x,y} = {}^Ab_B^x.{}^Ab_B^y, \quad {}^Ad_B^{x,y} = {}^Ad_B^x + {}^Ad_B^y - {}^Ad_B^x.{}^Ad_B^y$$
$$^Au_B^{x,y} = {}^Ab_B^x.{}^Au_B^y + {}^Au_B^x.{}^Ab_B^y + {}^Au_B^x.{}^Au_B^y$$

Consensus of Opinions - If A forms an opinion $^A\omega_B^x$ on B about the property x and C forms another opinion $^C\omega_B^x$ on B about the same property x, then the consensus ($\oplus$) of the two opinions is equivalent to the opinion $^{A,C}\omega_B^x$ formed on B about x by an imaginary system that represents both A and C.

$$^{A,C}\omega_B = {}^A\omega_B^x \oplus {}^C\omega_B^x$$
$$^{A,C}b_B^x = (^Ab_B^x.{}^Cu_B^x + {}^Cb_B^x.{}^Au_B^x)$$
$$^{A,C}d_B^x = (^Ad_B^x.{}^Cu_B^x + {}^Cd_B^x.{}^Au_B^x), \quad {}^{A,C}u_B^x = (^Au_B^x.{}^Cu_B^x)$$

Discounting Opinions - If A has an opinion on B and if B has an opinion on C, then A's opinion about C is computed by discounting B's opinion about C with A's opinion about B. Let $^A\omega_B = (^Ab_B, {}^Ad_B, {}^Au_B)$ and $^B\omega_C = (^Bb_C, {}^Bd_C, {}^Uu_C)$, then $^A\omega_C$ gives the discounted opinion ($\otimes$) of $^A\omega_B$ and $^B\omega_C$.

$$^A\omega_X = {}^A\omega_B \otimes {}^B\omega_C$$
$$^{AB}b_C = {}^Ab_B.{}^Bb_C, \quad {}^{AB}d_C = {}^Ab_B.{}^Bd_C$$
$$^{AB}u_C = {}^Ad_B + {}^Au_B + {}^Ab_B.{}^Bu_C$$

4   Trust Enhanced Security Model

In this section, we present the formalisation of our automated trust model (ATM) for property attestation. The trust model ATM for a Trusted Platform TP can be defined as $ATM = (E, TR, OP)$. E represents the set of entities that share one or more trust relationships, TR is the set of trust relationships between the entities and OP is the set of operations for the management of trust relationships. We now define each entity below.

4.1   Entities of the Trust Model - E

The entities of the trust model share one or more trust relationships with each other. The trust model includes three different entities. First, there is the Attestation Requester (AR). AR is the entity that requests a trusted platform to attest to a set of of properties. The second entity is the Attesting Platform (AP). AP is the trusted platform that attests its state to AR. The third entity is the Certification Authority (CA). CA is the trusted party that issues expected measurement certificates and property certificates for components that are installed on AP.

4.2   Trust Relationship - TR

TR defines the trust relationship that is shared between two entities for a given property under a given set of conditions. Though trust can be defined in many ways, in the context of this model, our definition is similar to the notion expressed in [7] where trust is described as the firm belief in the competence of an entity to act dependably, reliably and securely within a specific context. Based on this, we have the following definitions.

Definition 1. Property Trust - *Property trust is the belief that a component in AP will satisfy a given property that has been certified for that component.*

Definition 2. Certification Trust - *Certification trust is the belief on the honesty and competency of a certification authority to certify a given property of a component.*

Definition 3. Trust Relationship - *A trust relationship TR is defined as $TR = (A, B, C, P, K, \Theta, M, pos, neg, unc)$.*

The tuple states that an entity A trusts an entity B for a component C to satisfy the property P with trust class K at a given time Θ with experience held in pos, neg, unc and opinion held in M. Entities A and $B \in E$; C is a member of $\{C\}$, a finite set of all components in B; P is a member of $\{P\}$, a finite set of all properties satisfied by C; K is a member of $\{$satisfaction, certification$\}$ trust classes; Θ is the time at which experience values pos, neg, unc were last updated for this trust relationship i.e last update for this $\{TR\}$ occurred at time Θ; M is the evidence mapping operation on this trust relationship, which is presented as an opinion as defined in Definition 4; pos, neg, unc represent the total number of positive, negative and uncertain experiences respectively associated with this trust relationship.

4.3   Trust Management Operations - OP

This section outlines the different operations of the trust management system. The three main operations include evidence collection, opinion evaluation and opinion comparison. Each operation and its sub-operations are described below.

Evidence collection. Evidence collection is the process by which AR records the outcome of its experience with AP for a given property. Evidence collection is divided into two parts, evidence collection from past and present experience. The first part represents the collection of evidence based on past experiences that have occurred prior to the time of authorisation θ. Experience is recorded on how well a platform satisfied a property in the past. Evidence collection on property satisfaction is still susceptible to ambiguities. Therefore, one must ensure that correct evidence is collected without uncertainty. For this purpose, table 1 is used for evidence collection and the mechanism is described below. In the second part of the evidence collection mechanism, property presented at the time of authorisation is translated into opinions. This is explained in the latter part of this section.

Evidence collection from past experiences -   First, we describe the columns of the Table 1 below.

(i) Property Outcome - The property outcome column records if a property is satisfied by a platform or not. $p_s = 1$ indicates that a property is satisfied and $p_s = 0$ indicates that a property is not satisfied. Please note that this is the actual satisfaction of a property and not the property certificate validation outcome.

(ii) Events - The events column indicates if certain events have occurred in AP. A 'H-Event' can be considered as any change in AP that has occurred after the measurement time of a component and before the time of attestation report. A Pr-Event is an event that occurs in AP after property evaluation and certification but before property report. We combine both Pr-Events and H-Events events together as Pr/H Events. The value e = 0 indicates no events have occurred and the value e = 1 indicates one or more such events have occurred in AP. It must be noted that the occurrence of these events are not reflected in the attestation report as they occur after the time of measurement.

(iii) CA History - This represents the opinion about the honesty and/or ability of the CA to attest properties of a system in a correct manner.

(iv) Hash-History - This represents the opinion of AR on the validity of the hash measurement of a component in AP based on AR's past experiences with AP i.e how well a correct and current measurement was reported at the time of attestation.

(v) Experience recorded - This determines the experience recorded by AR about the satisfaction of a given property in AP. The main aim of the evidence collection operator is to populate this value given the other values in the table.

In table 1, we assume that all past experience outcomes recorded are absolute. AR either has complete belief, complete disbelief or complete uncertainty about a property. Correspondingly, belief (b), disbelief (d) and uncertainty (u) of hash H and certification authority CA are quantified as 0 or 1. Here, $b(ca) = 1$, $d(ca) = 1$ and $u(ca) = 1$ represent total belief, total disbelief and total uncertainty on the CA. Likewise, $b(ca) = 0$, $d(ca) = 0$ and $u(ca) = 0$ represent no belief, no disbelief and no uncertainty about CA respectively. Similarly, belief $b(h) = 1$, disbelief $d(h)=1$ and uncertainty $u(h)=1$ represent total belief, total disbelief and total uncertainty about the hash measurements of AP and $b(h) = 0$, $d(h)=0$ and $u(h)=0$ represent no belief, no disbelief and no uncertainty respectively. Table 1 has 4 categories. Each category defines a different condition in which experience is recorded.

(i) Category 1: An experience is recorded in the absence of CA history or hash history information. Here, when a property is satisfied, it is marked as a positive experience with respect to CA, property P and hash H. This is irrespective of whether events have occurred (that is, e=1) or events have not occurred in the system. When a property is not satisfied, it is marked

Table 1. Evidence collection I

Cat	Pr-Outcome	Pr/H-Events	CA-History	Hash-History	Experience-recorded
1	$p_s = 1$	$e = 0/1$	not available	not available	pos(ca,p,h)
	$p_s = 0$	$e = 0/1$			neg(p),unc(ca,h)
2	$p_s = 1$	$e = 0$	any b(ca),d(ca),u(ca)	any b(h),d(h),u(h)	pos(ca,p,h)
	$p_s = 1$	$e = 1$	any b(ca),d(ca),u(ca)	any b(h),d(h),u(h)	pos(ca,p,h)
3	$p_s = 0$	$e = 0$	b(ca) = 1	b(h) = 1	neg(p)
	$p_s = 0$	$e = 0$	b(ca) = 1	d(h) = 1	neg(p), neg(h)
	$p_s = 0$	$e = 0$	b(ca) = 1	u(h) = 1	neg(p), unc(h)
	$p_s = 0$	$e = 0$	d(ca) = 1	d(h) = 1	neg(p),unc(ca,h)
	$p_s = 0$	$e = 0$	d(ca) = 1	b(h) = 1	neg(ca,p)
	$p_s = 0$	$e = 0$	d(ca) = 1	u(h) = 1	neg(p),unc(ca,h)
	$p_s = 0$	$e = 0$	u(ca) = 1	u(h) = 1	unc(ca,h),neg(p)
	$p_s = 0$	$e = 0$	u(ca) = 1	b(h) = 1	unc(ca),neg(p)
	$p_s = 0$	$e = 0$	u(ca) = 1	d(h) = 1	unc(ca,h),neg(p)
4	$p_s = 0$	$e = 1$	b(ca) = 1	b(h) = 1	neg(p)
	$p_s = 0$	$e = 1$	b(ca) = 1	d(h) = 1	neg(p),unc(h)
	$p_s = 0$	$e = 1$	b(ca) = 1	u(h) = 1	neg(p),unc(h)
	$p_s = 0$	$e = 1$	d(ca) = 1	d(h) = 1	neg(p),unc(ca,h)
	$p_s = 0$	$e = 1$	d(ca) = 1	b(h) = 1	neg(p),unc(ca)
	$p_s = 0$	$e = 1$	d(ca) = 1	u(h) = 1	neg(p),unc(ca,h)
	$p_s = 0$	$e = 1$	u(ca) = 1	u(h) = 1	neg(p),unc(ca,h)
	$p_s = 0$	$e = 1$	u(ca) = 1	b(h) = 1	neg(p),unc(ca)
	$p_s = 0$	$e = 1$	u(ca) = 1	d(h) = 1	neg(p),unc(ca,h)

as a negative experience with respect to the property and uncertainty with respect to the CA and H. This is because, it is not possible to determine if H (hash being invalid) or CA (not certified correctly) contributed to the property being invalid.

(ii) Category 2: An experience is recorded when history information about CA and H is available but this history does not influence the outcome of the experience. When a property is satisfied, a positive experience pos(p) is recorded irrespective of the past experience with that platform. A satisfied property also increases belief in the hash and the certification authority and leads to a positive experience for both H and CA.

(iii) Category 3: In this category, an experience is recorded when a property is not satisfied and there have been no Pr/H-Events. In all these cases, because the property was not satisfied, outcome for P is marked as a negative experience. In order to record an experience for CA and H, we in turn use the history information associated with CA and H respectively. If b(ca) = 1 and b(h) = 1, then there is only a negative experience for P. However, if b(ca) = 1 and d(h) = 1, AR can ascertain based on its past experience of d(h)=1 that the most likely reason that the property failed is because the component's hash changed after boot time measurement. This leads to a negative experience for H. (We have taken a stronger approach and have

marked a negative experience for H. Alternatively, a more lenient approach
may be taken and H may be marked as uncertain.) If b(ca)=1 and u(h)=1,
then AR cannot determine if the property failed because of the component
hash as it is itself uncertain about the past experiences of H. This leads
to an uncertain experience for H. Alternatively, if AR totally disbelieves
CA (d(ca) = 1) and totally believes H (b(h) = 1), this records a negative
experience for CA as AR believes in H completely and will rule out H as a
possible reason (again a more lenient approach may be taken and CA may
be marked as uncertain, but we take a stronger approach). If d(ca) = 1 and
u(h) or d(h) = 1, then the platform is not certain if the property failed
because of the hash or CA. So it marks this as an uncertain experience for
both H and CA. Similarly, if AR is uncertain about CA, u(ca)=1 and the
property is not satisfied, then AR marks CA as uncertain again as it cannot
be sure if the property was not really satisfied or if the CA had wrongly
certified the property. Additionally, if AR does not have total belief in the
hash of the component, i.e. if d(h)=1 or u(h)=1, then a possible bad hash
measurement also adds to the existing uncertainty. Therefore, an uncertain
experience unc(h) is marked along with unc(ca).

(iv) Category 4: In category 4, an experience is recorded when a property is
not satisfied, when events have occurred, and when history of hash and CA
are available. Here as well, when a property is not satisfied, it is always
a negative experience with respect to P. In order to record values for CA
and H, we use the history information of CA and H respectively. The main
difference compared to category 3 is that the events introduce even more
uncertainty. For instance, when there is total belief in CA and total disbelief
in H, one cannot still record this as a negative experience with respect to H
as in the previous case. There is uncertainty as to whether the events lead to
the property being invalid or the hash value change after boot. Therefore, we
mark an uncertain experience for H and not a negative experience. Similarly,
when there is total belief in H and total disbelief in CA, one cannot record
this as a negative experience for CA. It is not clear if the events lead to the
property being invalid or if CA certified the property wrongly. Therefore,
we mark an uncertain experience for CA and not a negative experience. All
other experiences are recorded using similar judgement as in category 3 in
the table.

Evidence collection from present experience -   So far, we have discussed how
AR collects evidence about platform AP for a given property based on the past
behaviour. At the time of service request θ, AR presents property certificates
to AP to vouch for the current state of the platform. We believe that this information must also be taken into account while computing the overall opinion
of a platform. In order to take into account not only the past experiences but
also the present state of the platform, we record the successful validation of a
property certificate as a positive experience *pos* with respect to that property.
If the property certificate is verified, then the opinion formed at the time of attestation is considered as (1,0,0) where belief is $\frac{1}{1}$, disbelief and uncertainty are

$\frac{0}{1}$ as obtained from the evidence to opinion mapping operator given in section 3. Similarly, if a property certificate is not verified, then the opinion becomes (0,1,0). There is no uncertainty here as a property certificate either validates or does not validate.

Trust Evaluation. Section 3 describes subjective logic as the main context of this trust model. Subjective logic uses special belief functions called opinions to represent trust. An opinion metric is given by $\omega = (b, d, u)$ where b represents belief, d represents disbelief and u represents uncertainty for a given trust relationship. We adopt this representation of trust as an opinion metric in our trust model.

Definition 4. *Evidence Mapping*

The evidence mapping operator M (Definition 3) on a given trust relationship TR is used to represent the opinion of one entity on another entity. The main function of the mapping operator is to map the collected evidence in the form of positive, negative and uncertain experiences to an opinion value. This is achieved using the evidence to opinion mapping function of subjective logic as given in section 3.

Opinion Decay -   Trust is dynamic in nature and tends to change with time. Over a given time frame, the value of trust in the beginning of the period is different from the value in the end even when there are no underlying factors that affect the value of trust directly. Just as we humans tend to forget things or associate less importance to events that have occurred in the past, we model systems also to associate less importance to events that have occurred in the past compared to more recent events. In other words, the system is modelled to gradually become non-decisive about trust (and distrust) as time progresses. The decay operator is a function that is used to represent this nature of trust. Equation 1 shows the decay function $\Psi_{k,\Delta}$ used to calculate new opinion ω_{new} after decay from an old opinion ω_{old}.

$$\omega_{new} = \Psi_{k,\Delta}[\,\omega_{old}]\tag{1}$$

Where $\Psi_{k,\Delta}$ is gives as

$$b_{new} = b_{old}[1 - e^{-(k.\Delta)}]$$
$$d_{new} = d_{old}[1 - e^{-(k.\Delta)}]$$
$$u_{new} = u_{old} + [(b_{old} + d_{old}) - (b_{new} + d_{new})]$$

(i) k is the rate of decay and $k > 0$ & $k \leq 1$. For example, if the rate of decay is 1 %, then k = 0.01, if rate of decay is 10 %, then $k = 0.1$ and if rate of decay is 100 %, $k = 1$.

(ii) Δ is the difference between the current time θ at which service is requested and the time at which opinion for that property was last updated. The value of Δ is chosen such that ω_{new} does not decay rapidly. For example, if

$\Delta = 0$, then ω_{new} is same as ω_{old} and if $\Delta = \infty$ then ω_{new} tends to zero. In our model, we chose Δ as the number of years that have elapsed since the opinion was last updated. The minimum value of Δ is $0/365$ (zero days) and the maximum value is $730/365$ (2 years approximately). At $\Delta = 2$ and $k = 1$, b_{new} is 13 percent of b_{old}. This is the maximum decay possible for any opinion. Any time greater than 2 years is also assumed to be 2 years such that b_{new} decays at 100% to a maximum of $0.13(b_{old})$ and not more.

Total opinion on a property p_j of a component c_i -   Let $({}^A pos_{B,sat(c_i,p_j)}, {}^A neg_{B,sat(c_i,p_j)}, {}^A unc_{B,sat(c_i,p_j)})$ represent the evidence associated with a trust relationship TR of platform A about platform B for the satisfaction of a property p_j of a component c_i. Based on the evidence collected, the evidence mapping function M is used to calculate the opinion for this TR. This defines the opinion of A about platform B for the satisfaction of property p_i of component c_i at time Θ and is given as

$$ {}^A\omega^\Theta_{B,sat(c_i,p_j)} = \{ {}^A b^\Theta_{B,sat(c_i,p_j)}, {}^A d^\Theta_{B,sat(c_i,p_j)}, {}^A u^\Theta_{B,sat(c_i,p_j)} \} $$

Let ${}^A pos_{CA,cer(c_i,p_j)}, {}^A neg_{CA,cer(c_i,p_j)}, {}^A unc_{CA,cer(c_i,p_j)}$ represent the evidence associated with a Trust Relationship TR of a platform A about Certification Authority CA for the certification of the property p_j of a component c_i. Evidence mapping function M is used to calculate the opinion for this TR. This defines the opinion of platform A about CA for the certification of a property p_j of a component c_i at time Θ and is given as

$$ {}^A\omega^\Theta_{CA,cer(c_i,p_j)} = \{ {}^A b^\Theta_{CA,cer(c_i,p_j)}, {}^A d^\Theta_{CA,cer(c_i,p_j)}, {}^A u^\Theta_{CA,cer(c_i,p_j)} \} $$

The total opinion on the property p_j of the component c_i is calculated by combining the satisfaction opinion (how well the property was satisfied) and certification opinion (how well the CA certified that property) of that property. Equation 2 gives the conjunction (section 3) of both these opinions. The opinions are decayed using equation 1. Θ gives the time at which experience was last updated.

$$ {}^A\omega^\Theta_{B,c_i,p_j} = \Psi_{k,\Delta}[{}^A\omega^\Theta_{B,sat(c_i,p_j)}] \odot \Psi_{k,\Delta}[{}^A\omega^\Theta_{CA,cer(c_i,p_j)}] \tag{2} $$

Direct Trust -   Direct Trust is the belief one entity holds on another entity for a given context, based on its own past experiences with that entity. The direct trust on a component c_i and a property p_j is calculated by combining the total opinion formed at time of service request θ and the total opinion formed prior to service request at time $\theta - t$.

$$ {}^{A-dir}\omega_{B,c_i,p_j} = {}^A\omega^\theta_{B,c_i,p_j} \odot {}^A\omega^{\theta-t}_{B,c_i,p_j} \tag{3} $$

where, ${}^A\omega^\theta_{B,c_i,p_j}$ and ${}^A\omega^{\theta-t}_{B,c_i,p_j}$ are total opinions at times θ and $\theta-t$ respectively and $\theta, \theta - t \in \Theta$. The total opinions ${}^A\omega^\theta_{B,c_i,p_j}$ and ${}^A\omega^{\theta-t}_{B,c_i,p_j}$ are derived using equation 2.

$$^A\omega_{B,c_i,p_j}^{\theta-t} = \Psi_{k,\Delta}[^A\omega_{B,sat(c_i,p_j)}^{\theta-t}] \tag{4}$$

$$^A\omega_{B,c_i,p_j}^{\theta} = \Psi_{k,0}[^A\omega_{B,sat(c_i,p_j)}]^{\theta} \odot \Psi_{k,\Delta}[^A\omega_{CA,cer(c_i,p_j)}^{\theta-t}] \tag{5}$$

(i) In equation 3, the most recent opinion at θ is combined with all the previous experiences prior to time θ. Although the equation does not attach weightage to the opinions, clearly the opinion formed using the experience at time θ has more influence that any other individual experience prior to this time. If the opinion at time θ is (1,0,0), then the value of direct opinion is equal to the opinion at time $\theta-t$. An opinion (1,0,0) at θ is possible if the present experience is positive (evidence collection from present experience given in section 4.3) and the opinion of the privacy CA is (1,0,0). This is expected to be the usual case. If privacy CA is not completely trusted, then this reduces the value of the direct opinion dramatically due to the nature of the $\odot$ operator. The notion behind this is, if the CA is not trusted, then the certified property itself may not be trusted.

(ii) If a platform has had no direct experiences with respect to a property, $^A\omega_{B,sat(c_i,p_j)}^{\theta-t}$ is assumed as (1,0,0) in equation 3. This makes the direct opinion equal to opinion $^A\omega_{B,c_i,p_j}$ at θ.

(iii) Equation 5 is derived from equation 2. Here, the value of $^A\omega_{B,sat(c_i,p_j)}^{\theta}$ does not decay because it is computed based on the evidence recorded at the time of service request θ and the value of $\Delta = 0$. $^A\omega_{CA,cer(c_i,p_j)}^{\theta}$ represents the certification trust on CA that certifies the property p_i. When the past experience of this CA is unavailable, the value of $^A\omega_{CA,cer(c_i,p_j)}^{\theta-t}$ is assumed to be (1,0,0) which makes $^A\omega_{B,c_i,p_j}^{\theta} = \Psi_{k,0}[^A\omega_{B,sat(c_i,p_j)}^{\theta}]$

(iv) Equation 4 is derived from equation 2 where Θ is equal to $\theta - t$. Certification opinion on CA at time $\theta - t$ is removed from equation 4. This is because $^A\omega_{CA,cer(c_i,p_j)}^{\theta-t}$ is formed using a collection of certification outcomes for the property p_i. This property could have been certified by different certification authorities in the past. Therefore, it is not possible to attribute the certification opinion to any one single CA.

Recommended Trust - Recommended trust is the belief one entity holds on another entity for a given context, based on the recommendations obtained from its peer entities' past experiences. $^{A-rec}\omega_{B,c_i,p_j}$ represents the overall recommended opinion of A on B computed from the individual opinions of A's recommenders.

$$^{A-rec}\omega_{B,c_i,p_j} = (I_{R_1} \otimes \Psi_{k,t} [^{R_1}\omega_{B,sat(c_i,p_j)}^{\theta-t}]) \oplus .. \tag{6}$$
$$\oplus (I_{R_m} \otimes \Psi_{k,t} [^{R_m}\omega_{B,sat(c_i,p_j)}^{\theta-t}])$$

(i) A decay function is applied to each recommended opinion to ensure that the value of the recommenders' opinion decrements with time.

(ii) For each decayed opinion of a recommender, an importance factor I is attached to the respective recommendations. The importance factor determines how much platform A values each recommender. The importance factors of $I_{R_1}..I_{R_m}$ are attached to the decayed opinions of recommenders $R_1..R_m$ respectively using the discounting operator given in section 3. $I_R = (wt, 1 - wt, 0)$ where wt denotes the weight for a recommender R. The sum of the weights of all recommenders equals 1.

(iii) If there is more than one recommender, R_1 to R_m, then a consensus of every recommender's weighted decayed opinion is computed using the consensus operator $\oplus$ given in section 3.

Derived Trust -   Derived trust is the belief one entity builds on another entity for a given context, based on other atomic trust relationships such as direct trust and recommended trust. Derived opinion for a property p_j of component c_i is computed by combining the direct and recommended opinions for that property.

$$^{A-der}\omega_{B,c_i,p_j} = {}^{A-dir}\omega_{B,c_i,p_j} \oplus {}^{A-rec}\omega_{B,c_i,p_j} \qquad (7)$$

In equation 7, A computes derived opinion for property p_i of component c_i by combining its recommended opinion from equation 6 with its direct opinion from equation 3. If a recommended opinion is unavailable, then derived opinion is equal to the direct opinion. In the absence of direct opinion, derived opinion equals recommended opinion.

Derived Platform Trust - Derived platform trust is defined as the belief one platform holds on another platform for a given context based on the combined belief of the individual properties of that platform. Platform trust of A on B is computed by combining the derived opinions of all the properties in B.

$$^{A-der}\omega_B = I_{c_i,p_j} \otimes \Psi_{k,t} \left[{}^{A-der}\omega_{B,c_i,p_j} \right] \oplus I_{c_k,p_l} \otimes \Psi_{k,t} \left[{}^{A-der}\omega_{B,c_k,p_l} \right] \qquad (8)$$

Assuming that platform B has two properties - property p_j of component c_i and property p_l of component c_k where $p_j, p_l \in P$ and $c_i, c_k \in C$, then the derived platform opinion $^{A-der}\omega_B$ equals the consensus of the derived opinions $^{A-der}\omega_{B,c_i,p_j}$ and $^{A-der}\omega_{B,c_k,p_l}$ on properties p_j and p_l respectively. The opinion are decayed using the decay operator given in equation 1. An importance factor I is attached to each opinion. This importance factor determines how much A values each property to contribute to the overall trust of the platform. Sum of the importance factors is equal to 1 and $I = (wt, 1 - wt, 0)$ where wt denotes the weight for each property.

Trust Comparison. An opinion comparison operator $\geq_\omega$ that compares any two given opinions ω_1 and ω_2 is defined. Given two opinions ω_1 and ω_2, we define an opinion comparison operator $\geq_\omega$, whereby $\omega_1 \geq_\omega \omega_2$ holds if $b_1 > b_2$, $d_1 < d_2$ and $u_1 < u_2$. In such cases, we say that ω_1 is greater than the threshold presented by ω_2.

5   Authorisation Evaluation

We have previously defined a formal trust relationship TR. When a platform A (attestation requester) makes a request to another platform B (attestation provider) for some service, platform A must determine based on its existing trust relationship with platform B, if platform B will be allowed to access the service or not. Here, platform B presents a request to platform A with its measurement and property certificates that A requires in order to service the request. Using the property certificates and the trust relationship of A on B's properties, A can determine if it can trust platform B to really satisfy these properties.

An overall picture of the authorisation process can be given as follows. Initially, A computes its direct opinion of a property for platform B using the equation 3. If possible, A looks for recommenders that can provide recommendations for the properties satisfied by platform B. Each recommended opinion is decayed for the time elapsed since the last recommendation was recorded. It is possible that the decay time Δ is different for each recommender. Also note that A can define a different decay rate k and important rate I for each recommender. The final recommended opinion is then calculated using equation 6. Then the direct and recommended opinions are combined together using equation 7 to compute the derived opinion. Alternatively, A may compute B's overall platform trust using equation 8. For every service that is provided, A defines authorisation policies that include a threshold value ω_{th} as an opinion constant. A compares the derived opinion and threshold opinion using the comparison operator $\geq_\omega$. If the derived opinion is higher, then A services B's request.

A working architecture of the authorisation model has been implemented and several other design choices have also been made available. On the one hand, platform A may opt to make authorisation decisions using different trust groups; for example, with direct opinion alone, when recommendation trust is unavailable. Derived opinion is used as a default design choice. On the other hand, different authorisation parameters for soft trust may be defined. Opinion thresholds may be defined for an overall platform $(^A\omega_B)$ or for individual properties of components $(^A\omega_{B,c_i,p_j})$. In order to derive an overall threshold for a platform, individual $^A\omega_{B,c_i,p_j}$ are combined together using the consensus operator (section 3). Before consensus, weights for each $^A\omega_{B,c_i,p_j}$ may also be applied using the discounting operator, similar to the application of I in recommended opinion calculation. When thresholds for individual c_i, p_i are used, comparison operator is applied to each threshold and $^A\omega_{B,c_i,p_j}$ pair, and the outcomes are ANDed together for a final decision. A combination of both overall platform opinion and opinion on individual properties of components is also possible. A full description of the architecture and policy scenarios can be found in [5].

5.1 Example Scenario

In this section, we present an example scenario for the trust model. Here, a large number of past experience record is available but the number of recommendations that can be gathered is limited in number. Let us take the example of an online gaming system. In this system, the game provider must ensure that each of the participants is using the correct version of the gaming software that satisfies a required set of properties. Participants usually cheat the game provider by modifying the gaming software G to their advantage. By ensuring that a participant always plays with a software that is 'unmodified', the game provider can ascertain that all the participants are playing honestly and every participant has a fair chance to win. We assume that the game provider A has previous experiences with a participant X and has recorded all previous experience outcomes. The game provider is also able to obtain recommendations about X from two other game providers B and C that X has previously interacted with. Recommendations from both the recommenders are given equal weightage. The game provider is willing to allow X to participate if the derived trust on X for the given software is greater than a threshold opinion of $(0.5, 0.5, 0)$. Time of authorisation is November 12 2009, 14:00 hrs. Opinions are decayed at the rate of 100%. The following trust relationships are available in the trust base.

(a) $(A, X, G, unmodified, sat, Oct \ 01 \ 2009, 14 : 00 : 00, [0.789, 0.105, 0.105], 15, 2, 2)$
(b) $(A, X, G, unmodified, sat, Nov \ 12 \ 2009, 14 : 00 : 00, [1, 0, 0], 1, 0, 0)$
(c) $(A, CA, G, unmodified, cert, Oct \ 01 \ 2009, 14 : 00 : 00, [0.923, 0, 0.77], 12, 0, 1)$
(d) $(B, X, G, unmodified, sat, Oct \ 31 \ 2009, 14 : 00 : 00, [0.166, 0.833, 0], 3, 15, 0)$
(e) $(C, X, G, unmodified, sat, Oct \ 03 \ 2009, 14 : 00 : 00, [0.1, 0.90, 0], 2, 20, 0)$

Now we compute the opinions using these relationships.

(1) **Direct Trust**
  - Opinion $^A\omega^{\theta-42/365}_{X,G,unmodified}$ that software G is unmodified in X based on experience updated 42 days prior request (from eqn 4) $= (0.70, 0.09, 0.20)$
  - Opinion $^A\omega^{\theta}_{X,G,unmodified}$ that software G is unmodified in X based on experience recorded at the time of request (from eqn 5) $= (0.82, 0, 0.17)$
  - Direct $^{A-dir}\omega_{X,G,unmodified}$ opinion that software G is unmodified in X (from eqn 3) $= (0.57, 0.09, 0.32)$

2) **Recommended Trust**
  - Recommended opinion $^B\omega^{\theta-12/365}_{X,sat(G,unmodified)}$ of B based on evidence recorded 12 days prior request $= (0.16, 0.83, 0)$
  - Recommended opinion $^C\omega^{\theta-40/365}_{X,sat(G,unmodified)}$ of C based on evidence recorded 40 days prior request $= (0.09, 0.90, 0)$
  - Total recommended opinion $^{A-rec}\omega_{X,G,unmodified}$ after decay and with equal weights of 0.5 for both B and C (from eqn 6) $= (0.08, 0.55, 0.36)$

(3) **Derived Trust**
  Derived opinion $^{A-der}\omega_{X,G,unmodified}$ of A that software G is unmodified in platform X (From eqn 7) $= (0.42, 0.37, 0.20)$

The derived opinion is compared against the threshold opinion of $(0.5, 0.5, 0.0)$ using the comparison operator. The derived opinion is not greater than the threshold and the game player does not permit X to participate in the game. One can see that although the direct opinion of $(0.57, 0.09, 0.32)$ is greater than the threshold, the inclusion of the recommended opinions has yielded a different outcome with opinion $(0.42, 0.37, 0.20)$ being less than the required threshold.

6   Conclusion

Property based attestation is an extension of the TCG attestation mechanism where binary hash measurements are abstracted to meaningful properties of systems. Recently, property based attestation has gained considerable interest in the research community as properties of systems are more persistent and do not change like hash measurements for trivial changes in system configuration. In this paper, we have proposed a Trust Enhanced Security Model (TESM) that models dynamic trust for binary and property based attestation in trusted platforms. We have shown that both binary attestation and property based attestation introduce uncertainties in the attestation mechanism and due to this an attestation requester is unable to reason about the trustworthiness of an attesting platform with absolute certainty. To address this issue, we have proposed a trust enhanced security model that derives trust from property certificates and social control mechanisms like past experiences and recommendations of how well a platform behaved in the past. We have described how evidence about a platform is collected and how opinions are formed using the collected evidence. Using these opinions, an attestation requester is better able to gauge how well a platform will behave in the future with reduced uncertainty. We believe such a model is useful to enhance the attestation process and this will enable reasoning the trust on attesting platforms with greater confidence.

Acknowledgements. We would like to thank the anonymous reviewers and the program committee for their valuable comments and suggestions on the paper.

References

1. Trusted Computing Group: TPM Main - Part 1 Design Principles, Version 1.2, Revision 103 (July 2007)
2. Poritz, J., Schunter, M., Herreweghen, E.V., Waidner, M.: Property attestation-Scalable and privacy-friendly security assessment of peer computers. Technical report, IBM Research (May 2004)
3. Sadeghi, A.R., Stüble, C.: Property-based attestation for computing platforms: Caring about properties, not mechanisms. In: NSPW 2004: Proceedings of the 2004 Workshop on New Security Paradigms, USA, pp. 67–77. ACM, New York (2004)
4. Nagarajan, A., Varadharajan, V., Gallery, E., Hitchens, M.: Property based attestation and trusted computing: Analysis and challenges. In: Third International Conference on Network and System Security, Gold Coast, Australia (October 2009)
5. Anonymous: Title Suppressed. PhD thesis (2010)
6. Jøsang, A.: A logic for uncertain probabilities. Int. J. Uncertain. Fuzziness Knowl. Based Syst. 9(3), 279–311 (2001)
7. Grandison, T., Sloman, M.: A survey of trust in internet applications. IEEE Communications Surveys and Tutorials 3(4) (2000)

Towards Privacy-Enhancing Identity Management in Mashup-Providing Platforms

Jan Zibuschka, Matthias Herbert, and Heiko Roßnagel

Fraunhofer Institute for Industrial Engineering (IAO),
Nobelstr.12, 70569 Stuttgart, Germany
{first_name.last_name}@iao.fraunhofer.de

Abstract. Mashups empower users to easily combine and connect resources from independent Web-based sources and domains. However, these characteristics also introduce new and amplify existing security and privacy problems. This is especially critical in the emerging field of enterprise Mashups. Despite several contributions in the field of Mashup security the issue of protecting exchanged resources against the Mashup-providing Platform has generally been neglected. In this contribution we address the security challenges of server-side Mashup-providing Platforms with the aim of minimizing the required amount of trust. We achieve this by implementing a privacy-enhancing identity management system into the Mashup-providing Platform using Reverse Identity Based Encryption.

1 Introduction

Mashups empower developers to combine and connect resources from independent Web-based sources and domains. Mashups are dynamic and easy to create [1]. This combination of resources provides a considerable added value to both providers and end users, who can now manage a host of services inside one consistent environment. On the other hand, these characteristics also introduce new and amplify existing and arising security and privacy problems. These security shortcomings are especially relevant as Mashups are now moving into the enterprise space, where enterprise Mashups offer the compelling perspective of empowering business end users to compose business services as they are needed, allowing for a direct adaptation to changing business needs [2]. There have been several contributions in the field of Mashup security, such as De Keukelaere et al's SMash [3], Jackson and Wang's Subspace [4], Crites et al's OMash [5], or Zaradioon et al.'s OMOS [6]. However, the issue of protecting exchanged resources against the Mashup-providing Platform has generally been neglected. Providing the necessary privacy is a key issue for the broad success of enterprise Mashups [7], as especially smaller enterprises will not want to deploy their own Mashup infrastructure, and prefer to consume hosted services [8], allowing them minimum investment and maximum benefit from Mashups' ease of use. In this contribution we address the security challenges of server-side Mashup-providing

S. Foresti and S. Jajodia (Eds.): Data and Applications Security XXIV, LNCS 6166, pp. 273–286, 2010.

Platforms. In the spirit of multilateral security we aim at minimizing the required amount of trust of (enterprise and end) users in the platform. To achieve this we implement a privacy-enhancing identity management system as described in [9] into the Mashup-providing Platform. The further structure of this paper is as follows: First we present a generic architecture of a Mashup-providing Platform in section 2. We use this architecture to illustrate the security challenges in section 3 and provide an overview and discussion of related work in section 4. We present our approach to address the security challenges in section 5. We wrap up by discussing merits and limitations of our solution (section 6), before we conclude our findings.

2   Mashup Architecture

This section describes general assumptions we make about Mashups, including terminology, structure and API. We aim to give clear definitions based on earlier work, to ensure applicability of our results and readability of this work. Figure 1 (taken from [2]) gives an overview of the platform we are envisioning.

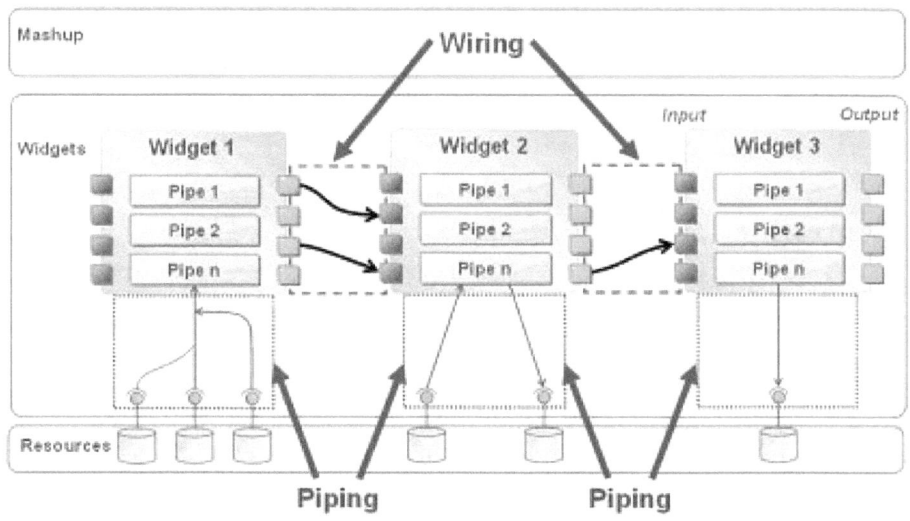

Fig. 1. Overview of Mashup-providing Platform [2]

2.1   Definitions

As Hoyer and Fischer [2] point out in the course of a comprehensive literature survey, there are various definitions of the term 'Mashup'. There seems to be a strong tendency of authors, even in scientific literature, to establish their own definition of Mashups without referring to earlier work. To make our work more readily comparable (and readable), we offer clear definitions based on earlier work of the terms we are using in this section.

Mashup. We slightly adapt the definition from [2] here, removing the enterprise aspect, as we think the definition is quite precise and convincing also outside of the enterprise setting, and in line with definitions used in other works, e.g. [3]. We define Mashup as: a Web-based resource that combines existing resources, be it content, data or application functionality, from more than one resource by empowering the actual end-users to create and adapt individual information centric and situational applications.

Widgets and Backend service. Still drawing on the definitions in [2], as well as [10] and others, we define Widgets as the visual representations of aforementioned Web-based resources that are combined into a Mashup. We refer to backend services when referring to the Web-based services piping those resources into the Mashup-providing Platform and to the Widgets.

Mashup-providing Platform (MPP). We define a Mashup-providing Platform as a Web-based server-side platform offering APIs and hosting functionalities that enable the creation of Mashups, specifically offering functionality for definition of Widgets and their Wiring as described in [2], and APIs such as the one described in [3].

Pipes and Wiring. We define Wiring as communication between Widgets within the platform, and Piping as the transfer of external resources into the platform via backend services and Widgets (Figure 1, [2]). Securing the Wiring-based communications (as discussed in [3]) is of special interest to us. We also address issues arising in the context of (cascaded) piping, as also described by [11].

Adapter (Backend) Services. We define an Adapter (Backend) Service as a Backend Service who does not have direct access to the resources it pipes into the Mashup. Consequently, it needs to cascade requests to other services which do have the necessary resources (but which usually do not integrate with the Mashup-providing Platform, making the adapter necessary). We are especially interested in the case where those services holding the resources are following a walled garden security model, requiring delegation of credentials to the adapter (as described by [11]).

2.2   API and Relevant Implementation Details

There are many Mashup-providing Platforms in the market, with many different approaches to communication between backend services. In this paper, we assume that the MPP implements an API and component model similar to the one presented in [3], using communication channels that respect the services home domain and thus do not break the browser security model, but still are embedded in and communicate via the Mashup-providing Platform using layered iFrames (see Figure 2). We deviate from the API presented in [3] in that we do not implement communication busses shared between different services, but use the Wiring model illustrated in Figure 1. This is a choice made for the sake of simplicity. As we use strong cryptography, shared busses would not be an issue

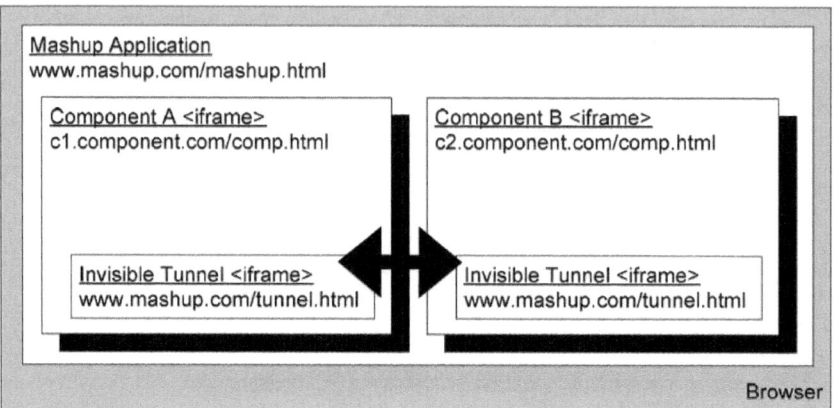

Fig. 2. Mashup Component Model (adapted from [3], now using direct tunneling)

from the security standpoint. However, they introduce an unnecessary level of complexity into the description of the system presented here. For simplicity, we assume a simple but flexible API, where the Wiring is managed using the API calls `requestValues()`, `requestPermits()` and `sendMessage()`, as illustrated by Figure 3. Table 1 gives an overview of the API we assume the MPP implements. This is an abstraction of APIs given in related work such as Hasan et al [12] and surveys of current Mashup systems [1][2]. It has also been verified by checking compliance with current approaches, such as the Enterprise Mashup Markup Language EMML [13] or JackBe Mashup Composer [14]. We also assume that the Piping is used mainly to integrate legacy services, accessed over HTTP, using passwords for authentication. However, we also demonstrate how access control to those backend services could be secured using mechanisms we describe in the context of the (more integrated) Wiring for Mashup Widgets.

3   Security Challenges of Mashup-Platforms

Since providing privacy is a key issue for the broad success of enterprise Mashups [7], the issue of protecting exchanged resources against the Mashup-providing

Table 1. Simplified Mashup API

API call	Description
`requestValues(serviceId, attributeId[], permit[])`	Request a set of attributes from a service
`sendMessage(serviceId, message)`	Send a message (e.g. attribute values) to another service
`requestPermits(serviceId[], attributeId[])`	Request permits to access a set of attributes from a service

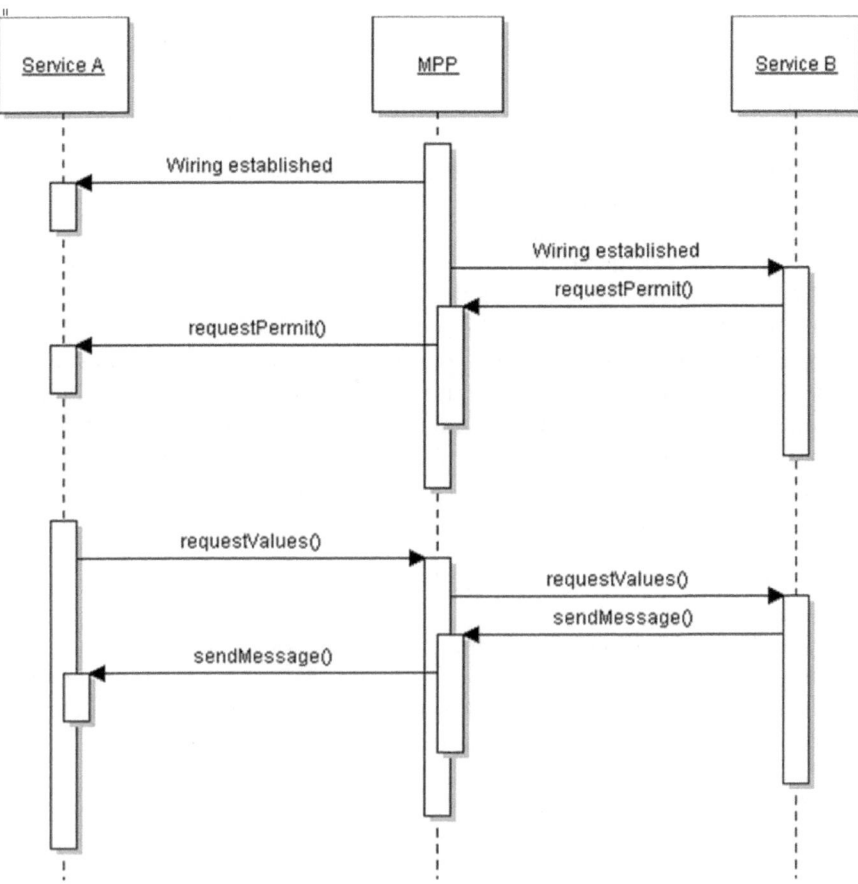

Fig. 3. Simplified Communication API High Level Overview

Platform is one of the major security challenges. In the component model we assume, the communication channels between Widgets (Wires) are embedded in and communicate via the Mashup-providing Platform. To protect these Wires against the MPP itself as well as other services or attackers, the traffic that is sent over the Wire should be encrypted. Therefore, we can formulate a first security requirement.

Requirement I: Resources transmitted via Wiring should be kept confidential against the MPP or other attackers.

The way contemporary Mashups combine their underlying resources, the established browser security model assumes that all services are from the identical source, as services are integrated in a MPP acting as a web proxy. This behavior of internet browsers is one of the most pressing security issues associated with Mashups, because this enables external services to freely retrieve information from other services inside the Mashup. A malicious service can read, write and modify the content and even the behavior of all other services [3]. To mitigate this problem some sort of data flow control under the supervision of the user should be established. This leads to a second security requirement:

Requirement II: A facility for controlling the flow of resources across the Wiring should be established.

Another example for the lack of security in contemporary MPPs concerns the user's authentication credentials. The user provides her personal data to the MPP or a service inside the MPP to enable it to access backend-services. Both the MPP and individual services acting as adapters between the MPP and external data sources may impersonate the user to those external backend-services [12]. Also, a malicious provider of this proxy-service could abuse the user's authentication information to gain access to services outside of the MPP if the user has reused his password [15]. Therefore, the amount of credentials that have to be stored at the adapter or proxy services should be minimized to reduce the risks of impersonation.

Requirement III: The amount of credentials stored at adapter services should be minimized.

One possibility to address Requirement III is to store all credentials on the user side. However, managing lots of different credentials can be very cumbersome and will most likely overburden the users [16] [24], reducing the benefits from Mashups' ease of use. Therefore, we formulate a usability requirement:

Requirement IV: The burden placed on users for the management of credentials should be minimized.

Requirements III and IV can be achieved by storing the credentials with a trusted third party on behalf and under the control of the user. This, however, requires (as suggested by the name) that the user trusts the third party. In the spirit of multilateral security we aim at minimizing the required amount of trust of users in the platform. Introducing a trusted third party will not minimize the required trust. It will only shift it to another stakeholder. This leads to another security requirement.

Requirement V: The required amount of trust in the system should be minimized, specifically, trust in third parties should be minimized.

What is needed is a method which addresses the described security and privacy problems associated with MPPs without restricting their role in creating useful and functional combinations of services, such as acting as an intermediary platform facilitating discovery of compatible services, and offering hosting of the Mashup infrastructure. The focus is an end-to-end encrypted communication between the services within the platform, without the help of an additional trusted third party, and without trust in the platform.

4   Related Work

We are not the first to address security in Mashup environments. Hasan et al [12] present a system for controlling data flow within a MPP, using an independent 'Permit Grant Service' that acts on behalf of the MPP. Crites et al [5] propose a new browser security model, while Jackson and Wang [4] describe a solution using the existing browser origin policies. Both are valuable contributions in fixing the proxy/security model problem, however, none of the systems offer protection versus the platform itself. In the same vein, Keukelaere et al [3] propose a secure channel communication model. We extend on their work, adding encryption to protect confidentiality of the users' information versus the MPP. Zarandioon et al [6][17] offer the most comprehensive approach to date, offering both a client-side identity management providing data flow control as well as a single-sign-on (SSO) solution. However, it requires that each user administers a specific identity-providing server outside the MPP, and understands a set of (non-trivial) mediating components. It also requires that inter-Widget (which are referred to as 'mashlets') communication is executed using specialized Widgets, which is a counterintuitive modification of Mashup programming practices, threatening Mashups' main selling point, namely their ease of modification by non-experts. We also build on Close's work [11], which describes transmitting fine-grained access credentials in HTTPS fragments, and provide additional protection in the cascading piping mechanism employed by adapter services.

5   Approach

We present an integrated approach, offering a comprehensive identity management system that can be integrated in today's mash-up platforms, while offering advanced security guarantees. This is realized by building on two main components: one system for securely delivering differentiated authorization tokens to backend services, building on the solutions presented in [11][12], meeting Requirements III, IV and V, and one system for preserving confidentiality and permitting data flow control of data exchanged within the Mashup-providing Platform, extending the work presented in [3][6][17], meeting Requirements I, II, IV and V. This section illustrates how the components are integrated within the platform, how data flows between them, and what functionality each component offers in the context of the larger system. It also gives details of the underlying system, specifically the cryptographic components used.

5.1   Key Management

To encrypt the Wiring-based communication between two Widgets in the Mashup, it seems logical to employ some sort of asymmetric cryptography to address the key distribution problem associated with n-to-n communication scenarios [18]. This approach has also been proposed in the context of Mashups by [17]. However, we want to avoid burdening the user with the management of a key server specifically for the purpose of using it in our Mashup platform. Studies have shown that it is hard for users to even use PKI systems [16], so having them manage key distribution seems like a long shot, especially in the context of Mashups, where the business value is in making things easier for users [1].

5.2   Identity-Based Encryption

Identity-based Encryption (IBE) [19] offers a possibility to reduce the complexity associated with key distribution and management, directly using identifiers (e.g. users' email addresses) as public keys. While early IBE systems were not feasible for Web usage, recently a system has been proposed that can even be used as a client side JavaScript implementation in the Web context (namely, Guan et al's WebIBC [20]). This should be sufficient to meet performance requirements associated with Mashups. Conventional IBE requires a trusted third party acting as a Private Key Generator (PKG) for the individual entities communicating within the system (usually users). We turn this system upside down in that in our approach, the user acts as a PKG for communicating Backend Services within a MPP, using service identifiers as public keys. This results in only the receiving Backend Service and the User being able to decrypt messages sent, which meets our confidentiality requirement (I). In addition, it is much more efficient to generate keys for the CPK cryptosystem used in WebIBC [20], than for RSA (as presented by Zarandioon et al [6]) as we do not need to perform primality tests, and even a relatively small CPK master key matrix scales to very high numbers of services (e.g. a 128x16 matrix supports 10^{32} services [20]). Thus, using asynchronous threads with native code embedded in JavaScript [6] is not necessary, and the system presented here stays much more responsive, and does not require native code running outside the browser sandbox, which adds a whole new layer of vulnerability [21]. Using this reversed approach to IBE (where the user acts as PKG for Backend Services) enables an initialization phase where, after mutual authentication between user and Backend Service, the key exchange can be executed in a non-interactive manner (see Figure 4). To avoid impact on the

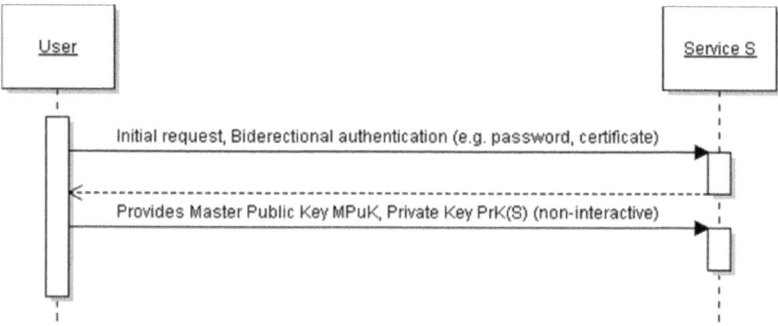

Fig. 4. Initial Setup and Key Exchange

user interaction, we employ a cryptographically secure pseudorandom function at the user side to derive the master key pair needed for IBE and the password for authenticating to the service from a master credential supplied by the user (e.g. a password, a cryptographic key on a smart card). In future usage, the specific algorithms used will depend on the available (enterprise and/or Web) infrastructure and Mashup-providing Platform, so the algorithms and identifiers given here should only be seen as a proof-of-concept realization based on to-day's systems. The detailed steps executed are: 1. If there is only one credential available (e.g. password supplied by user), harden it using e.g. iterated hashing using the method described by Halderman et al [22] for hardening the password, creating the hardened credential $cred_{hard}$. Apply PBKDF2 from PKCS #5 if expansion is needed [23]. Then derive from the hardened credential a Master Key Pair for Identity Based Encryption. Also derive a credential for mutual authentication with the Backend Service, using e.g. the method also described in [22] to derive a service specific password, using a deterministic pseudorandom function (PRF) [24]. If an enterprise smart card infrastructure can be used, the credentials may be stored directly on the smartcard, or passwords may be derived for interoperability with legacy services not supporting authentication by certificate, using e.g. the method proposed in [25]. Based on WebIBC, we use the revised CPK cryptosystem [20], which is based on elliptic curve cryptography, and generate keys as described in [24] [20], extracting them from matrices holding key pairs. We refer to them here as Master Public Key and Master Private Key $(MPuK, MPrK)$. Formalized in equations:

$$cred_{hard} = h^n(cred)$$

$$(MPrK, MPuK, base_{auth}) = PBKDF2(cred_{hard})$$

$$cred_{auth} = PRF(base_{auth}, id(S))$$

2. Perform mutual authentication of user and Backend Service (e.g. by using certificates on both sides, or the user authenticating to a Backend Service providing an SSL certificate, generically referred to here as $cred_{authSrv}(id(S))$). This step can be performed within the Mashup-providing Platform if (and only if) it provides direct contact to the backend service domains. Our architecture meets this requirement by using the iFrame approach given in section 2.2 [3]. In that case, direct communication with the service domain is possible, and e.g. SSL may be used normally. This is used to establish an encrypted communication channel between service and user (e.g. using SSL/TLS). Of course, more elaborate and reliable mutual authentication schemes for the web would be preferable, but how to realize them is still unclear, as pointed out by Dhamija and Dusseault [26], among others.

$$cred_{auth} < - - - - - - - - - - - - - - - - > cred_{authSrv}(id(S))$$
$$mutual\ authentication$$

3. Using the Master Private Key, the user extracts the service's private Key $PrK(S)$ based on the service's identifier also used as for the public key (e.g.

domain name or Widget identifier used for API calls within the MPP) (a detailed description of the extraction procedure from the master matrices in CPK/ WebIBC is given in [20]). He then sends Master Public Key and the Backend Service's private key he just generated to the service (across the established encrypted connection).

$$PrK(S) = extract(id(S), MPrK)$$

$$(PrK(S); MPuK) - - - - - - - - - - - - - - - - - >$$
$$encrypted\ transmission$$

5.3   Confidentiality of Personal Information (Wiring)

Using those keys, services can now establish encrypted communication channels via the platform. Sent messages are encrypted with the target Backend Service's public key, which is derived from the $MPuK$ and the service identifier $id(S)$. The extracted key may be cached when the credential certifying the receiving Backend Service's permission to access the data is received (as described in the next section).

$$sendMessage(id(S), enc_{extract(MpuK, id(S))}(message))$$

5.4   Data Flow Control

As already described in section 2.2, the data flow control is realized by requiring certification of the user's permission for the transaction from the requesting service. The sequence is generally similar to the one proposed by Hasan et al [12], but we remove the need for the trusted third party. The general sequence of the operation is given in Figure 5: Upon establishment of the Wiring, permits for access of the relevant information are requested from the user via the requesting Backend Service.

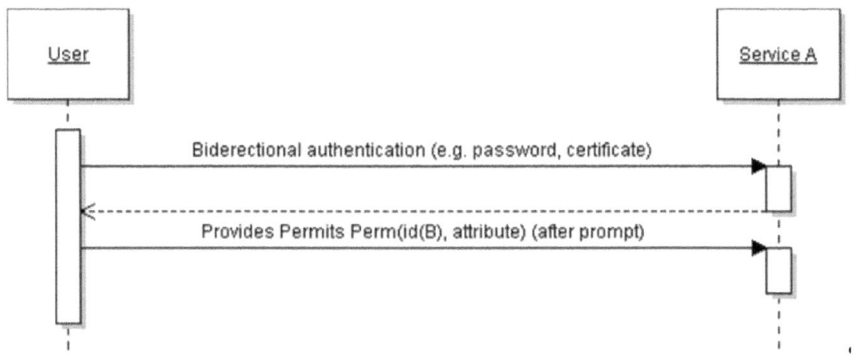

Fig. 5. Permit Granting Sequence

When a new Wiring is established (within the MPP's Wiring editor), the user is prompted to confirm (examples of Mashup permit dialogues are given in [12]). This is represented by the user's signature of a tupel consisting of requesting Backend Service, target Backend Service, and transmitted attributes. Using the terminology from 2.2:

$$Perm(id(A), id(B), attributes[]) =$$
$$Sign_{extract(id(U), MPrK)}(id(A), id(B), attributes[])$$

The pseudonymous communication via the MPP has the added advantage that the identity of Backend Services providing infomation resources is not necessarily revealed to consuming Backend Services.

5.5 Delegated Authentication and Authorization (Piping)

To minimize the credential exposure versus adapter services, we apply an approach consisting of two components. We address phishing and man in the middle attacks by employing PRFs to seed the credential (e.g. password) with the receiving domain (that is assumed to be able to authenticate itself using e.g. an SSL cert), an approach also employed in [22][25]. Our basic approach is to integrate with existing Single Sign On (SSO) systems to minimize credential exposure. In the context of the current web, this means providing some sort of Pseudo-SSO in the sense of de Clerq [27]. We chose to implement a password hashing approach, as several such systems exist, e.g. Halderman et al [22] or Zibuschka and Roßnagel [25], and are readily usable in all current browsers. To this end, we aim to establish direct channels within the MPP's Piping whenever possible. We use cascading iFrames for this, as proposed by [3], and illustrated in Figure 2. So, we derive the password, as already described in section 5.2, and implemented in [22][25]:

$$cred_{auth} = PRF(base_{auth}, id(S))$$

To further minimize risk of exposure, the next step would be to employ transmission in a HTTP fragment [5][11], which woild require minimal modifications of current practices. If the Backend Service behind the adapter supports it, finegrained permits (based on the permits described in 5.4) can also be used to further minimize exposure. However, this is not possible given the current state of the art of Web SSO.

6   Discussion and Limitations

Our system does not require trust into the MPP. It is the first solution to offer meaningful cryptographic security versus the MPP to end users of mashups. It still supports the current practice of integrating Mashup building blocks into a common MPP proxy, which is the basis of operations for current MPP providers.

Our solution goes beyond earlier work in that it provides strong security guarantees for the user, using strong cryptography, without requiring substantially modified user interaction, neither during authentication and identity management, nor during programming of Mashups. It integrates more readily into existing Mashup-providing Platforms, as it does not need client-side JavaScript Widgets. To realize this, we introduced the user as a private key generator within an identity-based encryption scheme securing Widget communication against the provider of a MPP. These mechanisms enable the providers of MPPs to complete their service with an efficient business model. Futhermore it makes mashups ready for enterprise use by offering a vector for integration in existing enterprise PKIs, while offering security across perimeter on individual level. To this end, we extend and integrate several earlier works, as well as propose new mechanisms like having the user act as a PKG in IBE systems for service communication. While the user-side components of our system may be implemented using JavaScript, this of course results in a high risk of phishing attacks. This is not specific to our solution, but a general weakness of systems using JavaScript and/or redirects [26][28]. In enterprise systems, which are our main focus, implementing e.g. Browser plugins is plausible, and also allows for integration of enterprise infrastructure, such as smart card infrastructures. Most of the MPPs (e.g. Yahoo Pipes, Intel Mash Maker or iGoogle) provide a free playground to the users, where they can combine several services. But thinking about the scenario where a company provides business-critical, sensitive data to the Backend Services in a Mashup, the necessity of an enduring security model can't be dismissed. Only an elaborated MPP which protects privacy and offers a secure encrypted and still usable communication, without making development and usability significantly more complicated, will be viable in the field of enterprise Mashups.

7   Conclusion

In this contribution we have presented a comprehensive privacy enhancing identity management system for implementation in the context of Mashup-providing Platforms minimizing required trust in the platform. We achieved this by using Reverse Identity Based Encryption to preserve the confidentiality of resources that are transmitted via Wiring. Our system does not require trust into the MPP. Our solution goes beyond earlier work in that it provides strong security guarantees for the user, using strong cryptography, without requiring substantially modified user interaction, neither during authentication and identity management, nor during programming of Mashups. Due to these advantages, it is now possible for providers of MPPs to adapt their services to the enterprise domain, where sensitive data will be processed. Having a robust security model is therefore a key prerequisite for developing business models in the context of enterprise Mashups.

Acknowledgements

This work was supported by the German Federal Ministry of Education and Research (BMBF) under Grant Number 01BS0824 (COCKTAIL).

References

1. Merrill, D.: Mashups: The new breed of Web app., IBM developerWorks (August 2006)
2. Hoyer, V., Fischer, M.: Market Overview of Enterprise Mashup Tools. In: Bouguettaya, A., Krueger, I., Margaria, T. (eds.) ICSOC 2008. LNCS, vol. 5364, pp. 708–721. Springer, Heidelberg (2008)
3. Keukelaere, F.D., Bhola, S., Steiner, M., Chari, S., Yoshihama, S.: SMash: secure component model for cross-domain mashups on unmodified browsers. In: Proceeding of the 17th international conference on World Wide Web, pp. 535–544. ACM, Beijing (2008)
4. Jackson, C., Wang, H.J.: Subspace: secure cross-domain communication for web mashups. In: Proceedings of the 16th international conference on World Wide Web, pp. 611–620. ACM, Banff (2007)
5. Crites, S., Hsu, F., Chen, H.: OMash: enabling secure web mashups via object abstractions. In: Proceedings of the 15th ACM conference on Computer and communications security, pp. 99–108. ACM, Alexandria (2008)
6. Zarandioon, S., Yao, D., Ganapathy, V.: OMOS: A Framework for Secure Communication in Mashup Applications. In: Proceedings of the 2008 Annual Computer Security Applications Conference, pp. 355–364. IEEE Computer Society, Los Alamitos (2008)
7. Mather, T., Kumaraswamy, S., Latif, S.: Cloud Security and Privacy: An Enterprise Perspective on Risks and Compliance. O'Reilly Media, Sebastopol (2009)
8. Brown, D.H., Lockett, N.: E-business, innovation and SMEs: the significance of hosted services and firm aggregations. International Journal of Entrepreneurship and Innovation Management 7, 92–112 (2007)
9. Hansen, M., Berlich, P., Camenisch, J., Clauß, S., Pfitzmann, A., Waidner, M.: Privacy-enhancing identity management, Information Security Technical Report, vol. 9, pp. 35–44 (2004)
10. Ennals, R.J., Garofalakis, M.N.: MashMaker: mashups for the masses. In: Proceedings of the 2007 ACM SIGMOD international conference on Management of data, pp. 1116–1118. ACM, Beijing (2007)
11. Close, T.: Web-key: Mashing with permission. In: W2SP 2008: Web 2.0 Security and Privacy 2008. IEEE Computer Society, Oakland (2008)
12. Hasan, R., Winslett, M., Conlan, R., Slesinsky, B., Ramani, N.: Please Permit Me: Stateless Delegated Authorization in Mashups. In: Proceedings of the 2008 Annual Computer Security Applications Conference, pp. 173–182. IEEE Computer Society, Los Alamitos (2008)
13. Open Mashup Alliance: OMA EMML Specification 1.0, http://www.openmashup.org/omadocs/v1.0/index.html
14. JackBe: JackBe Mashup Editor and Composer, http://www.jackbe.com/products/composers.php
15. Ives, B., Walsh, K.R., Schneider, H.: The domino effect of password reuse. ACM Commun. 47, 75–78 (2004)
16. Whitten, A., Tygar, J.D.: Why Johnny can't encrypt: a usability evaluation of PGP 5.0. In: Proceedings of the 8th conference on USENIX Security Symposium, vol. 8, p. 14. USENIX Association, Washington (1999)
17. Zarandioon, S., Yao, D., Ganapathy, V.: Privacy-aware identity management for client-side mashup applications. In: Proceedings of the 5th ACM workshop on Digital identity management, pp. 21–30. ACM, Chicago (2009)

18. Rivest, R.L., Shamir, A., Adleman, L.: A method for obtaining digital signatures and public-key cryptosystems. ACM Commun. 21, 120–126 (1978)
19. Shamir, A.: Identity-Based Cryptosystems and Signature Schemes. Advances in Cryptology, 47–53 (1985)
20. Guan, Z., Cao, Z., Zhao, X., Chen, R., Chen, Z., Nan, X.: WebIBC: Identity Based Cryptography for Client Side Security in Web Applications. In: International Conference on Distributed Computing Systems, pp. 689–696. IEEE Computer Society, Los Alamitos (2008)
21. Kemmerer, R.A.: Security issues in distributed software. SIGSOFT Softw. Eng. Notes 22, 52–59 (1997)
22. Halderman, J.A., Waters, B., Felten, E.W.: A convenient method for securely managing passwords. In: Proceedings of the 14th international conference on World Wide Web, pp. 471–479. ACM, Chiba (2005)
23. Kaliski, B.: PKCS #5: Password-Based Cryptography Specification Version 2.0 (2000)
24. Abadi, M., Bharat, K., Marais, J.: System and method for generating unique passwords, U.S. Patent 6141760
25. Zibuschka, J., Roßnagel, H.: Implementing Strong Authentication Interoperability with Legacy Systems. In: Policies and Research in Identity Management, pp. 149–160. Springer, Heidelberg (2008)
26. Dhamija, R., Dusseault, L.: The Seven Flaws of Identity Management: Usability and Security Challenges. IEEE Security & Privacy Magazine 6, 24–29 (2008)
27. de Clerq, J.: Single Sign-on Architectures. In: Proceedings of Infrastructure Security, International Conference, Bristol, UK, pp. 40–58 (2002)
28. Erlingsson, U., Livshits, B., Xie, Y.: End-to-end Web Application Security. In: 11th Workshop on Hot Topics in Operating Systems. USENIX Association, San Diego (2007)

An Access Control Model for Web Databases

Ahlem Bouchahda-Ben Tekaya[1,2], Nhan Le Thanh[1],
Adel Bouhoula[2], and Faten Labbene-Ayachi[2]

[1] I3S Laboratory, Nice-Sophia Antipolis University / CNRS,
Bâtiment Polytech'Sophia - SI 930 route des colles,
B.P. 145 06903 Sophia-Antipolis France Cedex
[2] Digital security research unit,
Higher communications school of Tunis,
Rte de Raoued Km 3, 5 2083, Ariana Tunisia

Abstract. The majority of today's web-based applications are based on
back-end databases to process and store business information. Containing valuable business information, these systems are highly interesting to
attackers and special care needs to be taken to prevent them from malicious accesses. In this paper, we propose ($RBAC^+$), an extension of the
NIST RBAC (Role-Based Access Control) standard with the notions of
application, application profile and sub-application session to distinguish
end users that execute the same application, providing them by only the
needed roles and continuously monitoring them throughout a whole session. It is based on business application logic rather than primitive reads
and writes to enhance the ability of detecting malicious transactions.
Hence, attacks caused by malicious transactions can be detected and
canceled timely before they succeed.

1 Introduction

Nowadays, Web applications depend more and more on the back-end database
to provide much more functionalities. Containing valuable business information,
these systems are highly interesting to attackers and special care needs to be
taken to prevent any malicious access to this database layer. Access control
is the primary means of attack prevention for databases. But as long as web
databases cannot identify their real users, they cannot supply them with proper
authorization. Database Views are another means of unauthorized access restriction as they can define the only part of a database relevant to a user. But for
web databases they are useless. In fact, web applications are run from the user's
browser windows. The browser does not directly connect to the database, but
instead transfer a request to a web server who processes the request and if an
access to the underlying database is needed, transfers it to the application server
which performs a transaction to the database. It implies that the database does
not identify the real user who accesses it and so, traditional identity-based mechanisms for performing access control are useless for web databases. Further, a
DBMS can not handle users who access it indirectly via the application server,
no user-based access control can be applied since the only recognized user is the

S. Foresti and S. Jajodia (Eds.): Data and Applications Security XXIV, LNCS 6166, pp. 287–294, 2010.
© IFIP International Federation for Information Processing 2010

user of the application server and for most of the web applications this is the user with very high privileges.

Databases can no longer differentiate between transactions of different application users. The principle of minimal privilege is violated. It is impossible to authorize the web application user with appropriate privileges at the database level: all application users have access to the same data. Restrictions on what authenticated users are allowed to do are not properly enforced. Attackers can exploit these flaws to view sensitive data, or use unauthorized functions. So, no more fine-grained access control to the database exists and authorization can be provided only at the application level.

To protect web databases from attacks, access control policies should be based on a strong model that is implemented by the DBMS. Checking for authorization should be done on every attempt to access secure information. For that end, we extend the NIST RBAC (Role-Based Access Control) standard [1]. The central idea of $RBAC^+$ is including the concepts of *application, application profile* and *sub-application session* when controlling the access to web databases. The application profile is necessary to track the user behavior throughout a whole session and mainly to prevent business logic violation attacks by enforcing access control. The $RBAC^+$ monitors transactions issued by users and malicious transactions are viewed as intrusion behaviors. If a malicious transaction is identified, the $RBAC^+$ cancels the transaction before it succeeds, thus minimize damage caused by malicious transactions.

The rest of the paper is organized as follows. We present the related work and discuss it in Section 2. In section 3, we present an overview of our model. We define formally and detail our model in Section 4. Access control policies are presented in section 5. We conclude our work and present future work in Section 6.

2   Related Work

The problem of access control to databases accessible over the web is very important one. This problem is well known to the web application developers and security consultants, but little existing work has addressed it. Gertz et al. in [2] pose this problem and presented some fundamental concepts and techniques that help administrators and security personnel to gradually evaluate and improve the security of a database. Also, Roichman in [3] proposed a method that uses the databases' built-in access control mechanisms enhanced with Parameterized Views and adapts them to work with web applications in order to prevent intrusions. He defines also the concept of session vector to represent the application fingerprints used in an application session in order to detect intrusions. This concept is similar to our application profile concept with the difference that the session vector represents the session profile while the application profile represents an execution way of the application. Beyond these two approaches, to protect web databases from attacks of malicious users, two main approaches exist. The first consist on using ad hoc tools specifically oriented to the detection of specific

kinds of attacks like SQL injection [4]. The second consists on using Intrusion
Detection Systems (IDSs). [5] presents a database IDS that uses the profile of the
transactions implemented by database applications (authorized transactions) to
identify user attempts to execute unauthorized transactions. Although we believe
that database IDSs should play an important role in database security, we have
to point out that the web application's access to databases remains untraceable.
Further, an IDS can not overcome the absence of web database internal access
control and the uselessness of views as a means of access restriction. Moreover,
with the assumption that the attack does not go unnoticed, IDSs focus on detecting attacks after the malicious user has accessed the DB with all the damage
it could cause. What we propose is strengthening access control and continuously
monitor users. Consequently, the majority of attacks can be stopped from the
access control stage and the IDS will be used to detect attacks that have escaped
the access control stage. Intrusion detection without enforcing access control is
not as efficient and effective. IDS is a complement but can not, alone, protect
DB from attacks.

3 Overview of Our Approach

As accesses to the data occur through several layers, starting with a person then
the application, which, in turn, performs operations on the database, correlat-
ing anomalous behaviors with a person is not a trivial task. To address these
problems, we propose $RBAC^+$, an extension of RBAC able to detect malicious
users and stopping the attack before it succeeds. Assuming that the database
management system (DBMS) has an RBAC model in place, the key idea of our
approach is as follows. We create application profiles that represent all the possible execution paths of the application. Given the permissions necessary to the
execution of an application and the set of roles that the underlying database
user (DBU) is authorized for, we calculate for each pair (application, DBU) the
subset of roles to activate in a web user session, called sub-application session.
It is called so because, in the context of a web application, a web user session
is included in a database session. Hence, a sub-application session contains only
the permissions really needed to fulfill exactly the tasks it was created for, and
so we take advantage of all RBAC assets such as least privilege and separation
of duty. A sub-application session allows to the DBMS distinguishing between
web users working with the database. It will also allow distinguishing between
the requests of different web users that belong to the same database session.
When the web user logs in, the SQL queries that he submits are associated with
a database session, an application and the underlying database user that issued
them. All queries belonging to a sub-application session must match an application execution path else the access is denied because the action to be executed
is illegitimate.

We assume that the user is identified at each tier. The recent tendency in the
architecture of web applications allows preserving the identity of the real user
through the middle tier As example, Oracle9i introduced n-tier authentication

[6], i.e., that is "lightweight session". Now, when an employee wants to attack enterprise resources, he, for example, can submit an SQL injection attack. But because his database privileges are limited only to legitimate actions, an SQL injection will be entirely mitigated or at least, its effect is strongly limited. The importance of our solution is that it enforces access control based on business application logic rather than primitive reads and writes. A user's ability to access and manipulate data is typically dependent of the application function the user executes thus reducing drastically attacks against databases and in particular, business logic violation attacks because an action may be legitimate on its own but illegitimate in the context of a whole session. Take the example of an online retailer application. If the intruder can submit the insert statement into the Orders table without submitting an insert into the Credit Card table, then he can buy goods without paying. This business rule violation can be detected only at the session level since each statement by itself is a legitimate one.

Databases cannot prevent them because the existing database access control can grant or revoke access to resources only according to the accessor identity/role. It cannot rely on the business logic of an organization.

4   The $RBAC^+$ Core Model

We, now, introduce a rigorous definition of the model. The purpose is to provide a comprehensive definition of the components, thus including all the aspects of the model. The general structure of the model is illustrated in Figure 1. We use the graphical representation adopted in RBAC. In particular, APPS, AP and SASES represent the sets of applications, application profiles and sub-application session respectively.

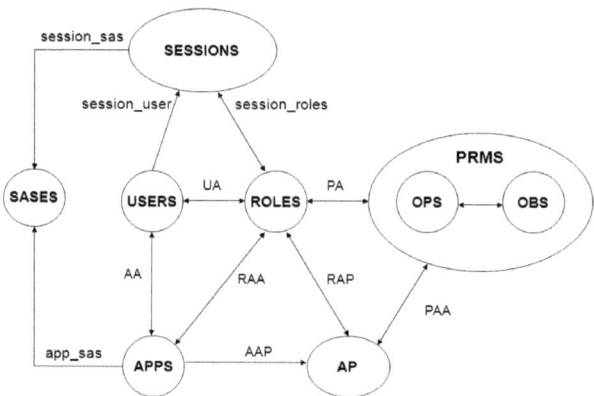

Fig. 1. Core $RBAC^+$

4.1 Application Profile

An application has many possible ways of execution each of which is called an application profile representing one valid execution sequence of the application (sequences of selects, inserts, updates, deletes). It consists of a sequence of nodes such that from each of its nodes there is an edge to the next node in the sequence. Each node in the path represent a SQL statement. It has one start node and one end node where the application execution starts and finishes, respectively. The other nodes in the path are called internal nodes. An application profile may include cycles representing the repetitive execution of sets of commands. Obviously, the set of application profiles must cover the different database application functionalities. To that end, we choose to analyze the application code which implicitly contains a policy that allows for distinguishing legitimate and malicious queries. Also, the source code contains enough information to infer models of the expected, legitimate sequences of SQL queries generated by the application.

Definition 1. *(Application Profile). An application profile AP is a binary vector with the length equal to the number of permissions (PRMS) in the DBMS, where the ith bit is 1 if the application profile needs the permission p_i , else bit i is 0. $p_i \in PRMS$.*

We also define :

- $AAP : APP \rightarrow AP$, the mapping of an application onto its corresponding application profiles. Formally,
  $APP\_profiles(app) = \{ap \in AP | (ap, app) \in AAP\}$.
- $RAP \subseteq ROLES \times AP$, a many-to-many mapping Role-to-Application profile Assignment relation.
- $AP\_roles : AP \rightarrow ROLES$, the mapping of an application profile to a set of roles. Formally, $AP\_roles(ap) = \{r \in ROLES | (r, ap) \in RAP\}$.
- $RAA \subseteq ROLES \times APP$, a many-to-many mapping Role-to-Application Assignment relation.
- $APP\_roles : APP \rightarrow ROLES$, the mapping of an application to a set of roles. Formally, $APP\_roles(app) = \{r \in ROLES | (r, app) \in RAA\}$.

Note that, $AP\_roles(ap) \subseteq APP\_roles(app)$ with $\{ap \in AP | (ap, app) \in AAP\}$

4.2 Sub-Application Session

An application session is composed of all the transactions that an application runs on behalf of all its users. A sub-application session (SASES) is the subset of transactions related to one user. Formally, we define :

Definition 2. *(Sub-application session) We define:*

- $app\_sas : APP \rightarrow 2^{SASES}$. *The mapping of an application onto a set of sub-application sessions.*
- $session\_sas : SESSIONS \rightarrow 2^{SASES}$. *The mapping of a session onto a set of sub-application sessions.*

4.3   Permissions

In our model, permissions are associated with roles and with application profiles. Applications are then associated with the appropriate roles based on the set of permissions assigned to application profiles.

Definition 3. *(Permissions) The set of permissions* PRMS *is defined as* $PRMS = 2^{(OPS \times OBJ)}$. *We also define:*

- $PAA \subseteq PRMS \times AP$, *a many-to-many mapping Permission-to-Application profile Assignment relation.*
- $AP\_perms : AP \to 2^{PRMS}$, *the mapping of an application profile onto a set of permissions. Formally,* $AP\_perms(ap) = \{p \in PRMS | (p, ap) \in PAA\}$.

4.4   Users

Each user is associated with a set of applications he/she is authorized to execute.

Definition 4. *(Users) We define:*

- $AA \subseteq APPS \times USERS$, *a many-to-many mapping application-to-user assignment relation.*
- $USER\_AssignedApps : USERS \to 2^{APPS}$, *the mapping of a user to a set of applications. Formally,*
  $USER\_AssignedApps(u) = \{u \in USERS | (app, u) \in AA\}$.

4.5   Sessions

When a user logs in, a new session is activated and a number of roles are selected to be included in the session role set. Formally:

Definition 5. *(Sessions): We define:*

- *session_user:* $SESSIONS \to USERS$, *the mapping from a session s to the user of s.*
- *session_roles :* $SESSIONS \to 2^{ROLES}$, *the mapping of session s onto a set of roles. Formally:* $session\_roles(s) \subseteq \{r \in ROLES | (session\_User(s), r) \in UA\}$.
- *session_applications :* $SESSIONS \to 2^{APPS}$, *the mapping of session s onto a set of applications.*
- *avail_app_roles :* $(SESSIONS, APPS) \to 2^{ROLES}$, *the mapping of a session and an application onto a set of roles. Formally,* $avail\_app\_roles(s, app) \subseteq \{r \in ROLES | r = session\_roles(s) \cap app\_roles(app)\}$
- *avail_app_prms :* $(SESSIONS, APPS) \to 2^{PRMS}$, *the permissions available to an application in a session. Formally,* $avail\_app\_prms(s, app) = \bigcup_{r \in avail\_app\_roles(s,app)} assigned\_permissions(r)$.

5   Access Control Policies

Application profiles representing valid application execution paths are used to detect unauthorized SQL statements, which are seen as invalid sequences of SQL commands.

Definition 6. *(Authorization control function): An access request ar is a tuple* $ar = \langle U, is, app, p, o \rangle \in USERS \times SASES \times APPS \times OPS \times OBJ.$ *ar can be satisfied if* $(p, o) \in avail\_app\_prms(s, a)$ *and is* $\in session\_sas(s)$.

An sql query is a set of permissions. the above function is repeated as many permissions as the sql query requires permissions to be executed.

To support a differentiated and adequate protection of the information stored in a database made available over the web, the access control policies must be flexible enough to support a spectrum of web-based applications, such as e-commerce web applications or health care web-applications. To that end, we specify two access control policies. The first consists on monitoring all the SQL statements submitted by an user and the second consists on monitoring only special statements that we call "critical points". A critical point may be an SQL statement manipulating sensitive data or an SQL statement modifying data (insert, delete, update). When a malicious transaction is detected, the transaction is rolled back.

5.1   Policy 1

Under this policy, every command executed must match a profile. When the first command of the transaction is executed the tool searches for all the application profiles starting with that same command, which are marked as candidate profiles for the current transaction. The next command executed is then compared with the second command of these candidate profiles. If it corresponds, the access is granted, either, access is denied. Only those who match remain candidate profiles. This process is executed over and over until the transaction reaches its end or there are no more candidate profiles for that transaction. In this latter case the transaction is identified as malicious. In practice, to detect malicious transactions, we implement the following generic algorithm over the application profiles:

1: **while** (1) **do**
2:    **for** each new command submitted **do**
3:       **if** user does not have any active transaction then {command is the 1st command in a new transaction } **then**
4:          obtain list of authorized application profiles starting with this command
5:       **else**
6:          **for** each valid (authorized) trans. for the user **do**
7:             **if** the current command represents a valid successor node in the application profile **then**
8:                the command is valid
9:             **else**

```
10:              mark the current transaction as a non valid trans.
11:         end if
12:         end for
13:         if there are transactions marked as non valid then
14:              a malicious transaction has been detected
15:         end if
16:     end if
17:     end for
18: end while
```

5.2 Policy 2

Under this policy, the SQL statements submitted by the user called *user context* are stored and the access is granted until he submits a critical point. In this case, the tool searches an application profile that corresponds to the user context. If one or more corresponding application profiles are found, the access is granted. Otherwise, the transaction is rolled back.

6 Conclusion and Future Work

Database security problems seriously persecute web-based applications that rely on web databases storing invaluable data. In this paper we have presented $RBAC^+$, an extension of the RBAC model addressing access control requirements for RBAC-administered web databases. We do not only monitor DB users to detect potential attacks, but timely stop the attacks when they are detected to minimize losses caused by the attacks. As future work, we will focus on the implementation of a prototype of the proposed system and its experimentation against a variety of simulated intrusions to prove its effectiveness and efficiency.

References

1. American national standard for information technology, role based access control. ansi incits 359-2004 (February 2004)
2. Gertz, M., Gandhi, M.: Security Re-engineering for Databases: Concepts and Techniques. In: Handbook of Database Security, pp. 267–296 (2007)
3. Roichman, A.: Intrusion prevention and detection for web databases (2008)
4. Halfond, W.G., Viegas, J., Orso, A.: A classification of sql-injection attacks and countermeasures. In: Proceedings of the IEEE International Symposium on Secure Software Engineering, Arlington, VA, USA (2006)
5. Vieira, M., Madeira, H.: Detection of malicious transactions in dbms. In: PRDC 2005: Proceedings of the 11th Pacific Rim International Symposium on Dependable Computing, Washington, DC, USA, pp. 350–357. IEEE Computer Society, Los Alamitos (2005)
6. Oracle corporation: Oracle9i database concepts release 2 (9.2). ch. 22: Controlling database access,
   http://download-west.oracle.com/docs/cd/B10501_01/
   server.920/a96524/c23acces.htm

Modelling Dynamic Access Control Policies for Web-Based Collaborative Systems*

Hasan Qunoo and Mark Ryan

School of Computer Science,
University of Birmingham, UK
{H.Qunoo,M.D.Ryan}@cs.bham.ac.uk

Abstract. We present a modelling language, called *X-Policy*, for web-based collaborative systems with dynamic access control policies. The access to resources in these systems depends on the state of the system and its configuration. The *X-Policy* language models systems as a set of actions. These actions can model system operations which are executed by users. The *X-Policy* language allows us to specify execution permissions on each action using complex access conditions which can depend on data values, other permissions, and agent roles. We demonstrate that *X-Policy* is expressive enough to model collaborative conference management systems. We model the EasyChair conference management system and we reason about three security attacks on EasyChair.

1 Introduction

Large conference management systems like iChair, WSAR, HotCRP and Easy-Chair are widely used to manage academic conferences. However, the size and the complexity of these systems make it hard to analyse their policies and their security properties. The policies of those systems are designed to preserve the system security and serve their desired purpose. Systems, however, can still fail some basic security properties. Users can compromise the system policy and its security properties by interactions of rules, co-operations between agents and multi-step actions. In EasyChair, the system is designed to collect a number (usually between 3 and 4) of reviewer's opinions of a submitted paper. These opinions determine whether a paper should be accepted or rejected. For the system rules to be fair, no single reviewer should be able to determine the outcome of a paper reviewing process by writing all three reviews of that paper. However, the intention of these rules can be breached by interaction of rules to allow a single user to write all the three reviews of a paper. For example, a single sub-reviewer manages to write all three paper reviews while all the agents still comply with the system rules.

In this paper, we present a simple yet expressive modelling language, called *X-Policy*, to model large web-based collaborative management systems. Our language enables us to:

---

* The long version[1] of this paper can be found at the authors' web pages.

S. Foresti and S. Jajodia (Eds.): Data and Applications Security XXIV, LNCS 6166, pp. 295–302, 2010.
© IFIP International Federation for Information Processing 2010

– model dynamic systems as a set of atomic multi-assignment write actions.
– specify read actions that gives us the ability to specify who can read what.
– specify action executing policy as preconditions which the user has to satisfy
  to execute the action.

We also use *EC* as a case study for our language. We model *EC* in *X-Policy*
and we reason about three security attacks on EasyChair using our model. The
long version of this paper is available at [1].

1.1 Paper Structure

We detail in Section 2 the related work. In Section 3, we present the *X-Policy*
language and the process of expressing the *EC* model using *X-Policy* language
and formalism. We introduce a selection of *EC* actions with their execution permissions statements which are used in the security attacks on *EC* and EasyChair
in Section 3.2. The conclusion and future work are in Section 4.

2 Related Work

Recently, there has been a plethora of languages and logics to express access
control policies. These logics and languages try to solve various issues arising
from decentralisation[2,3,4,5,6,7]. DeTreville was the first to propose a Datalog
based security language called Binder[4]. Since then Datalog has become the
foundation of recent logic-based access control policies like the RT family [7]
and SecPAL[2]. Researchers are mainly attracted to Datalog[8] as they can start
from a tractable and expressive language with the advantage of deducing trust
relations effectively based on well developed logic programming concepts and
deductive databases. Unfortunately, Datalog is stateless. Inherently, the ability of
datalog-based languages to express dynamic access control policies is restricted.
Cassandra[9], a Datalog-based language, has a separate mechanism to maintain
the authorisation state by inserting and retracting "hasActivated" facts according
to the policy rules.

Gurevich et. al. introduced Distributed Knowledge Authorisation Language
DKAL[5] and DKAL2[6] that extend SecPAL's expressiveness. However, Cassandra, SecPAL, DKAL, DKAL2 and other authorisation languages lack the ability
to express the dynamic aspect of access control where policies depend on and
update the system state like those we have in *EC*. They, also, cannot express
the effect of actions as part of the language and it has to be hard-coded in an
ad-hoc way. More recently, DyNPAL[3] aims to specify dynamic policies with
the ability to specify the effect of executing these actions. DyNPAL allows conditional bulk insertion and retraction of authorisation facts with transactional
execution semantics (either all or none are committed). However, DyNPAL's
declarative nature and minimalistic approach make it hard to follow the control flow of the actions. Also the lack of parameter typing does not allow us
to establish the relation between the agent who can execute an action and the

action itself. They tend to focus on answering the question "under what conditions can an action be executed?" rather than "under what conditions can an agent execute an action?". This is indeed necessary to enable us to define agent coalitions and establish which agent is executing an action. It allows us to detect attacks where we are interested in who can execute a set of actions rather than whether a set of actions can be executed regardless of the actors involved. RW framework[10], a precursor of *X-Policy*, can analyse the consequences of multi-agent multi-step actions by performing temporal reasoning. RW is both model checking based frameworks. However, RW, unlike *X-Policy*, cannot express the actions with multiple assignments needed to preserve the integrity constraints of the modelled system.

To the best of our knowledge, this is the first paper to model and analyse dynamic access control policy for a large web-based collaborative system with atomic actions like EasyChair.

3   Modelling EasyChair Conference Management System

We specify system operations as *X-Policy* programs[1] which can be either *write programs* that change the state of the system or *read programs* that give the user/agent the knowledge about the state of the system. Programs in *X-Policy* can not read and change the state of the system at the same time. Although this is formally a restriction, most actions in collaborative web-based systems are indeed either a read or write and rarely both. This is true for EasyChair in particular. We believe that this is a sensible heuristic for modelling web-based systems. Users are only enabled to perform only one operation per time.

A *read program* allows the user to know the value of a ground proposition by returning the value of that proposition to the user who executed the program. A *write program* allows the user to change the value of a set of ground propositions using assignment statements in the form $p(\overrightarrow{y}) := \top$; or $p(\overrightarrow{y}) := \bot$; where $p(\overrightarrow{y})$ is a ground proposition. We allow a proposition to occur at most once at the left of ":=". The assignment statements within the same program can be written in any order. Such an assumption result in making the programs effect independent from the state of the system and each program has the same effect at all the time. A program permission statement exec(g,u) defines the conditions for an agent u to execute a program g. These conditions are defined as propositional logic formulae using the ground propositions and logical connectors. The full syntax and semantics of *X-Policy* are details in the long version[1].

3.1   *EC* Model in *X-Policy* Formalism

In this section, we discuss the model *EC*. We build *EC*, a model of our understanding of EasyChair and restrict *EC* to a single conference system. We express the *EC* model in *X-Policy* formalism[1]. To model *EC*, we define a number of predicates P. For a,b of type Agent, p of type Paper, P includes:

Chair-review-en()	Review menu is enabled for Chair to manage the reviews of papers.
PCM-access-reviews-en()	PC members can access (view) other papers reviews.
PCM-review-editing-en()	PC members can add/modify reviews.
PCM-review-menu-en()	Review menu is enabled for PC members.
Review-assig-enabled()	Review assignments enabled.
Sub-anonymous()	Submissions are anonymous. The name of authors are obscured.
View-sub-title-permitted()	PC members can view the submissions title of all the papers.
Auth(p,a)	a is an author of p.
Chair(a)	a is the chair of the PC.
Conf-of-interest(p,a)	a has a conflict of interest with the p.
Decided-subrev(p,a,b)	b has accepted or rejected the subreviewing request for p issued by a.
PCM(a)	a is a PC member.
Requested-subrev(p,a,b)	a has requested b to be his subreviewer for p.
Reviewer(p,a)	p is assigned to PC member a for reviewing.
Submitted-review(p,a,b)	b's review of p has been submitted by a.
Subreviewer(p,a,b)	b has accepted the subreviewing request for p issued by a.

We now define the set of actions Actions and their execution permissions using the formula exec(act, u) for each action act ∈ Actions. The execution permission statements define whether or not u of type Agent is allowed to execute such an action and in what state. In the following, we list a sub-set of *EC* actions and their permission statements which are used in our properties analysis in X-*Policy*:

1. When the review menu is enabled and the submitted paper is not deleted: **(a)** A PC chair can read all the paper reviews. **(b)** A PC member can read a review for a paper p if she is a reviewer of that paper and has submitted her review. **(c)** A PC member can read a review for a paper to which she is not assigned, when PC members are permitted to access the titles and reviews of submitted papers. She also must have no conflict of interest with that paper.

Action ShowRev(p,a,b):- { return Submitted-review(p,a,b); }

$$
\text{exec(ShowRev(p,a,b),u)} \rightleftharpoons
\begin{pmatrix}
\begin{pmatrix} \text{Chair(u)} \land \text{Chair-review-en()} \\ \land \exists d : \text{Agent . Auth(p,d)} \end{pmatrix} \\
\lor \begin{pmatrix} \text{PCM(u)} \land \text{Reviewer(p,u)} \\ \land \text{PCM-review-menu-en()} \\ \land \exists c : \text{Agent . Submitted-review(p,u,c)} \\ \land \exists d : \text{Agent . Auth(p,d)} \end{pmatrix} \\
\lor \begin{pmatrix} \text{PCM(u)} \land \neg\text{Reviewer(p,u)} \\ \land \text{PCM-review-menu-en()} \\ \land \text{View-sub-title-permitted()} \\ \land \text{PCM-access-reviews-en()} \\ \land \neg\text{Conf-of-interest(p,u)} \\ \land \exists d : \text{Agent . Auth(p,d)} \end{pmatrix}
\end{pmatrix}
$$

2. When the review menu is enabled and the submitted paper is not deleted: **(a)** A PC chair can submit a review for any paper as himself. **(b)** A PC chair can submit a review for a paper as another PC member using "log in as another pc member" if the PC member is allowed to submit a review for that paper. **(c)** A PC member can review a paper if she is assigned to review that paper. **(d)** A PC member can review a paper to which she is not assigned when PC members are permitted to access the titles and reviews of submitted papers. She also must have no conflict of interest with that paper.

Action AddRev(p,a,b):-{ Submitted-review(p,a,b):=⊤;}

$$\text{exec}(\text{AddRev}(p,a,b),u)) \rightleftharpoons \left(\bigvee \left(\wedge \left(\begin{array}{c} \left(\begin{array}{c} \text{Chair}(u) \wedge \text{Chair-review-en}() \\ \wedge a = u \wedge \exists d : \text{Agent . Auth}(p,d) \end{array} \right) \\ (a = u \vee \text{Chair}(u)) \wedge \exists c : \text{Agent . Auth}(p,c) \\ \bigvee \left(\begin{array}{c} \left(\begin{array}{c} \text{PCM}(a) \wedge \text{Reviewer}(p,a) \\ \wedge \text{PCM-review-menu-en}() \\ \wedge \text{PCM-review-editing-en}() \end{array} \right) \\ \left(\begin{array}{c} \text{PCM}(a) \wedge \neg\text{Reviewer}(p,a) \\ \wedge \text{PCM-review-menu-en}() \\ \wedge \text{View-sub-title-permitted}() \\ \wedge \text{PCM-access-reviews-en}() \\ \wedge \neg\text{Conf-of-interest}(p,a) \end{array} \right) \end{array} \right) \end{array} \right) \right) \right)$$

3. When the review menu is enabled and the submitted paper is not deleted: **(a)** A PC chair can request another agent to subreview any paper. **(b)** A PC member can invite another agent to subreview a paper: (1) if she is the reviewer of the paper or (2) if the system is configured to give PC members access to the paper submission titles and reviews. The invited agent can decide whether to accept or reject the reviewing request as long as the paper has not been withdrawn. A PC member cannot cancel the subreviewing request but can accept or reject the request on behalf of the invited agent. Once the decision is made, only the PC member can change the decision.

Action RequestRev(p,a,b):- { Requested-subrev(p,a,b):= ⊤;}
Action AcceptRevRequest(p,a,b):-
         { Decided-subrev(p,a,b):=⊤; Subreviewer(p,a,b):=⊤;}
Action RejectRevRequest(p,a,b):-
         { Decided-subrev(p,a,b):=⊤; Subreviewer(p,a,b):=⊥;}

$$\text{exec}(\text{RequestRev}(p,a,b),u) \rightleftharpoons \left(\begin{array}{c} \left(\begin{array}{c} \text{Chair-review-en}() \wedge \text{Chair}(u) \\ \wedge \exists c : \text{Agent . Auth}(p,c) \end{array} \right) \\ \bigvee \left(\begin{array}{c} \text{PCM}(u) \wedge \text{Reviewer}(p,u) \\ \wedge \text{PCM-review-menu-en}() \\ \wedge \exists c : \text{Agent . Auth}(p,c) \end{array} \right) \\ \bigvee \left(\begin{array}{c} \text{PCM}(u) \wedge \neg\text{Reviewer}(p,u) \\ \wedge \text{PCM-review-menu-en}() \\ \wedge \text{View-sub-title-permitted}() \\ \wedge \text{PCM-access-reviews-en}() \\ \wedge \neg\text{Conf-of-interest}(p,u) \\ \wedge \exists c : \text{Agent . Auth}(p,c) \end{array} \right) \end{array} \right)$$

$$\text{exec}(\text{AcceptRevRequest}(p,a,b),u) \rightleftharpoons \left(\begin{array}{c} \text{Requested-subrev}(p,a,b) \\ \wedge \exists c : \text{Agent . Auth}(p,c) \\ \wedge \left(\neg\text{Decided-subrev}(p,a,u) \vee u = a \right) \end{array} \right)$$

$$\text{exec}(\text{RejectRevRequest}(p,a,b),u) \rightleftharpoons \left(\begin{array}{c} \text{Requested-subrev}(p,a,b) \\ \wedge \exists c : \text{Agent . Auth}(p,c) \\ \wedge \left(\neg\text{Decided-subrev}(p,a,u) \vee u = a \right) \end{array} \right)$$

4. Given that paper assignments are enabled, a PC chair can assign/de-assign a submitted paper to a PC member or a PC chair for reviewing, when she has no conflict of interest with that paper.

Action AddReviewerAssignment(p,a):-{ Reviewer(p,a) := ⊤; }

$$\text{exec}(\text{AddReviewerAssignment}(p, a), u) \rightleftharpoons \left(\begin{array}{l} \text{Chair}(u) \wedge (\text{PCM}(a) \vee \text{Chair}(a)) \\ \wedge \text{Review-assig-enabled}() \\ \wedge \neg \text{Conf-of-interest}(p, a) \\ \wedge \exists c : \text{Agent . Auth}(p, c) \end{array} \right)$$

3.2   Case Study: Analysis of *EC* Security Properties

In this Section, we will present three security properties in *EC*. We have discovered these issues while using EasyChair. In each case, we show an attack strategy to achieve an undesirable state. Each strategy is an execution sequence of read and write actions. A strategy can be executed by more than one agent where agents collaborate to reach the goal. These attacks can be derived using *EC* and have succeeded on EasyChair as of 1st of Spetember 2009. In the following, we report the results of each attack and make some suggestions on how to fix the system. For our *EC* model, we create the following configuration:

1. The system has five agents: Alice, Bob, Eve, Carol and Marvin. The system has two submitted papers: p1 and p2.
2. Alice is the Chair of PC. Bob and Carol are PC members. Paper p1 is submitted by the author Marvin while p2 is submitted by the author Eve.

The detailed configuration and the attacks derivation of the model *EC* can be found at [1].

Property 1: A single subreviewer should not be able to determine the outcome of a paper reviewing process by writing two reviews of the same paper. We show that we can derive an attack against *EC* involving 4 agents: Alice, Bob, Carol, and Eve. We explain the attack scenario as a sequence of actions executed by these agents as follows:

1. Alice acts as chair. She executes the actions: AddReviewerAssignment(p1,Bob) to assign Bob to review the paper p1. She also executes AddReviewerAssignment(p1,Carol) to assign Carol to review the paper p1.
2. Bob and Carol both assign Eve as their sub-reviewer for paper p1 by executing the actions RequestRev(p1,Bob,Eve) and RequestRev(p1,Carol,Eve) respectively.
3. Eve accepts the two paper subreviewing requests and sends Bob and Carol two similar reviews using AcceptRevRequest(p1,Carol,Eve) and AcceptRevRequest(p1,Bob,Eve).
4. Bob and Carol receive Eve's reviews and submit them to the system using AddRev(p1,Bob,Eve) and AddRev(p1,Carol,Eve).

EasyChair fails this property and allows Eve to submit two reviews for the same paper. One possible fix for this attack is as follows. Every time an agent a invites another agent b to subreview a paper, EasyChair should check whether agent b has been invited by another agent to subreview the same paper. We conjoin the condition $\neg\exists$ d : Agent . Requested-subrev(p, d, b) to the permission statement exec(RequestRev(p,a,b),u). This will prevent Carol from executing RequestRev(p1,Carol,Eve) as Requested-subrev(p1,Bob,Eve) is in the previous state.

Property 2: A paper author should not review her own paper. As before, we explain the attack scenario as a sequence of actions executed by the agents Alice, Bob and Eve:

1. Alice acts as Chair and assigns Bob, who is a PC member, to review the paper p2 submitted by Eve by executing the action AddReviewerAssignment(p2,Bob).
2. Bob executes the action RequestRev(p2,Bob,Eve) to assign Eve as his subreviewer as she is a good researcher in the field.
3. Eve accepts the request using AcceptRevRequest(p2,Bob,Eve).
4. Bob submits the review using AddRev(p2,Bob,Eve).

In this case, EasyChair fails the property and allows Eve to review her own paper. Note that the names of the authors and other reviewers are not known to the PC members. One possible fix for this attack is that every time an agent a invites another agent b to subreview a paper, EasyChair should check whether agent b is actually an author of that paper. We add the condition $\neg$Auth(p, a) to the permission statement exec(RequestRev(p,a,b),u). In this case Bob cannot execute RequestRev(p2,Bob,Eve).

Property 3: Users should be accountable for their actions. This property is violated in several ways, all of which involve the use of "log in as another pc member". For example, the system should not allow the chair to submit a review for a paper as another PC member without making it clear that it is actually the chair who has submitted the review and not the PC member. The following attack scenario involves Alice and Bob:

1. Alice is the chair. She executes AddReviewerAssignment(p1,Bob) to assign Bob to review the paper p1.
2. Bob submits his review using AddRev(p1,Bob,Bob).
3. Alice reads Bob's review of paper p1 by executing ShowRev(p1,Bob,Bob).
4. Alice submits a review for the paper p1 as if she is Carol who is a very famous and sought after academic by executing AddRev(p1,Carol,Carol).

EasyChair fails this property and allows the chair to read another reviewer's review for a paper and then submits a review for that paper as another PC member without being detected by the other PC members or the other chairs. This attack is possible because the system does not register the name of the user who updated the review. It will appear to others as if Carol has submitted the review herself. One possible fix for this attack is for AddRev() to have an additional parameter. Alice would then need to execute the action AddRev(p,a,b,c) where agent a is the chair acting on behalf of b who is the PCmember submitting the review written by agent c. The predicate Submitted-review() also has to be changed accordingly.

4   Conclusion and Future Work

We present a modelling language, *X-Policy*, to model the dynamic execution permissions of large web-based collaborative systems. We demonstrate the applicability of *X-Policy* to real-life web-based collaborative systems like EasyChair. Using *X-Policy*, we reason about the security properties of three security properties for EasyChair and described the possible attacks on these properties as well as ways the system could be changed to prevent these attacks. We have informed the developer of EasyChair of our findings. The full *EC* model is available at [11]. It contains 49 actions and permission statements. This is relatively concise given the size and complexity of EasyChair. The way the system functionality is split into actions is decided by our understanding of how the system is actually designed. Due to space restrictions, we detail the syntax and semantics of *X-Policy* and the traces for the discussed attacks in the long version of this paper [1]. In future work, we would like to model and analyse more systems, develop, and implement an algorithm to automate the analysis of these systems using model checking techniques.

References

1. Qunoo, H., Ryan, M.: Modelling dynamic access control policies for web-based collaborative systems - long version. Technical report, School of Computer Science, University of Birmingham, Available at the authors' webpage (April 2010)
2. Becker, M., Fournet, C., Gordon, A.: Design and semantics of a decentralized authorization language. In: 20th IEEE Computer Security Foundations Symposium, CSF 2007, pp. 3–15 (2007)
3. Becker, M.Y.: Specification and analysis of dynamic authorisation policies. IEEE Computer Security Foundations Symposium, 203–217 (2009)
4. DeTreville, J.: Binder, a logic-based security language. In: Proceedings of the 2002 IEEE Symposium on Security and Privacy (2002)
5. Gurevich, Y., Neeman, I.: DKAL: Distributed-knowledge authorization language. In: CSF 2008: Proceedings of the 2008, 21st IEEE Computer Security Foundations Symposium, Washington, DC, USA, pp. 149–162. IEEE Computer Society, Los Alamitos (2008)
6. Gurevich, Y., Neeman, I.: DKAL 2: A simplified and improved authorization language. Technical report, Microsoft Research - Cambridge (2009)
7. Li, N., Mitchell, J.C., Winsborough, W.H.: Design of a role-based trust management framework. In: Proc. IEEE Symposium on Security and Privacy, Oakland (May 2002)
8. McDermott, D., Doyle, J.: Nonmonotonic logic 1. Artificial Intelligence 13, 41–72 (1980)
9. Becker, M.Y., Sewell, P.: Cassandra: distributed access control policies with tunable expressiveness. In: 5th IEEE International Workshop on Policies for Distributed Systems and Networks, POLICY (2004)
10. Zhang, N., Ryan, M., Guelev, D.P.: Synthesising verified access control systems in XACML. In: 2004 ACM Workshop on Formal Methods in Security Engineering, Washington DC, USA, October 2004, pp. 56–65. ACM Press, New York (2004)
11. Qunoo, H., Ryan, M.: EC model in X-policy (December 2009), http://www.cs.bham.ac.uk/~hxq/X-policy/

Evaluating the Risk of Adopting RBAC Roles

Alessandro Colantonio[1,2], Roberto Di Pietro[2],
Alberto Ocello[1], and Nino Vincenzo Verde[2]

[1] Engiweb Security, Roma, Italy
{alessandro.colantonio,alberto.ocello}@eng.it
[2] Università di Roma Tre, Roma, Italy
{colanton,dipietro,nverde}@mat.uniroma3.it

Abstract. We propose a framework to evaluate the risk incurred when managing users and permissions through RBAC. The risk analysis framework does not require roles to be defined, thus making it applicable before the role engineering phase. In particular, the proposed approach highlights users and permissions that markedly deviate from others, and that might consequently be prone to error when roles are operating. By focusing on such users and permissions during the role definition process, it is possible to mitigate the risk of unauthorized accesses and role misuse.

1 Introduction

Access Control is a cornerstone of enterprise risk and security management. It represents the process of mediating requests to data and services maintained by a system, and determining whether the requests should be granted or denied [1]. Among all access control models proposed in the literature, *Role-Based Access Control* (RBAC) attracted the attention of many large-size organizations. According to this model, *roles* are created for various job functions, and permissions required to perform certain operations are assigned to specific roles. By deploying RBAC systems, companies obtain several benefits such as simplified access control administration, improved organizational productivity, and security policy enforcement. The definition of roles is one of the important issues that need to be more deeply addressed in order to increase interest toward RBAC. Role engineering [2,3] approaches can usually be classified in *top-down* and *bottom-up*. In the top-down case, a deep manual analysis is required to formulate roles that match the skills, tasks or duties of users. In the bottom-up case, also indicated with the term *role mining*, roles are automatically elicited from existing permission assignments. Several algorithms and models explicitly designed for role mining were proposed—see [4] for a brief survey on the subject. Once a role is created, its lifecycle will follow the evolution of the company: new users or new permissions can be added, old ones can be removed or replaced, users can change their job position, etc. This continuous modification of the access control system typically introduce "noise" within the data—namely, permissions exceptionally or accidentally granted or denied—, thus increasing the risk of making mistakes when managing the access control system. Moreover, it is important to create roles that administrators can easily understand and manage [5].

S. Foresti and S. Jajodia (Eds.): Data and Applications Security XXIV, LNCS 6166, pp. 303–310, 2010.
© IFIP International Federation for Information Processing 2010

In this paper, we introduce a risk analysis framework that allows to evaluate the risk incurred when managing users and permissions through RBAC. A distinguishing feature of our approach is that it can be used without having already defined roles, namely in a pre-engineering phase. By evaluating the risk level of a single user or a single permission, we make it possible to produce a ranking of users and permissions, highlighting those that most deviate from others in comparison to available user-permission relationships. Consequently, we are able to identify those users and permissions that represent the most (likely) dangerous and error prone ones from an administration point of view. Having this ranking available during the role engineering phase allows data analysts and role engineers to highlight users and permissions that are more prone to error and misuse when designed roles will be operating.

The the paper is organized as follows: In Section 2 a formal modeling of the problem is provided. Section 3 introduces our risk framework, mapping typical risk-related concepts to RBAC entities. Section 4 shows the results of a test on real data, while concluding remarks are provided in Section 5.

2   Problem Modeling

In this paper we use some concepts that were introduced in [6], where a three steps methodology to identify "stable" roles is thoroughly described. First, a weight is associated to roles; second, user-permission assignments that cannot belong to roles with a weight exceeding a given threshold are identified; and third, the role-finding problem is restricted to user-permission assignments identified in the second step. Differently from [6], this paper proposes a model that is not strictly bound with the role discovery within existing user-permission relationships, but it can be adopted in a pre-mining phase in order to evaluate the risk incurred to manage users and permissions.

Before introducing the formalism required to describe our risk evaluation model, we first review some concepts of the ANSI/INCITS RBAC standard [7] needed for the present analysis. Entities of interest are: $PERMS$, $USERS$, and $ROLES$, that is the set of all access permissions, users, and roles, respectively; $UA \subseteq USERS \times ROLES$, the set of all role-user relationships; and, $PA \subseteq PERMS \times ROLES$, the set of role-permission relationships. A RBAC $state$ is a tuple $\langle ROLES, UA, PA \rangle$, namely an instance of all the sets characterizing RBAC that is used to obtain a system configuration. We do not consider sessions, role hierarchies or separation of duties constraints in this paper, but in addition to RBAC concepts, we introduce: $UP \subseteq USERS \times PERMS$ to indicate the set of the existing user-permission assignments to analyze; $perms \colon USERS \to 2^{PERMS}$ to identify permissions assigned to a user, namely $perms(u) := \{p \in PERMS \mid \langle u, p \rangle \in UP\}$; and, $users \colon PERMS \to 2^{USERS}$ to identify users assigned with a permission, namely $users(p) := \{u \in USERS \mid \langle u, p \rangle \in UP\}$. Moreover, we define:

Definition 1 (Role Weight). *Given a role* $r \in ROLES$, *let* U_r *and* P_r *be the sets of users and permissions associated to* r, *that is* $U_r := \{u \in USERS \mid \langle u, r \rangle \in$

$UA\}$ and $P_r := \{p \in PERMS \mid \langle p, r \rangle \in PA\}$. We indicate with $w \colon ROLES \to \mathbb{N}$ the weight function of roles, defined as $w(r) := |U_r| \times |P_r|$.

Definition 2 (t-stability). Let Σ_{UP} be the set of all RBAC states that cover the user-permission assignments of UP, that is all $\langle ROLES, UA, PA \rangle \in \Sigma_{UP}$ such that $\forall \langle u, p \rangle \in UP \implies \exists r \in ROLES : \langle u, r \rangle \in UA, \langle p, r \rangle \in PA$. Given $\langle u, p \rangle \in UP$, let $\mathcal{R} \colon UP \to 2^{\left(\bigcup_{\langle ROLES, UA, PA \rangle \in \Sigma_{UP}} ROLES \right)}$ be the function that identifies the roles which could be used to manage $\langle u, p \rangle$, that is:

$$\mathcal{R}(\langle u, p \rangle) := \bigcup_{\langle ROLES, UA, PA \rangle \in \Sigma_{UP}} \{r \in ROLES \mid \langle u, r \rangle \in UA, \langle p, r \rangle \in PA\} .$$

We say that $\langle u, p \rangle$ is t-stable if it can be managed with at least one role r with weight $w(r) \geq t$, namely $\exists r \in \mathcal{R}(\langle u, p \rangle) : w(r) \geq t$.

If an assignment $\langle u, p \rangle \in UP$ is t-stable, it is also $(t - i)$-stable for each $i = 1, \ldots, t$. We are thus interested in the maximal stability of a given assignment, namely the maximum t that verifies the t-stability condition:

Definition 3 (Maximal Stability). The maximal stability of an assignment $\langle u, p \rangle \in UP$ is the maximum t such that the assignment is t-stable. It is identified by the function $t^* \colon UP \to \mathbb{N}$ such that $t^*(\langle u, p \rangle) := \max_{r \in \mathcal{R}(\langle u, p \rangle)} w(r)$.

The rational behind the introduction of the *stability* concept is that if an assignment can only be managed by roles with a limited weight, it represents an outlier. Indeed, only few users and permissions are involved in a role together with that assignment. System administrators are willing to manage roles with high weights—that is, which involve many users and many permissions—for several reasons. First, the benefits of using RBAC increase because there are fewer user-role and role-permission relationships to manage. Second, these roles represent relevant portions of the whole access control system of the company. Because of this relevance, they have a greater meaning for system administrators. Conversely, when an assignment cannot be managed with a high-weight role, it represents a portion of data which appears to be inconsistent with the remainder of that dataset. It might not be an error, but from the system administrator point of view, it is riskier than others. In other words, the risk of making mistakes when managing roles with a limited weight is higher: they are roles that are not used frequently, and are in some way obscure to administrators. We now introduce another function that will be used to evaluate the risk incurred when managing a single assignment:

Definition 4. The function $\mathcal{N} \colon UP \to 2^{UP}$ indicates the assignments of UP which can be managed together with the given assignment, namely:

$$\mathcal{N}(\langle u, p \rangle) := \{\langle u', p' \rangle \in UP \mid \langle u, p' \rangle, \langle u', p \rangle \in UP, \langle u, p \rangle \neq \langle u', p' \rangle\} .$$

The following Lemma relates $\mathcal{N}(\langle u, p \rangle)$ with the t-stability concept:

Lemma 1. Given an assignment $\omega := \langle u, p \rangle \in UP$, then $|\mathcal{N}(\omega)|$ is an upper bound for $t^*(\omega)$.

Proof. By definition, all the single assignments that could be managed in the same role together with $\langle u, p \rangle$ belongs to $\mathcal{N}(\omega)$. Hence, a role that contains more than $|\mathcal{N}(\omega)|$ assignments cannot exist, concluding the proof.   □

In [6] we proposed a practical approach to calculate $|\mathcal{N}(\omega)|$ for each $\omega \in UP$. We described two algorithms: a deterministic algorithm that is able to calculate the exact value for $|\mathcal{N}(\omega)|$ in $\mathcal{O}(|UP|^2)$ time, while a randomized algorithm offers an ε-approximated result with a computational complexity of $\mathcal{O}(k\,|UP|)$, where k is a parameter that can be arbitrarily chosen. Therefore, the joint usage of Lemma 1 and the algorithms described in [6] makes it possible to practically find an upper-bound for the maximal stability of each assignment belonging to UP. In the next section, we will show how to leverage this information to assign a risk level to a particular user or a particular permission.

3   The Risk Model

A typical risk management approach is made up of two parts: *risk analysis* (or *assessment*) and *risk control*. During risk analysis we identify potential risks and assess probabilities of negative events together with their consequences. With risk control we establish the tolerable level of risk for the organization, hence providing controls for failure prevention as well as actions to reduce the likelihood of a negative event. In a general risk management approach, aspects that need to be considered are: *vulnerabilities, threats,* and *risks.* When analyzing an access control system, possible vulnerabilities are represented by users that seem to behave differently from the majority of the users; threats are represented by errors and wrong administration actions that grant wrong permissions to users; and, risks correspond to either allowing users to execute operations that are not permitted, or to hamper their tasks by not granting required permissions.

Our target is to produce a *ranking* of users and permissions that is based on the risk of making mistakes when managing them in RBAC. By having this ranking available during a role engineering phase, it is possible to highlight users and permissions that are more prone to errors and misuse when roles are operating. At the same time, it is possible to check, and subsequently investigate the reasons why highlighted users and permissions behave as outliers. For instance, we can ask the manager of those users to confirm that the relative permissions have been granted correctly, or if there have been errors due to the omission of some internal rule. To evaluate such risks, in this paper we adopt a general risk formula that involves multiple factors with different probabilities [8], namely:

$$Risk := \sum_{i=1}^{n} P_i \times C_i \ , \tag{1}$$

where P_i denotes the probability of each risk factor i, and C_i quantifies the consequences of these risk factors.

In our model, risk factors are used to evaluate the degree of importance of users and permissions. Indeed, there could be users in charge of activities that are critical for the main business of the organization, while there could be other users with a marginal importance for the business. In the same way, there could be critical permissions, and others permissions that have marginal importance only. In general, we need to assign various degree of importance to each risk factor by taking the consequence of its execution into consideration. This process requires a thorough analysis of the organization. We assume that the impact evaluation is provided by experts.

We will use the t-stability concept to give to each user-permission assignment a probability of occurrence for each risk factor. In particular, given the assignment $\omega = \langle u, p \rangle \in UP$, we define the risk probability of ω as:

Definition 5 (Risk Probability of an Assignment). *Given an assignment* $\langle u, p \rangle \in UP$, *the risk probability of* $\langle u, p \rangle$ *is a function* ass_risk$\colon UP \to [0, 1]$ *such that:*

$$\text{ass\_risk}(\langle u, p \rangle) := 1 - \frac{t^*(\langle u, p \rangle)}{|UP|} \ .$$

The rationale behind the risk probability function is the following: The more $t^*(\langle u, p \rangle)$ is close to $|UP|$, the more the risk level of the assignment ω is close to 0. Indeed, if an assignment can be managed by a single role that covers almost all assignments in UP, the user-permission assignment reflects a permission granted to the majority of the users in the dataset. Note that we are not assuming the presence of such a role among those used in the RBAC configuration, but we are only saying that such a role can exist. This consideration allows us to use our risk model in a pre-mining phase, when roles have not yet been decided on.

According to Lemma 1, we can quickly estimate an upper bound for $t^*(\langle u, p \rangle)$, and therefore a lower bound for the risk function:

Lemma 2 (Lower-Bound for the Risk Probability of an Assignment). *Given an assignment* $\langle u, p \rangle \in UP$, *then*

$$\text{ass\_risk}(\langle u, p \rangle) \le 1 - \frac{|\mathcal{N}(\langle u, p \rangle)|}{|UP|} \ .$$

Proof. The proof immediately follows from Definition 5 and Lemma 1.   □

By leveraging the above concepts, we can evaluate the risk probability for users and permissions in the following way:

Definition 6 (Risk Probability of a User). *Given an user* $u \in USERS$, *the risk probability of* u *is a function* user_risk$\colon USERS \to [0, 1]$ *defined as:*

$$\text{user\_risk}(u) := \sqrt{\frac{\sum_{p \in perms(u)} \text{ass\_risk}^2(\langle u, p \rangle)}{|perms(u)|}} \ . \tag{2}$$

Definition 7 (Risk Probability of a Permission). *Given a permission* $p \in PERMS$, *the risk probability of* p *is a function* perm_risk$\colon PERMS \to [0, 1]$ *defined as:*

$$\text{perm\_risk}(p) := \sqrt{\frac{\sum_{u \in users(p)} \text{ass\_risk}^2(\langle u, p \rangle)}{|users(p)|}} \ . \tag{3}$$

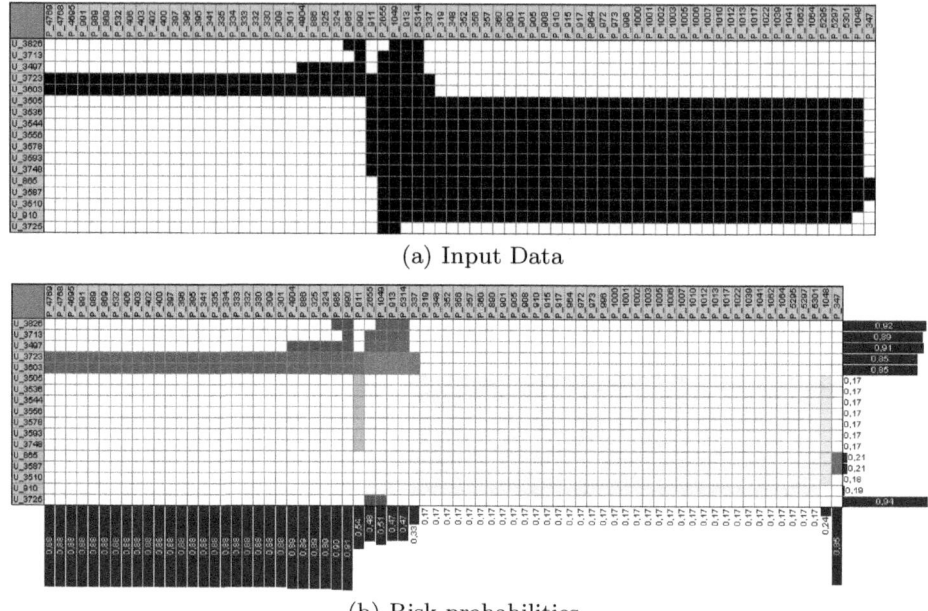

(a) Input Data

(b) Risk probabilities

Fig. 1. Risk probability of users and permissions in *UP*

By considering the root mean square instead of the arithmetic mean we give more importance to high risk values.

4   Experimental Results

We now show an application of our risk framework to a set of real data. Our case study has been carried out on a large private organization. Due to space limitation, we only report on a representative organization branch that contains 17 users and 72 permissions, counting 560 assignments.

Figure 1(a) depicts existing user-permission assignments in a matrix form, where each row represents a user, each column represents a permission, and a black cell indicates a user with a granted permission. Figure 1(b) depicts the same access control configuration, but the assignments colors indicate the corresponding risk probabilities. In particular, the cell color goes from red to white: Red means that the assignment has a high risk level when managed through RBAC; white means that it has a low risk level. Histograms on columns and rows borders respectively report the risk probability of managing permissions and users. Note that there are 6 users that are likely to be risky, mainly because they have a set of granted permissions that the majority of the other users do not have. This set is easily identifiable by looking at the permission histograms: Almost all the first half of the permissions are risky to manage. It is also possible

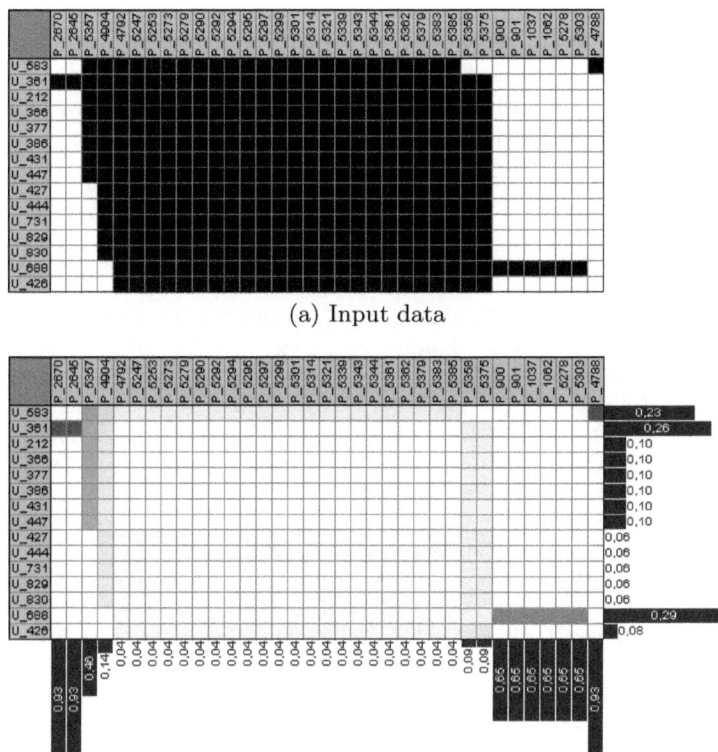

(a) Input data

(b) Risk probabilities

Fig. 2. Low risk users and permissions

to note that among the high risk users, two users have a slightly minor risk level
compared to the other four. Indeed, these two users have similar permissions
granted, and this is recognized as a kind of pattern within the data that reduces
the overall risk.

Figure 2(a) depicts another access control configuration relative to a different
branch of the same organization, while Figure 2(b) depicts the result of our risk
function applied to this branch. Here, the risk levels of all the users are lower
than 0.30. It means that, when adopting RBAC, the risk level is generally lower
than in the previous example. In other words, role administration should make
less mistakes in this second branch than in the first one.

5   Concluding Remarks

The risk management framework introduced in this paper allows role engineers
and system administrators of an RBAC system to highlight those users and
permissions that are more prone to error and misuse when roles are operating.

A distinguishing feature of our proposal, other than that of being rooted on sound theory, is that role definition is not an input parameter for the risk analysis to be performed; indeed, our model only needs to know the access control configuration of the organization, optionally enriched with other business information. Finally, it has been applied on a real case, and results obtained showed the usefulness and viability of the proposal.

References

1. De Capitani Di Vimercati, S., Foresti, S., Samarati, P., Jajodia, S.: Access control policies and languages. Int. J. Comput. Sci. Eng. 3(2), 94–102 (2007)
2. Coyne, E.J.: Role-engineering. In: Proceedings of the 1st ACM Workshop on Role-Based Access Control, RBAC 1995, pp. 15–16 (1995)
3. Coyne, E.J., Davis, J.M.: Role Engineering for Enterprise Security Management. Artech House (December 2007)
4. Molloy, I., Li, N., Li, T., Mao, Z., Wang, Q., Lobo, J.: Evaluating role mining algorithms. In: Proceedings of the 14th ACM Symposium on Access Control Models and Technologies, SACMAT 2009, pp. 95–104 (2009)
5. Colantonio, A., Di Pietro, R., Ocello, A., Verde, N.V.: A formal framework to elicit roles with business meaning in RBAC systems. In: Proceedings of the 14th ACM Symposium on Access Control Models and Technologies, SACMAT 2009, pp. 85–94 (2009)
6. Colantonio, A., Di Pietro, R., Ocello, A., Verde, N.V.: Taming role mining complexity in RBAC. Computers & Security Special Issue on Challenges for Security, Privacy & Trust (to appear, 2010)
7. American National Standards Institute (ANSI) and InterNational Committee for Information Technology Standards (INCITS): ANSI/INCITS 359-2004, Information Technology – Role Based Access Control (2004)
8. Colantonio, A., Di Pietro, R., Ocello, A., Verde, N.V.: A new role mining framework to elicit business roles and to mitigate enterprise risk. Decision Support Systems Special Issue on Enterprise Risk and Security Management: Data, Text and Web Mining (to appear, 2010)

Preserving Integrity and Confidentiality of a Directed Acyclic Graph Model of Provenance

Amril Syalim, Takashi Nishide, and Kouichi Sakurai

Department of Informatics, Kyushu University, Fukuoka, Japan
amr@itslab.csce.kyushu-u.ac.jp, {nishide,sakurai}@inf.kyushu-u.ac.jp

Abstract. This paper describes how to preserve integrity and confidentiality of a directed acyclic graph (DAG) model of provenance database. We show a method to preserve integrity by using digital signature where both of the provenance owner and the process executors (i.e. contributors) sign the nodes and the relationships between nodes in the provenance graph so that attacks to integrity can be detected by checking the signatures. To preserve confidentiality of the nodes and edges in the provenance graph we propose an access control model based on paths on the provenance graph because an auditor who need to audit a result normally need to access all nodes that have causal relationship with the result (i.e. all nodes that have a path to the result). We also complement the path-based access control with a compartment-based access control where each node is classified into compartments and the auditor is not allowed to access the nodes included in a compartment that can not be accessed by him/her (because of the sensitivity of the compartment). We implement the path-based access control by encrypting the nodes and later store encrypted encryption's keys in the children of the nodes. The compartment-based access control is implemented by encrypting the nodes in different compartments with different keys. We developed a prototype of the model and performed experiments to measure the overhead of digital signature and the double encryptions.

1 Introduction

In a system where we need to understand the processes that have been executed to produce a result we need to record provenance of the execution [1,2]. By recording provenance we may trace who have contributed to the creation of the result [3,4]. This feature is very important whenever we need to verify the process of result's creation, for example in a distributed system (i.e. a grid system), where a result may be produced by many parties in different computers [5]. Another real life example is in a hospital, a medicine prescription may be created by a doctor based on the examination result of another doctor. The result of the another doctor may be based on the examination results of the other doctors working in the same or other hospitals. Whenever there is something wrong with the prescription we need to trace who produce incorrect examinations. By using provenance of examination we can trace the process to create the prescription. To be useful,

S. Foresti and S. Jajodia (Eds.): Data and Applications Security XXIV, LNCS 6166, pp. 311–318, 2010.

312   A. Syalim, T. Nishide, and K. Sakurai

the process executors (i.e doctors) should not have ability to alter, delete or add the provenance of their examination results with intention to make errors go to other doctors. The doctors also can not deny their examination results.

For a sequential execution of processes, provenance can be represented in a form of chain [3,4]. A more expressive model that is suitable for a parallel execution is a directed graph model where nodes in the graph represent processes and the edges represent relationships between the processes (nodes) [6,7]. Because provenance is tightly associated with time, many models of provenance take the form of a directed acyclic graph (DAG) [8].

In this paper, we are focusing on securing a directed acyclic graph model of provenance in terms of integrity and confidentiality. To ensure integrity of the provenance graph (i.e. nodes and edges) we need to assure immutability and non-repudiation properties of each node and edge in the provenance graph. The contributors (i.e. the people or processes that contribute in the provenance graph) can not cheat for any purposes. The other parties in the provenance system (i.e. the manager of the provenance graph that we refer in this paper as the provenance owner), although powerful enough to manage access to provenance, also can not cheat (i.e by changing the provenance graph) without being detected. We propose a method to protect integrity of provenance by employing digital signature. Using this method, the contributors and provenance owner both sign the provenance's nodes and edges. To alter the nodes and edges without detected needs collusion from the two parties which means to repeat the process execution from beginning.

To support confidentiality of the provenance graph we need to define access control model to provenance and how to enforce the access control model. Provenance should only be accessed by the person who has the right to access, for example an auditor who need to audit the process [3,4]. The system should support restricting access to only some parts of the provenance [1]. Many access control models employ grouping mechanism to improve efficiency and security (i.e. by using groups, roles, security levels/compartments). We propose a grouping mechanism for access control to provenance by utilizing two grouping methods: grouping of entities in the provenance graph based on paths and grouping entities based on compartments. Grouping by paths is useful because the auditors who audit the process should be interested in the causal relationship in the provenance graph. However access control by paths alone is not expressive to enforce a more specific policies (i.e. an auditor only can access a part of nodes/edges in the paths). We complement the paths-based access control with a compartment-based access control so that we can enforce such policies. By using a compartment-based access control, each node is assigned with a compartment and the provenance owner grants access to the nodes in a compartment by granting access to that compartment.

2   Related Works

Hasan et al. [9,4,3] show a threat model to a chain model of provenance and the method to prevent/detect the attacks associated with the threats by using digital signature and broadcast/threshold encryption. Our method extends their method by applying the digital signature method to a directed acyclic graph model of provenance. While Hasan et. al need to sign the provenance record in the provenance chain and including checksum of previous provenance record in the chain to maintain the integrity of record and the chain structure, we need to sign the nodes in the provenance graph and including the signed checksum of the parent nodes. Hasan et. al use a broadcast and threshold encryption to support confidentiality so that they do not propose a specific access control model, while we propose a specific access control model based on paths and compartments.

Braun et.al. argue that provenance needs new security model [8]. They also propose a security model for provenance based on observation of the usage of provenance [10]. They focus on security model but do not deeply discuss how to guarantee integrity of provenance. Their main proposal is that we need to control access to edges (head and tail) and nodes (attributes). Their access control is more expressive because we can define access to the level of a head and tail of an edge. However, there is no analysis of efficiency of the model and the mechanism to implement the access control model.

3 Integrity Mechanism: Digitally Signing the Provenance Graph and Its Security Analysis

An example of provenance graph with six contributors is shown in the Figure 1. The Figure 1 shows that to produce the final result, the contributor C5 uses the outputs of contributors C1 and C2 while contributor C6 uses the output of contributors C3 and C4. Contributor C7 uses the output of C5 and C6 which later used by C8 and C9. The final process is executed by C10 that processes the outputs of C8 and C9. After each process is executed and the provenance of the process (i.e. node) is created/generated, the provenance is stored in the provenance database. The other papers [1,5,11,12,13] call the provenance database as a provenance store.

We identify three groups of active entities involved in a provenance system: provenance owners, contributors, and auditors. A provenance owner is the owner of provenance that mediates the provenance recording process and manages access to the provenance. The contributors are the people who execute process and contribute the results. Auditors are the people who need to access the provenance graph, for example for reviewing or auditing the process's execution.

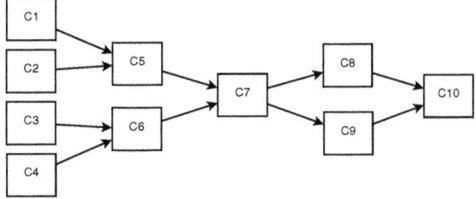

Fig. 1. Provenance graph

Provenance is recorded after each process is executed by the contributor. In a distributed system, before executing the distributed process, a worflow (i.e. a distributed execution plan) should be defined and sent to the provenance owner. The process to create a workflow may involve some or all of contributors. Based on the workflow, provenance owner sends each contributor information that is needed by the contributor to execute each process in the workflow (i.e inputs of the process). After a contributor execute a process, the contributor should produce outputs which we refer as a document. The provenance of the document is documentation of process execution to produce the document. The provenance can be automatically generated by the system where the contributor execute the process or manually created by the contributor. After execution of a process, the document and provenance of the document are sent to the provenance owner which later record them as a node in the provenance database. The provenance owner may also send the document to contributors that need the documents for their inputs.

After the provenance is recorded, there are some possible integrity problems with provenance. We identify four main problems: repudiation, alteration, deletion, and addition. A contributor may deny that she/he has contributed the document and its provenance. The document and provenance (i.e. nodes) may be altered by an attacker so that they do not reflect original process. Attacker may also delete a node or add a fake node.

The basic idea of the digital signature mechanism is whenever a provenance of a document is recorded, both of the contributor and provenance owner sign the document and the provenance before storing the provenance to the database. Whenever a contributor uses an output document of other contributor as an input, the contributor should create the hash/checksum of the input and store them as a provenance of the process executed by the contributor.

We assume that each contributor, auditor and provenance owner has a pair of public key and private key and each party can retrieve the public keys of the other parties securely. The private keys can only be accessed by the owner of the key. Let D_n is the document created by a contributor identified by n and P_n is a provenance of the document. The function $H(D_n)$ is a function that produce hash value of D_n. The function S_n is a signing function where $S_n(D_n)$ is a function that produce digital signature of contributor n to document D_n.

If a contributor n needs to use a document (i.e. D_{n-1}) produced by another contributor (i.e. contributor $n-1$) as input, before the contributor n executes the process, the provenance owner sends the input that has been signed by the provenance owner and the another contributor: $S_o(S_{n-1}(D_{n-1}))$. After verifying the document and the signatures, the contributor n execute the process. The contributor n signs the result D_n, its provenance P_n and hash of the input $H(D_{n-1})$. The signed result, its provenance and hash of the input is $S_n(P_n, D_n, H(D_{n-1}))$. The contributor sends them to the provenance owner. The provenance owner signs them and store them in the database.

This scheme supports integrity by preventing contributor deny a node after committing the node and detecting other attacks: alteration, deletion, and addition. A contributor cannot deny a node after committing the node because if the contributor deny a node means that the signature has been forged which is very unlikely. As for alteration, the possibilities are as follow:

1. A contributor alters the content of the nodes (i.e. documents or provenances) and create a new signature. The attack is not possible because the contributor cannot create a new signature of the provenance owner.
2. A provenance owner alters the content of the nodes and create the new signature. The attack is not possible because the provenance owner can not create a new signature for the contributor.
3. The other people accessing the system alter the nodes. The attack is not possible because they can not create the signatures of contributors and provenance owners.
4. The provenance owner and a contributor collude to alter a node, they still need to collude with all successors of the node because the children of the node include the hash of the parent's documents in their provenance. Colluding with all children mean repeating the process from the beginning.

As for addition, the possibilities are as follow:

1. If the provenance owner adds a new node, the provenance owner cannot create the contributor's signature of the new node.
2. If a contributor inserts a node between a parent and its children and change the references in the nodes so that the new node become the children of the parent and the previous children become the children of the new node, she cannot create the signature of the previous children so that the previous children are still refer to the original parent as their parent. The contributor also can not forge the signature of the provenance owner.

For deletion, the possibilities are as follow:

1. If a contributor or provenance owner deletes a node and want to change the relationship so that the children of the node become the children of any other nodes. They cannot change the signature consistently without colluding with all contributors of successors of the node.
2. The other people deletes the nodes. The attack is not possible because they can not create the signatures of contributors and provenance owners.

4 Confidentiality Mechanism: Path-Based Access Control and Encrypting the Provenance Graph

To protect confidentiality of provenance we need to prevent confidential provenance information be accessed by unauthorized people accessing the system. However, the system should also support authorized access to provenance (i.e. authorized auditors who need to access provenance to do audit and verify the process of object creation). We propose an access control model based on path on the provenance graph. The arguments of our proposal is that an auditor normally needs to access all nodes that have a path to the result because the nodes have causal relationship to the result. We believe that this model is more efficient and comfortable because the provenance owner can easily create access based on paths in the provenance graph.

However, by using path-based only access control, we can not create a more expressive policy (for example an auditor can only access a part of the paths). We combine path-based policy with another access policy based on compartments. Compartments define separation between nodes in different security level/classes and the auditors that can access those compartments.

We propose to implement the access control model by using cryptographic mechanisms (i.e. encryption). This method is especially important if we store the provenance in an untrusted server (i.e. the provenance owner wants to outsource the storage of provenance to a third party who may be not trusted). This method can also be used if the provenance owner wants to implement cryptographic-based access control (where the data is encrypted and access rights are granted by giving the encryption keys). The idea of our implementation for path-based access control is to encrypt the nodes and store the encryption keys in the children of the nodes. Below of the detail of the encryption process (see Figure 2).

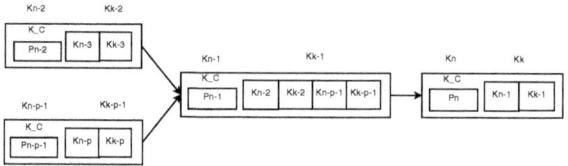

Fig. 2. Encrypting the Provenance Graph

Let P_n is the node that has been signed by the contributor n and the provenance owner o and let $E_k(P_n)$ is an encryption function that encrypt P_n with private key k. To encrypt the node P_n, the provenance owner define compartment of the node and find the parent nodes. The provenance owner retrieves the key associated with the compartment K_C, the keys to encrypt the parent nodes K_{n-1} and the key to encrypt the grandparent node K_{k-1}. The provenance owner generates two random keys: node's key K_n and parent-key's key K_k and store the keys in a key database managed by the provenance owner. The provenance owner encrypts the node P_n with key K_C. Then the provenance owner re-encrypts the node with the key K_n. After that the provenance owner encrypts the keys K_{n-1} and K_{k-1} with parent-key K_k. Encrypted form of the node is $E_{K_n}(E_{K_C}(P_n))|E_{K_k}(K_{n-1}|K_{k-1})$. The provenance owner stores encrypted form of the node in the provenance database.

The provenance owner may combine both path-based access and compartment access policy or only use a path-based access policy. To create a policy, the provenance owner first define the compartment of each provenance and encrypt the provenance with key K_C for that compartment. The provenance owner assigns which compartment that can be accessed by an auditor by giving the K_C to the auditor.

The provenance owner can define the policy of access of the auditor to the nodes based on the document that should be audited by the auditor. There are two keys in each node: K_n for encrypting provenance in the node and K_k is the key for encrypting the parent nodes (i.e. the nodes that have paths to the current node). By providing/not providing the keys K_n and K_k, there are four possible access policies of an auditor to a node:

1. The auditor cannot access any component of the node (provenance and the parent nodes). In this case the auditor is not provided any keys.
2. The auditor can access the node but not the parent node. In this case the auditor should be provided the key K_n.
3. The auditor cannot access the the node but can access the parent nodes. In this case the auditor should be provided with the key K_k.
4. The auditor can access the node and also the parent nodes. In this case the auditor should be provided both of the key K_n and K_k.

5 Experimental Results

We implemented the digital signature and encryption scheme and did two experiments to measure the overhead of the digital signature and encryption mechanisms. In the first experiment, we stored the provenance without first signing and encrypting the provenance. In the second experiment, we stored the identical provenance and used the digital signature and encryption scheme to sign and encrypt the provenance.

We performed experiments for workflows that produce provenance with the number of nodes 8, 16, 32, 64 and 128. The size of documents and provenance of the documents were between 100KB to 150KB. We measured the time to sign, encrypt, and store documents and provenance (the time to execute the process to produce the documents was not measured). The program was implemented with Java version 1.6 and used DSA for digital signature and AES for encryption. In the experiments, we executed the program on a Linux machine (Linux version 2.6.31) with Intel Core 2 Duo 2.00GHz processor and main memory 2GB. The documents and provenance were stored in a Postgresql database (version 8.4) run on another machine (a Linux version 2.6.31 with Pentium Dual-Core 2.50GHz

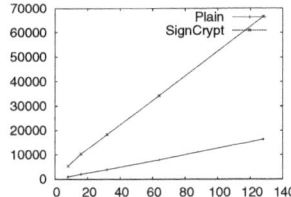

Fig. 3. Execution time (ms)

processor and main memory 2GB) connected by a Wireless Local Area Network (speed 54Mbps). For each experiment and the number of nodes we executed and measured the execution times three times.

The Figure 3 shows the experimental results. The X axis is the number of nodes, the Y axis is the times to store the provenance (in milliseconds). From the table we can find that the overhead to sign and encrypt provenance is about 5 times in compare to store provenance without signing and encrypting. This overhead shows that to sign and encrypt provenance graph takes time much higher than the process to store plain provenance graph to the database.

References

1. Groth, P., Jiang, S., Miles, S., Munroe, S., Tan, V., Tsasakou, S., Moreau, L.: An architecture for provenance systems. Technical report, University of Southampton (November 2006)
2. Buneman, P., Khanna, S., Tan, W.C.: Why and where: A characterization of data provenance. In: Van den Bussche, J., Vianu, V. (eds.) ICDT 2001. LNCS, vol. 1973, pp. 316–330. Springer, Heidelberg (2000)
3. Hasan, R., Sion, R., Winslett, M.: Preventing history forgery with secure provenance. ACM Transactions on Storage 5(4), 12:1–12:43 (2009)
4. Hasan, R., Sion, R., Winslett, M.: The case of the fake picasso: Preventing history forgery with secure provenance. In: Degano, P., Guttman, J., Martinelli, F. (eds.) FAST 2008. LNCS, vol. 5491, pp. 1–14. Springer, Heidelberg (2009)
5. Groth, P., Luck, M., Moreau, L.: A protocol for recording provenance in service-oriented grids. In: Higashino, T. (ed.) OPODIS 2004. LNCS, vol. 3544, pp. 124–139. Springer, Heidelberg (2005)
6. Moreau, L., Freire, J., Futrelle, J., McGrath, R.E., Myers, J., Paulson, P.: The open provenance model: An overview. In: Freire, J., Koop, D., Moreau, L. (eds.) IPAW 2008. LNCS, vol. 5272, pp. 323–326. Springer, Heidelberg (2008)
7. Bowers, S., McPhillips, T., Ludäscher, B., Cohen, S., Davidson, S.B.: A model for user-oriented data provenance in pipelined scientific workflows. In: Moreau, L., Foster, I. (eds.) IPAW 2006. LNCS, vol. 4145, pp. 133–147. Springer, Heidelberg (2006)
8. Braun, U., Shinnar, A., Seltzer, M.I.: Securing provenance. In: HotSec (2008)
9. Hasan, R., Sion, R., Winslett, M.: Introducing secure provenance: problems and challenges. In: StorageSS, pp. 13–18 (2007)
10. Braun, U., Shinnar, A.: A security model for provenance. Technical report, Harvard University (2006)
11. Paul Groth, S.M., Moreau, L.: Preserv: Provenance recording for services. In: UK e-Science All Hands Meeting 2005 (September 2005)
12. Altintas, I., Barney, O., Jaeger-Frank, E.: Provenance collection support in the kepler scientific workflow system. In: Moreau, L., Foster, I. (eds.) IPAW 2006. LNCS, vol. 4145, pp. 118–132. Springer, Heidelberg (2006)
13. Chapman, A., Jagadish, H.V., Ramanan, P.: Efficient provenance storage. In: SIGMOD Conference, pp. 993–1006 (2008)

When ABE Meets RSS

Yu Chen[1,*], Hyun Sung Kim[2], Jianbin Hu[1], and Zhong Chen[1]

[1] School of Electronics Engineering and Computer Science, Peking University, China
Key Laboratory of High Confidence Software Technologies, Ministry of Education
{chenyu,hujb,chen}@infosec.pku.edu.cn
[2] Department of Computer Engineering, Kyungil University, Kyungbuk, Korea
kim@kiu.ac.kr

Abstract. RSS (Really Simple Syndication) has been introduced as a response to the need of efficient information distribution and subscription. However, the current RSS standard does not provide privacy preservation and confidentiality protection. Independently, the emergence of ABE (Attribute-based Encryption) provides us a brand new cryptographic primitive for access control. This paper sets out to examine an unexplored area to date - how to apply ABE to RSS.

1 Introduction

As a widely used technique for information dissemination, RSS has been around for more than a decade. Starting from 1997 until 2007, RSS was keeping on popping with new versions. However, revisions are made to add some new features and make it backward-compatible, not for providing security mechanisms.

Most researches about RSS only focus on its applications. Cold [1] suggested that RSS can be used to enhance the efficiency of student research. Glotzbach *et al.* [2] discussed how to apply RSS to online education area. The security of RSS is neglected except in [3], Gregorio used Greasemonkey (a Mozilla Firefox extension) to encrypt and decrypt RSS feeds symmetrically. However, Gregorio's approach has many limitations and only works with Mozilla Firefox browser.

RSS works well when the feeds contents are public, but fails when the contents are only intended to a particular set of subscribers. The reason is that RSS lacks of basic security mechanism. Orthogonal to the development of RSS, ABE [4] [5] [6] is a fast emerging research area in cryptography. Messages are encrypted using a set of attributes describing the intended receivers. Only the principals processing appropriate attributes can recover the ciphertext. ABE allows encryption to inextricably bind expressive and enforceable access policy to data. It has enormous potentials for providing data security in distributed environment. Recently, Baden *et al.* [7] combined ABE and traditional public key cryptography to provide the functionality of existing online social networks with additional privacy benefits. RSS system may also be an example of such beneficiary. So given the emergence of ABE as a serious contender to access control

---

* This author is supported by China Scholarship Council (CSC).

S. Foresti and S. Jajodia (Eds.): Data and Applications Security XXIV, LNCS 6166, pp. 319–326, 2010.

mechanism based on conventional cryptographic techniques, it is important and timely to examine the suitability of ABE for securing RSS.

Our Contribution. First, we investigate the overlooked security issues of RSS. Then we explain the necessities of introducing security mechanism into RSS and outline the security targets RSS should achieve. After comparing with symmetric cryptography, public key cryptography and identity-based broadcast encryption, we conclude that ABE matches RSS best. We propose ABE-RSS, which can be viewed as an security enhanced version of RSS. By integrating ABE into RSS, ABE-RSS provides an excellent privacy preservation and confidentiality protection for RSS.

2 RSS and Its Security Issues

2.1 RSS Overview

RSS feed is an XML-based document which allows online information sources to be published once and viewed by many programs. An RSS feed includes full or summarized text, plus metadata such as publishing dates and authorship.

RSS reader is a program that helps users to view and manage their feeds. The RSS reader checks the user's subscribed feeds regularly for new items, fetches the updates it finds, and interprets the RSS feeds into human readable format. RSS reader can be browser-based (Google Reader) or desktop-based (FeedDemon).

RSS model consists of four entities: publisher, RSS server, RSS reader and subscriber. Generally speaking, publisher posts news on RSS server. RSS server automatically generate the RSS feeds of the news subsequently. Subscriber registers his interesting RSS feeds in RSS reader, RSS reader gathers the RSS feeds and shows them to subscriber.

2.2 Security and Privacy

RSS standard only focuses on the feed format. It provides no security mechanism itself, everyone can fetch and read it. When a publisher wants to publish some information via RSS feed only intended to particular set of subscribers, RSS fails to meet this demand. We describe the following two scenarios to illustrate why security and privacy are important for RSS.

Paid Resources. From [1] [2] we learn that many education institutions are trying to enhance the online education with RSS technique. By the advantages of RSS, the online education systems work well when the education resources are free to everyone, but when the online education charge, the RSS feeds shouldn't be readable to those who haven't paid for them. There are also many other examples. Now AppleMusic and YahooMusic provide RSS feeds containing the latest popular music on their sites. However, if the music needs to be paid in the future, the music can not be published via raw RSS feeds anymore.

Personal Blog. One of the most common usage of RSS is blog subscription. Blog is a widely used service through Internet. Many people treat blog as a platform to publish personal photos and diaries. As soon as a user submits a new post, blog service provider will generate and publish the corresponding RSS feed for it. This facilitates people viewing blogs by subscribing the corresponding RSS feeds. But when a blog entry is not public to everyone, for private concern, the blog service providers simply choose not to generate the corresponding RSS feed. However, this naive approach impedes the real intended readers from viewing the blogs by RSS feeds.

The above use cases show that for the lack of privacy and confidentiality protection, the current RSS standard is not appropriate for disseminating personal or confidential information. Users have to rely on the host trusted sites to protect their information security. Although the use of trusted sites allow for a relatively straightforward solution, there are some downsides to the approach:

1. User is unable to define his own access control policy on data but has to rely upon the less flexible mechanisms provided by the site. For instance, Alice writes a diary on facebook only intended to her female friend. If facebook does not support such kind of policy, Alice will fail to realize her desirable access control over the diary.

2. Different sites have different security mechanisms, which hinders users from obtaining information conveniently. e.g. Sarah is Alice's female friend, but she cannot read Alice's diary until she has registered as a legitimate user of facebook and passed the identity authentication. This will bring back the terrible user experiences.

3. Both the host sites must be trusted and remain secure. With the increasing number of attacks and intrusions, maintaining the security of any particular host is becoming increasingly difficult.

In order to meet the privacy and security demands as well as maintaining the convenience and openness of RSS, we expect RSS admits:

1. RSS feeds are still available to everyone, but only the subscribers with appropriate rights can read it.

2. Publishers can determine the intended readers by exerting describable and expressive access control policies over RSS feeds.

3. The contents of RSS feeds are transparent to the RSS server, which means RSS server just serves as a storage service provider.

4. Subscribers can delegate their rights further to RSS readers, thus enables RSS readers to aggregate the RSS feeds in a secure and automatic manner.

3 ABE and Its Properties

3.1 ABE Overview

After Sahai and Waters [4] introduced the concept of ABE, Goyal *et al.* [6] proposed key-policy ABE in which ciphertext is associated with a set of attributes and a user's private key can be associated with any monotonic tree-access structure over attributes. Subsequently, Bethencourt *et al.* [5] proposed ciphertext-policy ABE in which user's private keys are specified by a set of attributes and a principal encrypting data can specify a policy over these attributes indicating which users are able to decrypt.

3.2 Properties of ABE

We now identify the properties of ABE that distinguish it from traditional cryptographic techniques as follows.

1. Provide a natural mapping for target broadcast encryption.

2. Enable user to define any semantic access control policy over data.

3. Public keys are computable from self-describing attributes.

4. Allow user to further delegate his rights by issuing delegation private key.

It is clear that ABE happens to have the exact attractive properties which naturally meet the security demands of RSS.

4   Secure RSS with ABE

In this section, we propose ABE-RSS, in which ABE is used to secure RSS. Before presenting the concrete scheme, we first state that why ABE matches RSS best.

1. Why not symmetric cryptography?
   - The complexity of key management grows rapidly when the number of the subscribers increases.
   - When the number of the intended receivers is n, publisher has to encrypt one RSS feed n times.
   - It is impossible to exert any semantic access control policy over RSS feed.

2. Why not traditional public-key cryptography?
   - It requires the underlying PKI (Public Key Infrastructure) to be available.
   - Same as symmetric approach, publisher has to separately encrypt one RSS feed for every intended subscriber. Besides, public keys have to be authenticated before use.

3. Why not identity-based broadcast encryption [8] [9]?
   - The efficiency of identity-based broadcast encryption is dependent on the size of the authorized user set and the total number of users in the system.
   - Publisher must know the identities of all the intended subscribers each time a new RSS feed needs to be encrypted, which is inefficient and less flexible.

While using ABE, publisher only needs to describe the intended subscribers in terms of descriptive attributes and encrypt the RSS feed once. Additionally, ABE allows further delegation of private keys, which is useful in real use. We conclude that ABE is more efficient, flexible and suitable than other cryptographic techniques for RSS.

The choice of concrete ABE algorithm. There are two types of ABE algorithm, key-policy ABE [6] and ciphertext-policy ABE [5]. In key-policy ABE, user exerts no control over who can access to the ciphertext. If he wants to change the access control policy over the ciphertext in the future, he has to re-issue the private keys. The drawback is that private key generation and distribution are always time consuming and complex. In ciphertext-policy ABE, user's private key is associated with a set of attributes, ciphertext is associated with some access structure. When user wants to modify access control policy over the ciphertext, he just needs to re-encrypt the data using new access control policy without the need of re-issuing private keys. So we choose ciphertext-policy ABE as the underlying cryptographic primitive in order to ease the private key management and enable publisher to exert the access control policy over the RSS feeds. The following part of this section presents ABE-RSS, in which ciphertext-policy ABE is used to secure for RSS. We remark that ABE can also be used to enhance the security for Atom [10] in the same way, which is another syndication standard.

ABE-RSS. Figure 1 depicts the ABE-RSS model. In ABE-RSS, publisher enforces access control policy on RSS feed by encrypting it with ABE. We refer to the encrypted RSS feed as ABE-RSS feed, which has the same open nature as RSS feed, i.e. available to everyone by making a HTTP request. Note that in ABE-RSS model, RSS server only serves as a storage service provider. The contents of the feeds are totally transparent to the RSS server. We give a list of related notations in Table 1, then describe the main operations in ABE-RSS.

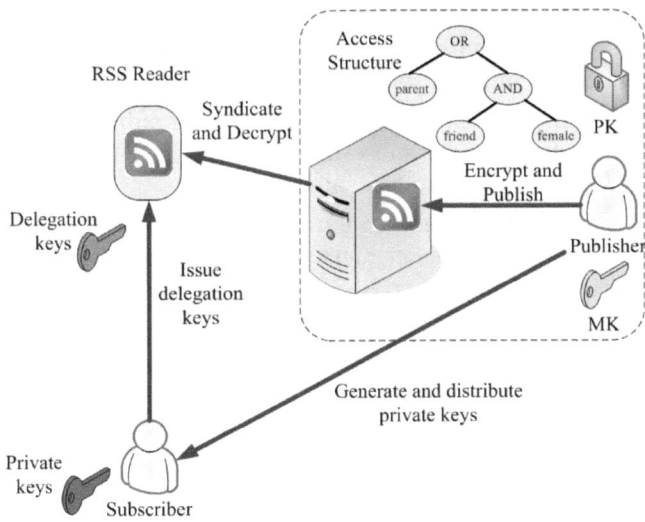

Fig. 1. ABE-RSS model

Table 1. Notation used in this paper

Term	Definition
PK	System public parameters
SK	Master secret
ASK	ABE user's private key
DSK	Delegation private key
$u.key$	Key created by u
$\mathbb{A}$	Access structure
ABESetup	Generate the public parameters PK and a master secret SK
ABEKeyGen(SK, R)	Generate private key ASK associated with attributes set R
ABEEncrypt$(PK, \mathbb{A}, M)$	Encrypt message M with public parameters PK and access structure $\mathbb{A}$
ABEDecrypt(PK, ASK, C)	Decrypt ciphertext C with public parameters PK and private key SK
ABEDelegate$(ASK, \widetilde{R})$	Further generate a delegation private key DSK of $\widetilde{R}$ taking ASK as the master secret, where $\widetilde{R} \subseteq R$
Publisher	The entity who publish new items in RSS format
Subscriber	The entity who subscribe RSS feeds
RSS Reader	The software syndicate and interpret RSS feed for subscribers
Key Authority	The trusted authority who set up the ABE system and act as Private Key Generator

DefineAttributes. Publisher acts as a key authority, invokes algorithm ABESetup and defines a set of attributes as $\{P_1, \ldots, P_n\}$. The resulting PK is public to everyone, while SK is only known to the publisher.

AssignAttributes. In order to entitle a subscriber, the publisher first assigns a set of attributes R to describe the subscriber, then runs ABEKeyGen to generate a private key of R and sends it to the subscriber.

Encrypt. Publisher run ABEEncrypt taking PK and $\mathbb{A}$ as inputs, encrypt <item> element into <EncryptedData> element. The encrypted data implicitly contains the access structure $\mathbb{A}$. Note that RSS feed is XML-based, we can perform encryption and decryption according to XML-Encryption specifications [11].

Delegate. ABEDelegate provides subscribers a refined manner to protect their private keys and achieve a faster decryption. Each subscriber acts as a local key authority and issues a delegation key DSK to his RSS reader using his private key ASK serving as the master key. Then the RSS reader can use DSK to decrypt ciphertext but unable to deduce subscriber's ASK from DSK. Note that $\widetilde{R}$ is a subset of R, so DSK is always shorter than ASK, which means that RSS reader decrypting the ABE-RSS feeds using DSK is faster than the subscriber himself decrypting the ABE-RSS feeds using ASK.

Decrypt. On fetching an ABE-RSS feed, RSS reader runs the ABEDecrypt which takes the public parameter PK and the delegation private key DSK of $\widetilde{R}$ as inputs to decrypt the <EncryptedData> element. RSS reader will be able to recover the <item> element if and only if $\widetilde{R}$ satisfies the access structure $\mathbb{A}$.

Hybrid Encryption. Compared to symmetric encryption, ABE is less efficient. As the size of RSS feed increases, it is wise to adopting hybrid encryption. Concretely, first use a symmetric key to encrypt the <item> element, then use ABE to encrypt the symmetric key. The encrypted element and the encrypted symmetric key are include in the <EncryptedData> as child elements.

5 Performance

The performance of ABE-RSS is evaluated on a desktop computer running GNU/Linux with Intel(R) Pentium(R) 4 CPU 3.00GHz and 1GB RAM. Hybrid encryption technique is adopted: using AES to encrypt the RSS feeds and using ciphertext-based ABE [5] to encapsulate the symmetric key. We use cpabe [12] library and their dependencies (pbc, gmp, glib, openssl) to implement ciphertext-policy ABE and AES.

ABESetup takes approximately 0.14 seconds. ABEKeyGen times average 0.16 seconds with one attribute and 0.06 seconds for each additional attributes. We assume that five attributes is enough to describe most access-control policy. Table 2 shows the times of encrypt/decrypt a 256 bits AES key when the number of attributes is from one to five. The value is the average time of 50 different experiments. The speed of AES-256 is around 0.03 millisecond for 1KB data. According to the results of Internet measurement, more than 80% of the RSS feeds are relatively small at less than 10KB. So the encryption and decryption times of AES-256 are negligible. Besides, thanks to the hybrid encryption technique, the ABE-RSS feed size is almost the same as the original size. The experiment results show that ABE-RSS scheme is feasible and efficient in practice.

Table 2. Desktop Performance

Number of attributes	1	2	3	4	5
ABEEncrypt	0.17s	0.21s	0.28s	0.34s	0.43s
ABEDecrypt	0.09s	0.12s	0.15s	0.18s	0.20s

6 Further Discussion

ABE-RSS focuses on the confidential and privacy issues of RSS, while neglects the validation issue. Next, we further discuss two unexplored problems.

Fake RSS feeds. Due to the open nature of RSS, attackers can easily generate fake RSS feeds. Even in ABE-RSS, attackers can still generate fake ABE-RSS feeds because the public key is available to everyone. So it is necessary for feeds subscriber to validate that RSS feeds really come from the right RSS publishers.

Malicious RSS feeds. Attackers may inject malicious scripts into RSS feeds, such as XSS (Cross-site script) [13]. RSS Reader should filter out the malicious scripts before interpretive execution.

A approach to eliminate the fake or malicious RSS feeds is applying digital signature to the RSS. Publisher signs the RSS feeds with his private key before publish them. Equivalently, on fetching new RSS feeds, the RSS readers first verify the contained signatures using the publisher's public key. If the verification passes, parse the feed, else reject the feed. In this way, RSS subscribers can make sure that the RSS feeds come from the trusted and real information source.

7   Conclusions

RSS brings unexperienced convenience and efficiency for information distribution, but it does not have any security mechanism. We propose ABE-RSS, an security enhanced version of RSS, in which ABE is used to secure RSS feeds. Experimental results demonstrate that ABE-RSS is efficient and feasible.

The study about ABE and RSS technique are still on the way, further research will unearth other potential advantages of attribute-based techniques and identify the associated practical and implementation issues.

References

1. Cold, S.J.: Using really simple syndication (rss) to enhance student research. SIGITE Newsl. 3, 6–9 (2006)
2. Glotzbach, R.J., Mohler, J.L., Radwan, J.E.: Rss as a course information delivery method. In: ACM SIGGRAPH 2007 educators program, pp. 16–21 (2007)
3. Gregorio, J.: Secure rss syndication (2005),
   http://www.xml.com/pub/a/2005/07/13/secure-rss.html
4. Sahai, A., Waters, B.: Fuzzy identity based encryption. In: Cachin, C., Camenisch, J.L. (eds.) EUROCRYPT 2004. LNCS, vol. 3027, pp. 457–473. Springer, Heidelberg (2004)
5. Bethencourt, J., Sahai, A., Waters, B.: Ciphertext-policy attribute-based encryption. In: IEEE Security and Privacy, pp. 321–334 (2007)
6. Goyal, V., Pandey, O., Sahai, A., Waters, B.: Attribute-based encryption for fine-grained access control of encrypted data. In: ACM CCS 2006, pp. 89–98 (2006)
7. Baden, R., Bender, A., Spring, N., Bhattacharjee, B., Starin, D.: Persona: an online social network with user-defined privacy. In: ACM SIGCOMM 2009 conference on Data communication, pp. 135–146 (2009)
8. Halevy, D., Shamir, A.: The lsd broadcast encryption scheme. In: Yung, M. (ed.) CRYPTO 2002. LNCS, vol. 2442, pp. 47–60. Springer, Heidelberg (2002)
9. Boneh, D., Gentry, C., Waters, B.: Collusion resistant broadcast encryption with short ciphertexts and private keys. In: Shoup, V. (ed.) CRYPTO 2005. LNCS, vol. 3621, pp. 258–275. Springer, Heidelberg (2005)
10. IETF: The atom publishing protocol,
    http://www.atomenabled.org/developers/protocol/atom-protocol-spec.php
11. Imamura, T., Dillaway, B., Simon, E.: XML Encryption Syntax and Processing (December 2002), http://www.w3.org/TR/xmlenc-core/
12. Advanced crypto software collection, http://acsc.csl.sri.com/cpabe
13. Grossman, J.: The origins of cross-site scripting, xss (2008)

PriMan: A Privacy-Preserving Identity Framework

Kristof Verslype[1], Pieter Verhaeghe[1], Jorn Lapon[2],
Vincent Naessens[2], and Bart De Decker[1]

[1] Katholieke Universiteit Leuven, Department of Computer Science,
Celestijnenlaan 200A, 3001 Heverlee, Belgium
`firstname.lastname@cs.kuleuven.be`
[2] Katholieke Hogeschool Sint-Lieven, Department of Industrial Engineering
Gebroeders Desmetstraat 1, 9000 Gent, Belgium
`firstname.lastname@kahosl.be`

Abstract. *PriMan* is presented; privacy-preserving user-centric identity management middleware which defines and groups the required functionality. It offers the
application developer a uniform technology-agnostic interface to use and combine different types of privacy enhancing technologies. Moreover, the *PriMan*
framework defines all the components and their functionality required to raise
the development of privacy enhanced client-server applications to a higher level.

1 Introduction

The digitalization of our society comes with a lot of benefits. However, privacy of the
user is increasingly at stake. The awareness of both citizens and companies is rising. In
fact, both can benefit from a higher level of privacy in applications.

Therefore, techniques are being developed to improve the user's anonymity; crowds
and mix networks at network level, and anonymous credentials w.r.t. personal user properties. The latter enable to prove only the required properties, e.g. that you are older than
18 if one of the credential attributes is your date of birth.

The privacy enhancing technologies (PETs) are heterogeneous in approach; e.g.,
pseudonym certificates are sent to the verifier, while Idemix credentials only send proofs.
Hence, it will cost the application developer much effort to develop a privacy-friendly
application, especially when multiple credential types must be supported. Also, chances
are that the privacy issues will be omitted or that the privacy is inadequately protected
due to incorrect use of PETs. Moreover, even in privacy-friendly applications, the user
remains in the dark about to whom and under which pseudonym personal properties have
been disclosed or, in short, about his degree of anonymity towards others.

Therefore, *PriMan*, a privacy-preserving user-centric identity middleware framework is designed and implemented. It facilitates the development of privacy-enhanced
applications. The different credential approaches are reconciled, resulting in a uniform
interface enabling the application developer to choose the most appropriate technology
and to easily switch to another one when e.g. the requirements change.

Three privacy-preserving applications in three different domains have been built on
top of this framework; an ePoll (eGoverment), an eTicketing (eCommerce) and an ePrescription (eHealth) application. The design of the presented framework has been reiter-
ated several times driven by the feedback received from the application developers.

S. Foresti and S. Jajodia (Eds.): Data and Applications Security XXIV, LNCS 6166, pp. 327–334, 2010.

The next section briefly sums up the relevant privacy preserving technologies supported by the framework. The requirements derived from the applications are presented in section 3. The general architecture, the generic credential representation and the validation are given in section 4, 5 and 6. Related work is discussed in section section 7 and the conclusions are given in section 8.

2 Building Blocks

The supported building blocks and the main credential systems are touched.

Mix networks (e.g. [1]) and **crowds** (e.g. [2]) guarantee anonymity at network level. A **commitment** scheme [3,4] allows an entity to commit to a set of values, while keeping these secret. The commitment hides the values towards the verifier, but allows the creator to prove properties of the committed values. A **verifiable encryption** scheme (e.g., [5]) also allows the creator to prove properties about the encrypted values, while the verifier is ensured that a known TTP will be able to decrypt the ciphertext if necessary. A **Pseudonym** is an identifier presumably unlinkable to a real identity.

An **X.509 certificate** is a set of personal attributes and other related properties signed by a certifier using a standard signing algorithm. The certificate owner needs the corresponding private key to prove ownership of it. Presenting it to others implies disclosing all the content in the certificate. X.509 certificates are revoked by adding their serial numbers on a revocation list. **Pseudonym certificates** [6] are standard certificates in which the identity information is replaced with a pseudonym. Different shows of the same certificate are linkable, potentialy undermining anonymity. The privacy can further be increased by substituting hashes or MACs for the actual attribute values. This way the certificate owner can decide which attributes to disclose. An **anonymous credential** [7,8] allows for selective disclosure of properties of credential attributes, while hiding the others. The credential itself with its values is not revealed, but instead, a zero-knowledge proof of knowledge that the disclosed properties were certified by the issuer. Usages of anonymous credentials can either be linkable (e.g. UProve) or unlinkable (e.g. Idemix). It is possible to prove membership of a set without revealing anything else. The disclosed properties can also involve attributes in other credentials, in verifiable encryptions and in commitments. Idemix credentials can be shown under a pseudonym to which the credential is not bound. The issuer of an Idemix credential can set a global limit on the number of times the credential can be used. Finally, a credential usage can optionally be deanonymized afterwards by a trusted party in case of abuse.

3 Requirements

The framework specific requirements are formulated (Fx) and are followed by the framework tasks derived from the applications (Tx). T1-T3 are indispensable. T4-T6 are needed to build a full-fledged privacy-preserving identity framework.

F1. User-centricity. The user controls the disclosure of his personal data.

F2. Usability. A technology agnostic, intuitive interface facilitates the development of privacy preserving applications and plugging in new implementations (e.g. UProve credentials) must be easy.

F3. Modularity. By loading only the required modules and implementations, *PriMan* can be run on portable devices; e.g. on a doctor's portable device to issue prescriptions on location in the ePrescription application.

F4. Protection of (highly) confidential information. Confidential data can be secret keys, but also personal data, since it can reduce users' anonymity.

T1. Setting up connections with various properties. An SSL connection might suffice for e.g. registration. However, a mix network might be a better choice to protect the user's anonymity for e.g. anonymous poll signing.

T2. Creation and usage of credentials. In all three applications, credentials of different types are issued and used. Proving properties during a credential show often requires commitments and verifiable encryptions.

T3. Secure storage of credentials & credential related data. Users often have many credentials, which must be stored and managed securely. Some credentials should always and everywhere be available and, hence, must be stored on a smartcard or on a remote server (e.g. ticketing).

[T4.] Anonymity set estimation. The user discloses mandatory properties in the ePoll and eTicketing plus potentially optional ones. The framework must estimate the consequences of these disclosures on the user's anonymity and give advice.

[T5.] Profile tracking. In the eTicketing application, multiple purchases by a user of tickets for the same event need to be linkable in order to be able to restrict the maximum number of tickets per customer. If the user discloses different properties when buying tickets at different occasions, his anonymity may decrease. Therefore, the framework has to securely and locally keep track of the properties disclosed under pseudonyms to other parties.

[T6.] Dispute solving. In the ePrescription and eTicketing application, abuse is possible. Hence, support for deanonymization must be provided.

4   General Architecture

The above-formulated requirements led to the *PriMan* architecture of which a high level overview is presented in figure 1. *PriMan* consists of abstract handler interfaces and concrete managers. A handler interface provides a uniform interface to a class of technologies such as credentials, connections or storage. A handler is in general a wrapper around an existing implementation of a technology (e.g. Idemix). A provider contains concrete handlers. Multiple providers can be plugged into *PriMan*. Each of the first six managers corresponds to one of the framework tasks T1-T6 and keeps track of and uses the underlying concrete handlers to offer higher level functionality, since the existing technologies are rather low level. A special manager is the policy manager to automate decisions. The `PriManFacade` is the application's entry point to the managers. Also, an appropriate GUI can be implemented and loaded; e.g. one GUI for PDAs and one for desktop computers.

A **connection hander** sets up, listens for and closes connections (T1). The **connection manager** allows the developer to specify connection properties such as integrity and/or anonymity properties. Based on these properties an appropriate handler is selected to set up the connection.

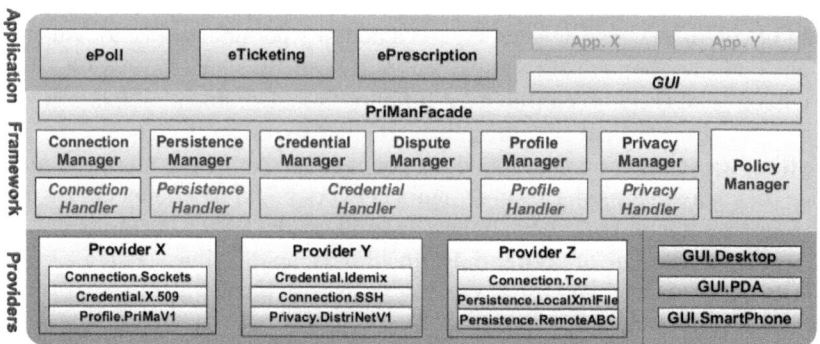

Fig. 1. High level architecture of *PriMan*

A **credential handler** provides the functionality to issue and receive credentials and pseudonyms as well as to authenticate or to sign messages with these credentials (T2). Three subhandler interfaces deal with revocation, commitments and verifiable encryptions. The service provider's access policy will define which credentials are to be used and which properties the user must or may disclose. Based on this request, the user's **credential manager** obtains the sets of credentials, commitments, pseudonyms and verifiable encryptions able to fulfill the request.

Storage of credentials and credential related data such as commitments (T3) is done by the **persistence manager**. It keeps track of where the different data objects are stored and which handler maintains them. Each **handler** defines a location type (e.g. smart card or server), an encoding structure (e.g. XML) and the protection mechanism (e.g. password based).

The **privacy manager** estimates the anonymity of pseudonyms towards other parties and the impact of disclosing certain properties (T4). Each **privacy handler** provides a concrete metric therefore.

Profile tracking (T5) is done by the **profile manager**. The **profile handler** keeps track of one or more profiles. Depending on the framework policy, authorization can be given to external entities to do certain types of queries on one or more profiles: adding or requesting for data which can be application or context specific (e.g. books bought). Also, a user can add data to a profile (e.g. books (s)he is interested in). The **profile manager** determines to which profile data are added. A **profile handler** also implements heuristics to probabilistically link profiles.

The **Dispute Manager** (T6) offers the means to file complaints in case of abuse. Complementary, evidence to protect against false accusations can be stored and later be disclosed to trusted third parties. These parties can do the deanonymization when certain conditions are fulfilled. Since deanonymization is credential type specific, an underlying credential handler is used.

Each provider consists of a set of concrete handlers (e.g. Credential.X509 and Connection.Tor). For each implementation, the provider maintains some bookkeeping information (names, properties, versions, ...)

5   Generic Credential Representation

The central concept in the framework are credentials. Therefore, this section presents a uniform, technology agnostic representation of credentials and related objects, which facilitates switching to other technologies. Credential technologies with heavily differing approaches such as passwords, X.509 certificates and Idemix credentials fit in the representation. Different object types are defined.

Credential template. It describes everything credentials of a certain category have in common (e.g. Belgian driving licenses with the same issuer public key): 1) technology specific *security parameters* such as key lengths; 2) *control settings* defining the credential's validity and usage rights such allowance to sign, the show limit, validity period and credential verification info; 3) the *issuer* data and 4) an *attribute specification* which specifies mainly the label and type of each of the attributes.

Credential. A credential consists of 1) a *credential template*, 2) *credential values*; i.e. credential's attribute values and the validity start date, 3) a *credential trace* containing all the information disclosed each time the credential is used (e.g. serial number and public key), and 4) (references to) *credential secrets* required to use the credential. Credentials never leave the framework. Credential secrets and values are sensitive data and the latter can only be exported by a framework protocol.

Show specification. This describes the properties to disclose or that were disclosed when a credential is/was used to sign, verify or issue a credential.

Disclosure. This contains the show specification and the involved objects required to either prove or verify the properties described in the show specification. Multiple credentials, commitments and verifiable encryptions and a pseudonym can be involved. In addition, deanonymization specifications can be added to specify the deanonymizers and deanonymization conditions (typically abuse). When a prover sends a disclosure to the verifier, information such as secrets and attribute values are removed from the contained objects, such that the received disclosure can only be used for verifications.

Entity. An entity represents a person or organisation and consists of a verifiable disclosure together with a proof (authentication or signature) of this disclosed information. Entities are useful to keep track of the information known to or about others. It allows to verify certification chains, which consist of entities.

Transcript. This is a framework protocol return value which contains all exchanged data and data required to rerun the protocol such as connection id or an entity representing the prover in case of an authentication verification. Transcripts are profile manager input.

The control settings in the templates allow for multiple issue keypairs in one credential and, hence, allow for issuing new credentials of different types with one existing credential; for instance, issuance of Idemix and UProve credentials with an X.509 credential. Similarly, multiple verifiable encryption keypairs can be included.

If the properties in the show specification are proven, the verifier knows in addition the credential trace. Hence, the less information in the credential trace, the better (which is technology dependent). This can be checked by the prover in advance.

As an example, an X.509 certificate without private key is represented as an entity since it represents a person or organization about which properties are certified. The corresponding verifier *disclosure* contains a credential trace and a credential template which contain all the information such as the attribute names and values and the certification signature to let an X.509 handler recompose the original X.509 certificate. An Idemix credential will have an empty credential trace.

6   Validation

In the ePoll application, citizens can participate in multiple polls using an anonymous credential, but can only vote once for each poll. Votes of the same user are unlinkable. The poll organizer can restrict the voter set and can invite voters to disclose some additional properties, enabling the generation of more significant poll statistics. For instance; the poll could be restricted to adults and optionally, they may disclose their gender. Poll signatures are published to allow everyone to verify the poll's correctness. In figure 2, a client and server application use different managers to build this application.

First, the client application creates an anonymous connection with the ePoll server (C1-C3,S1), which replies by sending a request (C4,S2). A `Request` object contains a description of the obligatory and optional properties to be disclosed and can contain a list of sign options. It also lists the templates of acceptable credentials. The received request thus contains the user's different personal property disclosure options and the different choices he can vote for. Based on the request, the client's credential manager is asked to give a description of each credential able to fulfill the request (C5); in the ePoll case, there is one such credential. Based on the request and the credential description, all the possible show specifications are returned (C6); i.e. all the sets of properties the user can disclose using that credential in order to cast a vote. The application could optionally ask the profile manager for the profile containing the information disclosed previously to that poll service (C7). Since the user never signed the poll, this profile will be empty. The privacy manager is asked for the impact on the privacy for each of the possible show specifications (C8). The returned `PrivacyInfo` object contains the relevant anonymity information for each of the show specifications if the contained properties were disclosed. Now, the application can decide which properties to disclose. Note that the policy manager can already filter out some possibilities.

The user selects the properties to disclose and the option to vote for (C9, C10). The client's credential manager is asked to create the `Disclosure` object corresponding to the show specification (C11). Therefore, it loads the corresponding credential (using the persistence manager) and creates the required pseudonym. The nym, credential and show specification are put in the disclosure, which is used to create the signature (C12). The disclosure, signature and choice are sent to the poll organizer (C13-15,S3-S5). The client's profile manager is informed that over `conn` a `disclosure` has happened, which was in fact a signature on `choice` and that the signature is published (C16).

After receiving a signature, disclosure and the corresponding choice (S3-S5), the server application asks the credential manager if the disclosure matches the request (S6) and if the signature is valid (S7) and it asks the profile manager if the pseudonym in the disclosure has not yet been used (S8). If these three conditions are met, the server application publishes the signature, disclosure and signed choice (9).

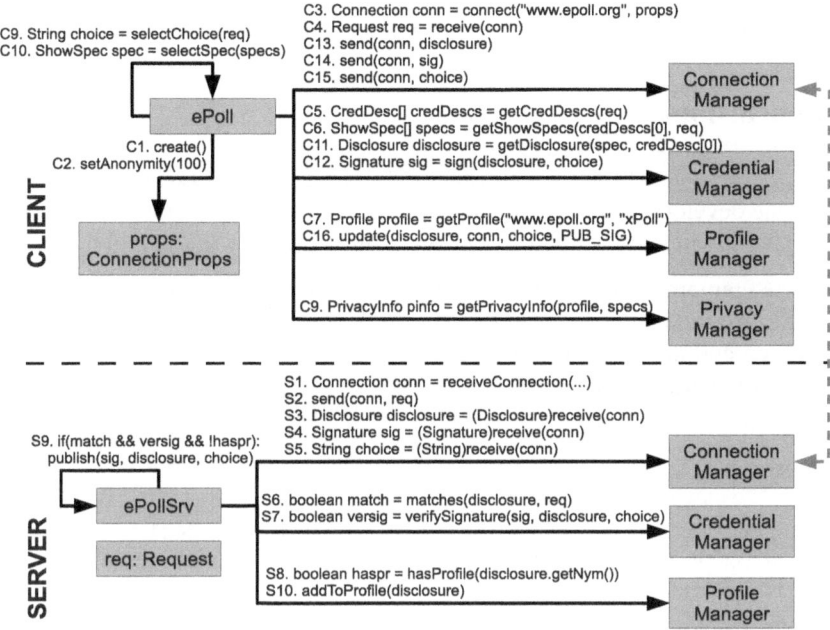

C9. String choice = selectChoice(req)
C10. ShowSpec spec = selectSpec(specs)

C3. Connection conn = connect("www.epoll.org", props)
C4. Request req = receive(conn)
C13. send(conn, disclosure)
C14. send(conn, sig)
C15. send(conn, choice)

Connection Manager

ePoll

C5. CredDesc[] credDescs = getCredDescs(req)
C6. ShowSpec[] specs = getShowSpecs(credDescs[0], req)
C11. Disclosure disclosure = getDisclosure(spec, credDesc[0])
C12. Signature sig = sign(disclosure, choice)

Credential Manager

C1. create()
C2. setAnonymity(100)

C7. Profile profile = getProfile("www.epoll.org", "xPoll")
C16. update(disclosure, conn, choice, PUB_SIG)

Profile Manager

props: ConnectionProps

C9. PrivacyInfo pinfo = getPrivacyInfo(profile, specs)

Privacy Manager

CLIENT

S9. if(match && versig && !haspr):
publish(sig, disclosure, choice)

S1. Connection conn = receiveConnection(...)
S2. send(conn, req)
S3. Disclosure disclosure = (Disclosure)receive(conn)
S4. Signature sig = (Signature)receive(conn)
S5. String choice = (String)receive(conn)

Connection Manager

ePollSrv

S6. boolean match = matches(disclosure, req)
S7. boolean versig = verifySignature(sig, disclosure, choice)

Credential Manager

req: Request

S8. boolean haspr = hasProfile(disclosure.getNym())
S10. addToProfile(disclosure)

Profile Manager

SERVER

Fig. 2. Example: signing an anonymous poll

Note that both client and server use the framework in a complementary way and also notice how easy it is to build applications on top of *PriMan*.

7 Related Work

Several federated identity management systems (FIMs) exist such as Shibboleth, Windows Cardspace, OpenId, Athens and Higgins. They all have in common that the user data is stored by a trusted identity provider (IdP). Some of the federated identity management systems allow the user to request the IdP a token containing only properties of the user, hence, improving the user's privacy. Still the IdP knows when what properties were requested by the user. None of the current FIMs offers real user-centric identity management, which is made possible using anonymous credentials. Also, none of the FIMs offers the user the possibility to keep track of disclosed properties, nor can they inform the user about his/her anonymity status. Since the IdP can always link an issued token to an identity, the FIMs do not need the possibility of deanonymization. Their tokens are typically based on SAML. Our approach is built upon the idea of real user-centric identity management, centered around the concept of anonymous credentials and offers support for the above-mentioned functionality. In addition, it can offer support for any credential type and is not limited to SAML tokens.

PriMan allows to use different concepts in a coherent way; credentials, connections, persistence, profiles, etc. Hence, the framework integrates current and future implementations and research in one aggregate. For instance, a high-level approach to control the information disclosure based on the sensitivity and the possibility that a user's identity is revealed was proposed [9] and could be implemented by a privacy handler.

8   Conclusions

This paper presented *PriMan*, a flexible middleware framework that considerably facilitates the development of privacy-preserving applications. Although not all building blocks have an implementation yet, *PriMan* is already a very useful tool for developers.

Acknowledgements. This research is partially funded by the Interuniversity Attraction Poles Programme Belgian State, Belgian Science Policy and the Research Fund K.U.Leuven and the IWT-SBO project (ADAPID) "Advanced Applications for Electronic Identity Cards in Flanders".

References

1. Camenisch, J., Mityagin, A.: Mix-network with stronger security. In: Danezis, G., Martin, D. (eds.) PET 2005. LNCS, vol. 3856, pp. 128–146. Springer, Heidelberg (2006)
2. Danezis, G., Díaz, C., Käsper, E., Troncoso, C.: The wisdom of crowds: Attacks and optimal constructions. In: Backes, M., Ning, P. (eds.) ESORICS 2009. LNCS, vol. 5789, pp. 406–423. Springer, Heidelberg (2009)
3. Pedersen, T.: Non-interactive and information-theoretic secure verifiable secret sharing. In: Feigenbaum, J. (ed.) CRYPTO 1991. LNCS, vol. 576, pp. 129–140. Springer, Heidelberg (1992)
4. Damgard, I., Pedersen, T., Pfitzmann, B.: Statistical secrecy and multi-bit commitments (1996)
5. Cramer, R., Shoup, V.: A practical public key cryptosystem provably secure against adaptive chosen ciphertext attack. In: Krawczyk, H. (ed.) CRYPTO 1998. LNCS, vol. 1462, pp. 13–25. Springer, Heidelberg (1998)
6. Asokan, N., Herreweghen, E.V., Steiner, M.: Towards a framework for handling disputes in payment systems. Technical Report RZ 2996 (1998)
7. Camenisch, J., Lysyanskaya, A.: An efficient system for non-transferable anonymous credentials with optional anonymity revocation. In: Pfitzmann, B. (ed.) EUROCRYPT 2001. LNCS, vol. 2045, pp. 93–118. Springer, Heidelberg (2001)
8. Brands, S.: Rethinking Public Key Infrastructures and Digital Certificates: Building in Privacy. MIT Press, Cambridge (2000)
9. Irwin, K., Yu, T.: An identifiability-based access control model for privacy protection in open systems. In: WPES 2004: Proceedings of the 2004 ACM workshop on Privacy in the electronic society, p. 43. ACM Press, New York (2004)

Detecting Spam Bots in Online Social Networking Sites: A Machine Learning Approach

Alex Hai Wang

College of Information Sciences and Technology,
The Pennsylvania State University,
Dunmore, PA 18512, USA
hwang@psu.edu

Abstract. As online social networking sites become more and more popular, they have also attracted the attentions of the spammers. In this paper, Twitter, a popular micro-blogging service, is studied as an example of spam bots detection in online social networking sites. A machine learning approach is proposed to distinguish the spam bots from normal ones. To facilitate the spam bots detection, three graph-based features, such as the number of friends and the number of followers, are extracted to explore the unique follower and friend relationships among users on Twitter. Three content-based features are also extracted from user's most recent 20 tweets. A real data set is collected from Twitter's public available information using two different methods. Evaluation experiments show that the detection system is efficient and accurate to identify spam bots in Twitter.

1   Introduction

Online social networking sites are becoming more popular each day, such as Facebook, Twitter, and LinkedIn. Among all these sites, Twitter is the fastest growing one than any other social network, surging more than 2,800% in 2009 according to Opera's State of the Mobile Web report [1]. Unfortunately, spam is becoming an increasing problem on Twitter as other online social network sites.

Spammers use Twitter as a tool to post multiple duplicate updates containing malicious links, abuse the reply function to post unsolicited messages to users, and hijack trending topics. Spammers also pushed offensive terms on to Twitter *trending topics*, which displays on Twitter's front page, for several times. This forced Twitter to temporarily disable the trending topic and remove the offensive terms.

Twitter tried several ways to fight spam, which include adding a "report as spam" feature to its service and cleaning up suspicious accounts. However, legitimate Twitter users complain that their accounts are getting caught up in Twitters anti-spam actions. Twitter recently admitted to accidentally suspending accounts as a result of a spam clean-up effort.

In this paper, the suspicious behaviors of spam bots are studied. My goal is to apply machine learning methods to distinguish spam bots from normal ones.

S. Foresti and S. Jajodia (Eds.): Data and Applications Security XXIV, LNCS 6166, pp. 335–342, 2010.
© IFIP International Federation for Information Processing 2010

The rest of the paper is organized as follow. In Section 2, the related works are discussed. In Section 3, novel content-based and graph-based features are proposed to facilitate spam bots detection. Bayesian classification method is applied in Section 4 to detect spam bots in Twitter. Section 5 introduces the two data set collecting methods. Experiments are also conducted to evaluate the performance of detection system.

2   Related Work

Spam detection has been studied for a long time. The previous work mainly focuses on email spam detection and Web spam detection. In [2], Sahami et al. first proposed a Bayesian approach to filter spam emails. Experiment results show that the classifier has a better performance considering domain-specific features in addition to the raw text of E-mail messages. Currently spam email filtering is a fairly mature technique. Bayesian spam email filters are implemented both on modern email clients and servers.

Not like email system, Web is massive, changes more rapidly, and is spread over geographically distributed computers [3]. It is a significant challenge to detect Web spam. [4] first formalized the problem and proposed a comprehensive solution to detect Web spam. The TrustRank algorithm is proposed to compute the trust score for a Web graph. Based on computed scores where good pages are given higher scores, spam pages can be filtered in the search engine results. In [5], the authors based on the link structure of the Web proposed a measurement Spam Mass to identify link spamming. A directed graph model of the Web is proposed in [6]. The authors apply classification algorithms for directed graphs to detect real-world link spam. In [7], both link-based features and content-based features are proposed. The basic decision tree classifier is implemented to classify spam. In [8], semi-supervised learning algorithms are proposed to boost the performance of a classifier which only needs small amount of labeled samples.

For spam detection in other applications, Wu et al. [9] present an approach for detection of spam calls over IP telephony called SPIT in VoIP system. Based on the popular semi-supervised learning methods, a improved algorithm called MPCK-Means is proposed. In [10], the authors study the video spammers and promoters detection in YouTube. By far this is the only work I found studying spam detection in online social network sites.

In [11], the authors collected three datasets of the Twitter network. The Twitter users' behaviors, geographic growth pattern, and current size of the network are studied.

3   Features

The features extracted for spam detection include three graph-based features and three content-based features. As a social networking site, Twitter allows users to build their own social graph. Three graph-based features are extracted from Twitter's social graph to capture the *"following"* relationship among users.

Twitter also allows users to broadcast short messages in 140 characters, known as "*tweet*", to their friends or followers. I extract three content-based features from the user's 20 most recent tweets.

3.1 Graph-Based Features

Following is one of the most important and unique functions about Twitter. Users can build their own social network by following friends and allowing others to follow them on Twitter. You can follow your friends' accounts to get their updates automatically on your Twitter homepage when you log in. And your friends can send your private messages, called *direct messages*, if you follow them. Spammers use the following function to take legitimate users' attention by following their accounts, since Twitter will send an email notification when someone follows your account. Twitter considers it as a spam bot, if this account "has small number of followers compared to the amount of people you are following".

Three graph-based features, which are the number of friends, the number of followers, and the follower ratio, are extracted to detect spam bots on Twitter. If someone follows your account, it becomes one of your followers. If you follow someone's account, then it becomes one of your friends. The number of friends and the number of followers are extracted for each individual Twitter account.

Furthermore, the follower ratio is computed based the number of followers and the number of to friends. Let N_{fo} denote the number of followers, N_{fr} denote the number of friends, and r_{ff} denote the follower ratio. To normalize the follower ratio, this feature is defined as the ratio between the number of people you are following and the number of people following you.

$$r_{ff} = \frac{N_{fo}}{N_{fo} + N_{fr}} \qquad (1)$$

Obviously if the number of followers is relatively small compared to the amount of people you are following, the follower ratio is relatively small and close to zero. At the same time the probability that the associated account is spam is high.

3.2 Content-Based Features

In this part, novel content-based features extracted from Twitter are introduced. Three features, which are the number of duplicate tweets, the number of HTTP links, and the number of replies/mentions, are extracted from the user's 20 most recent tweets.

First, an account may be considered as a spam if it posts duplicate content on one account. A sample Twitter spam page is shown in Figure 1. Usually legitimate users will not post duplicate updates. Duplicate tweets are detected by measuring the Levenshtein distance (also known as edit distance) between two different tweets posted by the same account. The Levenshtein distance is defined as the minimum cost of transforming one string into another through a

Fig. 1. A Twitter spam page (Duplicate tweets are circled in the same color rectangles)

sequence of edit operations, including the deletion, insertion, and substitution of individual symbols. The distance is zero if and only if the two tweets are identical.

To avoid detection and spam different accounts, spam bots often include different *@usernames* in their duplicates tweets. When the Levenshtein distances are computed between different tweets, I clean the data by deleting *@replies*, *#topic*, and HTTP slinks. In other words, the reply/mention, topic, and link information are ignored when I capture the duplicate tweet, instead only the content of the tweets is considereds.

Second, spam bots try to post malicious links in their tweets to allure legitimate users to click. Since Twitter only allows you to post a message within 140 characters, some URL shortening services and applications, such as bit.ly, become popular to meet the requirements. A shorten URL obscures the target address, and as a result it facilitates the spam accounts in pranks, phishing, or affiliate hiding. So Twitter considers it as a factor of spam if your tweets consist mainly of links, and not personal updates.

The number of links in one account is measured by the number of tweets containing HTTP links in the user's 20 most recent tweets. If a tweet contains the sequence of characters "http://" or "www.", this tweet is considered as containing a link.

Third, the number of replies/mentions is extracted from the user's 20 most recent tweets. On Twitter, users can use the *@+username+message* format to designate their message as a reply to another person . You can reply to anyone's tweet on Twitter no matter they are your friends or not. You can also mention another user name (*@username*) anywhere in the tweet, rather than just the beginning. Twitter collects all tweets containing your user name in the *@username* format in your replies tab. You can see all replies made to you, and mentions of your user name.

The reply and mention functions are designed to help users to discover each other on Twitter. However, the spam account utilize the service to draw other user's attention by sending unsolicited replies and mentions. Twitter also considers this as a factor to determine spamming. The number replies and mentions in one account is measured by the number of tweets containing the reply sign "@" in the user's 20 most recent tweets.

4 Spam Bots Detection

In this section, I apply different classification methods, such as decision tree, neural network, support vector machines, and k-nearest neighbors, to identify spam bots on Twitter. Among these algorithms, Bayesian classifier has the best performance for several reasons. First, Bayesian classifier is noise robust. Another reason that Bayesian classifier has a better performance is that the class label is predicted based on user's specific pattern. A spam probability is calculated for each individual user based its behaviors, instead of giving a general rule. Also, Bayesian classifier is a simple and very efficient classification algorithm.

The Bayesian classifier is based on the well-known Bayes theorem:

$$P(Y|X) = \frac{P(X|Y)P(Y)}{P(X)} \tag{2}$$

The conditional probability of $P(Y|X)$ is also known as the posterior probability for Y, as opposed to its prior probability $P(Y)$.

Each Twitter account is considered as a vector X with feature values as discussed in Section 3. I classify the vectors into two classes Y: spam and non-spam. To classify a data record, the posterior probability is computed for each class:

$$P(Y|X) = \frac{P(Y) \prod_{i=1}^{d} P(X_i|Y)}{P(X)} \tag{3}$$

Since $P(X)$ is a normalizing factor which is equal for all classes, we need only maximize the numerator $P(Y) \prod_{i=1}^{d} P(X_i|Y)$ in order to do the classification.

5   Experiments

5.1   Data Set

The data set is collected using two methods. First I use Twitter's API methods to collect user's detailed information. Second, a Web crawler is developed to extra a specific unauthorized user's 20 most recent tweets.

First I use the *public_timeline* API method to collect information about the 20 non-protected users who have set a custom user icon in real time. This method can randomly pick 20 non-protected users who updated their status recently on Twitter. I extract details of the current user, such as IDs, screen name, location, and etc. At the same time, I also use *social graph* API methods to collect information about user's friends and followers, such as the number of friends, the number of followers, list of friend IDs, list of follower IDs, and etc. The Twitter's *friends* and *followers* APIs can return maximum 5,000 users. If a user has more than 5,000 friends or followers, I could only extract a partial list of friends or followers. Based on my observation, the number of friends and followers of most users do not exceed 5,000, so this constraint does not affect my method significantly.

Another constraint of Twitter API methods is the number of queries per hour. Currently the rate limit for calls to the API is 150 requests per hour. To collect data from different time periods and avoid congesting Twitter Web servers, I crawl Twitter continuously and limit my request 120 calls per hour.

Although Twitter provides neat API methods for us, there is no method that allows us to collect a specific unauthorized user's recent tweets. The *public_timeline* API method can only return the most recent update from 20 different non-protected users (one update from one user). The *user_timeline* API method can return the 20 most recent tweets posted only from an authenticating user. The recent tweets posted by a user are important to extract content-based features, such as duplicate tweets. To solve this problem, I develop a web crawler to collect the 20 most recent tweets of a specific non-protected user based on the user's ID on Twitter. The extracted tweets are saved both as a XML file and into a relational database.

Finally, I collect the data set for 3 weeks from January 3 to January 24, 2010. Totally 25,847 users, around 500K tweets, and around 49M follower/friend relationships are collected from the public available data on Twitter.

5.2   Evaluation

To evaluate my method, I manually labeled 500 Twitter user accounts to two classes: spam and not spam. Each user account is manually evaluated by reading the 20 most recent tweets posted by the user and checking the friends and followers of the user. The result shows that there is around 1% spam account in the data set. The study [12] shows that there is probably 3% spam on Twitter. To simulate the reality and avoid the bias in my crawling method, I add more spam data to the data set.

As mentioned in Section 1, Twitter provides several method for users to report spam, which includes sending Twitter a direct message and clicking on the "report for spam" link. The most simple and public available method is to post a tweet in the "*@spam @username*" format where *@username* is to mention the spam account. I queried "*@spam*" to collect additional spam data set. Surprisedly I found that this service is abused by hoaxes and spam. Only a small percentage of *@spam* tweets is reporting spam. I clean the query results by manually evaluating each spam report. Finally the data set is mixed of containing around 3% spam.

The evaluation of the overall process is based on a set of measures commonly used in Machine Learning and Information Retrieval. Given a classification algorithm C, I consider its confusion matrix:

		Prediction	
		Spam	Not Spam
True	Spam	a	b
	Not Spam	c	d

Three measures are considered in the evaluation experiements: precision, recall, and F-measure. The precision is $P = a/(a+c)$ and the recall is $R = a/(a+b)$. The F-measure is defined as $F = 2PR/(P+R)$. For evaluating the classification algorithms, I focus on the F-measure F as it is a standard way of summarizing both precision and recall.

All the predictions reported in the paper are computed using 10-fold cross validation. For each classifier, the precision, recall, and F-measure are reported. Each classifier is trained 10 times, each time using the 9 out of the 10 partitions as training data and computing the confusion matrix using the tenth partition as test data. The evaluation metrics are estimated on the average confusion matrix. The evaluation results are shown in Table 1. The naïve Bayesian classifier has the best overall performance compared with other algorithms.

Table 1. Classification Evaluation

Classifier	Precision	Recall	F-measure
Decision Tree	0.667	0.333	0.444
Neural Networks	1	0.417	0.588
Support Vector Machines	1	0.25	0.4
Naïve Bayesian	0.917	0.917	0.917

6   Conclusion

In this paper, I focus on the suspicious behaviors of spam bots in online social networking sites. A popular micro-blogging service, called Twitter, is studied as an example. A machine learning approach is proposed to identify the spam bots from normal noes. Based on the spam policy on Twitter, graph-based features and content-based features are extracted from user's social graph and most recent tweets. Traditional classification algorithms are applied to detect suspicious behaviors of spam bots. A Web crawler using Twitter API is developed to collect real data set from Twitter public available information. Finally, I analyze the data set and evaluate the performance of the detection system. Several popular classification algorithms are studied and evaluated. The results show that the Bayesian classifier has a better overall performance.

References

1. Opera: State of the mobile web, `http://www.opera.com/smw/2009/12/`
2. Sahami, M., Dumais, S., Heckerman, D., Horvitz, E.: A bayesian approach to filtering junk e-mail. In: AAAI Workshop on Learning for Text Categorization (1998)
3. Arasu, A., Cho, J., Garcia-Molina, H., Paepcke, A., Raghavan, S.: Searching the web. ACM Trans. Internet Technol. 1(1), 2–43 (2001)
4. Gyöngyi, Z., Garcia-Molina, H., Pedersen, J.: Combating web spam with trustrank. In: Proceedings of the Thirtieth international conference on Very large data bases, pp. 576–587 (2004)
5. Gyongyi, Z., Berkhin, P., Garcia-Molina, H., Pedersen, J.: Link spam detection based on mass estimation. In: VLDB 2006: Proceedings of the 32nd international conference on Very large data bases, pp. 439–450 (2006)
6. Zhou, D., Burges, C.J.C., Tao, T.: Transductive link spam detection. In: Proceedings of the 3rd international workshop on Adversarial information retrieval on the web, pp. 21–28 (2007)
7. Castillo, C., Donato, D., Gionis, A., Murdock, V., Silvestri, F.: Know your neighbors: web spam detection using the web topology. In: Proceedings of the 30th annual international ACM SIGIR conference, pp. 423–430 (2007)
8. Geng, G.G., Li, Q., Zhang, X.: Link based small sample learning for web spam detection. In: Proceedings of the 18th international conference on World wide web, pp. 1185–1186 (2009)
9. Wu, Y.-S., Bagchi, S., Singh, N., Wita, R.: Spam detection in voice-over-ip calls through semi-supervised clustering. In: Proceedings of the 2009 Dependable Systems Networks, pp. 307–316 (2009)
10. Benevenuto, F., Rodrigues, T., Almeida, V., Almeida, J., Gonçalves, M.: Detecting spammers and content promoters in online video social networks. In: Proceedings of the 32nd international ACM SIGIR conference, pp. 620–627 (2009)
11. Krishnamurthy, B., Gill, P., Arlitt, M.: A few chirps about twitter. In: WOSP 2008: Proceedings of the first workshop on Online social networks, pp. 19–24 (2008)
12. Inc. Pear Analytics: Twitter study, `http://www.pearanalytics.com/wp-content/uploads/2009/08/Twitter-Study-August-2009.pdf`

Authentication Assurance Level Taxonomies for Smart Identity Token Deployments - A New Approach

Ramaswamy Chandramouli

National Institute of Standards and Technology Gaithersburg, MD, USA
mouli@nist.gov

Abstract. Authentication assurance level taxonomies that have been specified in many real-world smart identity token deployments do not fully reflect all the security properties associated with their underlying authentication mechanisms. In this paper we describe the development and application of a new methodology called SID-AAM (where the abbreviation stands for Smart Identity Token - Authentication Assurance Level Methodology) that identifies a new set of authentication factors appropriate for this technology, identifies all the security properties that need to be verified based on bindings between various entities involved in the authentication processes and then derives an authentication assurance level taxonomy based on the set of security properties verified in the various authentication modes specified in the deployment. The advantages of SID-AAM methodology compared to current approaches for determining authentication assurance levels for smart identity token deployments are highlighted.

1 Introduction

Smart Cards as identity tokens (or Smart Identity Tokens) are being increasingly deployed in the government and private sector. An authentication mode as specified in smart identity token deployments, consist of one or more authentication mechanisms. An authentication mechanism generally is classified as belonging to one of the following three types (also called Authentication Factors): (a) What you Know (b) What you Have and (c) What you Are. The authentication assurance level for an authentication mode is determined using a combination of the authentication factor coverage (one, two or three) and the strength of individual mechanism constituting that mode. In authentication processes involving smart identity tokens, the artifact that provides the "What you Have" factor can be stolen and hence a new methodology to analyze the authentication modes associated with Smart Identity Token deployments is needed and that is the main focus of this paper. The organization of the rest of the paper is as follows: In Section 2, we take a close look at the functionality of smart identity tokens and derive a new set of authentication factors that is appropriate for authentication processes enabled by that functionality. Section 3 describe the development of

S. Foresti and S. Jajodia (Eds.): Data and Applications Security XXIV, LNCS 6166, pp. 343–349, 2010.

our methodology for analyzing the strength of individual authentication modes (and hence designating an authentication assurance level) and by extension an authentication assurance level taxonomy for the entire smart identity token deployment, and is the main contribution of this paper. We use the acronym SID-AAM to refer to this methodology where the abbreviation stands for Smart Identity Token - Authentication Assurance Methodology. In Section 4, we outline the advantages of our methodology as compared to approaches based on traditional authentication factors for deriving authentication assurance levels.

2 Smart Identity Tokens - Functionality and Applicable Authentication Factors

In the context of this paper, a smart identity token is a plastic card with an ICC (integrated circuit chip) often called a smart card that has the capability to: (a) store a large identifier (SID-F1) (b) store other attributes associated with unique identifier (SID-F2) (c) store a tamper-proof cryptographic secret (SID-F3) and (d) control release of token secret through a secret shared between the token and holder (SID-F4). Based on these capabilities we find that authentication factors appropriate for smart token based authentication (we will them as SID authentication factors) are: (a) Authentication using credentials (SID-AF1) (b) Authentication using cryptographic secret (SID-AF2) and (c) Authentication using a digitally bound combination of credentials and cryptographic secret with or without user control of the secret (SID-AF4). Hence an authentication mode specified in a smart token deployment consists of one or more authentication mechanisms each based on one of the authentication factors listed above.

3 Methodology for Determining Authentication Assurance Level Taxonomies for Smart Identity Token Deployments (SID-AAM)

Next our goal is to develop a methodology by which any deployment authentication mode can be assigned an authentication assurance level and by extension an authentication assurance level taxonomy for the entire deployment scenario. To get to this goal we formulate the following strategic objectives: (a) identify a set of primitive authentication modes for smart identity tokens (called SID primitive authentication modes) and associate a set of security properties associated with each mode. Identify some partial orders among SID primitive authentication modes based on security property containment (b) Express any deployment authentication mode in terms of SID primitive authentication mode (c) Based on property aggregation (adding up all security properties satisfied by all SID primitive authentication modes within a deployment authentication mode) and partial orders among primitive authentication modes themselves, derive an authentication assurance level for a deployment authentication mode and (d) The assurance levels associated with all deployment authentication modes used in a particular deployment then provides the authentication assurance level taxonomy for that smart identity token deployment.

To realize our strategic objectives, our SID-AAM methodology adopts the following concrete steps. (a) SID-AAM - Step 1: View the entire spectrum of activities in a smart identity token deployment as consisting of two distinct phases - the token issuance phase and token usage phase. Perform a detailed review of all activities/sub tasks in the token issuance phase and derive the set of security properties introduced by each of the activities. (b) SID-AAM-Step 2: Using the set of SID authentication factors for smart identity tokens (derived in section 2) and the technology of smart token usage, derive a set of SID primitive authentication modes. (c) SID-AAM-Step 3: Identify the set of generic threats to SID entities. Also identify the set of security properties (that were introduced in the token issuance phase) that are verified by each of the SID primitive authentication modes and the adverse usage scenario that may result under each mode due to realization of those threats and (d) SID-AAM Step 4: Based on the set of verified properties associated with each SID primitive authentication mode, identify partial orders (dominance relationships) among the SID primitive authentication modes. Using these partial orders, derive the authentication assurance level for each of the SID primitive authentication mode. These levels can then be used for deriving an authentication assurance level taxonomy for any SID deployment based on the set of chosen authentication modes in that deployment.

3.1   Derivation of Security Properties Introduced in the Token Issuance Phase (SID-AAM Step 1)

The set of activities involved in a smart identity token deployment scenario can broadly be divided into two phases: (a) Token Issuance Phase and (b) Token Usage Phase. The list of token issuance activities are: (a) SID-I1: Identify Population & Eligibility - Target users eligible to receive tokens (b) SID-I2: Creating Credential Repository & Loading the Application on the token (c) SID-I3: Loading Credentials into the Token (d) SID-I4: Generating the token secret and digitally signing the token-secret related data (e) SID-I5: Populating Token Holder Data in Authentication Points and (f) SID-I6: Issue Token to the Legitimate Holder. These activities involve the following entities: (a) SID-E1: Credential Database (ECDB) - an electronic entity (b) SID-E2: Valid Credentials - Authentication Database (AUDB) at Authentication Points - an electronic entity (c) SID-E3: Token Issuer - (For the purpose of security property we treat this as the IT system that personalizes the token) - an electronic entity (d) SID-E4: The Valid Token -physical token issued to the legitimate user - a physical entity (e) SID-E5: The Token Credential - credentials on the token - an electronic entity (f) SID-E6: The Token Secret - an electronic entity and (g) SID-E7: The Token Holder - the legitimate user to whom the token is issued - a human entity. The token issuance activities introduce certain security properties in the form of bindings involving the entities and these security properties are the ones that have to be verified during the token usage phase. In the context of bindings, we treat the entities Token Secret (SID-E6) and Valid Token (SID-E4) as one entity since to obtain the token secret from the token without destroying the latter requires costly and sophisticated techniques. The list of security properties along with activities that introduces these properties and the participating entities are: (a) SID-AP1: Token Credential- Valid Credential Binding (SID-I5 involving SID-E5 & SID-E2) (b) SID-AP2: Token Credential-Token Issuer Binding (SID-I3 involving SID-E5 & SID-E3) (c) SID-AP3: Token Secret (Valid Token)-Token Issuer Binding (SID-I4 involving SID-E6/E4 & SID-E3) (d) SID-AP4: Token Secret (Valid Token)-Token Issuer-Token Holder Binding (Additional implementation feature under SID-I4 that enables user control of token secret and thus involves SID-E6/E4, SID-E3 & SID-E7)) (e) SID-AP5: Token Secret (Valid Token)-Token Issuer-Token Credential Binding (Another implementation feature under SID-I4 that digitally binds token secret and token credential and thus involves SID-E6/E4, SID-E3 & SID-E5) and (f) SID-AP6: Token Secret (Valid Token) - Token Issuer - Token Credential - Token Holder Binding (Another implementation feature under SID-I4 that digitally binds token secret and token credential as well as enables user control of token secret and thus involves SID-E6/E4, SID-E3, SID-E5 & SID-E7).

3.2 Deriving SID Primitive Authentication Modes (SID-AAM Step 2)

Each of the SID authentication factors for smart identity tokens (derived in Section 2) may have different implementations with different strengths and each implementation then becomes a SID primitive authentication mode. The list of SID primitive authentication modes are: (a) PAM-CR1: Verify that the credentials on the token are valid (SID-AF1) (b) PAM-CR2: Verify that the credentials on the token are Valid and Authentic (SID-AF1) (c) PAM-TS1: Verify that the token has a valid, authentic Secret (SID-AF2) (d) PAM-TS2: Verify that the token has a valid, authentic Secret and the user has control over the secret (SID-AF2) (e) PAM-CR-TS1: Verify that there is a digital binding of the Valid, Authentic Token Credential and a Valid, Authentic Token Secret (SID-AF3) and (f) PAM-CR-TS2: Verify that there is a digital binding of the Valid, Authentic Token Credential and a Valid, Authentic Token Secret and the user has control over the secret (SID-AF3. Now we that we have the set of security properties introduced in token issuance phase (from SID-AAM Step1) and the set of SID primitive authentication modes (from SID-AAM Step 2), our next task is to analyze the security property or properties that each SID primitive authentication mode verifies and the potential adverse usage scenarios that may affect the integrity of that property verification capability. To derive the latter, we need to look at the threats to SID entities. These threats along with the affected SID entities are: (a) SID-T1: A valid issued token (SID-E4) along with its embedded secret (SID-E6) may be easily stolen because of the small form factor of the artifact (b) SID-T2: The Token Credential (SID-E5) (along with its associated Digital Signature) may be duplicated on a cloned/illegal token and (c)

SID-T3: The Token Credential (SID-E5) may be altered/tampered on a valid issued token.

3.3 Security Properties Verified /Adverse Usage Scenario in Various SID Primitive Authentication Modes (SID-AMM Step 3)

We now proceed to analyze the security strength of each of the SID primitive authentication modes (under each of the SID authentication factors) in terms of the set of verified security properties as well as potential adverse usage scenario associated with its deployment. (a) PAM-CR1: Verify that the credentials on the token are valid with Token Credential - Valid Credential Binding (SID-AP1) as property verified with the Claimant with legitimate, stolen token with Valid Credentials (OR) Claimant with Cloned token with Valid Credentials as the potential adverse scenario. (b) PAM-CR2: Verify that the credentials on the token are Valid and Authentic Token Credential - Valid Credential Binding (SID-AP1) & Token Credential - Token Issuer Binding (SID-AP2) as verified properties with the Claimant with legitimate, stolen token with Valid, Authentic Credentials (OR) Claimant with Cloned token with Valid, Authentic Credentials as potential adverse scenario (c) PAM-TS1: Verify that the token has a valid, authentic Secret with Token Credential - Valid Credential Binding (SID-AP1) & Token Secret (Valid Token) - Token Issuer Binding (SID-AP3) as verified properties with Claimant with a legitimate, stolen token with or without tampered Credentials as potential adverse scenario. (d) PAM-TS2: Verify that the token has a valid, authentic Secret and the user has control over the secret with Token Credential - Valid Credential Binding (SID-AP1), Token Secret (Valid Token) - Token Issuer Binding (SID-AP3) & Token Secret (Valid Token)-Token Issuer-Token Holder Binding (SID-AP4) as verified properties with Claimant with a legitimate, owner-possessed token with tampered credentials as potential adverse usage scenario. (e) PAM-CR-TS1: Verify that there is a digital binding of the Valid, Authentic Token Credential and a Valid, Authentic Token Secret with Token Credential - Valid Credential Binding (SID-AP1), Token Credential - Token Issuer Binding (SID-AP2), Token Secret (Valid Token) - Token Issuer Binding (SID-AP3) & Token Secret (Valid Token) - Token Issuer - Token Credential Binding (SID-AP5) as verified properties with the Claimant with a legitimate, stolen token with Valid, Authentic Credentials as potential adverse scenario. (f) PAM-CR-TS2: Verify that there is a digital binding of the Valid, Authentic Token Credential and a Valid, Authentic Token Secret and the user has control over the secret with Token Credential - Valid Credential Binding (SID-AP1), Token Credential - Token Issuer Binding (SID-AP2) & Token Secret (Valid Token) - Token Issuer Binding (SID-AP3), Token Secret (Valid Token) - Token Issuer-Token Holder Binding (SID-AP4), Token Secret (Valid Token) - Token Issuer - Token Credential Binding (SID-AP5) & Token Secret (Valid Token) - Token Issuer - Token Credential - Token Holder Binding (SID-AP6) with no potential adverse usage scenario.

3.4 Deriving Authentication Assurance Level Taxonomy for SID-Based Authentications (SID-AAM Step 4)

Now that we have a set of verified security properties associated with each SID primitive authentication mode, our logic for deriving an authentication assurance level for each of these modes and by extension an authentication assurance level taxonomy for a smart identity token deployment should be based on property containment relationships between any pair of SID primitive authentication modes. Let us a choose a hierarchical chain of levels with number suffixes denoting the place in the chain - levels L0, L1, L2, L3 etc with L0 denoting the lowest level in the chain. By looking at the set of security properties verified by each SID primitive authentication mode in Section 3.1, 3.2 and 3.3, we arrive at the following dominance relationships. First we will look at dominance relationship between any two modes within a SID authentication factor and then look at such relationships between modes across authentication factors. The list of dominance relationships of the first category is as follows:

$$PAM\text{-}CR2 > PAM\text{-}CR1 (\text{within SID-AF1 factor}) \tag{1}$$
$$PAM\text{-}TS2 > PAM\text{-}TS1 (\text{within SID-AF2 factor}) \tag{2}$$
$$PAM\text{-}CR\text{-}TS2 > PAM\text{-}CR\text{-}TS1 (\text{within SID-AF3 factor}) \tag{3}$$

The list of dominance relationships between SID primitive authentication modes across SID authentication factors are as follows:

$$PAM\text{-}TS1 > PAM\text{-}CR1 \tag{4}$$
$$PAM\text{-}CR\text{-}TS1 > PAM\text{-}CR1 \tag{5}$$
$$PAM\text{-}CR\text{-}TS1 > PAM\text{-}CR2 \tag{6}$$
$$PAM\text{-}CR\text{-}TS1 > PAM\text{-}TS1 \tag{7}$$
$$PAM\text{-}CR\text{-}TS2 > PAM\text{-}CR1 \tag{8}$$
$$PAM\text{-}CR\text{-}TS2 > PAM\text{-}CR2 \tag{9}$$
$$PAM\text{-}CR\text{-}TS2 > PAM\text{-}TS1 \tag{10}$$
$$PAM\text{-}CR\text{-}TS2 > PAM\text{-}TS2 \tag{11}$$

By looking at the dominance relationships, we find that every SID primitive authentication mode dominates PAM-CR1 and that no mode dominates PAM-CR-TS2. Hence we can assign the lowest and highest authentication assurance levels respectively to these two modes. Let us start with assigning L0 to PAM-CR1 and look for assigning levels from the hierarchy. Using relationship 1 we can assign level L1 to PAM-CR2. By using relationship 4 and the fact that PAM-CR2 and PAM-TS1 do not have any dominant relationships between them, we can both assign them to level L2. By using this logic we arrive at the following authentication assurance levels for all SID primitive authentication modes as follows: Level L0: Qualifying SID primitive authentication mode: PAM-CR1 Level L1: Dominates PAM-CR1. Qualifying modes: PAM-CR2 and PAM-TS1 Level L2: Dominates any mode in Level L1 or involves more SID authentication factors but no mutual dominance relationship. Qualifying modes: PAM-TS2 and PAM-CR-TS1 Level L3: Dominates all modes. Qualifying mode: PAM-CR-TS2.

4   Advantages of SID-AAM Methodology

Published Literature for analyzing authentication assurance levels for smart identity token-based authentication processes concentrate either on strength of authentication protocols [1,2] or coverage of conventional authentication factors [3,4]. As far as we know SID-AAM is the only methodology that determines authentication assurance levels based on the set of security properties verified. The characteristics that makes this methodology robust are: (a) takes into account all technology-specific entities participating in the authentication processes (b) formulates a set of authentication factors that is specific to SID technology and (c) is based on verified security properties that involve binding between entities as well as consideration of the threats that can affect the integrity of these verifications.

References

1. Securing e-business applications using Smart Cards. IBM Systems Journal 40(3) (2001), http://www.research.ibm.com/journal/sj/403/hamann.html
2. Kumar, M.: New Remote User Authentication Scheme Using Smart Cards. IEEE Transactions on Consumer Electronics 50(2), 597–600 (2004)
3. FIPS 201 - Personal Identity Verification of Federal Employees and Contractors, http://csrc.nist.gov/publications/fips/fips201-1/FIPS-201-1-chng1.pdf
4. TWIC Reader Hardware And Card Application Specification, May 30 (2008), http://www.tsa.gov/assets/pdf/twic_reader_card_app_spec.pdf

A Secure RFID Ticket System for Public Transport

Kun Peng and Feng Bao

Institute for Infocomm Research, Singapore

Abstract. A secure RFID ticket system for public transport is proposed
in this paper. It supports security properties including secure authentication, unforgeability, correct billing and privacy and can prevent various
attacks. It consists of two protocols, both following three principles necessary for secure RFID ticket system. The first protocol is very efficient
and suitable for applications with critical requirement on efficiency. The
second protocol does not need any trust assumption and is suitable for
applications with critical requirement on security.

1 Introduction

RFID ticket system has been widely applied to public transport. Each user of the
public transport system holds a RFID card as his ticket. When the user enters
and leaves the public transport system, his card is read by a checking (verifying)
machine and his authentication is checked. Only valid users are allowed to enjoy
transport service. After each ride, a user's credit is charged. He can top up his
credit when necessary. Security of existing RFID ticket systems is weak and
needs improving. The existing RFID ticket schemes, including efficient solutions
without computation in RFID cards [3,5], solutions authenticating RFID cards
through an identity-linked key [9,1,6,7,8], solutions based on dynamic identity
[4,10] or more recent solutions like [11], cannot achieve strong enough security in
practical applications. Some of them are efficient, but need strong trust on the
participants; some of them are too inefficient when handling real-time tasks and
thus impractical; some of them ignore important security properties. In one word,
they cannot prevent the attacks at a practical cost in a practical environment.

In this paper, two new RFID ticket protocols are proposed. Both of them
follow three principles emphasized in this paper: one-time secret for authentication, secure database to store information and simple billing system to simplify
soundness and privacy. The first protocol does not need the RFID cards to carry
out any computation, so is very efficient. Although it is more secure than many
existing RFID ticket schemes, it needs to trust the vender machines, so still needs
to improve its security mechanism in applications with critical security requirements. The second protocol removes the trust assumption by letting the RFID
cards to carry out some necessary computations. Efficiency improving methods
like allocating costly computations to participants with greater computation capability and carrying out costly computations before hand guarantee that its
efficiency is high enough for its supposed applications.

S. Foresti and S. Jajodia (Eds.): Data and Applications Security XXIV, LNCS 6166, pp. 350–357, 2010.

2 New Schemes

Two new protocols for RFID ticket in public transport are proposed in this section. Before describing the two protocols, three designing principles are proposed and explained. We believe that they are necessary in secure RFID ticket schemes. Then the two protocols, denoted as Protocol 1 and Protocol 2 respectively, are proposed. Both of them follow the three principles. Protocol 1 is very efficient but depends on a trust assumption. Protocol 2 is less efficient but more secure and its efficiency is still practical.

2.1 Three Principles

There are three designing principles we think necessary in design of secure RFID ticket schemes. They are one-time secret, information stored in a database and simple billing mechanism.

Firstly, our analysis leads to a result: unless interactive asymmetric cipher based cryptographic techniques like zero knowledge proof is employed, a RFID card must use different secret information for each authentication operation in a RFID ticket based public transport system.

- If a RFID card uses the same symmetric cipher based secret information for each authentication, it can be linked to the unique authentication secret and thus can be traced.
- A unique authentication secret for a RFID card is liable to replay attack. The unique authentication secret may be reused.

As we stated before, with practical limitations to the computation capability, asymmetric cipher is too costly for authentication, which must be real-time. So to achieve privacy and prevent replay attack, one-time secret is necessary in authentication.

Secondly, we demonstrate that in a RFID ticket based public transportation system there must be a database.

- Although information in the system can be stored in the RFID cards, as stated before, it is difficult to prevent the card from being tampered with if the card owner colludes. Moreover, if the verifiers need to write some information (e.g. billing information) to the cards, a corrupted verifier may write invalid information to the RFID cards. So information on the IFID cards is not reliable and a database is needed to store some important information.
- As costly asymmetric cipher cannot be employed in authentication and one-time authentication secret must be employed, a database is needed to store some verification information, against which the one-time authentication secrets can be tested. For each valid one-time authentication secret, there is corresponding verification record in the database. A one-time authentication secret is accepted if and only if a corresponding verification record can be found in the database. After a one-time authentication secret is successfully verified, its corresponding verification record is deleted from the database so that it cannot be reused.

- If the credit and billing information of a RFID ticket is stored in the RFID card, it may be tampered with as stated before. So we suggest to store it in the same database together with the verification records. Various security mechanisms including access control, file protection, encryption, audit, encryption and sharing of power among multiple parties can be employed in the database to guarantee integrity (and privacy when necessary) of the credit and billing information.

Receiving an authentication query, the database searches its records for the corresponding verification information. The search must be efficient as it must be real-time. So computation in the search must be strictly limited although the database manager may have greater computation capability than the users. So the number of cryptographic operations should be strictly controlled and a large number of cryptographic operations like in [9] must be avoided.

Thirdly, we find that billing system should employ the so-called simple billing mechanism. In a simple billing mechanism, each trip in the public transport system is charged a same amount of credit no matter how long it is. As discussed before, the credit and billing information should be stored in a database. If charging of a RFID card is measured by the length of the trip, the authority in charge of the database must calculate the chargement according to the starting place and the ending place of the trip and thus can collect the card owner's location information and trace him. So for the sake of privacy of RFID card users and to prevent tracing attack, simple billing mechanism should be employed. Actually, this billing mechanism has been widely employed in public transport systems in many cities in the world.

2.2   Protocol 1

Protocol 1 is a simple and secure RFID based protocol for public transport especially suitable for low-capability RFID cards. In Protocol 1, a RFID card does not need to perform any computation. However, the vender machines must be trusted. The RFID card defined suitable for public transport is used. The three principles, one-time secret, database and simple billing mechanism are employed in Protocol 1. When a user buys a new RFID card or tops up his RFID card at a vender machine, the vender machine receives his payment and calculates how many times the user is allowed to use the public transport service according to the simple billing mechanism. Suppose the user's payment enables t times of service. The vender machine generates $2t$ verification tokens and stores them in the users' RFID card. The vender machine generates a verification record for each token and then stores the $2t$ tokens in the database, each in a random different place. Each trip costs a user two tokens in his card. Each of the two tokens is verified against the corresponding record in the database, which is deleted afterward. Detailed description of the protocol is as follows.

1. A database is set up. The vender machines have the right to insert records to the database. The check machines in the transport stations are verifiers and can query the database for a record. The database can automatically delete

a record after it matches a query. Necessary security measures like access control, file protection, encryption, audit, sharing of power are employed to guarantee that the data in the database is confidential and integrated.

2. A public one-way collision-resistent hash function $H()$ is set up to be used.
3. Initiation and top up

   A user accesses a vender machine to fill up a new RFID card or top up an old RFID card. The user pays money for t time usage of the public transport system. The vender machine operates as follows.

   (a) The vender machine randomly chooses $2t$ integers $a_1, a_2, \ldots, a_{2t}$ in Z_L where L is a security parameter decided by setting of $H()$ and system parameters like the number of users and the size of the public transport system.

   (b) The vender machine writes $a_2, a_3, \ldots, a_{2t}$ to the memory space for secret data in the RFID card. It writes a_1 to the outward readable memory space of the RFID card.

   (c) The vender machine separately inserts $H(a_1), H(a_2), \ldots, H(a_{2t})$ into the database. The vender machine does not send the records for the tokens of a card together in a batch so that neither the receiving database nor an eavesdropper can tell which records belong to the same RFID card. Instead some of the records of a newly updated RFID card is submitted, being mixed with the unsubmitted records of earlier updated RFID cards. The unsubmitted records of the newly updated RFID card will be submitted later, being mixed with the records of later updated RFID cards. This data insertion mechanism is called SMI (separate and mixed insertion). As no user will use up all his tokens just after buying them, SMI does not affect usability of the tokens.

4. Using the public transport

   (a) When a user enters the public transport system, he puts his RFID card on a checking machines (verifier or called reader). The checking machine reads the token in the outward readable memory space of the RFID card. Suppose the token it obtains is u.

   (b) The checking machine queries the database to search for $H(u)$. If $H(u)$ is a record in the database, the RFID card passes the authentication and the user is allowed to enter.

   (c) If the searched item is a record in the database, the database automatically deletes the record.

   (d) After being allowed in, the RFID card removes one token from its memory space for secret data and puts it in its outward readable memory to replace the used token.

   (e) When a user leaves the public transport system, he puts his RFID card on a checking machines. The checking machine reads the token in the outward readable memory space of the RFID card. Suppose the token it obtains is u'.

   (f) The checking machine queries the database to search for $H(u')$. If $H(u')$ is a record in the database, the RFID card passes the authentication the user is allowed to leave. Otherwise the user is punished.

(g) If the searched item is a record in the database, the database automatically deletes the record.
(h) After being allowed to leave, the RFID card removes one token from its memory space for secret data and puts it in its outward readable memory to replace the used token.

Protocol 1 can prevent some usual attacks.

- As one-time secret is used for authentication, replay attack cannot work no matter the attacker is the user himself or a third party.
- Forging credit attack is prevented as the credit information is stored in a secure database.
- Forging attack against authentication is difficult. With the assumption that the data stored in the RFID memory for secret information is unreadable without the card user's cooperation, the verifiers cannot obtain any token from any RFID card before it is used. As $H()$ is one-way, even if the communication between the vender machines and the database is intercepted by an attacker, it cannot find any token from the intercepted verification information. So unless the card owner or the vender machine is the attacker, forging attack against authentication cannot work. Even if a card owner launches a forging attack, takes out some tokens from his RFID card and copies it into a forged card, he does not benefit from the attack and cannot double use any of his tokens as the tokens are one-time secrets. So the only harmful forging attack is launched by the vender machine, who should be trusted not to record the tokens it generates and use them to launch a forging attack.
- As one-time secret tokens are used in authentication and submission of verification records from the vender machines to the database is through SMI, no one can link different tokens for a user unless a vender machine colludes with multiple verifiers. The only possible tracing attack is a collusion between a vender machine and multiple verifiers. The vender machine records the tokens of a user and share them with many verifiers. The verifiers look for the revealed tokens and record the locations they appear. If the vender machines are assumed to be trusted, no tracing attack can work.

2.3   Protocol 2

Protocol 1 is very efficient as it only employs hash function and does not need any asymmetric cipher. The RFID cards in it do not even need to carry out any computation. However, the vender machines must be trusted in it. Although techniques like tamper-resistent device may be applied to the vender machines to stengthen security and reduce the risk, the trust assumption is still too strong in some circumstances. So Protocol 2 is designed to remove the trust assumption. In Protocol 2, the RFID cards need to perform some computations when being filled up or topped up. As the computation does not need to be real-time and mostly depends on symmetric cipher, it is acceptable. Especially, some costly computation can be performed before hand so that when they are needed they are ready for use already. In protocol 2, a RFID card generates the tokens it buys itself using a hash chain. It then submits the end of the hash chain to the vender machine it uses, who forwards the end of the hash chain to the database. The vender machine helps the RFID card to encrypt the other nodes of the hash chain, which are stored in the RFID card as tokens. Detailed description of the protocol is as follows.

1. A database is set up. Multiple authorities are in charge of the database and for security they share the power of managing the database. The authorities receive records from the vender machines and insert them into the database. They also handle the verifiers' queries and search the database to answer them. As mentioned before, necessary security measures for database are employed to guarantee security of the database. The database authorities set up a Paillier encryption algorithm and they share the private key. Decryption is feasible only if the number of cooperating authorities is over a threshold. To learn more details about secure sharing of private key in Paillier encryption, interested readers are referred to [2].
2. A one-way collision-resistant hash function $H'()$ is set up and published.
3. Initiation and topping up
   A user accesses a vender machine to fill up a new RFID card or top up an old RFID card. The user pays money for t time usage of the public transport system. He and the vender machine operate as follows.

   (a) The vender machine generates $2k$ probabilistic random encryptions of 0 using the database authorities' public key: $e_0, e_1, \ldots, e_{2t-1}$. Note that although the generation needs $2k$ modulo exponentiations, it can be performed before hand so that when they are needed they are ready for use already. So it does not affect efficiency. The vender machine gives $e_0, e_1, \ldots, e_{2t-1}$ to the RFID card.
   (b) The RFID card chooses a seed s from the input space of $H'()$ and calculates tokens $a_i = H'(a_{i-1})$ for $i = 1, 2, \ldots, 2t$ where $a_0 = s$.
   (c) The RFID card calculates $b_i = a_i e_{\pi(i)}$ for $i = 0, 1, \ldots, 2t-1$ where $\pi()$ is a permutation of $\{0, 1, \ldots, 2t-1\}$. It stores $b_0, b_1, \ldots, b_{2t-2}$ in the memory space for secret data in his RFID card. $b_0, b_1, \ldots, b_{2t-2}$ are stored in their order. More precisely, the memory space for secret data is a stack such that b_0 is in the bottom of the stack, b_1 is on top of b_0, b_2 is on top of b_1, ..., b_{2t-2} is on top of b_{2t-3}. The RFID card stores b_{2t-1} in the outward readable memory space of the RFID card.
   (d) The RFID card submits a_{2t} to the vender machine.
   (e) The vender machines submits $(a_{2t}, 2t)$ to the database.
   (f) The database authorities store $(a_{2t}, 2t)$ in the database as a record.

4. Using the public transport

   (a) When a user enters the public transport system, he puts his RFID card on a checking machines (verifier or called reader). The checking machine reads the data in the outward readable memory space of the RFID card. Suppose the data it obtains is v.

(b) The checking machine sends v to the database.
(c) The database authorities cooperate to decrypt v and obtain the message
    in it r. Details of distributed Paillier decryption can be found in [2].
    If $H'(r)$ is in a record in the database and the other item in the same
    record (indicating the left credits the user has) is larger than zero,
       i. the RFID card passes the authentication and the user is allowed to
         enter;
       ii. the database aothorities replace $H'(r)$ with r;
       iii. 1 is subtracted from the other item in the same record.
    Otherwise, entry is rejected.
(d) After being allowed in, the RFID card removes one token on the top
    of its memory stack for secret data and puts it in its outward readable
    memory to replace the used token.
(e) When a user leaves the public transport system, he puts his RFID card
    on a checking machines. The checking machine reads the data in the
    outward readable memory space of the RFID card. Suppose the data it
    obtains is v'.
(f) The checking machine sends v' to the database.
(g) The database authorities cooperate to decrypt v' and obtains the mes-
    sage in it r'. If $H'(r')$ is a record in the database and the other item in
    the same record (indicating the left credits the user has) is larger than
    zero,
       i. the RFID card passes the authentication and the user is allowed to
         leave;
       ii. the database aothorities replace $H'(r')$ with r';
       iii. 1 is subtracted from the other item in the same record.
    Otherwise the user is punished.
(h) After being allowed to leave, the RFID card removes one token on the top
    of its memory stack for secret data and puts it in its outward readable
    memory to replace the used token.

Protocol 2 can prevent usual attacks

– As one-time secret is used for authentication, replay attack cannot work no
  matter the attacker is the user himself or a third party.
– Forging credit attack is prevented as the credit information is stored in a
  secure database.
– Forging attack against authentication is difficult. With the assumption that
  the data stored in the RFID memory for secret information is unreadable
  without the card user's cooperation, the verifiers cannot obtain any token
  from any RFID card before it is used. The tokens are generated by the
  RFID cards themselves and are unknown to the vender machines. So without
  any trust on the vender machines it is guaranteed that the tokens are not
  revealed. The vender machines only know the end of each hash chain, whose
  other nodes are the authentication secrets. As $H()$ is one-way, the vender
  machines cannot obtain any authentication secrets. For the same reason,
  even if an end of a hash chain sent from a vender machine to the database

is intercepted by an attacker, it cannot find any secret token. So unless the card owner is the attacker, forging attack cannot work. Even if a card owner launches a forging attack, takes out some tokens from his RFID card and copies it into a forged card, he does not benefit from the attack and cannot double use any of his tokens as the tokens are one-time secrets.

- As one-time secret used for authentication are in ciphertext, the verifiers cannot link the one-time tokens of the same user although they are in a hash chain. So even if a vender machine colludes with multiple verifiers, no tracing attack can work as none of them knows the plaintexts of the one-time tokens.

3   Conclusion

Each of the two protocols has its advantages and suitable application circumstance. Protocol 1 is suitable for applications requiring high efficiency and tolerating some trust assumption, while Protocol 2 is suitable of applications requiring high security and less critical with efficiency. The two protocols show that the three principles can be applied to design secure RFID ticket systems in practice. The two new RFID ticket protocols in this paper are secure and efficient and are respectively suitable for two different kinds of public transport applications.

References

1. Dimitriou, T.: A lightweight rfid protocol to protect against traceability and cloning attacks. In: ICSPEACN 2005, pp. 59–66 (2005)
2. Fouque, P., Poupard, G., Stern, J.: Sharing decryption in the context of voting or lotteries. In: Frankel, Y. (ed.) FC 2000. LNCS, vol. 1962, pp. 90–104. Springer, Heidelberg (2001)
3. Camenisch, J., Ateniese, G., de Medeiros, B.: Untraceable rfid tags via insubvertible encryption. In: ACM CCS 2005, pp. 92–101 (2005)
4. Henrici, D., Muller, P.: Hash-based enhancement of location privacy for radio-frequency identification devices using varying identifiers. In: IEEE CPCC 2004, pp. 149–153 (2004)
5. Juels, A., Pappu, R.: Squealing euros: Privacy protection in rfidenabled banknotes. In: Wright, R.N. (ed.) FC 2003. LNCS, vol. 2742, pp. 103–121. Springer, Heidelberg (2003)
6. Lim, C., Kwon, T.: Strong and robust rfid authentication enabling perfect ownership transfer. In: Ning, P., Qing, S., Li, N. (eds.) ICICS 2006. LNCS, vol. 4307, pp. 1–20. Springer, Heidelberg (2006)
7. Molnar, D., Wagner, D.: Privacy and security in library rfid: Issues, practices, and architectures. In: ACM CCS 2006, pp. 210–219 (2006)
8. Song, B., Mitchell, C.: Rfid authentication protocol for low-cost tags. In: ACM CWNS 2008, pp. 140–147 (2008)
9. Rivest, R., Weis, S., Sarma, S., Engels, D.: Security and privacy aspects of low-cost radio frequency identification systems. In: ICSPC 2003, pp. 50–59 (2003)
10. Tsudik, G.: Ya-trap: Yet another trivial rfid authentication protocol. In: IEEE PCCW 2006, pp. 640–643 (2006)
11. Sadeghi, A., Visconti, I., Wachsmann, C.: User privacy in transport systems based on rfid e-tickets. In: PILBA 2008 (2008)

Performance Evaluation of Non-parallelizable Client Puzzles for Defeating DoS Attacks in Authentication Protocols

Suratose Tritilanunt

Computer Engineering Department, Faculty of Engineering, Mahidol University
25/25, Salaya, Phuttamonthol, Nakornpathom, Thailand, 73170
egstl@mahidol.ac.th

Abstract. We provides an evaluation of non-parallelizable puzzles used to prevent DoS in authentication protocols. With an evaluation based on a simulation and performance analysis, this approach helps a responder to resist against DoS, as well as improves the throughput of services for legitimate clients. Another key strength is that the construction and verification at the responder is simple and fast.

1 Introduction

Client puzzles in computer network was first introduced by Dwork and Naor [1] for combating junk emails. Almost a decade, Juels and Brainard [2] adopted this technique to defeat denial-of-service (DoS) attacks in network protocols. Later on, many techniques have been proposed for constructing client puzzles, for examples, Hash-based Reversal Puzzles [2,3,4], Time-Lock Puzzles [5], and Diffie-Hellman based Puzzles [6].

Hash-based constructions meet many of the desirable properties of proofs of work [7], but they also have the property that exhaustive searching of a pre-image search space is a parallelizable task. Using such a technique in the presence of an adversary with access to distributed computing resources may leave authentication protocols exposed to DoS. Adopting alternate puzzle constructions, such as time lock puzzles that are inherently sequential and non-parallelizable, may need to be considered for protocols that are to be used in an environment where the adversarial model assumes that significant resources are available to the attacker.

A client puzzle is non-parallelizable if the solution to the puzzle cannot be computed in parallel. Non-parallelizable client puzzles can be used to defend against distributed denial-of-service (DDoS) attacks, where a single adversary can control a large group of compromised machines. This adversary could distribute puzzles to other compromised machines to obtain puzzle solutions faster than the time expected by the server. This kind of attack is identified as strong attacks [8].

Two examples of a puzzle construction which was implemented for preventing strong attacks are a *hash chain* [9,10], and a *modified repeated squaring* technique [11]. Because a nature of chaining requires a previous value for constructing

S. Foresti and S. Jajodia (Eds.): Data and Applications Security XXIV, LNCS 6166, pp. 358–365, 2010.
© IFIP International Federation for Information Processing 2010

the next consecutive items, the construction of hash chain can prevent parallel searching. In a repeated squaring puzzles, the developer improves a modular arithmetic calculation of Time-Lock Puzzles [5] to achieves a fast verification and a non-parallizable feature.

To address the problem of parallelizable client puzzles, this paper proposes a construction having characteristics comparable to time-lock and hash chain puzzles but the new scheme requires less computation in the puzzle construction and verification. Our new puzzle scheme including puzzle construction, puzzle solving, and puzzle verification, as well as the experimental results which are examined based on the performance analysis using CPN Tools are provided in this paper.

2 Non-parallelizable Puzzles Based on Subset Sum

Apart from a brute-force searching (that requires a running time of order $\mathcal{O}(2^n n)$, where n represents the number of decision variables) used to solve subset sum problems, an alternative technique used to successfully break subset sum problems is called a lattice basis reduction. There are several lattice reduction algorithms but the best method so far for breaking the subset sum problems is the LLL or L^3 algorithm developed by Lenstra et al. [12]. LLL algorithm has been widely used in breaking subset sum cryptosystems [13,14] because the algorithm is able to terminate in polynomial time. Moreover, it is highly sequential because the underlying program requires recursive computation. From this perspective, LLL is a promising technique to fulfill our requirement in terms of non-parallelizability and thwart coordinated adversaries from distributing the client puzzle to calculate the solution in a parallel manner. Details of L^3 lattice basis reduction is beyond our scope of this paper, so we encourage the reader interested in more detail to read the papers by Nguyen and Stern [14], and Joux and Stern [13].

2.1 Puzzle Construction, Solving, and Verification

To establish a secure connection to a responder R, I sends a request containing an identity (ID_I) along with a random nonce (N_I). The responder chooses a secret parameter s randomly to make the output unique for each communication, and decides a puzzle difficulty k depending on the workload condition. The value of k should be selected to be at least 25 in order to guarantee that the coordinated adversary requires over a thousand compromised machines to brute-force search or over a hundred compromised machines to run bounding algorithm on the subset sum puzzles at the equivalent time to the legitimate user performing LLL lattice reduction. As a practical choice we suggest to take a value of k between 25 and 100 and then if weights are chosen to be of length 200 bits we can ensure that the generated knapsack has density at most 0.5. Practical experimental tests can be found in [15] which support our proposal.

Figure 1 represents the *puzzle construction*. The responder R computes a hash operation $(H(\cdot))$, and computes $(LSB((\cdot), k)_2)$ to obtain k bits from the output

	I	R

		Precomputed parameters

Precomputed parameters
set of random weight w_n
$$w_n = H(w_{n-1})$$

1) send *request* $\xrightarrow{\quad ID_I, N_I \quad}$

choose *secret* $s \in_R \mathcal{Z}_n$
choose *puzzle difficulty* $k \rightarrow 25 \leq k \leq 100$
$$C = LSB(H(ID_I, N_I, ID_R, N_R, s)), k)_2$$
$$W = \sum_{i=1}^{k} C_i \cdot w_i$$
$$puzzle = (w_1, W, k)$$

2) verify ID_I, N_I $\qquad \xleftarrow[ID_R, N_R, puzzle]{ID_I, N_I,}$

generate $w_k = H(w_{k-1})$
form a Basis Set B
run *LLL Reduction* $\rightarrow$ get C'
check $W \stackrel{?}{=} \sum_{i=1}^{k} C'_i \cdot w_i$

3) return C' $\qquad \xrightarrow[N_R, puzzle, C']{ID_I, N_I, ID_R,}$

option 1) check $C' \stackrel{?}{=} C$
option 2) re-generate C
$$C = LSB(H(ID_I, N_I, ID_R, N_R, s)), k)_2$$
check $C' \stackrel{?}{=} C$

Fig. 1. Subset Sum Puzzles

of hash function. Finally, R forms a *puzzle* by computing a desired weight (W) that it wants a client to solve from a pre-computed set of random weight (w_n). To save on protocol bandwidth, weights can be generated given the initial random weight w_1 by iterative hashing. Hence, a puzzle contains an initial value of weight of the first item (w_1), a desired weight (W), and puzzle difficulty (k).

Considering the client's job for *solving a puzzle*, it begins to generate a series of random weights, $(w_1, w_2, \ldots, w_k)$, by computing a hash chain on an initial value w_1. Then, the client constructs a basis reduction set B as $b_1 = (1, 0, \ldots, 0, w_1)$, $b_2 = (0, 1, \ldots, 0, w_2)$, $b_k = (0, 0, \ldots, 1, w_k)$; and $b_{k+1} = (0, 0, \ldots, 0, -W)$. Finally, the client runs a LLL Basis Reduction [16] which is the most effective method to find moderately short lattice vectors in polynomial time. It is important to note that, the protocol does not limit the client to use LLL algorithm to solve the puzzles. However, using other techniques, such as brute-force search in traditional puzzles, might take an unreasonable interval to solve our scheme.

In terms of the puzzle granularity, there are two possible options for the responder to adjust the puzzle difficult; 1) adjusting the item size (n), or 2) adjusting the density (B). Both modifications affect the running time by a factor $(n^\alpha \cdot \log^\beta B)$, where α and β are real numbers dependent on the version of LLL basis reduction. Since the complexity of LLL basis reduction is a polynomial function, we conclude that our subset sum puzzles provide a polynomial granularity.

2.2 Comparison of Client Puzzle Properties

Based on the properties of good puzzles defined by Juels and Brainard [2]), only Repeated-squaring, Hash Chain, and Subset Sum puzzles can provide non-parallelization. Comparing our construction with the others, we find that both of them suffer from high computation at construction time which means that a responder using these puzzles would be susceptible to flooding attacks. Since our scheme has coarser granularity than Repeated-squaring and Hash Chain puzzles, this issue could be an interesting open problem for the research community to explore techniques providing both non-parallelization and linear granularity.

Table 1. Summary of Puzzles in term of Proposed Desirable Properties

Puzzle Type	Properties for Good Puzzles						
	Easy to Construct and Verify	Easy to Adjust	Not Require Specialised Client Hardware	Solution cannot be pre-computed	Server does not store solution	Non-parallelization	Granularity
Hash-based Reversal	✓	✓	✓	✓	✓	X	Exponential
Hint-Based Hash Reversal	✓	✓	✓	✓	✓	X	Linear
Repeated-Squaring	X	✓	✓	✓	✓	✓	Linear
DH-based	X	✓	✓	✓	X	X	Linear
Trapdoor RSA	X	✓	✓	✓	X	X	Linear
Trapdoor DLP	X	✓	✓	✓	X	X	Linear
Hash Chain	X	✓	✓	✓	✓	✓	Linear
Subset Sum	✓	✓	✓	✓	✓	✓	Polynomial

3 Performance Analysis on Subset Sum Puzzles

By replacing a hash-based reversal scheme with our subset sum puzzles, we set up a formal time-based model using CPN Tools as our formalism.

3.1 Tolerance of a DoS-Resistant Protocol

Evaluating tolerance of the server under DoS attacks is the major purpose of this experiment. We set up the experiment to measure tolerance of the server under two different workloads (Z); LOW for the light-load, and $HIGH$ for the heavy-load, from five types of adversaries as following

Type 1 adversary or ad1 computes a valid first message (may be pre-computed in practice), and takes no further action in the protocol.
Type 2 adversary or ad2 completes the protocol normally including searching a correct client puzzle solution C' until the third message is sent and takes no further action after this.
Type 3 adversary or ad3 searches for a correct client puzzle solution C' but randomly chooses the remaining message elements, then takes no further action in the protocol.
Coordinated Type 3 adversary or Co_ad3 is similar to Type 3 adversaries, except that Coordinated Type 3 adversaries are able to control a group of compromised machines to solve puzzles in parallel for obtaining the solution with a certain period.

Table 2. Percentage of Throughput with Hash-based Reversal and Subset Sum Puzzles

Adversaries	LOW		HIGH	
	Hash-based Reversal	Subset Sum	Hash-based Reversal	Subset Sum
ad1	100	100	100	100
ad2	71.60	80.65	42.05	48.25
ad3	62.95	70.50	31.45	33.20
Co_ad3	18.50	71.50	4.95	35.80
ad4	87.20	99.95	83.20	87.45

Type 4 adversary or ad4 is like an adversary type 3, except that the client puzzle solution C' is now also chosen randomly.

Table 2 summarizes experimental results as the percentage of a number of successful legitimate requests that the responder can serve under different adversarys abilities. While the output from Type 2 and Type 3 adversaries shows a slight improvement, the most contrast comes from Coordinated Type 3 adversary. Obviously, this is because hash-based reveral client puzzles have not been designed to tolerate the parallel computation from Coordinated Type 3 adversary.

3.2   Performance Analysis of Subset Sum Puzzles

To evaluate our mechanism, we apply a performance analysis to investigate our puzzles. By means of statistical analysis, we pay more attention to quantitative information about the performance including user processing time compared to server processing time, queue delay on the server at request messages and puzzle verification, as well as number of rejected packets of legitimate users. Table 3 represents our experimental result.

1) ad_Processing Time: This information represents how much computation is spent in the attack in comparison with the responder to defend such attacks as quantitative measurement in cost-based analysis of Meadows' proposal [17].

Table 3. Performance of Adjustable Subset Sum Client Puzzles

Performance Factors	Adjustable Subset Sum Puzzles									
	ad1		ad2		ad3		Co_ad3		ad4	
	LOW	HIGH	LOW	HIGH	LOW	HIGH	LOW	HIGH	LOW	HIGH
ad_Processing Time	50	500	75200	2645147.06	40638	2006222.03	150	1500	100	1000
responder Processing Time	42835	176260	69017	216540	103991.06	266340.90	107611.54	281906.65	42885	171704.86
Time Out at MSG1	0%	0%	0%	0%	0%	0%	0%	0%	0%	0%
Max Delay at MSG1	69	519	69	519	69	519	99.65	523.90	69	519
Max Delay at MSG3	0	0	1481	1494	1858.14	1716.35	2456.12	2265.87	0	1354.50

From Table 3, **ad2** takes the longest time because **ad2** computes puzzle solving and signature generation, while **ad1** spends less computation to mount DoS attack since they only create and flood bogus requests at step 1. However if we compare the result to Table 2, both **ad1** and **ad2** do not achieve their DoS attacks. From this point of view, other factors should be combined in the evaluation.

2) responder Processing Time: It has been used as a cost factor to compare with the adversaries' processing time for estimating the effect of DoS attacks. As shown in Table 3, the responder wastes maximum computation to **ad3** and **Co_ad3**, while spends lesser computation for **ad1**, **ad2**, and **ad4** approximately. This is because the responder can detect the attacks from **ad4** and disregard them very quickly. Considering the former case, **ad2** does not cause much destruction in comparison with **ad3** and **Co_ad3** because **ad2** requires to compute both puzzles and digital signature. Unlike **ad2**, **ad3** and **Co_ad3** do not compute the digital signature, so their bogus messages arrive to the responder quickly and those bogus packets have longer period to stay in the queue before puzzles expire. Although the responder is able to detect the attacks at signature verification, it is too late for serving legitimate users since the signature verification is an expensive operation which requires plenty of time.

3) Time Out at MSG1: It provides information regarding to how effective are flooding attacks from **ad1**, which is the most common and easiest DoS technique. Since most authentication protocols nowadays implement stateless connection and cookies to thwart TCP SYN flooding attacks, it is more difficult for adversaries to mount the attacks using this simple techniques. This factor also refers to the efficiency of the puzzle generation of the responder in order to deal with large numbers of flooding attacks. As shown in the table, there are no rejected messages at this state for any attacking strategies because our puzzle generation is very fast. The puzzle can therefore be a powerful defending approach as a first line of defense when we combine with other DoS-resistant mechanisms.

4) Max Delay at MSG1 and MSG3: These two values show the maximum time delay of incoming packets in the queue at protocol step 1 and step 3 on the responder. The delay at step 1 indicates the efficiency of the responder to generate the client puzzles, while the delay at step 3 can be referred to the efficiency of the puzzle validation. Not surprisingly the longer delay in the queue at step 3 is, the more degradation of overall services in the system will be. The reason is because the jobs at step 3, which primarily consists of puzzle and signature verification, requires longer time to execute than the job at state 1. In addition, the delay at state 3 might cause the increment of rejected messages at step 1 if the accumulation on the incoming messages at step 3 is increasing at a high rate and keeps the responder busy processing these packets until requests at state 1 have reached or exceeded the maximum time-out period. From the performance result, only **ad3** and **Co_ad3** are able to boost up the delay on both states in our puzzles.

In summary, our subset sum puzzles function properly at least under five proposed attacking strategies. Particularly, they can prevent users from gaining

advantages by searching valid puzzle solutions more quickly by parallel computation. Moreover, the performance of subset sum puzzle construction and puzzle
generation functions effectively as shown in the performance analysis. This leads
to the improvement of the tolerance under all defined denial-of-service techniques.

4 Conclusion

With regard to lacking of the parallelism characteristic in existing client puzzles,
we proposes a new puzzle construction based on the subset sum problem. Un-
doubtedly, the primary strength over others is non-parallelization. In addition,
the puzzle construction and verification requires simple and fast computation
on the responder as shown in the performance analysis. Evaluation by using
performance analysis under five performance parameters and the percentage of
successful service shows that our new approach improves the throughput in comparison with hash-based reversal technique.

References

1. Dwork, C., Naor, M.: Pricing via Processing or Combatting Junk Mail. In: Brick-
ell, E.F. (ed.) CRYPTO 1992. LNCS, vol. 740, pp. 139–147. Springer, Heidelberg
(1993)
2. Juels, A., Brainard, J.: Client Puzzles: A Cryptographic Defense Against Connection Depletion Attacks. In: the 1999 Network and Distributed System Security
Symposium (NDSS 1999), San Diego, California, USA, February 1999, pp. 151–165
(1999)
3. Aura, T., Nikander, P., Leiwo, J.: DoS-resistant authentication with client puzzles.
In: Christianson, B., Crispo, B., Malcolm, J.A., Roe, M. (eds.) Security Protocols
2000. LNCS, vol. 2133, pp. 170–181. Springer, Heidelberg (2001)
4. Feng, W.: The case for TCP/IP Puzzles. In: ACM SIGCOMM 2003 Workshops,
Karlsruhe, Germany, August 25-27, pp. 322–327. ACM Press, New York (2003)
5. Rivest, R.L., Shamir, A., Wagner, D.A.: Time-lock Puzzles and Timed-release
Crypto. Technical Report TR-684, Massachusetts Institute of Technology,
Cambridge, MA, USA (March 10, 1996)
6. Waters, B., Juels, A., Halderman, J.A., Felten, E.W.: New Client Puzzle Outsourcing Techniques for DoS Resistance. In: the 11th ACM Conference on Computer
and Communications Security (CCS 2004), USA. ACM Press, New York (2004)
7. Jakobsson, M., Juels, A.: Proofs of work and bread pudding protocols. In: The IFIP
TC6 and TC11 Joint Working Conference on Communications and Multimedia
Security (CMS 1999) (September 1999)
8. Bocan, V., Cosma, M.F.: Adaptive Threshold Puzzles. In: EUROCON 2005 - The
International Conference on Computer as a tool, Belgrade, Serbia and Montenegro,
November 22-24 (2005)
9. Ma, M.: Mitigating denial of service attacks with password puzzles. In: International Conference on Information Technology: Coding and Computing (ITCC
2005), vol. 2, pp. 621–626 (2005)
10. Groza, B., Petrica, D.: On Chained Cryptographic Puzzles. In: 3rd Romanian-
Hungarian Joint Symposium on Applied Computational Intelligence (SACI),
Timisoara, Romania, May 25-26 (2006)

11. Jeckmans, A.J.P.: Practical client puzzle from repeated squaring. Master's thesis (September 2009)
12. Lenstra, A.K., Lenstra Jr., H.W., Lovász, L.: Factoring Polynomials with Rational Coefficients. Mathematische Annalen 261(4), 515–534 (1982)
13. Joux, A., Stern, J.: Lattice Reduction: A Toolbox for the Cryptanalyst. Journal of Cryptology: the journal of the International Association for Cryptologic Research 11(3), 161–185 (1998)
14. Nguyen, P.Q., Stern, J.: Lattice Reduction in Cryptology: An Update. In: Bosma, W. (ed.) ANTS 2000. LNCS, vol. 1838, pp. 85–112. Springer, Heidelberg (2000)
15. Tritilanunt, S., Boyd, C., Foo, E., Nieto, J.M.G.: Toward Non-Parallelizable Client Puzzles. In: Bao, F., Ling, S., Okamoto, T., Wang, H., Xing, C. (eds.) CANS 2007. LNCS, vol. 4856, pp. 247–264. Springer, Heidelberg (2007)
16. Coster, M.J., Joux, A., LaMacchia, B.A., Odlyzko, A.M., Schnorr, C., Stern, J.: Improved low-density subset sum algorithms. Computational Complexity 2(2), 111–128 (1992)
17. Meadows, C.: A Cost-Based Framework for Analysis of DoS in Networks. Journal of Computer Security 9(1/2), 143–164 (2001)

Secure Location Verification
A Security Analysis of GPS Signal Authentication

Georg T. Becker[1,2], Sherman C. Lo[3], David S. De Lorenzo[3],
Per K. Enge[3], and Christof Paar[1]

[1] Horst Görtz Institute for IT Security, Ruhr University Bochum, Germany
[2] University of Massachusetts Amherst, USA
[3] Stanford University, USA

Abstract. The use of location based services has increased significantly over the last few years. However, location information is only sparsely used as a security mechanism. One of the reasons for this is the lack of location verification techniques with global coverage. Recently, a new method for authenticating signals from Global Navigation Satellite Systems(GNSS) such as GPS or Galileo has been proposed. In this paper, we analyze the security of this signal authentication mechanism and show how it can be used to establish a secure location verification service with global coverage. This new security service can be used to increase the security of various different applications, even if they are not directly connected to navigation or positioning.

1 Introduction

The use of location based services has grown tremendously in recent years. One of the reasons is that the GNSS receivers have become very small and cheap. Many mobile phones, for example, already have GPS capability. There has also been research in the area of location based access control, mainly for wireless networks. However, there has been a lack of technologies that can provide location verification services with global coverage. But location has great potential to be used as a cryptographic primitive. In many cases, a communication partner can be identified primarily by its location. In other cases the location can be used as an additional authentication parameter to increase the strength of an authentication protocol. In [1] the idea of using GPS to establish a location verification service was first introduced. However, this approach relied on the fact that the verifier as well as the user both have a trusted GPS-authentication device. Furthermore, this approach is vulnerable to spoofing, especially since the selective availability was turned off. Recently, Lo et al. introduced a new way to authenticate GPS signals in [2] called SAGA. In this paper we analyze the security of this new signal authentication mechanism and evaluate its usability. The advantage of this mechanism is that it does not only increase the security of location *self-verification*, but it can also be used for location *verification*. Previous approaches of location verification either relied on trusted devices or on bidirectional systems with only local coverage such as distance bounding [3]. In SAGA

S. Foresti and S. Jajodia (Eds.): Data and Applications Security XXIV, LNCS 6166, pp. 366–373, 2010.

on the other hand, the location and time of the reception of any GPS signal can be securely determined. This enables a location verification service that does not need any trusted devices and that does not need to have a bidirectional communication with any location service provider. Therefore, SAGA can be used as a building block to set up different secure location based services, ranging from traditional applications such as secure positioning and secure tracking to new applications such as location based access control. The main difference between this paper and [2] is that in [2] SAGA is described from a technical and navigational point of view. It includes a proof of concept implementation and complexity estimations but does not explain any possible attacks on the system nor states any security assumptions. In this paper we will look at SAGA from the computer security point of view. The second chapter is aimed to provide enough information so that non-navigation experts can understand the functionality of SAGA and our security analysis. In the third chapter we then come to the security analysis of SAGA by explaining the possible attacks on the system. From this threat analysis we then derive the security assumptions under which the system is secure. The conclusions from this security analysis are drawn in the last section. As location verification is not commonly defined in the literature yet, we start this paper with a definition of location verification and location self-verification: In secure *location verification from A to B*, B can be sure that entity A was at location L_A at time t. In secure *location self-verification for A*, A can be sure that A was at location L_A at time t.

2   Secure Authentication for GNSS Applications (SAGA)

In this section, we give an overview how Secure Authentication for GNSS Applications (SAGA) works. A more technical description of SAGA with test results can be found in [2]. In this paper we explain SAGA using GPS, but as other GNSS systems such as GALILEO or COMPASS work similarly, they can be used with SAGA as well.

GPS Background

In GPS, the position is determine by measuring the arrival times of signals from different GPS satellites. With these arrival times, pseudo ranges between the receiver and the satellites are determined. Trilateration is used to calculate the position of the receiver out of these pseudo-ranges. Signals from four different satellites are needed to solve the trilateration equations, three to determine the 3-dimensional position and one to determine the accurate time. In the current GPS constellation (typically 24-32 satellites), all satellites transmit signals on at least two frequencies: L1 and L2 (at 1575.42 MHz and 1227.60 MHz, respectively). The GPS satellites transmit a civilian signal on the L1 frequency. This C/A-code sequence (for Coarse Acquisition) is publicly available free-of-charge to any user worldwide. GPS satellites also transmit a secret military signal on both L1 and L2. This P-code (for Precision) sequence is encrypted to deny access to

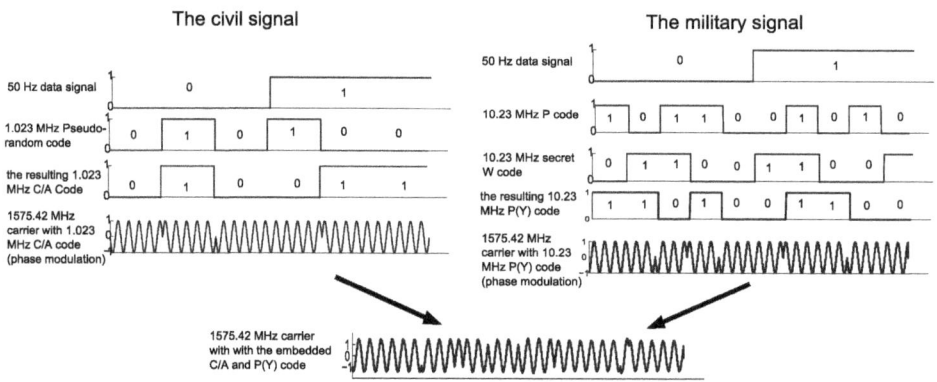

Fig. 1. The GPS signal structure on the L1 frequency

unauthorized users, becoming the P(Y)-code. As all satellites transmit on the same frequency, code-division multiple access is used to ensure that the satellites do not interfere with each other. Figure 1 illustrates the GPS signal structure. The 50 Hz data signal gets added (XOR) with the 1.023 MHz C/A code sequence. This C/A code is a pseudo-random code sequence with a length of 1023 bits (also called chips). Each satellite has its own unique pseudo-random code sequence. The resulting combination of the 50Hz data message with the 1.023 MHz C/A code is transmitted using binary phase modulation on a sinusoidal 1575.42 MHz carrier frequency. By adding the 50 Hz data signal with the 1.023 MHz C/A code, the signal is spread over a wider bandwidth. In this way, the signal can be recovered, although the signal is transmitted roughly 20 DB below the thermal noise floor. To recover the signal, a code replica of the C/A code is correlated with the received signal. A correlation peak shows the presence of the C/A code in the received signal. A positive correlation peak indicates that the currently transmitted data bit is a '0', a negative correlation peak indicates a '1'. The military P(Y) code works in nearly the same way. Instead of the 1.023 MHz C/A code, a 10.23 MHz P code is used. This has the effect that the code is hidden deeper in the noise. To restrict access to this signal, the P code gets encrypted to the P(Y) code by adding a secret and very long pseudo-random sequence W to the P code. Both the length of the code and its hidden nature make it very hard to discover the P(Y) code. The C/A and P(Y) code are both transmitted on L1 with a frequency of 1575.42 MHz. The P(Y) code is shifted by 90 degree ($\pi/2$) in phase compared to the C/A code,(also called phase quadrature) so that the C/A code has its minimum and maximum when the P(Y) code is zero and vice versa.

Functionality of SAGA

We now describe how the military P(Y) signal can be used to securely authenticate the GPS signal, even without the knowledge of the secret W code.

The main idea is to exploit the fact that the P(Y) code sequence received at location 1 is identical to the sequence received at location 2, except for the difference in satellite-to-receiver signal travel time (and some frequency differences due to the receiver clock and Doppler effect). The idea is to cross-correlate the samples taken at location 1 and location 2 with each other. This will result in a correlation peak when the phases of the P(Y) codes of the two samples are aligned with each other. The presence of this peak indicates the verifier that the same code is hidden in both samples. Of course, the C/A code in both samples can create a correlation peak as well. But keep in mind that the C/A and P(Y) code are orthogonal to each other. Hence, the verifier knows exactly where the P(Y) code should be located in the noise. The verifier takes sample points when the sine term of the C/A carrier goes to zero, so that the carrier of the P(Y) signal goes to one or minus one.[1] Hence, only the P(Y) code creates a correlation peak. The C/A code is known for each satellite. This enables the verifier to match each correlation peak to the different satellites, as the P(Y) code is in phase with the C/A code of the same satellite.

The verifier can precisely measure the time offsets between the satellite signals of the two samples to determine the arrival times of the different signals. If the verifier knows the arrival times of at least four satellites, the verifier can determine the exact location and time at which the sample was taken using the same trilateration methods that are used for the normal location determination in GPS. Hence, this system can be used to provide location verification from A to B. To provide location verification, the verifier B needs a signal S_B that is valid and has not been spoofed. When A sends a signal S_A to B, B can use the reference signal S_B and the signal S_A to verify the location and time at which S_A was received.

The accuracy of this methods lies within a magnitude of the normal GPS positioning determination. Hence, the verifier can determine the position where the signal was received with an accuracy in the meter range.

3   Threat Model against Location Verification Using SAGA

In this section, the possible attacks on location verification using SAGA are described.

Signal-synthesis attacks using the secret code. The hidden signals are generated using a secret code. In the case of GPS, this code is the military P(Y) code. An attacker who possesses this code can generate valid signals for every position he wants. Therefore, the system is only secure as long as the code is kept secret. If the attacker does not know the secret code used to generate the signals, he can try to guess the code. However, if the code is long enough and pseudo-randomly generated, it is computational infeasible for an attacker to

---

[1] In communication jargon, the verifier separates out the quadrature (sine) component from the in phase (cosine) component of the signal.

successfully guess the secret code (which is true for the P(Y) code). It might be possible to use high-gain steerable antennas to raise the P(Y) code above noise. However, for every satellite one expensive and big (more than 10 meters) high-gain steerable dish antenna is needed. Note that if the P(Y) code is revealed, the anti-spoofing capability and the restricted use of the military GPS signals would be broken. Hence, the same security assumption is needed for the military GPS anti-spoofing mechanism.

Signal-synthesis attack without the secret code. An attacker can try generating and transmitting his own navigation signals. Such an attack is called signal-synthesis attack. However, the attacker does not know the secret P(Y) code and therefore the attacker's signals will not match with the verifier's signals. Hence, the attacker would need to attack the verifier's reference signal as well. An attacker can try a signal-synthesis attack by inserting a hidden signal h into the verifier's reference signal. To be successful, the attacker needs centimeter knowledge of the verifier's antenna. The attacker sends a hidden signal h to the verifier's antenna that is buried deep in the noise so that it does not interfere with the GPS signals. As the C/A code is not changed at all, and the hidden signals are buried well below the thermal noise floor, a verifier cannot detect the existence of these hidden signals. The attacker can now create a signal that the verifier falsely accepts as valid. To do this, the attacker first generates the C/A codes for the different satellites like they are expected at the wanted spoofing position. With the knowledge of the location of the verifier's antenna, the attacker can determine the travel time of the hidden signal to the verifier's antenna and therefore the offset between the hidden signal h and the C/A codes of each satellite in the verifier's data sample. Using the same offsets, the attacker aligns a copy of the hidden signal h with the C/A code of each satellite in his data sample. When the verifier correlates the data sample of the attacker with his data sample, the hidden signal h in the attacker's data sample and in the verifier's data sample correlates. The verifier cannot distinguish a correlation peak that is generated by the hidden signal h from a correlation peak that is generated by the P(Y) code and will therefore falsely accept the signal as valid. Without knowing the P(Y) code, the verifier will not be able to detect this attack. Signal observation techniques of the C/A code will be useless, as the original GPS signals are kept untouched by this attack. Using directional antennas to get the reference signal and shielding the antenna can make the attack much more complicated, as it would be more difficult for the attacker to insert the hidden signal into the verifier's signal. The insertion of the hidden signal can also be mitigated by collecting data samples from antennas at closely related locations (e.g. 3-5 meters). The attacker would need to align a hidden signal h_i for each used antenna i. Furthermore, each antenna would receive the hidden signals h_i with a different phase. Using cross-correlation techniques the presence of these signals is detectable. The verifier can also use reference signals from different places to increase the security. By using signals from different locations a web-of-trust can be build. This would significantly increase the attack complexity as the attacker would need to spoof each of these locations. Note that signal-synthesis attacks become very complicated in case an attacker needs to attack a receiver over-the-air, e.g. when he attacks location self-verification. In this case the attacker needs to somehow get rid of the original C/A code and P(Y) code (if cross-correlation is used to detect spoofing), which can be very complicated without physical access to the user's receiver.

Delay attack. In a delay attack, the attacker delays the incoming signals for the same amount of time. If all signals are delayed for the same amount of time, this has no impact on the position computation. However, this results in a clock offset at the receiver. B can still validate at which time A was at the location L_A. But the clock of A and B are not synchronized. Therefore, delay attacks are very powerful against time synchronization, but do not have a direct impact on secure location verification. But if B's clock is not synchronized to a standard time reference such as UTC (from US Naval Observatory, GPS, etc.), e.g. because B is being attacked by a delay attack as well, B might falsely accept an old signal as fresh. Hence, as a requirement B's clock must be securely synchronized if B needs to decide whether the signal is fresh or not.

Selective-delay attack. In a selective delay attack, the attacker delays each satellite signal for a different amount of time so that a false position is calculated. This is a very powerful attack against navigation systems.[4] However, to be able to delay each signal for a different amount of time it must be possible to separate the signals from each other. But this is very difficult for the P(Y) signals as they are hidden in the noise. It might be possible to separate the signals by using high gain directional antennas for each satellite. Using a directional antenna pointing at one satellite, the C/A and P(Y) code of the target satellite are stronger than the signals from the other satellites.(But might be still below the thermal noise floor) If you combine signals from two directional antennas that target different satellites, a verifier might be able to detect the signals of the two satellites, while the signals of the other satellites might be too weak. Using this method the C/A and P(Y) signal from one satellite can be separated from the signals from the other satellites. But note that this attack needs at least four very good high-gain directional antennas and quite some knowledge in signal processing. Furthermore, this attack needs to be done in real-time, as the verifier can precisely determine the freshness of the signal. Whether this attack is successful depends on the verifier's ability to detect the signals from the not-targeted satellites. This strongly depends on the attacker's as well as the verifier's antennas and the verifier's effort to find these signals.

Relaying attack (wormhole attack). This is the most powerful attack against location verification with SAGA. In a relaying attack, the attacker relays the signals S_v received at location L_v to the attacker's location L_A. As S_v is a valid signal, B will falsely validate A's position as L_v. This kind of attack is the biggest problem for all passive location verification techniques, as these techniques only verify the location of the received signal, and not of the receiver. So in passive location verification services that use GNSS techniques, it will only be possible to proof that an entity has access to a receiver (signal) at the claimed location, but not that he is actually there. As the exact reception time (less than a millisecond) of the signal is known these relay attacks can be made more difficult by setting up sharp bounds of the freshness of the signal. Note, that the accuracy of SAGA lies within the low meter range, hence, an attacker can only collect valid signals if he is within a few meters from the valid location.

Security Assumptions for Location Verification

We will now summarize the needed security assumptions in order to provide location verification services with SAGA.

1. *B can be sure that the signals he has received are valid and no other signal than the P(Y) code is hidden in the noise.*
2. *An attacker does not have a signal from the claimed location L_A for the claimed time period.*
3. *It is impossible to separate the signals from the different satellites from each other, so that they cannot be delayed for different amounts of time.*
4. *The attacker does not possess the secret code needed to generate the hidden signals.*
5. *Additional security assumption for location self-verification.* To prevent delay attacks, A either needs to be securely synchronized with GPS time or A needs to be sure that B's signal S_B is fresh.

4   Conclusion

The new mechanism to authenticate GPS signals is very promising to enable secure location verification services. As GNSS signals cover great areas, only about 6 reference stations can provide reference signals that enable location verification with global coverage. However, looking at the security assumptions it is clear that careful consideration is needed for every application to decide whether or not secure location verification is possible with SAGA. The key assumption for SAGA is assumption number 2, that an attacker does not have a signal from a valid location. This assumption is not just limited to SAGA but is rather a general shortcoming of location verification: If a malicious user has a collaborator at the claimed location, the verifier cannot distinguish whether the received location signals are the user's or the collaborator's signal. Hence, he will not be able to know whether the user is at the claimed location or some collaborator. Therefore, SAGA should be used in applications where it is very unlikely that an attacker has access to a signal at a valid location at the claimed time. As an example application, a server with confidential information might restrict its access only to the company area and maybe the home of some employees that sometimes work from home. In this case, SAGA can be used for location based access control as an additional security mechanism for this server. Of course an attacker could try to circumvent this security mechanism by collecting a location signal at a valid location during the attack. However, this would significantly increase the complexity of the attack, especially as in many cases an attacker could be living far away from the target, e.g. in another country. Furthermore, the fact that the verifier will have meter knowledge of the attackers position, as well as the fact that he needs to be very close (in the meter range) to a specific location increases the chance that the attacker gets caught significantly. So location verification would not make the system unbreakable, but it could significantly increase the complexity of an attack. Hence, for many real-world systems, the proposed location verification techniques can significantly increase security. Furthermore, location verification can be a security tool that provides security in situation where traditional security mechanism such as passwords often fail. The main reason for this is that the security of location verification with SAGA does not rely on any secret information that can be lost and reused for later attacks. If a location signal is not fresh it is of no use for an attacker.

If SAGA needs to be resistant against very sophisticated attackers, the assumption that the P(Y) signals cannot be separated from each other might not be true, as an attacker could use very sophisticated high-gain steerable antennas. But in most cases, a possible adversary does not have access to such technology.

It should be further noted, that there currently does not exist any alternative to SAGA for using civil GNSS signals for location verification. Civil GNSS signals do not have any security mechanism so that spoofing can easily be done.[5] Hence, the security of SAGA far exceeds the security of normal civil GNSS services. Especially in applications, such as tracking, where location verification is the primary goal there is no alternative right now to SAGA with a comparable level of security when using GNSS. SAGA is also currently the most secure civil system for using GPS for location self-verification.

References

1. Denning, D.E., MacDoran, P.F.: Location-based authentication: grounding cyberspace for better security. Computer Fraud & Security, 12–16 (February 1996)
2. Lo, S.C., De Lorenzo, D.S., Enge, P.K., Akos, D., Bradley, P.: Signal authentication - a secure civil gnss for today. In: inside GNSS, September 2009, pp. 30–39 (2009)
3. Chandran, N., Goyal, V., Moriarty, R., Ostrovsky, R.: Position based cryptography. In: Halevi, S. (ed.) Advances in Cryptology - CRYPTO 2009. LNCS, vol. 5677, pp. 391–407. Springer, Heidelberg (2009)
4. Kuhn, M.G.: An Asymmetric Security Mechanism for Navigation Signals. In: Fridrich, J. (ed.) IH 2004. LNCS, vol. 3200, pp. 239–252. Springer, Heidelberg (2004)
5. Humphreys, T., Ledvina, B., Psiaki, M., O'Hanlon, B., Kintner, P.: Assessing the Spoofing Threat. GPS World, 28–38 (January 2009)
6. Scott, L.: Anti-Spoofing & Authenticated Signal Architectures for Civil Navigation Systems. In: Proc. ION GPS/GNSS, pp. 1543–1552 (2003)

Author Index

GPSR Compliance

The European Union's (EU) General Product Safety Regulation (GPSR)
is a set of rules that requires consumer products to be safe and our
obligations to ensure this.

If you have any concerns about our products, you can contact us on
ProductSafety@springernature.com

In case Publisher is established outside the EU, the EU authorized
representative is:

Springer Nature Customer Service Center GmbH
Europaplatz 3
69115 Heidelberg, Germany

Batch number: 09473985

Printed by Printforce, the Netherlands